SOUTH CHINA IN THE SIXTEENTH CENTURY

BIBLIOTHECA ORIENTALIS

CHINA

Tractado em que se cõtam muito por estẽso as cousas da China, cõ suas particularidades, e assi do reyno dormuz cõposto por el. R. padre frey Gaspar da Cruz da ordẽ de sam Domingos. Dirigido ao muito poderoso Rey dom Sebastiam nosso senhor.

Impresso com licença. 1 5 6 9.

The title-page of the first European book on China
(The *Tractado* of Caspar da Cruz, Evora, 1569)

SOUTH CHINA IN THE SIXTEENTH CENTURY

Being the narratives of
Galeote Pereira
Fr. Gaspar da Cruz, O.P.
Fr. Martin De Rada, O.E.S.A.
(1550-1575)

Edited by
C. R. Boxer

Orchid Press
Bangkok 2004

C.R. Boxer
SOUTH CHINA IN THE SIXTEENTH CENTURY

First published: 1953
Reprinted: 2004

ORCHID PRESS
P.O. Box 19,
Yuttitham Post Office,
Bangkok 10907, Thailand

www.orchidbooks.com

Cover illustration : *Portrait of the Ming Hongzhi Emperor*, Ming Dynasty, 16th century, hanging scroll, ink and colour on silk
© National Palace Museum, Taipei, Taiwan, Republic of China

Printed in Thailand

ISBN 974-524-043-5

To Jack Braga
*As a small acknowledgement
of many kindnesses*

PREFACE

THIS volume contains three narratives describing South China as it appeared to Portuguese and Spanish visitors to that country in the years 1550–1575. The narratives and their writers are discussed in the introduction, this preface being concerned only with the editing of the volume.

The translation of the narrative of Galeote Pereira is based on Richard Willis' translation in the *History of Trauayle in the West and East Indies and other countreys lying eyther way towards the fruitfull and ryche Moluccas* (London, 1577), leaves 237–251 [misprinted 253], which, in its turn, was taken from the Italian version printed in the *Nuovi Avisi delle Indie di Portogallo . . . Quarta Parte* (Venice, 1565), pp. 63–87. I have carefully compared Willis' version with the Portuguese manuscript copies of Pereira's original report which are preserved in the Archives at Lisbon and Rome, and made such additions and alterations to Willis' text as proved to be necessary.

Similarly, the translation of the *Tractado* of Gaspar da Cruz is based on Samuel Purchas' pioneer English translation, 'A Treatise of China and the adjoining regions, written by Gaspar da Cruz a Dominican Friar, and dedicated to Sebastian, King of Portugal: here abbreviated,' printed in *Purchas his Pilgrimes* (London, 1625), III, pp. 166–198. I have restored Purchas' omissions (amounting to about one-third of the original text) and corrected and amplified his translation where a careful comparison with the original Portuguese edition of 1569–70 showed this to be justified. Since this present edition is not a textual reprint of Willis' and Purchas' pioneer efforts, I have not adhered slavishly to their spelling and punctuation. I have modernised the spelling of other than proper names, and corrected the punctuation where this was necessary for the sense; but apart from this, I have not altered their wording or their idiom except where they had mistaken the meaning of their often obscurely worded Portuguese originals.

There was no contemporaneous English translation of Fr. Martín de Rada's 'Relación' of 1575, on which I could base my own version and thus give the latter the authentic flavour of the original. I have accordingly made my own translation from a comparison of three sixteenth-century Spanish versions, only one of which has been hitherto available in print—and that in the files of an obscure Spanish religious periodical (*Revista Agustiniana*, Vols. VIII and IX, Valladolid, 1884–1885). I have tried to pay due regard not only to the sense but to the idiom of the sixteenth-century Spanish texts; but obviously this translation does not have the Elizabethan or Jacobean flavour of the other two.

In preparing the footnotes, I have done my best to confine them to such points as are necessary to elucidate the text, in accordance with the Society's present practice. Most of the bibliographical references given in the introduction and notes are abbreviated: the full titles of the works so cited will be found in the Bibliography.

The transcription and transliteration of Chinese names presents a problem which cannot, in the present circumstances, be solved to the entire satisfaction of all concerned. No two Sinologues hold identical views on this matter, and no two authors have followed identical methods of using even the more generally accepted systems outside France where the use of the Vissière system is *de rigueur*. After much cogitation, I have decided to use a slightly modified form of the Wade-Giles system, in the belief that it is likely to be the one most familiar to my readers, and because it is the one which is used in most of the standard works on China which are quoted in the footnotes. I admit that one Sinologue, in discussing the various European systems of transcribing Chinese, wrote that 'it is not easy amidst these fantastic systems to pick out the least objectionable; but there can be no possible doubt as to which is absolutely the worst; and the palm here must be given to that introduced into the British service on the authority of the late Sir Thomas Wade, and to which, owing to its having been adopted by the Imperial Maritime Customs, wide prominence has been given by modern writers on China'.[1] I further admit that H. A. Giles, whose use of this system in his great *Dictionary* (1892) gave it a quasi-official sanction, described it as 'anything but scientifically exact. In some respects it is cumbersome; in others inconsistent'. Nor am I forgetful that the Wade-Giles system was

[1] *Journal of the North China branch of the Royal Asiatic Society*, XXXIX, 163–4

designed for the Pekingese or North Mandarin language, whereas this book deals with South China. But the Canton, Amoy, and Foochow languages (or 'dialects' as they are often if incorrectly called) are as far removed from each other as they are from Pekingese. On balance, therefore, it is probably less confusing for the reader to use one admittedly imperfect system throughout the book, than three or four widely-differing systems,—particularly as almost all English works dealing with China use the Wade-Giles system or close approximations to it.

Departures from the Wade-Giles system have been kept to a minimum, but the following principal modifications should be noted. In accordance with the usual practice in works intended for a public which does not know Chinese, all tonal marks and superior tone numbers have been omitted. Aspirates and diacritical marks have been retained, except in words which have become household usage without them. Similarly, common geographical names such as Peking, Canton, and Foochow, which have become anglicised in the same way as have Lisbon, Rome, and Copenhagen, are retained in their familiar forms. Capital letters and hyphens have also been employed (or dispensed with) at times more in accordance with the dictates of common sense than with strict adherence to the unmodified Wade-Giles system.

The sound of a Chinese word can, as a rule, only be rendered very approximately in the letters of our alphabet, and the correct tone and pronunciation can only be learnt from a Chinese. In the Wade-Giles orthography, broadly speaking, the consonants are sounded as in English and the vowels as in Italian. The chief exception is the letter *j*, which represents something between the French *j* and an *r*. The initial *hs* is a compromise between *h* and *sh*, so that the word *hsi*, for instance, is neither quite *he* nor *she; e* is pronounced more or less as in 'lens'; *ê* the vowel-sound in 'lurk'; *ou* as in 'soul'; *ih* like the *i* in 'shirt'; and *ü* in the same way as the French *u*. The aspirate is an expulsion of breath between the consonant and the vowel. Further details will be found in H. A. Giles' monumental *Dictionary*, in E. T. C. Werner's prefatory note to his *Dictionary of Chinese Mythology* (Shanghai, 1932), pp. xv–xvii, and in the School of Oriental Studies' *Handbook of Oriental History*, pp. 157–165. Chinese emperors are designated, conveniently if incorrectly, by their *nien-hao* or year-period, thus the Emperor Yung-lo, instead of 'the Yung-lo emperor'. The translation of Chinese official titles presents a more difficult problem, since in most cases there is no exact (or even approximate) European equivalent. Generally speaking, I have retained the explanations given by my original authorities, save where these are manifestly misleading. The reproduction of all Chinese names which occur in this book, in a special section at the end (by Mr. Ch'ên Chih-jang) greatly facilitates their identification.

ACKNOWLEDGEMENTS

My own knowledge of Chinese being limited to a few characters, I have drawn freely on the knowledge of this language possessed by others. I am, however, solely responsible for the identifications made from Carstairs Douglas, *Dictionary of the Amoy vernacular*, which I had to use on my own.

Mr. Ch'ên Chih-jang and Mr. Lo Hsien-hau kindly translated many relevant passages from the Chinese works which are listed in the bibliography. Professor K. Enoki of Tokyo University, and Mr. O. B. van der Sprenkel of the School of Oriental Studies (London University) gave me some useful hints and indications, and kindly checked a number of references. Miss J. M. Stead, of the same institution, suggested identifications of some Cambodian Buddhist terms which I could not find in the works of Aymonier and Leclère. Padre António da Silva Rego of the Escola Superior Colonial at Lisbon, and the Rev. F. E. Croydon of King's College, London University, helped me to find some Biblical references. D. Virginia Rau, of the University of Lisbon, secured for me accurate transcripts of the relevant documents in the Portuguese archives. Fr. G. Schurhammer, S.J., and Fr. M. Batllori, S.J., were equally obliging in furnishing me with copies and photostats of relevant material in the Jesuit archives at Rome. I am indebted to Mr. Stephen Rickert for assistance in procuring photostats and microfilms of documents in the Spanish archives, and to Snra. Mercedes Mendoza for typing others. Mr. James Cummins has kindly checked and re-checked my translation of Fr. Martín de Rada. Mr. R. A. Skelton, Hon. Secretary of the Society, has been most helpful in his capacity as editor. Mr. G. S. Holland of the Royal Geographical Society kindly drew the sketch-maps with his customary skill. To none, however, am I under a greater obligation than to Mr. J. V. Mills, who has never wearied in searching for relevant material in Chinese books and maps.

Mistakes, no doubt, will be found in this book. As Mr. Mills writes, 'I distrust all translations: I have just come across one by an ex-Professor of Chinese at King's College, London: he has translated "[written by] Tëĕ-Tseen-yun" instead of "[written in] the same rhyme as before": Hirth and Rockhill translated "Ta Shih" as "a great feast" instead of "the Arabs".' Where such Sinologues have faltered, it is certainly not in me to command complete success. I trust, however, that such errors have been reduced to a minimum by the kindness and assiduity of the friends mentioned above, and the cross-checking which has been applied wherever practicable.

The majority of the illustrations are taken from books in my own library; but special acknowledgement is due to Professor K. Enoki for securing permission to reproduce the very rare map of Canton in 1558 (Pl. 3) from the original in the Research Institute of Humanistic Science, Kyoto University, Japan, and to the Council of the Royal Asiatic Society for the loan of the blocks for Plates 4, 8 and 10.

1 *January*, 1953   C. R. B.

CONTENTS

ILLUSTRATIONS

SKETCH MAPS

INTRODUCTION

ONE of the outstanding 'best-sellers' of the sixteenth century was Juan González de Mendoza's *Historia de las cosas más notables, ritos y costumbres del gran Reyno de la China*, first printed at Rome in 1585. By the end of the century, thirty editions of this book had been published in the principal European languages.[1] Translations of Mendoza's *Historia* continued to appear down to 1656, although its place as the standard work on China was taken first by Nicholas Trigault's *De Christiana Expeditione apud Sinas* (Augsburg, 1615),[2] and later by Martino Martini's *De Bello Tartarico* (Antwerp, 1654),[3] both of which enjoyed a comparable popularity. The reading public in those days was small, and it is probably no exaggeration to say that Mendoza's book had been read by the majority of well-educated Europeans at the beginning of the seventeenth century. Its influence was naturally enormous, and it is not surprising to find that men like Francis Bacon and Sir Walter Raleigh derived their notions of China and the Chinese primarily, if not exclusively, from this work. Even travellers who, like Jan Huighen van Linschoten, had themselves been in Asia, relied mainly on Mendoza's *Historia* for their accounts of China, although Mendoza himself had gone no further than Mexico. As G. F. Hudson has observed, 'Mendoza's book reaches the very essentials of the life of Old China, and its publication may be taken to mark the date from which an adequate knowledge of China and its institutions was available for the learned world of Europe.'[4]

The English translation of Mendoza's book, which appeared in

[1] 'Juan Gonzalez de Mendoza, Historia de las cosas mas notables, ritos y costumbres del gran Reyno de la China and El viaje que hizo Antonio de Espejo', by H. R. Wagner, reprinted from *The Spanish Southwest* (Berkeley, 1924), is the best bibliographical survey in English. See also R. Streit, *Bibliotheca Missionum*, IV, nr. 1972, pp. 531–533.

[2] Eleven editions in the decade between 1615 and 1625. Streit, *Bibliotheca Missionum*, V, 716–717.

[3] Twenty-one editions in twenty years, 1654–1674. Streit, *Bibliotheca Missionum*, V, 796–797.

[4] G. F. Hudson, *Europe and China* (London, 1931), p. 242.

the year of the Armada,[1] was reprinted by the Hakluyt Society in two volumes edited by Sir G. T. Staunton and R. H. Major a century ago.[2] It has long been out of print and is one of the most difficult to find (and costly to buy) of the volumes in the first series, although the editing left a great deal to be desired. No effort was made to disentangle Mendoza's sources from his own interpolations and observations, and little trouble was taken over the identification of Chinese names and terms, many of which were left unexplained. This was probably because Staunton was then an old and tired man (he died in 1859 at the age of seventy-eight), and Major did not claim to be a Sinologue.[3]

Since Mendoza himself was never in China, the principal value of his work lies in the eyewitness accounts which he used. The two most important of these were the *Tractado em que se cõtam muito por estẽso as cousas da China*, by the Portuguese Dominican friar, Gaspar da Cruz, printed at Evora in 1569–1570, and the 'Relación de las cosas de China que propriamente se llama Taybin' written by the Augustinian friar, Martín de Rada, after his visit to Fukien in 1575. Rada's 'Relación' was all his own work, but Cruz's *Tractado* was partly based on the narrative of Galeote Pereira who had been a prisoner in South China from 1549 to 1552. It is these three basic sources which form the staple of this book, but, before considering them separately, it will be as well to survey the course of Portuguese and Spanish contacts with China down to 1575. This need be done only in broadest outline, since the subject has been treated by previous writers in some detail, although the published material admittedly leaves several gaps and doubtful episodes in the story.[4]

[1] *The Historie of the great and mightie kingdome of China, and the situation thereof: Together with the great riches, huge citties, politike governement, and rare inventions in the same. Translated out of Spanish by R. Parke* (London, 1588).

[2] *The History of the great and mighty kingdom of China and the situation thereof. Compiled by the Padre Juan Gonzalez de Mendoza. And now reprinted from the early translation of R. Parke.* Edited by Sir G. T. Staunton, Bart., with an introduction by R. H. Major, 2 vols., Hakluyt Society, First Series, Vol. XIV (1853), and Vol. XV (1854).

[3] A facsimile (and unauthorised) reprint of the 1853–1854 Hakluyt Society edition was published by Henri Vetch of Peking shortly before World War II, but it is now as rare as the 1853–1854 edition.

[4] D. Ferguson, *Letters from Portuguese captives in Canton, written in 1534 and 1536* [alias 1524 for both]. *With an introduction on Portuguese intercourse with China in the first half of the sixteenth century* (Bombay, 1902); E. A. Voretzsch,

1. THE COMING OF THE FRANKS

(a) The Portuguese

At the time (1498) when the Portuguese opened the maritime route round the Cape of Good Hope to India, the emperors of the Ming dynasty, reversing the expansionist policy of the third emperor, Yung-lo (1403–1424), which had carried Chinese fleets as far as the Persian Gulf and the Somali coast, officially forbade their subjects from emigrating or trading overseas, on pain of death.[1] This ban was not very strictly observed, and junks from Fukien and Kuangtung visited Malayan, Indochinese and Indonesian harbours with fair regularity, but they seldom went further west than Malacca. The Portuguese established friendly contacts with Chinese junk-masters on their first arrival at and subsequent occupation of Malacca, whose dispossessed Muslim sultan vainly appealed to his nominal suzerain at Peking for help against the *Feringhi* (*Fo-lang-chi*) or Frankish intruders.[2] The first contacts of the Portuguese with China itself were made by individual merchant-adventurers who sailed from Malacca for the South China coast in native junks, and they found that there was

'Documento acêrca da primeira embaixada Portuguesa á China', in *Boletim da Sociedade Luso-Japonesa*, I (Tokyo, 1929), pp. 50–69; J. Yano, 'Comércio dos Portugueses em Tamau e as circunstâncias em que frequentaram Lampacau', in *Ibidem*, pp. 70–77; T. T. Chang, *Sino-Portuguese Trade from 1514 to 1644. A synthesis of Portuguese and Chinese sources* (Leiden, 1934), pp. 32–99, and P. Pelliot's lengthy review of this work in *T'oung Pao*, Second Series, XXXI, 58–94; H. Bernard-Maître, S. J., *Aux Portes de la Chine. Les missionaires du seizième siècle, 1514–1583* (Tientsin, 1933); *Ibid.*, *Les Iles Philippines du grand archipel de la Chine. Un essai de conquête spirituelle de l'Extrême-Orient, 1571–1641* (Tientsin, 1936), pp. 1–51; A. Kammerer, *La Découverte de la Chine par les Portugais au XVIème siècle et la cartographie des portulans* (Leiden, 1944); A. Cortesão, *The Suma Oriental of Tomé Pires and the Book of Francisco Rodrigues*, Vol. I, (Hakluyt Society, Ser. II, N⁰ LXXXIX, 1944), pp. xxvii–lxiii; J. M. Braga, *The Western Pioneers and their discovery of Macao*, (Macau, 1949); W. H. Chang's monograph (in Chinese), *A commentary on the four chapters on Portugal, Spain, Holland and Italy in the History of the Ming Dynasty*, in the *Yenching Journal of Chinese Studies*, Monograph Series No. 7 (Peking, 1934), pp. 5–82, cited hereafter as W. H. Chang, *Commentary*.

[1] This subject is discussed by J. J. L. Duyvendak, *China's discovery of Africa* (London, 1949), and G. B. Sansom, *The Western World and Japan* (London, 1950), pp. 42–53, 147–151.

[2] For the connection between 'Franks', *Feringhi*, *Fărangī*, and *Fo-lang-chi* see P. Pelliot, 'Le Hōjă et le sayyid Husain de l'histoire des Ming', in *T'oung Pao*, Second Series, XXXVIII, 86–87, 204–206.

'as great profit in taking spices to China as in taking them to Portugal'.[1]

In 1517, a Portuguese squadron commanded by Fernão Peres de Andrade, carrying Tomé Pires as ambassador, anchored in the Pearl River off Canton. After some hesitation on the part of the Chinese, Tomé Pires was eventually allowed to proceed to Peking, and Fernão Peres de Andrade established peaceful and profitable relations with the local officials at Canton. A detachment of this

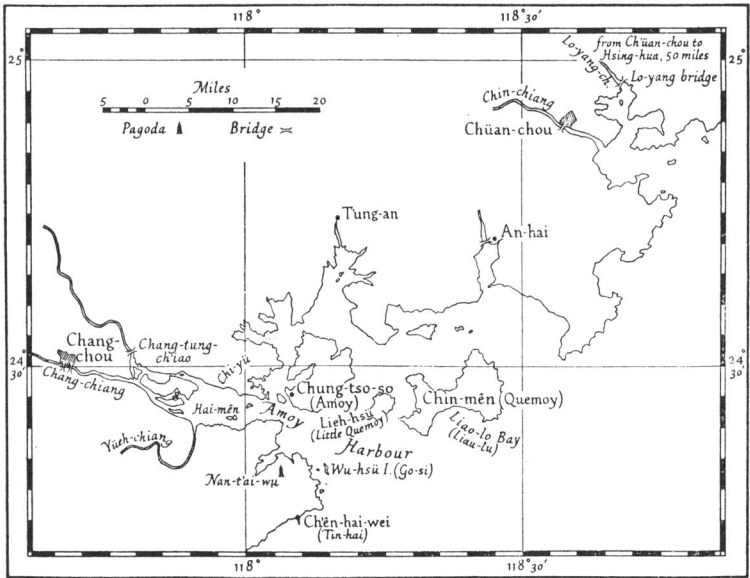

Fig. 2. The Region of the Bay of Amoy

squadron, under Jorge Mascarenhas, was sent to discover the Liu-chiu (Ryūkyū) islands, but got no further than Fukien, where, however, they drove an exceedingly profitable trade at the port of 'Chincheo', (probably the Bay of Amoy),[2] before rejoining Fernão Peres at Canton. All seemed 'set-fair' for the smooth development of Sino-Portuguese commercial intercourse when

[1] Andrea Corsali to Duke Giuliano de Medici, Malacca, 6 January 1515, quoted in D. Ferguson, *Portuguese captives in Canton*, pp. 4–5. Duarte Barbosa, writing about the same time, states that pepper could be sent from Malacca to China at a profit of 300%; *Book of Duarte Barbosa* (ed. Longworth Dames, Hakluyt Society), Vol. II, p. 215. Cf. also Diogo do Couto, *Decada IV*, Livro 3, cap. 1.

[2] Cf. Appendix I 'Chincheo'.

Fernão Peres left Canton for Malacca, 'very prosperous in honour and wealth, things rarely secured together', as his friend and chronicler, João de Barros, wrily commented. This prospect was blighted by Fernão Peres' brother, Simão de Andrade, who was the commander of the next royal squadron which visited Chinese waters. He behaved in so outrageous and high-handed a way[1] that credence was now given to the complaints of the envoys of the fugitive Sultan of Malacca. The position was further aggravated by the death of the Ming emperor, Chêng-tê, who had apparently agreed to receive Tomé Pires, and by the inability of the Portuguese to realise that Chinese etiquette demanded the temporary cessation of foreign trade during the period of Imperial mourning. Tomé Pires and his suite were sent back to Canton, where they were arrested, tortured and imprisoned. Some of them were executed; others, including the ambassador himself, died of the hardships to which they were subjected, but two of the survivors succeeded in smuggling out letters which recorded their plight and give us, incidentally, a wonderful 'worm's-eye' view of Ming China.[2] The Portuguese ships which attempted to renew the trade in 1521–1522 were forcibly expelled from the Kuangtung coast, and an imperial decree was promulgated, banning all dealings with the 'barbarian devils' or *fan-kuei*, as well as with other foreigners.

The China trade was too valuable for the Portuguese to give up this new and promising market without a struggle. The Fo-lang-chi accordingly continued to visit the China coast for the next

[1] Cf. the Chinese records quoted by S. F. Balfour, 'Hong Kong before the British' in *T'ien Hsia Monthly*, XI, 40.

[2] The letters of Christovão Vieira and Vasco Calvo, discussed at length in the works of Ferguson, Voretzsch, and Cortesão quoted on pp. xviii–xix. Cortesão has shown that both letters must have been written towards the end of the year 1524, and not in 1534–1536, as erroneously ascribed by some early copyist, who thereby misled Ferguson and Voretzsch. I cannot, however, follow Cortesão in his surmise that Tomé Pires did not die in May 1524 (as stated by the writer of the letters and accepted by João de Barros), but lived in exile for years in the interior, where his daughter subsequently met Fernão Mendes Pinto. To my mind, the arguments of Ferguson (*op. cit.*) and of Schurhammer (*Fernão Mendes Pinto und seine 'Peregrinacam'*, Leipzig, 1927, and in *Anais da Academia Portuguesa da História*, II series, Vol. I) against the authenticity of Fernão Mendes Pinto's travels in China and Tartary, are far stronger than the elaborate and unconvincing defence of his veracity advanced by Cortesão in his edition of the *Suma Oriental*, I, xlix–xliii, and by the Visconde de Lagoa in his *A Peregrinação de Fernão Mendes Pinto. Tentativa de reconstituição geográfica* (Lisbon, 1947).

thirty years, sometimes trading with the connivance of the local officials and sometimes in despite of them. As the imperial ban on their trade was originally enforced fairly strictly in Kuangtung, the Portuguese turned their attention to the more northerly maritime provinces of Fukien and Chekiang, where they wintered in

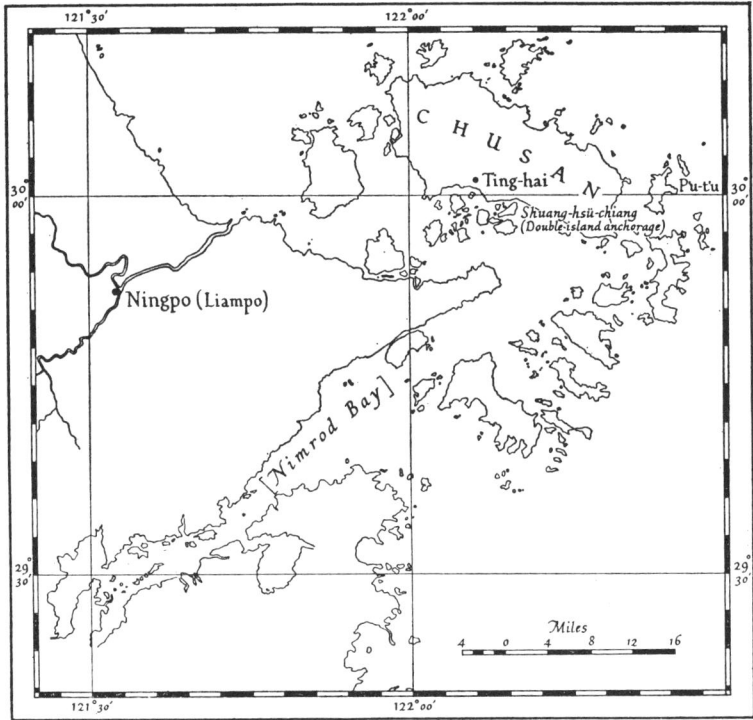

Fig. 3. Ningpo and Double-island anchorage

various sheltered but obscure islands and anchorages. The most flourishing of these temporary settlements were the Shuang-hsü-chiang (Double-island anchorage) near Ningpo, and Wu-hsü island[1] and Yüeh-chiang (Moon anchorage)[2] on the southern

[1] According to the *Ch'ou-hai-t'u-pien* of 1562 (ch. 4, p. 10), Wu-hsü water-station was then subordinate to Ch'üan-chou prefecture. At an unascertained later date, it was transferred to that of Chang-chou. Cf. map on p. 316.

[2] The *Chang-chou-fu-chih*, as quoted in W. H. Chang, *Commentary*, p. 40, states 'Hai-têng district was originally the territory of Pa-chiu-tu in Lung-ch'i district; its old name was Yüeh-chiang'; and 'Yüeh-chiang is in sub-district 99; on the exterior it goes out to the tidal waters of the sea; on the interior it abuts on

edge of the vast Bay of Amoy. Despite Fernão Mendes Pinto's traveller's tales, there is no reason to suppose that these settlements were anything more than temporary affairs, where the Portuguese erected matsheds to house themselves and their goods on shore during the trading-season, and which were burnt or dismantled when they sailed away in their ships. This was the way in which the trade was conducted in later years at Saint John's island (Shang-ch'uan), at Lampacau (Lang-pai-kao) and, for the first couple of years, at Macao.[1] Even if the Portuguese had begun the construction of more permanent buildings at Shuang-hsü-chiang, Wu-hsü and Yüeh-chiang, they could not have progressed very far before their embryo settlements at these places were broken up by the Chinese in 1548–1549.

It is clear from Chinese records that the Portuguese smuggler-traders who frequented the China coast in 1521–1551 met with a good deal of sympathy and support from Chinese of all classes who were anxious to do business with them. As one of these records expressed it, 'the Fo-lang-chi who came, brought their local pepper, sappan-wood, ivory, thyme-oil, aloes, sandal-wood, and all kinds of incense in order to trade with our borderers. Their prices were particularly cheap. Every day they consumed supplies of drinks and eatables which they got from our people, such as quantities of rice, flour, pigs and fowls. The prices which they paid for them were double the usual amount, and therefore our borderers gladly provided them with a market.'[2] Another contemporaneous record states that 'the officials in each territory, directly the foreigners entered the anchorage, were unable to restrain the local people from trading. They felt that the Court was far away, and they once more took the foreigners' illicit presents and allowed them to moor their ships. The foreigners employed the wicked rascals in the locality and carried on their traffic without

the fresh waters; its shape is like that of the moon, hence its name'.

[1] Cf. Cruz, Ch. XXIX p. 224 (n) (4) *infra*, and Gregorio Gonçalves' eyewitness account of the origin of Macao in P. Pastells, *Catálogo de los documentos relativos las islas Filipinas existentes en el archivo de Indias de Sevilla*, I, cclii–ccliii. Cf. also the *Ao-men chih-lüeh*, II, p. 226, quoted in T. T. Chang, *Sino-Portuguese trade*, p. 91, and P. Luis Frois, S.J., letter of 15 December 1555, *apud* J. M. Braga, *Western Pioneers*, p. 83.

[2] The passage from the collected works of Lin Hsi-yüan, quoted in W. H. Chang, *Commentary*, p. 44. Cf. J. M. Braga, *Western Pioneers*, p. 68, for a slightly different version of this passage

restraint'.¹ In short, as the *Chang-chou Gazetteer* put it, 'the
literati and the people privately went out to sea to bribe the
foreigners and entice the pirates; prohibitions did not deter them.'²
Local smugglers and merchants, or even petty officials, 'tipped-
off' the Portuguese as to what harbours it would be safe for them to
frequent, and at what times. Expatriate mariners and local fishermen acted as pilots to the Portuguese ships and junks; but, as
T. T. Chang remarks, this smuggling-trade along the coast of
Fukien and Chekiang could never have achieved the proportions it
did, if it had not been actively encouraged by the scholar-gentry.³

Portuguese smugglers were not the only ones who frequented
the China coast at this time. Even more serious, from the point of
view of the Ming Court, were the depredations of the 'dwarf
robbers' or Japanese pirates. Japan at this time was in the throes
of the *Sengoku-jidai* (or 'country at war period'), with the *daimyō*
or feudal barons contending among themselves for local supre-
macy in a bewildering series of ever-changing combinations and
fluctuating fortunes. Raiding the China coast was a favourite
occupation of many of the *samurai* from southwest Japan, who
behaved as pirates or as traders as the occasion offered. In the
words of the official history of the Ming dynasty, 'the Wa [Japanese]
were shrewd by nature; they carried merchandise and weapons
together, and appeared here and there along the sea-coast. If
opportunity arrived, they displayed their weapons, raiding and
plundering ruthlessly. Otherwise they exhibited their merchandise,
saying that they were on their way to the Court with tribute. The
southeastern coast was victimised by them.'⁴ These bands of
'dwarf-robbers' (*Wakō* in Sinico-Japanese) were often organised
and equipped by the daimyō of Kyūshū, Shikoku and the Inland Sea

¹ *Ming-shih-lu*, ch. 363, quoted in W. H. Chang, *Commentary*, p. 42–43.
² *Chang-chou-fu-chih*, ch. 31, p. 7, quoted in W. H. Chang, *Commentary*, p.
40. Cf. also *China Review*, XIX (1891), p. 50.
³ T. T. Chang, *Sino-Portuguese trade*, pp. 69–70. The close association
between foreign traders and local pirates persisted in the minds of the Chinese
authorities for centuries. Commenting in 1880 on the Ch'ing criminal code
(based with trifling exceptions on that of the Ming), a Sinologue wrote, 'It is
curious to observe, too, in some places, how pirates and foreigners are classed
together, as if the distinction between them was so small as not to be worth
noticing' (*China Review*, VIII, 5n.).
⁴ *Ming-shih*, ch. 322 of the 1739 edition, quoted in R. Tsunoda & L. C.
Goodrich, *Japan in the Chinese Dynastic Histories, Later Han through Ming
Dynasties* (South Pasadena, 1951) p. 117.

region, whose origin was not usually very distinguished. According to a noted Japanese historian, 'their manners were rude, their lives loose, their thoughts low, their tempers hot, and their strength great, while they all suspected and were jealous of one another.'[1]

To guard against the ravages of the Japanese pirates, which had begun in the Mongol (Yüan) dynasty, but greatly increased in scope and ferocity during the early Ming period, the Ming created the so-called *Wei* or military guards. These Wei were regional military establishments located at strategic places along the sea coast, and also on the Northwestern frontier against the Mongols and Manchus. Each Wei originally consisted of about 5600 men, subdivided into smaller formations known as *ch'ien-hu-so* and *po-hu-so*, or garrison posts of 1120 and 112 men respectively. These figures were subsequently modified on different occasions in later years, and the garrisons were often under strength. They were recruited on a local hereditary militia basis, and came under the direct command of regional high commanderies, which in their turn came under the military board (*ping-pu*) at Peking.[2] In addition to the forces stationed ashore, there were also provincial coastguard fleets in the southern maritime provinces which were supposed to keep the coast clear of Japanese and other pirates, although at this time they seldom did so. It was the Kuangtung division of this coastguard fleet which had driven off the Portuguese ships after the closure of Canton to foreign trade in 1522, but the Chekiang and Fukien formations were not so efficient. As the *Fukien Gazetteer* put it, 'Evil people recklessly went out and traded illicitly with the Dwarfs [Japanese], the Fo-lang-chi [Portuguese] and others. At that time our coast defences in Chekiang and Fukien had for a long time been obsolete. Only one or two in every ten fighting-ships and revenue-vessels had been retained. . . . The Japanese robbed with violence, and at once realised their ambitions; there was nothing which they hesitated to do. They followed closely on each other, and started all sorts of trouble on the seas.'[3]

[1] Y. Takekoshi, *The economic aspects of the history of the civilization of Japan*, Vol. I (London, 1930), p. 292.

[2] For the organization of the *Wei*, see the *Ch'ou-hai-t'u-pien* (1562), ch. 4 and maps; *Ming-shih*, chüan 90; E. Hauer, *K'ai-kuo Fang-lüeh* (Berlin, 1926), p. 618 n. (53); F. Michael, *The origin of Manchu rule in China* (Baltimore, 1942), pp. 30–31.

[3] *Fukien t'ung-chih*, ch. 267, p. 14, quoted by W.H. Chang, *Commentary*, p. 38.

We know from Ming Chinese records that Portuguese smugglers and Japanese pirates sometimes co-operated with each other along the China coast, although there are remarkably few references to their joint activities in European works.[1] The Portuguese discovery of Japan, 1542–1543, gave them direct access to the land of the Rising Sun, whose inhabitants were, like themselves, prohibited by the Ming rulers from visiting China on pain of death. The extension of Portuguese trade to Japan led to an increase in their activities along the China coast, which coincided (whether fortuitously or otherwise is not clear) with an increase in the depredations of the Wakō.[2] The Imperial Court at Peking was finally roused to one of its spasmodic displays of energy. An honest and capable Censor named Chu Wan was appointed Viceroy and commander-in-chief of Fukien and Chekiang in 1547, and the provincial authorities were ordered to prepare a fleet to clear the coast of Japanese pirates, Portuguese smugglers and Chinese collaborators.

As the account given by Gaspar da Cruz (Chapter XXIII and XXIV *infra*) agrees substantially with such Chinese records as are available in print, save for one important point, only the briefest summary of subsequent events need be given here. The Chinese coastguard fleet mobilised in Fukien was directed in the first place against the notorious pirate settlement at Shuang-hsü-chiang (Double-island anchorage) near Ningpo, where some Chinese pirates and the Fo-lang-chi had been making themselves particularly obnoxious, as Gaspar da Cruz frankly admits. Our friar alleges that owing to contrary winds the Chinese fleet could not reach its objective, and was consequently diverted southwards against the Portuguese smugglers off the Fukien-Kuangtung coast, but the Chinese records tell a different story. According to

[1] One such reference will be found in González de Mendoza's *Historia*, Part I, Book I, Ch. XXVI (pp. 95–96 of Vol. II of the Hakluyt Society edition).

[2] The standard Chinese monograph on the ravages of the Wako is M. H. Ch'en, *The invasion of China by Japanese pirates during the Ming Dynasty*, in the *Yenching Journal of Chinese Studies*, Monograph Series nr. 6 (Peking, 1934). There is also an extensive Japanese work covering the subject by K. Akiyama, *Nisshi kōshō-shi kenkyū* (Tokyo, 1939). Cf. also R. Tsunoda-Goodrich, *Japan in the Chinese Dynastic Histories*, pp. 106–161. There is a good book in German by P. A. Tschepe, S.J., *Japans Beziehungen zu China seit den ältesten Zeiten bis zum Jahre 1600* (Jentschoufu, 1907), but although based almost entirely on Chinese sources, such as the provincial gazetteers, it does not give specific references to these in the text.

them, the Chinese commander, Lu T'ang, attacked the pirate stronghold at Shuang-hsü-chiang in June 1548, under cover of a dark night and thick weather. The assault was completely successful, but estimates of the pirate casualties range from fifty-five to a few hundred only.[1] No mention whatever is made of the presence of Portuguese among the pirates who were killed and captured, so there can hardly have been very many of them. Probably the majority were among those pirates who escaped and fled southwards to Fukien, whither they were pursued by Lu T'ang. In any event, Pinto's fantastic story of a 'blood-bath' which exterminated the settlement near 'Liampo' with the loss of thousands of lives, must be dismissed as one of his many fabrications. When the pursuing Chinese fleet finally came up with the Portuguese ships in the region of the bay of Amoy, there was some desultory skirmishing off Wu-hsü island and elsewhere, but the Portuguese were apparently able to do some trading at night by bribing the subordinate Chinese commanders. This concluded matters for the trading-season of 1548, but news was sent via Malacca to India that 'the ports of China were all up in arms against the Portuguese'.[2]

Despite this warning, some adventurous spirits, of whom Galeote Pereira was one, resolved to try their luck along the China coast in 1548–1549. The coastguard fleet was more active than ever, but (as Gaspar da Cruz explained), the coast is so studded with islands and inlets that the Portuguese adventurers were able to run the blockade in a few places near the Kuangtung-Fukien border. They could not dispose of all their cargoes, however, before they returned to Malacca. They therefore left a couple of junks with the unsold goods at anchor off Tsou-ma-ch'i,[3] a deep water

[1] Cf. Ch'ou-hai-t'u-pien, chüan 4, page 12, and chüan 5, page 19; ch. 8, p. 22.

[2] Letter of St. Francis Xavier, S.J., to Padre Simão Rodrigues, S.J., Cochin, 25 January, 1549, in G. Schurhammer, Epistolae S. Francisci Xaverii (Rome, 1945), II, 56–57; Gaspar da Cruz, Tractado, ch. XXIII, pp. 192–193 infra.

[3] 'Tsou-ma-ch'i is on the sea-coast of the 5th sub-district of Chao-an; on the inside it has Tung-ao, also called Ts'ê-ao [Pirate Bay], because the estuary is a place which is sheltered from the winds, and the pirate ships coming and going all anchor there.' Chang-chou-fu-chih, Ch. 22, p. 47, quoted in W. H. Chang, Commentary, p. 41. This place may well be identical with either the 'enseada preta' or the 'enseada de Rui Lobo' of the sixteenth-century Portuguese charts and sailing directions. Cf. A. Kammerer, La Découverte de la Chine par les Portugais au XVIme siècle et la cartographie des portulans (Leiden, 1944), pp. 168–169, 222–223.

inlet situated about half-way between Swatow and Amoy. These two junks were surprised and captured by the Chinese coast-guard commander, Lu T'ang, in the circumstances described by Gaspar da Cruz in Chapter XXIII *infra*. The prisoners were taken via Ch'üan-chou to Foochow, after some of them had been killed out of hand. About ninety-six of the survivors, mostly Chinese apparently, were later executed by order of the Viceroy Chu Wan, and the remainder were thrown into prison at Foochow, where some of them died from the treatment to which they were subjected.

Chu Wan's vigorous enforcement of the anti-smuggling and foreign-trade laws evoked the active opposition of the local scholar-gentry. As the Viceroy stated in one of his memorials to the throne, 'It is easy to exterminate robbers from foreign lands, but it is difficult to get rid of those from our own country. It is comparatively easy to extirpate the robbers of our coast, but it is indeed difficult to eliminate those who belong to the "robe and cap class" of our own country.'[1] His enemies in the maritime provinces intrigued against him at Court, where their accusations found a ready hearing from the influential Censor, Ch'ên Chiu-tê, who was a personal enemy of Chu Wan.[2] Ch'ên Chiu-tê impeached Chu Wan for having exceeded his authority in putting to death the prisoners taken at Tsou-ma-ch'i without having obtained confirmation of their sentence from the throne. After some discussion of this matter among government boards at the capital, the Emperor dispatched the Supervising Censor, Tu Ju-chên, together with some other high officials to investigate the affair on the spot. Gaspar da Cruz comments that it was lucky for the Portuguese prisoners that the Imperial commissioners' investigations took them to Ch'üan-chou prefecture, where the Portuguese were known as relatively peaceful (if illegal) traders, and not to Chekiang province, where their high-handed behaviour in the Ningpo region had raised the countryside against them.

The result of the commission of enquiry's investigations is fully recorded by Gaspar da Cruz in Chapters XXV–XXVI *infra*, and

[1] *Ming-shih*, ch. 205, p. 2, *apud* T. T. Chang, *Sino-Portuguese Trade*, p. 83. Cf. also *Ch'ou-hai-t'u-pien*, Ch. 4; K. Akiyama, *Nisshi Kōshō-shi kenkyū*, pp. 585–602.

[2] W. H. Chang, *Commentary*, p. 41; R. Tsunoda-Goodrich, *Japan in the Chinese Dynastic Histories*, pp. 127–128.

his account tallies remarkably well with the more fragmentary references to this affair in the *Ming Shih-lu* and other Chinese records.[1] In brief, many of the charges against the Portuguese were declared to be unfounded, and most of the survivors were released from prison at Foochow and sent into what was clearly a not very onerous exile in the province of Kuangsi.[2] Here they were split up into small groups and distributed in the principal provincial cities. Four of the less lucky ones were convicted of killing Chinese soldiers when unlawfully resisting arrest at Tsou-ma-ch'i; they received either long-term or death sentences. Chu Wan and many of his subordinates were found guilty of unjustifiably executing traders, embezzling their goods, and concealing the truth from the Court. After the findings of Ch'ên Chiu-tê's commission had been presented to the Court, an imperial decree (summarized at some length by Gaspar da Cruz) was promulgated, dealing out punishment to the guilty according to the gravity of their offences. The luckless Chu Wan committed suicide in order to avoid a shameful punishment, and several of his principal naval and military subordinates were sentenced to death. Many other officials involved in this affair were banished, demoted or degraded, and a few were promoted for having protested against the summary execution of the Portuguese and other prisoners.

In view of this outcome, it is not perhaps surprising that the Portuguese survivors, despite the hardships which they had suffered during their imprisonment, lauded Chinese justice to the skies, and stated outright that accused persons in a similar position could never have had such a fair trial in Europe. Galeote Pereira went so far in this commendation of Chinese justice at the expense of European, that the Jesuit censor at Rome made large cuts in this section of his report before it was sent to the printer.[3] On turning to the Chinese records, however, one is forced to the conclusion that the Imperial Commissioner and his fellow-investigators were actuated not by motives of sympathy for the

---

[1] Summarized by W. H. Chang, *Commentary*, pp. 40–48, and T. T. Chang *Sino-Portuguese Trade*, pp. 81–85; Tsunoda-Goodrich, *op. cit.*, pp. 125–128.

[2] As will be seen from the account of Galeote Pereira (pp. 34ff *infra*), T. T. Chang is mistaken in identifying the city of 'Cãsi' with Hangchow in his *Sino-Portuguese Trade*, p. 84.

[3] Cf. Galeote Pereira's report on pp. 20–21 *infra*, and in *Archivum Historicum Societatis Iesu*, Vol. XXII, pp. 57–92.

plight of the Portuguese, or even by strict impartiality, but by the desire to secure at all costs incriminating evidence against the Viceroy Chu Wan.[1] This argument does not apply, of course, to the Imperial edict which was promulgated, confirming the findings of the commission of enquiry and dealing out rewards and punishment; but it is difficult to avoid the conclusion that Chu Wan was the victim of a Court intrigue and thus of a miscarriage of justice, and that the Portuguese were lucky to escape as lightly as they did. This suspicion is strengthened by the fact that after Chu Wan's suicide, Lu T'ang, K'o Ch'iao, and others who had been sentenced to death were reprieved, and their sentences commuted in whole or in part.

It is interesting to contrast the encomiums lavished by Galeote Pereira and (to a lesser extent) by Gaspar da Cruz on the impartial administration of justice by the Ming mandarinate as a whole, with the criticisms of other Portuguese who had similar experiences. Judging from the accounts of Pereira and Cruz, one would be justified in assuming that the Ming government was functioning exceptionally well at this period, and that the empire as a whole was rich and prosperous. This no doubt was so in comparison with the other Asian states which were known to the Portuguese, but it does not convey the whole truth. Calvo and Vieira, writing from their Canton prison in 1524, paint a vivid picture of the harsh rule of the provincial mandarins. Whereas our writers (and the great chronicler João de Barros in their footsteps) extol the system of appointing provincial officials who had no ties of family relationship with the districts in which they ruled, Christovão Vieira claims that this practice led to oppression and extortion. 'Hence it comes that no judge in China does equity, because he does not think of the good of the district, but only of "squeeze", because he is not a native of it, and does not know when he may be transferred to another province. Hence it comes that they form no ties and are of no service where they govern, nor have they any love for the people; they do nothing but rob, kill, beat and torture the people. The people are worse treated by these mandarins than by the devil in hell. Hence it comes that the people have no love for the king and for the mandarins, and every

---

[1] Cf. W. H. Chang, *Commentary*, pp. 40–48; T. T. Chang, *Sino-Portuguese Trade*, pp. 81–85; Tschepe, *Japans Beziehungen zu China*, pp. 216–224.

day they go on rising and becoming robbers; and because the
people who are robbed have no vineyards nor any source of food,
they too are forced to become robbers. Of these risings there are a
thousand. In places where there are no rivers, many people rise;
those that are between rivers where they can be caught remain
quiet; but all are desirous of every change, because they are
placed in the lowest depths of subjection. It is much worse than
I have said.'[1]

Another feature of Chinese life which greatly impressed
Galeote Pereira (echoed by Gaspar da Cruz) was the great hereditary estates of the princes of the blood, particularly the *wang-fu* or
palace of the Chin-chiang princely family at Kueilin, whose
exalted occupant showed great kindness to the exiled Portuguese.[2]
Later historians have condemned the formation and extension of
these vast imperial benefices, as one of the main causes of the
internal decline of the Ming, and, for that matter, contemporary
critics among the literati were not wanting. These estates enjoyed a
wide range of tax-exemptions, and they occupied a great deal of
valuable agricultural land whose revenues did not reach the provincial or central government but were squandered by their
spendthrift (and often absentee) proprietors. Their abolition by
the Manchus on the collapse of the Ming empire was a popular
move which helped to reconcile the Chinese peasantry to their
new masters.[3]

The fate of Chu Wan naturally gave no inducement to other
high officials in the southern maritime provinces to enforce the
existing laws against trading with the Portuguese, and must have
encouraged the latter to renew their efforts. According to the
Ming-shih, 'after the death of Wan, the prohibition against sea-

[1] Cf. Christovão Vieira's letter in D. Ferguson, *Portuguese captives*, pp. 71–74,
124. The wording of my translation differs slightly from that of Ferguson.
[2] Cf. pp. 41–42 *infra*.
[3] For accounts of these vast hereditary estates and their development under the
Ming, see H. Maspero, *Mélanges posthumes sur les religions et l'histoire de la Chine*,
III, *Etudes Historiques* (Paris, 1950), pp. 170–174, 185–189, 212; T. Shimizu,
'A study on the manors of the Ming period', in *Tōyō Gakuhō*, XVI (1927), pp.
334–350, 463–544; K. T. Wan, 'Royal and official estates in the Ming dynasty', in
the *Nanking Journal*, III (1933), pp. 295–310. These last two articles are in
Japanese and Chinese respectively.

trading was again relaxed, and the Fo-lang-chi subsequently sailed over the seas fearing nothing.'[1] They were, however, sufficiently impressed by the events of 1548–1549, to transfer their efforts from Chekiang and Fukien back towards their old haunts in Kuangtung province. The general prohibition on overseas trade, which had been imposed at Canton at the time of the expulsion of the Portuguese in 1522, was apparently the cause of widespread hardship and discontent in Kuangtung, which led the local high officials repeatedly to petition Peking for leave to reopen the port. This was finally granted in 1530, but it was expressly stipulated that the Fo-lang-chi should not be allowed to return with the other foreigners but should still be refused leave to trade.[2] It may be asked why foreign trade was so important to China—or at any rate to Kuangtung—that the Imperial Court was forced to reopen Canton. Friar Gaspar da Cruz noted in 1556, after the Portuguese were allowed to come to Canton along with other foreigners, that China's overseas trade 'is so little in comparison of the great traffic of the country, that it almost remaineth as nothing and unperceived'. He added that the shipping engaged in foreign trade was an infinitesimal fraction of that engaged in the coastal and inland navigation. The principal Portuguese imports at this period were ivory and pepper, and these, as the worthy Dominican noted, 'a man may well live without'.[3] But, as in contemporary Europe, spices were in great demand at the Court of Peking. In addition to spices, ivory and aromatic woods were imported by the Portuguese in exchange for Chinese silk, porcelain and musk. In other words, the trade was a luxury trade; and if small in volume it was great in value by contemporary standards.

With the development of Portuguese trade with Japan, and the opening of new silver-mines in the island-empire, a change came over the nature of Portuguese commerce with China, which now became primarily a matter of exchanging Chinese silks and gold for Japanese silver bullion. As noted above, the Portuguese were able to get a firm grip on this valuable trade owing to the international repercussions of the ravages of the Wakō. Writing from Malacca on the 1 December 1555, the Jesuit Luis Frois recorded

[1] *Ming-shih*, ch. 325, quoted in W. H. Chang, *Commentary*, p. 48.
[2] T. T. Chang, *Sino-Portuguese Trade*, pp. 63–75; J. M. Braga, *Western Pioneers*, pp. 78–84.
[3] Cf. Gaspar da Cruz, ch. IX, p. 112 *infra*.

that 'Last year we learnt from the ships that came here from China that there were very great quarrels and disputes between China and Japan. A great fleet from Camgoxima [Kagoshima] had destroyed many places in China which were situated along the sea coast, including a very populous city [T'ai-ts'ang] where the Japanese had wrought great destruction and captured some very great lords who were in it. They say that these wars are so fierce that they will not be appeased for many years. This discord between China and Japan is a great help to the Portuguese who want to go to Japan; for as the Chinese do not go thither to trade with their merchandise, the Portuguese merchants have a great advantage in negotiating their worldly business.[1]' This profitable commerce reached its apogee after the Portuguese had secured a firm base in China at Macao (1557), and another in Japan at Nagasaki (1571), but there is no need to treat this development in detail here.[2] We may conclude this survey of early Sino-Portuguese relations by outlining the circumstances which enabled the Fo-lang-chi to establish themselves at Macao.

Within a year or two of their expulsion from Fukien, we find the Portuguese frequenting the islands of Shang-ch'uan (São João or Saint John's as Europeans called it) and Lampacau or Lang-pai-kao off the coast of Kuangtung, apparently with the connivance of the local mandarins.[3] As hitherto, they merely erected matsheds ashore for the duration of the trading-season, and sailed away to Malacca or to Japan when they had concluded their business. The precarious nature of their tenure, and the rapid development of the Japan trade, rendered it increasingly urgent for the Portuguese to get a firm base on the South China coast within easy reach of Canton. This was at last secured in 1554 by the Captain-major, Leonel de Sousa, who after prolonged negotiations concluded a verbal agreement with Wang Po, the acting commander of the coastguard fleet (*Hai-tao-fu-shih*), whereby the Portuguese were

[1] Letter of Luis Frois, S.J., d. Malacca, 1 Dec. 1555, in Jordão de Freitas, *Fernão Mendes Pinto. Sua ultima viagem á China (1554–1555)*, reprinted from *Archivo Historico Portuguez*, III (Lisbon, 1905); cf. also Tsunoda-Goodrich, *Japan in the Chinese Dynastic Histories*, pp. 129–130.

[2] For details see C. R. Boxer, *The Christian Century in Japan 1549–1650* (Berkeley, 1951), pp. 91–121, 425–427, and Delmer M. Brown, *Money economy in medieval Japan* (New Haven, 1951), pp. 56–66, 72–77.

[3] Yano's article in *Boletim da Sociedade Luso-Japonesa*, I, 70–77; T. T. Chang, *Sino-Portuguese trade*, pp. 86–88; J. M. Braga, *Western Pioneers*, pp. 80–84.

c

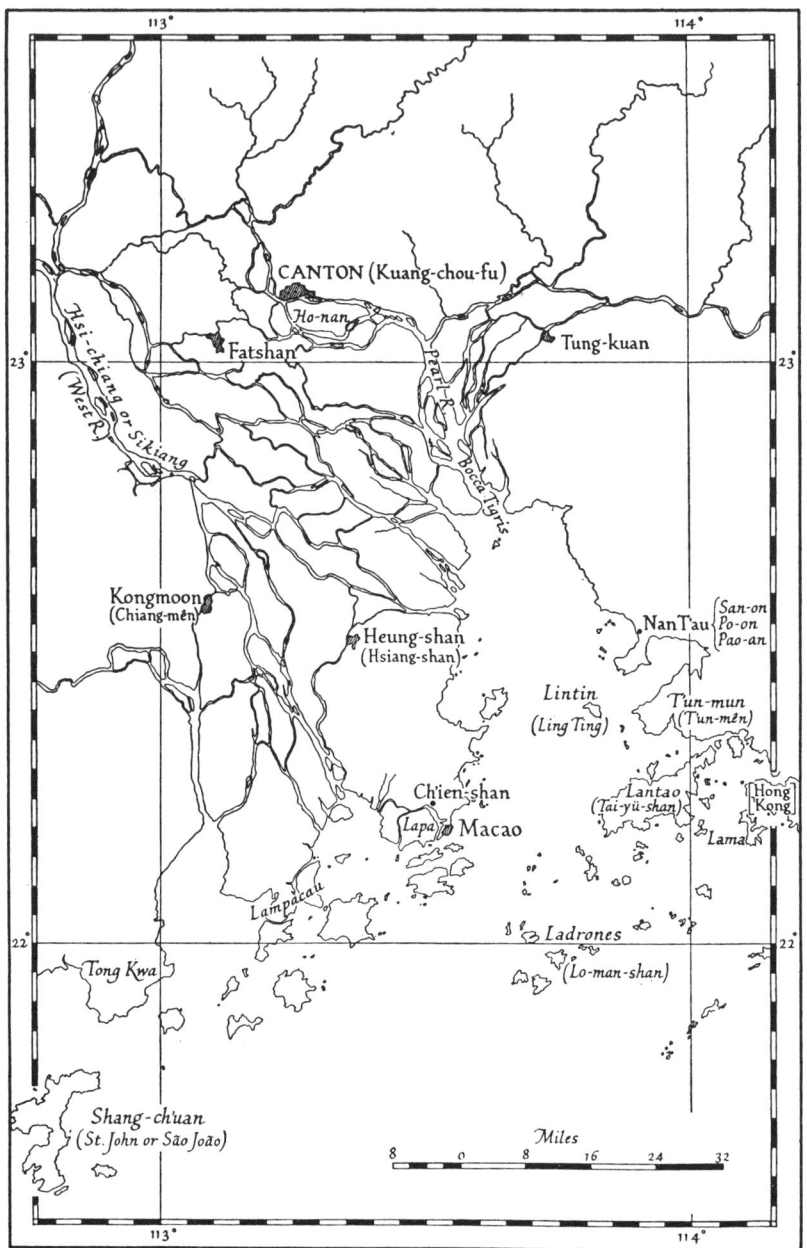

Fig. 4. The Pearl and the West River estuaries

allowed to trade in Kuangtung on the same terms as the Siamese.[1]
It is clear from De Sousa's own account of this arrangement, that
it was a verbal one; and it also seems that the Portuguese were not
admitted as Fo-lang-chi, but as Siamese, or as foreigners belonging to some other of China's tributary states. However this
may be, the agreement suited both parties, and consequently had
a much longer lease of life than one would expect from an oral
arrangement made after much junketing on board the Portuguese
ships.[2] At first the Portuguese frequented Shang-ch'uan island
where St. Francis Xavier had died in December 1552, but they
afterwards transferred their embryo settlement to the smoother and
more sheltered waters of Lang-pai-kao, and then, in 1557 or thereabouts, to the 'Bay (or shrine) of the goddess A-ma', or Macao.[3]

Much has been written on the origins of the settlement at Macao
itself, but nothing definite has been established.[4] The Portuguese
certainly frequented the place prior to 1557, as we know by the
letters written there by some Jesuits in 1555.[5] It has been suggested that the 'water-lily peninsula' was given to the Portuguese
in return for their help in suppressing piracy in the Pearl River
estuary; and if there is no definite proof of this, neither is it
inherently improbable.[6] I only wish to draw attention here to one
contemporary source which has been overlooked by most writers on
the subject. This is an undated Spanish transcript of a document
written about 1570 by Gregorio Gonçalves, 'presbitero secular', addressed to Don Juan de Borja, the Spanish ambassador in Portugal.[7]

[1] Leonel de Sousa's letter of 15 Jan. 1555, which is the only contemporary
piece of evidence for the existence of this agreement, has often been published,
most recently by J. M. Braga, *Western Pioneers*, pp. 84–86, 202–208.

[2] 'foram de mim muyto bem hagasalhados, e banqueteados com algũas
dadivas que elles tomaram escondido', as Leonel de Sousa wrote in this letter of
15 January 1555. (Braga, *op. cit.*, p. 205.)

[3] For the origin of the name of Macao, and a list of its numerous other Chinese
names, cf. J. J. L. Duyvendak in *T'oung Pao*, Second Series, XXXIX, 188–190
and J. M. Braga, *Western Pioneers*, pp. 103–105.

[4] The latest and fullest discussion is in J. M. Braga, *Western Pioneers*, pp.
102–139.

[5] *Cartas que os Padres e Irmãos da Companhia de Jesus escreverão dos Reynos de
Iapão e China . . . desdo anno de 1549 ate o de 1580* (Evora, 1598), fls. 32 verso.

[6] This point is fully discussed in Braga, *Western Pioneers*, pp. 109–118.

[7] Archivo de Indias de Sevilla, 67-6-27. Printed by P. Pastells, *Catálogo de los
documentos relativos a las islas Filipinas existentes en el archivo de Indias de Sevilla*,
I, cclii–ccliii.

The writer claims that he stayed ashore in the year that Leonel de Sousa concluded his agreement with the Chinese, and built a church thatched with straw. After the departure of the Portuguese ships, he and his few Chinese converts were seized by the officials and 'scattered in different places, without one knowing the whereabouts of the other, the Chinese shouting at me that I was staying on shore to hatch some treason, and they detained us until the next year. We then came together again and I built another church and the Portuguese some houses'. He goes on to say that the Chinese, having thus got to know him, let him alone, and he was able quietly to continue his missionary work. Within twelve years the Portuguese had built 'a very large settlement on a point of the mainland, which is called Macao, with three churches and a hospital for the poor, and a house of the Santa Misericordia,[1] which nowadays forms a settlement of over five thousand Christian souls'. This is the only piece of evidence by a participant in the actual founding of Macao that we have, and unfortunately he mentions no dates. Nothing is said therein about Portuguese services in suppressing piracy, although it is very likely that they had done this locally, if only for their own benefit. In any event, it seems that the beginnings of the settlement were very similar to those previously established elsewhere along the Kuangtung and Fukien coast.

Finally, it should be added that the verbal agreement made between Leonel de Sousa and the provincial authorities at Canton was not reported to the Court of Peking, which was not aware of the establishment of the Portuguese at Macao until long afterwards. An ex-governor of the Philippines reported in 1582, that the Portuguese of Macao 'are still nowadays without any weapons or gunpowder, nor justice, having a Chinese mandarin who searches their houses to see if they have any such. And because it is a regular town with about five hundred houses and there is a Portuguese governor and a bishop therein, they pay every three years to the incoming viceroy of Canton about 100,000 ducats to avoid being expelled from the land, which sum he divides with the grandees of the household of the king of China. However, it is constantly

---

[1] A Charitable Brotherhood, for whose history at Macao cf. C. R. Boxer, *Fidalgos in the Far East, 1550–1770*, pp. 217–221; J. C. Soares, *Macau e a Assistência; panorama médico-social* (Lisbon, 1950).

affirmed by everyone that the king has no idea that there are any such Portuguese in his land'.[1]

(b) The Spaniards

In the period which elapsed between the discovery of Hispaniola by Columbus in 1492 and the conquest of Mexico by Cortés in 1521, the advantages reaped by the Spaniards from their American possessions did not seem so alluring as those derived by the Portuguese from their control of the Asian spice-trade. When the Spaniards finally realised that Columbus and his immediate successors had discovered neither Cathay nor the real Indies, one of their chief preoccupations was to find a way round the American barrier to the coveted spice islands of the Eastern seas. This was achieved by the voyage of Magellan in 1519–1521, and crowned by the return of Del Cano with a cargo of spices from the Moluccas, after Magellan had perished with many others in the fighting around Cebú. The spices brought to Seville in the little *Victoria* sufficed to recoup the initial cost of the whole expedition.

The Portuguese had been established in the Spice Islands since the pioneer voyage of António de Abreu and Francisco Serrão in 1512,[2] and they were not disposed to tolerate Spanish intruders in what was then regarded as the most profitable trade in the world. By the terms of the Treaty of Tordesillas in 1494, the boundary line between Spanish and Portuguese spheres of exploration and conquest had been fixed along the meridian running 370 leagues west of the Cape Verde islands. With the appearance of the Spaniards in the Moluccas, the problem arose as to where the Atlantic line of demarcation ran when continued on the other side of the globe. In fact, it followed approximately the meridian near which Tokyo in Japan and Adelaide in Australia are now situated, so that both the Moluccas and the Philippines were really on the

---

[1] Dr. de Sande to Conde de la Coruña, Mexico, 25 January 1582, in P. Pastells, *Catálogo*, II, lviii. Cf. A. P. Van den Wyngaert, *Sinica Franciscana*, II, 134, for confirmation of Dr. Sande's remarks. Fr. H. Bernard-Maître, S.J., in his valuable *Aux portes de la Chine*, p. 102 misunderstood the final phrase of this letter, 'el Rey no sabe que aya tal gente portuguesa en su tierra', which he mistranslates as 'le Roi de Chine lui-même ne sait pas qu'il se trouve tant de Portugais dans son royaume', thereby missing the point of Sande's remark.

[2] For this voyage and its results cf. A. Cortesão, *Suma Oriental* (Hakluyt Society ed.), I. lxxix–lxxxiv, and H. Leitão, *Os Portugueses em Solor e Timor de 1515 a 1702* (Lisbon, 1948), pp. 25–52.

Portuguese side of the line.[1] But the sixteenth-century Spanish and Portuguese cosmographers had very different ideas about where the Tordesillas line ran when continued in the Eastern hemisphere. The Portuguese confidently claimed that the Moluccas were well within their sphere, whereas the Spaniards as obstinately maintained that not merely the Moluccas but China and even Malacca fell within the Spanish sphere. Clashes were therefore inevitable, and speedily occurred when the Spaniards attempted to follow up Magellan's voyage with similar expeditions. Portuguese opposition in the Moluccas proved too strong for such exhausted Spanish forces as survived the long Pacific crossing. In 1529 the Emperor Charles V recognised the strength of the Portuguese position by renouncing his claim to the Spice Islands in return for a cash indemnity in the Treaty of Zaragoza.

Spanish interest in this part of the world now shifted to the Philippines, with which they had hitherto been only casually concerned. Magellan had originally christened this island group after San Lázaro, since they were first sighted on that saint's day. Later navigators called them the Islas del Poniente—the Islands of the West, or Islands of the Sunset. Their present name was given them in 1542 by Ruy López de Villalobos, in honour of the Infante Felipe who later became King Philip II. Villalobos was ordered to keep clear of the Portuguese-occupied Spice Islands, and to investigate the possibilities of trade, conquest and colonisation in the Philippines, where it was reported that the Chinese went 'to trade for gold and precious stones'.[2] This expedition proved to be a failure like those which had been directed to the Moluccas. Most of the survivors became prisoners of the Portuguese, and Villalobos died in the arms of Saint Francis Xavier in Amboina. The eighty-ton *Victoria's* cargo of spices in 1522 was still Spain's only tangible return for all the sacrifices she had made in this part of the world. Then the exploitation of the immensely rich silver mines of Mexico and Peru, which were discovered in the years 1545–1548, diverted Spanish attention from the Spice Islands and the Philippines for the best part of two decades. However, the Iberian *conquistadores*

[1] W. L. Schurz, *The Manila Galleon*, p. 17.
[2] W. L. Schurz, *The Manila Galleon*, p. 21. These early expeditions to the Philippines are fully documented in E. H. Blair and J. Robertson (eds.), *The Philippine islands, 1493–1803*, Vols. I–III, and P. Pastells, S.J., *Catálogo*, I–II, *passim*.

were not the kind of men to abandon an enterprise on which they had once embarked, and, in spite of so many failures, the Spaniards still had hopes of breaking the Portuguese monopoly of the spice trade. Another and this time more lasting effort was made in 1564.

The commander of the expedition which left Mexico under sealed orders for the Philippines was Miguel López de Legazpi, a Basque gentleman from Guipúzcoa, who had long been settled in New Spain. Cebú was reached in April 1565, exactly forty-four years after Magellan's death on neighbouring Mactan. Legazpi founded a settlement on Cebú, but his high hopes of finding spices in this region soon faded, although some reputed cinnamon was obtained from Mindanao. Small quantities of gold were found in possession of the natives, but not enough to suggest that the Philippines might rival the wealth of Mexico and Peru. The relatively modest trade of the islands was mostly in the hands of the Moros, whose commercial activities Legazpi described in a letter written from Cebú to King Philip on 23 July 1567.[1] 'To the north of where we are, or almost to the northwest, not far from here, are some large islands which are called Luzón and Vindoro [=Mindoro], whither the Chinese and Japanese come yearly to trade. The goods which they bring are silks, webbed stuffs, bells, porcelain, aromatics, tin, printed cotton cloths, and other trifles, and they receive in return gold and wax. The people of these two islands are Moros,[2] and when they have bought what the Chinese and Japanese bring, they trade throughout this whole island archipelago. Some of them have come here, although we have not been able to go thither, since we have too few people to detach them in so many places.'

The Chinese of Fukien had been trading intermittently with the Philippines for centuries before the arrival of the Spaniards, although historical notices of the islands before the Ming period are few and vague.[3] A work published in 1575 observes that

[1] Printed in P. Pastells, S.J., *Catálogo*, I. ccxciv.

[2] The Moros, as their name implies, were tribes who had accepted Islam, then creeping up from the south, their strongholds being in Mindanao and the Sulu archipelago.

[3] They are discussed by B. Laufer, 'The relations of the Chinese to the Philippine islands', reprinted from the *Smithsonian Miscellaneous Collections* (*Quarterly Issue*), Volume 50 (1907), pp. 248–284, and by S. Wada, 'The Philippine Islands as known to the Chinese before the Ming period', in *Memoirs of the Research Department of the Toyo Bunko*, No. 4 (Tokyo, 1929), pp. 121–166,

'Luzón produces gold, which is the reason of its wealth; the people are simple-minded, and do not like to go to law'.[1] The growth of Chinese influence on Luzón is described in Chapter 323 of the *Ming-shih* as follows. 'Tens of thousands of Fukien people came here for the purpose of trading, because the country was both near and wealthy. Some of them stayed for good and brought up their children there.'[2] As regards the Japanese, most of those who frequented Luzón seem to have been connected with the Wakō, but they were not averse from peaceful trading. Captain Juan Pacheco Maldonado, writing about 1572, noted that 'Every year merchant ships come to this island from Japan, their principal trade being the bartering of gold for silver, at the ratio of 2 marks or $2\frac{1}{2}$ marks of silver for one of gold'.[3] Their numbers and influence were not so great as those of the Chinese. The 'tens of thousands' of Fukienese who frequented Luzón according to the *Ming-shih* need not be taken too literally; Maldonado's more modest estimate of twelve or fifteen junks a year trading between Fukien ports and Manila is obviously nearer the truth.

Rumours of the wealth of the China trade at its source were not long in reaching the ears of the Spaniards. Andrés de Mirandaola, the Royal Factor in the Philippines, wrote to King Philip II from Cebú in 1569 that he had been told by the Portuguese on that island 'how they traded and trafficked along the coast of China and Japan, and how this was the commerce which supported them, for it is the greatest and most profitable trade which has been seen hitherto'.[4] The reports of the Portuguese were partly confirmed by two stray Chinese traders whom Mirandaola interrogated; but they assured him that the Emperor of China did not allow the Portuguese to settle ashore because he was nervous of potential foreign aggression. Like a true conquistador, Mirandaola concluded his letter by forecasting that the conquest of China would

---

[1] Quoted in B. Laufer, 'Relations', p. 257.

[2] Quoted in S. Wada, 'Philippine Islands', p. 151. I have followed Wada's translation as being more accurate than that of B. Laufer (*op cit.*, p. 50), but a comparison of these two versions with the original text shows the difficulty of translating Chinese into a Western language. Cf. also W. H. Chang, *Commentary*, p. 81.

[3] Cf. Pastells, *Catálogo*, I, ccxcviii–ccxix; Blair and Robertson, *Philippine Islands*, III, 298–9.

[4] P. Pastells, *Catálogo*, I, ccxiii–ccxix; Blair and Robertson, *Philippine Islands*, III, 33–43.

prove an easy matter for the Spaniards if the King would sanction this enterprise in due time. So tempting were the reports of the wealth of the little-known lands on the other side of the China Sea, that several stalwarts said there was no point in wasting time in attempting to conquer or convert half-savage Filipinos. They urged the abandonment of the islands, and an advance to the countries where the real riches lay, 'such as China, Lequios [Liu-chiu], Java and Japan'.[1]

In 1570 Legazpi moved his headquarters from Cebú to Panay, where supplies were easier to obtain, and whence he dispatched Martín de Goyti to make a reconnaissance in force in the island of Luzón. Goyti's subsequent report on the advantages of Cavite near Manila as a site for a future Spanish base, led Legazpi to consider another move. He wrote to the Viceroy of Mexico, pointing out that, if the King still had his eye on the Moluccas, then Cebú was better situated as a base. If, on the other hand, the King supported the advocates of an advance northwards and to the China coast, then it would be better to transfer his head-quarters to Luzón.[2]

After further consideration and consultation with his officers, Legazpi finally decided that the pacification of the Philippines could best be effected by the seizure of the Moro settlement at Manila which was the principal place on Luzón. Accordingly he left Panay for Luzón on the 15 April 1571. Manila was occupied without any difficulty in the following month, the submission of the local chiefs being speedily followed by that of most of the others on the island. Legazpi was justly proud of his new conquest, and urged the King to colonise Manila as soon as possible, since the place was ideally situated for trade with 'Japan, China, Java, Borneo, the Moluccas and New Guinea, as one can go to any of those parts in a short time'.[3]

A few days before his unexpected death from a heart-attack in August 1572, Legazpi wrote to the Viceroy of Mexico summarising

[1] Fr. Diego Herrera to Philip II, Mexico, 16 January 1570, in P. Pastells, *Catálogo*, I, ccxlvii; Blair and Robertson, *Philippine Islands*, III, 72.

[2] Legazpi to the Viceroy of Mexico, Panay, 25 July 1570, in P. Pastells, *Catálogo*, I, ccxcvi.

[3] Legazpi's letter of 1572, in P. Pastells, *Catálogo*, I, ccxcviii–ccxix. For details of the occupation of Manila see Fr. Gaspar de San Agustín, O.E.S.A., *Conquistas de las Islas Philipinas* (Madrid, 1698), pp. 218–231.

the information which he had been able to gather about China since his occupation of Manila.[1] On his way to that place in April 1571, he had ransomed fifty shipwrecked Chinese from the Filipino tribesmen at Mindoro and sent them back to China, in pursuance of his policy of giving all Chinese traders good treatment. He had considered sending two friars to China in one of the returning junks, hoping that they could make 'a treaty of peace and perpetual friendship' with the Emperor, but the Chinese refused to take them. The Chinese explained that the friars would not be allowed to land without a licence, but they promised to try to obtain one from the Fukien provincial authorities.[2] They gave Legazpi a rough sketch-map of the China coast from Canton to Ningpo, 'which they drew in front of me, without a compass, or order of altitude or degrees'. The voyage to Fukien was a matter of eight or ten days only, and the distance could not be more than 150 leagues. He had dropped his idea of sending some Spaniards back with them, so as to avoid causing alarm and despondency among the provincial authorities. This decision was the easier to take, since the Chinese would come and trade freely in the Philippines of their own accord. One of the Chinese castaways rescued from the Filipinos had returned to Manila after having been in Canton, where he saw and spoke with some Portuguese from Macao. This Chinese said that, when he told the Portuguese how well the Spaniards had treated him and his compatriots, the Portuguese replied that 'he should not trust us, for we were pirates who roved around plundering and robbing, and that they would come and throw us out of here. But he, without taking any notice of what they told him, came straight back here'.[3]

On Legazpi's death, the government of the colony was assumed

[1] Legazpi to the Viceroy of Mexico, Manila, 11 August 1572, in P. Pastells. *Catálogo*, I, ccci–cccii. Legazpi died on the night of the 20 August. Cf. also Colin-Pastells, *Labor Evangelica*, I, 133.

[2] Rada, in his letter to the Viceroy of Mexico, dated Manila, 10 August 1572 states just the opposite, *i.e.* that the Chinese offered to take two friars along with them, but that Legazpi refused to allow it without authorisation from the Viceroy or the King. P. Pastells, *Catálogo*, I, ccxcv; Gaspar de San Agustín, *Conquistas*, pp. 251–253.

[3] Cf. Gaspar de San Agustín, *Conquistas*, pp. 224, 246. The earlier futile efforts of the Portuguese to expel Legazpi and his companions from the Philippines are narrated at length in the *Conquistas*, pp. 177–182, 189–193, 201–210. For the Portuguese version cf. Diogo do Couto, *Decada VIII*, Cap. 25 (ed. Lisbon, 1673).

by another Basque, Guido de Lavezares, who had first come out to the Philippines in 1543 with Villalobos. Carping critics subsequently alleged that he was an old and tired man, devoid of enterprise and ambition. They instanced his abandonment of Juan de la Isla's projected voyage of discovery along the coast of China and Tartary, and thence back to Mexico by way of North America, which had been sanctioned by Legazpi. They also claimed that there were more quarrels and dissensions among the colonists during the first nine months of Lavezares' rule than there were during the nine years when Legazpi was at the helm.[1] These accusations were unfair. Lavezares was certainly an old man of over seventy, but he was active, intelligent and ambitious. He fostered the trade with China no less carefully and tactfully than had his predecessor; and at one time he even advocated the conquest and conversion of the Ming empire. In order that King Philip II could appreciate the situation in East Asia, he sent him (in July 1574) a manuscript chart of the island of Luzón and the China coast, together with a Chinese printed geographical compendium, including relevant information about Japan and the Liu-chiu.[2] In other dispatches of the same month, he described the welcome growth of the Fukien junk-trade with Manila, despite the damage caused by 'the numerous pirates who infest the coast of China'.[3]

One moonlit night towards the end of November 1574, a Spanish soldier on the coast of Ilocos descried a large and well-gunned fleet steering southwards in an orderly formation. The soldier's first impression was that this was a Portuguese armada, come to make good their threat of dislodging the Spaniards from the Philippines once for all. He reported this alarming news to his commander, Juan de Salcedo, Legazpi's Mexican-born grandson and the *encomendero* (feudatory) of Vigan, who likewise sighted the armada.[4] Though puzzled as to the identity of this mysterious

[1] Cf. the documents printed in extract in P. Pastells, *Catálogo*, II, xi–xiv; Blair and Robertson, *Philippine Islands*, III, 260–276.

[2] Lavezares to King Philip II, 30 July 1574, in P. Pastells, *Catálogo*, II, xxii. This Chinese book 'en que se hallaba escrito y figuredo de molde todo este Reino' may have been one of the early editions of the Ming Atlas, *Kuang-yü-t'u*, but I can trace no further reference to it in the Seville archives.

[3] Lavezares' letters of 16 and 17 July, 1574, in P. Pastells, *Catálogo*, II, xv; Blair and Robertson, *Philippine Islands*, III, 276.

[4] Juan de Salcedo came out to the Philippines in 1567. He has been called the 'Cortés of the Philippines', and was undoubtedly the greatest *conquistador* of

fleet, Salcedo realised that Manila must be its objective, and he lost no time in repairing thither with a force of fifty arquebusiers in seven oared vessels. He reached the city in the nick of time on 1 December, after a six day voyage of 180 miles on a rough sea. Salcedo found that Manila had barely staved off a surprise attack on the night of 30 November by the invaders, who turned out to be Chinese corsairs under the leadership of a Cantonese adventurer named Lin [Ah] Feng, subsequently known to the Spaniards as Limahon. The Chinese renewed the attack on 2 December, but were repulsed after a fierce fight in which the Japanese leader of the assaulting columns was killed. Limahon, being unable to induce his men to renew the battle for the third time, sailed back along the west side of Luzón to Pangasinán, where he fortified himself on a hill overlooking the river of that name. Here he was blockaded by the indefatigable Juan de Salcedo with a force of 250 Spaniards and 1,500 Filipinos, at the end of March 1575.[1]

The blockade of the pirate stronghold had only lasted a few weeks when an Imperial Chinese war-junk arrived off Pangasinán. The commander of this vessel was the *Pa-tsung* (coastguard garrison commander) Wang Wang-kao,[2] who had been sent by the Viceroy of Fukien and Chekiang to find the whereabouts of Limahon, one of the worst piratical scourges of the China coast for some years past. Wang Wang-kao was well received by Salcedo who sent him on to Manila, together with a Chinese merchant called (by the Spaniards) 'Sinsay'[3] who acted as adviser and interpreter to the Camp-master and Governor. Guido de Lavezares gave Wang a

them all, having pacified most of Luzón and the adjacent islands before he was twenty-five years old. After saving Manila from the Chinese in 1574–1575, he returned to Ilocos, where he died suddenly on 11 March 1576. For his biography see W. E. Retana's edition of Dr. Antonio de Morga, *Sucesos de las Islas Filipinas* (Madrid, 1909), pp. 569–970 (cited hereafter as Morga-Retana).

[1] The campaign of 1574–1575 is very fully documented. For the Spanish side cf. Gaspar de San Agustín, *Conquistas*, pp. 275–302; P. Pastells, *Catálogo*, II, xxiv–xlix; Blair and Robertson, *Philippine Islands*, IV, 1–97; González de Mendoza, *History* (Hakluyt Society ed., Vol. II, pp. 3–118). For the Chinese side, cf. *Yenching Journal of Chinese Studies*, No. 8 (December 1930), pp. 1473–1491; *ibid.*, No. 9 (June 1931), 1869–1871; No. 10 (December 1931), pp. 2061–2081.

[2] *Yenching Journal of Chinese studies*, No. 10, pp. 2064–2065.

[3] 'un Chino de mucha capacidad y buena intención', according to Fr. Gaspar de San Agustín, *Conquistas*, p. 294. I have not been able to identify this man in the Chinese records.

warm welcome and promised him that when Limahon was killed or captured he would hand him over, whether dead or alive, to the Chinese authorities. The governor also gave Wang a number of Chinese prisoners (mostly women) who had been carried off by the rover from the Fukien coast and recaptured by the Spaniards at Pangasinán. The Chinese commander was so delighted with Lavezares' chivalrous co-operation that he offered to take some Spaniards as envoys from Manila to the provincial authorities of Fukien. This was the chance for which the Spaniards had long been waiting, and Lavezares at once accepted the offer. The envoys selected were two Augustinian friars, Martín de Rada and Jerónimo Marín,[1] accompanied by two military men, Miguel de Loarca, *encomendero* of Otón,[2] and Pedro Sarmiento, *encomendero* of Buracay.[3] The soldiers were to return to Manila with news of the embassy, leaving the friars in Fukien if (as was hoped) the Chinese authorities would allow them to stay there.

Lavezares instructed the envoys to present the letters and presents which he was sending to the Chinese authorities at Ch'üan-chou and Foochow. The friars were to give these Chinese officials ample assurances of Spanish friendship, and to request that missionaries should be allowed to preach the Gospel freely. They were to ask for a Fukien port to be assigned to the Spaniards for trade, as the Portuguese had at Macao. They were also to find out all they could about the character, habits and commerce of the

[1] Fr. Jerónimo Marín was born at Mexico City of conquistador parents. He became an Augustinian friar in 1556, and worked as a missionary in the Philippines and Mexico before his death in that latter country in 1606. Cf. Gaspar de San Agustín, *Conquistas*, pp. 524–525, for further biographical details. For Rada's biography see pp. lxvii ff. below.

[2] Miguel de Loarca was an old companion in arms of Legazpi. His account of the embassy to China is the fullest and best which is extant, and has been freely used in my notes to the text of Rada's 'Relación'. In later years he was magistrate of Arévalo (Panay) and wrote a very valuable account of the Filipino Indian tribes, extracts from which will be found on pp. 371–392 of J. Delgado, S.J. *Historia General . . . de las islas del Poniente llamadas Filipinas* (Manila, 1892). Cf. also Pastells, *Catálogo*, IV, 150, nr. 5812, and *Boletín de la Academia de la Historia*, Vol. XCVIII (Madrid, 1931), p. 424, for the location of Loarca's manuscripts, none of which has yet been published in full.

[3] Pedro Sarmiento was Alguacil Mayor of Cebú, and commanded an expedition of 100 men to help the Portuguese in Tidore against the Sultan of Ternate in 1585. In 1588 he was responsible for uncovering many of the Filipino plotters who were scheming to overthrow the Spaniards with the aid of the Japanese. Colin-Pastells, *Labor Evangelica*, I, 169–173; II, 672–673.

Chinese, together with 'all the other matters and secrets of the country which can be found and learnt'. If the provincial authorities insisted on referring the Spanish requests to Peking, then the friars were to ask for leave to stay in the country until the imperial decision was made known.

In view of what is often written (and often true) about sixteenth-century Spanish intolerance, it is worth noting that Lavezares expressly enjoined the friars that neither they nor any of their suite should mock or laugh at the idols, temples, or religious ceremonies of the Chinese, 'for it is said that this is something which they greatly resent'. They were not to manifest wonder or delight at anything they were shown, but neither were they to criticise or to slight it. No Spaniard was to be allowed to speak or deal with Chinese women, 'because the men are said to be very jealous, and it is a dangerous thing; great loss and inconvenience might result therefrom, thus affording a reason or pretext for opposing our plan'. To avoid the risk of brawls and quarrels, no Spaniard or Filipino should be allowed to walk the streets by night. Finally nothing should be asked of the Chinese without making prompt cash payment,—'so that they may realise the benefit which will result to them from allowing the Spaniards to go and trade with them there.' All in all, Lavezares' instructions of the 12 June 1575, can be fairly described as a model of their kind.[1]

The voyage of Fr. Martín de Rada and his companions to China, their reception by the provincial authorities of Fukien, their travels in that province, and their return voyage with the Chinese commanders to Manila, are described in the friar's own account which is translated on pp. 243–260 below. There is no need to repeat this information here, but I must mention two important events which occurred in the Philippines during Rada's absence in Fukien, and which had a decisive effect on the hitherto promising development of Spanish relations with China.

The Spaniards were convinced that the capture of Limahon was merely a matter of time, since the corsair's junks had been burnt by Salcedo's punitive column when this force reached Pangasinán at the end of March. It seemed, therefore, that Limahon had no

[1] Printed in Gaspar de San Agustín, Conquistas, pp. 306–308, together with Guido de Levazares' letter to the Emperor of China, which was translated into Chinese by Sinsay, 'very curiously written and sealed'. Loarca's version of this letter is transcribed in P. Pastells, Catálogo, II, xxxviii–xxxix.

chance of escape by sea even if he broke through his besieger's lines; but in making this natural assumption, Salcedo seriously underestimated his enemy's resource and audacity. By skilful use of camouflage, Limahon secretly built thirty-three small craft in his improvised stronghold, and managed to slip away down the river to the open sea on the night of 2/3 August, to the surprise and consternation of the Spaniards, whose tardy pursuit of him proved fruitless.[1] Three weeks after this disaster, a new governor arrived from Mexico and took charge of the colony on the 24 August. The replacement of the tactful and experienced Guido de Lavezares by the learned and conceited Dr. Francisco de Sande at this juncture proved to be singularly unfortunate.

Rada and his companions returned to Manila in a Chinese squadron of ten war-junks whose commander, 'Siahoya Oxiaguac' (?), was entrusted with the task of co-operating with the Spaniards in the final liquidation of Limahon. The news of the pirate's escape, which reached the squadron off the Pescadores, naturally shook the confidence of the Chinese commander in the Spaniards' good faith, and relations deteriorated still further after the arrival of the party at Manila. The Chinese officers carried rich presents from the provincial authorities of Fukien for the governor of Manila, but they insisted on delivering them to Lavezares, for whom they had been originally intended, instead of to his successor. Dr. de Sande's pride was obviously piqued by this incident, and he subsequently displayed a consistent antipathy to China and the Chinese.[2]

Juan González de Mendoza in his celebrated *History* states that the Chinese commander stayed for six months in Manila, and that he and his Spanish hosts parted with mutual respect and esteem.[3] In this, however, Mendoza has seriously misrepresented his authorities, for contemporary records tell a very different story. Over five hundred Chinese were lodged in the little settlement (not yet recovered from Limahon's attack), many of them in the Spaniards' own houses, from November 1575 to May 1576. It is not surprising that this influx proved too much for the scanty food-

---

[1] Fr. Gaspar de San Agustín, *Conquistas*, pp. 301–302.

[2] Fr. Gaspar de San Agustín, *Conquistas*, p. 310. I cannot identify the proper name of the Chinese commander, 'Siahoya Oxiaguac.'

[3] González de Mendoza, *History*, Part II, Book I, Ch. XXXII, (Hakluyt Soc. ed. Vol. II, pp. 119–123).

supply and for the short tempers of their hosts. Consequently, the Chinese 'suffered hardships and left very discontented and very angry with the governor'.[1] Some eyewitnesses attributed their discontent not so much to their short commons as to the fact that Sande had not given them rich presents as they expected and as Chinese etiquette demanded.

Sande, in his turn, explained that it was decided not to give them presents lest they might take these as tribute;[2] but he claimed that he treated them generously at the expense of the royal exchequer, so as to induce them to take back two friars to Fukien. He added that the real reason for their annoyance was that 'As they were informed that Limahon had escaped them, and they are as weak as Indians, they wanted me to write to China that Limahon was dead; for this purpose they collected many human heads (for many natives of this country keep them as jewels)[3] in order to say that they were those of Limahon and his men. They made a false seal, saying that it was that of Limahon and had been taken from him; and they wanted me to write from here to China in the same sense. I always told them when they raised this matter, that we Castilians neither could nor would tell lies, and that they should give over such childishness.'[4] It may be added that the real fate of Limahon is uncertain. After effecting his spectacular escape from Pangasinán, he made a fleeting appearance on the China coast where he was apparently worsted in an encounter with the provincial naval forces, after raiding a few villages in Kuangtung and Fukien. One account adds that he escaped to Siam; but the only thing that can be said with certainty is that he was never again a menace to either the Philippines or the China coast.[5]

Disgusted at the escape of Limahon, and annoyed with De Sande for his churlish refusal to give them any presents for themselves or their superiors, the Chinese commanders finally left

[1] D. Salvador Diaz de Ceballos to the Viceroy of Mexico, Manila, 4 June 1576, in P. Pastells, *Catálogo*, II, xlv.

[2] In this, of course, he was quite right.

[3] For the head-hunting proclivities of some of the Filipino tribes at this period cf. Morga-Retana, *Sucesos*, p. 175.

[4] Dr. de Sande to King Philip II, Manila, 7 June 1576, in P. Pastells, *Catálogo*, II, xlvi–xlvii; Blair and Robertson, *Philippine Islands*, IV, 61–62.

[5] For different accounts of Limahon's end cf. Gaspar de San Agustín, *Conquistas*, pp. 325–326; P. Pastells, *Catálogo*, II, xlii; *Yenching Journal of Chinese Studies*, No. 10 (December 1931), pp. 2075–2081.

Manila for Fukien on the 4 May 1576. At the insistence of the
governor, they had taken on board Fr. Martín de Rada and Fr.
Agustín de Albuquerque; but they had no intention of taking the
friars to China without the head of Limahon or some valuable
presents to impress the provincial authorities. A few days later,
they dumped the two Augustinians ashore on a beach in Ilocos,
'which was the least harm they could have done them, . . . but
they beat a Chinese interpreter whom the Religious were taking
with them within an inch of his life. They killed the Chinese whom
they took from here, and who were Limahon's men, so that there
would be nobody left to tell the truth about what had happened to
the tryant, and for other barbarous reasons which moved them.'[1]
Such was the ignominious end of the promising relations which the
Spaniards had established with the Chinese authorities a year
previously.

A comparison of the contemporary accounts of the events of
1575-1576, makes it fairly clear that if Salcedo had killed or captured
Limahon, then in all probability the Spaniards would have been
allowed a settlement in the Bay of Amoy, similar to that which the
Portuguese had obtained at Macao, for their help (so it seems) in
bridling local piracy. When Rada and his companions started on
their return voyage from Amoy in September 1575, they were
shown from the ship's deck the place which would be given the
Spaniards for a trading-post if all went well. This was evidently
the island of Wu-hsü, or some place on the shore at the foot of the
hill on which stands the old stone tower of Nan-t'ai-wu, at the
southern entrance to the Bay of Amoy.[2] Owing to Salcedo's
tactical blunder at Pangasinán and to Dr. Francisco de Sande's
offended vanity, the Spaniards never occupied this site, but the
tradition that they had done so evidently lingered for long in the
Amoy region.[3]

[1] The Cabildo of Manila to King Philip II, 2 June 1576, in P. Pastells,
Catálogo, II, xlvii–xlviii. For further details see pp. lxxiv *infra*.
[2] Miguel de Loarca, 'Verdadera Relación', Part I, Ch. XII, '. . . un cerro muy
alto que está en la tierra firme al entrar de la enseada que tiene una hermita en la
cumbre donde ellos dicen que han de poblar los españoles si se hacen las paces,
se llama Taibu y la punta baxo de este cerro se llama Gontzu.' 'Gontzu' is of
course a corruption of Gosí, the local pronunciation of Wu-hsü. Cf. Appendix I,
pp. 318–319 *infra*.
[3] M. Pitcher, *In and about Amoy* (ed. Shanghai, 1912), p. 43, *apud* H. Bernard-
Maître, *Les Iles Philippines*, p. 18; cf. also *China Review*, XIX, p. 48.

D

Possibly one reason for Sande's cavalier attitude towards the Chinese, was his conviction that they could easily be conquered by a Spanish expeditionary force from Manila with the assistance of Japanese and Filipino auxiliaries, 'who are much braver than they are'. The bellicose governor begged his royal master seriously to consider the prospect of the conquest of China, 'for it is very right that such a just and great king's hands and laws should encircle the globe'.[1] This crazy project received plenty of support from clerical and military hotheads at Manila; but, unlike the men on the spot, the Crown councillors at Madrid clearly saw the monstrous folly of such an undertaking. Their opinion was echoed by King Philip II who sharply rebuked his headstrong governor, 'As regards the conquest of China which you think should be undertaken forthwith, it has seemed to us here that this matter should be dropped; and that, on the contrary, good friendship should be sought with the Chinese. You should not act or collaborate with the piratical enemies of the said Chinese, nor give them any excuse to have just cause of complaint against our people.'[2]

2. THE WRITERS AND THEIR NARRATIVES

(a) Galeote Pereira

The seventeenth-century Portuguese genealogist, Belchior de Andrade Leitão, states that Galeote Pereira belonged to the Pereiras of Gege, lords of the manor of Castro Daire in the province of Beira.[3] He was the third son of Henrique Pereira, *Alcaide-Mór* of Arraiolos, and went out to India in 1534. He embarked in

[1] Proposal of Dr. Francisco de Sande and Diego Garcia de Palacios to attempt the conquest and conversion of China, Manila, 2 June 1576, in P. Pastells, *Catálogo*, II, xlviii–xlix. Cf. also Blair and Robertson, IV, *passim*, for this and other wild-cat schemes for conquering China. Sande's dreams of expansion were not limited to the Middle Flowery Kingdom. He also advocated the conquest of Achin in Sumatra, where the local rajah had recently received an auxiliary force of 500 or 600 Turkish arquebusiers, with whose aid he was rapidly extending the boundaries of his kingdom. Sande had small confidence in the co-operation of the Portuguese of Malacca. 'Waiting for the Portuguese to do something is a weariness to the flesh, for they are a poor people at best. Nearly all the inhabitants were born in India, and are children of Indians.'

[2] King Philip II to Dr. F. Sande, 29 April 1577, in P. Pastells, *op. et loc. cit.*

[3] I owe this reference to the kindness of Fr. G. Schurhammer, S.J., who also points out that Barbosa Machado (*Bibliotheca Lusitana*, Tomo II, Lisbon, 1747, *in voce* Galeote Pereira) and later Portuguese writers are mistaken in their assertion that Galeote Pereira was a son of Fernão Pereira and half-brother of the first Count of Feira. This Fernão died in 1467 and was a 'Dom'.

the ship *São Miguel*,[1] in the India-fleet of Captain-Major Martim Affonso de Sousa, whose *físico-mór* or chief physician, was the celebrated Garcia d'Orta. Galeote Pereira served with Pero de Faria, the patron of Fernão Mendes Pinto, at Malacca in 1539,[2] and was present at Saint Francis Xavier's sermon on the victory over the Achinese, at the end of October 1547.[3] He evidently made one or more trading voyages to the China coast between 1539 and 1547, but details of these are lacking. In 1548, he accompanied Xavier's great friend, Diogo Pereira, to Siam, where he fought in the Portuguese contingent which helped to defend the Siamese capital of Ayut'ia against the army of the Pegu king Tabinshweti.[4] He then went with Diogo Pereira to China, where the Portuguese found that Chu Wan, the recently appointed viceroy of the pro-vinces of Chekiang and Fukien, was determined to break up the smuggling-trade which they had enjoyed intermittently with the inhabitants of that coastal region since their forcible exclusion from Kuangtung in 1522.[5]

Diogo Pereira returned to Malacca towards the end of 1548 or early in 1549, leaving two junks laden with the bulk of the unsold goods and about thirty Portuguese, including Galeote Pereira, off the coast of Fukien. In March 1549, these two junks were captured by the Chinese coast-defence commanders, as described on pp. 194–195 *infra*, at Tsou-ma-ch'i or 'running horse creek', in the Chao-an district at the extreme southern tip of Fukien province, adjoining the Kuangtung provincial border. From here the Portuguese and other captives were taken to the city of 'Chincheo', which in this instance was evidently Ch'üan-chou, as it is stated to have been seven or eight days journey from the

---

[1] With '2,000 reis de moradia', according to the so-called 'D. Flamínio' codex, printed in *Ethnos*, II, 165, where his father's name is wrongly given as Galeote; or with 2,400 reis according to the Pombal Codex 123, folio 44, in the National Library at Lisbon.

[2] Letter of Pero de Faria to King D. João III, d. Malacca, 25 November 1539, in G. Schurhammer, S.J., *Die zeitgenössischen Quellen zur Geschichte Portugie-sisch-Asiens und seiner Nachbarländer zur Zeit des hl. Franz Xaver* (Leipzig, 1932), p. 34, nr. 437.

[3] *Monumenta Xaveriana*, II (Madrid, 1912), pp. 274–5.

[4] Diogo do Couto, *Decada VI*, Livro vii, cap. 9. There were several Diogo Pereiras in Asia during this period, but this one was a celebrated fidalgo from the Azores whose spectacular career in the East is outlined in my *Fidalgos in the Far East*, pp. 32–35.

[5] Cf. pp. xxi–xxvi above and pp. 190–193 below.

provincial capital of Foochow.[1] It is not clear from Galeote
Pereira's description of their journey and his confused references
to the great stone bridges which they passed on their way,
whether the captives were taken via Chang-chou and T'ung-an to
Chüan-chou, or whether they went all or part of the way by sea.
It is possible that in the first instance they were taken to Chang-
chou, as this city was the administrative headquarters of the border

(a) *From the Ch'ou-hai-t'u-pien*, 1562   (b) *From an Admiralty chart*

Fig. 5. T'ung-shan Bay

region in which they were captured. On the whole, however, it
seems likely that they were taken overland from some point on the
Bay of Amoy to Chüan-chou; and it is clear that they were taken
thence to Foochow by land, and that they remained in the provincial capital for over a year.[2] As mentioned previously, some of
the Portuguese and their slaves, together with nearly all of their
ninety-odd Chinese smuggler-confederates, were summarily
executed, and the remainder naturally expected to share their fate.
Fortunately for them, Chu Wan's enemies at the Court of Peking
now impeached him for carrying out the death sentences without

[1] '... formos trazidos a Funcheo (que he hũa comarca) outo dias de caminho
de Chincheo',—letter of Affonso Ramiro (or Ramirez) dated 1555. (Bibl. de
Ajuda, Lisbon, Codex 49–IV–49 fol 234, and Bibl. da Academia das Sciencias,
Codex 'Cartas do Japão' Vol. I, fl. 255*v*–257). The Spanish embassy of 1575 took
seven days to cover the distance between Ch'üan-chou and Foochow. Cf.
Appendix I, p. 318 *infra*.

[2] Twenty-two months, according to Affonso Ramiro's letter of 1555.

awaiting confirmation from the Imperial Court. This was a serious
offence in Ming China, where capital punishment could only be
inflicted in peace time at the annual autumn assizes after confirmation of the death-sentence by the Dragon Throne,—at any rate in
theory.[1] The dispatch of an imperial commission of enquiry to
Foochow, the interrogation of the captive Portuguese, the disgrace
of Chu Wan and many of his subordinates, and the exiling of the
Portuguese survivors to Kuangsi are described elsewhere in this
work (pp. 199–211). Here we have only to consider the route taken
by Galeote Pereira and his companions from Foochow to
Kueilin.

It is not clear from the confused and scrappy accounts of their
journey to Kuangsi, whether the Portuguese were taken through
Kiangsi and Kuangtung provinces, or through Kiangsi and
southern Hukuang to their destination. If the former, then they
presumably went over the 'ambassadors' road' through the
Meiling pass, down the North River (Pei-kiang) to its junction
with the West River (Hsi-chiang or Si-kiang), and thence via
Wuchow up the Cassia River (Kuei-kiang) to Kueilin. If the latter,
then they presumably went via the Siang-kiang and the Kuei-
kiang to Kueilin. Galeote Pereira makes confusion worse con-
founded by implying that they went direct from Kiangsi province
into Kuangsi, which is, of course, impossible. They must have
passed either through northern Kuangtung or through southern
Hukuang in order to get to Kuangsi, as a glance at the map will
show. It is pretty clear that at one stage of their journey Galeote
Pereira and his companions went up (or down) the Cassia River, as
his account of this river tallies remarkably well with those of later
travellers.[2] This is on the assumption that Pereira's 'rio Camcim'
is identical with the Kuei River, at least in part. Phonetically the
Chang-shui River in southern Kiangsi is nearer the mark, but it
would be a mistake to attach too much importance to this name.
Apart from possible copyist's corruptions, Chinese rivers are
often known locally by different names along different stretches of

[1] Cf. *Ming-shih*, chüan 94; *China Review*, XIII, 401; *ibid.*, II, 173–175, 230–
244; Couling, *Encyclopedia Sinica*, p. 467.

[2] Cf. for instance, A. S. Bickermore, 'Sketch of a journey [in 1866] from Canton
to Hankow through the provinces of Kwangtung, Kwangsi, and Hunan', in
JNCBRAS, pp. 4–12, especially pp. 5–8, and W. E. Geil, *Eighteen Capitals of
China* (London, 1911), pp. 104–111.

the same river. Pereira may have asked the name of the river along which he was travelling, and been told by his guards or the boat-men some name of purely local significance. His statement that on entering Kuangsi province, they went mostly downstream towards the south,[1] is more applicable to the normal route down the North River in Kuangtung (*not* Kuangsi) province. Moreover, his re-mark that 'the nearest port of the sea which it has is Canton where this river enters it',[2] implies that at some stage of his journey he travelled along either the West or the North River. He nowhere makes mention of any portages, although there must have been at least one of these, whichever route he took from Kan-chou-fu in Kiangsi. The muddled and self-contradictory nature of his account is obvious to anyone who tries to follow his route on the map. In the circumstances, one is reduced to guess-work; and my guess is that Pereira and his party probably went from Fukien via Ning-tu to Kan-chou-fu in Kiangsi, and thence up the Chang-shui river and over the Meiling pass into Kuangtung province to Shao-chou-fu.[3] I suggest that from here they went down the North River to its junction with the West River at San-shui, and thence via Chao-ch'ing[4] and Wuchow up the Cassia River to the Kuangsi provincial capital of Kueilin.

Whatever his route, it is certain that Pereira spent some time in Kueilin, which he calls the 'city of Kuangsi', and he also visited Wuchow. Soon after their arrival in Kuangsi province, the Portuguese prisoners, or rather exiles as they might now be more accurately termed, were divided into small groups and distributed among various towns in this province, enjoying thenceforward relative freedom of movement.[5] Several of them were thus able to get in touch with their compatriots trading at the island of Shang-ch'uan, through the intermediary of Chinese merchants. The Portu-

---

[1] 'Sendo o nosso caminho assi por este rio abaixo, comessou ser logo ao sul.' Cf. p. 34 *infra*.

[2] 'o mais perto porto do mar que tem he Cantão onde vay este rio entrar.' Cf. p. 35 *infra*.

[3] Also called Shiu-chow; or Ch'ü-chiang (Ku-kong) on some maps.

[4] Also called Shiu-hing on modern maps.

[5] Affonso Ramiro in his letter of 1555 wrote 'fomos trazidos a esta comarca de Conquedis [?!], e fomos juntos a principal cidade Consi, não podendo nos os Mandarins fazer maior mal, que repartir nos em mujtas partes sem sabello El Rej ... todavia fomos tratados honestamente graças a Deus nosso senhor'. Cf. also pp. 40–41 *infra*.

guese traders offered large rewards to any Chinese who would help
the exiled Europeans to escape to the coast, with the result that a
number of them were smuggled out to safety. Among the lucky
ones was Galeote Pereira, who reached Shang-ch'uan about the
time of Xavier's death, since he was among those present when
the saint's body was exhumed on the 27 February 1553.[1] Four
years later, he was one of the witnesses in the process for the
beatification of Xavier at Cochin.[2] I have not been able to ascertain
the date and place of his death. During his service in India he was
captain of Damão; and by his wife, Philippa Pacheco, daughter of
the secretary to the Archbishop of Braga, he had a son, Manuel,
who predeceased him.[3]

Galeote Pereira presumably jotted down his recollections of
his captivity in South China soon after his escape, but the oldest
surviving draft of his narrative dates from nearly a decade later.
As can be seen from the endorsement by Padre Luis Frois, S.J.,
on the contemporary *via* preserved in the Jesuit archives at Rome,
it was hurriedly copied by the children of the seminary attached
to the College of São Paulo at Goa at the end of 1561,[4] and included
as an appendix to the annual Jesuit missionary reports to their
headquarters in Europe. Allowing for the copyists' errors made by
half-trained native neophytes, the narrative does credit to Galeote
Pereira's reliability and acumen. He carefully distinguishes between what he saw and what he was told, nor did the hard conditions of his captivity warp his judgement or dull his interest in his
surroundings. His narrative is one of many which could be cited to
disprove the common allegation that the Portuguese pioneers in
Asia made no efforts to understand the people with whom they
mixed.[5]

[1] *Monumenta Xaveriana*, II, 276.
[2] *Monumenta Xaveriana*, II, 272 ff.
[3] Letter of Fr. G. Schurhammer, S.J., d. 20 Dec. 1950.
[4] '. . . somente hir mal trasladado pelos meninos da terra do Colegio por não
aver tempo.'
[5] For example, G. E. Harvey, *History of Burma* (London, 1925), p. 342, on
Fernão Mendes Pinto, . . . 'like a true Portuguese of his age, he makes no effort
to understand the customs and religion of the races with which he mixed', and
my refutation of this standpoint in 'Three Historians of Portuguese Asia,
Barros, Couto and Bocarro', reprinted from the *Boletim do Instituto Português de
Hongkong* (Macau, 1948).

Galeote Pereira's account of South China attained a fairly wide
circulation in its time, being translated (in a slightly abridged form)
into Italian and published in the *Nuoui Auisi Delle Indie Di
Portogallo, Venuti nuouamente dalli R. padri della compagnia di
Giesu & tradotti dalla lingua Spagnola nella Italiana, Quarta parte;*
printed at Venice in 1565.[1] It was from this version that the rene-
gade Dorset Jesuit, Richard Willis, made his English translation
which was first printed in the *History of Travayle in the West and
East Indies*, (London, 1577), and subsequently reprinted in the
well-known collections of Hakluyt and Purchas.[2] The Portuguese
draft of 1561 remained unprinted until its publication by the present
editor in the *Archivum Historicum Societatis Iesu*, Vol. XXII, (1953)
pp. 57–92.

Galeote Pereira was not the only one of the Portuguese captured in 1549 who wrote an account of his experiences, although
his account is certainly the longest and best. Another narrative
which found its way into print and at an earlier date was the
anonymous 'Enformação da China, que hum homem honrado que
là esteue catiuo seis annos, contou no collegio de Malaca ao Padre
Mestre Belchior' ('Information of China, which an honourable
man who was captive there for six years, related in the college of
Malacca to Father Master Belchior'), dated 3 December 1554.[3]
This was first printed in a slightly abridged Spanish translation in
the *Copia de unas Cartas de algunos padres y hermanos dela compañia de Jesus que escriuieron dela India, Iapon, y Brasil a los padres
y hermanos dela misma compañia, en Portugal trasladadas de portugues en castellano. Fuerõ recibidas el año de mil y quinientos y*

---

[1] Barbosa Machado, *Bibliotheca Lusitana* (Lisbon, 1747), Vol. II, *in voce*
'Galeote Pereira' has misled many subsequent bibliographers into believing that
Pereira's narrative was published at Venice as a separate work in 1565. But the
*Alcune cose del paese della China sapute da certi Portughesi che ivi furon fatti
schiavi; e questo su cavato de un trattato che fece Galeotto Perera gentil huomo
persona di molto credito il quale stette prjgione nel sudetto luogo per alcuni anni*,
which Barbosa quotes in a confused and inaccurate way, was in fact merely the
explanatory heading of the Italian translation printed on fls. 63–87 of the *Nuovi
Avisi . . . Quarte parte* (Venice, 1565), of which it forms an integral part. I
examined the copy in the British Museum (pressmark 867. d. 4, 5). Cf. also
Streit, *Bibliotheca Missionum*, IV, p. 238, nr. 913.
[2] For the chequered career of Richard Willis (fl. 1558–1578) see *Dictionary of
National Biography*, XXI (1909), p. 288.
[3] Biblioteca de Ajuda, Lisbon; Codex Ulyssiponensis, I, (49–1V–49) fls.
193v–197v; Schurhammer, *Die zeitgenössischen Quellen*, nr. 6062.

cincuenta y cinco, published at Lisbon in 1555.[1] This account was subsequently reprinted in several of the collections of Jesuit missionary reports from the East which were published in Italian, Spanish and French versions between 1556 and 1561,[2] including Francisco Alvares, S.J., *Historia de Ethiopia* (Zaragoza, 1561). It was from the Spanish version printed in this last-named work that R. H. Major made the English translation which will be found on pp. xxxix–li of his introduction to the Hakluyt Society's edition of Mendoza. Father Belchior Nunes, S.J., did not give the name of his informant, but Father G. Schurhammer, S.J., who has studied the records of this period with such thoroughness and care, tentatively identifies him with Manuel de Chaves who escaped to Shang-ch'uan (where he met Saint Francis Xavier) in 1552.[3] Against this theory must be set the fact that the 'Enformação' states explicitly that the informant had been a prisoner for six years in China, whereas Manuel de Chaves, like Galeote Pereira, escaped after three or four years captivity.

The accounts of Gaspar Lopes, Affonso Ramiro and Amaro Pereira need not detain us here. They will be found listed in the Bibliography at the end of this book (pp. 347–348), and in Father Schurhammer's monumental *Zeitgenössischen Quellen*.[4] Due use has been made of them in annotating the text of Pereira's narrative, but unfortunately they throw no light on one of the most difficult problems posed by this text, namely the route taken by the Portuguese prisoners from Foochow to Kueilin. It is of course possible, perhaps even probable, that the prisoners were not sent together in one group by the same way, but in different groups by different ways. The evidence on this point is conflicting. The writer of the 'Enformação' was chiefly impressed by the highways in the interior of the country, and infers that most of his journey of 120 days was made by road.[5] Galeote Pereira, on the other hand, waxes

[1] Streit, *Bibliotheca Missionum*, IV, nrs. 777 and 1918.

[2] Cf. the editions listed in Streit, *Bibliotheca Missionum*, IV, nrs. 805, 806, 807, 808, 850, and 880.

[3] Schurhammer, *Die zeitgenössischen Quellen*, nr. 6062; Schurhammer-Wicki, *Epistolae S. Francisci Xaverii*, II, pp. 499, 506.

[4] Schurhammer, *Die zeitgenössischen Quellen*, nrs. 4694, 6107 and 6159.

[5] 'They took us from this city where we were prisoners to another region, and we were one hundred and twenty days on the road without crossing the kingdom, and all the roads were paved and made even: and sometimes when we

eloquent over the network of China's inland waterways, and infers that the whole journey was made by boat from the time that they entered Kiangsi province. Affonso Ramiro implies that the Portuguese prisoners were not split up into small groups until they had reached Kuangsi province, but the evidence on this point is not conclusive. Nevertheless, despite these and other differences between the above-quoted narratives written by Portuguese prisoners (or ex-prisoners) in 1554–1562, they are sufficiently in agreement to prove that their authors were all originally captured with the two junks of Fernão Borges and Lançarote Pereira in 1549.

In compiling the present text, I have carefully collated the two oldest surviving copies of the Portuguese text, preserved respectively at Rome and Lisbon, with the printed Italian version of 1565 and Willis' English translation of 1577. I have thus been able to correct some of Willis' mistakes and to restore a number of passages omitted in the printed Italian and English texts. Such obscurities as remain, must be ascribed (as Padre Luis Frois explicitly stated on the endorsement of the original draft) to the haste of the children who copied the correspondence in the Jesuit College at Goa. It is only fair to their memory to add that the errors are not, on the whole, very numerous or very important.

Galeote Pereira's narrative was confessedly one of the chief sources of the Dominican friar Gaspar da Cruz's *Tractado*, so that a certain amount of duplication and overlapping between the two texts is inevitable. It will be found, however, that Gaspar da Cruz did not reproduce more than about a third of Pereira's narrative, and that the two, taken together, furnish a completer picture than either one of them taken by himself. The most valuable part of Galeote Pereira's narrative is his account of the administration of Chinese justice and prison economy. As Samuel Purchas judiciously noted when reproducing Pereira's account: 'You shall have a more full description of the country by later authors: who yet could not so well as this, tell their proceedings, severity, prisons, executions etc.'

(b) Fr. Gaspar da Cruz O.P.

Gaspar da Cruz was born at Evora, but neither the name of his parents nor the date of his birth is recorded by his biographers.
went by rivers, we asked if the other roads which went on further were similar, and they told us that they were.'

He was admitted into the Order of Saint Dominic at the convent of Azeitão, but the year in which he became one of the Friars Preacher is likewise unknown.[1] The first recorded date in his life is the year 1548, when he sailed for Goa as one of the band of twelve Dominican missionaries who went out to Asia under the leadership of their Vicar-General, Fr. Diogo Bermudes. A few other Dominican friars had gone to India before this time, but as chaplains to work among the Portuguese: the arrival of Fr. Diogo Bermudes and his companions marks the official beginning of the Asian missions of the Order.

Friar Gaspar da Cruz seems first to have worked in organising the mission on the west coast of India, and then at Malacca, where he tells us in passing that he founded a convent of his Order. This was evidently shortly before his abortive effort to found a mission in Cambodia in 1555–1556, which he describes in the first chapter of his work. Disillusioned by his lack of success in this country, he transferred his efforts to Canton, which city he visited in the winter of 1556.[2] Most of his biographers, who obviously did not trouble to read his book thoroughly, absurdly claim that he spent many years in China as a pioneer missionary spreading the gospel. He himself makes no such claim in his *Tractado*, and it is obvious from his own account that he spent only a few weeks in Canton, and that the Jesuits had preceded him to that city. It is evident that he spent a little time on the China coast on his way to and from Canton,[3] but it is quite clear that he was not more than a few months in China altogether.

Having met with no greater success at Canton than he had in Cambodia, owing to the reasons which he explains in Chapter XXVIII of his book, he returned, presumably, to Malacca, but almost nothing is recorded of his movements during the next twelve years. From a few passing allusions in his book, we know that he spent some time in Ormuz, and Fr. João dos Santos states that he went there after his return from

[1] Barbosa Machado, *Bibliotheca Lusitana, in voce* Gaspar da Cruz, gives the standard biography and a list of the works on which it is based.
[2] Cf. Ch. X of his Treatise, and p. 122 *infra*.
[3] Ch. XXIX, pp. 221, 224. For Gaspar da Cruz's Jesuit predecessors and contemporaries in Canton, cf. B. Biermann O.P., *Die Anfänge der neueren Dominikanermission in China* (Münster im Westphalen, 1927), pp. 2–5; H. Bernard, *Aux Portes de la Chine*, pp. 59–71.

China.[1] He gives no authority for this statement, but it may well be true, and there is every likelihood that he is the translator of the chronicle of the Kings of Ormuz which is included as a kind of afterthought or appendix to his treatise on China. The printer's heading to this chronicle merely states that it was 'summarily translated into the Portuguese tongue by a Religious of the Order of Saint Dominic who founded a house of his Order in the island of Ormuz'; but if Fr. João dos Santos' statement is correct, then the translator can hardly have been anyone else than Fr. Gaspar da Cruz.

Our friar apparently returned to Portugal in 1569, and embarked in the same fleet which carried the historian Diogo do Couto.[2] If this was so, Friar Gaspar must have sailed in the ship *Santa Catarina*, as this was the only one which reached Portugal this year, her three consorts being forced back by stress of weather off the Natal coast to winter in Mozambique. The *Santa Catarina* reached Lisbon 'at the height of the great pestilence', and Fr. Gaspar, despite the hardships of his voyage, lost no time in volunteering for work among the plague-stricken populace. When the force of the plague began to diminish in Lisbon, he immediately moved to Setúbal where it was still raging. Here he remained 'until the plague was over, and at the end of it he sickened of the same disease and died, as he himself had prophesied when alive, saying that he would be stricken and would die of the same plague, and that after his death nobody else would get ill from the disease, as happened: so that he was the last one who sickened and died of the plague in Setúbal, whence they carried him for burial in the convent of Saint Dominic of Azeitão, of which he was a son'.[3]

Fr. João dos Santos further assures us that 'a person of credit' had informed him that King Sebastian had decided to appoint Fr. Gaspar da Cruz as Bishop of Malacca, but that his death 'deprived him of this dignity in this miserable life, by God giving him other

[1] Fr. João dos Santos, O.P., *Ethiopia Oriental* (Evora, 1609), Part II, Book II, Ch. II. fls. 28–29.
[2] Diogo do Couto, *Decada VIII* (Lisbon, 1673), Ch. 28. From the accounts of Fr. Gaspar da Cruz's biographers, it is not quite clear whether he returned to Lisbon in 1569 or shortly before, but most of them give 1569 as the date of his return.
[3] Fr. João dos Santos, *Ethiopia Oriental*, Book II, fl. 29.

and greater ones in life eternal'.[1] Other writers give a slightly different version of this story, claiming that Fr. Gaspar da Cruz refused the proffered episcopal dignity out of modesty. His death on the 5 February 1570, virtually coincided with the publication of his book, the colophon of which is dated Evora, 20 February, 1570.

Fr. Gaspar da Cruz was obviously a missionary of more than ordinary zeal and energy, and a perusal of his book gives us the impression that we have to do with an exceptionally honest if at times rather naïve man. He frankly acknowledges his debt to Galeote Pereira and the kindnesses which he received on several occasions from the Chinese. He is not content with simply copying Pereira, but adds much information from his own experience, particularly about Chinese social life at Canton which clearly fascinated him. Among many more important things, he does not forget to describe his pet Cantonese song-birds, who turned December into April with their singing.[2] He naturally had his share of the prejudices of his age and nation, but he shows an astonishing broad-mindedness in many ways. He is the first recorded (and for a long time the only) European to appreciate Chinese music, and he found Chinese practices in husbandry and navigation in many ways superior to those of Europe.[3] He made good use of his eyes and ears during his short stay in Kuangtung; and he took the trouble to obtain translations of Chinese state documents and private letters which greatly enhance the value of his work. The unbounded admiration which (in common with his countryman Galeote Pereira) he expressed for many aspects of Chinese life and work forms an interesting contrast to the more critical attitude of Fr. Martín de Rada, as we shall see in the next section.

Apart from occasional lapses into religious bigotry, such as

[1] Fr. João dos Santos, op. et loc. cit. George Cardoso, Agiologio Lusitano dos Sanctos e varoens illustres em virtude do Reino de Portugal e suas conquistas, Vol. I (Lisbon, 1652), p. 353, adds that King Sebastian's selection of Fr. Gaspar as Bishop of Malacca was in recognition of the devoted courage which he had shown in succouring plague victims.

[2] 'eu tive dous, macho e femea, e em dezembro cantavam como fora em abril.' Cf. Ch. X, p. 122 infra. Gaspar da Cruz was luckier with his songsters than was Peter Mundy with his pet Cantonese goldfish nearly a century later. Cf. Travels of Peter Mundy (Hakluyt Society ed.), III, 267–268.

[3] Ch. IX and X, pp. 111–121 infra.

the iconoclastic scene in the temple at Canton described on p. 217, he reveals himself as an earnest missionary whose own high standards and character probably impressed many of those whom he failed to convince of the error of their ways. Perhaps he may be quoted as an exemplar of Sir George Sansom's observation that 'the record of missions in many Asiatic countries shows that the soundness of a doctrine is often less important than the character of its exponent'.[1]

The *Tractado em que se cõtam muito por estêco as cousas da China*, printed at Evora in 1569/1570, may fairly be claimed as the first book devoted to China which was printed in Europe, if we except the work of Marco Polo, which, after all, dealt rather with the 'kingdoms and marvels of the East' in general than with the wonders of medieval Cathay in particular.[2] Accounts of China had already been published by the Portuguese historians Fernão Lopes de Castanheda,[3] João de Barros[4] and Damião de Goes,[5] in their general histories dealing with the rise of the Portuguese power in Asia: but these accounts, like the narrative of Galeote Pereira and others which were embodied in the Jesuit annual relations, were not books on China, but only parts of books which dealt incidentally with China. Nine-tenths of Cruz's *Tractado* is directly concerned with China, and it is clear from his preface that he intended the book to be entirely devoted to that country. The inclusion of a few sheets relating to Ormuz at the end of the book is obviously an afterthought of the printer, as Cruz makes no allusion to this appendix in the preface in which he outlines the scope of his work.[6] To this humble Dominican friar, therefore, must be given the honour (if that is the right word) of writing the first book on China which was published in Europe.

[1] G. B. Sansom, *The Western World and Japan*, 104.

[2] H. Cordier, *Bibliotheca Sinica* (2nd edition), cols 1964–1987, lists the early printed editions of Polo's famous book.

[3] Fernão Lopes de Castanheda, *Os livros quarto & quĩto da historia do descobrimento & cõquista da India pelos Portuguezes* (Coimbra, 1553), Book IV, Ch. xxvii–xxxi.

[4] João de Barros, *Decada Terceira* (Lisbon, 1563), Book II, Ch. vii–viii.

[5] Damião de Goes, *Quarta e vltima parte da chronica do felicissimo Rei Dom Manuel* (Lisbon, 1567), Ch. xxv.

[6] Translated on pp. 56–57 *infra*.

Apart from its priority as the first European book on China, the treatise of Gaspar da Cruz has another claim on the reader's interest. Marco Polo's great editor rightly observed that 'in no respect is his book so defective as in regard to Chinese manners and peculiarities. The Great Wall is never mentioned, though we have shown reason for believing that it was in his mind when one passage of his book was dictated. The use of tea, though he travelled through the tea districts of Fo-kien, is never mentioned; the compressed feet of the women and the employment of the fishing cormorant (both mentioned by Friar Odoric, the contemporary of his later years), artificial egg-hatching, printing of books (though the notice of this art seems positively challenged in his account of paper-money) besides a score of remarkable arts and customs which one would have expected to recur to his memory, are never alluded to. Neither does he speak of the great characteristic of the Chinese writing. It is difficult to account for these omissions, especially considering the comparative fulness with which he treats the manners of the Tartars and of the Southern Hindoos; but the impression remains that his associations in China were chiefly with foreigners.'[1]

A perusal of the text of Gaspar da Cruz will show that the same criticisms cannot be made of his treatise. All the omissions of Marco Polo are there made good, and our friar has many observations on Chinese life and customs which anticipate those of the later Jesuit writers who are usually credited with first revealing China to Europe. It might, perhaps, be going too far to claim that Gaspar da Cruz made better use of his few weeks' stay in Canton than did Marco Polo of all the years he spent in Cathay; but there can be no doubt that the Portuguese friar gives us a better and clearer account of China as he saw it than did the more famous Italian traveller. Writers on the history of the Far East too often assume that nothing noteworthy about China was published in Europe between the accounts of Marco Polo and those of Juan González de Mendoza and Matteo Ricci.[2] Woeful ignorance of

[1] Yule-Cordier, *The Book of Ser Marco Polo*, I, 110–111.

[2] Cf. for instance, W. A. Appleton, *A Cycle of Cathay. The Chinese vogue in England during the seventeenth and eighteenth centuries* (New York, 1951), pp. 3–10; A. H. Rowbotham, *Missionary and Mandarin. The Jesuits at the Court of China* (Berkeley, 1942), pp. 29–51. The statement on p. 49 of this last-named work that Padre Melchior Nunes 'left a short account of the country and its institutions which is perhaps the first book on China to have been composed by

Portuguese and Spanish historical literature is probably responsible for this erroneous impression, at any rate in English-speaking
countries. I think that most people who have had the opportunity
of travelling in China and of reading the *Tractado* of Gaspar da
Cruz, will agree that this Portuguese account will stand comparison with any of those printed in Europe before 1625—and with
many of those printed much later.

One reason why Gaspar da Cruz's *Tractado* was not more often
quoted by subsequent writers was doubtless its rarity. Published
in Portugal in the great plague year, it never seems to have circulated widely. I have only been able to trace the undermentioned
ten recorded copies at the time of writing, and it will be seen that
only two or three of these are now in private hands. British
Museum (2 copies); Bibliothèque National, Paris; Biblioteca
Nacional, Lisbon (2 copies); Biblioteca de Ajuda, Lisbon; Casa de
Bragança, Vila-Viçosa; Livraria Coelho, Lisbon; Fischer Collection, Shanghai (in 1941); C. R. Boxer (the Christie-Miller &
Leicester Harmsworth copy).[1]

Portuguese writers in the vernacular never had much of a
circulation outside Portugal, since their works could not compete
elsewhere with those published in Spanish, French or Italian.
This is one reason why so much of their early work on China was
ignored. For example, the scholarly Italian trader, Filipo Sassetti,
on reading the *Decadas* of João de Barros at Lisbon about 1580,
observed that it was a great pity they were not written in some
language other than Portuguese.[2] Diogo do Couto, writing about

a European since the fantastic work of Fernand Mendez Pinto', is doubly
erroneous. The *Avisi Particolari Del Aumento Che Iddio Da alla sua Chiesa
Catholica nell' India, et spetialmente nelli regni di Giappon con informatione della
China* (Rome, 1558), quoted by Prof. Rowbotham (*op. cit.*, pp. 308–309) in support
of his assertion, is not 'the first book on China', but a collection of Jesuit letters
relating mainly to Japan, as stated in the title. Nunes' brief account of China,
written at Macao on 23 November 1555, occupies only fls. 16–27 of this work.
It was in any event preceeded by the lengthier 'Enformação' which was
embodied in earlier Italian, Spanish and French editions, as mentioned on p.
lvi–lvii above. Cf. Streit, *Bibliotheca Missionum*, IV, 215, nr. 837. Fernão Mendes
Pinto's celebrated *Peregrinaçam* was not composed (in its final form) until the
fifteen-eighties and it was not published until 1614.

[1] For further bibliographical details cf. *Early Portuguese books in the Library of
H.M. the King of Portugal* (London, 1935), III, nr. 121, where, however, only
four copies are listed.

[2] Sassetti was evidently unaware that the first two volumes of the *Decadas*
had already been published in an Italian translation in 1562.

twenty years later at Goa, doubted if there were then ten copies of Barros' work left in Portugal or one in India. Richard Hakluyt, in his 'epistle dedicatorie' of October 1601 to his translation of Antonio Galvão's *Tratado* printed at Lisbon in 1563, complained that he had vainly sought for a copy of the original edition for over twelve years.[1] Nor would it be difficult to adduce many other examples of the rarity of such Portuguese works and of the appreciation in which they were held (usually through the medium of some translation) by a few discerning foreigners.[2]

Among these discerning few may be numbered our John Frampton, who translated Bernardino de Escalante's *Discurso de la Navegacion que los Portugueses hazen á los Reinos y Provincias del Oriente, y de la noticia que se tiene de las grandezas del Reino de la China* (Seville, 1577)[3] into English under the title of *A Discourse of the Navigation which the Portugales doe make to the Realmes and Provinces of the East partes of the world, and of the knowledge which grows by them of the great things which are in the dominions of China* (Imprinted at London at the three cranes in the vine-tree, 1579).[4] As the Spanish Augustinian chronicler Fr. Jerónimo Román noted twenty years later, Escalante's *Discurso* was, for the most part, a thinly-disguised paraphrase of Fr. Gaspar da Cruz's pioneer *Tractado*.[5] It reflected Gaspar da Cruz's enthusiastic appreciation of the Chinese accurately enough, for in the English translation the Chinese are said to be 'endued with so great wisdom and discretion

[1] ' In all which space though I have made much inquirie, and sent to Lisbon, where it seemeth it was printed, yet to this day I could never obtaine the original copie; whereby I might reforme the manifold errours of the translator' (Hakluyt Society ed., 1862, p. vi).

[2] Cf. C. R. Boxer, 'Three historians of Portuguese Asia', reprinted from the *Boletim do Instituto Português de Hongkong*, I, 21–22, and *idem*, 'The Portuguese in the East, 1500–1800', in *An Introduction to Portugal and Brazil* (ed. H. Livermore, Oxford University Press, 1953), pp. 241–243 for further examples.

[3] Streit, *Bibliotheca Missionum*, IV, nr. 970.

[4] John Frampton had lived for years as an English merchant at Seville, before occupying his retirement in England in translating works from the Spanish. Cf. *Dictionary of National Biography*, VII, 599, and Streit, *Bibliotheca Missionum*, IV, nr. 982, pp. 257–258.

[5] Fr. Jerónimo Román, O.E.S.A., *Tercera Parte de las Republicas del Mundo* (Salamanca, 1595), p. 211, 'Este es propriamente, aunque disfraçado el librito que hizo Bernardino de Escalante que se intitula *Discurso de la navegacion*.' Escalante also made a good deal of use of the references to China in the *Decadas* of João de Barros.

E

in natural things, and in the government of their commonwealth, that no other nations (be they never so politic) seem to pass them, or have therein the advantage of them, nor yet to have the like wits for all manners of arts'.[1]

Escalante's work appears to have been little read and John Frampton's Elizabethan translation still less so; much more important for the diffusion of Gaspar da Cruz's work was the publication of Juan González de Mendoza's *Historia de las cosas mas notables, ritos y costumbres del gran reyno de la China* at Rome in 1585. As mentioned in the beginning of this introduction, this work had an enormous success with the reading public of Western Europe, and in it Mendoza frankly admitted his debt to 'Frier Gaspar de la Cruz a Portugall of the order of Saint Dominicke, who was in the citie of Canton, where he did write many things of this kingdome, and with great attention, whom I do follow in many things in the process of this historie'.[2] But although Mendoza generously gave credit to da Cruz in general terms, he seldom quoted chapter and verse, so that it is not always easy to determine where his indebtedness to Gaspar da Cruz ends and his reliance on Fr. Martín de Rada (his other principal authority) begins. After reading all three works, I consider that he relies on Cruz almost as much as he does on Rada for the chapters in which he discusses the social life of the Chinese.[3]

Fr. Jerónimo Román, whose *Republicas del Mundo* (Salamanca, 1595) will be discussed in the next section, likewise drew heavily on Gaspar da Cruz's *Tractado* for his account of China and the Chinese, and, unlike Mendoza, he usually gives the relevant chapter references. Román's excellent and conscientious work did not, however, attain anything like the popularity of Mendoza's 'best-seller', so general knowledge of Cruz's work was not much advanced thereby.[4] Of more importance in the history of travel literature was the inclusion of an abridged translation of Cruz's

---

[1] John Frampton, *Discourse of the Navigation*, quoting Escalante's original dedication to the Archbishop of Seville.

[2] *Historie of the great and mightie kingdome of China* (ed. 1588), p. 25; or Vol. I, p. 38 of the Hakluyt Society edition.

[3] Part I, Ch. I–XXII; pp. 7–156 of Vol. I of the Hakluyt Society edition.

[4] The first edition of the *Republicas* (2 vols., Medina del Campo, 1575), got Román into serious trouble with the Spanish Inquisition, and this may have adversely affected the circulation of the revised and enlarged edition of 1595.

Tractado in Samuel Purchas' *Pilgrimes*, Part III (London, 1625), pp. 166–198. As explained in the preface, it is this version which forms the basis of my own, which is not, however, a textual reprint of Purchas but one corrected and amplified after confrontation with the original Portuguese.

(c) Fr. Martín de Rada O.E.S.A.

Martín de Rada was born at Pamplona, capital of the Spanish (and Basque) province of Navarre on the 20 July, 1533. His parents, Don León Rada and Doña Margarita Cruzat, were both scions of noble families which traced their origins back to García Ramírez, one of the medieval kings of Navarre (1134–1150). At the early age of eleven years, accompanied by his elder brother, he was sent to study in Paris, where, according to his biographers, he particularly distinguished himself in mathematics, geography, astronomy and languages. After a stay of about five or six years at the University of Paris, Martín and his brother were compelled to return to Spain, on account of the unsettled conditions in France with the strife between Protestants and Catholics. Shortly after his return home, Martín de Rada entered the University of Salamanca, then at the zenith of its fame and justly proud of its motto: *Omnium scientiarum princeps, Salamantica docet*.[1]

A brilliant secular career lay open before him, but Martín felt that he had a religious vocation, and despite evident reluctance on the part of his parents—or at any rate of his father—he took the habit of Saint Augustine in the Augustinian convent at Salamanca

---

[1] The chief sources for the biography of Fr. Martín de Rada are (i) Fr. Gaspar de San Agustín, O.E.S.A., *Conquistas de las Islas Philipinas*, pp. 362–372, who claims to have had access to original papers in the Mexican headquarters of his Order; (ii) P. Gregorio de Santiago Vela, O.E.S.A., *Ensayo de una Biblioteca Ibero-Americana de la Orden de San Agustín*, Tomo III (Madrid, 1917), pp. 226–231, VI (1922), pp. 444–459; (iii) Fr. Manuel Merino, O.S.A., 'Semblanzas misioneras: Fr. Martín de Rada, Agustino', a well-documented article on pp. 167–212 of *Missionalia Hispanica*, Año I (Madrid, 1944). A full list of secondary sources will be found in the footnote appended to pp. 168–169 of Fr. M. Merino's article. A few documents by Fr. Martín de Rada are also translated in Blair and Robertson, *The Philippine Islands*, III, 253–259; XXXIV, 223–228, 286–294, and a (modern) portrait of him is reproduced as the frontispiece to Vol. III of that series. Cf. also P. Pastells, S.J., *Catálogo*, I, ccxcv, 184–185; II, xiii–xiv, xxiv–lvii; C. Sanz Arizmendi, 'Un capítulo para la historia de Felipe II (Relaciones entre España y China)', in *Actas y Memorias, Congreso de historia y geografía Hispano-Americanas, Sevilla, Abril 1914* (Madrid, 1914), pp. 447–449, 456–457; Streit, *Bibliotheca Missionum*, IV, 311–312.

on the 20 August 1553, making solemn profession of his final vows fifteen months later (21 Nov. 1554) at the age of twenty-one. He then continued his theological studies at Salamanca, matriculating in 1554–1556, after which he went to the convent of San Esteban at Toledo. How long he stayed at Toledo is uncertain. His early biographers are unanimous in asserting that he volunteered for the mission-field and went to Mexico in 1557; but Fr. Santiago Vela later discovered a document in the Augustinian archives which implies that he was still at Toledo in the spring of 1560.[1]

Whatever the date of his departure for Mexico, it was certainly before 1563. In May of that year he is listed in a catalogue of missionaries drawn up at Mexico city as being confessor in the Otomí Indian language—one of the most difficult and complicated of that country, and which was formerly believed to resemble (or to be derived from) Chinese. So successful was his work amongst these highland Indians that, in 1561 or 1562, he was offered the bishopric of Jalisco de Guadalajara in New Galicia; an honour which he declined since he did not wish to abandon his converts. Two years later, he was one of a numerous band of friars who volunteered to accompany Miguel López de Legazpi and Fr. Andrés de Urdaneta on their expedition to the Philippines, being one of those finally selected by his Superiors in February, 1564. The news that he had volunteered for the new mission-field greatly disturbed his Father-Provincial in Spain, who wrote post-haste to the Superiors in Mexico, peremptorily forbidding them to allow Fr. Martín de Rada to proceed on his projected voyage to 'China',[2] but this letter arrived when Rada was already on the Pacific.

Legazpi's expedition reached Philippine waters in February 1565, and anchored off Cebú two months later. During the next few years Martín de Rada was one of the most tireless missionaries

---

[1] He signed his name 'de rrada', and is often called Martín de Herrada in contemporary documents and later works. The difficulty caused by the document of 1560 is discussed in *Missionalia Hispanica*, I, 174–176.

[2] 'Tengo entendido que, entre otros religiosos que van a la China, envían V. R. R. al P. Fr. Martín de Rada' . . . At this period the word China was used to cover the Philippines whose new name had not yet taken root. However, other documents of the same year give the impression that the missionaries *did* intend to go to China sooner or later; cf. *Missionalia Hispanica*, I, 180. The Chinese were often referred to as 'Indios de China', 'Indios Chinos' and the like, as may be seen from the documents printed in P. Pastells, *Catálogo*, I–II.

INTRODUCTION lxix

in these islands, evangelising almost single-handed Cebú and Panay. The linguistic attainments which he had displayed at Paris and in Mexico stood him in good stead, and the Visayan language proved easy to him after the Otomí. Apart from catechising and converting the natives, he did much charitable work amongst the famished Spanish soldiery, and even found time to make numerous astronomical observations and calculations with an instrument 'for verifying the longitude' which he had brought with him from Mexico. His most valuable work was, however, undoubtedly his frequent intervention on behalf of the Filipino Indians against the excesses and oppression to which they were sometimes subjected by the Spaniards.[1] Rada was well supported in this attitude by his colleagues, and it was indeed the peaceful persuasion of the friars as much as the weapons of the conquistadores which was responsible for the relatively rapid and easy conquest of Cebú, Panay and Luzón. As his friend, Fr. Jerónimo Román, observed some thirty years later, the Spaniards and Portuguese could never have made the conquests which they did, nor kept them when made, but for the missionaries who accompanied the expeditions and tempered the violence and greed of the conquistadores, 'by reminding them that they were not sent to rob nor to kill, but to gain souls and to trade honestly, according to the most Christian instructions which their kings had given them'.[2]

[1] Cf. his letters and reports of 8 July 1569, 21 July 1570, 1 June 1573, 21 June and 30 June 1574, printed in whole or in part in P. Pastells, *Catálogo*, I, 184, 188; II, xiii; *Missionalia Hispanica*, I, 195; Blair and Robertson, *The Philippine Islands*, III, 253–259; XXXIV, 223–294; Colin-Pastells, *Labor Evangelica*, I, 134; II, 665.

[2] J. Román, O.E.S.A., *Tercera Parte de las Republicas del Mundo*, 210. This claim was echoed by the Bishop of Cebú, writing to the King in May, 1636, who praised the friars in the Philippines for 'endeavouring not only to gain souls for God by Christian means, but loyal vassalls for Your Majesty'. This prelate emphasised that so few Spanish soldiers could not have conquered such extensive regions 'if the ministers of religion had not, with their blandishments and gentle ways, attracted the natives to the yoke of the church. And still less would it have been possible, with the many vexations and forced labour inflicted on people who were not used to such, nor accustomed to recognise superiors, to keep them in obedience to your Majesty, if it had not been for the presence and care of the ministers of Religion, whom the natives venerate and esteem, since they find in them, in all their spiritual and temporal needs, the protection of true fathers' etc. (*Missionalia Hispanica*, I, 360–363, where the Bishop's letter is printed in full). It may be added that the missionaries were not always the models of decorum and moderation which they are portrayed as being here, and that sometimes the King or the Crown officials had to intervene to curb their bigotry

During the Portuguese blockade of the Spaniards on Cebú in 1568, Fr. Martín de Rada, as the recognised scientific expert of his side, spent much time in demonstrating to the Portuguese commander, Gonçalo Pereira, that the Philippines lay on the Spanish side of the Tordesillas line of demarcation.[1] As we have had occasion to observe, this archipelago was really on the Portuguese side; and the Spaniards evidently had some secret doubts as to their exact position, since they spared no efforts to obtain Portuguese charts of the China Sea and the adjacent regions. One of the paragraphs of Legazpi's original sailing-orders, on his departure from Mexico in 1564, stressed the desirability of his maintaining good relations with the Portuguese and enjoined him to try 'to see the sea-cards ("cartas de marear") which they use in their navigation, and if you can get hold of some of them, even by buying them you should do so, or at least obtain the copy of one of them'.[2] The instructions of the Mexican authorities to the pilot, Juan de la Isla, for his projected voyage of discovery along the coast of China and Tartary, likewise stressed the desirability of keeping on friendly terms with any Portuguese ship or ships he might meet, adding that if it came to a fight and the Spaniards proved victorious, they should take particular care to seize the Portuguese charts.[3] That the Spaniards did obtain—whether by fair means or foul—Portuguese charts of the China Sea, is evident from Miguel de Loarca's narrative of the embassy to China in 1575, where it is stated that the Portuguese charts showed 'Chincheo' to be in 24° degrees of latitude.[4]

We noted previously (p.xl) that the Spaniards soon heard about the riches to be gained in the China trade from the Portuguese whom they met in the Philippines, but Rada's first recorded references to China occur in a letter written by him to the viceroy

and intolerance. On the whole it can be said, however, that their influence at this period was mainly exerted for good, and in defence of the Filipino Indians against the excesses of their colonial masters.

[1] Gaspar de San Agustín, *Conquistas*, pp. 365–366; Santiago Vela, *Ensayo*, VI, 459.

[2] Presidente y Oidores of Mexico, instructions to Legazpi dated 1 September, 1564, in Pastells, *Catálogo*, I, cclix–x.

[3] Instructions of the Viceroy of Mexico for Captain Juan de la Isla, dated 1 February 1572, printed in Sanz y Arizmendi, 'Capítulo', pp. 450–455.

[4] Miguel de Loarca, 'Verdadera Relación', Parte I Cap. 4. Cf. Appendix I *infra*, and Diogo do Couto, *Decada VIII*, ch. 25.

of Mexico on the 8 July 1569. In this letter he gave a brief description of China, advocated its conquest, and explained that the missionaries hesitated to baptize as many Filipino natives as they otherwise could, since it was thought likely that the king might order the evacuation of the Philippines and the concentration of all Spanish efforts against China.[1]

Rada apparently did not take part in the expedition against Manila in 1571, but remained in Cebú until April of the following year, when he went to the new capital to attend a meeting of the Augustinian provincial chapter at the beginning of May 1572. He was elected Provincial by his colleagues and accordingly stayed in Manila. One of his principal preoccupations during his three-year term of office was the possibility of the conversion of China. Writing to the Viceroy of Mexico on the 1 July 1572, he stated that he had volunteered to go to China to verify the reports which he had received of its wealth—and weakness—from a Chinese named 'Canco', whom he had kept for some months in his house on Cebú. He added that the governor was unwilling to let him go until he had obtained authorisation from either the King or the Viceroy of Mexico; and concluded by saying that it would be a good thing if a couple of friars were sent—'for besides that this might well open a great door to the Gospel and the service of our Lord, it will also serve to give us thence a true notion of what there is, and they will tell the Chinese about the grandeur of our king and give them to understand that it is their duty to serve his Majesty, since he sends them missionaries at his cost and charges to teach them. And even if these should only serve as interpreters and to establish trade with them, their going will be of no little importance; and as for me, if I should be one of those to be sent, I would esteem it a particular favour and do it very willingly.'[2]

A few days after writing this letter, Fr. Martín de Rada was summoned to attend Miguel López de Legazpi in his last hours, (20 August 1572) and it was he who preached the redoubtable old conquistador's funeral sermon next day. The scene round Legazpi's death-bed in some ways recalls the death of the great

[1] Printed in Blair & Robertson, *Philippine Islands*, XXXIV, 223–228.

[2] Printed in Sanz Arizmendi, 'Capítulo', pp. 456–457. M. Merino, who prints it in extract from the same source (Archivo de Indias, Seville, Pat. 1–1–24, num. 22), dates it 10 August 1572. Cf. pp. xlii above for Legazpi's attitude to Rada's request.

Portuguese viceroy of India, Dom João de Castro, in the arms of Rada's fellow-countryman, Saint Francis Xavier, at Goa twenty-four years before. The new governor, Guido de Lavezares, likewise proved a good friend to the Augustinian friar, who busied himself during the next two years in supervising the conversion of Luzón and the neighbouring islands. Rada took an active part in the epic defence of Manila against Limahon, and subsequently accompanied Juan de Salcedo in his expedition against the pirate's stronghold at Pangasinán. His term of office as Provincial ended in April 1575, when he was elected prior of the convent of Ogtón in Panay; but it is unlikely that he assumed this post, since a few weeks later he was selected to head the mission to China which resulted from the meeting with Wang Wang-kao as narrated on pp. xlv–xlvi above, where Lavezares' instructions to Rada and his companions are also briefly commented upon. It will be recalled that the missionary motive was naturally placed first and foremost in these orders;[1] but more mundane matters were not forgotten, and two of the paragraphs dealing with trade are worth quoting in full: '*Item.* If the Viceroy and the governors agree that there may be trade between one kingdom and the other, for which they say that they have authority, or at any rate from the viceroy, you will ask them to designate a port for us, where our merchant ships can enter and leave securely, like the one that the Portuguese have. '*Item.* You will try to learn the quality of the people of the land, and understand their manners and customs, and what trade and commerce they have; and if they keep their word and speak the truth in what they promise, and what merchandise can be taken from here and brought from there, so that the trade may be profitable to both parties, together with all the other matters and secrets of the country which can be found and learnt. And if you are allowed to stay there, you will send us a full and lengthy report of everything by the two Spaniards, Miguel de Loarca and Pedro Sarmiento, who go in your company; and if they do not let you stay there, then you will give it us when you return.'

It was evidently in obedience to these instructions that Rada drew up after his return to Manila not one but several reports of what he and his companions had seen and learnt during their two months in Fukien. Nor was Rada the only one who wrote an

[1] Printed in extenso by Fr. Gaspar de San Agustín, *Conquistas*, pp. 304–306.

account of this embassy, for an extensive narrative by Miguel de Loarca has survived in numerous copies, and there is every reason to suppose that Fr. Jerónimo Marín and Pedro Sarmiento recorded their impressions as well.[1] The nature and fate of these various manuscripts are discussed below, and it will be sufficient to state here that the version which is translated and printed in this present work is evidently Rada's preliminary report. Anyone who reads this report, together with the *Historia* of González de Mendoza and the *Republicas* of Jerónimo Román (both of whom had access to Rada's later and fuller papers which have since disappeared), will agree that the friar certainly carried out Lavezares' instructions to the letter.

Although, owing to the unexpected escape of Limahon (pp. xlvi–xlvii above), Rada's expedition had not secured for the Spaniards all the advantages for which they had hoped, the door did not seem entirely closed against further efforts to get a secure religious and commercial footing in China. Whatever prospects of success there were, however, were ruined by Dr. Francisco de Sande's churlish behaviour to the Chinese officers at Manila in the spring of 1576, and Rada openly voiced his doubts that another attempt would prove less successful. Writing to the King of Spain and the Viceroy of Mexico a few days before his second departure for Fukien in May 1576, he alluded to the discontent of the Chinese with Sande's behaviour and added, 'With all this, the Governor Doctor Sande was of the opinion that two Religious should return thither; and therefore Fr. Agustín de Albuquerque[2] and myself are going; may it please God that we will be able to do something for his holy service. I believe that it would have been a very great help in this case, if there had not been any change in the government, for as Guido de Lavezares began the affair and the Chinese captains already knew him, I think that it would then have been carried on more earnestly and willingly by them.'[3] But

[1] Cf. the bibliographical details given in Santiago y Vela, *Ensayo*, III, 229–231; VI, 453–456, and on pp. 345–348 below.

[2] Agustín de Albuquerque, born at Badajoz, entered the Augustinian order at Salamanca, and went out to the Philippines in 1571. Like Rada, he had previously volunteered to go to China as a slave with the junk-masters of returning Chinese ships, if they would not take him otherwise. He died in 1580. Cf. Streit, *Bibliotheca Missionum*, IV, 315; *Missionalia Hispanica*, I, 196, 211.

[3] Rada's letters of 1 and 4 May 1576, printed in Santiago Vela, *Ensayo*, VI, 453–454; *Missionalia Hispanica*, I, 203; *Revista Agustiniana*, I (Valladolid, 1881), pp. 55–57.

Rada naturally put the salvation of souls above all other considera-
tions, so he embarked on the returning Chinese fleet in spite of his
forebodings.

Rada's early biographers and most later writers in their footsteps, paint this return voyage in the blackest colours. They allege
that, shortly after leaving Manila, the Chinese treacherously
turned on the unfortunate friars, brutally killed their servants and
interpreter, and, after beating the two Spaniards within an inch of
their lives, left them tied to a tree, stark naked and bleeding, on
an island infested by hostile cannibals. Here they were found by
pure chance some days later by a passing Spaniard who took them
to Manila in his boat.[1] This story is wildly exaggerated, and Rada's
own account of what happened is much less dramatic. The
Chinese fleet left Manila on 7 May 1576, and the commander lost
no time in trying to persuade Rada and his companions to abandon
their project, pointing out that they would be ill-received by the
Fukien authorities and might even be killed. When entreaties and
threats failed to move the friars from their intended purpose, the
Chinese finally lost patience and set them ashore in a region inhabited by savage Zambale tribes, it is true, but who were then at
peace with the Spaniards. No harm was done them by the savages
or by anyone else; and they were picked up, safe and sound, by a
Spanish officer five days later. The Chinese commander did beat-
up their interpreter; and the men whom he killed were not the
friar's servants, but some of Limahon's men who had been taken
prisoners previously.[2]

After his return to Manila from this abortive expedition, Martín
de Rada was elected prior of the recently-founded convent of
Calumpit in the province of Bulacán, but it was not long before he
was transferred once again to Manila, and later on back to Cebú.
Wherever he was, he busied himself in writing religious, linguistic and mathematical works, besides continuing to exercise his
charge of protector and advocate of the Filipino Indians. The

[1] This is the essence of the story as related by Gaspar de San Agustín (*Conquistas*, pp. 327–328), Joseph Sicardo, O.E.S.A., (*Christiandad del Japon*), and
numerous other seventeenth–eighteenth century chroniclers, but which is flatly
contradicted by Rada's own letter of 3 June 1576, and by the letter of the
Cabildo Secular of Manila to Philip II (2 June 1576), quoted on p. xlix *supra*.

[2] Rada's letter and that of the Cabildo of Manila, June 1576, printed in
Revista Agustiniana, I, 55–57; Pastells, *Catálogo*, II, xlvii–xlviii; *Missionalia
Hispanica*, I, 203–205.

above-quoted letter which he wrote to a colleague on the 3 June 1576, gives some idea of his manifold scientific activities, He states that he had compiled 'un libro de recta Hidrografiae ratione', presumably in Latin, and was then actively engaged on a *Geometría Práctica*, which he was writing in Spanish, 'for it seems to me that nothing has appeared in Spanish on this subject which is worth reading, and it is divided into seven books'. He also intended to write another seven books of 'Cosmography and Astronomy', having already compiled a manuscript work on 'Astrología Judiciaria', and another on 'all the ways of making clocks'. He complains that he had lost many of his books at sea, and during Limahon's attack on Manila, when the Augustinian convent was burnt; he asks his correspondent to send him mathematical works, 'since I believe that the Lord gave me a special ability and inclination for this, despite my lack of books. For of geometry I have here only the works of Euclides and Archimedes; of astronomy, Ptolemy and Copernicus; of perspective, Vitelión;[1] of judicial astronomy, Hali-abenragel.[2] I likewise have the book *De Triangulis*, and the 'directions' of Monte Regio[3] and the Ephemerides of Cipriano Leontio,[4] as well as the Alfonsian and Prutenical tables.'[5] It is most unfortunate that none of Rada's scientific works have hitherto come to light, although the possibility remains that one or another of them may be lying forgotten in some Spanish or monastic archive. In any event, it is high time that he was given the credit which is his due for being the first Euro-

[1] Witelo (fl.1250–1270), whose mathematical works were first published in 1535.

[2] Abû al Hasan 'Ali Ibn abî al-Riğal al Saybânî al Kātib al Mağribî, a noted Spanish-Arab astrologer who died at Tunis about the year 1040. The book to which Rada refers is evidently the *Praeclarissimus liber completus in judicio astrorum quem edit Abohazen Haly filius Abenragel*, first published at Venice in 1485, and several times reprinted. Cf. A. Mieli, *La Science Arabe et l'évolution scientifique mondiale*, Leiden, 1938, p. 181.

[3] Regiomontanus, whose real name was Johann Müller (1436–1476), so called from his birthplace of Königsberg in Franconia. The works cited here are evidently the *De Triangulis Libri Quinque*, first published in 1533, and the *Tabulae Directionum* (Nuremberg, 1475), which contains a table of tangents.

[4] ? Cyprian of Lentini (a town on the coast of Sicily between Augusta and Catania, formerly called Leontini), though I can trace no mathematician of this name.

[5] The Alfonsian tables of Alfonso X (King of Castile, 1252–1284), were first published at Venice, 1483. The original tables of Copernicus were revised and enlarged some years after his death by Erasmus Reinhold under the title of *Prutenicae Tabulae Coelistium Motuum* (Tubingen, 1551), in honour of his Patron the Duke of Prussia.

pean writer on China who clearly and correctly identified this country with Marco Polo's Cathay.

Apart from his scientific works, his output in other spheres of knowledge was also considerable. Omitting all mention of the religious and linguistic works which he wrote when in Mexico, we have the titles of two linguistic works which he compiled when in the Philippines; 'Arte y Vocabulario de la lengua Cebuana', and 'Arte y vocabulario de la lengua China'. These no longer appear to be extant, although references to their existence were made during the last century. The gist of the former work was embodied in Fr. Alonso de Méntrida's *Bocabulario de lengua Bisaia . . . de la isla de Panai y Sugbu* (Manila, 1637). The existence of the second has never been fully established; but there seems little reason to doubt that Rada with his linguistic gifts and tireless energy at least made a start with such a work, even if (as is probable) it never got beyond an imperfect draft.[1]

Martín de Rada was busily engaged in compiling some astronomical and nautical tables from the stellar observations which he had made in the Philippines, when he was summoned from the studious quiet of his cell to take part in Dr. Francisco de Sande's expedition to Brunei in 1578. This expedition was undertaken at the request of a fugitive brother of the reigning rajah, who claimed that he had been forcibly deposed by his brother, and offered to acknowledge Philip II as his suzerain if he was restored to the throne.[2] The expedition achieved initial success; but so many of the Spaniards sickened and died in the unhealthy climate, that Sande broke off the campaign and ordered the expedition to return to Manila, at the entreaty of Fr. Martín who was acting as his chaplain and confessor. Many of the soldiers died on the return voyage, and Fr. Martín de Rada himself caught the contagion and died on board ship, at some unascertained date about the middle of June 1578. His body was buried at sea—which provoked some adverse criticism of the governor after the latter's return to Manila—and thus ended the career of this singular

[1] Cf. the extensive biography of Rada's works in Santiago Vela, *Ensayo*, VI, 448–459, especially 448–452. For Méntrida's *Bocabulario* of 1637, cf. W. E. Retana, *Orígenes de la imprenta Filipina* (Madrid, 1911), pp. 119–121; Streit, *Bibliotheca Missionum*, V, 271–273.

[2] For details of the Brunei campaign see Morga-Retana, *Sucesos de las Islas Filipinas*, pp. 388–390; Gaspar de S. Agustín, *Conquistas*, pp. 357–362.

man when he was in the prime of life, being then forty-five years old.[1]

Even when the hyperbole of his clerical panegyrists is discounted, it is clear that Friar Martín de Rada was an uncommonly gifted man, and such he was acknowledged to be during his lifetime with a unanimity which was rare amongst his countrymen and contemporaries. The General of his Order conferred on him the title of Master (equivalent to that of Doctor) on the 7 March 1575, on account of his 'learning, upright life and the toils he had undergone for the faith and religion'. Philip II twice considered presenting him to a bishopric, and only desisted from offering him one on the second occasion because he knew the modest friar would refuse it. Captain Juan de la Isla, one of the pioneer navigators and pilots of the Pacific, whose scheme for a systematic survey of the China coast has been previously mentioned, described Rada as a 'very great mathematician, geometrician and astrologer, so much so that they say he is one of the best in the world'. Another contemporary wrote from the Philippines, 'we have here the flower and phoenix of the mathematical arts of Spain, who is one Friar Martín de Herrada, who has found out many things which were hidden from the Spaniards, as time will disclose in due course'.[2] His advocacy and support of the Filipino Indians has led to his being termed the 'Las Casas of the Philippines'; and although this may be an exaggeration, none who have read his original reports can doubt that he was sincerely their protector and their friend.

It cannot be said that he nourished an equal sympathy for the Chinese, although his opinion of them may have been adversely affected by the fiasco of May 1576. Coming as he did from a warlike stock which included a member of the church militant who was one of the heroes of the battle of Las Navas de Tolosa,[3] Rada had scant sympathy with the inherently peaceful character of the Chinese.[4] Like Saint Francis Xavier, his fellow-countryman from

[1] *Missionalia Hispanica*, I, 206–208, for further details.

[2] *Missionalia Hispanica*, I, 209–210, for the relevant documents.

[3] D. Rodrigo Ximénez de Rada, Archbishop and first *Adelantado* of Cazorla. The battle of Las Navas de Tolosa (16 July 1212), gained by the allied Christian princes of Spain against the Almohades, marks the turning-point of the reconquest of the Iberian peninsula.

[4] Rada in his letter about China d. 1 July 1572, stigmatised the Chinese as being 'la gente mas vil para la guerra que ay en el mundo'; but, even so, he never

Navarre, he probably found the bellicose Japanese more to his liking. Be this as it may, we can agree with his seventeenth-century biographer that to Rada belongs the credit of being the first Spanish friar 'who set foot in the lands of that Empire without any preparation, either in the language of that people or with expert interpreters who could help him to get some knowledge of the much that is to be learnt about so old and politic a nation. Yet despite these difficulties, the narratives which Friar Martín wrote about China are so full and detailed that they make us wonder how he could have acquired such extensive information in so short a time; by this we realise his great ability, which, according to all those who knew him, was outstanding even in that golden age.'[1]

The report of Fr. Martín de Rada on his mission to Fukien in 1575, falls naturally into two parts. The first deals with the voyage to China, journey in Fukien, and return to Manila; and the second part consists of a short description of China, divided into twelve chapters or sections. Both parts were used by Fr. González de Mendoza in writing his *Historia* (1585), and by Fr. Jerónimo Román in the revised edition of his *Republicas del Mundo* (1595); but the first part was first printed as an integral whole by Fr. Gaspar de San Agustín on pp. 313–323 of his *Conquistas* (1698). Fr. Gaspar tells us that he scrupulously followed Rada's own manuscript text, 'without making any alteration other than that of a few words which were not quite clear'.[2] He did not publish the second part, since Mendoza and Román had already drawn upon it so heavily for their own works, to which he referred the interested reader. The second part remained unpublished in its original form until 1884, when it was printed in the files of an Augustinian magazine *Revista Agustiniana* (Valladolid, 1884–1885), Vols. VIII–IX, together with the first part which the editor of this magazine did not realise (or did not state) had already been printed by Fr. Gaspar de San Agustín nearly two centuries previously. The

---

went so far as Fernando Riquel, who wrote to Philip II (in January, 1574), that China, notwithstanding its great population, could be subjected 'with less than sixty good Spanish soldiers'! Cf. Sanz Arizmendi, 'Capítulo', p. 456; Blair & Robertson, *Philippine Islands*, III, 22.

[1] Gaspar de San Agustín, *Conquistas*, p. 323.

[2] 'sin mas mutacion que la de algunas palabras algo confusas', *Conquistas*, p. 313. Cf. Bibliography, p. 346 below.

complete version, which thus appeared for the first time in its original form, was taken from a sixteenth-century copy in the Bibliothèque National at Paris (Cod. 325 fol. 16–31v. *Fonds Esp.*), but I have not had the opportunity of examining this codex myself.[1] For the translation which is printed in this present work, I have utilised the version of the first part printed by Fr. Gaspar de San Agustín, and the second part as printed in the *Revista Agustiniana* from the copy at Paris. Comparison of this latter version with that printed in the *Conquistas* in 1698 shows clearly that both were taken from the same original, which may (or may not) have been that first written or dedicated by Rada himself. Rada's original draft does not appear to have survived, but several copies are extant, and details of those which are known to me will be found in the Bibliography.

The reader now has before him Fr. Martín de Rada's report of his mission to Fukien and description of China, as nearly as possible in the same form as when he first put his signature to it. Comparison of this account with the *Historia* of González de Mendoza shows that although the latter relied heavily on this report, he obviously had other and more detailed accounts in front of him. We have already mentioned (p. lxvi) that he quoted extensively from Fr. Gaspar da Cruz's *Tractado*, acknowledging his obligations to the Portuguese author with the same frankness as he does to Fr. Martín de Rada. González de Mendoza also tells us that he obtained much information from Rada's companion, Fr. Jerónimo Marín, whom he met in Mexico, and it is also clear that he used the '*Verdadera Relación*' of Miguel de Loarca which will be discussed shortly. His chief source of additional information was, however, other papers and MSS. which had belonged to Rada, and which he had opportunities of studying in Spain and in Mexico.[2] Comparison of Mendoza's *Historia* with the narratives of Fr. Gaspar da Cruz and Fr. Martín de Rada as they are printed here, prove that Mendoza was a careful and conscientious editor

[1] Santiago Vela, *Ensayo*, I, 525 and VI, 454–455, states that this codex comprises a collection of papers relating to the Philippines and Mexico compiled by Fr. Alonso de Veracruz, O.E.S.A., who was a friend and contemporary of Rada, and an active missionary on both sides of the Pacific.

[2] Cf. the dedication and preface to the Spanish editions of González de Mendoza's *Historia* (1585 et seq.), which have been omitted from the English translations of 1588 and 1853, being substituted by Robert Parke's dedication to the circumnavigator, Thomas Cavendish.

who made the best possible use of his material. Allegations of mendacity and plagiarism which were made against him as early as 1585 by D. Juan Fernández de Velasco, the Constable of Castile,[1] are utterly unjustified. They merely serve to reveal the ignorance of the writers who first made them and the parrot-like tendencies of some bibliographers who repeat them. These allegations have been convincingly demolished by the erudite Santiago Vela with a wealth of detail (*Ensayo*, III, pp. 201–237).

I mentioned above (pp. lxxv–lxxvi) that most of Rada's voluminous papers seem to have been lost, and this subject merits further investigation. Writing to King Philip II a few days after Rada's death, Fr. Agustín de Albuquerque, his companion on the abortive expedition of 1576, observed that the manuscript works of Fr. Martín de Rada were then in 'the monastery where he was living, a hundred leagues from this port' of Manila, which would imply that Fr. Martín was living in Cebú prior to his joining the expedition to Borneo.[2] Albuquerque added that it was intended to 'collect them all together in the state in which he left them and send them to your Majesty' at the first opportunity. Apparently, many of them were in fact sent to Madrid by the hand of Fr. Jerónimo Marín in August of that year. But Rada's preliminary report on China must, of course, have been sent to Spain long before his death. We learn from Fr. Gaspar de San Agustín that Fr. Jerónimo Marín embarked for Mexico in 1577, in the ship *San Felipe* which was shipwrecked off Catanduanes. This disaster forced Fr. Marín to return to Manila, where 'having written with his own hand the relation of the China journey which Friar Martín dictated to him, and which had been sent to Spain, he returned to Mexico and was elected prior of the convent of Guadalajara of Jalisco'.[3] From this passage it is clear that Fr. Martín de Rada had already sent one copy of his report to Spain

<hr/>

[1] The Constable's embittered 'Invectiva del Soldado de Caceres contra el Maestro Mendoza y su Historia de la China' (dated Naples, 7 August 1585), and Mendoza's rather laboured 'Apologia de el Cura de Arganda a el soldado de Caceres' (dated 1589), circulated in manuscript until printed at Seville in 1870. The best edition will be found in Pérez Pastor, *La Imprenta en Medina del Campo* (Madrid, 1895), pp. 271–292.

[2] Letter of Fr. Agustín de Albuquerque, O.E.S.A., d. Manila, 22 June 1578 in *Missionalia Hispanica*, I, 210.

[3] Gaspar de San Agustín, *Conquistas*, p. 525. Cf. also Pastells, *Catálogo*, II, lii–lvii.

before he dictated another to Fr. Marín in 1577.[1] It is, in fact, obvious that he must have sent his preliminary report to Spain (and in all probability a copy to the viceroy of Mexico) in the interval which elapsed between his return from Amoy in November 1575, and his departure on the abortive expedition of 7 May 1576. Since, as we shall see, some material translated from Chinese books was included in this 'Relación', it can hardly have been ready before the end of 1575, and was probably sent some time in the spring of the next year. Santiago y Vela suggests that it was sent along with a letter which Fr. Martín wrote to King Philip II on 1 May 1576, a week before his second departure for China, and this date gives us in any case a probable *terminus ad quem*.[2] Rada also alludes to this preliminary report in his letter of 3 June 1576 to Fr. Alonso de Veracruz, where he writes 'After having written to your paternity and sent with the letters the relation of the journey which we made last year to China' . . . ,[3] from which it seems likely that he originally sent the report to Spain and Mexico through the intermediary of Veracruz. However this may be, the original 'Relación' addressed to King Philip II does not seem to have survived but to have gone the way of so many of Rada's manuscripts.

Apart from Marín, Veracruz, and González de Mendoza, another contemporary writer who had access to some of Rada's papers, including his account óf China, was the Augustinian chronicler, Fr. Jerónimo Román, whose *Republicas del Mundo* has already been referred to, and whose evidence is worth quoting in more detail. Alluding to Rada's first journey to China, Román observes, '. . . since he did not wish to remain idle while he was in China, he resolved to read divers books in that Chinese language,[4] and among them many of those which treat of their antiquities; and studying attentively the rites and customs of those peoples, he recorded them in a small treatise which came into my hands, and

---

[1] This seems to have been virtually identical with the first draft of 1575–1576. Cf. Santiago Vela, *Ensayo*, VI, p. 453.

[2] Streit, *Bibliotheca Missionum*, IV, 519, nr. 1927, evidently errs in assuming that Rada's 'Relación' was first written in 1577.

[3] Printed in *Revista Agustiniana*, I, 55–56.

[4] This is of course a gross exaggeration. From the tenour of Rada's own 'Relación' it is clear that he knew no Chinese worth mentioning at this time; and personally I feel very doubtful if he ever attained to more than a superficial smattering.

F

somebody or other took it from me and never would give it back to me, which greatly vexed me, because I was desirous of writing the republic of this people. However it turned out all the better for me; since searching where I could find papers for this matter, I turned to where it seemed to me that I could find most plentifully what I wanted, and thus I asked the illustrious gentleman, the Licentiate Juan de Rada, Judge of the High Court (*Alcalde de la corte mayor*) of the kingdom of Navarre, brother of the said Friar Martín de Rada, and he, displaying his great generosity, sent me [the account of] what had happened on the journey to China and other very interesting papers, although he himself complained that he had been deprived of some others which were very important.' Fr. Jerónimo Román added that he could personally vouch for Fr. Martín de Rada's virtue, intelligence and reliability, since they had been together for some time in the same monastery at Toledo. He even claimed that Rada's report on China had been framed with the wishes of the editor of the *Republicas* in mind; but this would appear to be an exaggeration, as the first edition of the *Republicas* only appeared in the summer of 1575. It is possible that Román had previously circulated manuscript drafts among his friends; but personally I feel that the tenour of Rada's report was rather dictated by the principles laid down in the instructions of Guido de Lavezares.

From the above it will be seen that Fr. Jerónimo Román had access (at different times) both to a version of Rada's original report and to another copy and other relevant papers sent him by Fr. Martín's elder brother.[1] Curiously enough, Román's only mention of Mendoza's work, which was published ten years before the second edition of the *Republicas*, is a veiled allusion in the preface to Vol. III. After describing his use of Rada's papers in compiling his own account of China, Román adds: 'Whereby, after considering what is said here, and what an[other] author has written of the things of China, which he told us as though he were some oracle, it will be seen which of the two of us is nearer the mark'. Although no names are mentioned, this invidious comparison can only refer to Fr. González de Mendoza and his celebrated

---

[1] He certainly made as extensive use of Rada's account in his 'Republica del Reyno de la China' (*Tercera Parte de las Republicas del Mundo*, fls. 210–235), as did González de Mendoza in his *Historia*.

Historia which had already run through numerous editions by this time.

Although González de Mendoza and Jerónimo Román both had access to some at least of Rada's original papers and reports, it is not clear what happened to these manuscripts after they had finished with them. Several contemporary copies remain, but all trace of the originals seems to have been lost at a relatively early date. Four years after Rada's death, Don Gonzalo Ronquillo, the governor of the Philippines, informed the government at Madrid that none of Rada's papers were left in those islands,[1] which indicates that everything had then been sent to Mexico and Spain, as forecast in Fr. Agustín de Albuquerque's above-quoted letter of 22 June 1578. It is true that, as previously mentioned, some writers claim to have seen the originals of some of Rada's linguistic works in Philippine convents during the nineteenth century; but, as Fr. Santiago y Vela points out,[2] these statements are not altogether convincing; and, I may add, they may have confused copies with originals. That some copies were available after 1582 is indisputable. I myself possess a codex compiled at Manila about 1590, which contains a transcript of Rada's account of China, which has been used for this present edition;[3] and Fr. Gaspar de San Agustín tells us that he had access to some of Rada's papers in the convent of San Pablo at Mexico City about the end of the seventeenth century.[4]

Not only have most of Rada's original manuscripts been lost, but also the collections of Chinese books which he brought back from Fukien in 1575, and some of which were subsequently translated in whole or in part (mostly the latter, one may safely presume) from Chinese into Spanish by 'Sangleys' at Manila. This collection was obviously so important, and the extracts from these books which were embodied in Rada's report are so interesting, that it is worth while reproducing here the list of these

[1] D. Gonzalo Ronquillo to King Philip II, Manila, 15 June 1582, in P Pastells, *Catálogo*, II, 106. This was in reply to a query from the court which implies that the papers could not then be found at either Madrid or Valladolid.

[2] Santiago Vela, *Ensayo*, VI, 448–452, for a full discussion of this matter.

[3] Described and illustrated in *JRAS April, 1950*, pp. 37–49.

[4] 'aviendo yo visto lo que escrivió vno, y otro, y diferentes papeles en la Libreria de nuestro Colegio de San Pablo de Mexico, hallandome en èl por Lector de Sagrada Escritura, y de Prima de Theologia' (Gaspar de San Agustín, *Conquistas*, p. 362).

works as given in the Elizabethan translation of González de
Mendoza's *Historia*.[1]

'*The substance and manner of those bookes that Friar Herrada and his
companions brought from China.*

They brought with them a great number of bookes, as wee have
said, that did intreate of divers matters, as you shall perceive in the
sequele.

Of the description of all the whole kingdome of China, and the
placing of the 15 provinces, and the length and bredth of every
one of them, and of other kingdomes bordering vppon them.

Of all tributes and rentes belonging vnto the king, and of all the
orders of his royall pallace, and of his ordinarie pensions that hee
giveth, and the names of all officers in his house, and how far
every office doth extend.

How many tributaries eurie province hath, and the number of such
as are free from tribute, and the order and time, how and when they
are to be recouered.

For the making of ships of all sorts, and the order of nauigation
with the altitudes of euery port, and the quantitie[2] of euery one in
particular.

Of the antiquitie of this kingdome of China, and of the beginning
of the world, and in what time and for whome it beganne.

Of the kings that have raigned in this kingdome, and the order of
their succession and gouernment, with their liues and customes.

Of the ceremonies they vse in doing sacrifice vnto their idols
(which they hold as gods), and the names of them: of their beginnings, and at what time they shoulde make their sacrifices.

Their opinions of the immortalitie of the soule, of the heauen, of
hell, of the manner of their funerals, and of their mourning
apparel that euery one is bounde to weare, according as he is
alianced unto the dead.

Of the lawes of the kingdome, and when and by whome they were
made; and the punishment executed on those which violate the
same, with manie other matters touching their good government
and policie.

---

[1] Part I, Book III, Chapter xvii. I have checked Parke's translation with the
Spanish original.
[2] 'calidad' ('quality') in the Spanish original.

Manie herbals, or bookes of herbes, for phisitions, shewing how they should be applied to heale infirmities.

Many other bookes of phisicke and medicine, compiled by authors of that kingdome, of antiquitie and of late daies, containing in them the manner how to use the sicke, and to heale them of their sickness, and to make preservatives against all sicknesses and infirmities.

Of the properties of stones and mettals, and of things natural that have vertue of themselues; and wherefore pearles, gold, and silver, and other metals, may serve for the vtility of man, comparing with the one and the other the vtilitie of euerie thing.

Of the nomber, and moouings of the heauens: of the planets and stars, and of their operations and particular influences.

Of such kingdomes and nations as they have notice off, and of particular things that are in them.

Of the life and behauiour of such men, whom they holde for saints, where they lead their liues, and where they died and were buried.

The order howe to play at the tables, and at the chests [=chess?], and how to make sports of legerdemaine and puppets.

Of musicke and songs, and who were the inuentors thereof.

Of the mathematicall sciences, and of arithmeticke, and rules how to use the same.

Of the effectes that the children doo make in their mothers wombs, and how they are euery moneth sustained, and of the good and bad times of their birth.

Of architecture, and all manner of buildings, with the bredth and length that euerie edifice ought to have for his proportion.

Of the properties of good and bad ground, and tokens how to know them, and what seede they will beare euery yeare.

Of astrologie naturall, and judiciarie, and rules to learne the same, and to cast figures to make coniectures.

Of chiromancia and phisiognomia, and other signes and tokens,[1] and what euery one doth signifie.

The order how to write letters, and how to giue euerie one his title, according to the dignitie of his person.

How to bring vp horses, and to teach them to runne and trauaile.

---

[1] This category presumably includes books relating to *fêng-shui*, or the 'wind and water' system of geomancy which played such an overwhelmingly important part in Chinese life. Cf. Dyer Ball, *Things Chinese* (ed. 1925), pp. 269–271.

How to deuine vpon dreames, and cast lottes when they beginne any iourney, or take any thing in hande, whose ende is doubtfull. Of apparell worne in all the kingdome, beginning with the king, and of the ensignes or coates of armes of such as doo gouerne. How to make armour and instruments of warre, and howe to firme[1] a squadron.

These bookes, and many others that the fryers brought, out of the which (as afore saide) have been taken all such thinges as have beene and shall be declared in this historie, interpreted by persons naturally borne in China, and brought up in Philippinas with the Spaniards that dwell there,[2] who affirme that they have seene great libraries in cities where they abode, but especially in Auchea and Chincheo.'[3]

It may be safely presumed that some of these books were sent to Europe, and possibly a few of them may still survive in neglected monastic libraries, but none have hitherto been identified to my knowledge. The celebrated French essayist, Montaigne, on his visit to the Vatican Library at Rome (6 March 1581), was shown 'a book of China, in outlandish characters, the leaves of some material much softer and more pellucid than our paper, and, as they cannot bear the stain of ink, only one side of the leaf is written upon, and the leaves are all double and folded at the outside edges, by which they hold together; they think it is the membrane of some tree'.[4]

It is tempting to identify this book as one of those from Fr. Martín de Rada's collection, but this is only one possibility out of several which are equally likely. The great Portuguese historian, João de Barros (1498–1570), acquired several Chinese books and maps (and a Chinese slave to translate them), some of which he subsequently sent to the Italian historian, Paolo Giovio.[5] The book

---

[1] 'form'.   [2] The so-called 'Sangleyes', or 'Sangleys'.

[3] Foochow and Ch'üan-chou.

[4] E. J. Trechmann [ed.], *The Diary of Montaigne's Journey to Italy in 1580 and 1581* (London, 1929), pp. 142–143. Dr. G. Loehr of Princeton University kindly drew my attention to this interesting passage. Mendoza (Part I, Book III, Ch. xiii) mentions having seen Chinese books in the Vatican Library and in King Philip's library at the Escorial. The latter, at least, were probably those sent home by Rada.

[5] For the Chinese books and 'card geographical' collected by João de Barros see Escalante-Frampton, *Discourse of Navigation* (London 1579), pp. 17, 19, and my articles in *T'ien Hsia Monthly*, IX (Shanghai, 1939), pp. 451–453, and *Boletim do Instituto Português de Hongkong*, I, 19–22.

which Montaigne saw in 1581, might well have come from this collection; or possibly from that of the Dowager Queen Catherine of Portugal, whom Escalante recorded as possessing two printed Chinese chronicles in 1577.[1] But in any case, the ultimate fate of the books is not so important as the fact that Rada had the intelligence and enterprise to collect them in the first place, and that he was able to find some Chinese who could translate them, even if imperfectly, at Manila. Most of the books probably perished in the damp and insect-ridden climate of the Philippines; but the point I wish to make here is that both Barros and Rada preceded Ricci and his Jesuit successors in the systematic acquisition and study of Chinese books. It may be suggested that only Rada's untimely death in 1578, prevented his making a more thorough and effective use of the books brought back from Fukien in 1575, although the inadequacy of his interpreters evidently handicapped him, as we shall see.

González de Mendoza claims—or rather implies—that he had seen Rada's original report and papers at Madrid; but it is more likely that, as Santiago Vela points out, he made greater use of those documents—whether originals or copies—which he found at Mexico during his stay there on his abortive embassy to China in 1581.[2] Despite the fiasco of Rada's second expedition in May 1576, and the opposition of Dr. de Sande, there were a number of people in the Philippines who wrote to Philip II, urging the importance and desirability of sending an embassy to China, both for religious and for commercial reasons. The King himself had read Rada's original 'Relación' with great interest, and despite his preoccupation with the preparations for the conquest of Portugal, decided on the dispatch of an embassy to China in June, 1580. One of the prime movers in this matter was Fr. Juan González de Mendoza, who had lived for some years in Mexico, although he had never been either in China or in the Philippines, and a patron at court secured his appointment as one of the envoys.[3] The friar was authorised to take a number of presents,

---

[1] Escalante-Frampton, *Discourse of Navigation* (1579), p. 30.

[2] Santiago Vela, *Ensayo*, III, 229.

[3] Juan González de Mendoza was born at Torrecilla de Cameros near Toledo in 1545, and became an Austin Friar some twenty years later, when serving as a soldier in Mexico. He returned to Spain in 1574, and after the failure of his abortive embassy in 1581–1582, went back again from Mexico to Europe. In

including pictures, clocks and watches, arms and armour, personal clothing and accoutrements from Philip II to the Emperor Wan-li. It is interesting to compare the list of these gifts with those sent by our King George III to the Emperor Ch'ien-lung just over two hundred years later.[1] Fr. González de Mendoza was not the sole envoy, as he was associated with Fr. Francisco de Ortega, O.E.S.A.; the party was to be joined in Mexico by Fr. Jerónimo Marín, whose experience of the 1575 mission would prove invaluable.

Mendoza and Ortega left San Lucar in February 1581, with a party which included a painter and a watch-maker, reaching Mexico in June. Mendoza states that when they first arrived the Viceroy, Conde de Coruña, was very keen about the embassy, but changed his mind later from reasons of personal pique; finally it was decided to await the arrival of Dr. de Sande, the returning governor of the Philippines, before proceeding further with the matter. Sande arrived at Mexico in January 1582, and strongly opposed the project as a waste of time and money. A similar line was taken by Fr. Jerónimo Marín, who argued that the presents could not be made large enough to suit the cupidity of the Chinese, and that Chinese friendship was not essential to the security of the Philippines anyway. The viceroy therefore referred the matter back to Madrid, where, as a seventeenth-century chronicler observed, 'these reasons seemed so sound that an order was given to put the embassy in silence, and the silence was so great that up to the present time we have not returned to talk about it'.[2]

Ortega went back to Madrid when the embassy first ran into difficulties in 1581, before the arrival of Dr. de Sande. Mendoza

1593 he was appointed Bishop of Lipari (Sicily), and then successively Bishop of Chiappa (1607), and Popayán (1608) where he died in February, 1618. Full biographical details will be found in Santiago Vela, *Ensayo*, III, 201–237.

[1] King Philip's letter to the Emperor Wan-li (Badajoz, 11 June 1580), and the list of presents as proposed by Rada, and of those actually sent, will be found in Sanz Arizmendi, 'Capítulo', appendices G–H, pp. 465–470. When the embassy was abandoned, Philip II ordered (*cédula* or decree of 27 May, 1583) that his presents should be sold in Mexico. In 1586 some were still on hand, including six of the clocks and watches, an equestrian portrait of Charles V and another of Philip II, a painting of Our Lady of the Conception, two velvet girdles embroidered with gold, and four boxes in which the presents had come. The presents sent from George III to Ch'ien-lung will be found listed in *T'oung Pao*, XXXI, 34, and E. H. Pritchard, *The crucial years of early Anglo-Chinese relations, 1750–1800* (Washington, 1936), pp. 306, 339.

[2] H. R. Wagner, 'Juan González de Mendoza', pp. 22–23, for further details.

remained for some time in Mexico, preaching the *Bula de Cruzada* in the provinces, and copying the papers of Martín de Rada, before returning to Spain after the definitive abandonment of the embassy in 1582. While in Mexico he had frequent conversations with Fr. Jerónimo Marín, who is undoubtedly the source of much of the additional material which is incorporated in Mendoza's *Historia*, and which cannot be found in the much briefer report of Fr. Martín de Rada. Another source concerning the 1575 mission to which Mendoza had access, either in Mexico or in Spain, was the 'Verdadera Relación' of Miguel de Loarca, one of the two soldiers who accompanied Rada and Marín. Loarca's narrative is much more extensive than any of Rada's accounts which have survived. From many passages which are virtually identical in both accounts, it is obvious (and quite natural) that Rada and Loarca made use of each other's drafts when writing their own reports.[1]

Soon after his return to Spain, González de Mendoza went on to Rome where he put the final touches to his celebrated *Historia*, which was first printed there in 1585. The great success which

[1] Part II, Book II of Mendoza's *Historia* is concerned with the narratives of two parties of Franciscan friars from the Philippines who made abortive attempts to found missions in China in 1579–1580 and in 1582 respectively. We are not concerned with these expeditions here, as Mendoza made but little use of them for his general account of China, relying almost entirely on the *Tractado* of Gaspar da Cruz and the reports of Fr. Martín de Rada and his companions. For the Franciscan expeditions of 1579–1582, see A. Van den Wyngaert [ed.] *Sinica Franciscana*, II, 1–213, and Pelliot's article in *T'oung Pao*, XXXIV, 191–222. In this connection mention may be made of an excessively rare little work, of which I have only been able to trace one other copy besides that in the British Museum (press-mark 1312. c. 1), *Libro y Relacion de las grandezas del Reyno de la China. Hecho por un frayle descalço de la Orden de Sant Francisco, de seys que fueron pressos en el dicho Reyno, en la isla de Haynam. en el año de 1585*, (no place or date of publication, but presumably printed in Spain in 1586 or 1587). This very curious account of China does *not* contain the narrative of Fr. Martín Ignacio de Loyola, O.F.M., as stated by Streit, *Bibl. Miss.*, IV, p. 534, nr. 1974, and has nothing to do with him. It is written by one of the party of Franciscan friars headed by Fr. Diego de Oropesa, O.F.M., who were shipwrecked on the coast of Hainan island at the end of May, 1583. They were taken to Canton where the Jesuits, Ricci and Ruggiere, found them in September and were instrumental in securing their release. None of the bibliographers who mention this account apparently have troubled to examine it, with the exception of Madrolle. It gives a most laudatory account of China, and incorporates whole passages from the letter of the Crown Factor, Juan Bautista Román, which was appended to Ricci's letter of September, 1584. Cf. *Fonti Ricciane*, I, 142, 179–180; *Missionalia Hispanica*, I, 347–352; Colin-Pastells, *Labor Evangelica*, III, 448–452; Cordier, *Bib. Sin.* (ed. 1904), col. 7–8.

this work achieved has been mentioned at the beginning of this introduction, but there is one point connected with Mendoza's use of Rada's material which may be mentioned here.

A perusal of Martín de Rada's narrative in its original form, reveals that he was a good deal more critical of the Chinese than either Galeote Pereira or Gaspar da Cruz had been, as we have already had occasion to observe (p. lxi). Apart from the use which he made of the statistics he found in the *Kuang-yü-t'u* and other similar Chinese works, Rada does not seem to have been very impressed by the contents of the books which he had so carefully collected in Fukien. He scornfully dismisses most of them as containing only the name or the smell ('olor') of the subjects with which they dealt. He is very contemptuous of Chinese achievements in astronomy, mathematics, and natural sciences; only making an exception for Chinese herbals, which he found were as well illustrated as the contemporary European editions of Dioscorides. He even went so far as to rate the knowledge of the Chinese in the field of natural science as not much higher than that of the half-savage Filipino Indians. His unfavourable views may, however, have been partly due to the inadequacy of his translators; for it may be doubted whether he could rely on anybody better educated than the semi-literate itinerant 'Sangley' smugglers from Fukien who were the only Chinese who frequented the Philippines at that time.

Rada's critical attitude is not, however, readily apparent from a first reading of Mendoza's book. Most of Rada's asperities are there either omitted or watered down, and the more admiring tone of his Portuguese predecessors seems to have strongly influenced Mendoza's attitude as an editor when compiling his famous *History*. This is of great importance, as these pioneer Portuguese and Spanish eye-witness accounts, when skilfully dovetailed together by González de Mendoza, can be said to have formed in Europe a new tradition of Marco Polo's Cathay. China now became to the reading public of Europe an enviable country, where justice was well administered, where the people were all prosperous and hard-working, peaceable and self-controlled. Art and industry were developed to unsuspected heights; and even the invention of printing on which Europe so prided itself, was found to have been anticipated in China. Only in the all-important matter of revealed religion did the Chinese fall short of the highest achievements of the West, but God would doubtless remedy this defect in due time. Meanwhile, what may be termed the 'China Legend', so industriously fostered by the Jesuits in the next two centuries, and which influenced Leibniz and other European thinkers of the 'Enlightenment' so profoundly, was off to a good start.[1]

[1] For the development of this tendency to idealise the government of China, largely as the result of the publication of Mendoza's *History*, cf. G. Atkinson, *Les nouveaux horizons de la Renaissance française* (Paris, 1935), pp. 59–60, 174–177, 194–195; C. S. Ch'ien, 'China in the English literature of the seventeenth century', in the *Quarterly Bulletin of Chinese Bibliography* (English edition), New Series, Vol. I (1940), pp. 353–354, 358–364.

TEXT OF GALEOTE PEREIRA

Certain reports of China,[1] *learned through the Portugals there imprisoned, and chiefly by the relation of Galeote Pereira, a gentleman of good credit, that lay prisoner in that country many years. Done out of Italian into English by R[ichard] W[illis]*

THIS land of China is parted into 13 shires, the which sometimes were each one a kingdom by itself, but these many years they have been all subject unto one king.[2] Foquiem[3] is made by the Portugals the first shire, because there their troubles began, and had occasion thereby to know the rest.

In this shire be viii cities, but one principally more famous than others, called Fucheo,[4] the other seven are reasonably great, the best known whereof unto the Portugals is Chincheo.[5] in respect of a certain haven below it,[6] whither in time past they were wont for merchandise to resort.

Cantão[7] is the second shire, not so great in quantity, as well

[1] 'Certain reports of the province China', in the original English; 'the province' is Willis' translation of the Italian 'del paese', which is itself a gratuitous interpolation, the original Portuguese title commencing simply 'Algũas cousas sabidas da China'. Willis' later references to 'the province China' have likewise been abridged by me to 'China'.

[2] Ming China was divided into two metropolitan provinces, Pei-Chihli and Nan-Chihli (or Kiangnan), commonly known from their respective capitals as Peking and Nanking, and thirteen 'ambulatory' provinces, Shantung, Shansi, Shensi, Honan, Hukuang, Kiangsi, Fukien, Chekiang, Kueichou, Ssǔch'üan, Yünnan, Kuangsi, and Kuangtung,—an arrangement which dated from the Yüan or Mongol dynasty. The fifteen provinces of Ming China became the eighteen provinces under the succeeding Ch'ing or Manchu dynasty, when Kansu was constituted from a part of Shensi, Kiangnan was divided into Anhuei and Kiangsu, and Hukuang split into Hupei and Hunan. Cf. Couling, *Encyclopedia Sinica*, (London, 1917), p. 157; *Handbook of Oriental History*, pp. 173, 190.

[3] Fukien (Fu-chien), 'happily established' or 'happy establishment'. The number of cities given here refers to the *fu* or prefectual cities, of which there were in fact eight at this time.

[4] Foochow (Fu-chou), the provincial capital. Cf. Appendix II.

[5] Either Ch'üan-chou or else Chang-chou. Cf. Appendix I, 'Chincheo.'

[6] . . . 'abaixo della' in the original Portuguese text. Willis' text of 1577 renders this rather freely (through the Italian) as 'joyning thereunto'. As argued in Appendix I *infra*, it is clear that the Bay of Amoy, in the widest sense of the term, is intended.

[7] Kuangtung, 'broad East'. It then contained ten prefectual cities.

accounted of, both by the king, and also by the Portugals, for that it lieth nearer unto Malaqua [Malacca] than any other part of China, and was first descried by the Portugals before any other shire: this shire hath in it seven cities.

Chequeam[1] is the third shire, the chiefest city therein is Ocho,[2] therein also standeth Liampo,[3] with other thirteen or fourteen boroughs: country towns therein are too many to be spoken of.

The fourth shire is called Xutianfu,[4] the principal city thereof is great Pachim,[5] where the king is always resident. In it are fifteen other very great cities: of other towns therein, and boroughs well walled and trenched about, I will say nothing.

The fifth shire hath name Chelim;[6] the great city Nanquim,[7] chief of other fifteen cities, was herein of ancient time the royal seat of the kings of China. From this shire, and from that aforesaid Chequeam forward, bare rule the other kings, until the whole region became one kingdom.[8]

[1] Chekiang, 'crooked river', so called because of the bore or tidal wave of its north river, which drives back, and as it were bends its waters. Cf. L. Richards, *Comprehensive Geography of the Chinese Empire*, (Shanghai, 1908), p. 227. It contained eleven *fu* cities.

[2] Ōchō, or d'Ōchō ('of Ōchō') has become *Dochion* in Willis' text. Presumably a corrupted form of Hangchow, the provincial capital.

[3] Ningpo.

[4] Shun-t'ien-fu, the 'city obedient to Heaven', or 'region enclosing the imperial capital' as it is sometimes more prosaically translated. The expression dates from the Mongol dynasty. Another term for the city and prefecture of Peking.

[5] Peking, (Pei-ching), 'northern capital', so called to distinguish it from Nanking, the 'southern capital'. The Emperor Yung-lo (1403–1425) of the Ming dynasty transferred the national capital from Nanking to Peking in 1416–1420 but it had previously occupied this position in Mongol times, being then called Ta-tu and Khanbalik.

[6] Chihli 'direct rule', more correctly Nan-Chihli or 'southern direct rule' to distinguish it from Pei-Chihli, or 'northern direct rule' *alias* Peking province.

[7] Nanking (Nan-ching), 'southern capital', was the national capital from the establishment of the Ming dynasty in 1368, until the seat of the imperial residence was transferred to Peking in 1416–1420. It was also called Kiang-ning-(Chiang-ning-)fu, and was the provincial capital of Nan-Chihli, (see last note), or Kiangnan (Chiangnan), 'south of the river', province. Cf. note (1) on next page.

[8] Nanking was the capital of the Wu principality in the second century A.D., but the implication that the Chinese race originated in this region is erroneous. Modern research has shown that the Yellow River (Huang-ho) valley and the plains of North China were the seat of a flourishing civilization over three thousand years ago. Cf. H. G. Creel, *The birth of China. A study of the formative period of Chinese civilization* (New York, 1937).

The sixth shire beareth name Quianssi,[1] as also the principal city thereof, and it is that in which all the fine porcelain is made from Culio upwards, without any being made elsewhere and from Culljo downwards in all the cities of China;[2] and as this city of Quiansi lieth nearer to Liampo, the Portugals being ignorant of this country, and finding great abundance of that fine porcelain to be sold at Liampo, and that very good cheap, thought at the first that it had been made there, howbeit in fine, they perceived that the standing of Quiansi more near unto Liampo than to Chincheo or Cantão, was the cause of so much fine porcelain at Liampo. Within the compass of Quiansi shire be other 12 cities.

The seventh shire is Quichio,[3] the eighth Quansi,[4] the ninth Confu,[5] the tenth Vrnan,[6] the eleventh Sichuan.[7] In the first hereof there be six cities, in the next fifteen; how many towns the other three have, we are ignorant as yet, as also of the proper names of the twelfth and thirteenth shires, and the towns therein.[8]

[1] Kiangsi, 'west of the river', a most inappropriate name nowadays, as the province lies south of the Yangtse river. During the T'ang dynasty, most of the country between this river and the two Kuang provinces (Ling-nan) was one enormous Tao or circuit called Kiang-nan (Chiang-nan), 'south of the river.' In Sung times, this circuit was sub-divided into provinces, two of which were called Kiang-nan-tung (east) and Kiang-nan-hsi (west) respectively. These in turn were later abbreviated to Kiangnan (capital, Nanking) and Kiangsi (capital, Nanchang).

[2] This passage defeated Willis who discreetly abridged it in his translation from the Italian. The original Portuguese text is no help, as some words or lines are obviously missing. The centre of porcelain manufacture was the celebrated city of Ching-tê-chên, but the identity of 'Culio' baffles me.

[3] Kueichou, 'precious region.'

[4] Kuangsi, 'broad West.'

[5] I cannot identify Confu in this context; but the name is vaguely reminiscent of Marco Polo's 'Ganfu', or 'Canfu', the sea-port of Kan-p'u in Chekiang. Father G. Schurhammer, S.J., suggests that Hukuang province is meant.

[6] It is not clear whether 'Urnan' here stands for Honan, or for Yünnan.

[7] Ssǔch'üan (Szechwan), 'four rivers.'

[8] The omissions from Pereira's list, apart from the alternatives given in the penultimate note are Hukuang ('broad lake'), Shantung ('east of the mountains'), Shansi ('west of the mountains') and Shensi ('west of the pass'). João de Barros gave a full list of the fifteen provinces of Ming China in his Decada III, Book 2, Ch. vii, which, though published in 1563, is more accurate than those of Galeote Pereira and Gaspar da Cruz. The allusions to cities, boroughs and towns in Pereira's text evidently reflect the Chinese system of fu, chou, and hsien, of which there are no exact equivalents in English. The terms 'prefectural' (fu), 'departmental' (chou) and 'district' (hsien) cities are generally used, but for a more

G

This finally may be generally said hereof, that the greater shires in China, may be compared with mighty kingdoms.

In each one of these shires be set Ponchasis[1] and Anchasis,[2] before whom are handled the matters of the other cities. There is also placed in each one a Tutão,[3] as you would say a governor, and a Chaem,[4] that is a visitor, as it were, whose office is to go in circuit, and to see justice exactly done. By these means so uprightly things are ordered there, that it may be worthily accounted one of the best governed lands in all the world.

The king maketh always his abode in the great city Paquim, which is, according to what I was told, the name of the kingdom. This kingdom is so large, that under five months you are not able to travel from the towns by the sea-side to the Court and back again, no not under three months in post at your urgent business. The post-horses in this country are little of body, but swift of foot. Many do travel the greater part of this journey by water in certain light barks, for the multitude of rivers commodious for passage from one city to another.[5]

exact definition of their respective categories see *Handbook of Oriental History*, pp. 181, 184, 190–191. Pereira's figures are hopelessly garbled, but Chinese statistics of 1579 give the totals as 159 *fu*, 234 *chou* and 1,114 *hsien*. Cf. *Fonti Ricciane*, I, 15 *n* (4).

[1] *Pu-chêng-shih*, civil governor and comptroller, whose functions became later essentially those of a provincial treasurer. The post dates from 1376. Cf. Abbé Delamarre, *Histoire de la dynastie des Ming composée par l'empereur Khian loung* (Paris, 1865), p. 57.

[2] *An-ch'a-shih*, provincial judge or Chief Justice. Also translated as criminal judge, judicial commissioner, etc.

[3] *Tu-t'ang*, abbreviated from the title *Hsün-fu-tu-t'ang*, Viceroy, Governor or Inspector-General. This was a temporary provincial appointment conferred on a high official of the central government who was detached for the duration of some regional emergency. Mainly owing to the depredations of Japanese pirates and their Chinese collaborators, such appointments were made for the two Kuang provinces, with a general-headquarters at Wu-chou, and for Fukien and Chekiang conjointly known as the Minchê. These 'viceroys' as the Portuguese and Spaniards called them, were civil officials, but often exercised supervisory control over the armed forces in their provinces.

[4] *Ch'a-yüan*, abbreviation of *Tu-ch'a-yüan*, the Censorate or court of censors at the capital. Here as elsewhere applied to the censors or imperial commissioners who toured the provinces in various capacities.

[5] The old Chinese proverb, *Nan-chuan Pei-ma*, 'ship in the south, horse in the north', well exemplified the basic difference between travel and communications south and north of the Yangtse, respectively. Horses or donkeys were the chief means of conveyance on the plains of North China, whereas the numerous rivers and canals in South China greatly facilitated travel by river and boat.

The king, notwithstanding the hugeness of his kingdom, hath such a care thereof, that every moon (by the moons they reckon their months) he is advertised fully of whatsoever thing happeneth therein, by these means following.

The whole kingdom being divided into shires, and each shire having in it one chief and principal city, whereunto the matters of all the other cities, towns and boroughs, are brought: there are drawn in every chief city aforesaid, intelligencies of such things as do monthly fall out, and be sent in writing to the Court. If haply on one month every post is not able to go so long a way, yet doth there notwithstanding once every month arrive one post out of the shire. Whoso commeth before the new moon, stayeth for the delivery of his letters until the moon be changed. Then likewise are dispatched other posts back into all the thirteen shires again.[1]

Before that we do come to Chincheo[2] we have to pass through many places, and some of great importance. For this country is so well inhabited near the sea side, that you cannot go one mile but you shall see some town, borough, or hostelry, the which are so abundantly provided of all things, that in the cities and towns they live civily. Nevertheless such as dwell abroad are very poor, for the multitude of them everywhere so great, that out of a tree you shall see many times swarm a number of children, where a man would not have thought to have found any one at all.

From these places in number infinite, you shall come unto two cities very populous, and being compared with Cinceo, not possibly to be discerned which is the greater of them. These cities are as well walled as any cities in all the world. As you come into either of them, standeth so great and mighty a bridge, that the like thereof I have never seen in Portugal nor elsewhere.[3] I heard one of my fellows say, that he told in one bridge forty arches. The occasion wherefor these bridges are made so great, is for that the country is toward the sea very plain and low, and over-whelmed ever as the sea-water increaseth. The breadth of the

---

[1] For the working of the *chi-ti-p'u* or government courier express service at a slightly later date, see S. K. Fairbank and S. Y. Têng, 'On the transmission of Ch'ing documents', in *Harvard Journal of Asiatic Studies* (April, 1938), pp. 14–46, especially pp. 28–29. The Manchu system there described was closely modelled on that of the Ming. Cf. *Ming-shih*, chüan 75.

[2] Probably Ch'üan-chou in this context, as argued in Appendix I.

[3] For details of these bridges see Appendix III *infra*.

bridges, although it be well proportioned unto the length thereof, yet are they equally built, no higher in the middle than at either end, in such wise that you may directly see from the one end to the other; the sides are wonderfully well engraved after the manner of Roman works. But that we did most marvel at, was therewithal the hugeness of the stones, the like whereof as we came into the city, we did see many set up in places dishabited by the way, to no small charges of theirs, howbeit to little purpose, whereas nobody seeth them but such as do come by. The arches are not made after our fashion, vaulted with sundry stones set together; but paved, as it were, whole stones reaching from one pillar to another, in such wise that they lie both for the arches heads, and gallantly serve also for the highway. I have been astunned to behold the hugeness of these aforesaid stones; some of them are twelve paces long and upward, the least an eleven good paces long and an half.

The ways eachwhere are gallantly paved with foursquare stone, except it be where for want of stone they use to lay brick. In this journey as far as Fucheo, wheresover it was necessary, the road was cut with a pickaxe, and in many places no worse paved than in the plain ground.[1] This causeth us to think, that in all the world there be no better workmen for buildings, than the inhabitants of China.

The country is so well inhabited, that no one foot of ground is left untilled: small store of cattle have we seen this way we went to the city of Fucheo, save only certain oxen wherewithal the countrymen do plough their ground. One ox draweth the plough alone, not only in this shire, but in other places also, wherein is greater store of cattle. These countrymen by art do that in tillage, which we are constrained to do by force. Here be sold the voidings of close-stools, although there wanteth not the dung of beasts: and the excrements of man are good merchandise throughout all China. The dung-farmers seek in every street by exchange to buy

[1] Galeote Pereira's account of the excellence of the Fukien coastal highway agrees with that of Cornelis Reyersen who travelled over the same ground in 1623 (cf. W. P. Groeneveldt, *De Nederlanders in China*, p. 160). Under Manchu rule, the condition of the highways gradually deteriorated, and nineteenth-century travellers are very scornful of the roads in South China (cf. Dukes, *Everyday Life in China*, Ch. 2); but it must be remembered that European highways in the sixteenth century were generally very bad, and not least in the Iberian peninsula.

this dirty ware for herbs and wood.[1] The custom is very good for keeping the city clean.[2] There is great abundance of hens, geese, ducks, swine and goats, but wethers have they none. The hens are sold by weight, and so are all other things. Two pound of hen's flesh, goose, or duck, is worth two *foi* of their money, that is one penny sterling.[3] Swine's flesh is sold at a penny the pound. Beef beareth the same price, for the scarcity thereof, howbeit northward from Funcheo, and further off from the sea coast, there is beef more plenty and sold better cheap. Beef only excepted, great abundance of all these viands we have had in all the cities we passed through. And if this country were like unto India, the inhabitants whereof eat neither hens, beef, nor pork, but keep that only for the Portugals and Moors, they would be sold here for nothing. But it so falling out, that the Chins are the greatest eaters in all the world, they do feed upon all things, specially on pork, the fatter that is, unto them the less loathsome. The highest price of these things aforesaid, I have set down, better cheap shall you sometimes buy them for the great plenty thereof in this country. Frogs are sold at the same price that is made of hens, and are good meat amongst them, as also dogs, cats, rats, snakes, and all other unclean meats.

The cities be very gallant, specially near unto the gates, the which are marvelously great, and covered with iron. The gatehouses built on high with towers, the lower part thereof is made of brick and stone, proportionally with the walls; from the walls upward, the building is of timber, and many stories in it one above the other. The strength of their towns is in the mighty walls and ditches, artillery have they none.[4]

[1] A practice noticed by most Western travellers to (and residents in) China. 'Throughout China human manure is collected and treasured up, as a native said one day, "like precious jewels"; and is used in agriculture with a most jealous economy, being valued by them as the best manure.' (W. C. Milne, *Life in China*, p. 317). Cf. also F. H. King, *Farmers of Forty Centuries* (ed. 1926), pp. 171–190.

[2] Pereira was doubtless thinking of contemporary Lisbon, where, in common with many other European cities, visitors complained 'of the stench of the ordure that is continually thrown out; for not only the dust of the houses is cast into the streets, but chamber-pots and close-stools, for in all the city there are no houses of office', (J. Stevens, *The Ancient and Present State of Portugal*, London, 1706, p. 182).

[3] *fên* (*fun*). The hundredth part of a *tael* or Chinese ounce of silver. Also called *candarin* or *candareen*.

[4] This last observation is quite wrong, although the Chinese artillery of this period was admittedly inferior to the best European variety. Cf. p. 274, n. (2) *infra*.

The streets in Chincheo, and in all the rest of the cities we have seen are very fair, so large and so straight, that it is wonderful to behold.[1] Their houses are built with timber, the foundations only excepted, the which are laid with stone; in each side of the streets are pantils or continual porches for the merchants to walk under: the breadth of the street is nevertheless such, that in them fifteen men may ride commodiously side by side. As they ride, they must needs pass under many high arches of triumph that cross over the streets, made of timber and carved diversely, covered with tile of fine clay: under these arches the mercers do utter their smaller wares, and such as list to stand there, are defended from rain and the heat of the sun.[2] The greater gentlemen have these arches at their doors, although some of them be not so mightily built as the rest.

I shall have occasion to speak of a certain order of gentlemen that are called Loutea. I will first therefor expound what this word signifieth. Loutea is as much to say in our language as 'sir', and when any of them calleth for his servant, he answereth 'Loutea', as we 'sir';[3] and as we do say that the king hath made some gentleman, so say they, that there is made a Loutea. And for that amongst them the degrees are divers both in name and office, I will tell you only of some principals, being not able to advertise you of all.

The manner how gentlemen are created Louteas, and do come to that honour and title, is by the giving of a broad girdle not like to the rest, and a cap, at the commandment of the king. The name Loutea is more general and common unto more, than equality of

---

[1] A rather surprising statement when compared with the remarks of nineteenth-century travellers on the narrowness and inadequacy of Chinese streets, (Dukes, *Everyday Life in China*, Ch. 1). But it must be remembered that (as with the roads) the narrow and tortuous alleys of sixteenth-century European towns were nothing to boast about, and that Pereira was probably referring to the main streets of Chinese cities.

[2] *P'ai-lou* (*pailow*), an ornamental gateway or arch, erected in honour of some person of outstanding loyalty, filial piety, chastity, etc. Cf. H. A. Giles, *Glossary of Reference* (ed. 1878), p. 101; J. J. de Groot, *The Religious System of China*, II, 789–794, and the accompanying illustrations.

[3] 'Loutea is verbatim "old father", and roughly equivalent to the cockney "guv'ner"' (C. S. Chien, 'China in the English Literature of the seventeenth century', p. 353). This word is derived from the Amoy vernacular *ló-tia*, or the Chüan-chou form *lāu-tia* (Carstairs Douglas, *Dictionary of the Amoy vernacular*, pp. 315, 493).

honour thereby signified, agreeth withal. Such Louteas that do serve their prince in weighty matters for justice, are created after trial made of their learning: but the other which serve in smaller affairs, as captains, constables, sergeants by land and sea, receivers and such like, whereof there be in every city, as also in this, very many, are made for favour; the chief Louteas are served kneeling, although the caps and names of all the others are the same as theirs.[1]

The whole land of China is divided, as I have said, into thirteen shires; in every shire is one governor called Tutão, save where there are some of these who govern in two.[2]

Chief in office next unto them be certain other named Chacins that is, high commissioners as you would say, or visitors, with full authority in such wise, that they do call unto an account the Tutões themselves, but their authority lasteth not in any shire longer than one year. Nevertheless, in every shire being at the least seven cities, yea, in some of them fifteen or sixteen, besides other boroughs and towns not well to be numbered,[3] these visitors, where they come, are so honoured and feared, as though they were some great princes. At the year's end their circuit done, they come unto that city which is chief of others in the shire, to do justice there: finally busying themselves in the searching out of such as are to receive the degree of Louteas, whereof more shall be said in another place.

Over and besides these officers, in the chief city of each one of these aforesaid thirteen provinces, is resident one Ponchaçim,[4] captain thereof, and treasurer of all the king's revenues. This magistrate maketh his abode in one of the four greatest houses that be in all these head cities. And although the principal part of his function be, to be captain, to be treasurer of the revenues in that province, to send these revenues at appointed times to the Court,

---

[1] There is no satisfactory translation of this passage, since the original Portuguese (*Jap-Sin.* 123, fol. 35) is defective and consequently neither the Italian nor the English translator was able to make sense of it. 'Captains' and 'constables', are interpolated by Willis.

[2] Willis mistranslated this passage as 'in some shires there be two' which is the exact opposite of the original 'senão que ha allgũs destes que governão em duas'. For the *Tutão, Tu-t'ang*, viceroy or governor-general cf. p. 6 note (3) above.

[3] Evidently another groping after the distinction between *fu, chou* and *hsien*, for which see p. 5 note (8) above. For the *chaems* or censors see p. 6 note (4) above.

[4] *Pu-chêng-shih*, provincial civil governor and comptroller,

yet hath he notwithstanding by his office also to meddle with matters appertaining unto justice, as they are of great importance.

In the second great house dwelleth another magistrate called Anchassi,[1] a great officer also, for he hath dealings in all matters of justice. Who although he be somewhat inferior in dignity unto the Pomchassi, yet for his great dealings and general charge of justice, whosoever seeth the affairs of the one house and the other, might judge this Anchaçi to be the greater.

Tuzi, another officer so called, lieth in the third house, a magistrate of importance, specially in things belonging unto warfare, for thereof hath he charge.[2]

There is resident in the fourth house a fourth officer, bearing name Taissu.[3] In this house is the principal prison of all the city. Each one of these magistrates aforesaid may both lay evil-doers in prison, and deliver them out again, except the fact be heinous and of importance: in such a case they can do nothing, except they do meet together and confer at length. And if the deed deserveth death, all they together cannot determine thereof, without recourse made unto the Chian wheresoever he be, or to the Tutão; and eftsoones it falleth out, that the case be referred unto higher power. In all cities, not only chief in each shire, but in the rest also, are means found to make Louteas. Many of them do study at the prince his charges, wherefor at the year's end they resort unto the head cities, whither the Chacims do come, as it hath been erst said, as well to give these degrees as to sit in judgement over the prisoners.

The Chaçims go in circuit every year, but such as are to be chosen to the greatest offices, meet not but from three years to three years, and that in certain large halls appointed for them to be

---

[1] *An-ch'a-shih*, provincial judge or chief justice.

[2] Probably the *Tu-ssŭ*, title of a senior provincial army commander, of whom there were two in Fukien, but only one in most of the other provinces. Alternatively, the word may be connected with *Tu-chih*, which formed part of the title of many senior military officers, (E. Hauer, *K'ai-kuo Fang-lueh*, p. 645 note (44) and p. 618 note (57)); or possibly it may be derived from *Tê-si, Tosi*, in the Amoy vernacular, although this title was applied to a military officer of comparatively junior rank (major) in the Manchu period (Carstairs Douglas, *Dictionary*, pp. 420, 517).

[3] I cannot identify this official, but it has been suggested that the word is a corruption of *T'ai-shou* or *T'ai-tsun*, the epistlory style for a *Chih-fu* or prefect. Cf. Mayers, *Chinese Government*, nr: 281.

examined in. Many things are asked them, whereunto if they do answer accordingly, and be found sufficient to take their degree, the Chaçim by and by granteth it them; but the cap and girdle whereby they are known to be Louteas, they wear not before that they be confirmed by the king. Their examination done, and trial made of them, such as have taken their degree wont to be given them with all ceremonies, use to banquet and feast many days together (as the Chinese fashion is to end all their pleasures with eating and drinking) and so remain chosen to do the king service in positions which depend on learning. The other examinates found insufficient to proceed, are sent back to their study again. Whose ignorance is perceived to come of negligence and default, such a one is whipped, and sometimes sent to prison, where we lying that year that this kind of act was, we found many thus punished, and demanding the cause thereof, they said it was for that they knew not how to answer unto certain things asked them.[1]

It is a world to see how these Louteas are served and feared, in sort that in public assemblies at one shout they give, all the servitors belonging unto justice tremble thereat. At their being in these places, when they list to move, be it but even to the gate, these servitors do take them up, and carry them in seats of beaten gold.[2] After this sort are they borne when they go in the city, either for their own business abroad, or to see each other at home. For the diginity they have, and office they do bear, they be all accompanied: the very meanest of them all that goeth in these seats is ushered by two men at the least, that cry unto the people to give place, howbeit, they need it not, for that reverence the common people hath unto them. They have also in their company certain sergeants, with their maces either silvered, or altogether silver, some two, some four, other six, other eight, conveniently for each one his degree. The more principal and chief Louteas have going orderly before these sergeants, many other with staves, and a great

[1] The beating of state-aided candidates whose performance did not satisfy the examiners is mentioned by E. Biot, *Essai sur l'histoire de l'instruction publique en Chine . . . d'après les documents chinois* (Paris, 1847), p. 452. Pp. 422–491 of this work give an excellent account of the Chinese civil service examination system, and of educational practice during the Ming dynasty. The prevalence of purchasing degrees and so side-stepping the competitive literary examinations in the second half of the sixteenth century is described on pp. 480–483.

[2] . . . 'cozido em ouro' in the original, which might, perhaps, be better rendered as 'gilded'.

many catchpoles with rods of Indish canes [bamboos] dragged on the ground, so that the streets being paved, you may hear afar off as well the noise of the rods, as the voice of the criers. These fellows serve also to apprehend others, and the better to be known they wear livery red girdles, and in their caps peacocks' feathers.[1] Behind these Louteas come such as do bear certain boards hanged at staves' ends, wherein is written in silver letters the name, degree, and office of that Loutea whom they follow.[2] In like manner they have born after them umbrellas agreeable unto their titles.[3] If the Loutea be mean, then hath he brought after him but one umbrella, and that may not be yellow; but if he be of the better sort, then may he have two, three, or four: the principal and chief Louteas may have all their umbrellas yellow, the which among them is accompted great honour. The Loutea for wars, although he be but mean, may notwithstanding have yellow umbrellas. The Tutans and Chaçims, when they go abroad, have besides all this before them led three or four horses with their guard in armour.

Furthermore the Louteas, yea and all the people of China, are wont to eat their meat sitting on stools at high tables as we do, and that very cleanly, although they use neither table-cloths nor napkins. Whatsoever is set down upon the board, is first carved, before that it be brought in: they feed with two sticks,[4] refraining from touching their meat with their hands, even as we[5] do with forks, for the which respect, they less do need any table-cloths. Neither is the nation only civil at meat, but also in conversation, and in courtesy they seem to exceed all other. Likewise in their dealings, after their manner, they are so ready, that they far pass

[1] Cf. Giles, *Glossary*, p. 103; Couling, *Encyclopedia Sinica*, p. 426. Under the Manchus, the peacock feather was a badge of merit conferred on high officials, the raven's or 'blue feather' serving for lower officials, although both kinds were known to foreigners under the former name. Contrary to what Giles and Couling assert, a similar practice evidently prevailed under the Ming.

[2] The *p'ai* or official rank board. Cf. *Travels of Peter Mundy*, III, 171, 259.

[3] *Sombreiro* in the Portuguese original. For the application of this word, which originally meant 'hat', to the state-umbrellas of the East cf. *Hobson-Jobson*, p. 851; *Travels of Peter Mundy*, III, 259, 288.

[4] Chopsticks, *k'uai-tzŭ*, 'hasteners'. Cf. Giles, *Glossary*, p. 26; Dyer Ball, *Things Chinese* (ed. 1925) p. 149.

[5] 'We, that is, the Italians and Spaniards', Willis explains in a marginal note, oblivious that the original writer was a Portuguese. This comment implies that forks were still a rarity in Elizabethan England.

all other gentiles and Moors, and have little reason to envy us.[1] The greater states are so vain that they line their clothes with the best silk that may be found.

The Louteas are an idle generation, without all manner of exercises and pastimes, except it be eating and drinking. Sometimes they walk abroad in the fields, to make the soldiers shoot at pricks with their bows, but their eating passeth; they will stand eating even when the other do draw to shoot. The prick is a great blanket spread on certain long poles; he that striketh it, hath of the best man there standing a piece of crimson taffeta, the which is knit about his head: in this sort the winners honoured, and the Louteas with their bellies full, return home again.

The inhabitants of China be very great idolaters, all generally do worship the heavens; and as we are wont to say 'God knoweth it', so say they at every word *Tien xautee*,[2] that is to say, 'The heavens do know it.' Some do worship the sun, and some the moon, as they think good, for none are bound more to one than to another. In their temples, the which they do call Meãos,[3] they have a great altar in the same place as we have; true it is that one may go round it. There set they up the image of a certain Loutea who in that region where they put him (and hold him in this veneration) has done something notable.[4] At the right hand standeth the devil, much more ugly painted than we do use to set him out, whereunto great homage is done by such as come into the temple to ask council, or to draw lots: this opinion they have of him, that he is malicious and able to do evil.[5] If you ask them what they do think of the souls departed, they will answer, that they be immortal, and that as

[1] The words 'and have little reason to envy us' are omitted in the Italian, and hence in the original English, translation.

[2] *T'ien hsiao tê*, 'Heaven knows'.

[3] *Miao*, generic word for a wayside shrine, and a Buddhist temple not inhabited by priests. Cf. Couling, *Encyclopedia Sinica*, p. 553; Giles, *Glossary*, p. 146.

[4] Willis here has a marginal note, 'After the Dutch fashion', the relevance of which is not apparent to me. Pereira probably alludes here to the practice of awarding minor canonization to the memory of local worthies or officials who had benefited the people (*T'u T'i Lao Yeh*). Cf. Werner, *Dictionary of Chinese Mythology*, pp. 528–529.

[5] Pereira is obviously thinking of either Buddhist or Taoist temples, but his description is too vague to enable one to identify the deities concerned. Cf. Sir Charles Eliot, *Hinduism and Buddhism*, III, 325–327, for a description of a typical Chinese Buddhist temple.

soon as any one departeth out of this life, he becometh a devil[1] if he have lived well in this world; if otherwise, that the same devil changeth him into a buffalo, ox, or dog. Wherefor to this devil do they much honour, to him do they sacrifice, praying him that he will make them like unto himself, and not like unto other beasts.

They have moreover another sort of temples, wherein both upon the altars and also on the walls do stand many idols well pro-portioned, but bare-headed. These bear name *Omithofom*,[2] accompted of them spirits, but such as in heaven do neither good nor evil, thought to be such men and women as have chastely lived in this world in abstinence from fish and flesh, fed only with rice and salads. Of that devil they make some accompt; for these spirits they care little or nothing at all. Again they hold opinion that if a man do well in this life, the heavens will give him many temporal blessings, but if he do evil, then shall he have infirmi-ties, diseases, troubles, and penury, and all this without any knowledge of God. Finally, this people knoweth no other thing than to live and die, yet because they be reasonable creatures, all seemed good unto them we spake through our interpreter, though it were not very sufficient. Our manner of praying especially pleased them, and truly they are well enough disposed to re-ceive the knowledge of the truth. Our Lord grant in his mercy all things so to be disposed, that it may some time be brought to pass, that so great a nation as this is, perish not for want of help.

Our manner of praying so well liked them, that in prison im-portunately they besought us to write for them somewhat as con-cerning heaven, the which we did to their contentment with such reasons as we knew, howbeit not very cunningly. As they do their idolatry they laugh at themselves. If at any time this country might be joined in league with the kingdom of Portugal, in such wise that free access were had to deal with the people there, they might all be soon converted. The greatest fault we do find in them is sodomy, a vice very common in the meaner sort, and nothing

---

[1] *Kuei* (*kwei*); strictly speaking, the disembodied spirits of dead people. Cf. Giles, *Glossary*, p. 35; Werner, *Dictionary of Chinese Mythology*, p. 231.

[2] Buddha Amitābha, the *Omitofe* of Ricci, the Buddha of Boundless Light. Werner, *Dictionary of Chinese Mythology*, pp. 130–137, 336–338.

strange amongst the best.[1] This sin were it left of them, in all other things so well disposed they be, that a good interpreter in a short space might do there great good, if, as I said, the country were joined in league with us.

Furthermore the Louteas, with all the people of China, are wont to solemnize the days of the new and full moons in visiting one each other, and making great banquets, for to that end, as I erst said, do tend all their pastimes and spending their days in pleasure; but before they go to make their visits, they go to pay their respects to their elders and these to the temple, and afterwards they spend these days in pastimes.[2]

They are wont also to solemnize each one his birthday, whereunto their kindred and friends do resort of custom, with presents of jewels or money, receiving again for their reward good cheer. They keep in like manner a general feast with great banquets that day their king was born. But their most principal and greatest feast of all, and best cheer, is the first day of their new year, namely the first day of the new moon of February, so that their first month is March, and they reckon the times accordingly, as the philosophers of old time reckoned before the birth of Christ, respect being had unto the reign of their princes; as when any deed is written, they date it thus, made such a day of such a moon, and such a year of the reign of such a king. And their ancient writings bear date of the years of this or that king.[3]

Now will I speak of the manner the which the Chins do observe in doing justice, that it may be known how far these Gentiles do herein exceed Christians, that be more bounden than they to deal justly and in truth. Because the king of China maketh his abode continually in the city Pachim, his kingdom so great, the shires so

[1] The prevalence of pederasty in Ming China was frequently mentioned in the accounts of European travellers and missionaries. A study of contemporary Chinese literature shows that the practice was neither condemned nor encouraged, but regarded with indifference. Cf. R. H. Van Gulik, *Erotic colour-prints of the Ming period* (Tokyo, 1951), I, p. 9.

[2] For details of the celebration of the lunar feasts in Fukien province, cf. J. Doolittle, *Social Life of the Chinese*, (London, 1866), II, pp. 1–90; J. J. de Groot, *Les Fêtes annuellement célébrées à Emoui (Amoy)*, 2 vols. (Paris, 1886). For comparison with those elsewhere in China, see J. Bredon, *The Moon Year. A Record of Chinese customs and festivals* (Shanghai, 1927).

[3] For a concise account of Chinese calendars and systems of dating, see *Handbook of Oriental History*, pp. 196–200.

many, as tofore it hath been said: in it therefore the governors and rulers, much like unto our sheriffs, be so appointed suddenly and speedily discharged again, that they have no time to hatch ill. Furthermore to keep the state in more security, the Louteas that govern one shire, are chosen out of some other shire distant far off, where they must leave their wives, children and goods, carrying nothing with them but themselves.[1] True it is, that at their coming thither they do find in a readiness all things necessary, their house, furniture, servants, and all other things in such perfection and plenty, that they want nothing. Thus the king is well served without all fear of treason.

In the principal cities of the shires be four chief Louteas, before whom are brought all matters of the inferior towns, throughout the whole shire. Divers other Louteas have the managing of justice, and receiving of rents, bound to yield an accompt thereof unto the greater officers. Others do see that there be no evil rule kept in the city; each one as it behoveth him. Generally all these do imprison malefactors, cause them to be whipped and racked, a thing very usual there, and accompted no shame. These Louteas do use great diligence in the apprehending of thieves, so that it is a wonder to see a thief escape away in any town, city, or village. Upon the sea near unto the shore many are taken, and look even as they are taken, so be they first whipped, and afterward laid in prison, where shortly after they all die for hunger and cold. At that time when we were in prison, there died of them above threescore. If haply any one, having the means to get food, do escape, he is set with the condemned persons, and provided for as they be by the king, in such wise as hereafter it shall be said.

Their whips be bamboos, cleft in the middle, in such sort that they seem rather plain than sharp. He that is to be whipped lieth groveling on the ground. Upon his thighs the hangman layeth on blows mightily with these bamboos, that the standers-by tremble at their cruelty. Ten stripes draw a great deal of blood, twenty or thirty spoil the flesh altogether, fifty or threescore will require a

---

[1] João de Barros, *Decada* III, Livro 2, cap. vii (Lisbon, 1563), compares this system to 'a maneira que neste Reyno de Portugal se vsam os juizes que chamam de fóra', which was instituted in Portugal with the same object of preventing magistrates being influenced by ties of local kinship or friendship. Other Portuguese contemporaries were more critical of this practice. Cf. introduction, pp. xxx–xxxi.

Fig. 1

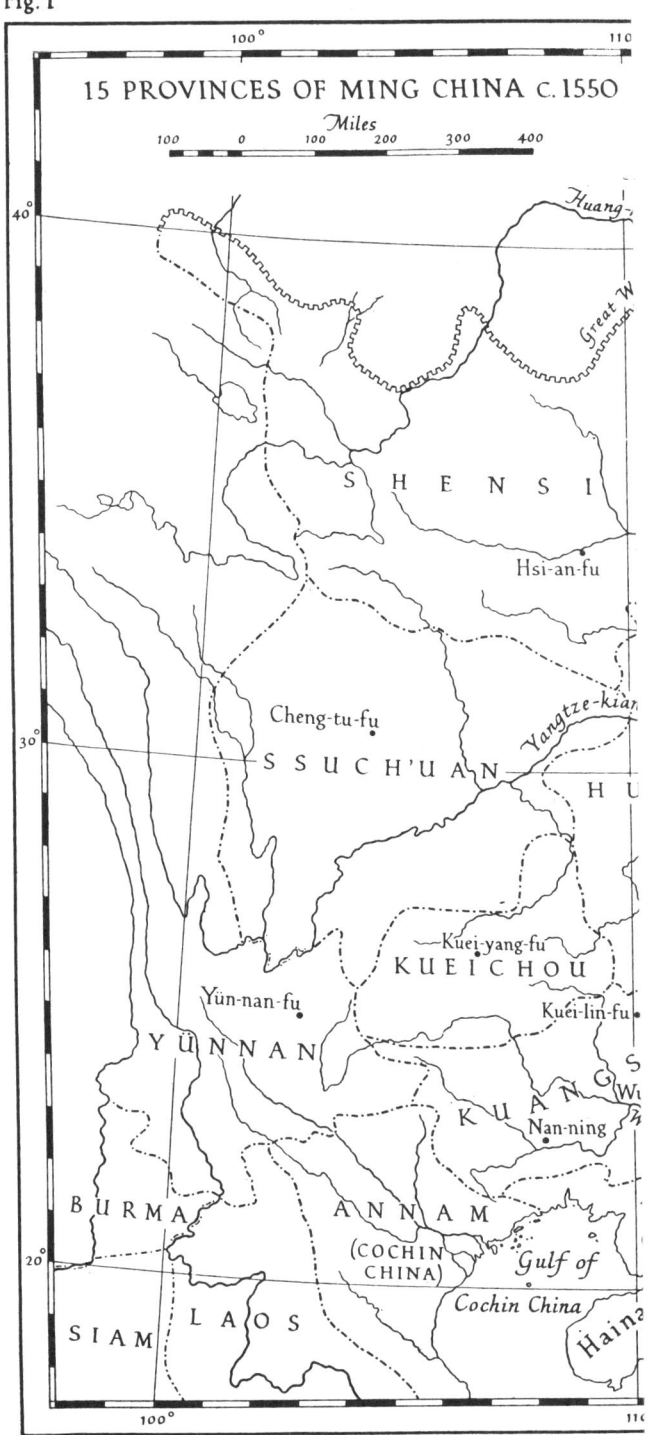

15 PROVINCES OF MING CHINA C. 1550

Miles

100   0   100   200   300   400

40°

Huang-

Great W

S   H E N S I

Hsi-an-fu

Yangtze-kian

30°

Cheng-tu-fu

S S U C H' U A N

H U

Kuei-yang-fu

K U E I C H O U

Yün-nan-fu

Kuei-lin-fu

Y U N N A N

K U A N G S

Wu

K U A N G

Nan-ning

B U R M A

A N N A M

20°

(COCHIN
CHINA)

Gulf of

Cochin China

Haina

S I A M

L A O S

100°

long time to be healed, and if they come to the number of one hundred, then are they incurable—and they are given to whosoever hath nothing wherewith to bribe these executioners who administer them.[1]

The Louteas observe moreover this: when any man is brought before them to be examined, they ask him openly in the hearing of as many as be present, be the offence never so great. Thus did they also behave themselves with us. For this cause amongst them can there be no false witness, as daily amongst us it falleth out, whence it often happens that men's goods, lives and honours are imperilled by being placed in the hand of a dishonest notary.[2] This good cometh thereof, that many being always about the judge to hear the evidence, and bear witness, the process cannot be falsified, as it happeneth sometimes with us. The Moors, Gentiles, and Jews, have all their sundry oaths; the Moors do swear by their *moçafa*[3] the Brahmans by their sacred thread,[4] the Jews by their *Torah*,[5] the rest likewise by the things they do worship. The Chins though they be wont to swear by heaven, by the moon, by the sun, and by all their idols, in judgement nevertheless they swear not at all. If for some offence an oath be used of anyone, by and by with the least evidence he is tormented; so be the witnesses he bringeth, if they tell not the truth, or do in any point disagree, except they be men of worship and credit,[6] who are believed

[1] Descriptions of beating with the bamboo, and of the various types of bamboo used, will be found in *The Punishments of China* (London, 1804), Pl. IV; G. Staunton, *Ta Tsing Leu Lee . . . The penal code of China* (London, 1810), p. lxxiv; and in the *Ta Ming Hui-tien*, chüan 178. The Ming practice was not radically different from that obtaining under the Manchus.

[2] This unfavourable comparison of European with Chinese justice was drastically abridged by the Italian censor, and so appears in a very truncated form in the previously printed versions. The practice of trial in open court lapsed under the Manchu dynasty. Cf. Gray, *China*, I, 32–33.

[3] *Mushaf*, a volume or book; hence the Koran. Cf. Dalgado, *Glossário Luso-Asiático*, II, 58.

[4] The sacred thread or *Janeu*, which is, however, not the monopoly of the Brahmans but is shared by the first three castes. Cf. Dalgado, *Glossário Luso-Asiático*, I, 527–529; S. Sen, *Indian Travels of Thevenot and Careri* (New Delhi, 1949), p. 385 *n* (15).

[5] The Torah or Pentateuch, the first five books of the Old Testament regarded as a connected group, and whose authorship was often ascribed to Moses.

[6] The *Shên-shih*, or 'girdled scholars', otherwise known as the 'scholar-gentry'. Defined by Morse as 'unemployed officials, men of family, of means and of education, living generally on inherited estates, controlling the thoughts and feelings of their poorer neighbours and able to influence the action of the

without any further matter; the rest are made to confess the truth by force of torments and whips.

And as for questioning the witnesses in public, besides not confiding the life and honour of one man to the bare oath of another, this is productive of another good, which is that as these audience chambers are always full of people who can hear what the witnesses are saying, only the truth can be written down. In this way the judicial processes cannot be falsified, as sometimes happens with us, where what the witnesses say is known only to the examiner and notary, so great is the power of money, etc. But in this country, besides this order observed of them in examinations, they do fear so much their king, and he where he maketh his abode keepeth them so low, that they dare not once stir; in sort that these men are unique in the doing of their justice, more than were the Romans or any other kind of people.

Again, these Louteas as great as they be, notwithstanding the multitude of notaries they have, not trusting any others, do write all great processes and matters of importance themselves. Moreover one virtue they have worthy of great praise, and that is, being men so well regarded and accompted of as though they were princes, they be patient above measure in giving audience. We poor strangers brought before them might say what we would, as all to be lies and falacies that they did write, neither did we stand before them with the usual ceremonies of that country, yet did they bear with us so patiently, that they caused us to wonder, knowing specially how little any advocate or judge is wont in our country to bear with us. And if the wand of office were taken from any one of our judges they could very well serve any one of these Chins,— disregarding the fact that these are heathen, for it is obvious that a Christian cannot demean himself to serve a heathen; and as for their being heathen, I do not know a better proof of praising their justice than the fact that they respected ours, we being prisoners and foreigners. For wheresoever in any town of Christendom should be accused unknown men as we were, I know not what end the very Innocents' cause would have; but we in a heathen country, having for our great enemies two of the chiefest men in a whole

officials'. Couling, *Encyclopedia Sinica*, p. 511. The exemption from torture probably referred more specifically to the 'eight privileged classes'. Cf. clause 404 of the Ch'ing penal code in Staunton's *Penal Code of China*, 1810, and Mayers, *Chinese Reader's Manual* (ed. 1910), p. 353.

town, wanting an interpreter, ignorant of that country language, did in the end see our great adversaries cast into prison for our sake, and deprived of their offices and honour for not doing justice, yea not to escape death, for as the rumour goeth, they shall be beheaded,—now see if they do justice or no?[1]

Somewhat is now to be said of the laws that I have been able to know in this country, and first, no theft or murder, is at any time pardoned: adulterers are put in prison, and the fact once proved, condemned to die; the woman's husband must accuse them. This order is kept with men and women found in that fault, but thieves and murderers are imprisoned as I have said, where they shortly die for hunger and cold. If any one haply escape by bribing the gaoler to give him meat, his process goeth further, and cometh to the Court where he is condemned to die. Sentence being given, the prisoner is brought in public with a terrible band of men that lay him in irons hand and foot, with a board at his neck one handful thick, in length reaching down to his knees, cleft in two parts, and with a hole one handful downward in the table fit for his neck, the which they enclose up therein, nailing the board fast together; one handful of the board standeth up behind the neck. The sentence and cause wherefor the fellon was condemned to die, is written in that part of the table that standeth before.[2]

This ceremony ended, he is laid in a great prison in the company of some other condemned persons, the which are found by the king as long as they do live. The board aforesaid so made, tormenteth the prisoners very much, keeping them both from rest, and eke letting them to eat commodiously, their hands being manacled in irons under that board, so that in fine there is no remedy but death.

In the chief cities of every shire, as we have erst said, there be four principal houses, in each of them a prison: but in one of them

[1] This long eulogy of Chinese justice was drastically abridged by the Italian censor, and hence in the English version of 1577. Cf. p. 19 note (2) above, and p. xxix of the introduction.

[2] The portable pillory or cangue (*chia* in Chinese), illustrations of which will be found in the accompanying woodcuts from a Ming book. The efforts of English lexicographers to derive the word 'cangue' from the Portuguese *canga* (ox-yoke), receive no support from Dalgado who points out that none of the old Portuguese writers on China use such a word before *c.* 1640. He suggests that it was probably derived from the Annamite *gang*. Dalgado, *Glossário Luso-Asiático*, I, 203–204.

H

where the Taissu maketh his abode, there is a greater and a more principal prison than in any of the rest; and although in every city there be many, nevertheless in three of them remain only such as be condemned to die. Their death is much prolonged, for that ordinarily there is no execution done but once a year, though many die for hunger and cold, as we have seen in this prison.[1] Execution is done in this manner. The Chaem, to wit the High Commissioner or Lord Chief Justice, at the year's end goeth to the head city, where he heareth again the causes of such as be condemned. Many times he delivereth some of them, declaring that board to have been wrongfully put about their necks. The visitation ended, he chooseth out seven or eight, not many more or less, according to his good or ill disposition, of the greatest malefactors, the which to terrify and keep in awe the people, are brought into a great field, where all the great Louteas meet together, and after many ceremonies and superstitions, as the use of the country is, are beheaded. This is done once a year: whoso escapeth that day, may be sure that he shall not be put to death all that year following, and so remaineth at the king's charges in the greater prison. In that prison where we lay were always one hundred and more of these condemned persons, besides them that lay in other prisons.[2]

These prisons wherein the condemned catiffs do remain are so strong, that it hath not been heard that any prisoner in all China hath escaped out of prison, for indeed it is a thing impossible. The prisons are thus builded. First, all the place is mightily walled about, with its watch-tower above, the walls be very strong and high, the gate of no less force. Within it three other gates, before you come where the prisoners do lie; there many great lodgings are

---

[1] 'The real tortures of a Chinese prison are the filthy dens in which the unfortunate victims are confined, the stench in which they have to draw breath, the fetters and manacles by which they are secured, the absolute insufficiency even of the disgusting rations doled out to them'; Giles, *Glossary*, p. 155. On the other hand, sixteenth-century European jails were little (if at all) better in many respects, and it is noteworthy that Pereira does not write of his experiences in an embittered tone.

[2] Theoretically, capital punishment could only be inflicted at the annual autumn assizes, after confirmation of the death-sentence had been received from Peking. This practice dated from the reign of the first emperor of the Sung dynasty. In the nineteenth century, the provincial authorities were allowed much more latitude. Cf. *Ming-shih*, chüan 94; Staunton, *Penal Code of China*, pp. 451–452, 460; *Chinese Repository*, IV, 174; *China Review*, II, 173–175; XIII, 401; Gray, *China*, I, 31–32.

to be seen of the Louteas, Notaries, Parthions,[1] that is, such as do
these keep watch and ward day and night; the court large and
paved, on the one side whereof standeth a prison, with two mighty
gates, wherein are kept such prisoners as have committed cruel
crimes. This prison is so great, that in it are streets and market-
places wherein all things necessary are sold. Yea some prisoners
live by that kind of trade, buying and selling, and letting out beds
to hire. Some are daily sent to prison, some daily delivered, wherefore this place is never void of seven or eight hundred men that go
at liberty.

Into one other prison of condemned persons shall you go at three
very low iron gates, one after another, the court paved and vauted
round about, and open above as it were a cloister. In this cloister
be eight rooms with iron doors, and in each of them a large gallery,
wherein every night the prisoners do lie at length, their feet in the
stocks, their bodies hampered in huge wooden grates that keep
them from sitting, so that they lie as it were in a cage, sleep if
they can; in the morning they are loosed again, that they may go into
the court. Notwithstanding the strength of this prison, it is kept
with a garrison of men, part whereof watch within the house, part
of them in the court, some keep about the prison with lanterns and
watch-bells answering one another five times every night, and
giving warning so loud, that the Loutea resting in a chamber not
near thereunto, may hear them. In these prisons of condemned
persons remain some fifteen, others twenty years imprisoned, not
executed, for the love of their honourable friends that seek to pro-
long their lives. Many of these prisoners be shoemakers, and have
from the king a certain allowance of rice. Some of them work for
the keeper, who suffereth them to go at liberty without fetters and
boards, the better to work. Howbeit when the Loutea calleth his
check-roll, and with the keeper vieweth them, they all wear their
liveries, that is, boards at their necks, ironed hand and foot.

When any of these prisoners dieth, he is to be seen of the Loutea
and Notaries, brought out at a gate so narrow, that there can but
one be drawn out there at once. The prisoner being brought forth,
one of the aforesaid Parthions striketh him thrice on the head with

[1] *Parthianous* (Japsin), *Partilõs* (Ajuda). Probably derived from the colloquial
Pu-t'ing, (*Pō-thia*ⁿ in the Amoy vernacular), district police-masters and jail-
wardens. Cf. Carstairs Douglas, *Dictionary*, pp. 379, 551, and Mayers, *Chinese
Government*, nr: 294.

an iron-tipped stave; that done, he is delivered unto his friends if he have any, otherwise the king hireth men to carry him to his burial in the fields.

Thus adulterers and thieves are used. Such as be imprisoned for debt once known, lie there until it be paid. The Taissu or Loutea calleth them many times before him by the virtue of his office, who understanding the cause wherefor they do not pay their debts, appointeth them a certain time to do it, within the compass whereof if they discharge not their debts being debtors indeed, then they be whipped and condemned to perpetual imprisonment. If the creditors be many, and one is to be paid before another, they do, contrary to our manner, pay him first of whom they last borrowed, and so ordinarily the rest, in such sort that the first lender be the last receiver. The same order is kept in paying legacies; the last named receiveth his portion first. They accompt it nothing to show favour to such a one as can do the like again, but to do good to them that have little or nothing, that is worth thanks. Therefore they pay the last before the first, for that their intent seemeth rather to be virtuous than gainful.

When I said that such as be committed to prison for theft and murder were judged by the court, I meant not them that were apprehended in the deed doing, for they need no trial, but are brought immediately before the Tutan, who out of hand giveth sentence. Others not taken so openly, and do need trial, are the malefactors put to execution once a year in the chief cities, to keep in awe the people: or condemned, do remain in prison, looking for their day. Thieves being taken, are carried to prison from one place to another in a chest which is a little longer than a sitting man, upon men's shoulders, hired for this purpose by the king. The chest is six handfulls high, the prisoner sitteth therein upon a bench, the cover of the chest is two boards, amid them both a pillory-like hole, for the prisoner his neck; there sitteth he with his head without the chest, and the rest of his body within, not able to move or turn his head this way or that way, nor to pluck it in. The necessities of nature he voideth at a hole in the bottom of the chest; the meat he eateth is put into his mouth by others. There abideth he day and night during his whole journey: if haply his porters stumble, or the chest do jog, or be set down carelessly, it turneth to his great pains that sitteth therein, all such motions being unto him hanging as it were. Thus were our companions brought to this city of Funcheo in seven days journey, never taking any rest as afterward they told us, and their greatest grief was to stay by the way. As soon as they came, being taken out of the chests, they were not able to stand on their feet and two of them died shortly after.

Of Fucheo [Foochow]. When we lay in prison at Fucheo, we came many times abroad, and were brought to the palaces of noblemen, to be seen of them and their wives, for that they had never seen any Portugal before. Many things they asked us of our country, and our fashions, and did write everything, for they be curious in novelties above measure. The gentlemen show great courtesy unto strangers, and so did we find at their hands; and because that many times we were brought abroad into the city, somewhat will I say of such things as I did see therein, being a gallant city, and chief in one of the thirteen shires aforesaid.

The city of Fucheo is very great, and mightily walled with square stone both within and without, and as it may seem by the breadth thereof, filled up in the middle with earth, the watch-towers covered with tiles and with galleries very well made, that one might dwell therein. The stairs they use, are so easily made, that one may go them up and down a-horseback as eftsoons they do. The streets are paved, as already it hath been said. There be a great number of merchants; every one hath written in a great board at his door such things as he hath to sell. In like manner every artisan painteth out his craft. The market-places be large; great abundance of all things there be to be sold. The city standeth upon water, many streams run through it, the banks pitched, and so broad that they serve for streets to the city's use. Over the streams are sundry bridges both of timber and stone, that being made level with the streets, hinder not the passage of the barges to and fro, the channels are so deep. Where the streams come in and out of the city, be certain arches in the wall; there go in and out their *paraos*, that is a kind of barges they have,[1] and this only in the day-time.

[1] *Parau, paró* etc., a generic term for small ships approximating in size and burthen to the *fustas* (foists) and *galeotas* (galliots) of the contemporary Portuguese. Dalgado, *Glossário Luso-Asiático*, I, 170–172, derives the term from the Dravidarian *padavu* which passed into the languages of the Indian Archipelago and Malaya under such forms as *parahu, parāu*, whence *prauw* and *prow*. Cf. also *Hobson-Jobson*, p. 733.

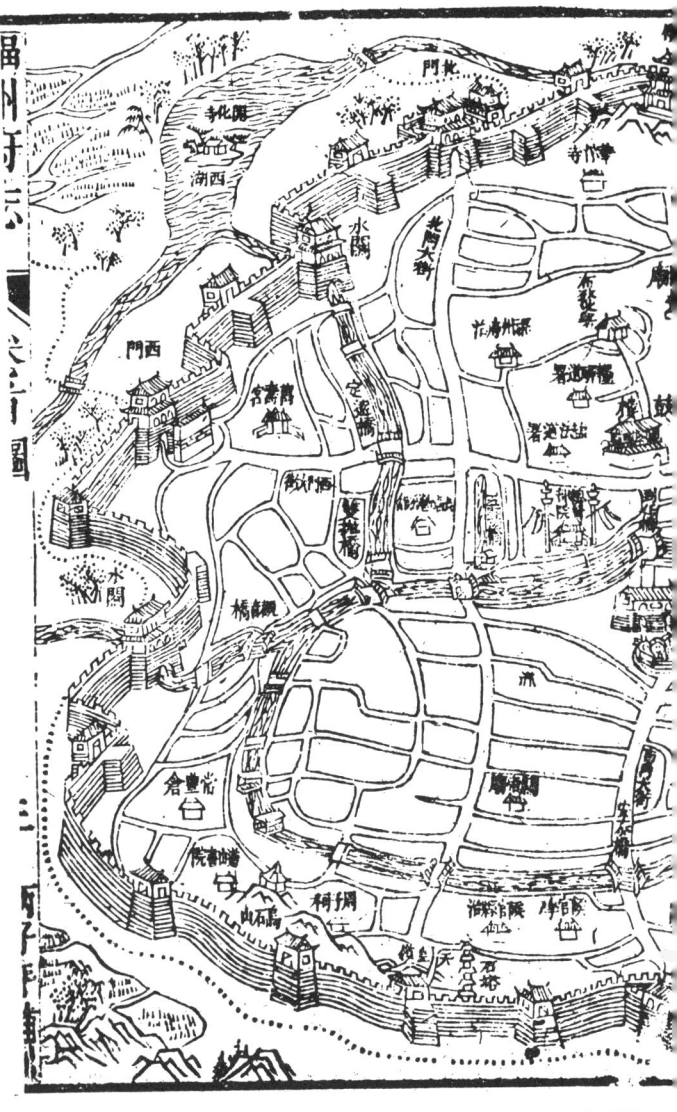

II. The
(From t

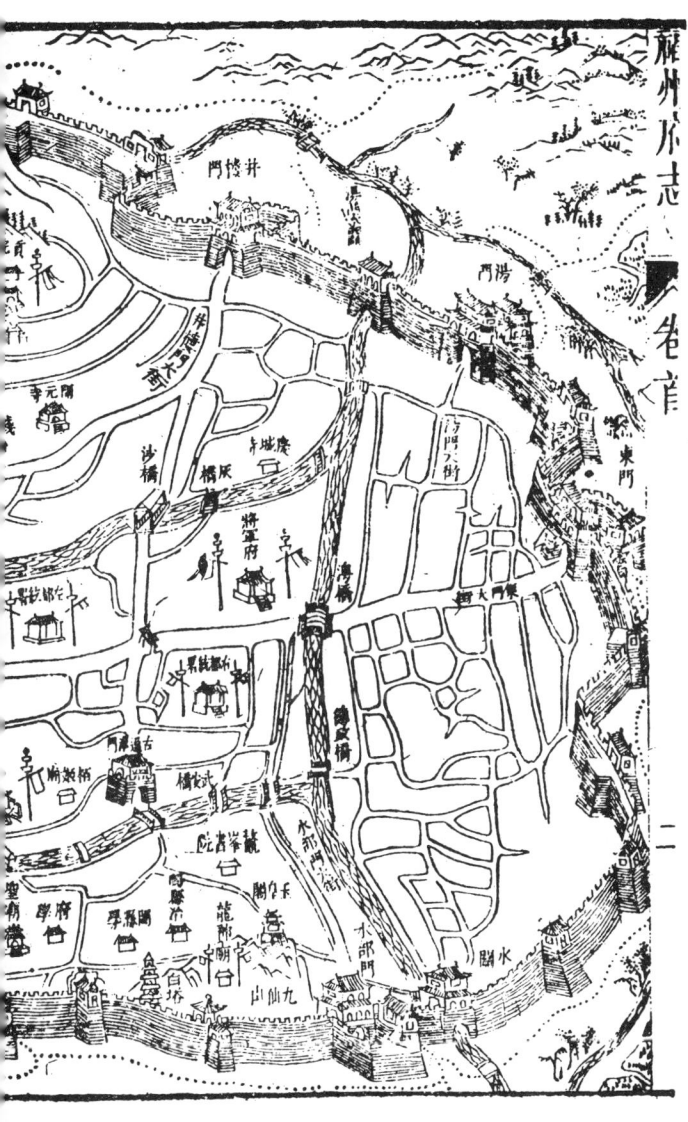

OW

-chih, 1754)

At night these arches are closed up with gates, so do they shut up all the gates of the city. These streams and barges do ennoble very much the city, and make it as it were to seem another Venice.[1] The houses are all low but well made, not lofted except it be some wherein merchandise is laid. It is a world to see how great these cities are, and the cause is, for that the houses are built low, as I have said, and do take a great deal of room. And albeit the cities are so large as I say, yet the people are so weak (although inumerable) that with very little, one could in this country in a very short time do a great deal of service to God and to our lord the king.[2] One thing we saw in this city that made us all to wonder, and is worthy to be noted; namely, over a porch at the coming in to one of the aforesaid four houses, the which the king hath in every shire for his governors as I have erst said, standeth a tower built upon forty pillars, each one whereof is but one stone, each one forty handfulls or spans long: in breadth or compass twelve, as many of us did measure them. Besides this, their greatness such in one piece, that it might seem impossible to work them. They be moreover cornered, and in colour, length, and breadth so alike, that the one nothing differeth from the other. This thing made us all to wonder very much.

We are wont to call this country China, and the people Chins; but as long as we were prisoners, not hearing amongst them at any time that name, I determined to learn how they were called, and asked sometimes by them thereof, for that they understood us not when we called them Chins.[3] I answered them that all the inhabitants of India called them Chins, wherefore I prayed them that they would tell me for what occasion they are so called, whether peradventure any city of theirs bear that name, like the Portugals had derived their name from [Porto, Oporto] the oldest city in Portugal, and similarly with other nations which had taken their names from kingdoms. Hereunto they always answered me, to have

[1] This comparison is discussed in Appendix II, pp. 330–331.

[2] This paragraph, implying that the conquest of China would be a relatively simple matter, is omitted in the Italian (and other) printed version(s). Cf. Ferguson, *Letters from Portuguese captives in Canton*, pp. 47, 122, 133, for more open advocacy of the conquest of Kuangtung.

[3] It is commonly accepted that the word was derived from the Ch'in or Ts'in dynasty which flourished in the third century B.C., and became widely known in India, Persia, and other Asian countries. Cf. *Fonti Ricciane*, I, 8–9, *note*, for a detailed discussion.

no such name, nor ever to have had. Then did I ask them what name the whole country beareth, and what they would answer being asked of other nations what countrymen they were. It was told me that of ancient time in this country had been many kings, and though presently it were all under one, each kingdom nevertheless enjoyed that name it first had; these kingdoms are the provinces I spoke of before. In conclusion they said, that the whole country is called *Tamen*, and the inhabitants *Tamenjins*,[1] so that their name China or Chins, is not heard of in that country. I do think that the nearness of another country thereabout called Cochinchina,[2] and of which the Jaos [Javanese] and Siames [Siamese] must needs have had first notice and knowledge as lying nearer to Mallaqua, did give occasion both to the one nation and to the other of that name Chins, as also to the whole country to be named China. But their proper name is that aforesaid.

I have heard moreover that in the city of Nanquin remaineth a tablet of gold, and in it written a king his name, as a memory of that residence the kings were wont to keep there. This tablet standeth in a great palace, covered always, except it be in some of their festival days, at what time they are wont to let it be seen; covered nevertheless as it is, all the nobility of the city goeth of duty to do it every day reverence.[3] And by this can be seen how feared is this king, whose very name is worshipped; and likewise this is done in Pachim and in all the head cities of all the other shires in the houses of the Pomchaçins, wherein these aforesaid tablets do stand, with the king his name written in them, although no reverence be done thereunto but in solemn feasts. But in this city of Nanquim there is this custom which there is not in the others, in memory of the kings having resided therein of ancient time. On these tablets are written the names of the kings who succeed each other.

I have likewise understood that the city Paquim where the king

[1] *Ta Ming*, 'Great Ming'; and *Ta Ming Jên*, 'Great Ming person (or people).' Cf. also Cruz, Ch. I, p. 64, note (1).

[2] The 'Cochinchina' of the Portuguese was not the Mekong delta region which is now called by that name, but Tongking and Northern Annam. Cf. Gaspar da Cruz, Ch. I, p. 64, n. (2) *infra*.

[3] The Wan-shou-kuan, or 'Hall of Ten Thousand Ages', where a ceremony of this nature took place on certain festival days, including New Year's Day, and the Imperial birthdays. Cf. B. C. Henry, *Ling-nam*, pp. 40–41; Doolittle, *Social Life of the Chinese*, II, 218; Gray, *China*, I, 253; *China Review*, VIII, 61.

maketh his abode, is so great, that to go from one side to the other, besides the suburbs, the which are greater than the city itself, it requireth one whole day a-horseback, going hackney pace, and judging by what we have seen I can well believe it.[1] In the suburbs are many more wealthy merchants of all kinds of merchandise and richness in the world. They told me furthermore that it was moated about, and in the moats great store of fish, whereof the king maketh great gains.

It was also told me that the king of China had no king to wage battle withal, besides the Tartars, with whom he had concluded a peace more than fourscore years ago.[2] Nevertheless their friend-ship was not so great, that the one nation might marry with the other. And demanding with whom they married, they said, that in old time the kings of China when they would marry their daughters, accustomed to make a solemn feast, whereunto came all sorts of men. The daughter that was to be married, stood in a place where she might see them all, and look whom she liked best, him did she chose to husband, and if haply he were of a base condition, he became forthwith a grandee; but this custom hath been left long since.[3] Nowadays the king marrieth his daughters at his own pleasure, with great men of the same kingdom. The like order be observed in the marriage of his sons.

They have moreover one thing very good, and that which made us all to marvel at them being gentiles: namely, that there be hospitals in all their cities, always full of people; we never saw any poor body beg.[4] We therefore asked the cause of this: and answered

---

[1] This story of the size of Peking was repeated by many later European writers on China, including Juan González de Mendoza and Fernão Mendes Pinto. Cf. Gaspar da Cruz, Ch. V, p. 90, n. (1) below.

[2] Probably a confused reference to the Emperor Ying-tsung, who was cap-tured by the Mongol Tartars in 1449, but released a few years later. He re-nounced the throne at this time, but was persuaded to re-ascend it under a new reign-title (T'ien-shun) in 1457.

[3] Someone was pulling Pereira's leg, but this fable is reminiscent of the story told about a celebrated T'ang statesman, as related on p. 450 of Giles' *Bio-graphical Dictionary*. Cf. Cruz, Ch. XXII, p. 186 infra.

[4] 'Did it ever strike you that an able bodied beggar is seldom or never seen in China', wrote an English Sinologue in 1875, pointing out that it was the family-system which took the place of governmental, religious, or organised charity in the main. *China Review*, III, 51–57. Cf. W. C. Milne, *Life in China*, pp. 49–61; Gray, *China*, II, pp. 46–63, for accounts of pauper relief and Chinese hospitals in later (and more degenerate) days.

it was, that in every city there is a great circuit, wherein be many
houses for poor people, for blind, lame, old folk, not able to travel
for age, nor having any other means to live. These folk have in the
aforesaid houses, ever plenty of rice during their lives, but nothing
else. Such as be received into these houses, come in after this
manner. When one is sick, blind, or lame, he maketh a supplica-
tion to the Ponchassi, and proving that to be true he writeth, he
remaineth in the aforesaid great lodging as long as he liveth.
Besides this they keep in these places swine and hens, whereby
the poor be relieved without going a-begging.

I said before that China was so full of rivers that only someone
who had seen it could believe it, but now I mind to confirm the
same anew, for the farther we went into the country, the greater we
found the rivers. Sometimes we were so far off from the sea, that
where we came no sea-fish had been seen, and salt was there very
dear; withal from the rivers alone we found the bazars full of
saveis [shads] and *garoupas, bagres* and *peixe-pedra, robellos, raya*
[rays] and such a great quantity of fish as to amaze us, and likewise
much shell-fish.[1] We did not know how to explain this, since it was
as I say so far from the sea, and although the fresh-water shell-fish
was quite tasteless, the fish is most excellent good, and what is
more it is mostly from fish-ponds; and throughout the interior of
this country they keep it good after this manner. Where the rivers
do meet, and so pass into the sea, there lieth great store of boats,
specially where no salt water cometh, and that in March and April.

[1] *Saveis*, plural of *savel = Alosa alosa* (Linnaeus); *garoupa = Serranellus
Cabrilla* (Linnaeus); *bagres = boga = Boopo* Voopo (Linnaeus); *peixe-pedra =
peixe-espada*, [sword-fish] *= Lepidopus Candatus* (Euphrasen); *roballos = Hemi-
barbres dissimilis* (Chinese variety), and *rayas* [rays] are too numerous to mention
here. I owe these identifications to the kindness of my friends Cdte. Gervasio
Leite, and Cdte. Valente de Araujo of the School of Fishery Investigation at
Lisbon. These identifications do not, however, always agree with those suggested for some of the corresponding names in Ambrosio Fernandes Brandão's
sixteenth-century *Dialogos das Grandezas do Brasil* (ed. J. Cortesão and R.
Garcia, Rio de Janeiro, 1943), pp. 237 and 266. In this work, *peixe-pedra*,
described by Brandão as 'a small fish thus called because it has a stone in the head
instead of brains; and as it is very healthful and enjoyed by invalids, it is fished in
great quantity', is there identified with the '*camorim* or *camurim*, of the Percidos
family, *Oxylabrax undecimalis*, Bl., the well-known *robalo* of Rio de Janeiro',
(*op. cit.*, p. 266); the *peixe-espada* is here identified with the *Xiphias gladius* of
Linnaeus. It will be seen that Pereira distinguishes between *robalo* and *peixe-
pedra*. For Chinese fishes in general see Couling, *Encyclopedia Sinica*, pp.
180–183; Y. T. Chu, *Index Piscarum Sinensium* (Shanghai, 1931).

These boats are so many that it seemeth wonderful, neither serve they for other than to take small fish. By the rivers' sides they make fish-ponds of fine and strong nets, that lie three handfulls under the water, and one above, to keep and nourish their fish in, until such time as other fishers do come with boats, bringing for that purpose certain great baskets lined with paper, able to hold water, wherein they carry their fish up and down the river, every day renewing the chest with fresh water, and selling their fish in every city, town, and village where they pass, unto the people as they need it; most of them have fish-ponds to keep fish in always for their provision. Where the greater boats cannot pass any farther forward, they take lesser, and because the whole country is very well watered, there is so great plenty of divers sorts of fish, that it is wonderful to see. Assuredly we were amazed to behold the manner of their provision. Their fish is chiefly nourished with the dung of buffaloes and oxen, that greatly fatteneth it. Although I said their fishing to be in March and April at what time we saw them do it, nevertheless they told us that they fished at all times, for that usually they do feed on fish, wherefore it behoveth them to make their provision continually.

When we had passed Foquiem, we went into Quiancy shire, where the fine porcelain is made, as I said before; and we came to a city built at the foot of the mountains on the other side, whereby passeth a river navigable.[1] There we took boat, and went down stream. On each side of the river we found many cities, towns and villages, where did we land by the way to buy victuals and other necessaries, and wherein we saw great store of merchandise, principally porcelain, for it was the most we had seen since the time when we were captured. Going down this river southward, we were glad that we drew near unto a warmer country, from whence we had been far distant: this province of Quiançi we passed through in eight days, for our journey lay down the stream. Before that I do say anything of that province we next came into, I will first speak of the great city of Quamchefu,[2] wherein always remaineth a Tutan, that is a governor, as you have seen, though some Tutans do govern two or three shires.

---

[1] Possibly the city of Ningtu, as argued in the introduction.
[2] Presumably Kan-chou-fu in Kiangsi province, which was also the seat of a Tu-t'ang in Martini's time. Cf. Thevenot, Relations, III, 115.

That Tutão that hung himself for our cause, of whom I spake before, was born in this country, but he governed Foquiem shire.[1] Nothing it availed him to be so great an officer. This country is so great, that in many places where we went, there had been as yet no talk of his death, although it had happened nearly a whole year before. At the city of Quanchefu whither we came, the river was so great that it seemed a sea, though it were so little where we took water that we needed small boats. One day about nine of the clock, beginning to row near the walls with the stream, we came at noon to a bridge made of many barges, over-linked all together with two mighty chains. There stayed we until it was late, but we saw not one go either up thereon or down, except two Louteas that about the going down of the sun, came and set them down there, the one in one side, the other in the other side. Then was the bridge opened in many places, and barges both great and small to the number of 600 began to pass: those that went up by the stream at one place, such as came down at another. When all had thus shot the bridge, then was it shut up again.[2]

We hear say that every day they take this order in all principal passages of merchandise, for paying of the custom unto the king, specially for salt, whereof the greatest revenues are made that the king hath in this country. The passages of the bridge where it is opened, be so near the shore, that nothing can pass without touching the same. To stay the barges at their pleasure, that they go no further forward, are used certain iron instruments. The bridge consisteth of 112 barges; there stayed we until the evening that they were opened, loathsomely oppressed by the multitude of people that came to see us, so many in number, that we were enforced to go aside from the bank until such time as the bridge was opened, howbeit we were nevertheless thronged about with many boats full of people. And though in other cities and places where we went, the people came so importunate upon us, that it was

[1] Chu Wan was born at Ch'ang-chou in Nanking (Kiangnan) province, according to his biography in the *Ming-shih*, Ch. 205: 1a–3b.

[2] This pontoon bridge of boats also impressed many later European travellers as can be seen from *Fonti Ricciane*, I, 343; J. Nieuhof, *Embassy from the East-India Company of the United Provinces to the Grand Tartar Cham, Emperor of China* (London, 1669), pp. 62–63. For Chinese pontoon bridges in general, cf. Fugl-Meyer, *Chinese Bridges*, pp. 49–51.

needful to withdraw ourselves,[1] yet were we here much more molested for the number of people; and this bridge is the principal way out of the city to the other bank, which was so populous that were it walled about, it might be compared to the city. When we had shot the bridge, we kept along the city until it was night, then met we with another river which joined with this; we rowed up that by the walls until we came to another bridge gallantly made of barges, but lesser a great deal than that other bridge over the greater stream. Here stayed we that night and other two days with more quiet, being out of the press of the people. These rivers do meet without at one corner point of the city. In either of them were so many junks and *somas* great and small, that we all thought them at the least to be above three thousand; the greater number thereof was in the lesser river where we were. Amongst the rest here lay certain greater vessels, called in their language *Parau*,[2] that serve for the Tutão, when he taketh his voyage by other rivers that join with this, towards Pachin, where the king maketh his abode. For, as many times I have erst said, all this country is full of rivers. Desirous to see those parau we got into some of them, where we found some chambers set forth with gilded beds very richly, other furnished with tables and seats, and all other things so neat and in perfection, that it was wonderful.

Quanci shyre,[3] as far as I can perceive, lieth upon the south, and it is the end of this kingdom; for as soon as we began to enter therein, we went always in a southerly direction for most of the time, travelling not far from the high mountains we saw there. Asking what people dwelleth beyond those mountains, it was told me that they be robbers, and men of a strange language. And because that unto sundry places near this river, the mountains do approach, whence the people issuing down do many times great harm, this order is taken at the entry into Quanci shire. As this city of Quanci and the cities, towns and villages of the whole province

---

[1] Later travellers had similar experiences at this place. Cf. J. Nieuhof, *Embassy*, pp. 62–63; A. E. Van Braam Houckgeest, *Voyage de l'ambassade de la Compagnie des Indes Orientales Hollandaises, vers l'Empereur de la Chine, 1794–1795* (Philadelphia, 1797–1798), I, pp. 60–61, II, pp. 117–118; G. Staunton, *Notes of proceedings and occurences during the British Embassy to Peking in 1816* (Havant, 1824), pp. 409–410.

[2] As explained on p. 25, note (1), this word is not a Chinese term.

[3] Kuangsi province, as is apparent from the context. Willis (through the Italian) has *Quiacim*.

are all situated at the extremity of the kingdom on this side, and so far from the coast, and their sites seem to have been chosen rather from necessity than from choice in so dry and sterile a region, so it is surprising to find so many and such large towns as we found all along this river and the adjacent mountains. But the reason therefore, as we were told and as we saw from the manner and order of their guarding this river, seems to be (as I have said) that it is one of the bounds of the kingdom, and borders with these people who obey nobody.[1]

As this region is so far the land inward, and as there are so many and such large cities therein, and the nearest seaport thereto is Cantão, where this river enters the sea, it is continually a highway of large and small paraos laden with salt, salted fish, and pepper and other things which this region lacks; the which, in order that they may be taken to and fro securely along the river Camçim,[2] (a month's voyage), at each of their leagues (which are ten in one of ours) they have a watch consisting of three or four large armed somas and small paros, which watch all the night long on both sides of the river;[3] and the paros which spend the night under guard of these watchers are secure, apart from the fact that they never voyage except in close convoys. And in each one of these watches there are from thirty to two hundred men, as the passage requireth.

This guard is kept usually until you come to the city of Ucheo, where continually the Tutão of this shire, and eke of Cantão, maketh his abode.[4] From that city upward, where the river waxeth more narrow, and the passage more dangerous,[5] there be always armed from forty to fifty paraos, to accompany other vessels fraught with merchandise, and all this at the king his charges. This seemed to me one of the greatest things I did see in this country.

[1] Banditry was endemic in Kuangsi province for centuries. All this section is much abridged in the Italian and English translations.

[2] The route taken by Pereira and his companions is discussed in the introduction, pp. liii–liv, as is the doubtful identification of the river 'Camçim'.

[3] I think Pereira must mean that these guard-boats were stationed at every ten *li*. Cf. Gray, *China*, II, 101.

[4] Presumably Wu-chou, the most populous city in Kuangsi and the commercial centre of the province, owing to its excellent position. The headquarters of the two Kuang provinces were established here in 1469. Cf. Appendix II, p. 328.

[5] Here at any rate the Kuei or Cassia river must be intended. Cf. JNCBRAS (1867) pp. 5–8, and Geil, *Eighteen capitals of China*, pp. 104–111.

Forasmuch as in all this time we were able to wander at leisure about this city, and I saw therein some things worth recording here, I will relate some of them, beginning with these Moors whom we found here, and of how Moors came to be in China.[1]

When we lay at Fuquiem, we did see certain Moors, who knew so little of their sect, that they could say nothing else but that 'Mahomed was a Moor,[2] my father was a Moor, and I am a Moor,' with some other words of their Alcoran, wherewithal and in abstinence from swine's flesh, they live until the devil take them all. This when I saw, and being sure that in many Chinish cities the relics of Mahomed are kept, I concluded that there came by way of Siam some Moors who converted other people to their sect,— until we reached this city[3] where we found these fellows, from whom I informed myself and learnt the truth.

These Moors, as they told me, in times past came in great nailed ships with topsails[4] fraught with merchandise from Pachinward,[5] to a port granted unto them by the king, as he is wont to all them that traffic into this country, where they being arrived at a little town standing in the haven's mouth, in time converted unto their sect the greatest Loutea there. When that Loutea with all his family was become Moorish, the rest began likewise to do the same. In this point of religion the Chins be at liberty, every one to worship and follow what liketh him best. Wherefore nobody took heed thereto, until such time as the Moors perceiving that many followed them in superstition, and that the Loutea favoured them, they began to forbid wholly the eating of swine's flesh. But all this countrymen and women, chosing rather to forsake father and mother, than to leave off eating of pork, by no means would yield to that proclamation. For besides the great desire they all

---

[1] For the introduction of Islam into China, its subsequent vicissitudes, and the position of its adherents during the Ming dynasty, cf. E. Bretschneider, *Medieval Researches from Eastern Asiatic sources*, I, 264–274; M. Broomhall, *Islam in China* (London, 1910), pp. 5–80; *Fonti Ricciane*, I, 110–113; JNCBRAS, LX, 42–78.

[2] Muslim.

[3] Apparently either Wu-chou or else Kueilin is intended here.

[4] '. . . naos pregadiças e de gaveas,' in the original.

[5] '. . . por aquella banda de Paquim' in the original. Apparently Pereira had a confused idea that river (or sea?) communication between the Caspian Sea and the Great Wall was possible. Cf. p. 38 note (1) below.

have to eat that kind of meat, many of them do live thereby;[1] and therefore the people complained unto the magistrates, accusing the Moors of a conspiracy pretended betwixt them and the Loutea against their king. In this country, as no suspicion, no not one traitorous word is long borne withal, so was the king speedily advertised thereof, who gave commandment out of hand that the aforesaid Loutea should be put to death, and with him the Moors of most importance; the others to be laid first in prison, and afterwards to be sent abroad into certain cities, where they remained perpetual slaves to the king as we were.

In this city of Quançy[2] came by hap men and women threescore and odd, who at this day are brought to five men and four women, for it is now twenty years ago this happened.[3] Their offspring passeth the number of two hundred and they in this city, as the rest in other cities whither they were sent, have their mosques, whereunto they all resort every Friday to keep their holiday. But, as I think, that will no longer endure, than whiles they do live that came from thence, who are more Moorish than Mahomed himself; for their posterity is so confused, that they have nothing of a Moor in them but abstinence from swine's flesh, and yet many of them do eat thereof privily. They tell me that their native country hath name Çamarquão,[4] a firm land, wherein be many kings, and the Indish country well known unto them. It may so be; for as soon as they did see our servants (our servants were Guzerates)[5] they judged them to be Indians. Many of their words be founded upon the Persian tongue, but none of us could understand them.

[1] Chinese fondness for pork and pig-breeding is described in Gray, *China*, II, 165–170.

[2] Here again it is not clear whether Kueilin or Wu-chou is meant, but probably the former. In any event, Muslims are still relatively numerous in Kuangsi.

[3] There is no trace of such a legend in the works quoted, p. 36 note (1) above, nor in M. G. Devéria's article 'Origine de l'Islam en Chine' in the *Centenaire de l'Ecole des Langues Orientales Vivantes*, Paris, 189(5), pp. 305–355, nor in M. C. Schefer's article on Chinese and Muhammadan relations on pp. 1–30 of the same work. How this fantastic sort of story can gain currency may be seen from H. Muller's note on 'Mohammedans and Chinese common opinion', in *T'oung Pao*, XXXIX, 108–121.

[4] 'Camarian' in Willis; Samarkand. Cf. Bretschneider, *Medieval Researches*, II, 256–271.

[5] Gujarātis. Willis has 'Preuzaretes', and a marginal note 'It should seem by their voyage to be Cardandan in Ortelius'.

I

I asked them whether they converted any of the Chins unto their sect. They answered me, that with much ado they converted the women with whom they do marry, yielding me no other cause thereof, but the difficulty they find in them to be brought from eating swine's flesh and drinking of wine. I am persuaded therefore, that if this country were in league with us, forbidding them neither of both, it would be an easy matter to draw them to our religion from their superstition, whereat they themselves do laugh when they do their idolatry.

I have learned moreover that the sea whereby these Moors that came to China were wont to travel is a very great gulf, that falleth into this country out from Tartaria and Persia, leaving on the other side all the country of China, and land of the Mogores, drawing always toward the south.[1] And of all likelihood it is even so, because that these Moors, the which we have seen, be rather brown than white, whereby they show themselves to come from some warmer country than China is near to Pachin, where the rivers are frozen in the winter for cold, and many of them so vehemently that carts may pass over them.

We did see in this city many Tartars, Mogores, Bramas and Laos,[2] both men and women. The Tartars are men very white, good horsemen and archers, confining with China on that side where Pachin standeth, separated from thence by great mountains that are betwixt these kingdoms. Over them be certain ways to pass, and for both sides, castles continually kept with soldiers. In time past, the Tartars were wont always to have wars with the Chins, but these fourscore years past they were quiet, until the second year of our imprisonment.[3] The Mogores be in like manner white and heathen.[4] We are advertised that of one side they border upon these Tartars, and confine with the Persian Tartars on the other side, whereof they made us some signs, [?imitating] both their manner of clothes, and that kind of hat the Saracens do wear, but

[1] Willis adds a marginal note 'It seemeth they came by the river from the Caspian Sea'. Cf. p. 36 note (5) above.

[2] 'Tartares, Mogorites, Bremes and Laoynes' in Willis.

[3] For the great Mongol Tartar raid of 1550, under Altan (Anda or Yenta) Khan, into the region of Peking and Paoting-fu, see De Mailla, *Histoire Générale*, Paris, 1779, X, pp. 317–319; S. Wada, *Tōā-shi ronsō*, Tokyo, 1942, pp. 338–348.

[4] It is difficult to make out whether Pereira is here thinking of the Mongols of Mongolia, or of the so-called Mughals from Central Asia, a branch of whom were then engaged in the conquest of Northern India.

we did not see any.[1] The Moors affirmed, that where the king lieth,[2] there be many Tartars and Mogores, that brought into China certain blues of great value, and we all thought it to be *anil* of Cambaya,[3] wont to be sold at Ormuz. So that this is the true situation of that country, not in the north parts, as many times I have heard say, confining with Germany.[4]

As for the Bramas[5], we have seen in this city of Quançi certain men and women, amongst whom there was one that came not long since, having as yet her hair tied up after the Pegus' fashion. This woman, and others more with whom a blackmoor damsel[6] in our company had conference, and did understand them well enough, had dwelt in Pegu. This new come woman, imagining that we meant to make our abode in that city, bid us to be of good comfort, for that her country was not distant from thence above five days journey, and that from there we could go into our own. Being asked the way, she answered that the first three days the way lieth over certain great mountains and wilderness, afterward people to be met withal again. Thence two days journey more to the Bramas country.[7] Wherefore I do conclude that Quançi is one of the confines of this kingdom, and as I have said, it is divided by these huge mountains which run thence due north and south. And westwards lies the land of the Bramas, of which we found such sure signs as I relate here; and in those mountains which are on the south side beyond these frontier ranges, lies the whole land of Sião [Siam] and of the Laos (whome we also found here) and the lands of Camboja and Champa, and Cochinchina.[8]

[1] This sentence is corrupt both in Willis' version and in the original Portuguese.

[2] Probably Peking is intended here, but the wording of the original text is far from clear.

[3] Indigo from Cujarāt. This commodity was 'carried by land from Agra to the Cambay ports or across the frontier to Persia, the export value of the commodity being exceptionally high in proportion to its bulk', (W. H. Moreland, *India at the death of Akbar. An Economic Study*, London, 1920, p. 105).

[4] Galeote Pereira was more accurate in this respect than was Fr. Gaspar da Cruz. Cf. pp. 71 *infra*.

[5] Burmese. Cf. Dalgado, *Glossário Luso-Asiático*, I, 149.

[6] ... 'hũa negra' in the Portuguese original. Neither term in this context implies a Negress, and probably some Indian, Indochinese or Malayan slave-girl is meant.

[7] The slave-girl was, of course, far too optimistic in her estimate of the time it would take the Portuguese to get from Kuangsi to Pegu, which would have been a matter of months and not of days.

[8] This passage was drastically abridged by the Italian translator and consequently by Willis.

I have said that the cities, towns and villages through which we passed in this province of Quançi were all situated in a dry and barren land, but this city,[1] which is the head and chief of other sixteen, is situated in a pleasant plain, abounding in things necessary, sea-fish only excepted, for it standeth far from the sea. Of fresh [water] fish so much store, that the market-places are never empty. The walls of this city are very strong and high, and so broad that one day did I see the Louteas thereof go upon the walls, to take the view thereof, borne in their seats I spake of before, accompanied with a troop of horsemen that went two and two. It was told me they might have gone three and three. These walls are so high and broad, and their circuit is so great that walking along them at our leisure as we did, we could never see the end thereof.

We have seen moreover, that within this aforesaid city the king hath more than a thousand of his kin lodged in great palaces, in divers parts of the city. Their gates be red, and the entry into their houses that they may be known, for that is the king his colour;[2] and the city is so large that even these thousand great houses do not make it look as if it were brightly painted. These gentlemen, according to their nearness in blood unto the king, as soon as they be married, receive their place in honour. This place neither increaseth nor diminisheth in any respect, as long as the king liveth. The king appointeth them their wives and servants, allowing them by the month, all things necessary abundantly, but they have to receive it from the grandees who rule the cities and the provinces. Howbeit, not one of these hath as long as he liveth, any charge or government at all. They give themselves to eating and drinking, and be for the most part burly men of body, insomuch that espying any one of them whom we had not seen before, we might know him to be the king his cousin. They be nevertheless very pleasant, courteous, and fair conditioned; neither did we find, all the time we were in that city, so much honour and good enter-

---

[1] Kueilin, the capital of Kuangsi province is presumably meant here, but the description is not a very good one. Kueilin is (or was) a charming city set like a hobgoblin town in a ring of hills connected by walls.

[2] Yellow was the imperial colour *par excellence* but Red was the dynastic colour of the Ming emperors. Cf. *Ming-shih*, chüan 67, p. 1*b*; Schuyler Camman, *China's Dragon Robes* (New York, 1952), pp. 16-17, 19, 24, 112-114; *China Review*, XV, 253.

tainment anywhere, as at their hands. They bid us to their houses, to eat and drink, and when they found us not, or we were not willing to go with them, they bid our servants and slaves, causing them to sit down with the first. Notwithstanding the good lodging these gentlemen have so commodious that they want nothing, yet are they in this bondage, that during life they never go abroad. The cause, as I did understand, wherefor the king so useth his cousins, is that none of them at any time may rebel against him; and thus he shutteth them up in three or four cities.[1] Most of them can play on the lute; and to make that kind of pastime peculiar unto them only, all others in the cities where they do lie be forbidden that instrument, the courtesans and blind folk only excepted, who be musicians and can play.[2]

This king furthermore for the greater security of his realm, and the avoiding of tumults, letteth not one in all his country to be called lord, except he be of his blood. Many great estates and governors there be, that during their office are lodged lordlike, and do bear the port of mighty princes; but they be so many times displaced, and others placed anew, that they have not the while to become corrupt. True it is that during their office they be well provided for, as afterwards also lodged at the king's charges, and in pension as long as they live, paid them monthly in the cities where they dwell, by certain officers appointed for that purpose. The king then is a lord only, not one besides him as you have seen, except it be such as be of his blood. A nephew likewise of the king, the king his sister's son, lieth continually within the walls of the city, in a strong palace built castle-wise, even as his other cousins do, remaining always within doors, served by eunuchs, never dealing with any matters. Their festival days, new moons, and full moons the magistrates go there to make him reverence, and so do all his relatives, and his name is Vão Folli.[3] His palace is walled

[1] On the status of the princes of the blood in Ming China, cf. *Fonti Ricciane*, I, 54-55, 101-102; and for their extensive manors and country estates, H. Maspero, *Mélanges Posthumes*, III, 185-189, 212.

[2] *Ch'in*, or Chinese lute, alternatively translated as 'horizontal psaltery. Contrary to what Pereira alleges, courtesans were not supposed to play the lute, although this rule was certainly disregarded in practice. Cf. R. H. Van Gulik, *The lore of the Chinese Lute. An essay in Ch'in ideology* (Tokyo, 1940).

[3] Pereira has here confused the name of the palace with that of its occupant. *Wang-fu* means 'imperial palace', this particular one at Kueilin being the seat of the hereditary princes of Chin-chiang during the Ming dynasty.

about, the wall is not high but four-square, and in circuit nothing inferior to the walls of Goa.[1] The outside is painted red, in every square a gate, and over each gate a tower, made of timber excellently well wrought. Before the principal gate of the four, that openeth into the high street, no Loutea, be he never so great, may pass on horseback, or carried in his seat. Amid this quadrangle standeth the palace where that gentleman lieth, doubtless worth the sight, although we came not in to see it. By report the roofs of the towers and house are glazed green, the greater part of the quadrangle set with savage trees, as oaks, chestnuts, cypress, pineapples, cedars, and other such like that we do want, in sort that it forms as fresh and singular a wood as can be seen anywhere, wherein are kept stags, gazelles, oxen and cows, and other beasts, for that lord his recreation, since he never goeth abroad as I have said.

One pre-eminence this city hath above the rest where we have been, and it of right as we do think, that besides the multitude of market-places wherein all things are to be sold, through every street continually are cried all things necessary, as flesh of all sorts, fresh fish, herbs, oil, vinegar, meal, rice, *in summa*, all things so plentifully, that many houses need no servants, everything being brought to their doors. Most part of the merchants remain in the suburbs, for that the cities are shut up every night as I have said. The merchants therefore the better to attend their business, do chose rather to make their abode without in the suburbs than within the city. I have seen in this river a pretty kind of fishing, not to be omitted in my opinion, and therefore will I set it down.

The king hath in many rivers good store of barges full of sea-crows,[2] that breed, are fed, and do die therein, in certain cages, allowed monthly a certain provision of rice. These barges the king bestoweth upon his greatest magistrates, giving to some two, to some three of them, as he thinketh good, to fish therewithal after this manner. At the hour appointed to fish, all the barges are brought together in a circle, where the river is shallow, and the crows, tied together under the wings, are let leap down into the

---

[1] According to Andrea Corsali, the circuit of Goa in the early sixteenth century was not more than a mile. Another authority estimates that the city was then ¾ mile in length and ¼ in breadth. Cf. J. N. Fonseca, *Historical and Archeological sketch of the city of Goa* (Bombay, 1878), p. 133.

[2] Cormorants.

water, some under, some above, worth the looking upon. Each one as he hath filled his bag, goeth to his own barge and emptieth it, which done, he returneth to fish again. Thus having taken good store of fish, they set the crows at liberty, and do suffer them to fish for their own pleasure. There were in that city, where I was, twenty barges at the least of those aforesaid crows. I went almost every day to see them, yet could I never be thoroughly satisfied to see so strange a kind of fishing.[1]

[1] Cf. E. W. Gudger, 'Fishing with the Cormorant in China', in *The American Naturalist*, Vol. LX (New York, 1926), pp. 5–41; C. B. Laufer, 'The domestication of the cormorant in China and Japan', reprinted from the *Field Museum of Natural History Anthropology Series*, No. 3 (Chicago, 1931), pp. 205–262. Galeote Pereira's account is particularly interesting as Marco Polo does not mention this practice, Friar Odoric of Pordenone being the first to describe it. Pereira's description is the second oldest by a European traveller that we have, and the first one to mention community fishing.

Tractado em que se

cõtam muito por estẽso as cousas
da China, cõ suas particulari·
dades, e assi do reyno Dormuz
cõposto por el. M. padre frey
Galpar da Cruz da ordẽ
de sam Domingos.
Dirigido ao muito poderoso Rey dom
Sebastiam nosso senhor.

Impresso com licença. 1 5 6 9.

Treatise in which the things of China are
related at great length, with their particularities, as likewise of the kingdom of
Ormuz. Composed by the Rev. Father Fr.
Gaspar da Cruz of the Order of Saint Dominic.

Dedicated to the most powerful King Dom
Sebastian Our Lord.

Printed with licence, 1569.

LIST OF THE CHAPTERS
WHICH ARE CONTAINED IN THIS
TREATISE[1]

[1] There is no list of contents in the original edition of 1569–1570, but this is supplied here from the chapter headings of that work

Prologue of André of Burgos, printer to the very high and mighty King Dom Sebastian, first of this name, King of Portugal and of the Algarves etc.[1]

IT is natural that men of profound understanding should take great pleasure and contentment in learning noteworthy matters, when these are written by wise men, who may be expected not to deviate from the reality of truth. It would further seem that this pleasure and contentment must be even greater in kings and princes; because the greater the height of their estate, the more they are expected to have a supreme and penetrating understanding. And because I know that your highness excels all in this, and desires to see new things, especially those of China (whereof there is so much to say that it astonishes the hearers, and whereof Dom Francisco Henriques, captain of Malacca,[2] gave a brief relation to your highness), I resolved to print this treatise wherein are related the particularities and grandeurs thereof, written by a Religious of the order of Saint Dominic, a learned and God-fearing man, who may be expected not to deviate from the truth, since he was an eyewitness thereof. I beg your highness to receive this little service of mine, and to take it under your royal protection. For being favoured by such an exalted prince, it will remain secure from detractors and slanderers. Our Lord increase the days and the life and the royal estate of your highness for His service and the protection of these kingdoms.

[1] André de Burgos was a Spaniard, native of Granada, who first worked as a printer at Seville between 1542 and 1549, before establishing himself at Evora on the invitation of the Cardinal-Infant, Dom Henrique, whose household printer he became. In 1559, he was sentenced to a year's banishment from the city, on suspicion of having taught the manufacture of playing-cards, but was pardoned two months later, presumably on the intervention of his princely patron. His books are, like the *Tractado*, carelessly printed on coarse paper and with old-fashioned and inferior types. Some forty-three works were issued under his imprint between 1552 (?) and 1579, before his death in 1580 or thereabouts. For further details see A. J. Anselmo, *Bibliografia das obras impressas em Portugal no século XVI* (Lisbon, 1926), p. 102. Dom Sebastian, to whom the book is dedicated, was King of Portugal from 1557 until his defeat and death at the hands of the Moors on the field of Alcáçer-el-Kebir, 4 August, 1578.

A certain Dom Francisco Henriques was captain of Malacca from November 1573, until his death there a year later (Couto, *Decada IX*, Cap. 14 and 17); but I cannot trace another with this name before the publication of the *Tractado* in 1569–1570. Cf. *Archivo Portuguez Oriental*, fasc. 5 (1865), pp. 670–671.

PROLOGUE OF THE WORK

IN order that the peoples might be summoned to hear the gospel as they ought to be before the end of the world (according to Saint Paul and according to Christ through Saint Matthew[1]), God ordained the discoveries made by the Spaniards in the New World, and that done by the Portugals in the navigation of India. By these means God through his servants has converted many peoples newly to the faith, and continues converting and will convert them, until the coming (as Saint Paul the Apostle says) of the overflowing of the peoples;[2] Israel being saved by conversion, Jews and Gentiles forming one flock, and thus all will be in one pale of one holy and catholic Church, and under one pastor as Christ says.[3] The peoples that the Portugals have summoned, and of whom many have been converted to the faith, are the Brasis,[4] and those of all the Guinee coast, where there are many multitudes of Christians made in diverse ways beyond the Cape of Good Hope, and all along the coast to Milinde, including Sofala and Moçambique.[5] There are many Christians dwelling among the Portugals in Ormuz and its lands (which are in the coasts of Arabia and Persia), for Ormuz is an island wherein is a very noble and wealthy city, and this island is in the midst of the sea.[6] There are also many Christians on the borders of Persia and Arabia, but as these peoples are Moors, fewer of them are converted than are of idolaters. Along all the coast of India, namely from Diu to Cape Camorim,[7] where are the principal strongholds of the

[1] Matthew, xxiv. 14, and xxviii. 18–20.

[2] Romans, XI. 25–26.

[3] John X. 16.

[4] Brazilians, Amerindians of Brazil. The name Brazil was derived from *braza* (or *brasa*) a live coal, and was applied to the country because it produced a dyewood having the colour of live coal.

[5] The Guinea coast here means the African coast from Cape Nun on the West to C. Guardafui on the East.

[6] See the Chronicle of the Kings of Ormuz translated and annotated at the end of this work.

[7] More usually spelt Comorim or Comorin. The name is derived from the Tamil *Kumāri*, a young girl, a princess; a name of the goddess Durgā, whose temple at the extremity of the Indian peninsula has given to the adjacent cape and coast this name since high antiquity. Cf. *Hobson-Jobson*, pp. 238–239.

Portugals and their principal habitations, there are many thousands of Christians in all the regions possessed by the Portugals, where many temples of idols have been demolished, and where idolatry has been largely destroyed; many churches have been founded (many of them very noble) and many monasteries of religious.[1] In all these lands baptism is carried on unceasingly; and even though many of the peoples who are converted in these parts are bad Christians or apostates who leave the faith, yet I can affirm from my own experience that many of them live better than commonly do the Portugals who frequent those regions. The principal Christian communities are those in the lands of Bacana and at the end of the island of Tana opposite Bacaim, called Salsete,[2] where the fathers of Saint Francis have churches in various places, and fathers who take care of them for doctrine and administration of the Sacraments, which are well cultivated and taught in doctrine. The fathers of the Company have likewise contributed their share in the christianising of the city proper.[3] And now that those of Saint Dominic have founded a house there, they have likewise begun to lend a hand with the others, both in baptising as in catechising. The fathers of the Company have also a good harvest of new Christianity in Tana, where they have a dignified house and church. And the said fathers have under their charge an island near Goa called Chorão, a little island, where they

[1] A. da Silva Rego, *História das missões do Padroado Português do Oriente*. *India, 1500–1542* (Lisbon, 1949), gives the latest and best survey of Portuguese missionary activities in India during this period. It is based on the same author's monumental *Documentação para a história das Missões do Padroado Português do Oriente. India*, of which, at the time of writing, seven volumes have been published, covering the years 1499–1559.

[2] I cannot identify *Bacana*, as the name does not occur in any work which I have consulted. Probably it is a misprint for some place near Bassein. The Sultan of Gujarāt, Bahādur Shah, ceded Bassein (Hindu *Wasai* or *Vasai*, Muslim *Bassai*, Portuguese *Baçaim*), and the neighbouring districts of Thana and Salsette or Salcete (this last not to be confused with the district of the same name adjoining Goa) to the Portuguese in 1533. The ruins of the old fortified Portuguese city of Bassein are situated some twenty-three miles north of Bombay, and Christianity's roots in this corner of India are deep. The region round Bassein is still thickly inhabited by Roman Catholics, whose women may be distinguished from those of the Hindus by the long sleeves which they wear on their otherwise purely Indian costume. Cf. J. Gerson da Cunha, *Notes on the history and antiquities of Chaul and Bassein* (Bombay, 1876), pp. 117–251; Silva Rego, *História das Missões*, I, 463–476; Father Hull, S.J., *A short guide to Bassein* (Bombay, 1941).

[3] The first missionaries of the Company of Jesus reached Goa with St. Francis Xavie   1542.

have a good church and a good and populous Christian community.[1] They have made in the course of time many thousands of Christians in their noble house in the city of Goa, and they instruct well those of their converts who are under their wing.[2] The fathers of Saint Dominic have made many thousands of Christians, both in their house at Goa as in five churches which are entrusted to them, and wherein they teach and administer the Sacraments, teaching their converts thoroughly.[3] The fathers of Saint Francis have made many Christians in Cranganor, five leagues from Cochim, and in other places such as Vaipi and Our Lady of Grace, but chiefly in Cranganor, where they have a good breed of youths in an institution.[4] The fathers of Saint Dominic have made many Christians in Cochim at Reis Magos, which is at the end of the island where the Portugals have a fortress. They have also increased the cult and devotion of Our Lady in the said Cochim, through a confraternity of Our Lady of the Rosary, founded there by Malabar nobles, very rich and noble, whereby her devotion is increased and the faith augmented. The fathers of Saint Francis at Coulão[5] have likewise made great fruit in the new Christian community there, helped by those of the Company. These are the chief and new fruits of the coast of India, besides which there are many Christians everywhere in great number. Christianity in Diu began a short time ago to increase greatly, both through the fathers of Saint Dominic, as through the others. In the island of Ceilam, I saw many and large Christian communities (even after they had been greatly reduced by the wars) cultivated

[1] The island of Chorão, some three miles north of Goa, between the rivers Mapuçá and Naroa. Cf. A. Valignano, S.J., *Historia del principio y progresso de la Compañía de Jesús en las Indias Orientales, 1542–1564*, ed. J. Wicki, S.J., pp. 380–381.

[2] The Confraternity of the Holy Faith (Santa Fé) and the college of St. Paul (São Paulo) was founded shortly before the arrival of the Jesuits in India but was taken over by them soon after. Cf. J. N. da Fonseca, *Historical and Archeological sketch of the city of Goa* (Bombay, 1878), pp. 260–266; Silva Rego, *História das Missões*, I, 279–286.

[3] Although a few stray Dominicans worked in India as early as the first decade of the sixteenth century, this Order was only officially and permanently established in Asia with the arrival of the group of twelve friars (of whom Gaspar da Cruz was one) at Goa in 1548.

[4] For the Franciscan missions at Cranganore, Vaipin (an island opposite Cochin) and the adjoining region of the Malabar coast, see Silva Rego, *História das Missões*, I, 103–153, 379–398.

[5] Quilon, or Koylang, on the Travancore coast, about halfway between Cochin and Cape Comorin. Cf. Silva Rego, *História das Missões*, I, 399–410.

K

by the fathers of Saint Francis, who are distributed among several churches in different parts of the island, catechising and baptizing continually, and administering the sacraments.[1] And whereas this was the aspect of the new Christianity which most pleased me in India, it is all now lost through the disorder and ill government of the Portugals, which is a great pity. From Cape Comorim in the direction of São Thomé, where the apostle suffered martyrdom and where exists to this day the church he founded there, there are many thousands of Christians living among the Portugals. The fathers of the Company reside continuously among those of the district called the Fishery; and these, although a very bad and inferior race, are yet so firm in the faith and so averse from their idols, that in the regions where there are no fathers, they themselves catechize the children, and on Sundays they decorate the altars and churches, and go to pray there. And when a father goes there from time to time, they take him their children to be baptized.[2] The fathers of the Company in Japan have made many Christians in several regions (I think in three at the least; this was when I went to China in the year fifty-six, and I do not know if they have increased since) and those of them who are under their wing are good Christians.[3] The same fathers have made many thousands of Christians in Maluco besides others that they have made by other means in the island of Amboino, and in the same regions.[4] A friar of Saint Dominic has made over five thousand Christians in the island of Timor whence comes the sandalwood, and also many in the island of Ende;[5] and other friars of the same order likewise do

[1] The history of the early Roman Catholic missions in Ceylon is very fully documented. Cf. G. Schurhammer, S.J., and E. A. Voretzsch, *Ceylon zu Zeit des Königs Bhuvaneka Bahu und Franz Xavers, (1539–1552). Quellen zur Geschichte der Portugiesen, sowie der Franziskaner-und Jesuitenmission auf Ceylon* (2 vols., Leipzig, 1928); P. E. Pieris and M. A. H. Fitzler, *Ceylon and Portugal. Kings and Christians, 1539–1552* (Leipzig, 1932); Léon Bourdon, *Les Débuts de l'évangélisation de Ceylon vers le milieu du XVIᵉ siècle* (Lisbon, 1936).

[2] For the Jesuit mission among the Paravas of the Fishery Coast see Silva Rego, *História das Missões*, I, 359–377.

[3] For the early history of the Jesuit mission in Japan, see G. Schurhammer, S.J., and E. A. Voretzsch [eds.], *Die Geschichte Japans, 1549–1578, von P. Luis Frois, S.J.* (Leipzig, 1926).

[4] The standard work on the Jesuit mission in Amboina is by C. Wessels, S.J., *De Geschiedenis der R. K. Missie in Amboina, 1546–1605* (Utrecht, 1926).

[5] For the Dominican Mission in the Lesser Sunda islands see Humberto Leitão, *Os Portugueses em Solor e Timor de 1515 a 1702* (Lisbon, 1948). Ende is a small island off the south coast of Flores.

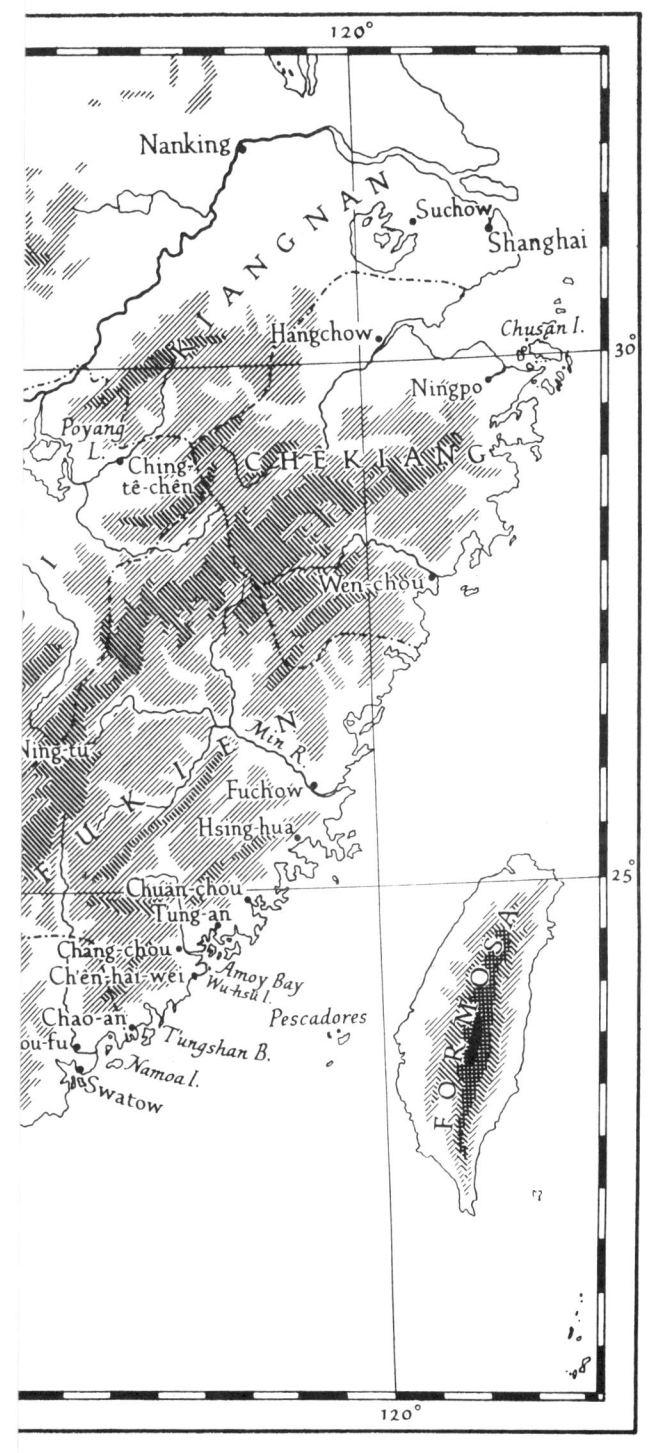

good work in the island of Panaraca which is in Jaoa.[1] Besides these principal Christian communities, there is a great multitude of Christians living with the Portugals in all places where these do dwell, consisting of all nations, such as Bengallas, Pegus, Malacos, Jaos, Chinas, from the Maldiva islands and from many other parts; but the most of the Christians who are converted in these parts are gained through slavery; for neither in Bengala, nor Pegu, nor in Jaoa, nor in China do the Portugals have any fortress or land of their own, nor have any Religious dwelt among these and other peoples in order to make Christians. And because among all these peoples whom I have mentioned, the Chinas exceed all the others in populousness, in greatness of the realm, in excellence of polity and government, and in abundance of possessions and wealth (not in precious things such as gold and jewels but in wealth, dispositions and goods which chiefly minister to bodily needs), and because these peoples have many very memorable things, I resolved to give a general survey of their affairs as best I could, both from what I saw, as from what I read in a compendium composed by a gentleman who was a prisoner the land inward,[2] and from what I heard from trustworthy people. [My intention being] that both by the things which are related herein, those which are as yet unknown could be conjectured, as also that those who read this work should give praise to God for His greatness and likewise feel compassion for such a vast multitude of lost souls who are ignorant of the truth,—praying God to spread His holy Catholic faith among this people as the others, rescuing them from their ignorance and blindness in which they live idolatrously, and opening up a road for His servants to lead these (and the others whom we have mentioned) by way of baptism into the fold of His church. And above all, because seeing so many and such blind peoples, being withal so politic, the reader may give thanks to his Redeemer because although He has not called these, or not brought them into the fold of His Church (because this is the gift of God) He has yet brought the reader and given him the light of faith and knowledge of Himself; and so the reader while making an act of grace may feel inspired to further His love and service.

[1] Panarukan (Panaroekan) is a seaport, not an island, on the north-east coast of Java. This region was still under Hindu control, being finally conquered by the Muslim ruler of Surabaya between 1597 and 1600.

[2] The treatise of Galeote Pereira, translated on pp. 3–43 of this work.

NOTICE TO THE READERS

THE reader must not expect an abundance of eloquence from me, nor ornament in the choice of words, but must content himself with my being faithful and truthful in a plain narration. Lest the reader should be displeased on reading the work at first blush, thinking there are defects in it, I thought good to show him here the order in which I proceed in this work. Firstly, I will treat of China in general, both of the land as of the people; and I will forthwith descend to details in describing the kingdom and its provinces. And afterwards I will speak of the buildings and ships; and after this, of the cultivation of the land and occupations of the men, of the dress of the men and of the women, and of some of their manners and customs. I will treat at length further on of those who rule the country and of its government. And at the end of all, I deal with the cults and religious worship, and of the disposition which I found in the land favouring the propagation of Christianity, and of the obstacles which there are against this. And although this epilogue is necessarily dealt with summarily, I will deal with the things of China in detail. I know that the curious will find many things which they will like to read: and even if someone when reading finds something which he does not much like, he should not on this account fail to read what follows on, thinking that all the rest is like that. I say this because in reading travel stories, things that are not well understood sometimes annoy the reader, and it sometimes happens that on account of some small misunderstanding he may despise all the rest of the book, which he should not do. He should not lose the enjoyment of the most and chiefest part out of annoyance with a small part. I also hereby give readers a necessary warning by which they can conjecture the greatness of the things of China, viz.—that whereas distant things often sound greater than they really are, this is clean contrary, because China is much more than it sounds and the sight thereof makes a very different impression from what is heard or read about it, as has been verified by myself and others after we have seen the things of China. This must be seen and not heard, because hearing it is nothing in comparison with seeing it. What happens in this case, is what happened to the Queen of Sheba with Solomon, when moved by the fame which she had heard of his widsom, she wished to prove it by experience, and going from her country to Jerusalem, and after hearing many things from Solomon and seeing his house and the government thereof, she said, 'Blessed be God who loved Israel and made you King over it; what I have seen is incomparably greater than what they told me of you.'[1] The reader ought to feel the same way about the things which I relate of China herein (which are much greater than what I have said), so that he may read this work with greater pleasure.

[1] I Kings, X. 7, for the Authorised Version rendering.

CHAPTER I

In which is set forth the reason why the author felt moved to go to China, and of this name China, and of the name of the country.

BECAUSE some curious reader, seeing at the beginning of the book that I had gone to China, might like to know the reason which induced me to go there (as some persons have told me) it seemed good to me not to leave him in suspense, but to satisfy him in part straightway in the beginning of the book. Know then that I, being in Malacca building an house of my Order, and preaching, was informed that in the kingdom of Camboja (which is subject to the King of Siam, and lieth toward the parts of China, and doth confine with Champa,[1] whence cometh the most precious Calambuco, or Calambach as they call it[2]) was great opportunity to preach the Gospel, and to reap some fruit. And the information was such, that although everyone in Malacca was opposed to my going, working to prevent my departure in every way they could, yet my conscience forbade me from failing to undertake the journey thither, for it seemed to me that I would be guilty of a grave sin if I failed to do it, having leave of my prelate as I did, and so I took the journey in hand.

And after passing many troubles and hunger in the journey, with dangers and sicknesses, I came ashore, and after I had reasonably informed myself by a third person, conversing with the people and with the fathers, even before I knew it I found all to the contrary of that which they had told, and that all were deceits of the

---

[1] Cambodia (more correctly Kamvuja or Camboja) was not at this time tributary to Siam, although it was before and later, but the reigning King, Ang Chan I, successfully disputed the right of Siam to treat him as a vassal. For details of Cambodia and Champa at this period, see Aymonier, *Le Cambodge*, I, 749–755; A. Leclère, *Histoire du Cambodge depuis le 1er siècle de notre ére* (Paris, 1914), pp. 262–281, and G. Maspero, *Le Royaume de Champa* (Paris, 1928), pp. 239–241. The name 'Champa' is derived from the Sanskrit *Campâ*, which was the name of an ancient Indian kingdom in what is now the district of Bhagalpur.

[2] Calambac, the finest kind of aloes-wood. Cf. *Hobson-Jobson*, (ed. 1903), p. 144 Dalgado, *Glossário Luso-Asiático*, I, 180–182.

simple laity, which of light matters were moved to presume of the people that which was not in them. And besides this I found many hindrances for the obtaining of my desires and intent, for first the King is a Bramene, and the Bramenes are his principal men and his favourites, and most familiar, because they are wizards, for they are much given to be pleased with witchcrafts, and they do nothing without consulting with the Devil, through the wizards and Bramenes that are in the kingdom (who thrive by this means).[1] And so the first thing that the King asked me was if I were a wizard.

Forasmuch then as the Bramenes are the most difficult people to convert, since they are very attached to their rites and idolatries, while the King is a Bramene and his favourites and closest advisers are likewise Bramenes, this is a very great obstacle to the propagation of Christianity in that country. Moreover, the Bramenes do worship among others one God, whom they call Probar missur[2] (which they said made the heavens and the earth, having been given leave to do so by another god called Pralocussar,[3] this god also having obtained power of another whom they call Praissur,[4] for to give this licence to Probar missur), and I showed them that not only he had not made the heavens and the earth, but that he had been a very wicked man and a great sinner; wherefore these priests said, that they would worship him no more, having worshipped him hitherto with their god Praput prasar metri.[5]

[1] Under Siamese influence, Hinayanist Buddhism gradually supplanted the earlier Mahayanist form of that faith and Brahmanism, which previously had flourished side by side without mutual hostility in Combodia (as elsewhere) from about 400 to 1400 A.D. During the fifteenth and sixteenth centuries Brahmanism in Cambodia became what it now is, a court ritual without roots among the people. The narrative of Fr. Gaspar da Cruz is particularly interesting because it shows that Brahman influence was still very powerful as late as 1556. His account is all the more welcome since we have very few notices about Cambodian religion at this period. It escaped the notice of Sir Charles Eliot in his discussion of this problem in *Hinduism and Buddhism. An historical sketch*, III, 112–132, and was also overlooked by Leclère, Aymonier, and other French *savants* who have studied this period of Cambodian history.

[2] Préas Baram Eysaur, or Préas Barmeysaur (Barma-Içvara) one of the titles of Siva. Leclère, *Le Buddhisme au Cambodge* (Paris, 1899), p. 40.

[3] Préas Lok Eysaur, title of a Bodhisatta in Cambodia, as Miss J. M. Stead informs me.

[4] Préas Eysaur, another Cambodian title of Siva. Leclère, *Buddhisme*, p. 40.

[5] Miss J. M. Stead suggests that this must be Préas Put Préas séar Metrei, title of the future Buddha; the second Préas (=sacred, eminent) being inserted into the usual form Préas Put séar Metrei.

Whereupon the hatred of the Bramenes increased towards me, and from thence forward I had disfavours of the King, who was moved for the zeal of his god and the god of his Bramenes.

An additional hindrance was the priests of the idols, and all of their troupe, who go for priests and hold themselves for religious men, and in their conversation and life they are separated from all other people, who to my thinking are the third part of the people of the land; the King thereof setting an hundred thousand men in the field. This religious people, or that holds itself for such, are exceedingly proud and vain, and alive they are worshipped for gods, in sort that the inferior among them do worship the superior like gods, praying unto them and prostrating themselves before them: and so the common people have a great confidence in them, with a great reverence and worship: in sort that there is no person that dare contradict them in anything, and their words among them are held for so sacred, that in no wise will they endure to be gainsaid. Insomuch that it happened sometimes while I was preaching, many round about me hearing me very well, and being very satisfied with what I told them, that if there came along any of these priests and said, 'This is good, but ours is better,' they would all depart and leave me alone. Further, they being very ignorant presume to be very wise, and the common people hold them for such, though all their knowledge is ignorance and heathenish follies. They make seven and twenty heavens,[1] some where there is meat and drink and fair women, whither they say all living things do go, even the flea and the louse, for they say that as they have souls, that they must live in the other world. And to these, they say, all do go that are not religious men as they are. They place others higher, whither they say, do go in an ascending scale their holy priests that do live in the wildernesses; and all the felicity they give them there, is to sit refreshing themselves with the wind. They place others yet higher, the gods of the which, they say, have round bodies like balls; the honour which they give those that go to these heavens is to give them round bodies as the gods themselves have.

[1] Twenty-six according to the description with schematic plan in Leclère, *Buddhisme au Cambodge*, pp. 97–102; possibly our friar confused these with the twenty-seven 'maisons lunaires ou constellations' described on pp. 79–82 of this same work. For a comparison of Buddhist with Brahman ideas, see E. T. C. Werner, *Dictionary of Chinese Mythology*, p. 123.

And even as they make many heavens, so they do many hells, for they make thirteen,[1] to the which they go either higher or lower according to the greviousness of the sins of every one. They have these and other greater ignorancies in which they did not fail to persevere, although I sometimes convinced them of their folly.

They have a division of their religious men, for some they call Massancraches,[2] who are as supreme, and who sit above the King. Others they call Nacsendeches, who are as our bishops here.[3] These sit equal with the King. Others they call Mitires,[4] who are in the common degree of priests, and who sit under the King. Under these there are yet two degrees, whom they call Chapuzes[5] and Sazes,[6] And all these as they ascend in degree, so they do in vanity and pride, and are more reverenced. Turn, then, wise fools from their opinion, especially when they are fortified therein with pride and veneration, esteem and credit, and see what chance there is of winning over the rest of the people, if the former are not convinced of their errors and follies! This is, therefore, a very great obstacle to the propagation of Christianity in this country.

Besides all this, there is another very great inconvenience, that except the priests and all those that hold themselves for religious men, all the rest are slaves of the King; and when the owner of the house dieth all that is in it returneth to the King, and the wife and children hide what they can, and begin to seek a new life.[7] The King acquired this right in the land, because the people rebelled against one of his brothers who was then King, and he subdued

[1] The *Norok* are rather purgatories than proper hells. There are 8 great hells or *mâha norok*, and 16 small *noroks* to each of these. Cf. Leclère, *Buddhisme au Cambodge*, pp. 103–109.

[2] Maha Sângréach (or Sankharéach), title of the High Priest of Cambodia, according to Miss J. M. Stead. Leclère (p. 45) has the form Sámdach Sângréach for this dignitary. Cf. Dalgado, *Glossário Luso-Asiático*, II, p. 572.

[3] Neak Sámdach, the title of a religious dignitary lower in rank than the foregoing.

[4] Miss Stead suggests the derivation *methéa*, 'a wise man' from the Sanskrit *medhira*, 'intelligent'. The ordinary term for ordained Buddhist monks nowadays is *Bhikkus* or *Phikkus*. Cf. Leclère, *Buddhisme au Cambodge*, pp. 389 ff.; Eliot, *Hinduism and Buddhism*, III, 130–131. The Brahman priests are known as *Bakus*.

[5] Presumably derived from *chipôr*, the monk's robe invariably worn when outside the monastery. Leclère, *Buddhisme au Cambodge*, p. 413.

[6] Miss J. M. Stead tentatively derives this from *sak*, meaning 'grade', 'honours.'

[7] Cf. Chapter X, pp. 119–20 below.

them, wherefore his brother made over the kingdom to him.[1] Hence it is that they dare do nothing of themselves, nor accept anything new without leave of the King, which is why Christians cannot be made without the King's approval. And if some of my readers should say that they could be converted without the King knowing it, to this I answer that the people of the country is of such a nature, that nothing is done that the King knoweth not; and anybody be he never so simple may speak with the King, wherefore everyone seeketh news to carry unto him, to have an occasion for to speak with him; whereby without the King's good will nothing can be done, and we have already showed before that he is unwilling in the matter of Christianity.

To all these things were joined some disorders of the Portugals so that in every way I found crosses and inconveniences for to obtain my desires and my pretence. Wherefore I having been in the country about a year, and seeing that I could make no fruit therein beside the passing of grievous sicknesses, I determined to leave this country. And because they told me many things of China, and the people of it to have a disposition to Christianity, and that they loved reason, I resolved, seeing I did no good in this country, nor baptized more than one gentile whom I left in the grave, to go to China in a ship of Chinas which was then in the country, in which they carried me with a very good will, giving me the best room in the ship, not taking any advantage of me, yea, they dealt very charitably with me.[2] This was the reason and by this means I resolved to go to China.

[1] This passage is particularly important as showing that Ang Chan I was still reigning in 1556, although some authorities give 1555 as the year of his death. Gaspar da Cruz' account of his rise to power is rather garbled, but there can be little doubt but that he refers to Ang Chan. This monarch was the younger brother of Srey Sokonthorbat, who had been deposed and killed by Sdach Kân in 1512. Ang Chan was then a refugee in Siam, and only drove out the usurper many years later. The chronology of the Cambodian kings at this period is largely tentative, De Moura, Aymonier, Leclère and other authorities all differing in their assignment of dates. Cf. Aymonier, *Le Cambodge*, I, 749–755; Leclère, *Histoire du Cambodge*, pp. 235–278.

[2] It is interesting to compare the different opinions of European missionaries who took passages in Chinese junks. Da Cruz's favourable impression is echoed by St. Francis Xavier (making due allowance for his dislike of Buddhist services held on board ship) in 1549, and by the Spanish Franciscan friars, Jaime Tarin and Lucas Estevan, in 1680–1688. Cf. Schurhammer-Wicki, [eds.] *Epistolae S. Francisci Xaverii aliaque eius scripta*, II, 179–185, 230; *Sinica Franciscana*, IV, 74–75, 439. On the other hand, the celebrated French Jesuit, Jean de Fontaney,

What I did therein, and the disposition that I found there for the hearing of the word of God, and the obstacles which I found against making fruit therein, I will say at the end of this book, where I describe the rites of the Chinas, and to which I refer the reader.

Now that I have satisfied what could be expected of me at the beginning of the book, it is time that I began to put hand to the work. And for a start thereof, you must know that this name China is not the proper name of the people of this country, nor of the country itself, neither is there commonly in the country notice of such a name; only among all the people of India, and among those who dwell in the Southern regions, such as Malacca, Siam and Jaoa, this denomination of China goeth current, and also among those Chinas who do traffic and deal among us.

The proper name of the country is Tame, the *e* not well pronounced, but almost drowning it; and the name of the people of the country is Tamgin.[1] Whence this name China doth come which is current among the strangers we know not; but it may be conjectured that the people which in old time did sail to those parts, because they passed by the coast of a kingdom which is called Cauchim China,[2] and likewise traded in it and victualled and refreshed themselves there for the journey to the country that lieth further on, which is that of China (in the which kingdom they live after the manner of the Chinas, to whom it is subject), it seemeth that these voyagers, omitting Cauchim from the denomination of this other kingdom, they called all the country that lieth

was of the contrary opinion in 1687, and his unfavourable view was shared by his Spanish Franciscan contemporary, Fr. Miguel Flores. Cf. H. Bernard-Maître, S.J., *Le Voyage du Père de Fontaney au Siam et à la Chine, 1685-1687 d'après des lettres inédites* (Shanghai, 1942), pp. 47-48, reprinted from the *Bulletin de l'Université l'Aurore*. Série III, Tome III, No. 2; O. Maas, *Cartas de China* (Seville, 1917), p. 158.

[1] Probably a corruption of Ta Ming and Ta Ming Jên. Cf. n. (1) on p. 29 above. Possibly, however, it is a corruption of T'ang and T'ang-jên, as the Cantonese often referred to themselves as 'men of T'ang', in the same way as 'men of Han' is (or was) used in the rest of China,—both these dynasties being among the most glorious in Chinese history. The T'ang dynasty flourished 618–907 A.D.

[2] As noted previously, Cochinchina was the name applied by the Portuguese to the country corresponding to the modern Tongking and northern Annam. The name is probably derived from the Arabic *Kawči min Čīn*. Cf. L. Aurousseau, 'Sur le nom de Cochinchine', in BEFEO, XXIV (1924), pp. 551–579.

further along China.[1] However this may be, the truth is that the
name of the country is Tame as we have said, and that of the people
thereof is Tamgin.

[1] This suggestion found no favour with later writers, most of whom on the
contrary thought that China had given its name to its southern neighbour. The
Jesuit Borri, for example, derived the word from the Sino-Japanese pronunciation (Kōchi) of the Sino-Annamite Giao-chi (Chinese Chiao-chih),—'But the
Portugals which traffique in *Anam*, are they which of the Japonian word *Coci* and
of *China*, have made and compounded this word *Cochin-China*, being as much
as to say, as *Cochin* of *China*, to distinguish it from *Cochin* a city of *India* frequented by them'. R. Ashley, *Cochin-China: containing many admirable rarities
and singularities of that country. Extracted out of an Italian relation, lately presented to the Pope by Christophoro Borri, that lived certaine years there* (London,
1633), Ch. I.

CHAPTER II

In which it is shown what country China may be, and what sort of people the Chinas are.

HINA is a great part of Scythia; for as Herodotus saith, Scythia extendeth itself unto India, which may be understood in one of two ways.[1] Either because the Chinas did possess many parts of India and did conquer them of old time, whereof at this day there are some vestiges,[2] as in the coast of Choromandel, which is on the opposite coast of the kingdom of Narsinga,[3] on that side which we call São Thomé, because there is the house built by the apostle, and the relics of his body.[4] There is at this day a great temple of idols, which is a mark for the navigators to know the coast, which is all very low, the which as the men of the country affirm, was made by the Chinas, of whom there remained among them a perpetual memory, and therefore they call it 'Pagoda of the Chinas', which is to say Temple of the Chinas.[5] And in the kingdom of Calequu, which is the head of Malabar, there be very ancient fruit trees which the men of the country say were planted by the Chinas; and on the shoals of Chilão,[6] which

[1] For a discussion of the connection between Scythia and China, and of Herodotus' references thereto, see G. F. Hudson, *Europe and China. A survey of their relations from the earliest times to 1800*, pp. 27–52.

[2] For a succinct survey of the great Chinese voyages to Ceylon and Southern India in Yüan (Mongol) and early Ming times see J. V. Mills, 'Notes on early Chinese voyages' in JRAS (1951) pp. 3–25, which contains a select bibliography of the numerous works dealing with these voyages.

[3] A Portuguese name for the great Hindu empire of Vijayanagar (Bisnaga) in South India, derived from the name of the Prince of Telugu origin, Vira Narasimha, who ruled 1505–1508. *Hobson-Jobson*, pp 618–619; *Handbook of Oriental History*, p. 85.

[4] For the legend of Saint Thomas in Meliapor (Mailapur) see João de Barros, *Decada* III, Book vii, Ch. 11; A. E. Medlycott, *India and the Apostle Thomas. An enquiry. With a critical analysis of the Acta Thomae* (London, 1905); J. Dahlmann, S.J., *Die Thomas-Legende* (Freiburg, 1912); Silva Rego, *História das Missões*, I, 411–435.

[5] Presumably the so-called 'Chinese pagoda' at Negapatam, which was pulled down in 1867, at the petition of the local Jesuit fathers, being then in a ruinous condition. Yule-Cordier, *Marco Polo*, II, 336–337, 391–392; III, 113–114.

[6] Salábham in the vicinity of Adam's Bridge and the gulf of Manar, where there was a famous pearl-fishery. Yule-Cordier, *Marco Polo*, II, 337; *Hobson-Jobson*, p. 195.

do run from the island of Ceilam toward the coast of Choromandel, is affirmed, by the men of the country, a very great armada of the Chinas to be cast away which came for India, which was lost because the Chinas were but young in that navigation.

And so the men of the country say the Chinas were lords of all Jaoa [Java] and of Jantana,[1] which is the kingdom of Malacca, and of Siam and of Champa, as it is commonly affirmed in those parts. Wherefore some do affirm many of these peoples to be like the Chinas, that is having small eyes, flat noses and broad faces, for the great commixture that the Chinas had with all of them, especially with the Jaos who are commonly more China-like.

But the King of China, seeing that his kingdom went to decay, and was in danger by their seeking to conquer many other foreign countries, he withdrew himself with his men to his own kingdom, making a public edict that under pain of death none of the country should sail out of the kingdom of China; the which lasteth to this day.[2] These vestiges show that the Chinas not only had dealings with the regions of India, but conquered and ruled many parts of it, whereby Herodotus said that Scythia reached as far as India. As for China, it reached to the end of Scythia, or, as it seems that Herodotus more truly said, that Scythia reached to India; for some people speak of three Indias, and the third and last they call Jantana, which is in the kingdom of Malacca, and which they call the end of the earth. The people of those regions, because the land in the straight of Cimcapura[3] makes a great bend into the sea like a cape, call the region which extends from this cape and straight to China the third India. According to this, China lies in the third Indian region and the last of all the Indies, and so likewise at the extremity of Scythia; and thus it is true that, as Herodotus says,

[1] Ujong Tanah, 'Land's End', an old name for Johore. I cannot trace that it was ever used in the wide sense which Fr. Gaspar da Cruz alleges; but it is noteworthy that the same assertion was made by Gaspar Barzeu, S.J., in a letter of 1553, where he states that Siam, Patani and Achin were included in this 'imperio de Jantanaa que hé hum grande senhorio que tem debaixo de sy o rei de Cyon, Patanes e Achens'. Silva Rego, *Documentacão*, VII, 171–172.

[2] For the imperial edicts prohibiting overseas navigation see *T'oung Pao*, XXXIV, 388–389. The reasons for this drastic reversal of the Emperor Yung-lo's policy are discussed on pp. 395–399 of this article by Prof. J. J. L. Duyvendak and in G. B. Sansom, *The Western World and Japan*, 147–152.

[3] Singapore. The old Portuguese form is close to the Malay *Singapura*, which in its turn was derived from the honorific Sanskrit title of *Sinhapura*, or 'Lion-city'.

Scythia reaches as far as India, because it is the furthest region of India, or to say better of the Indies. Likewise Jacobo Filipo Bergonense, in his supplement of the Chronicles,[1] after stating that there are two Scythias, one Northern and another Eastern, explains that the Eastern one ends in a point and that Asia lies behind it.

And as to what he says about the Eastern Scythia ending in a point, it seems to me that both he and those from whom he took this are mistaken; and that this mistake arose from seeing it thus depicted in a world-map, which was for lack of true information. Because the point which they show as containing the country and people of the Liquos[2] is not continued with the mainland, but it is an island which standeth in the sea of China, little more or less than thirty leagues from China itself. In this island live this people, which is a well-disposed people, more to the white than brown.

It is a cleanly and well attired people; they dress their hair like women, and tie it up on the side of their head, fastened with a silver bodkin. Their land is fresh and fertile, with many and good waters; and it is a people that sail very seldom although they are in the midst of the sea. They use weapons and wear very good short swords. They were in times past subject to the Chinas, with whom they had much communication, and therefore are they very like the Chinas.[3]

Now this island lying in the China Sea, as we have said, the coast of China runneth winding from the province of Cantão[4] and from its coast to the coast of the province of Namquim,[5] whither the Portugals have sailed, the coast making never a point as the maps do make, the which may be seen well delineated in the sea-cards of the Portugals, and in the maps which they do make.[6]

---

[1] Jacobus Philippus Bergomensis (Foresti), an Italian Augustinian friar, author of the *Supplementum Chronicarum*, of which many editions and several translations were published 1483–1553.

[2] Liu-chiu (Ryūkyū) islands and their inhabitants. The forms Lequeos, Liquios, etc., occur in old Portuguese and Spanish texts.

[3] Compare the account of these islanders given by Tomé Pires in 1512; Pires-Cortesão, *Suma Oriental*, I, 128–131.

[4] Kuangtung (Kwangtung) province. Cruz uses the forms Cantam, Cantão indiscriminately.

[5] Nanking, also called Kiangnan (Chiangnan) and Nan-Chihli. Cf. p. 4 above.

[6] For the representation of the Liu-chiu islands in early sixteenth century Portuguese maps see Pires-Cortesão, *Suma Oriental*, I, 120 (note); A. Cortesão, *Cartografia e Cartógrafos Portugueses dos séculos XV e XVI* (Lisbon, 1935), II, Plates XIV, XVII, XIX, XXII–III, XXVII–VIII, LI.

And thus Jacobo Philipo is mistaken as to what he says about Scythia ending in a point; but as to what he says about having all Asia behind it, there can be no doubt that this is China, of which this can truly be said as we will clearly show below. And in saying that Scythia ends in a point, even though erroneously, he shows us clearly that he is speaking of China, since those of old time held this mistaken opinion.

Jacobo Philipo further says that Scythia contains seventeen provinces, and that the river Thanas[1] runs by the last one which is called Thisageta. By the word 'last' is meant last in respect of us, which ends on our side, that is on the side of Europe, bordering on the edge of Asia; and the river Thanas is that which divides Asia from Europe, and it runs as far as lake Meothis.[2]

Of the river Thanas, running along the boundary of China, I was informed by a rich Venetian merchant of good understanding, who had been for some days trading in Cantam which is one of the principal cities of China, where the Portugals do trade, and in whose company he had gone thither. This man told me that he had trustworthy information from the Chinas that they had heard from the remotest region of China that a river called Thanas ran along the edge of that frontier region. This shows that the kingdom of China has two extremities, which front with the extremities of Scythia whichever it is,—one at the end of Asia major, on the extremity of India, and the other at the end of the same Asia major, but which reaches as far as the confines and frontier of Europe, from which it is divided [by the river Thanas]. Besides this, [Scythia] is shown to have Asia behind it, as Jacobo Philipo says, since on one side thereof lies nearly all India until all of Tartary, which borders along all around of it, as we will further show in the next chapter.

And even though some may object that it is not a good conjecture to infer all the foregoing from the name of the river Thanas, since different regions can have different rivers of the same name, the conjecture will not be found insufficient after reading what is said in the next chapter.

And there is also another good argument to corroborate it, which is that the Tartars reach as far as lake Meothis on the East,

---

[1] Tanais, Tanas, Tana, an old name for the river Don.

[2] The Sea of Azov. Ptolemy greatly exaggerated the extent of this sea, which he at the same time misrepresented as having its direction from south to north.

L

and extend above it as far as the river Thanas, whence the lake receives its waters. These Tartars are likewise reckoned among the Scythians, and extend as far along the border of China, with the which they have continual war; and it is commonly affirmed that between the Chinas and the Tartars there is a wall of a hundred leagues in length, and some will affirm it to be more than a hundred leagues.[1]

Well, if this is true, what doubt can there be, or rather how can it not be possible that the lake which is the origin of the river Thanas lies in the country of the Chinas, and that their land runs for some distance down alongside this river until the country of the Chinas divides from that of the Tartars?

I myself find no doubt in this theory, and I find good indications and proofs that it is indeed so. And thus there can be no doubt that China is really a very large part of Scythia.

---

[1] The Great Wall of China extended from the Gulf of Chihli about 1,500 miles to the westward along its actual length. For descriptions and photographs see W. E. Geil, *The Great Wall of China* (London, 1909), and L. Newton Hayes, *The Great Wall of China* (Shanghai, 1929).

CHAPTER III

Of the kingdoms which border on China; in which notice is given of its greatness; and it is declared to border on the edge of Almayne[1] for it treats of two Russias, and of how one of them confines with China.

AMONG the many and great kingdoms which adjoin China, running along it from above the lake whence originates the river Thanas on the European side, one is Russia, where Europe ends, which belongs to Scythia and is part of it. This Russia lies at the end of Almayne, and it either borders on China or is part thereof; and it seems rather to be a part of China, because, as I was informed by some Portugals who were captive there, the Chinas know of Almayne and call the people thereof Alimenes;[2] and the King of China has many mercenaries who guard the weak passes along the border of Tartary, and these are said to be big men, ruddy, and heavily bearded, wearing cuthose and blunt swords.[3]

[1] 'ho ultimo dalemanha' in the 1569 text. 'Almayne' in Purchas whose Elizabethan rendering I have retained here since it is closer to the Portuguese 'Alemanha', and the English 'Germany' is not applicable to the arguments advanced by Fr. Gaspar da Cruz.

[2] This assertion is not so incredible as it sounds. The characters representing the sound of the word Alemannia (A-lu-mang-ni-a) are shown in the extreme north-west corner of Europe on a Chinese world-map of about 1300. They presumably appeared on later maps as well. Cf. W. Fuchs, *The Mongol Atlas of China by Chu Ssu-pen and the Kuang-yü-t'u* (Peking, 1946), p. 11. The idea that China, or at any rate Tartary, bordered on Germany was evidently widespread among the Portuguese in Asia at that time, although Galeote Pereira (cf. p. 39 above) had more accurate notions on this subject. Gaspar da Cruz's opinion finds an echo in the Flemish Jesuit Gaspar Barzeu's letters of 16 December 1551, (... 'Pareçe-me que a China, que comquista com Alemanha, principalmente a Tartaria mayor' ...), and 12 January 1553, ('Do imperio da China ... dizem que conquista de huma banda com Alemanha, e pola muita frialdade não descobrem a terra' ...); Silva Rego, *Documentacão*, VII, 83, 172–173. I presume that 'comquista' is here used in the sense of 'confina' which is the word that Cruz uses.

[3] This implies that these men were either Russian or German mercenaries, which is highly improbable, although a few stray individuals (mostly prisoners) were to be found in China in Mongol (Yüan) times. Cf. E. Bretschneider,

And thus it seems clear that China borders on the end of Almayne; and that whereas Russia is part of Scythia on its European side, the end of it seems clearly to be a part of China. And it is also pertinent to this argument, that as we have said that Russia includes the greater part of Scythia,[1] and it is certain that beyond Almayne are peoples who have not received the faith, and are idolaters and heathens, then these must be the Chinas since they border with the Russians. Because it must be understood that there are two Russias, one of which runs between [sic] Poland and Almayne and which abuts on lake Meothis, on which it has a very good harbour where is a noble city called Capha;[2] concerning which I was told, when I was in Ormuz, by people who had come from those regions to trade at Ormuz, that the King of Russia had come with a great army to take it, having already taken two other cities which the Turk held in his lands.[3]

The other Russia is at the end of Almayne, and it belongs to Scythia and is the end of Europe, and it is of this one that we treat here.

In this way, Almayne lies between the two Russias, on the side which runs to Lake Meothis to the end thereof, forming the final boundary of Europe. And by what has been said above, the doubt is dissolved as to whether China can be said to border on the end of Almayne; and that it does in fact confine with it is clearly shown by the greatness thereof, and the vast extent of territory which it

Medieval Researches from Eastern Asiatic sources (London, 1910), II, 79–81, 84–90, 154–155 (where Pinto's statement is probably an embroidered version of the information given by Cruz's informants at Canton); A. C. Moule, *Christians in China before the year 1550* (London, 1930), pp. 260–264; Hudson, *Europe and China*, pp. 151–153.

[1] The classical Scythia was, broadly speaking, the South Russian steppes and country north of the Black Sea. The true Scythians had disappeared before the birth of Christ, and Gaspar da Cruz uses their name as a designation for a remote and little-known Central Asian people of whom he had no personal knowledge and confuses them with the Russians.

[2] Kaffa, or Theodosia, on the S.E. coast of the Crimea, where the Genoese established themselves in 1263–1267. It was later incorporated in Krim Tartary and hence became tributary to Turkey after the conquest of the Krim Tartars by Sultan Muhammad II in 1475.

[3] Probably a garbled allusion to the campaigns of Ivan the Terrible against the Golden Horde of Mongol Tartars along the Volga, culminating in the capture of Kazan and Astrakhan in 1552–1555. The Czar's subsequent operations against the Krim Tartars were not so successful as Gaspar da Cruz implies. Their Khan burnt 'the Mosco every stick', as an English resident of the Russian capital wrote after the great Mongol raid of 1571.

comprises, besides the great sea coast which it has on the side where it adjoins India and forms part thereof.

And the first kingdom that doth confine with it on the sea-side of India, is one that is called Cauchim China, which hath about an hundred leagues little more or less along the sea-coast.[1] The sea maketh a great gulf between it and the isle of Ainão,[2] which is of fifty leagues in length, and is already of the Chinas. And at the end of this gulf this kingdom abutteth with the kingdom of China, and is subject to the king of China.[3]

The people of this kingdom in their apparel, policy and government, do use themselves like the people of China. The country is much inhabited and of much people; it is also a very plentiful country, as can be seen from the fact that although they do not deal with other peoples outside of their own kingdom, and living with good polity, they feed and dress themselves very well, as they likewise furnish their houses, having many good buildings, all of which argues the fertility, abundance and prosperity of this country. They have the same writing that the Chinas have, although their speech be different; and while they can understand each other in 'writing, they cannot understand each other's speech.

And do not let anyone think that I am deceiving him, because in China there are many differences of language, for the which reason many of them do not understand each other's speech, yet they understand each other's writing, as do likewise the inhabitants of the islands of Japan, who understand the Chinas through their writing although they have a different language. And how this can be and may be we will explain in its due place.

Beyond this kingdom of the Cauchins-chinas lieth another very

[1] Tongking (Annam). See Ch. I p. 64, n. (2) above.

[2] Hainan. The Portuguese spelt this indifferently 'Hainão' or 'Ainão', but when the preposition de (=of) happens to come before it, Fr. Gaspar da Cruz combines the two words thus 'Dainão', as he and his contemporaries often did with 'Hormuz', 'Ormuz', 'Dormuz'.

[3] The monarchs of the later Lê dynasty of Annam and Tongking at this period only effectively controlled the country between Langson on the Chinese frontier and Thanh-hoa on the Champa frontier, according to some authorities (BEFEO, XXIV, 573), but others extend effective Annamite control as far south as Cape Varella (Maspero, Royaume de Champa, pp. 239–240). Both Annam and Champa acknowledged Chinese suzerainty, but the former consistently ignored repeated Chinese demands to return the provinces conquered from Champa to the rightful owner.

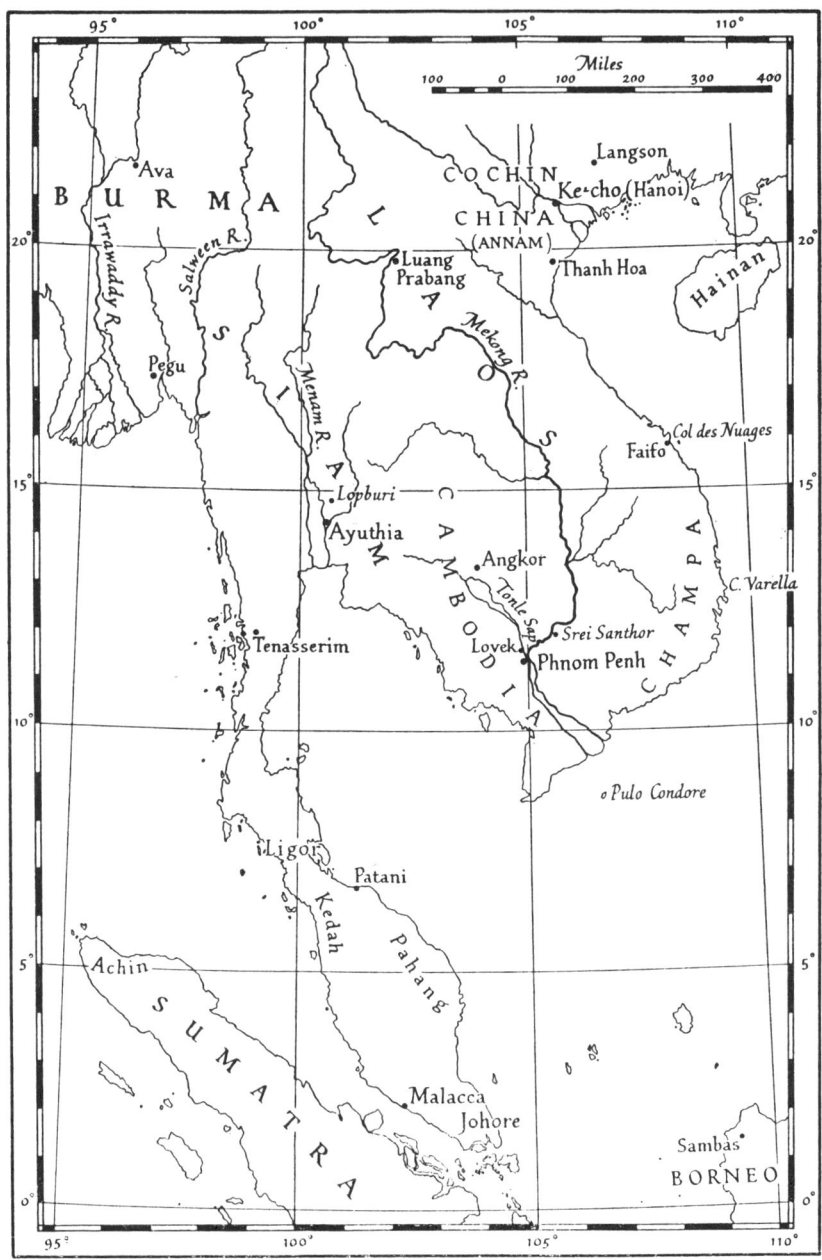

Fig. 7. Indo-China and Malaya, *c.* 1550

great kingdom, which runneth within the land along China, which some do call Laos, and others Siões mãos.[1] This by the other side towards India, doth confine with the kingdom of Camboja, and with the great kingdom of Siam, and with the very rich kingdom of Peguu,[2] with all the which kingdoms it hath traffic; in sort that there remaineth to this kingdom towards the sea of India, all the coast from Peguu unto the ends of the kingdom of Champa, which doth confine with Cauchim-china.[3] And so on the side of these Laos towards the Indian Sea, there lie the great kingdom of Peguu, and that of Tanaçarim,[4] and that of Quedaa,[5] and that of Malacca, and the kingdom of Pão,[6] and that of Patane,[7] and that of Siam, and that of Camboja, and that of Champa[8] which abutteth upon the Cauchins-chinas.

And lest this may seem strange and wonderful, you must know that Siam and Peguu confine with one another in the hinterland, having great wars between themselves, each ruler holding himself as an emperor,[9] being from one to the other a great number of leagues by sea, while the other kingdoms which we have named remain to seaward of them.[10] The reason for this is that the land, running from Peguu to Malacca and thence to Siam, juts out a long way into the sea, and goes along withdrawing from either side, in such wise that Peguu lies as it were on one side and Malacca on

[1] Siamese Mons. For the kingdom of Laos (Lang-Xang, or Luang Prabang) as it was at this period see P. Le Boulanger, *Histoire du Laos français*, pp. 71–89.

[2] The Mon kingdom of Pegu was conquered by the Burmese King Tabin-shwehti in 1539 and Pegu became the capital of the united country until 1635, when the capital was transferred to Ava.

[3] Gaspar da Cruz has become hopelessly confused here, as a glance at the map opposite will show. Laos or Lang-Xang was an inland kingdom, and the coast-line which he allots to Laos was really shared by Siam and Cambodia.

[4] Tenasserim was at this time and for long afterwards a Siamese province, but was finally conquered by the Burmese in 1760.

[5] Kedah in the Malay peninsula also acknowledged Siamese suzerainty.

[6] Pahang, which paid tribute to China in the early Ming dynasty, and later to Siam.

[7] Patani was another Siamese vassal state, and usually ruled by a Queen.

[8] Cf. G. Maspero, *Le Royaume de Champa*, pp. 239–241.

[9] For the wars between Burma and Siam at this period, see G. E. Harvey, *History of Burma*, pp. 153–179, 343; W. A. R. Wood, *History of Siam*, pp. 108–138. Portuguese mercenaries played prominent parts on both sides, although the Burmese usually came off best.

[10] This is very confusing, but he presumably means that it was a long way by sea round the Malay peninsula from Pegu to Siam, as implied in the following sentence.

the other, with the land jutting out a great space into the Indian Sea, wherein lie the aforementioned kingdoms.

Hence it is clear how the Laos or Siões mãos have on the side of the Indian Ocean so many kingdoms running along towards China, and confining with the said kingdoms, and consequently trading with the same.

This kingdom of the Laos, or Siões mãos, was subdued by the Bramas (of whom we will speak presently) in the year of fifty-six;[1] and among some which they brought captive to Peguu they brought some Chinas which the Laos held captives, as one Jorge de Mello, who went for Captain of the voyage to Peguu, affirmed unto me. And though commonly there be no wars between these Laos and the Chinas, because of the great mountains that are between them, on the which the Chinas have good strongholds on that side in the province of Camsi,[2] which doth confine with these and with the Bramas; and in the strongholds they have continually men in garrison for the defence of those parts; there be notwithstanding, continually assaults on the one side and on the other; whereby the Laos might have some Chinas captives.

Before that these Laos were subdued by the Bramas, they carried to Siam, and to Camboja, and to Peguu some very good musk[3] and gold, whereof is affirmed to be great store in that country; and these people having musk, makes us conjecture that the great store of musk which the Chinas have, they get it from the many beasts that are in the confines of this kingdom, in the province of Camsi, from whence they bring it.

The musk is the flesh and blood of certain beasts, which they say to be as big as foxes,[4] the which beaten with strokes and killed, they tie the skin with the flesh together in lumps, the which they cut after the flesh is rotten, and so they sell it, which the Portugals

---

[1] Burmese. Cf. Dalgado, *Glossário Luso-Asiático*, I, 149. For the Burmese invasion of Laos in 1556, cf. Harvey, *History of Burma*, pp. 165–166; Le Boulanger, *Histoire du Laos Français*, pp. 76–80.

[2] Kuangsi.

[3] Portuguese *almiscle*, from the Arabic *al-misk*, derived in its turn from the Persian *muishk* or Sanskrit *muska* (*mushka*), 'testicle.' *Hobson-Jobson*, p. 599; Dalgado, *Glossário Luso-Asiático*, II, 27.

[4] The musk-deer whose principal habitat is the Himalaya and the mountainous regions of Western China (*Moschus moschiferous*, L.). Musk is an excretion of the navel of this animal and Cruz's traditional account of how it was obtained is erroneous.

do call musk-cods. And when it cometh fresh, presently it appeareth to be rotten flesh and blood; the rest they sell loose, holding these cods for the finer musk.

Returning to the Laos, whereof we were speaking, this is the ware which they brought to the above said kingdoms, carrying in return cotton-cloths and other things they had need of.

This people is not very brown; they wear their hair all cut round underneath, and all the rest above ruffled, raising it many times upwards with their hands, that it remaineth to them like a cap, and serveth instead of one, for they wear nothing on their heads. They go naked from the middle upward; and from the thighs downwards they wear certain cotton-cloths girt about them and all white. The women go covered from the breasts to the half leg; they have their faces somewhat like the Chinas; they have the same heathenish ceremonies as do the Pegus, the Siões and the Cambojas; the priests of their idols do wear yellow clothes girt about as the rest of the people, with certain folds and seams in which they hold their superstitious charms. I saw many of this people in Camboja, who had remained there from the year before by the way of traffic; and that year that I was there, they came not because of the wars wherein (as I said) they were subdued by the Bramas.[1]

These Laos came to Camboja down a river many days' journey, the which is very large and they say has its origin in China, as do many others which run into the sea of India.[2] It hath eight, fifteen and twenty fathom of water, as I myself saw by experience, in a great part of it. It passeth through many untilled and deserted countries of great woods and forests, where there is innumerable elephants and many buffaloes, of which I saw many wild in that country, and Merus,[3] which are like good mules, and certain great cattle which in that country they call Badas,[4] of the which the male have a pointless and blunt horn in their forehead, and some of the horns are spotted with singular colours, and others all black,

---

[1] The Burmese occupation was a short-lived one. Le Boulanger, *Laos Français*, pp. 76–80.

[2] Mekong river which rises in Thibet and has an estimated length of about 2,800 miles.

[3] Meru, a species of deer, *Rusa Aristotelis*. Dalgado, *Glossário Luso-Asiático*, II, p. 50.

[4] *Bada* (*Abada*), an old Portuguese name for the rhinoceros. *Hobson-Jobson*, p. 1; Dalgado, *Glossário Luso-Asiático*, I, pp. 1–4. From the Malay *bādak* which is pronounced *bāda* by the Bugis and Makassars.

others of a wax colour; but they have no virtue, but only for the hemorroides or piles; and after the elephant there is no other greater beast; the hair of it is brown and it is footed like an elephant, the head like a cow, and on the chest a great lump of flesh that falls from around the nape, whereof I did eat when travelling in those parts. There are also many other wild beasts.

There be some thorny trees, like lemons and oranges, and many wild grapes through those woods.

When these Laos do return to their country, it takes them three months, as they go against the stream. This river causeth a wonder in the land of Camboja, worthy of reciting.

Coming near to a place which they call Chudurmuch,[1] which is twelve leagues from the principal city of Camboja, it maketh a passage to another river which cometh from a great lake that is in the uttermost parts of Camboja, and that hath Siam on the other side; in the middest of the which, its bigness being great, you can see no land on neither side; and this river passeth by Loech,[2] which is the principal city of Camboja, unto Chudurmuch. The waters of this river, which is also very great, the most of them do pass to the river that cometh from the Laos, near to Chudurmuch, and the rest do run down the river directly to the sea, when the great winter floods do come, which happen when it rains not in the lands of Camboja. The many waters which do come by the river that cometh from the Laos, which there they call the river of Sistor,[3] do make a passage right against Chudurmuch, to the river that passeth through Loech, with so great fury, that where the waters of Loech did run downward, by multitude of the other that entreth into it, they are turned back and run upward with a great current; in sort that it overfloweth all the country of Camboja, whereby all the country is not travelled in the time of these floods, but in boats, and they make their houses all with high lofts, and

---

[1] Khmer *Chademuk, Chordemuko*, from the Sanskrit *Caturmukha*, 'the four faces', arms or ways, an old name for Phnom Pénh. Admirably situated at the junction of the Tonlé Sap and of two arms of the Mekong, it is the great market for all the products of Cambodia. Cabaton, *Relation du Cambodge*, p. 95, n. (3).

[2] Lovek, on the Tonlé Sap river, a little above Phnom Pénh. It was fortified and ornamented by Ang Chan I, who made it his capital, the old Khmer capital of Angkor Thom being too exposed to Siamese raids.

[3] Sithor, Srei Chor (contraction of Srei Santhor), a town and province of the region of the Tonlé Tôch (an arm of the Mekong), 32 km. NE. of Phnom Pénh. A. Cabaton, *op. et loc. cit.*

underneath they are all overflown; and often these floods are so
high that they are forced to make higher rooms with canes, to
keep their household stuff in, and to lodge themselves. This river
runneth upwards from July to September, and with the passing
from the river that cometh from the Laos (or from the river Sistor,
which is its proper name) of so many waters to the river of Loech,
it doth not fail to run to the sea, making below very great arms, and
goeth very high, overflowing many countries downward, but not so
much as above.[1] The Portugals did show me in Loech a great hill
of earth in a field, over the which they affirmed that in the time of
the floods a great ship that was made in the country did pass
without touching, which ship might well have sailed from India to
Portugal.

The cause of this miracle in my opinion is that these rivers are
very large and big, whereby in the season of the spring-tides of the
sea, such a mass of sea waters enters with the tides upstream that it
repels somewhat the currents which run in the river Loech above,
since its current is not so impetuous as is that of the river of
Sistor and of the two of Chudurmuch downwards, for which
reason it runs sometimes with more force and sometimes with less,
according to the state of the tides.

And even though this digression hath made us depart from our
theme, it did not seem good to me to fail to record it as a notable
thing. And returning to our chief intent, and sufficing what is said
above of the Laos, who after the Cauchins-chinas confine with
China, beyond these Laos follow the Brames, who are a great
people, and very rich of gold and precious stones, chiefly of rubies.
It is a proud nation and valiant. These are now lords of Peguu, the
which they subdued by force of arms some years before they subdued the Laos.[2] They are men of good complexion, well made,
and brown. They have Peguu and a part of Bengala[3] adjoining the
Indian Ocean. It is a country very scarce of victuals. They apparel
themselves as we said of the Laos, but that their clothes are fine,

[1] The Mekong, like the Nile, is subject to an annual flood. The waters begin
to rise in May, attain their maximum in October, and then decrease until March.
At some places the difference between flood-mark and ordinary level is as much
as forty feet.

[2] The Burmese conquest of Pegu was completed in 1539.

[3] Bengal was frequently raided by the Arakanese and occasionally by the
Burmese.

and many do wear them painted or wrought. They are also some-what like the Chinas in the faces. They have very rich and gallant ships garnished with gold, in the which they sail along the rivers. They use vessels of gold and of silver. Their houses are of timber, very well wrought. The kingdom is very great. They have not commonly war with the Chinas, because of the great mountains that are between the one and the other, and because the Chinas are well fortified on that side.

Notwithstanding this, sometimes there are robbers on the one side and on the other that do make assaults, whereby the Chinas have some Bramas captives, as some Portugals who were prisoners in those parts and who saw them did affirm, and did speak with them in the great city of Camsi:[1] and these captives told them, that from thence it was not very far to Brama, and that they had seen Portugals in Peguu. And lest this chapter should become too prolix, we will put what remains of this matter in the next.

[1] Kueilin. Compare the account of Galeote Pereira on p. 39 above.

CHAPTER IV

In which the subject of the confines of China is continued.

THERE followeth along the border of China beyond the Bramas, the kingdom of the Patanes,[1] who are now lords of Bengala, who dominate all that portion of India towards the Indian Ocean that lies between Bengala and Cambaya[2] which is the kingdom of Guzarate[3] and which they have sometimes raided.[4] They are a warlike people, use bows and arrows on horseback, and have good short broad-swords.

This people is as one with the Mogores,[5] and they were of the same kingdom and generation, and they were divided into different kingdoms as a result of civil broils amongst them. Their kingdom reaches from Bengala to Cambaya, the former being in the middle of India and the latter almost at the end; for the kingdom of Cam-

[1] Pathāns. The Afghān dynasty which ruled Western Bengal at the time when Gaspar da Cruz wrote, was destroyed with the defeat and death of Daud Khan Kararānī, by the armies of the Mughal Emperor Akbar in 1576.

[2] Cambay (Kanbāyat, Kambáya), famous port and principal residence of the Sultans of Gujarāt. Cf.

> 'The Prince of Cambay's daily food
> is asp, and basilisk, and toad:
> which makes him have so strong a breath,
> each night he stinks a queen to death.'
> (Samuel Butler, *Hudibras*. Part II, canto i.)

[3] Gujarāt, then an independent Muhammadan kingdom, was conquered by Akbar in 1572.

[4] Our author evidently confuses the Afghān rulers of Bengal with the sultans of the Afghān Sūr dynasty of Delhi, who disputed the possession of Northern India with the Mughals until their final overthrow in 1555.

[5] Moguls, Moghuls or Mughals. 'This name should properly mean a person of the great nomad race of Mongols, called in Persia and elsewhere *Mughals*; but in India it has come, in connection with the nominally Mongol, though essentially rather *Turk*, family of Bābur to be applied to all foreign Muhammadans from the countries on the west and north-west of India except the Pathāns' (*Hobson-Jobson*, p. 570). The Timurid rulers of India were of Central Asian Turki origin, and Bābur himself usually wrote disparagingly of the Mughals, although his mother was a Mughal princess.

baya reaches to that of Sinide,[1] where India ends or begins with the Indo[2] river which is called Sinide.

From Bengala to the kingdom of Sinide runs the Ganges, which encloses all India from behind and by which ships bring sugar from Bengala to Sinide, whence they are trans-shipped from Sinide to Ormuz, as I saw in the time when I was living there.

Along the China border after the Patanes lie the Mogores, whose kingdom is very great and exceedingly populous. This people is very warlike. They fight with bows and arrows on horseback, using breast-plate and helmets and short broad-swords. They often waged war against Cambaya and made many raids therein. They are now lords of Sinide and of the kingdom of Delli,[3] which is a very great kingdom in the interior beyond Sinide and which extends the land inward to the confines of Cambaya.

The capital of their kingdom is called the great Samarcam,[4] which is called 'capital of Tartary' in the maps. These are counted among the Scythians, as Josephus testifies in the first book of Antiquities, the which, according to him, are descended from Japhet, the son of Noah, by Magog.[5] These are the Scythians who are very celebrated by the historians, and are called Masagetas[6] to distinguish them from the other Scythians.

It is affirmed of them that they were never conquered by any other nations. These are they of whom it is written that they made Vejoim, King of the Egyptians,[7] fly in a very cowardly manner, and

[1] Sindh, Sind, Scinde, etc., the territory on the Indus below the Punjab. It was annexed by Akbar in 1590.

[2] Indus.

[3] Delhi, capital of the kings of Delhi of the house of Timur, who were later known as the Grão Mogor or Great Mogul.

[4] Samarkand or Samarquand. The first Mughal emperor of India, Bābur, had been driven out of this city by the Uzbegs in 1512, and contrary to what Gaspar da Cruz implies, the Mughals never regained their ancestral capital.

[5] Josephus Flavius (Joseph ben Matthias) who flourished A.D. 38–100, wrote (in Greek) a comprehensive history of the Jews, which is the work quoted here.

[6] The Massagetae appear from Herodotus to have lived east of the Aral and north of the Oxus; Hudson, *Europe and China*, pp. 28, 45. Their name is probably reflected in the 'Sagatai' who are shown north of the Caspian in 'Hondius his map of Tartary' reproduced in Purchas, *Pilgrimes*, III, 234, and *Pilgrimage*, p. 407 of the 1625–1626 edition.

[7] King Psemthek or Psametik (Psammeticus) of Egypt who reigned c. 666–610 B.C., and was the founder of the 26th dynasty. He allegedly bought off Scythian invaders who had advanced as far as Philistaea.

they did the same to Darius,[1] King of the Persians. They killed Cyrus, likewise King of the Persians;[2] they destroyed Cyfiriona captain of Alexander the Great,[3] and subjugated Asia three times by force of arms, and held it tributary for many years.

From these descended the most famous captain called the great Tamorlam,[4] who gained many victories in Asia and conquered many lands by force of arms. These confine on one side with the Persians with whom they have now a great league and much trade, and every year many of them come with wares to Ormuz; they also confine with the Caspian Sea, and on one side with the Tartars. And even though the Greeks called these people Scythians, throughout all of Asia Major and Minor they are called Mogores,[5] thus retaining their first name which they took from father Magog, from whom they are descended and were named.

Pedraza says of them in the Treatise which he made about Antichrist,[6] that they are Scythians and live beyond the Caspian Sea, and that there are many of them, and that they are to come and help Antichrist, which I mention to show that it agrees with what I have said previously.

And as for this people coming to the help of Antichrist, Saint

[1] Darius' expedition over the Bosphorus and Danube into Scythia was unsuccessful.

[2] Cyrus was commonly believed to have fallen in battle against the Massagetae on the river Jaxartes.

[3] Zopyrion, the Macedonian Antipater's general in Thrace. He crossed the Danube, perhaps reached Olbia, and was killed by the Scythians in the course of his attempt to link Thrace with Bactria. W. W. Tarn, *Alexander the Great* (London, 1948), I, 71.

[4] Timur had been wounded in the hand and foot in Seistan in 1363, hence his Persian sobriquet of *Timur-lenk*, 'Timur the lame', whence the Tamerlane of European literature. Bretschneider, *Medieval Researches*, II, 257, n. 1059.

[5] As noted previously, the designation of Mughal was a very vague one. The French traveller in India, Bernier, observed a century later that 'to be considered a *Mogol*, it is enough if a foreigner have a white face and profess Mahometanism'. S. N. Sen, *The Indian Travels of Thevenot and Careri*, p. 280.

[6] Fr. Juan de Pedraza, O.P., was author of a *Suma de casos de Consciencia*, which was first published at Coimbra in 1567 and several times reprinted in Spain during the next decade. He was also author of a *Confessionario* (Lisbon 1546), but I cannot trace his treatise on Antichrist. Authorities differ as to whether he was a Portuguese or a Spaniard by birth, but he was Professor of Scripture at Coimbra from 1537–1540, and apparently spent the remainder of his life at Lisbon. Palau y Dulcet, *Manual de librero Hispano-Americano*, VI (1926), p. 55; *Enciclopédia Portuguesa e Brasileira* in voce 'Pedraza'. He should not be confused with the Segovian poet of the same name and time who wrote a *Danza de la muerte* which was printed in 1551.

Jerome states in his Commentary on Ezekiel[1] that some are of the opinion that these Mogores in bygone times had dealings the land inward with the Chinas; and owing to a certain occurence which took place in China on their account, as we will relate below, many of them were made captive and distributed through different regions of China, while others were killed, and now only the children of those who were spared are left.[2] Withal, the Portugals who were prisoners in the great city of Cansi, found one very old Moor among the former, who told them that he was a native of great Samarcham, which was near Persia.

In the city of Cantam, I saw one of the descendents of these survivors who had with him his own son, a very fine gentleman. This people is very well made and proportioned, big men, well set up, and white for the most part; for they live in a cold country towards the North-east and North from the direction of the Holy Land. Beyond these Mogores there runneth along the China border the Tartars,[3] who do extend themselves from Mogor to the lake Meothis[4] and the river Thanas,[5] which is a very great kingdom and of much and innumerable people.

This people are commonly red and not white; they go naked from the waist upward; they eat raw flesh, and anoint themselves with the blood of it; whereby commonly they are stinking and have a foul smell. An old man of China did affirm unto me, that sometimes when they came against the countries of China, if the wind blew from that side whence they came, they were discerned by their smell.[6] When they go to war, they carry the flesh raw under them for to eat. They eat it in this manner and anoint themselves with the blood to make themselves the more sturdy and strong, and to provoke themselves to cruelty in the war. These also fight on horseback with bows and arrows, and use short swords.

---

[1] I cannot find this reference in J. P. Migne, *Patrologiae Latinae*, XXV (Paris, 1884), pp. 15–490, which contains St. Jerome's commentary on Ezechiel.

[2] Here he is confusing, deliberately or otherwise, the Mogores with the Chinese Muslims.

[3] Mongol rather than Manchu Tartars at this period and in this connection. Cf. Bretschneider, *Medieval Researches*, II, 160.

[4] Sea of Azov.

[5] River Don.

[6] For Chinese notices of the Mongols at this period, cf. Bretschneider, *Medieval Researches*, II, 159–173; H. Howorth, *History of the Mongols* (London, 1876), I, 372–378.

With these is the continual war of the Chinas; and as I have said, the Chinas have an hundred leagues (others saying there are more) of a wall between them and the other, where are continually garrisons of men for defence against the raids of the Tartars.[1] It may be believed that this wall is not continuous, but that some mountains or hills are intermixt between; for a Persian lord affirmed to me that the like works were in some parts of Persia, intermixed with some hills or mountains.

It was affirmed to the Portugals who were captives and imprisoned in dungeons in the year of 1550, that some years ago a truce was made between the Chinas and the Tartars; and in that year of fifty the Tartars made a great raid into China, when they took a very principal city thereof; but a great number of Chinas coming and besieging the city, and not being able to enter it by force of arms, by the council of a man of low degree, they had a means whereby they killed them and their horses and remained lords again of the city.[2] The same Portugals who afterwards were set at liberty, affirmed that all the prisoners rejoiced exceedingly and made a great stir in the jails when the Tartars made this raid, in the hope of being set at liberty by the means of the Tartars, if they did possess China.[3]

In the city of Cantam I saw many Tartar captives who have no other captivity than to serve for men-at-arms in other places far from Tartary; and they wear for a difference red caps, being otherwise dressed like the Chinas with whom they live.[4] They have for their maintenance a certain stipend of the King, which they have paid them without fail. The Chinas call them Tatos, for they cannot pronounce the letter r.[5]

Above the lake where Thanas hath its origin, they do confront with the skirts of High Almayne, on the edge of Europe, although between them and Almayne are hills that do divide

[1] Cf. Ch. II, p. 70 above.

[2] This is a garbled version of the great Mongol raid in 1550, under the leadership of Altan Khan (1507–1583), when the country around Peking and Paotingfu was thoroughly devastated. See De Mailla, *Histoire*, X, 317–319.

[3] Compare Galeote Pereira's account, p. 38 above.

[4] For the use of convicted criminals, prisoners of war, and political exiles as frontier garrison troops by the Ming see *T'oung Pao*, XXXIV, 392–394.

[5] For the application of the word *Tatz* (*Tatsz'*) or *Ta-Ta-erh*, whence 'Tartar', by the Chinese, the Russians and others to the Mongols, cf. Bretschneider, *Medieval Researches*, I, 318; II, 160; Couling, *Encyclopedia Sinica*, p. 549.

M

them.[1] And of these people of the skirts of the mountains, the Chinas say that the King of China hath many men of war in pay, that do keep the weak passes and the walls on the side of the Tartars. They say that they are great men with great beards, and wear cut-hose and caps and blunt swords. And a Portugal that was carried captive the land inward, told me that he had heard the Chinas say that they called these men Alimenes [Germans].[2] Some will have it that China runs above this as far as High Russia, which is included in Scythia, for there are two Russias, one betwixt Poland and Almayne, and another, lower down from the North, at the extremity of Almayne. And it is not impossible that China extends as far as this last one, because, as we have already said, it is clearly shown that China comprises the larger part of Scythia, since it includes that within the Ismaos mountains[3] as beyond them. And if these Russians are regarded as Scythians within the bounds of Europe, then there is no great objection to saying that China extends as far as them. And if this is true, as also what we have stated previously, it is clear that what we said about the river Thanas in the second chapter is true; and it is likewise after all the foregoing clearly proved that China lies behind all Asia, as we mentioned above that Jacobo Philipo stated.

For by what has been said, it is shown that China reaches the extremity of Asia, since it is situated in the last India and forms part thereof, and on the other side it extends to the river Thanas which forms the European boundary of Asia.

Besides all this, consider how the people of China must be all of one kind, as may be judged from the inhabitants who come from one extremity thereof to the other, and how they go from one end

---

[1] Possibly the Carpathian mountains are those intended here, but Fr. Gaspar da Cruz's desperate attempts to reconcile Ptolemaic geography with sixteenth-century cartography lead him into hopeless confusion and self-contradiction.

[2] Cf. Ch. III, pp. 71–72 above.

[3] Imaos or Imaus was the name given by Ptolemy to the Pamir mountains which he depicted as running north and south across Scythia, dividing that region into two distinct portions, which he termed *Scythia intra Imaum* and *Scythia extra Imaum* respectively. The Pamirs were thus grotesquely misplaced by Ptolemy, being transferred to 140° E. longitude or 80° East of Alexandria, whereas the real interval between the two is just over 40°. Ptolemy's fancies had a remarkably long life, despite the rapid progress of geographical knowledge during the sixteenth century. His *Scythia extra Imaum montem* can be found on 'Hondius his map of Tartary' reproduced in Purchas, *Pilgrimes* (1625), being there shown as running from Burma (Bramas) to Northern Siberia.

to another of Scythia. As for what the Ancients said of the Pigmies who were Scythians, who lived in the extremity of Scythia, very small men who fought with griffins for gold,[1] this has been proved a fable like other things which they related of the peoples who were said to inhabit India,—that they had very small mouths, and sucked up their food through a tube after it had been well pounded, and of others who had one enormous foot which gave them shade when lifted up over their head. These and other things which they affirmed of those parts, were proved to be fables after that India had been discovered by the Portugals.

True it is, that commonly the staple food of India, which is rice, is eaten after being pounded with pestles, and after it has been hulled, but their mouths are like those of all the other peoples in this world.

True it is that there are men in Malabar, of the noble caste called Panicaes, some of whom have a leg very disformly swollen, and others who have both legs in the usual shape.[2] The others have only one leg swollen, and it is not in such wise that they can use the leg to give shade to the head.

Thus both these and the Pigmies should be regarded as fabulous; and from all what has been conjectured above, it can be inferred how great a King is that of China, and how extensive the said China is in its territories.

[1] Such fables are another echo of Herodotian and Ptolemaic tradition, having been given a new lease of life in the later middle ages by the *Travels of Sir John Mandeville* and similar works.

[2] Malayālam *perikkāl*, 'great leg', or elephantiasis, a disease very common in Cochin, hence called 'Cochin leg' in old Anglo-Indian parlance. Fr. Gaspar da Cruz is evidently confusing the name of the disease with the word *Panikar* (*Panikan*, *Panical*, plural *panicaes* etc.) which formerly designated the fencing-masters of the warrior Nairs in old Malabar. It is nowadays more used in the sense of 'astrologer(s)'. *Hobson-Jobson*, p. 669; Dalgado, *Glossário Luso-Asiático*, II, 160–162.

CHAPTER V

Of the provinces into which China is divided.

THOSE of the country affirm generally that China has thirteen provinces,[1] and each province has as its capital a city very great and very populous, with very noble buildings. The first one on the side towards India is the province of Cantão,[2] and the capital of this province is the city of Cantão, from which the province takes its name.[3] This province has eleven cities, including the capital, and eighty walled towns, each one of which would be considered a city elsewhere, for they are very noble and well peopled.[4] The townships which are not walled (and many of them are very large) are innumerable, for these lands are very populous.

Another province is called Camsi,[5] which is much more noble than that of Cantão, and the capital city thereof is likewise called thus.[6] There are seventeen cities in this province; and there are many walled towns, as likewise unwalled places.

There is another province called Fuquem,[7] whose capital is called Fucheo.[8] This province has ten cities, but they are very great and very noble, because this is one of the largest and noblest provinces.[9] It has a very large number of walled towns. The unwalled townships are beyond counting. How much larger this

[1] For a list of the thirteen 'ambulatory' and two 'metropolitan' provinces of Ming China, see Galeote Pereira's account, p. 3, n. (2). It will be seen that this chapter of Cruz is partly based on Pereira.

[2] Kuangtung. Elsewhere spelt Cantam, Cantan, etc., and used indifferently for the name of the province and the provincial capital. Cf. *China Review*, XIII, 225.

[3] Actually the reverse; the official name of the city was Kuangtung-shêng-ch'eng, 'Kuangtung-province-city.'

[4] The reference is to *fu*, *chou* and *hsien* cities. Gaspar da Cruz's figures are not very far out, if we realise that he lumped the last two categories together. The corresponding figures given in the *Ming-shih* are 10 *fu*, 8 *chou* and 75 *hsien*.

[5] Kuangsi. Elsewhere he also used the form 'Cansi', as does Pereira.

[6] Compare nn. (2) and (3) above. Kueilin-fu was its other and more usual name.

[7] Fukien. The forms Foquien, Fuquiem and variants also occur in Cruz and his contemporaries.

[8] Foochow (Fuchou-fu). Cf. Appendix II, 'Aucheo'.

[9] On the contrary, Fukien was one of the smallest and most backward.

88

province is than that of Cantão and that of Camsi, is shown by the fact that it has only one governor, whereas Cantão and Cansi have both together one governor.[1] And it can further be seen from the province of Cantam including the island of Ainão,[2] which could be a kingdom in itself, because it is very thickly peopled and has fifty leagues of coastline in length, and the mainland of the coast of Cantão has as many leagues or more than the island [of Ainão].

And if this is the smallest province, or one of the smallest, whereas Fuquem on the contrary is one of the largest, you can judge the size of this latter.[3] In this province is the city of Chincheo,[4] wherein the Portugals traded in times past.

Another province is called Chaqueam,[5] of which the great city of Omquom[6] is the capital. This province has fourteen cities, including the city of Liampoo,[7] where formerly the Portugals likewise had trade, but now everything has gone to Cantão.

There is another province called Xuteafim,[8] whose capital is the great city of Paquim, where the King continually resides. This province has seventeen cities, which in greatness and nobility exceed those of many other provinces. It is said that the city of Paquim[9] is so large that a man on horseback can hardly ride straight

[1] The fact that the 'Two Kuang' were ruled by a viceroy or commander-in-chief (usually known to the Portuguese as Tutão, Tutam, Tutan, etc., from an abbreviated part of his official title, Tu-t'ang), was nothing to do with their size as compared with that of Fukien. It was primarily the prevalence of banditry in Kuangsi and piracy in Kuangtung which led to the establishment of a joint headquarters for the Two Kuang at the city of Wu-chou, just over the Kuangsi side of the border, in 1469. Cf. Galeote Pereira's narrative, p. 6, n. (3).

[2] Hainan island. Dainão in the original, as explained in Ch. III, p. 73, n. (2).

[3] This is quite wrong. Fukien, with an area of 46,332 square miles is one of the smallest provinces; whereas Kuangtung province with 100,000 square miles was not only much larger but more populous. Cf. L. Richards, Comprehensive Geography, pp. 202, 218.

[4] Either Ch'üan-chou or Chang-chou, as explained in Appendix I below.

[5] Chekiang. The Portuguese also used 'Chequeam' and other variants.

[6] 'Omquom' in this context, like Galeote Pereira's 'Dŏchŏ' p. 4, n. (2), can only be the Chekiang provincial capital of Hangchow (Hang-chou-fu). I suspect, however, that somewhere along the line of transmission 'Omquom' originally stood for the Ming province of Hukuang.

[7] Ningpo. Also appears as 'Liampo' and variants in Cruz and Pereira.

[8] Shun-t'ien-fu. An official name for Peking. See Galeote Pereira, p. 4, n. (4) above.

[9] Peking. Elsewhere romanised as Pachim, Paquim, etc. Cf. p. 4, n. (5) above.

across it between sunrise and sunset (for the streets are straight and run from gate to gate), and this only within the walls, for even the suburbs are very large.[1]

There is another province called Chilim,[2] whose capital is the great city of Namquim.[3] This province has sixteen cities, and of old time the King dwelt therein as it is a very fertile, fresh and beautiful country; and he moved the court to Paquim so as to be nearer at hand for the Tartarian wars.[4] This province was anciently with that of Chaqueam, a kingdom of its own, which was gradually extended over the other provinces until China was made all one kingdom.[5] They say that this city is as large as that of Paquim. In memory of the fact that the King used to reside in this city in times past, there is, in the house of the Pouchasi,[6] who is the comptroller of the revenue of that province, a golden tablet on which is inscribed the name of the reigning King. This is covered with a rich cloth, and all the high officials who rule this province and who dwell in this city are compelled to go there daily and reverence it as if it was the King himself. This tablet is exhibited publicly on all the festival days of the Chinas, which are principally those of the new moons. There are other tablets like these in all the provinces, in the houses of the Ponchasis, but these are not reverenced, save only when they are exhibited during the festivals, whence it may be seen how venerated are the Kings in these countries.

There is another province called Sanxi,[7] and this is likewise the name of the city which is the capital of the province. This province

---

[1] This exaggerated estimate of the size of Peking had a long life in Western works, being repeated by González de Mendoza, Fernão Mendes Pinto and many others, until finally exposed by the (posthumous) publication of Padre Gabriel de Magalhães, S.J., 'Doze excellencias da China', under the French title of *Nouvelle Relation de la Chine* (Paris 1688), where a very full and detailed description of the city was given.

[2] Chihli, 'direct rule'. In this context the province of Nan-Chihli or Kiangnan, *alias* Nanking. Cf. Galeote Pereira, p. 4, n. (6) above.

[3] Nanking. 'Lamquin' and 'Lamquim', and variants, are also found in the old Portuguese and Spanish accounts, doubtless derived from the Amoy vernacular form of this word. Cf. Martìn de Rada's 'Relación', p. 268 *infra*.

[4] Correct. The transference of the national capital from Nanking to Peking was effected by the third Ming emperor, Yung-lo, in 1416–1420.

[5] Incorrect. The unification of China started from the Yellow River valley.

[6] *Pu-chêng-shih*, civil governor and comptroller. The post dates from 1376.

[7] Shansi is the nearest phonetically, but from the context it is clear that Kiangsi province is the one meant here. Kiangsi had in fact 13 *fu* cities and was the centre of the porcelain industry.

has thirteen cities. Porcelain is made only in this province,[1] and because it is near to Liampoo, where a great quantity is sold, very good and very cheap, the Portugals thought that it was made in Liampoo itself.

There is another province called Quichio.[2] This province has eleven cities. There is another called Fuquom.[3] Another called Quinsi.[4] Another called Vinan.[5] Another called Siquam.[6] Another called Siensi.[7] The number of the cities in these last-named provinces was not known for certain.[8]

[1] Incorrect, although the best and most famous porcelain was made here at the celebrated imperial factories of Ching-tê-chên.

[2] Kueichou province, which had 8 *fu* cities, and not 11 as stated here.

[3] Hukuang province, which under the Manchus was split into Hupeh and Hunan.

[4] In view of what is stated on p. ˹90, n. (7) above, 'Quinsi' must here stand for Shansi province, and not Kuangsi or Kiangsi as would otherwise be likely.

[5] Yünnan; or possibly Honan.

[6] Ssŭch'üan (Szechwan).

[7] Shensi.

[8] Shantung is omitted from this list, as is either Yünnan or Honan, depending on which of the two is to be identified with 'Vinan' in n. (5). João de Barros had already given a full and more accurate list of the fifteen provinces of Ming China in his *Decada* III, Book iv, Ch. 7, printed at Lisbon in 1563, but Cruz apparently did not know of this work.

CHAPTER VI

In the which the city of Cantam is particularly described.

EING to treat of the city of Cantão, I give first a warning to the readers, that among the noble cities, Cantão is one of the less noble than many of China, and far inferior in buildings than many others, although it be more populous than many. This is said by all them that saw it and travelled within the land, where they saw many others.

This advice presupposed, it is to be noted that Cantam in its compass, is of very strong walls, very well made, and of a good height; and to the sight they seem almost new, being eighteen hundred years since they were made, as the Chinas did affirm.[1] They are very clean, without any cleft, hole, or rift, or anything threatening ruin. The cause of their being thus, is that they are of free-stone for just over a man's height, and from thence upward of bricks made of a clay like unto that of the porcelain dishes, whence it causeth them to be so strong, that I, building a chapel in Malacca, found that one like these (which was brought from China) could scarcely be broken with a good pickaxe.[2] Add to this, that there is in this city and in all the rest, an officer of the King whose only care is to oversee the walls, for the which he hath a good stipend. And every year, when the regional governor comes to visit the province, he doth visit this as well as the other officers, to know if he doth his office well and carefully. And if he is found in any fault or negligence, he is put from his office and punished. And if he standeth in need of any expence for the mending of the walls, the Comptroller of the Revenue is bound to give him that which is necessary, under pain that if the mending remaineth undone, he likewise

---

[1] The Chinese were boasting. The city wall, as it was in our author's day, dated only from the early Ming period, although the 'City of Rams' itself was founded as early as the fourth century B.C., according to the traditional account.

[2] These particularly tough bricks may have been made with *chunam*, a kind of lime obtained from pounded oyster-shells. *Hobson-Jobson*, pp. 218–219; Dalgado, *Glossário Luso-Asiático*, I, 282–283.

shall be well punished. For this cause the walls of all the cities are continually kept very sound and in very good repair.

These walls are within the city little more than the walk of the same city in their height, which is the cause of being much more cooler.[1] The walls have in compass 12,350 paces, and it hath eighty-three bulwarks. Some Portugals who saw it, tried to maintain that this circuit was about the same compass as that of Lisbon, and it seemed larger to others.

The foregoing enumeration of the paces and bulwarks was made very exactly; others tried to estimate it by the distance between the bulwarks, but as they are not all at an equal distance from each other, but some are more and others less distant, their estimate cannot possibly be correct.[2] This city (and so all the rest) hath on the one side the river,[3] along the which, this (like the others) is built, almost as if in an entrenchment, for it hath round it on the other sides a good broad moat full of water. Between this moat and the wall remaineth a good space where a good troop of people may assemble together; and the earth that was taken out of the moat was cast between it and the wall, whereby the ground at the foot of the wall is a great deal higher than the rest. Beyond the moat, not-withstanding, this wall hath a great blemish, for it hath on the opposite side to the river,[4] without the walls and moat, a little hill that discovereth all the city within the walls. This wall hath seven gates. The entries of the gates are very sumptuous and high, strong and very well made, with battlements above, not square but made like steps. The other parts of the walls have no battlements. The bulk of the wall at the entrance gates is twelve paces thick; the

---

[1] Bad as Purchas' translation is, I cannot improve on it here, as the original Portuguese text is clearly corrupt at this point and does not make better sense.

[2] The walls of old Canton city were extended southwards in 1563 to include the southern suburb which then became the 'new city'. Cf. *Kuang-tung-t'ung-chih* (ed. 1731), chüan 14, pp. 2a–2b. João de Barros, *Decada* III, Book ii, Ch. 7, relates that Antonio Fernandes, one of the Portuguese who visited Canton with Fernão Peres de Andrade in 1517, took the opportunity one night when the populace were occupied with a feast of lanterns (evidently the autumnal or harvest-moon festival in this instance) to climb the city wall and run right round it, counting ninety towers thereon. Gaspar da Cruz's bulwarks (*baluartes*) are doubtless the equivalent of these towers. The city walls were demolished in 1920–1921.

[3] The Kiu-kiang (Chiu-chiang), or Pearl River, a branch of the Si-kiang (Hsi-chiang) or West River.

[4] The North side.

III. The c
(From the *Kua*

Canton
(-t'ung-chih, 1558)

gates are all plated with iron from top to bottom; and all of them have very strong portcullises in front, which are always up and never let down, but are ready against they be needfull.

All the gates have breastworks at their entrances; and the breastworks that are on the side of the suburb which lieth along the river[1] have every one three gates, one in front and two at the sides which are for the service of the streets that lie along the wall. The walls of the breastworks are almost of the height of them within. The gate which is in the front of the breastwork is like unto that of the walls within, and it hath also a portcullis. The gates which are in the sides of the breastwork are small. The breastworks which are on the other side of the field, where no suburb is, have no more than one gate, and this is not right against that of the walls, but stands on the one side.

The streets of the city are all drawn by a line very straight, without any manner of making a nook or winding. The principal streets are something broader than the Rua Nova dos Mercadores 'dos ferros' of Lisbon.[2] All the cross ways are as straight as the streets; in sort that there is neither street nor traverse that maketh any turning. All the streets and traverses are very well paved, the paving going higher along by the houses, and lower in the middle for the course of water. The principal streets have triumphant arches which do cross them, high and very well made, which make the streets very beautiful and ennoble the city.[3] The principal streets have along the houses close portals, in the which and under the arches many things are sold.

The houses of the magistrates[4] are very sumptuous at the entrances, with high portals, great and well wrought of mason's work. They have in the fore-front very great gates like the gates of a city, with two giants painted with clubs in their hands. I saw four

---

[1] Nam-kuan or southern suburb. Compare the detailed description of the walls and gates of Canton in Ljungstedt, *Historical sketch*, pp. 229–232. He was not nearly so impressed by their strength as Gaspar da Cruz had been.

[2] The *Rua Nova dos ferros* was the most famous street of Lisbon and the mercantile centre of the capital before the great earthquake of 1755. For its exact situation and description, cf. the plans in J. de Castilho, *Lisboa Antiga*, (ed. 1936), VII and VIII; *Guia de Portugal* (Lisbon, 1924), I, 197.

[3] *P'ai-lou*, ornamental arch or gateway. Cf. Galeote Pereira, p. 10, n. (2) above.

[4] Mandarins' or magistrates' *yamens* (*yamuns*). Cf. Giles, *Glossary*, p. 166.

in one pagoda (which is a temple of idols)[1] drawn naturally from some which they say the King hath to keep the weakest passes from Tartary. They are of great members, of about twelve or thirteen spans high. On the street side, it hath right against the principal gate a reception court, not very great. It hath built along the street a good wall of a good height, right against the gate, that when the gate is open they that are within may not be gazed on by them that go by in the street.[2] This gate serveth not, neither is it opened but for dispatching of matters of Justice, and the principals of the house go in and out of it, and others that are as honourable or more than they.

At the one side of this principal gate is another very great gate, but not so big as the principal, which is for the service of the house and of the prisoners when the principal gate is shut. And when this principal gate is shut, they set a glued paper across over both the doors, on which is written the name or firm of the principal of the house; and for to open it again, an officer of the house bringeth the same firm or mark on a plastered board to the porter, that he may open it, without the which token he may not open it under pain of a very great punishment. Entering by this gate there is a great court and almost square, which is almost a horse-race;[3] and in the middle it hath a gallery which is a little less than the width of the gate, and which leadeth straight from the gate to a very great platform that stands at the end of the court. This gallery is all paved with square flagstones and has balustrades as high as a man's waist; and it is high at the entrance gate and there remaineth only one step from the end of it to the platform; and the court at the sides of this gallery is low, so that they go down to it by steps. This middle gallery is of such respect among them, that in no wise is it lawful for anyone to pass through it, but only some of the chiefest of the house, and others as great or greater than they. And those that go to negotiate with the officer of the house when they enter in at the

[1] For the derivation of the word *pagoda*, and its various meanings at different times, cf. *Hobson-Jobson*, pp. 562–567; Dalgado, *Glossário Luso-Asiático*, II, 129–137; Giles, *Glossary*, p. 101.

[2] The 'shadow-wall', or isolated wall placed before the entrance-gate as a bar to all noxious influences, which are supposed to travel only in straight lines. Giles, *Glossary*, p. 166. What follows is the description of a great mandarin's yamen. Cf. the ground-plan of such a mansion in De Groot, *Religious system of China*, I, 16.

[3] 'quasi de carreira dũ cauallo' in the original. Cf. Ch. 8, p. 107, n. (2) *infra*.

gate, they must go presently to one side, going down to the court which hath very great trees for shadow, and they go up again by steps unto the platform abovesaid, which is at the end of the court, which is very great.

At the back of this platform there is a step which runs along the whole width thereof, and further beyond the step a very great covered way, all paved with great square flagstones, as is the platform without it, and very high and all wrought with mason's work. In the middle thereof, leaning against the front wall are two chairs with two tables before them, a little distant the one from the other. One of them, which stands on the left hand, serveth for the governor of that house; and that of the right hand is void, for if there should come another of a higher dignity than he, to sit him down. On each one of the sides there are two spaces which run behind this governor, and are of a good breadth, having placed along the sides of these two spaces in every one five chairs with five tables before them, and as the distance from them to the principal is good, they remain though behind, in sight of the principal governor. These serve for ten assistants who are with the principal at the dispatching of weighty matters.

From these galleries inwards are great lodgings, as well for the governor of the house as for the assistants, and for all the other ministers and officers of the house, who are many, as we shall show in their place. On every side of the court are very great prisons and great lodgings, as well for the jailers (who are also of great authority) as for the watches that watch by night and by day; but neither these prisons, nor the chambers of the ministers of them, nor the lodgings of the chiefs of the house are seen from outside, for they are served of all things behind closed doors which have continually their porters[1].

There are in Cantam four of these houses for four principal officers, and in the capital city of every province there are five of these houses. In Cantam there are but four; for as the governor of Cantam is also the governor of Cansi, he is not resident in Cantam, but in a city that is on the border of one of the provinces,[2] that the

---

[1] 'A mandarin's residence is a perfect Chinese puzzle of gateways, courtyards, lanes, temples and shops, often covering several acres of ground, yet without a single comfortable room' (*Chinese and Japanese Repository*, III, 464).

[2] Wu-chou (Wuchow), where the seat of the headquarters of the Two Kuang had been established in 1469. Delamarre, *Histoire de la Dynastie des Ming*, p. 348.

recourse in the affairs of both the provinces may be the easier. Besides these principal houses of the chief governors, there are many others in Cantam of other inferior officers the which though they be not of so great majesty as these, they are notwithstanding very great, and chiefly those of the chief jailer which are very great.

There is on the walls of Cantam on the contrary side of the river, a high tower all closed behind, that they who are in it may not be seen nor gazed on from the hillock which we formerly said was without the walls; and it is built in length along the wall, so that it is longer than broad, and it is all made in galleries very sumptuous, from whence they discover all the city, and the cultivated grounds and fields beyond the river, which serveth for the recreation of them that rule.[1] In the other cities are also such buildings which serve for recreation, many and very sumptuous, and of singular building.

The houses of the common people in the outward show, are not ordinarily very fair, but within are much to be admired; for commonly they are white as milk, that they seem like burnished paper; they are paved with square stones; along the ground of a span little more or less, they are dyed with vermilion, or almost black. The timber is all very smooth and very even, and very finely wrought and placed, that it seemeth to be all polished, or dyed, or in white; and some there is in white so fair and pleasant to the sight, waved damask-like, as it were almost the colour of gold, and so bright that they should do it an injury in painting it. I confess, in truth, that I never saw so fine timber as that.

It hath after the house that is at the entry, a court with solaces of small trees and bowers with a very fair little fountain. And then, at the entry of the house where the women do withdraw themselves, it hath a certain kind of covered way, open in front towards the court, where they have very great cupboards finely wrought, which take up the curtain-wall of the house, and wherein they have their oratories or gods made of wood, or of clay; these oratories are more or less curious according to the ability of everyone.

All the houses are tiled with very good tiles, better and more durable than ours are; for besides they being very well made, they

[1] The famous 'five-storied pagoda', described by most subsequent visitors to Canton. Ljungstedt, *Sketch*, p. 234, J. G. R., *Guide to China* (1924), p. 405.

are of very good clay. Those which receive the water are broad and short, and the uppermost that close the others are narrower, and at the ends towards the street side they are garnished with fine works made of lime. For many years they have no need to be tiled again, for as the clay is very good they are not as porous as ours, or so rough, but they are very smooth and warm, and being so well set they breed no dirt.

There be many houses very fair within, and very few are storied, the most being low houses.[1] They have in the middest of the city, a temple of idols with high towers, the walls of the which we will speak of hereafter.[2] They have their mosque with Alcoram very high and with its pinnacle on the top.[3]

The suburbs without are very great and of many households, in such sort that some Portugals would have compared them in size with those of Lisbon, but to me and to others they seemed less, though they be bigger and of more houses than the city within the walls.[4] It is very populous, and the people is so much, that at the entering of the gates on the river side you can scarce get through. Commonly the people that goeth out and in, do cry and make a great noise to give place to them that carry burthens.[5]

And the rulers of the city commanding to enquire what victuals were spent every day, it was found to spend of pigs alone five or six thousand, and ten or eleven thousand ducks; besides which, they

[1] Our friar's account of Cantonese houses is much more enthusiastic than those of foreign visitors in Manchu days. The city was savagely sacked by the Manchus in 1650, when most of the Ming houses were destroyed.

[2] He does not mention this temple again, unless it was the one where he created a scene as related at the end of Ch. XXVII below. He may have been alluding to the temple dedicated to the tutelary god of Canton city, popularly known to foreigners as the 'temple of horrors' from its representations of the Buddhist Hells.

[3] The Kuang-t'a (Cantonese, Kwong-tap), near the western gate of the old city. This celebrated Muhammaden mosque with its minaret (Cruz's *alcoram*) was built during the T'ang dynasty, over a thousand years ago, and repaired in 1468. It was (and is?) the first object to be seen in the city by anyone approaching from a distance.

[4] The suburbs of Tung-kuan, Hsi-kuan and Nam-kuan (East, West and South). Honam, on the south side of the river, was also usually reckoned as a suburb of Canton.

[5] 'The motley crowd that throngs these streets is very great indeed. At a busy hour of the day, the stout, half-naked, vociferating porters, carrying every description of merchandise, and the nimble sedan-bearers, in noise and bustle make up for the deficiency of carts and carriages.' Ljungstedt, *Historical Sketch*, p. 232.

eat great store of beeves and buffaloes, and many hens, and an infinite deal of fish, whereof the markets and streets are full, and many frogs and shell-fish, great store of fruits and other pulse. Hereby little more or less may be seen what people are in Cantam, and whether it may be compared with Lisbon.[1]

The rows of houses in the suburbs are like those of the walls within; the streets are likewise as well laid out and straight as are those within, and all for the most part likewise very well paved, and some of them are very broad and have triumphal arches, but few. Some streets, as well without as within the walls, on the one side and the other along the houses, have trees for to give shade. In all the streets of the suburbs at the ends of them are gates with special porters, whose office is to lock them every night under pain of sore punishment if they neglect this, and every street hath a constable and a jail. He stands bound, either to yield the malefactor who by night doth any harm in the street, or to pay for him; wherefore all the streets have every night a watch, the neighbours dividing themselves in quarters; and they make every night six quarters or watches, and for a sign that they are awake, in every street they sound a drum, where they have all the night a lanthorn with a light.[2] The gates of the city are all shut as soon as it is night, and on the folding doors is glued a paper with the chief captain's mark on every one of them; and they are opened at sunrise, with a token from the same captain to them all, with his mark written on a plastered board. Every gate hath a captain, a very honourable man, and every one hath certain soldiers who continually do watch every one of the gates by day and by night.

What more there is to be told of Cantam, will be told together with what is common to the rest of China, concerning some things in particular places.

[1] Figures for the consumption of country produce at Lisbon, at a slightly later date, will be found in Nicolau de Oliveira. *Livro das grandezas de Lisboa* (Lisbon, 1620), pp. 90–92, 100–102.

[2] Cf. Ljungstedt, *Historical sketch*, p. 249.

N

CHAPTER VII

Of some buildings which there are the land inward.[1]

MANY of the cities of China, which as I have said are very much more noble than Cantam, have over the gates of the walls up to the height of the walk of the wall, galleries made of stone or of very strong brick, high and very well wrought, with battlements on top, and all very fair, something which greatly embellishes and ennobles the cities.

The walls in many cities are very broad, in such wise that three or four men abreast can walk along them; and in some parts they are all paved on top with bricks, and all made with covered galleries, and the bulwarks all with high galleries and battlements, all very well wrought and exceeding fair; and very often the magistrates go there to pass the time.[2] And the upper works and galleries are made in such sort that they can all be lived in.

In the city of Fucheo, which, as we have said, is the capital of the province of Fuquem, there is at the gate of the Comptroller of the Revenue,[3] a tower well worth seeing, built upon forty pillars, each composed of a single block of octagonal stone, each of which measured twelve spans round and a little more or less than forty spans long,—for the Portugals could not measure the length exactly but this is what it seemed to them that the pillars could measure.[4] They were connected and joined above with very large and very thick beams on top of which was a very high and very

---

[1] Purchas has abridged this chapter to a few lines.

[2] Cf. Ljungstedt, *Historical sketch*, p. 230, 'A line of battlements, with embrasures at intervals of a few feet, are raised on the top of the wall round the whole city; these the Chinese call *ching-jin* [*ch'eng-jên*], literally *city-men*; and on the rear of them there is a broad pathway'. Fr. Gaspar da Cruz's account of the width and solidity of Chinese city-walls is not exaggerated. Three centuries later, Archdeacon Gray noted that they were remarkable 'both for the extent of their circumference and for their massive appearance, their width affording space sufficient for two carriages travelling abreast'. Gray, *China*, I, 5.

[3] *Veedor da Fazenda* in the original. Presumably the Pu-chêng-shih.

[4] Galeote Pereira's account states that they *did* take exact measurements, (cf. p. 28 above). I have not been able to identify this building, but Fukien province was noted for its great stone works. Cf. Appendix III.

beautiful tower, all wrought with very fair galleries and very well carved; but this upper-work is nothing to wonder at, since there are many such works all over China. Only the stone base is worthy of note, as being built of so many and such large pillars, all equal, and each worked from one stone block, each one being a marvel in itself.

In many of the principal cities, chiefly from the quay, where the mandarins and magistrates disembark, to the house of the Comptroller of the Revenue, the streets are so noble and broad, that ten or fifteen men on horseback can ride abreast along them, although there are very good covered ways along the sides, where live many merchants trading in many and diverse wares, and under the same covered ways are sold many fruits and many other things. All the broad and principal streets of all the cities have these covered ways, the which serve for what we have already said.

In all the streets of the principal cities, which are royal or main highways, there are very many and very sumptuous triumphal arches,[1] whereas Cantão has but few and not sumptuous. These arches in the principal cities, besides being very fair, sumptuous and very well wrought, in such wise that the Portugals (who were carried captives through the land inward) thought that each one of these had cost three thousand crowns,[2] are erected upon eight columns, very large and very thick; and they are placed in such sort that they form three arches crossing the street, that in the middle being larger than the two at the sides, the eight columns being arranged in pairs. They are topped by a very fair and curious edifice of wood. It is roofed with very fair porcelain tile, which gives it much grace and beauty; and these arches are made of such width and in such wise that many people can stand underneath protected from the rain and the sun; wherefore underneath them are sold many fruits and toys and a great variety of wares. And even though in some parts these arches may be built upon timber, in many others they are all of stone, very good and very well wrought. These arches make the cities look very proud, noble and beautiful. When new officers come to the region, and likewise when the Chinas celebrate their general feast-days, these arches are

---

[1] *P'ai-lou.* Cf. Galeote Pereira, p. 10, n. (2) above.
[2] *Cruzados* in the original. A *cruzado* was then worth between three and four English shillings.

decked with silken hangings, and at night, which is the chief time for their feasts, they hang many lanterns on them, the which make them very fair and large, the silken stuffs being very well coloured and in the light of the candles they look very well. Thus these arches at night with these lanterns and with these silken tapestries are very beautiful and look very fine.[1] The chief magistrates make these arches so that perpetual memory may remain of themselves, wherefore they place their inscriptions thereon.[2]

This invention of memorials seems to have been stolen from the Romans, as does the government polity and laws with which they govern and rule the country, and eating at high tables, and likewise other similar things which none of the other peoples of Asia have; by which it seems that Ovid, when he was exiled to the Scythians, was placed among those of the region of the river Thanas, and introduced in this way politic manners and customs among them. For he says in his *De Tristibus*, 'I made good use of my stay among these Scythian barbarians whither they exiled me, for I made them live in the Roman manner.'[3]

Almost all the cities are built along the banks of rivers. On the rivers which are not very high and impetuous, these cities have for service over the river, very noble and very well wrought bridges of stone; and the butments are not made in arches until after they have been very securely founded and built to a good height. They are connected one with another above by very large and very solid flagstones. The Portugals measured them and found them to be some of eleven and some of twelve paces long. These bridges are very wide, and as the rivers are very broad, they are likewise very long. The Portugals counted the butments on one side of one bridge, and found them to be forty-nine; and as they are made without arches and all level in a straight line, you can see directly

[1] Gaspar da Cruz was probably thinking of the *Teng-chieh* feast of the first lunar month, later called by foreigners the 'feast of lanterns'. It marks the official ending of the New Year holidays. Cf. J. Bredon, *The Moon Year*, pp. 133–141.

[2] This, of course, is not correct. *P'ai-lou* were normally erected to commemorate outstanding exemplars of filial-piety, chastity, loyalty, etc., and required imperial sanction or command.

[3] Ovid was exiled to Tomi on the Danube, and not to the Don. My colleague, Prof. W. S. Maguinness, to whom I referred this problem, writes, 'I can find nothing at all like this either in the *Tristia* or the *Epistulae ex Ponto*, although I have glanced through them all. The poet seems everywhere to regard the Scythians as complete savages and his genius as completely wasted among them.'

from one end to the other.[1] The parapets on both sides are very fairly engraved.

These bridges form the chief market-place of the cities, where all kinds of eatables are sold. What is to be wondered at in China, is that there are many bridges in uninhabited places throughout China, and these are not less well built nor less costly than those which are nigh the cities, but rather they are all costly and very well wrought. In some cities where the rivers are very high and impetuous, principally in times of great floods when they will not bear stone bridges, they make wooden bridges built on boats, the which are ranged in two rows, and connected with stout chains of iron, with wooden stays on both sides, very fairly wrought. The Portugals counted the boats of one of these bridges, and found them to be one hundred and twelve.[2] These bridges likewise form the chief market-place of the city, where all kinds of things are sold, but chiefly food; and a great multitude of boats laden with provisions comes to either side of the bridge, where they offer for sale what they bring.

When the winter season comes, and the river runs furiously, they break up these bridges, chaining one row of boats along one bank of the river and the other row on the other bank. They then make use of ferry-boats, the which the magistrates are compelled to provide for the service of the city, paid at the cost of the public revenues of the King. There are many of these bridges in many parts of China.

In some cities the water runneth through almost all the streets, and on the one side and the other of the street are landing-places made of free-stone for the common service of the people; and over all the streets are very good and well wrought bridges for to pass from one side to another; and through the middest of the streets is very great traffic of boats that go from one place to another.

In those places whereby the water entereth into the city, they have made very good portals in the walls, which have very strong iron gates for to shut by night. And the most of the roads in the land inward are very well paved with stone, and where there is no stone, with tiled brick, which is what we described above in Chapter Six.

[1] For these famous stone bridges of Fukien see Appendix III.
[2] Presumably the Kan-chou-fu pontoon bridge described by Galeote Pereira (cf. pp. 33–34), from whose account most of this chapter is taken.

In all the mountains and hills where there are paths, they are very well made, cut out with the pickaxe, and paved where it is needfull. This is one of the good works of China, and it is very general in every place of it. Many hills on the side of the Bramas and of the Laos,[1] are cut in steps, very well made; and at the top of the hill is made a low place, very well cut, in the which is a very high tower, whose top is level with the summit of the hill, and which is very strong. The wall of one of the towers was measured at the entering of the gate, and it was six fathom and a half thick. There are on this side many of these works, and so there may be in other places.

In the unwalled villages, there are some houses of rich husbandmen, the which when a man sees them from afar, (for they are among very fresh tree groves, so you cannot see any other houses but these), on account of the groves of trees a man might think that he is looking at country manors in Portugal,[2] noble and high. Many of these can be seen in many regions, which at first seem to be uninhabited, but on coming nearer them, some very large villages and of many households are to be seen, very well divided into streets, although the streets are commonly narrow. These houses are very high, with three or four stories. The tiled roofs cannot be seen, because the walls run up above them, very well finished, and water is thrown outside by projecting gutter-pipes. These are strong holds and have great and noble portals of stonework, and at the entrance a reception-court surrounded with good and high walls. They make these houses strong in this manner and with these courts, because it happens that sometimes bands of robbers assemble and go about pillaging these unwalled villages; and as these men are rich, they make the houses in this way, for to have their refuge therein, withdrawing their people inside for defence against the robbers.

Entering in the first of these houses (which is large) it has therein some huge cupboards very well wrought and carved, but the work is more for strength and durability than for show. They have likewise chairs with shoulder-backs, all made of a very strong wood and very well made, in such wise that their furniture is durable and of great repute and credit, which endures for their sons and grandsons.

---

[1] He refers here to the Chinese frontier posts on the marches of Kuangsi and Yünnan.
[2] 'Quintas em Portugal' in the original.

CHAPTER VIII

Which treats of the nobility of the houses of the kinsmen of the blood royal, and likewise of the magistrates who are in the principal cities.[1]

IT has already been stated how noble are the houses of the magistrates of the city of Cantam, and we said that among the principal cities, Cantam was one of the least noble. Thus, like as many cities exceed Cantam in nobility, so do the houses of their magistrates surpass in nobility those of the city of Cantam.

The houses of the magistrates in the principal cities, before one reaches where these magistrates are, have two very wide and long courts, each one of which would be about the size of a large horse-race.[2] In these courts are planted very fresh gardens wherein are many fruit trees; and there are high galleries in the middle, through which the magistrates walk; and on both sides of the galleries, between gardens and galleries, there is a space for the use of the people who have business, and for the other service of the house-hold. And because there are commonly in these houses very great lodgings, as well for the magistrate as for his assistants, and great prisons with lodgings for the jailers and the watches, they have within great kitchen-gardens with their ponds, in which they have many fish, not so much for a pastime as for eating. Each one of these houses has about as large a compass as that of a modest town. In the city of Cansi, which as we said is the capital of the province of Cansi,[3] there are a thousand houses in which the kinsmen of the King are lodged, and they are very great and much superior in

---

[1] This chapter is omitted in Purchas' translation, as most of it was to be found in Galeote Pereira's account which he likewise reprinted in his *Pilgrimes*, III, 199–209, in an abridged form.

[2] 'de grande carreira de cavallo' in the original. The expression also occurs in the penultimate chapter where I have, with some hesitation, retained Purchas' translation, 'horse-race'. Obviously this was nothing like the size of a modern race-course. Perhaps what Cruz had in mind was the kind of small private open-air bull-ring such as is sometimes found attached to the old mansions of Iberian grandees. The Castle at Oropesa (Spain) provides an example.

[3] Kueilin-fu. Kuei-lin means 'Cassia forest' or 'Cassia grove'.

nobility and beauty to the houses of the magistrates. As a mark of distinction, they have their fronts and doors coloured red. One who has seen it affirms that the palace of one of these, belonging to a kinsman of the King's wife named Vã folim, has as great a circuit as a large town.[1] They are square and have four gates for four principal streets, very sumptuous and very well made, with high towers above the gates, made with very fair galleries. Within this enclosure, he has very fresh and large gardens, with many fruit trees, and with great ponds where there are a multitude of fishes, both for a pastime as for sustenance of his household. He has there borders of all kinds of small flowers, and pinks and scented herbs; and within he has groves of wild trees, where he keeps many deer and wild boars and other beasts of the chase. In sort, that he has pastimes of every kind within his gates, for he can never leave his estate, both because of the greatness of his condition, as because this is a law of the kingdom, since the King wishes thereby to secure his kingdom, by depriving those of the blood royal of any opportunity to revolt. All the magistrates of the city are obliged to go and pay their respects to him on all the feast-days of the year. The other kinsmen of the King sometimes go abroad in the city, but on no account whatsoever may they go outside the walls, for if they try to do so, they are forthwith inexorably seized and punished with the supreme penalty which is death.

The lodging of these is Cansi [Kuangsi], because it is at the extremity of the kingdom, which is a region where they could not make themselves powerful even if they wished to do so, because the King takes care of the kingdom in such wise that it is not possible to raise a rebellion therein. And thus in all China there is no titled nobility, because these kinsmen of the King and those who are of the blood royal, are given lodgings when they marry; and then, accordingly as they are more or less closely related to the King, so are they given in marriage, and the servants and retainers and women who are to form their own household; and for him and his wife, and for all the people of his household, he is given a fixed revenue which suffices him very well, the which is paid every month without fail from the public revenue of the King. In sort

[1] Gaspar da Cruz here follows Galeote Pereira ('one who has seen it') in confusing the generic term for a palace of a prince of the blood, *wang-fu*, with its occupant, in this case one of the hereditary princes of Chin-chiang, whose seat was at Kueilin. This particular prince was Pang Ning (1525–1572).

that those of the blood royal are always administered and provided for in this fashion, in which there is no want.

Those who govern the country, who are principals in the kingdom,[1] have each a revenue fixed in accordance with the quality of their person and the needs of their office; in sort that nothing is wanting to him and to his, but neither is there enough surplus to enable him to enrich himself therewith. As for patrimonies, either they have none because their brothers enjoy them, or else they are so small that they are not enough to make them powerful. Add to this, they are commonly great spenders, given to enjoying life, to eating and drinking heavily, for which reasons they usually do not save from their pay.[2]

In this way the land is governed by all these means in such sort that there cannot be any rebellions therein. The houses of these of the blood royal are commonly very noble and large, in the which are great enclosures and ponds, kitchen-gardens and pleasaunces; for as they cannot go outside of the city, everything needful for their pastimes is provided for them within their estate. And when the magistrates pass by the gate of these nobles, whether they go on horseback or in a litter, they have to dismount out of respect until they have passed the gate; and while their retainers are passing it they cannot go along shouting to clear the way as they are wont to do, but they must pass silently and without pomp.

I heard say from a gentleman of good credit named Galeote Pereira, brother of the Governor[3] of Arraiolos, who had been in this city of Cansi as a captive, that (with the houses of these kinsmen of the King, being so many and so great) the city was so big that it seemed they occupied very little of it, and make a very little show in it; and so he had it written in a rutter of his, whence I took

[1] 'Os que regem ha terra, que sam principaes no reyno' in the original. The provincial mandarins, and the high officials who staffed the various departmental boards in the capital, most of whom had likewise had considerable administrative experience in the provinces. The Mandarinate.

[2] An interesting observation on the character of Ming high officials, when compared with those of Galeote Pereira and Martín de Rada, and taken in conjunction with the remarks of R. van Gulik, *Erotic colour-prints of the Ming dynasty*, I, xiii.

[3] *Alcaide-Mór* in the original, which Purchas translates as 'Chief-Justice'. 'Military governor' would be a more accurate rendering, but the post was mainly an honorary (and lucrative) one at this time, with few responsibilities. It will be noted that Fr. Gaspar da Cruz, here as elsewhere, makes full acknowledgment of his indebtedness to Galeote Pereira.

a great deal of that which is here spoken of; in such sort that the greatness of the city did hide in itself the multitude and greatness of these houses. And as it would seem that this man did not lie in this matter since he saw it, it therefore would seem to be equally true what is commonly affirmed of the grandeur of the city of Paquim and of that of Namquim, that a pacing horse can scarcely cross the walled city between sunrise and sunset, as these are royal cities and the chiefest of all China.[1]

These of the blood royal are commonly musical, and pride themselves on their skill in playing the viol,[2] and since they have little opportunity for exercise and are given to good living, they are commonly very fat, and they are in consequence very good natured, affable, and sociable, and of very good understanding, very courteous, and very well educated. In sort that the Portugals, after being let out of the jails, and having some freedom, did not find in anybody such hospitality, honour and favour, as in these, because they took them to their houses and ate and drank with them; and when the Portugals excused themselves, or they did not find them at home, then they took their servants (who had been captives with them and who did not forsake them after their release but on the contrary accompanied and served them) and showed as much honour unto the servants as to the masters.[3]

It must be noted here with how much care and consideration this country is governed, how great pains are taken to keep it in peace, nipping in the bud any attempt to raise a rebellion. This is the reason why China has maintained and governed itself securely for so many years, and is in peace without any internal wars.

[1] Cf. Ch. V, p. 90n. (1). Although this is an exaggeration, these cities were certainly very large. Archdeacon Gray, writing about 1870, noted that the walls 'which inclose the city of Nanking are eighteen English miles in circumference. At all events, it took me six hours to walk round them; and I walked, without stopping once, at a rate exceeding three miles per hour'. Gray, *China*, I, 5.

[2] 'hūa viola' in the original, which is, of course, taken from Galeote Pereira. Probably the *ch'in* or horizontal psaltery, also called the Chinese Lute, is intended here, as this was the scholar-aristocrat's musical instrument *par excellence*. Cf. R. van Gulik, *The Lore of the Chinese Lute* (Tokyo, 1940). Cf. also Ch. XIV, pp. 144–145.

[3] The same thing happened in Japan about this time. Jorge Alvares, the Portuguese sea-captain who wrote an interesting account of his visit to Yamagawa at the southern tip of Satsuma in 1547, states that the Japanese went out of their way to entertain the Negro slaves of the Portuguese—somewhat, it may be presumed, to the embarrassment of their masters. C. R. Boxer, *The Christian Century in Japan*, p. 35.

CHAPTER IX

Of the ships and vessels which there are in the country.

A S in this country there is great store of timber and very cheap, and much iron and cheap, and it is very good, there is an immense number of ships and vessels, for throughout the country are infinite groves of fir-trees and of other trees, whereby it is easy for any one though of a little substance, to make a ship and own a vessel, and this causeth the great profit and gain that is of them with the necessity the country hath of them; for it hath not only a great number of islands along the coast, but also a very great coast where they navigate. And besides this, all China within is navigated, and run through with rivers which do intersect and water it all, which are many and very great, so that you may sail and navigate in boats unto the ends of the land.[1]

Any captain along the coast may in a little space join two hundred, three hundred, even to a thousand ships, if he stand in need of them for to fight. And there is no small town along the river that is not plentiful in small and great ships. Along the city of Cantam, more than half a league by the river, is so great a multitude of ships that it is a wonderful thing to see them;[2] and that which is most to wonder is that this multitude never decreaseth nor faileth almost all the year, for if thirty, forty, or an hundred go forth one day, as many do come in again. I say, the multitude never to diminish nor fail, for though sometimes there be more, some less, always there remaineth a marvellous multitude; and what is more, all those that go forth, go laden, and all that come in, come laden, taking goods and bringing goods.

And that which showeth much the nobleness of the country, the plenty and riches thereof, is, that all these ships bringing great store of merchandise of cloths, silks, provisions and other goods,

---

[1] On the ubiquity of shipping in South China, cf. D. Ferguson, *Letters from Portuguese captives in Canton*, pp. 119, 156; Galeote Pereira, p. 6, n. (5) above; *Travels of Peter Mundy*, III, 184; Gray, *China*, II, 246–287.

[2] Their number was estimated at about 84,000 in the early nineteenth century. Ljungstedt, *Historical sketch*, p. 285.

some do go into the land, others come from within the land, and nothing cometh from without China, neither goeth out of it. And that which the Portugals do carry, and some that they of Siam do carry, is so little in comparison with the great traffic of the country, that it almost remaineth as nothing, and unperceived; seeing that out of China there goeth no more but that which the Portugals and they of Siam do carry; the which is, though much, as though they brought nothing out of China, five or six carracks coming laden with silk and porcelain.[1] The great plenty and riches of the country doth this, that it can sustain itself alone.

Pepper and ivory which is the principal that the Portugals do carry, a man may well live without it.[2]

And the traffic of the merchandise that is in this country is in all the cities within the land, which as we have said, are almost all built along the rivers.

The Chinas have a common saying for to show the nobleness of their kingdom, that the King of China can make a bridge of ships from China unto Malacca, which are near five hundred leagues, the which though it seemeth it cannot be, yet by metaphor it signifieth the greatness of China, and the multitude of ships that of itself it can make.[3] The greatest ships they call junks,[4] which are ships fit for war, made like great carracks, in the which they make great forecastles and high, and likewise abaft, to fight from them in such

---

[1] We have so few details about the nature and extent of early Sino-Portuguese trade, that even this rather general statement is very welcome. It can be added to the arguments advanced by J. C. van Leur, *Eenige beschouwingen betreffende den ouden Aziatischen handel* (Middelburgh, 1934), pp. 157–180, where he seeks to show that the advent of Europeans in East Asian waters made relatively little difference to the extent and operation of the existing sea-borne trade. A Portuguese carrack (*não, nau*) of that period seldom exceeded 500 tons, but by the end of the century they were often twice that tonnage.

[2] Japanese silver bullion soon became the mainstay of the Portuguese imports into China, and remained so until the end of the Macao-Nagasaki trade in 1640. Silk (raw and manufactured) and gold were their principal exports from Macao to Japan. C. R. Boxer, *The Christian Century in Japan*, pp. 91–121; Delmar M. Brown, *Money economy in medieval Japan*, pp. 61–93.

[3] The seventeenth-century Jesuit, Martin Martini, relates that the Fukienese once offered to facilitate a projected invasion of Japan by bridging the interval with their shipping. Thevenot, *Relations de divers voyages curieux*, III, 151. Christovão Vieira, in 1524, wrote that Fukien province possessed junks 'to the number of millions'.

[4] *juncos* in the original. It is not certain whether the word is of Chinese or Malay origin. *Hobson-Jobson*, pp. 472–473; Dalgado, *Glossário Luso-Asiático*, I, 497–499.

IV. A Cantonese war-junk
(From the *Ch'ou-hai-t'u-pien*, 1562)

manner that they over-master their adversaries.[1] And because they use no ordnance, all their use is to come many together, and com-passing the adversary ship, they board it; and at the first onset they cast a great deal of lime to blind the adversaries, and as well from the castles as from the tops they cast many sharp pikes burned at the end, which serve for top-darts, of a very stiff wood. They use also great store of stone, and the chiefest they labour for, is to break with their ships the dead-works of their adversaries, that they may be masters over them, having them under them, and being destitute of anything to shelter them; and as soon as they can enter they come to the pike or handy-blows, for the which they have long lances, and broad-swords hanging at their sides.[2] There be other junks for lading of goods, but they are not so high as those of war, though there be some very great. All these ships as well of war as of burthen use two oars ahead.[3] They are very great, and four or five men do row each one of them, laying them along-side the ship they move them with such a sleight, that they make the ship go forward, and they help very much for to go out and in at a bar, and setting upon the enemies for to board them. They call these oars *Lios lios*; in all manner of their vessels they use the *Lios lios* neither do they use any other manner of oars in any kind of shipping.[4]

There be other lesser vessels than junks, called Bancões,[5] they bear three oars on a side, and row very well, and load

[1] Cf. the remarks on Chinese naval tactics by the Portuguese prisoners at Canton in 1524, in Ferguson, *Letters from Portuguese captives at Canton*, pp. 137, 164. For a brief account of Cantonese war-junks during the Ming dynasty, see J. V. Mills, 'Notes on early Chinese voyages' in JRAS (1951), pp. 12, 24–25. Readers who can cope with Chinese will find further details in M. H. Ch'en's article, 'The invasion of China by Japanese pirates during the Ming dynasty' in the *Yenching Journal of Chinese studies*, monograph series No. 6, (Peking, 1934) especially pp. 142–147. Original woodcuts in the *Ch'ou-hai-t'u-pien* (1562).

[2] The firearms and other weapons used in Chinese war-junks are illustrated in the *Ch'ou-hai-t'u-pien* (1562). Cf. also E. T. C. Werner, *Chinese Weapons*, extra volume of the *JNCBRAS* (1932), and L. Carrington Goodrich & C. S. Feng's articles in *Isis*, XXXV (1944), pp. 177, 211–213, XXXVI (1946), pp. 114–123, 250–251, XXXIX (1948), pp. 63–64.

[3] 'dous remos por proa'. Purchas has mistakenly translated 'two oars astern'.

[4] Chinese *lu* (Cantonese (*lô,*) a scull, oar, or sweep. The Chinese develop-ment of sculling, which is nowadays termed *yuloh* (*yaolu*) by foreigners, is well described by Sir F. Maze, 'Notes on the Chinese Yuloh', *Mariner's Mirror*, XXXVI (1950), pp. 55–57.

[5] Plural form of *Bancão*, *Vancão*, *Wankan*, etc., from the Malay *vankan*.

a great deal of goods. There be other less, called Lanteas,[1] which have six or seven oars on a side, which do row very swift, and bear a good burthen also; and these two sorts of ships, viz. Bancões and Lanteas, because they are swift, the pirates do commonly use. The rowing of these oars is standing, two men at every oar, every one of his side, setting one foot forward, another backward.[2] In the junks go four, five, or six men at an oar.

They use also certain vessels very long, like unto gallies without oars or beak-head, which do lade great store of goods. And they make them so long because being laden with a great burden they may sail the better by the rivers, which sometimes are not rough.[3]

They have many other vessels of burthen, which is superfluous to tell of every one. There be many small boats of poor people, in which are husband and wife and children, and they have no other dwelling but in their boat in the half-deck, for defence of the sun and of the rain, as also have the Bancões and Lanteas, and others which we said were like gallies; and these decks are in such sort, that under them are very good lodgings and chambers in the great ships; in these of the poor, they are much inferior. There they breed their little pig, their little hen, and there they have also their poor little garden, and there they have all their poor state and harbouring.[4] The men go to seek work about the city to help to maintain their little house; the women go in the boats, and with a long cane that reacheth well to the bottom of the river (at the end of which there is a little basket made of rods, wherewith they get shell-fish) with their industry and with ferrying people from one side to the other, they help to sustain their household.

The term was chiefly applied to what Peter Mundy (in 1637) called 'skulling junks', particularly used for patrol work along rivers. *Travels of Peter Mundy*, III, 203–204; Dalgado, *Glossário Luso-Asiático*, II, 402.

[1] A word of uncertain origin. Although described by Fr. Gaspar da Cruz as a type of vessel noted for its speed, the word was later applied to the large lighter-like barges which brought down goods by the inland waterway from Canton to Macao. C. R. Boxer, *Macao three hundred years ago*, pp. 35, 217.

[2] The sculling or yuloh action described and illustrated in the article quoted on p. 113 n. (4) above.

[3] It was to this type of lighter or barge that the name *lantea* was applied in the seventeenth century.

[4] The *Tanka* (lit. 'egg-people') or boat-people of the Canton (Pearl) river delta, for whom see Giles, *Glossary*, p. 142; Ljungstedt, *Historical sketch*, p. 285; C. S. Balfour in *T'ien Hsia Monthly*, XI, pp. 332–334. It can be seen from these accounts how little the Tanka have changed since Da Cruz's time.

These poor people notwithstanding do not live so poorly and beggarly in their apparel as do those who live poorly in Portugal.[1]

There are other great vessels wherein is the stock of them both [the husband's merchandise and the wife's housewifery],[2] which have great lodgings where they may bestow a great deal of stuff; these have a great stock; they have certain cages made all the length of the ship with canes, in which they keep two or three thousand ducks, more or less as the vessel is. Some of these belong to lordships, and their servants go in them; they feed these ducks as followeth. After it is broad day, they give them a little sodden rice, but not till they have had enough; and when they have given it them, they open a door to the river where is a bridge made of canes, and it is a wonderful thing to see them when they go forth, tumbling one over another for the great abundance of them, and the time they take in going out. They feed all the day until night among the fields of rice, and those who have charge of these vessels do receive a fee of them that own the rice-fields, for letting them feed in them, for they do cleanse them, eating the weed that groweth among them. When night cometh, they call them with a little tabor, and though there be sundry barks together, yet every one knowns their own by the sound of the tabor and goes unto it.[3] And because there are always in time some which remain out and return not again, there are everywhere many flocks of wild ducks, and likewise of geese. When I saw such a great multitude of ducks in each one of these barks, and all of one bigness, and thinking they could not be hatched by ducks or hens, for if it were so, some would have been bigger and others smaller, seeing so many could not be hatched in one, two, or fifteen days, I was willing to know how they hatched them; and they told me it was in one of two sorts.

In summer, laying two or three thousand eggs in the dung, and with the heat of the weather and the dung, the eggs are hatched. In

---

[1] A similar comparison between the very poor of England and of China, likewise to the advantage of the Chinese, is made in the anonymous *Diary of a journey overland, through the maritime provinces of China, from Manchao, on the south coast of Hainan, to Canton in the years 1819, and 1820* (London, 1822), p. 30. 'We made it a general remark, that people of the poorest sort here, are better clothed than the same class of persons even in England.'

[2] Words in square brackets are supplied from Purchas' marginal note.

[3] This description closely tallies with that of the Cantonese duck-boats and flocks given over three centuries later by B. C. Henry, *Ling-nam* (London, 1886), pp. 61–63.

winter, they make a hurdle of canes very great, upon the which they lay that great number of eggs, under the which they make a slack fire, continuing it of the same heat for a number of days till the eggs be hatched.[1] And because they are hatched in this sort, there are so many of one bigness; and all along the river are many of these barks, whereby the lands are well provided of this food.

It is a very pleasant thing to see by the river the multitude of vessels, some going and others coming, some under sail and others with oars. And as the rice-fields stretch as for as the eye can see, it looks as if many of the vessels under sail afar off, are coming as it were through the land, until you go in their direction and they in yours, when you see the great hulls which they have (not having seen before anything more than the sails), and at the same time see the great arms of the rivers along which they come. There are some ships wherein the magistrates do sail, which have very high lodgings, and within houses very well made, gilt, rich, and very sumptuous; and on the one side and the other they have great windows, with their nets woven of silk hanging from very fine small rods set before them, that they within seeing all them without, may not be seen of them. Whereas the vessels of the nobles of Peguu are very rich and fair, those who have seen both of them, affirm that those of the Chinas are vastly superior.

Towards the side of the Laos and the Bramas, are continually watches and wards in the rivers in many ships, even a whole month's journey in length unto the city of Cansi.[2] These ships are in the places where the rivers make some arms, because of the many pirates who commonly are in these parts, being the uttermost part of the kingdom; and because the rivers have many arms, many vessels are placed in those parts. In every place where these vessels are, there be two small vessels which continually do go night and day from one watch to another, because they are very swift; and those of the great vessels do divide themselves into watches at their quarters for to watch; and this is also done in the small and swift as in the great ones. The ships of passage go always a great number together, that they may defend themselves and one

---

[1] Cf. the accounts of Chinese egg-hatcheries given by W. C. Milne, *Life in China*, pp. 318–321; Gray, *China*, II, 182–184; F. H. King, *Farmers of forty centuries*, pp. 157–161.

[2] It is not clear whether the West river or the Cassia river is indicated here. See Galeote Pereira, p. 35 above.

another until the ships of war and the watches do come to their help. And at the watch which they reach at nightfall, there they stay till the morning, and by the small boats they are delivered safe to the next watch forward, and so from watch to watch they are accompanied of the small vessels till they be set in safety.

From the city of Oucheo, that is where the governor of Cansi and Cantam is resident,[1] unto the bounds of the province of Cansi, which are the most dangerous places, there are continually armadas of forty or fifty vessels. All these guards and watches are paid from the common revenues of the kingdom. From this it can be clearly seen how well China is governed, and how much trouble is taken to make the ways safe for merchants and travellers.

[1] 'Oucheo' here is obviously Wu-chou, just over the Kuangsi border, and not (as in some other sixteenth-century narratives) Aucheo or Foochow. Cf. Appendix II.

o

CHAPTER X

Of the husbandry of the land and the occupations of the people.

CHINA is almost all a well husbanded country; for as the country is well inhabited, and people in abundance, and the men spenders, and using themselves very deliciously in eating and drinking and apparel, and in the other services of their houses, especially that they are great eaters, every one laboureth to get a living, and every one seeketh ways to earn their food, and how to maintain their great expenses. A great help to this is that idle people be much abhorred in this country, and are very odious unto the rest, and he that laboureth not shall not eat, for commonly there is none that do give alms to the poor;[1] wherefore, if any poor man did ask alms of a Portugal, and he did give it to him, the Chinas did laugh at him and asked him mockingly, 'Why givest thou alms to this which is a knave? Let him go and earn it.'

Only some jesters have some reward, standing on some high place where they gather the people around them and tell them some fables to get something. The fathers and priests of their idols are commonly abhorred and not esteemed, because they hold them for idle people, and the magistrates for any light fault do not spare them but give them many stripes.[2] Wherefore, a magistrate whipping once before a Portugal a priest of theirs, and he asking him wherefore he did use their priests so ill and held them in so little esteem, answered him, 'These are idle and abandoned knaves.'

One day, I, and certain Portugals entering into the house of the Comptroller of the Revenue,[3] about the delivery of certain Portu-

---

[1] Fr. Gaspar da Cruz is obviously exaggerating here, but it is interesting to note that the Chinese anticipated Lenin's dictum that 'He who does not work, shall not eat'.

[2] The dislike and contempt in which Buddhist and Taoist priests were held by the governing class in China was noted by all foreign visitors. It formed a particularly striking contrast to the privileged position of the clergy in Portugal and Spain. Cf. De Groot, *Fêtes*, II, 735–737.

[3] *Pu-chêng-shih*, civil governor and comptroller.

gals that were in prison, because the matter belongs to him for the great profit that came thereof to the King, much people came in with us to see us, among the which there was a priest; as soon as the magistrate said, 'Set them down,' all of them ran away in great haste, the priest running as all the rest, for fear of the whip.

From this it can be seen that idle people are abhorred in this country, and that he who doth not earn doth not eat; wherefore it behoves every one to seek a way and manner of livelihood by which he can support himself. Every one laboureth to seek a living, for that which he earneth he enjoyeth freely, and spends it as he will, and that which is left him at his death remains to his children and grandchildren, paying only duties royal, as well of the fruits that they gather, as of the goods they deal in, which are not heavy. The greatest tribute they have, is every married man, or whosoever is head of a household, payeth for every person in his house two mace, which are sixty reis.[1] No further exaction is made from him than only the levy of the royal dues. Their goods and all that they can amass remain free for them to enjoy at their own will, wherefore they all strive to gain a livelihood and to cultivate the land and profit from it.

From Champaa, which as we said, doth confine with Cauchim-china, unto as far as all India there are many unprofitable grounds, and made wildernesses and woods, and the men are generally little curious to get or gather together; for they never gain or get so much but it is tyrannized from them, for that which they have is only theirs as long as the King listeth and no more. In such sort that as soon as the Kings knoweth that any of their officers hath much money, they command him to be put in prison, and they use him so hardly, that they make him disgorge all that he hath gotten.[2]

Wherefore there are many in those parts, who if they get any-thing or money one day or one week, they will not labour until after they have consumed all that they have earned in eating and drinking; and they do it because if any tyranny should chance to

---

[1] *Maz* or *mace* from the Malay-Japanese *mas* and Sanskrit *māsa*. It denoted the $\frac{1}{16}$ part of a Malay *tael* and the $\frac{1}{10}$ part of a Chinese *tael* or *liang*, which latter was also about this time roughly equated with the Portuguese *cruzado*. *Hobson-Jobson*, p. 530; Dalgado, *Glossário Luso-Asiático*, II, 45; Boxer, *Christian Century*, pp. 107–108. For this householder's tax, cf. Martín de Rada, p. 275, n. (3) *infra*.

[2] Cf. Ch. I, p. 62 above.

come, they may find nothing to take from them. From hence it cometh, as I say, that they have in India many grounds in divers places unprofitable; which is not so in China, for every one enjoyeth the fruits of his labour.[1] Hence it cometh that all the ground in China which can yield any kind of fruit after receiving seed, is husbanded. The high ground which is not so good for corn hath very fair groves of pine trees, sowing also between them some pulse where it may be.

In the dry lands and stiff, they sow wheat and pulse. In the low lands which are overflowed, which are many and very extensive, they sow rice; and some of these low lands do yield two or three crops a year.[2] Only the mountains that are high and beaten with the weather, and are not fit to plant any thing, remain unprofitable. There is nothing lost in the country be it never so vile; for the bones as well of dogs as of other beasts, they do use, making toys, and carving them instead of ivory, they inlay them in tables, beds, and other fair things. They lose not a rag of any quality, for as well of the fine as of the coarse, that are not of wool, they make fine and coarse paper; and they make paper of barks of trees, and of canes, and of silken rags, and in the paper made of silk they write; the rest serveth for to roll between the pieces of silk.

Even the dung of men yields profit, and is bought for money or

[1] The Jesuit Father Le Comte made the same comparison nearly two centuries later. 'Si les terres de la Chine n' estoient aussi-fertiles, et les habitans aussi-laborieux qu'ils le sont, l'Empire ne seroit bientost qu'une assemblée de gueux et de misérables, comme la plus part des Royaumes des Indes.' (*Nouveaux Mémoires de la Chine*, II, 93, *apud* G. Atkinson, *Les relations de voyage du XVII*[e] *siècle et l'évolution des idées*, p. 87). On the other hand, the Portuguese captives at Canton in 1521–1524, and Padre Gabriel de Magalhães, S.J., in the middle of the seventeenth century sharply criticised the tyranny of the provincial mandarins and asserted that the people were unbearably oppressed by them. See the quotations from the former in the introduction (p. xxx above); and G. Magalhães, *A New History of China*, (London, 1688), p. 135, . . . 'So that it is a common proverb in China that the King unwittingly lets loose so many hangmen, murderers, hungry dogs and wolves to ruin and devour the poor people, when he creates new mandarins to govern them.' On the whole, however, I am inclined to think that Gaspar da Cruz's comparison was justified. Cf. W. H. Moreland, *India at the death of Akbar* (London, 1920), pp. 31–52, 253–280, for conditions in contemporary India.

[2] In South China two crops of rice are obtained annually in most low-lying districts, but three only in a few exceptionally favoured localities. Further north, one annual crop is the rule. Cf. Couling, *Encyclopedia Sinica*, p. 483; Dyer Ball, *Things Chinese*, pp. 561–563; F. H. King, *Farmers of forty centuries*, pp. 238–272 for facts and figures on Chinese rice cultivation and production.

in change of vegetables, and they carry it from the houses,[1] in sort
that they give money or money's worth, to suffer them to cleanse
their houses of office, though it smelleth evil through the city.
When they carry it on their backs through the city, in order to
avoid the evil smell, they carry it in tubs very clean without, and
although they go uncovered, notwithstanding it showeth the
cleanliness of the country and cities. In some cities these tubs used
to go covered in order not to annoy. This dung serves them for to
manure their kitchen-gardens, and they say that with it the vegetables can be seen to grow;[2] they mix it with earth and bake it in
the sun.

And like as they use this, so do they use in all things more
sleight than force; whereby they plough with one ox, making the
plough in such fashion that it cutteth well the earth, though the
furrows are not so big as among us.[3] A ship be it never so big, and
have it never so great a leak, the pumps are made by such sleight
that one man alone sitting moving his feet as one that goeth up a
staircase, in a very little space he pumps it out. These pumps are of
many pieces made in the manner of water-wheels, laid alongside
the side of the ship, between rib and rib, every piece having a piece
of wood of half a yard [a] little more or less, one quarter well
wrought; in the middest of this piece of wood is a square little
board, almost of a hand's breadth, and they join one piece into
another in such manner as it may double well. The joints, which are
all very close, whereby this manner of pump doth run, is within
of the breadth of the little boards of every one of the pieces, for
they are all equal; and this manner of pump bringeth so much
water as may be contained between the two little boards.[4] The
Chinas also use puppets, with the which they make artful representations, as some foreigners do with them in Portugal for to gain
money, and the Chinas use them for the same purpose of gaining
money. They bring up nightingales in cages, and teach them to

[1] 'Manure is valued as if it were gold.' (Couling, Encyclopedia Sinica, p. 8).
Compare also Galeote Pereira's remarks on pp. 8–9 above.

[2] Manure is applied more to the roots of the growing plant than to the soil, as I
can vouch from personal experience in 1943–1945.

[3] Dyer Ball gives a clearer but less flattering description of the Chinese plough,
in Things Chinese, pp. 19–20.

[4] For more coherent descriptions of Chinese endless-chain pumps see
Doolittle, Social Life of the Chinese, I, 53–54; Gray, China, II, 291; F. H. King,
Farmers of forty centuries, pp. 78, 262–264; Fugl-Meyer, Chinese Bridges, pp. 53, 63.

make representations with divers kinds of dresses of men and women, and they make tricks and turns very mirthful for to see. It is only this kind of little birds which they breed in cages, very well made, for to sing; and they commonly keep the male and the female in different cages, and in order to make them sing they separate the male from the female in such sort that they can feel but not see each other; and in this way the male melts himself in music and sings all the year round. I kept two males and a female, and they sang in December as if it had been in April.[1] They feed them with cooked rice wrapped in the yolk of an egg, somewhat on the dry side, which deceives them into thinking they are eating little insects.

I said above that they did not give alms to the poor in this country, and forasmuch as some readers might ask what remedy had the poor who could not earn their bread, through being maimed, crippled or blind, I thought it good to satisfy them. It is a thing worth noting that the blind have a labour appointed them for to get their food, which is to serve in a horse-mill, like horses grinding corn; and commonly where there is one horse-mill there are two, because one blind man going in each mill, they may recreate themselves in talking one with the other, as I saw them treading the wheel with fans in their hands, fanning themselves and talking very friendly.

The blind women are the common women,[2] and they have nurses that do dress them and paint them with vermillion and ceruse, and receive the wages of their evil use. The lame and the cripple, which either have no kindred within a certain degree, or if they have them and they do not provide for them that which is necessary, or are not able to help them, they make their petition to the Comptroller of the King's Revenue;[3] and their kindred being examined by his officers, if among them are any that can maintain them, they do bind the nearest to take them to their charge and maintain them; and if their kindred be not able to maintain them,

---

[1] This passage implies that Gaspar da Cruz visited Canton in December. As a later passage (Ch. XXVIII, p. 221 *infra*) indicates that he was just over a month in the city, it is most likely that his stay in Canton was in December 1556–January 1557. For larks and other song-birds favoured by the Cantonese, see Dyer Ball, *Things Chinese*, pp. 322–324.

[2] Prostitutes.

[3] *Pu-chêng-shih*, civil governor and comptroller.

or if they have no kindred in the country, the Comptroller of the Revenue commandeth they be received into the King's Hospital; for the King hath in all the cities great hospitals which have many lodgings within a great enclosure. And the officers of the hospital are bound to administer to those that are bed-ridden all things necessary, for the which there are very sufficient rents appointed out of the King's exchequer.

The lame that keep not their bed, have every month a certain quantity of rice, with the which, and with a little hen or a little pig which they bring up in the hospital, they have sufficient to maintain themselves; and all these things are very well paid, without fail. And because commonly those who are received into these hospitals are incurable, they receive them for life. And all those who are received by commandment of the Comptroller of the Revenue are enrolled, and every year the officers of the hospital do yield account of the expences, and of the provision for the poor sick; and if any fault or negligence be found in them of that which they are bound to do, without remission they are well punished for it.[1]

[1] If our friar's account can be taken at its face value (and I do not see why not), conditions in the provincial alms-houses and hospitals must have sharply deteriorated under the Manchu régime. Cf. Ljungstedt, *Historical sketch*, pp. 269–270. Even so, Chinese hospitals were not invariably so bad as is often alleged, even under the Manchus, as may be seen from the discussion of these institutions in W. A. Milne, *Life in China*, pp. 49–61, and the *China Review*, VIII, 362–363.

CHAPTER XI

Of the mechanical craftsmen, and of the merchants.

THERE are in this country many workmen of all trades, and great abundance of all things necessary for the common use, and so it is requisite, for the people is infinite. And because shoes are the thing that most is spent, there are more workmen of shoemakers than of any other trade. In Cantam are two particular streets of shoemakers very long, one where they sell rich shoes and of silk, another where they sell common shoes of leather;[1] and besides these two streets, there are many workmen scattered about the city.

The rich boots and shoes are covered with coloured silk, embroidered over with twisted thread of very fine work; and there be boots from ten crowns to one crown price, and shoes of two crowns and thence downward, and in some places are shoes of three pence.[2] So that the rich and the very poor may wear shoes, and the rich as they list. The shoes of three pence, or of a rial, are of straw, and I say of three pence, for there is money that answereth our three pence. There be many rich husbandmen that set men by the ways with many of these straw shoes for the poor travellers, and it is no wonder to have this charity among these infidels, for in the regions of India are many rich gentiles which have very great houses, wherein they spend continually much rice, giving food to all the poor of what quality soever that will come thither to eat, and by the ways they have men set to give drink to the poor travellers.[3] There be also good carpenters and very good workmen of all manner of work. They have continually many boxes made of many sorts,

---

[1] 'It is a feature of Canton trade that as a rule shops selling the same kind of goods are found in distinct locations, so that one street is known for its shops dealing in one or two articles, another street for goods of a different kind.' J. G. R., *Guide to China*, p. 393.

[2] These prices are Purchas' equivalents of the original *cruzado* and *meio-real*.

[3] Purchas has here a distinctly unfair marginal note, whose carping tone is not justified by any reading of the original Portuguese text: 'Alms not alms; the fruit of vainglory not of mercy.' I am not clear whether Cruz is referring to Hindu or to Buddhist organised charity, but both were inspired by merciful motives.

some varnished with a very fair varnish,[1] others painted, others lined with leather, and likewise of other sorts. They have continually a great number of chairs made, some of very fair white wood, and others fairly gilt and silvered, very finely wrought.

They have also chairs wherein the magistrates are carried on men's backs through the city, which are very rich, of a great price and very fair. They have another manner of chairs which are high, very rich and pleasant, all close with a little window on each side very fair with a net made of ivory, or of bone or of wood, through the which they that go within do see on the one side and on the other of the street, without being seen.[2] These serve for to carry the women about the city when they go abroad. The seat is of the height of one of our chairs where they go sitting with their legs at length. There be many of these chairs very rich, and of a great price; and there are some plain, and have pinnacles on the top very fair.

There are also many bedsteads very pleasant and very rich, all close round about, of wood finely wrought. I being in Cantam, there was a very rich one made wrought with ivory, and of a sweet wood which they call Cayolaque,[3] and of sandalwood, that was priced at four hundred crowns.[4]

Of little boxes gilt, and platters, and baskets, writing-desks and tables, as well gilt as with silver, there is no count nor better. Goldsmiths, silver-smiths, copper-smiths, iron-smiths, and of all other trades, there be many and perfect workmen, and great abundance of things of every trade, and very perfect.

They use infinite vessels of brass; and from China they furnish all Jaoa[5] and Siam with these vessels which in India they call

[1] Lacquer-ware. Cf. Couling, *Encyclopedia Sinica*, pp 283–284; Dyer Ball, *Things Chinese*, pp. 312–325.

[2] The *chiao-tzu*, origin of the European sedan-chair. Giles, *Glossary*, p. 21; Couling, *Encyclopedia Sinica*, p. 86.

[3] Crawfurd's Malay dictionary identifies this as the name of a 'redwood used as incense, *Myristica iners*', but the real Malayan derivation seems to be uncertain. *Hobson-Jobson*, p. 177; Dalgado, *Glossário Luso-Asiático*, I, 175.

[4] Compare González de Mendoza's enthusiastic appreciation of a Chinese bed which was brought from Manila to Europe some years later,—'I did see my selfe, one that was brought unto Lysborne in the yeare 1582, by Captaine Ribera, chiefe sergant of Manila, that it was to be wondred at the excellence thereof: it caused the king's maiestie to have admyration and he [Philip II] is a person that little wondreth at things. All the people did wonder at it: yea the famous imbroiderers did marvaile at the curiousnesse thereof.' *History* (Hakluyt Society ed.), I, 32.

[5] Java.

Bategaria,[1] and they are in every kind very perfect. They use skillets, and chafing-dishes, and other vessels of cast iron, and not only they do cast these vessels of iron, but after they are broken, they buy them again for to recast them.

There are many merchants of pieces and cloths of silk, because they spend many in the same country, and in India and in Siam; and there are pieces of damask and taffeta among themselves so rich that they bring them not to us, because we cannot give for them what they are worth within the land. They also sell fine and coarse serge of sundry colours. There are many merchants of white and dyed linen cloth, for it is that which is most spent in the country. They gave me a piece of linen cloth of about ten cubits, which was valued at ten crowns; and there is both fine and coarse as every one will have it.[2]

And howsoever the porcelain which is used in all the country of China, and in all India, is of common clay, notwithstanding, there is very much coarse porcelain, and other very fine; and there is some that is not lawful to be sold commonly, for the magistrates only use it, because it is red and green, and gilt, and yellow. Some of this is sold, but very little, and that very secretly.[3]

And because there are many opinions among the Portugals

---

[1] Generic term for metal basins, dishes and so forth. An Indo-Portuguese word of uncertain origin. Dalgado, *Glossário Luso-Asiático*, I, 103–104.

[2] Linen was later superseded by cotton, which was first extensively grown in China under the Yüan (Mongol) Dynasty. Couling, *Encyclopedia Sinica*, pp. 134–135; Dyer Ball, *Things Chinese*, pp. 161–163. The change over from linen to cotton as the staple of clothing for the masses, seems to have taken place about this time. Cruz does not mention cotton; Rada, writing in 1575, states that it was then widely grown and used; Trigault, writing in 1615, alleges that the Chinese used cotton to the exclusion of linen.

[3] Gaspar da Cruz is mistaken in his assertion that certain kinds of porcelain were reserved for the use of high officials; he is probably confusing this with the fact that the porcelains made for the Palace by the imperial kiln at Ching-tê-chên could not be sold to outsiders, and some of the glazes could not be made for anyone but the Court. Mr. Soame Jenyns, of the Department of Oriental Antiquities at the British Museum, points out that in the early part of Chia-ching's reign, the imperial kiln was in great difficulties and the custom had arisen of putting out to contract a great proportion of the imperial wares to outside firms. This must have made it easier for the Portuguese at Canton to acquire such pieces. Cruz's account is important because it shows that the Chinese porcelains exported to Europe at this time, through the medium of the Portuguese, were not all inferior wares made expressly for this export market, as is often assumed. For conditions at Ching-tê-chên during this period see G. R. Sayer, *Ching-tê-chên T'ao Lu* (London, 1951), pp. 41–48.

who have not been in China, about where this porcelain is made, and touching the substance of which it is made, some saying of oyster-shells, others of dung rotten for a long time, because they were not informed of the truth, I thought it convenient to tell here the substance whereof it is made, according to the truth told by them who saw it.

The substance of the porcelain is a white and soft stone, and some is red which is not so fine; or in better speaking, it is a hard clay, the which after well beating and grinding it, and laying in cisterns of water (which they have very well made of free-stone, and some plastered and they are very clean) and after it is well stirred in the water, of the cream that remaineth on the top they make the very fine porcelain, and so the lower the coarser; and of the dregs they make the coarsest and base, which the poor people of China do use. They make them first in this clay, as the potters do any other vessel; after they are made they dry them in the sun, and after they are dried they paint them as they list with azure, which is so fine as we see. After these pictures are dried, they lay on the glaze, and then bake them when glazed.[1]

The principal streets of the merchants are the most principal streets, which have covered ways on the one side and on the other; notwithstanding the chiefest sale of the porcelain is at the gates of the cities; and every merchant hath at his door written on a board all that is sold within his shop. Those which sell simples for medicines, have at their doors tied and hanging from a string a piece of every thing.

There is in China great store of rhubarb, but it is not brought to Cantam save when it is dressed; there is none found raw.[2]

As the goods of China are very great and many, so the revenues which the King of China hath in every part of his kingdom are very great. Some China merchants did affirm that Cantam did yield every year to the King three thousand piculs of silver. Every three piculs make one bahar, every bahar hath four quintals, every

[1] For an eye-witness account of the manufacture of porcelain at Ching-tê-chên, see Gray, China, II, 231–243.
[2] The best rhubarb was brought to Canton from its natural habitat in NW. Ssüch'üan and the adjoining regions. Cf. the curious reference to rhubarb from N.W. China which had been brought overland to Ormuz, and was sent by the Jesuit Gaspar Barzeu to St. Ignatius Loyola in 1551, in Silva Rego, Documentação, VII, p. 83.

quintal hath four arrobas. So that one bahar is sixteen arrobas, and as three thousand piculs make one thousand bahars, by consequence one thousand bahars make sixteen thousand arrobas;[1] and we speak of weight, for in China is no money of gold or silver, but only of copper.[2] The gold and silver goeth by weight.[3]

But these as they are common people, though occupied in the traffic of the country, it seems that they cannot well know the truth of this, and that the sum which is collected from the royal revenues must be greater, for the country is very great, and the merchandises many and very substantial. I was informed by means of the magistrate, which is a more certain information because the revenues do pass through their hands, that the rent of the salt in Cantam alone[4] did yield to the King three hundred piculs of silver, which do make one hundred bahars, which are four hundred quintals, which are sixteen hundred arrobas of silver.[5]

And as we have already said, there is no gold or silver money in China, but only current weight of gold and silver, and everything is bought and sold by weight; wherefore every man hath a pair of scales and weights in his house, which all are exceedingly perfect. The weights that they commonly have, are from ten crowns to one, and from ten tangas to one (a tanga being nine pence).[6] By the

[1] The *bahar* was originally an Indian weight (Sanskrit, *bhāra*) spread throughout Asia by the Arabs under the form *bahār*. Its weight varied according to the localities in (and the commodities for) which it was used, but the equivalents given by Gaspar da Cruz seem to have been the most widespread. A picul (Malay-Javanese *pikul*, 'a man's load') was 133⅓ lb. avoirdupois; and the bahar described here was thus approximately 400 lb. avoirdupois. The *quintal* was generally equivalent to 100 lb., and the *arroba* to about 25 lb. Cf. *Hobson-Jobson*, pp. 47–48, 690; Dalgado, *Glossário Luso-Asiático*, I, 78–79, II, 208; G. Ferrand, *Les poids, mesures, et monnaies des mers du Sud aux XVIᵉ et XVIIᵉ siècles* (Paris, 1921), p. 90; Pires-Cortesão, *Suma Oriental*, I, 82; II, 277. Purchas, who trans-ates *quintal* as *quarter*, gives the total value as '400,000 pound weight of silver', in a marginal note.

[2] *Cobre* in the original. Perhaps Purchas' translation of 'brass' would be better here, as the Chinese so-called 'copper cash' were in fact made of an alloy of copper and lead. *Hobson-Jobson*, pp. 167–168; Dalgado, *Glossário Luso-Asiático*, I, 175–176; *Travels of Peter Mundy*, III, 310.

[3] This refers to the universal Far Eastern system of bullion currency and trading by weight of bullion. *Travels of Peter Mundy*, III, 309.

[4] Salt gabelle. Cf. Couling, *Encyclopedia Sinica*, p. 494; D'Elia, *Fonti Ricciane*, I, 24, nn. 9 and 10.

[5] 'which is 40,000 pound weight of silver' (marginal note in Purchas).

[6] Crown = *cruzado*, and ninepence = *tres vintens* in the original. The *tanga* mentioned here by Gaspar da Cruz as weighing six to the Chinese tael, is

name of their country, the lesser great weight is of one tael,[1] one tael is six mace;[2] one mace is the same as a tanga.[3] Of the small weights, the smallest is one conderin;[4] ten conderins make one tanga, or one mace. One conderin hath ten cash, which are moneys of copper, and one mace hath one hundred cash.[5] And because the common that goeth instead of money is silver by weight, every one hath scales of his own, as abovesaid. For each one laboureth by all means he can to deceive the other, so none do trust the scales and weights of the other, and every one that goeth to buy in the market carrieth a weight and balance and broken silver. The balance is a little beam of ivory with a weight hanging at the one end with a string, and on the other end a little scale, and the string of the weight runneth along the beam which is marked from one con-derin to ten, or from one mace to ten.[6] These scales serve for to buy

probably the same as the *tanga larin* which Antonio Nunez calculated at $7\frac{1}{2}$ to the Chinese tael in 1554, (G. Ferrand, *Les poids, mesures, et monnaies*, p. 90). The tanga was also an Indo-Portuguese money of account prior to 1569, when the first issue of a silver tanga (with a fixed value of 60 *reis*) was ordered to be struck by the viceroy at Goa. However, the earliest known specimen of such a coin dates from 1594, so there is some doubt whether the 1569 issue materialised. *Hobson-Jobson,* pp. 896–897; Dalgado, *Glossário Luso-Asiático*, II, 355–357; H. T. Grogan, 'The silver issues of Goa', in Spink & Sons' *Monthly Numismatic Circular*, Sept. 1912, col. 13865–13872.

[1] In point of fact, the proper Chinese name for 'tael' was not *tael* but *liang*. Lexicographers derive the word *tael* from the Malay *tahil*. It was used both for the trade-name for the Chinese ounce, and also for the Chinese money of account, often called 'the ounce of silver'. *Hobson-Jobson*, p. 888; G. Ferrand, *Les poids, mesures et monnaies*, pp. 255–256.

[2] *Mas* or *mace*, $\frac{1}{16}$ of a Malay Tael and $\frac{1}{10}$ of a Chinese (silver) tael.

[3] The *tanga larin* presumably. Cf. n. (6) above.

[4] *Conderim, Candarim, Candareen*, etc., from the Malay *kandūrī*. A term applied to $\frac{1}{100}$ part of a Chinese ounce or weight (*tael, liang*), there being thus 10 conderins to the mace. *Hobson-Jobson*, p. 155; Dalgado, *Glossário Luso-Asiático*, I, 303.

[5] *Caixa* in the original. Cf. p. 128 n. (2).

[6] The *tu-ch'eng* (*dachem, dotchin*, etc.,) or steelyard. Compare Peter Mundy's description in 1637: 'I think a Dachein is a little stillyard, which usually China men carry aboutt them to wey their monies, there beeing great ones to way commodities, off which if one will not serve to wey whatt you require, then they hang uppe 2 stillyards, waying one thing with both waightts at once.' Mundy's editor explains that 'the difference between a crossbeam or balance and a dotchin or steelyard is that the former apparatus consists of a beam made to move freely on a central pivot with a scale pan at each end, while the latter is a balance consisting of a lever with unequal arms which moves on a fulcrum': *Travels of Peter Mundy*, III, 311–312. Cf. also Giles, *Glossary*, p. 37; *Hobson-Jobson*, p. 298; Dalgado, *Glossário Luso-Asiático*, I, 340–341.

by retail; for to buy by gross they have perfect scales very curious and fine, with very perfect weights. They carry the silver commonly full of alloy; and because they increase it with the alloy, from hence it cometh that he who will make good market in the country of China, and that it may be cheap, carrieth silver rather than goods; for by the increase which the Chinas make in the silver with the alloy, they give the merchandise good and cheap for the silver. The merchants are commonly false and liars, and labour as much as they can to have hidden defects in their wares, with which they deceive the buyers. For they have no conscience which reproaches them therewith as they are long since habituated to this ill.[1]

---

[1] It is perhaps needless to add that the faults were not all on one side.

CHAPTER XII

Of the fullness of the land, and of its abundance.

FORASMUCH as we have said the lands are all well husbanded, and the men though they be great eaters and spenders are withal diligent in seeking their livelihood, there is much fullness in the land, and great abundance of all things necessary for food and for sustaining life, for of the chief provision of the country which is rice, there is great abundance of it in all the country, for there are many great rice-fields which yield two or three crops every year.[1]

There is also much and very good wheat,[2] whereof they make very good bread, which they learned to make of the Portugals; their use before were cakes of the same wheat. There be many French beans and other pulse; there is great store of beef, and of buffaloes' flesh which is like beef. There are many hens, geese, and innumerable ducks. There are infinite swine which is the flesh they love most.[3] They make of the hogs very singular flitches, whereof the Portugals carry an infinite number to India, when they go thither by way of traffic. The Chinas do esteem pork so much, that they give it to the sick. They eat frogs also, which are sold in great tubs full of water at the gates, and they that sell them are bound to flay them. In a very short time they can skin a hundred, and they strip off the skin from behind, giving them a tap which strips them of all the skin.[4]

[1] As noted previously, two crops of rice a year are quite common in South China, but three are secured only in a few exceptionally favoured localities. Fr. Gaspar da Cruz may be confusing this with multiple cropping, which in the form of two rice crops and one (or even two) crops of vegetables, is quite common. Cf. F. H. King, *Farmers of Forty Centuries*, pp. 23, 73, 87–92, 233–237.

[2] *Trigo*: Chinese, *hsiao-mai*. Wheat is grown in every province of China, but is a crop of far more importance in the north than in the south, where it merely supplements rice as a winter crop. Couling, *Encyclopedia Sinica*, p. 600.

[3] 'Pork is the chief meat of the Chinese in the south—in fact, in some of the southern languages of China, the word meat is used to mean pork'; Dyer Ball, *Things Chinese*, p. 246. Cf. also Galeote Pereira, pp. 36–37 above.

[4] 'The edible frog—*Rana Esculenta*—is an article of European diet in Hong-king as well as of Chinese'; Dyer Ball, *Things Chinese*, p. 255.

All flesh is sold by weight alive, except beef and buffaloes' flesh and pork, which commonly is sold by the pound,[1] except if they do buy it whole, for then they are to weigh it whole. And in order that they may weigh the more, they fill them first with food and drink. The hens to make them weigh the more, they fill them likewise with water, and their crops full of sand and other things.[2] The pound of the hen, goose, duck and frog, is all at one price; the pork, beef and buffalo flesh is worth less, and all at one price.

The fish is exceeding much, and of many kinds, all very good, and it never wanteth in the markets.[3] There be many crabs and oysters and other shell-fish, and all very good, and of all these things the markets are full. The markets are commonly at the gates of the cities, and under the triumphal arches which are in the large and principal streets, as we said before, and along the covered ways of the same streets; but not to sell here fish nor flesh, for there are special streets for these things, excepting quick flesh which can be sold everywhere.

There are many kitchen-garden herbs, viz. turnips, radishes, cabbage; and all smelling herbs, garlics, onions, and other herbs in great abundance. There are also many fruits, viz. peaches, damsons, and another kind of plums which we have not, with long, wide stones, sharp at both ends, and of these they make prunes.[4] There are many nuts and very good, and many chestnuts, both *culharinhas* and wild, very big and very good, and the wild ones are better than ours, because they cast the shell altogether, which ours do not. The culharinhas are as good as the best of ours, but there are few and they grow in the woods; they do not know how to plant and till them.

There are many and very good oranges. There are three kinds of sweet oranges of which the best are some that have a very thin

[1] 'aos arrates' in the original. The Portuguese pound, *arratel*, derived from the Arabian pound, *ratl*; *Hobson-Jobson*, p. 770. Cortesão notes that the weight of the *arratel* was liable to vary according to the merchandise for which it was used; *Suma Oriental*, II, 277. It usually varied between 14 and 16 ounces.

[2] A practice quite common at the present day, and by no means confined to China.

[3] 'The consumption of fish, both fresh and salt, is enormous'; Dyer Ball, *Things Chinese*, p. 246. For lists of Chinese fishes see Couling, *Encyclopedia Sinica*, pp. 180–183; Y. T. Chu, *Index Piscarum Sinensium*, Shanghai, 1931.

[4] The principal fruits of South China are enumerated by Dyer Ball, *Things Chinese*, pp. 255–258, and Archdeacon Gray, *China*, II, 194.

skin and that taste almost like grapes; others that have the skin thick and wrinkled, somewhat like very tasty pomegranates, which they eat skin and all. Others, larger than the rest, that have the skin middling, neither very thick nor very thin; these are inferior because they are very sweet.[1]

There are some figs which cannot be eaten when ripe, save only one or two, but they are very good when dried, and are carried to India.

There is a kind of apples that in the colour and rind are like grey pears, but in smell and taste better than they.[2]

There is a fruit whereof there are many orchards, and it groweth on great and large-boughed trees; it is a fruit as big as a plum round, and a little bigger; it casts the husk and is a very singular and rare fruit. None can have his fill of it, for always it leaveth a desire for more, though they eat never so much, yet it does no hurt. Of this fruit there is another kind smaller, but the biggest is the best; they are called Lechias.[3] There are many other fruits which it were too long to recite.

And though there be particular streets of victualling houses, yet there are victualling-houses in almost all the streets of the city.

[1] Probably the pommelow, grape-fruit, and *Kumquat* are included in these so-called 'oranges', although our friar's description is not rigorously exact for any one of them. Compare Peter Mundy's description of these fruits in his *Travels*, III, 306. It is often said that the Portuguese introduced the sweet China orange into Europe about 1548, but there is nothing in Gaspar da Cruz's account to indicate this. Yule (*Hobson-Jobson*, pp. 642–643) has shown that the orange was cultivated at Cintra in the fourteenth century, which would account for the name of *portogallo* given to the large sweet orange in Sicily and Italy. On the other hand, the Portuguese certainly did transplant a variety of the China orange to Europe at a somewhat later date. Dom Francisco Mascarenhas, the first captain-general of Macao (1623–1626), succeeded in transplanting this fruit to Lisbon, some years after his return to Europe. Duarte Ribeiro de Macedo, the seventeenth-century Portuguese statesman and economist, referred to this fact about 1675—'Finalmente as laranjas da China são o exemplo mais moderno e visivel, a que mais nos pode persuadir. Dom Francisco Mascarenhas trouxe a Lisboa no ano de 1635, uma laranjeira que mandou vir da China a Goa, e de aí para o seu jardim de Xabregas, onde a plantou.' Cf. A. Sérgio, *Antologia dos Economistas Portugueses* (Lisbon, 1924), p. 382. For the varieties of the sweet orange in South China see Couling, *Encyclopedia Sinica*, p. 410, and Dyer Ball, *Things Chinese*, p. 256.

[2] Crab-apples rather than ordinary apples. Cf. Couling, *Encyclopedia Sinica*, p.31.

[3] *Lichi* or *Lychee*. Compare Peter Mundy's description of this fruit in 1637— 'They are nott offensive to the stomacke, allthough a man eat many of them. . . . And to speak my own mynde, it is the prettiest and plesauntest Fruit thatt ever I saw or tasted'. *Travels of Peter Mundy*, III, 162. Cf. also Couling, *Encyclopedia Sinica*, p. 307; Dyer Ball, *Things Chinese*, p. 257.

P

In these victualling houses is a very great store of meat dressed. There are many geese and hens and ducks roasted and cooked, and store of other flesh and fish dressed. I saw at one door hanging, a whole hog roasted; and let one ask where he will, for all is very cleanly dressed. The show of all the meat that is dressed is at the door, almost inciting them that pass. At the door is a vessel full of rice, well reddened and very well arranged. And because the matters of justice are commonly almost from ten of the clock forward, and many have their houses far away because the city is very great, or because they are people who come from out of town with business, as well citizens as strangers do eat in these houses. When any man meeteth any acquaintance of his that cometh from outside, or that he hath not seen'him for some days, saluting one another, he asketh him presently if he hath dined,[1] and if he answereth no, he carrieth him to one of these victualling-houses, and there they eat and drink privily, for there is great store of wine and better than in any place in India, which they make adulterated;[2] and if he answereth that he hath dined already, he carrieth him to a victualling-house where they have only wine and shell-fish, wherewith they drink, of which houses there are also many, and there doth he entertain him.[3]

There is also in Cantam along the wall on the outside, a street of victualling-houses, in all of which they sell dogs cut in quarters, roasted, boiled and raw, with the heads pulled, and with their ears, for they scald them all like pigs.[4] It is a meat which the base people do eat, and they sell them alive about the city in cages. It is a very pleasing thing to see the entrances of the city gates, the clamour of those who enter and leave, some carrying dogs, others sucking-pigs others vegetables, others with divers things, each one crying for to give him room.[5]

[1] 'To eat rice' is synonymous with taking a meal; and the equivalent of 'How do you do?' is 'Have you eaten your rice yet?' (Dyer Ball, *Things Chinese*, pp. 559–560.) Cf. p. 140 below.

[2] Chinese wines (*chiu*) are more properly spirits got from rice and other grains by fermentation or by distillation. Couling, *Encyclopedia Sinica*, p. 603; *Travels of Peter Mundy*, III, 194.

[3] Very similar descriptions of tea-houses and eating-houses in China three centuries later are given by W. C. Milne, *Life in China*, pp. 69–70, and Gray, *China*, II, 64–74.

[4] For the chow or edible dog of China, and ways of cooking and eating it, see Dyer Ball, *Things Chinese*, pp. 189, 246; Gray, *China*, II, 75–77.

[5] Compare Ch. VI, p. 100 n. (5) above.

This land has one great nobleness, which is that through every street they sell flesh, fish, vegeatables, fruit, and all things necessary, crying that which they sell; in such sort that everything needfull passes their doors and they have no need to go to the market-place.

There are in the country, two hundred, three hundred, four hundred leagues and more from the sea by the land inward, a great abundance of sea fish, in sort that every day all the market-places are newly full of fresh sea fish, which seems a wonderful thing. But it is no longer a wonderful thing, on seeing the wonderful diligence which they use to provide themselves in the following way. You must know that in the end of February, in March, and part of April, when the great flowings are, there cometh great store of fish from the sea to spawn in the mouths of the rivers along the sea, whereby there breedeth infinite small fish of many sorts in the estuaries of the rivers. To get these spawns in this time, all the fishers along the sea coast do meet in their boats, and there meet so many that they cover the sea, and they lie together off the estuaries.[1] In sort, that the ships which come from seaward when they see them think that it is all firm land, until they come closer and can see what it is, and they marvel at the multitude of boats. I heard say that two thousand assembled together, little more or less. I do not affirm it, because I know that I will not be believed; but forasmuch as the people are many and the vessels that there are in the country are also many, this does not sound an incredible thing to those men who have seen China and been there, chiefly because in the districts which are along the sea coast there is an innumerable multitude of fishers. These fishers, then, do take a very great quantity of this small fish, and cast it in cisterns which they have made with stakes, and a very strong net made of wire, where they do feed them until the end of the fishing time. And at this time there are wont to come a great number of barks from all places of China within the land (for I said already that all China is navigable by rivers, for it is all cut up and watered with great rivers), and these barks do bring a great many baskets within and without, which are all lined with oiled paper, which does not let the water through but on the contrary holds it, and every one of these barks do buy the fish they have need of. Then they carry this

[1] All this is taken from Galeote Pereira. Cf. pp. 31–32 above.

fish in these baskets through all the country inward, changing every day the water; and all men of any possibility, within their grounds and enclosures have great store of fish in ponds, for the which they buy the baskets they have need. They bring up this fish in the ponds in a very short time with cow dung and buffalo dung, wherewith it groweth very fast.[1] In all the moats of the cities likewise they breed great store of fish in the same sort, of which the magistrates are served. In this way it can be understood how in the country many leagues distant from the sea, the market-places are daily filled with fresh fish of the sea.

In all the cities, which as I said already are built along the rivers, the King hath many sea-crows in coops, in which they breed, with the which they make royal fishings many times. All the barks that are bound to go a-fishing with these cormorants, do meet and form a circle in the river. Those that have charge of the birds, do tie them about the crops, so that they cannot swallow the fish, and thus tied they cast them to fish in the river. They fish till they fill their crops with middling fish, and if it be great they bring it in the beak; and they come to the bark where they cast all the fish from their crops, the fishers forcing them to cast it. And in this manner they fish the quantity they will, till they have to their contentment. After the cormorants have finished fishing for the bark, the fishers untie them and let them go fish for themselves; after they be full, they come to the boats, and are put in the coops. These birds do fish very much. The King doth give for a favour to the magistrates one or two of these barks, according as the person is of quality, for the maintaining of his house with fresh fish.[2]

[1] Cf. Gray, *China*, II, 290–293, for a very similar account of how fish are artificially reared.

[2] Although Gaspar da Cruz may have seen fishing with cormorants, his account reads as if it was probably based on that of Galeote Pereira, q.v. above, pp. 42–43.

CHAPTER XIII

Of the apparel and customs of the men.

ALTHOUGH the Chinas commonly are ill-favoured, having small eyes, and their faces and noses flat, and are beardless, with some few little hairs on the point of the chin, notwithstanding there are some who have very good faces, and well proportioned, with great eyes, their beards well set, and their noses well shapen.[1] But these are very few, and it may be that they are descended from other nations which of old times were mixed up with the Chinas when they communicated with different peoples.

Their ordinary apparel is long gowns with long plaits after our good ancient use; they curve over the breast and are tied down the side, and they all in general have very long sleeves to their gowns.[2] They wear commonly black gowns of linen, or of fine or coarse serge of diverse colours. Some wear gowns of silk, and many do wear silken gowns on feast-days. The magistrates wear commonly fine serge, and on their feast-days they use very fine silks, chiefly crimson, which none in the country may wear but they. The poor people wear commonly gowns of white linen,[3] because it costs but little.

On their head they wear a high round cap made of very thin little wands covered over with woven black silk, very well made.

[1] Peter Mundy wrote almost word for word the same in 1637. *Travels*, III, 261–262.

The inadequacy of Chinese beards constantly intrigued early western visitors, Edward Barlow going so far as to write (in 1672), 'their beards growing thin and straggling, like to Salisbury Plain, here a bush and there a thief, whereof ariseth the old saying of a Chinaman having but nine hairs in his beard' (*Barlow's journal of his life at sea in King's ships, East and West Indiamen and other merchantmen from 1659 to 1703*, I, 222, London, 1934).

[2] For contemporary representations of Ming costume, see the illustrations in the *Jên-ching-yang-ch'iu* and similar works published during the Ming dynasty. Peter Mundy's sketches taken at Macao in 1637, form a useful check (*Travels*, III, 256–262), and a detailed description will be found in R. Van Gulik, *Erotic colour-prints of the Ming period*, I, 170–172.

[3] 'linho branco' in the original. Cf. Ch. XI, p. 126 n. (2) above.

They wear their stockings whole-footed, which are very well made and stitched; and they wear boots or shoes, as the curiosity or ability of every one is, either of silk or of leather. In winter they wear stockings of felt, either fine or coarse, but the cloth is made of felt. They wear also in winter their garments lined with marten's fur, chiefly about the neck. They wear quilted jackets, and some do wear them of felt in winter under their gowns.

They wear long hair like women, which they have very well brushed and combed, and they comb it many times a day. They wear it tied on the crown of the head, and the top-knot thrust through with a long thin silver pin. Those who are not married, to wit the young bachelors, do wear it for a device parted very well on the forehead, their cap remaining above the parting that it may be seen.[1] They have a superstition about their hair, wherefore they wear it so long, holding that by it they shall be carried to Heaven.

The common priests do not let their hair grow long, but are shaven, for they say that they need no help to carry them to Heaven. Yet among them are some priests of the temple of the idols, who among the Chinas are more reverenced than the rest; these let their hair grow and wear it tied up on the top of the head, thrust through with a stick, very curiously wrought like a closed hand, varnished with a very fine varnish, which they call Acharam,[2] and these priests do wear black gowns, the others wearing white gowns.

The Chinas are very courteous men. The common courtesy is, the left hand closed, they enclose it within the right hand, and they move their hands repeatedly up and down towards the breast, showing that they have one another enclosed in their heart;[3] and to this motion of the hands, they join words of courtesy, though the words of the common sort is to say one to another, *chifã*

[1] The reader will perhaps hardly need reminding that the Ming dandies attention to their complicated hairdressing was anterior to the imposition of the pigtail or queue by the Manchus.

[2] Apparently derived in some way from the Cantonese *ts'at* or the Amoy vernacular *chhat,* meaning 'lacquer', 'varnish', 'to varnish', etc., but the second part of the word baffles me. The etymology advanced by Dalgado, *Glossário Luso-Asiático,* I, 262, is quite untenable. The word is still used at Macao to distinguish polished as opposed to unvarnished lacquer, Mr. J. M. Braga informs me. The priests referred to here are, of course, Taoists. Buddhist monks were invariably shaven.

[3] Saluting with clasped hands and a bow is (or at any rate *was*) the Chinese equivalent of a handshake, but does not bear the symbolic meaning alleged here. Cf. Dyer Ball, *Things Chinese*, p. 221.

V. Chinese method of greeting
(From the *Jên-ching-yang-ch'iu*, 1600)

mesão, which is to say 'Have you eaten or no,'[1] for all their good in this world is resolved in eating.

The particular courtesies between men who have some breeding, and who have not seen one another for some days, are the arms bowed and the fingers clasped one within another, they stoop and speak with words of great courtesy, each one labouring to give the hand to the other to make him rise; and the more honourable they are the longer they stand in these courtesies. The honourable and noble people do use also many courtesies at the table, the one giving drink to the other, and each one laboureth to give the hand to the other in their drinking, for at the table there is no other service than that of drinking.[2]

If there come any guest newly to his friend's or to his kinsman's house, if the master of the house be not apparelled in holiday clothes, when the guest cometh in, he maketh no account of him nor any mention, till he commandeth to bring his festival apparel and foot-wear; and after he is so apparelled, he goeth to the guest, and receiveth him with many compliments, and courtesies. For they hold it not convenient that a new-come guest and of reverence be received with common apparel, but clothed in festive apparel, for in this he showeth him that his entering into his house is a feast-day to him.

Whatsoever person or persons come to any man of quality's house, it is customary to offer him on a fair tray in a porcelain cup (as or many cups as there are persons) a kind of warm water which they call *cha*, which is somewhat red and very medicinal, which they use to drink, made from a concoction of somewhat bitter herbs; with this they commonly welcome all manner of persons that they do respect, be they acquaintances or be they not, and to me they offered it many times.[3]

---

[1] 'Breakfast is *ch'ao-fán* (Cantonese, *chiú-fán*), "morning rice" and *yeh-fán* or *mán-fán* (Cantonese, *wan-fán*), "late rice" or "evening rice" stands for dinner.' Dyer Ball, *Things Chinese*, pp. 561–562. *Mesão* is probably a misprint for *mefão* which would be very easy in the gothic type used for the *Tractado*.

[2] For comparison of Ming with more modern practice, cf. Francisco Varo, O.P., *Arte de la lengua Mandarina*, (Canton, 1703), Cap. XVI, 'De las palabras corteses inter loquendum, y cortesias de las visitas, y combites,' pp. 91–99; S. Kiong, S.J., *Quelques mots sur la politesse Chinoise* (Shanghai, 1906); Dyer Ball, *Things Chinese*, pp. 217–225.

[3] For the origin of tea-drinking in China, and its use in later times, cf. *Fonti Ricciane*, I, 26, 75–77; Dyer Ball, *Things Chinese*, pp. 222, 637–638.

The Chinas are great eaters and they use many dishes. They eat at one table fish and flesh, and the base people dress it sometimes all together. The dishes which are to be eaten at one table, are set all together on the board, that every one may eat which he liketh best. The noble and gentle folk have much polity in their dealings, conversation and apparel.[1] The common people have some gross things.

Certain noble Portugals went to show me on a day at Cantam a banquet which a rich merchant made, which was worth the sight. The house where it was made was storied and very fair, with many fair windows and casements, and it was all great sport.[2] The tables were set in three places of the house, for every guest invited there was a table and a chair very fair and gilt, or with silver, and every table had before it a cloth of damask down to the ground. On the tables was neither cloth nor napkins, as well because the tables were very fine, as because they eat so cleanly that they need none of these things. The fruit was set along the edges of every table, all set in order, which was, roasted chestnuts and peeled, and nuts cracked and shelled, and sugar-canes clean and cut in slices, and the fruit we spoke of before called Lichias, great and small, but they were dried. All the fruit was set in small heaps like turrets very well made, crossed between with certain small sticks very clean, whereby all the tables in a circle were very fairly adorned with these little turrets. Presently after the fruit, all the services were placed in fine porcelain dishes, all very well dressed and neatly carved, and every thing set in good order; and although the sets of dishes were set on top of the other, all were beautifully set; in such sort that he who sat at the table might eat what he would without any need of stirring or removing any of them. And presently there were two small sticks,[3] very fine and gilt, for to eat with, holding them between the fingers; they use them like a pair of pincers, so that they touch nothing of that which is on the board with their hand. Yea, though they eat a dish of rice, they do it with those sticks, without any grain of the rice falling.

[1] More detailed accounts of Ming manners and courtesies will be found in *Fonti Ricciane*, I, 71–79; Trigault-Gallagher, *The China that was*, pp. 98–112.

[2] 'toda era hũ brinco'. Purchas translates 'and all of it was a mirror'. *Brinco* has a wide range of meanings in Portuguese, including 'bauble', 'play-thing', etc., but I take it that the sense here is that a good time was had by all.

[3] Chopsticks. See p. 14, n. (4) above.

And because they eat so cleanly, not touching with the hand their meat, they have no need of cloth or napkins. All comes carved and well ordered to the table. They have also a very small porcelain cup gilt, which holdeth a mouthful of wine, and only for this is there a waiter at the table. They drink so little because at each mouthful of food they must take a sip of drink, and therefore the cup is so small. There are some Chinas who wear very long finger-nails, from half a span to a span long, which they keep very clean; and these finger-nails do serve them instead of the chop-sticks for to eat withal.[1]

[1] For the affectation of long finger-nails, cf. Couling, *Encyclopedia Sinica*, p. 179; Dyer Ball, *Things Chinese*, pp. 220–221.

CHAPTER XIV

Of some feasts that the Chinas do make, and of their music and burials.

THE Chinas do use on their birthdays to make great feasts, continuing yet in them the custom of the old gentiles.[1] In these feasts are wont to meet all the kinsmen and friends, and all do help the host to bear the charges of the feasts by sending him presents, so that when they do celebrate their own birthdays they are repaid in the same sort; and because they have these helps, they make great expence and solemnity. The feast lasteth all night long, for all the gentiles as they walk in darkness, living without the knowledge of God, so all their feasts through all the regions of India and in China particularly are made by night. In these feasts is great abundance of meat and great store of wine; all the night they spend in eating and drinking, and in music, playing on divers instruments.

Their priests offer their sacrifices to their gods, apparelled very richly. They apparel themselves in divers sorts of garments, and the priests do sing their songs in a very tunable voice; among these sacrifices, playing and singing, the tables are always furnished with sundry meats, every one taking what he liketh best. The priests when singing like all the rest, do make in the street at their door triumphal arches, very well made of paper, and scaffolds with divers representations of figures, statues and pictures, and certain high trees, and of broken boughs, very well wrought and painted, where they put many lighted candles, and in every place many lanthorns very new and fair, all alight.

In the general feast-days of all the people, chiefly on the first day of the year,[2] all the streets and doors are very richly dressed, and chiefly they do endeavour and labour to deck the triumphal arches, covering them with many cloths of damask and other silk, and with many lanthorns. There is much playing of sundry

[1] Ricci made the same observation later. *Fonti Ricciane*, I, 87.
[2] For descriptions of the New Year and other Chinese feast-days, see the works of Bredon, De Groot, Doolittle, and Gray listed in the Bibliography.

instruments, and singing, and jointly with this great store of meat of sundry kinds, and great abundance of wine. They use many times representations of plays, the which are very well acted and to the life, the actors having very good apparel, and well ordered and fitting as is requisite for the persons whom they represent; and whosoever representeth a woman's part, besides the apparel that is necessary for the part of a woman, likewise goeth painted with stibium and ceruse. Those who do not understand what the actors say are sometimes wearied, but whosoever understandeth them doth delight very much to hear them; and one whole night, and two, and sometimes three, they are continually busied in representations, one after another. While these representations do last, there must be a table set with great store of meat and drink. They have in these plays two great blemishes. The one is, that if one man represents two parts, and has to change his attire, he doth it before all the beholders. The other is, that the actor, as well as he that speaketh alone, do speak in a very high voice almost singing.[1] Sometimes they go to the carracks to play, that the Portugals may give them money.

The instruments that they use for to play on, are certain bandoraes like ours, though not so well made, with their pins to tune them; and there be some like gitterns which are smaller, and others like a viol de gamba which are less. They also use dulcimers and rebecks, and a certain kind of hoboyse, closely resembling those which we use.[2] They use a certain manner of harpsichord that hath

[1] It is interesting to note that Gaspar da Cruz despite his criticisms of the Chinese theatre thought more highly of it than did Matteo Ricci (Cf. *Fonti Ricciane*, I, 33.) For a European translation of a typical Ming light comedy, see *T'ien Hsia Monthly*, VIII, 357–372; and for a succinct discussion of the Chinese theatre in general, Dyer Ball, *Things Chinese*, pp. 656–660.

[2] I have retained Purchas' equivalents of the Portuguese terms in the 1569 text, which are as follows. Bandoraes =*violas*; gitterns =*guitarras*; viol de gamba =*viola darco*; dulcimers =*doçainas*; rebecks =*rabecas*; hoboyse =*charamela*. Mr. Kenneth Robinson, whom I consulted about the identification of these instruments, has favoured me with a long note on the subject, from which I venture to abstract the following. Gaspar da Cruz seems to have understood music and to have attempted to describe the instruments accurately, whereas Purchas was evidently not always clear about what was intended. The upshot of this description seems to be (i) the Chinese had instruments which resembled the sixteenth century European viol family. (ii) They were smaller than their European counterparts. (iii) One sort resembled the guitar, i.e. it was plucked, and was probably the *p'i-p'a*. (iv) Another sort resembled the ancestor of our violin, i.e. was played with a bow, e.g. the *hu-ch'in*. Then comes the reference to

many wire strings, upon which they play with their finger-nails for which purpose they let them grow long. They have a great sound, and make a very good harmony.[1] They play many instruments together sometimes, consorted in four voices which make a very good consonancy.

It happened one night by moonshine, that I and certain Portugals were sitting on a bench at the riverside by the door of our lodging, when a few young men came along the river in a boat passing the time, playing on divers instruments; and we, being glad to hear the music, sent for them to come near where we were, and that we would invite them. They as gallant youths came near with the boat and began to tune their instruments, in such sort that we were glad to see them fit themselves that they might make no discord; and beginning to sound, they began not all together, but the one tarried for to enter with the other, making many divisions in the process of the music, some staying, others playing; and the most times they played all together in four parts. The parts were two small bandoraes for tenor, a great one for counter-tenor, a harpsichord that followed the rest, and sometimes a rebeck and sometimes a dulcimer for treble.[2] And they used a good policy in not playing more than two strains, so that we might remain desirous for more. We begged them to return there the next day with music of singers' voices, and although they promised that they would do so they did not; but at daybreak one morning they came

dulcimers. The dulcimer was played by striking the strings with hammers (ancestor of our piano). This is un-Chinese, and the reference is probably to the shape and spread of strings over a flat surface, hence (v) instruments of the dulcimer-zither-psaltery group, i.e. the *ch'in*, *shê*, and/or *chêng*. The rebeck is an early instrument played with a bow and is therefore included in category (iv) above. The hoboye or oboe makes (vi) an end-blown reed pipe, i.e. *kuan*, and the Elizabethan oboe does very closely resemble it.

[1] This reference to the harpsichord indicates that the *chêng* or zither is the instrument intended here, in the opinion of Mr. Kenneth Robinson; and not the *ch'in*, horizontal psaltery or Chinese Lute, as I had supposed. For a description and illustration of the *chêng*, see A. C. Moule, 'A list of the musical and other sound-producing instruments of the Chinese.' in JNCBRAS, XXXIX, 111 and Plates X and XI.

[2] Mr. Kenneth Robinson suggests that the concert party on the water used 3 instruments of the *p'i-p'a* type, one of which was bigger and deeper than the others; 1 *chêng*, that followed the rest; 1 *hu-ch'in*, and 1 *ch'in* or *shê*, that joined in sometimes. For an illustration and description of such a Cantonese concert party, see J. A. van Aalst, *Chinese Music* (Shanghai, 1884), pp. 36, 64–67.

with the same instruments to give us a dawn-song, so as not to disappoint us altogether.[1]

They are commonly very ingenious and cunning with their hands. They have many inventions in every kind of work, chiefly in masonry-work and in drawing; and they are very good at painting pictures, chiefly of foliage and small birds, as can be seen in the tapestries which come to us from China.[2]

They are very cunning and clever in all things, for they have a great natural vivacity and ingeniousness. And thus in warfare they make greater use of strategy and of numbers than they do of strength, albeit they attack bravely.[3] They use shirts of chain-mail and helmets, and the other weapons which we said formerly. It is not lawful for any man in all the country to carry any manner of weapon, no not a knife; therefore when one quarrels with another, they go to buffets and pulling by the hair. Only the soldiers and ministers of the captains of war do wear swords on their hangers.

When any man dieth that hath house, kindred and children, after he hath given up the ghost, they wash the corpse and put on his best apparel, and his good footwear and his cap on his head, and set him on a chair, and then cometh his wife and kneeleth down before him, and with many tears and lamentable words she taketh her leave of him; and after the wife, come the children in their order doing the like, and after the children the rest of the

---

[1] This recalls (or anticipates) the impromptu concert given by a similar boating-party to some of Lord Amherst's embassy near Kan-chou-fu on 13 December 1816. Cf. Staunton, *Notes of proceedings and occurences durinq the British Embassy to Pekin in 1816* (Havant, 1824), I, 418.

[2] Chinese brocades and textiles found a ready market among the Portuguese and Spaniards at this period. Luis Frois, S.J., describing the festivities connected with the opening of the Jesuits' scholastic year in their seminary at Goa on the 21 October 1559, states that the Church was decorated with 'panos de China dourados' (Silva Rego, *Documentação*, VII, 320). Cf. also González de Mendoza's remarks in 1585: 'The women as well as the men be ingenious; they doe vse drawne workes and carved works, excellent painters of flowers, birds and beasts, as it is to be seene vpon beddes and bords that is brought from thence' (*History*, Hakluyt Society ed., I, 32). For the curious hybrid productions which sometimes resulted from this European interest in Chinese textiles, cf. *Chinese Art. An introductory handbook to painting, sculpture, ceramics, textiles, etc.* (London 1949), pp. 42–45.

[3] Another unusual compliment from a European at this period. For centuries most Western writers were never tired of denouncing Chinese cowardice, and ascribed Chinese victories solely to overwhelming numbers, although the Korean campaigns of 1592–1598 should have taught them better.

kindred and all the rest of the household and friends.[1] These ceremonies ended, they put him in a coffin made for him of camphor
wood, which is preservative for dead bodies, and smelleth well,
and they close it and pitch it well that no smell may come out of it.[2]
They then set it upon two little forms, and cast over it a cloth to
cover the coffin down to the ground, whereon the portrait of the
man deceased is pictured drawn from life. They make a little
house before the coffin of white raw cloths, with a portal right
against the corpse, wherein a table is set with lighted candlesticks
and candles, and set thereon bread and all the fruits of the country.
And all this they do only for ceremony, and there they keep the
corpse eight or fifteen days, in the which the priests of their gods
come continually by night to offer their sacrifices and to pray their
heathenish inventions.[3] There they bring many pictures of men and
women, and burn them with many ceremonies. Finally they have
some pictures of men and women in paper hanging on cords, and
with moving these pictures by the cords, and with great praying
and shouting, they say that they are sending the dead man to
Heaven. All day and all night while they are in these ceremonies,
there is a table set with great store of meat and drink. These ceremonies ended, they take the coffin and set it in a field where the
dead are, and there it consumes with time.[4]

The mourning which they use is the sharpest that ever I saw,

[1] A very full description of Chinese burial and mourning customs, with special
reference to Fukien, will be found in J. de Groot, *Religious System of China*,
I–III. Shorter but adequate surveys of Cantonese customs will be found in
Gray, *China*, I, 278–307, and Dyer Ball, *Things Chinese*, pp. 403–408.

[2] The wood of the camphor tree (*chang*) is superior to most other kinds of
timber in resisting insects and *fungi*. For its use in coffining and for the methods
of caulking and sealing coffins, see De Groot, *Religious System of China*, I, 95,
106, 287–288, 301.

[3] A full description of these recitations from the Buddhist scriptures will be
found in De Groot, *Religious system of China*, I, 120–127. Funeral ceremonies in
China have always formed the major part of religion, and the services of the
priesthood are consequently most in requisition on these occasions. C. Eliot,
Hinduism and Buddhism, III, 318, 333.

[4] In most cases where coffins were left exposed, this was because the burial-
day had been found to be an unlucky one by a soothsayer, or because the sooth-
sayers could not agree on a propitious site in accordance with the dictates of the
pseudo-science of *fêng-shui* (lit. 'wind and water') or geomancy. Otherwise, only
the very poor, who could not afford a tomb, would leave the coffin unburied, as a
last resort. Cf. De Groot, *Religious system of China*, I, 127–139, 267–268; Doré,
Manuel des superstitions chinoises (Shanghai, 1926), p. 71.

for they wear gowns after the common sort of very coarse wool next to the flesh, and girt with great cords, and on their head a cap of the same cloth made like the caps that are used in the country, saving that these have some flaps that fall over their eyes. Notwithstanding, that as they are nearest in kindred, so they wear the rougher mourning weed. The rest wear sackcloth and not so coarse.[1] For father or mother, they mourn three years; and if he be Louthea, as soon as he heareth the news presently he leaveth the office he serveth, and goeth to mourn to his own house for three years, which being ended he goeth to the Court to demand an office.[2]

It is said in China that it is over nine hundred years since the Chinas have used printing, and that they not only make printed books but also different figures.[3]

[1] This mourning-sackcloth is illustrated and described in detail by De Groot, *Religious system of China*, II, 585–589. Cf. also Gray, *China*, I, 286.

[2] The mourning duties of mandarins and their resignation of office are fully explained by De Groot, *Religious system of China*, II, 571–585. Twenty-five or twenty-seven months was the usual period in practice.

[3] For Ming printing and woodcuts, see K. T. Wu, 'Ming printing and printers' in *Harvard Journal of Asiatic studies*, VII, 203–260; and for Chinese priority, T. F. Carter, *The invention of printing in China and its spread westward* (New York, 1931).

CHAPTER XV

Of the apparel and customs of the women, and whether there are slaves in China.

THE women commonly, excepting those of the sea coast and of the mountains, are very white and gentlewomen, some having their noses and eyes well proportioned. From their childhood they squeeze their feet in cloths, so that they may remain small,[1] and they do it because the Chinas do hold them for finer gentlewomen that have small noses and feet. This withal is the custom among the well-bred people, and not among the basest.

They wear their hair very well combed, drawn back and tied at the crown of the head, and bound from the roots to the top with a broad riband very well placed. And the riband is garnished with jewels and pieces of gold round about.

They wear long petticoats like the Portugal women, which have the waist in the same manner that they have. They wear upper-bodices with long sleeves. They commonly spend more silk in their attire than do their husbands, but in their common apparel they are clothed in white linen cloth.[2]

They make curtseys as our women do, but they make three together and very hastily. They use painting their faces with vermillion and white ceruse very well set. They commonly keep themselves close, so that through all the city of Cantam, there appeareth not a woman, but some light huswives and base women.[3]

[1] For the practice of foot-binding, which is of uncertain origin, see Giles, *Glossary*, p. 133, and *Adversaria Sinica* (Shanghai, 1914), p. 282; Couling, *Encyclopedia Sinica*, pp. 186–187.

[2] For details of the dress of Chinese women in the Ming dynasty see R. van Gulik, *Erotic colour-prints of the Ming period*, I, 170–172. It did not differ greatly from the costume described by Dyer Ball, *Things Chinese*, pp. 195–201.

[3] This was not always so. 'To one accustomed in Canton and neighbourhood to the constant presence of women in the fields and streets and on the river and sea, busy with various kinds of manual labour, it is strange to note their entire absence, with but trifling exceptions, in the country round Swatow' (Dyer Ball, *Things Chinese*, p. 718). Rada and his companions noticed women working in the fields of Fukien in 1575. Cf. p. 283 below.

And when they go abroad they are not seen, for they go in close
chairs (whereof we spake before); neither when anybody cometh
into the house doth he see them, except for curiosity they chance
under the door-cloth to look on them that come in when they are
foreigners. Commonly the men have one wife, whom they buy for
their money, more or less, according as they are, from their
fathers and mothers.[1] Yet may every one have as many wives as he
is able to maintain; but one is the principal with whom they live,
and the others he lodgeth in sundry houses.[2] And if he hath
dealings in divers regions, he hath in every one a wife[3] and house
with entertainment. If the wife committeth adultery, and the
husband accuseth her and the adulterer, both suffer the penalty of
death. And if the husband do suffer the wife to play the adulteress,
he is greviously punished.[4]

I being in Cantam, saw a merchant go from justice to justice,
very sharply handled for suffering his wife to play the adulteress.

The common women[5] are in no wise permitted to dwell within
the walls. And in the suburbs without they have their proper
streets where they dwell, out of the which they may not live,—
something which goes against the grain with us. All the common
women are slaves, being brought up for this purpose from their
childhood; they buy them of their mothers, and teach them to
play the viols and other instruments of music and to sing. And
those that can best do this, because they gain most, are worth more.
Those which cannot do that, are worth less. The masters either
deflower them or sell them. And when they are to be set in the

---

[1] Gaspar da Cruz is here confusing the 'earnest money' sent with the betrothal
presents (ch'a-li) from the bridegroom's family to that of his legitimate bride,
with the purchase money paid for a concubine or secondary wife. Cf. Dyer
Ball, *Things Chinese*, pp. 70–73, 367–373; *China Review*, VI, 66–67; VIII, 75–76,
87; X, 78.

[2] More often, under one roof but in separate rooms. 'Only one woman in a
man's household holds the position of a proper wife; all the others—and he
may take as many as he likes—are not principal wives, or legal ones; but secondary wives or concubines, though their children are on an equality with those
of the first wife. The women who are taken as concubines are sometimes told
by their husbands, in order to humour them, that they are to be considered as
equal wives with the first.' Dyer Ball, *Things Chinese*, p. 372. Cf. also *China
Review*, VIII, 19; X, 80; XXI, 29, for further particulars about concubines.

[3] That is, secondary wife or concubine.

[4] Compare Gray, *China*, I, 224–228.

[5] Prostitutes. Cf. Dyer Ball, *Things Chinese*, pp. 589–590.

street of the common women, they are written by an officer of the
King in a book, and the master is bound to come every year with a
certain fee to this officer; they are bound to answer their master with
so much every month. When they are old, they make them seem
young girls with painting and rouge. And after they are not for
that trade, they are altogether free, without any obligation to the
master or anybody, and then they feed upon that which they have
gotten.

I spake so particularly of this matter, for to come to say that in
this country of China there is no greater servitude than that of these
wenches.[1] And let no man say or affirm any other thing, for about
the examining of it I laboured somewhat in Cantam, because some
Portugals would affirm it otherwise. The servitude in this country
is in the manner following.

If any woman by the death of her husband remaineth a widow,
and hath nothing to maintain herself with, neither that the children
that are left her are such as are able to get their living, neither hath
she anything to give her children, this woman in this necessity
cometh to a rich man, and agreeth with him for six or seven crowns,
for a son or a daughter; and the price received, she delivereth the
child.[2] If it be a daughter, she serveth as above said for a common
woman, and is brought up for that purpose. If it be a son, he
serveth his master for some time. And when he is of age to marry,
the master giveth him a wife, and all the children that are born to
him remain free and without any obligation; notwithstanding, this
servant is bound to give his master so much by the year, having a
household of his own; for when he marrieth they give him a house,
and he laboureth either at a trade, or by his industry, to earn his
living.[3] And no man may sell any of these slaves to the Portugals,
having great penalties for it.

The women, as by their being common, they look for great

---

[1] I.e. this is the worst form of slavery which exists in China.

[2] Fr. Gaspar da Cruz evidently is here thinking not only of the prostitute
slaves, but of the *mui-tsai* or domestic slaves (indentured servants) of both sexes,
although girls formed the majority. Cf. Doolittle, *Social life of the Chinese*, II,
209–213; Dyer Ball, *Things Chinese*, p. 588–592; C. R. Boxer, *Fidalgos in the Far
East*, pp. 222–241, for the *mui-tsai* and their treatment in South China.

[3] Either this is a mistake, or their position deteriorated under the Manchus.
Dyer Ball (*Things Chinese*, pp. 590–591), noted that 'the cases of little boys sold
to be servants is even worse than that of the servant-girls, as they do not have
marriage to look forward to, to set them free and end their life of servitude'.

profit of them, in no wise will they sell them, besides the running into great penalties also.

Now let each one who reads this judge, if some Chinas should sell to some Portugals one of these slaves, whether such a slave would be lawfully acquired,—how much more when none of them are sold. And all those who commonly are sold to the Portugals are stolen, and they carry them deceived and secretly to the Portugals, and so they sell them.[1] If they were perceived or taken in these stealths, they would be condemned to death. And if it should happen that some Portugal might say that he bought his China slave in China with the permission of some justice, even this would not give him lawful authority to own him. Because such an officer would have done what he did for the sake of the bribe given him for that purpose. And if the judge was caught in such a delinquency, he would not escape without a severe punishment, for transgressing the laws of the kingdom.

The laws of China give authority to the women for to sell their children, and not to the men; for as the men are bound to seek a living for themselves and their children, if a man lacks a livelihood, they hold that he is in the fault for that. And likewise that men may the better labour for to get their own living and their children's. So far is China from having slaves who are entirely slaves, that not even those whom they take in war are enslaved; only they are bound to the King, and are placed for soldiers in districts far from their native lands where they were taken, eating from the wages which they have of the King.[2] These do wear for device a red cap, as I saw the Tartars wear in Cantam, who had been taken in the wars.

---

[1] 'Though to keep a free man or lost child as a slave, or to give or take in hire a wife or daughter, are severely punishable, the adoption of stolen or lost children, and the sale of free children and inferior wives are daily transactions in China. Inundations and famines are the chief cause.' Dyer Ball, *Things Chinese*, p. 591. Cf. also *Chinese Repository*, Vol. XVIII, 348 ff. where a form of contract for the sale of a *mui-tsai* is translated on p. 363.

[2] Prisoners of war were, in fact, State slaves. There is, however, no need to dispute the accuracy of Gaspar da Cruz's main contention viz. that Chinese domestic slaves were in a very different category from the Negro and other slaves who were bought and sold like cattle in the Portuguese colonies—and that consequently the Portuguese had no legal or moral right to purchase either *mui-tsai* or kidnapped children for use as slaves.

CHAPTER XVI

Of the number and different degrees of the officers of the provinces.

FORASMUCH as we have spoken many times hitherto of the magistrates[1] of China, and of the officers of justice, and henceforward we have to treat particularly of them and of their government, it will be good to know the name by which they are commonly called in the country, so that from here onwards we may use it. Everyone that in China hath any office, command or dignity by the King, is called Louthea, which is to say with us 'sir'.[2] How this title is given him, we will in its place make mention of it.

There are in each province of China one thousand Louthias, or according to others three thousand, besides those that are resident in the court, by whom are ordained all matters of the kingdom, and to whom come all the weighty matters of the realm. And because they must dispatch with the King, and converse with him within doors, and it is not lawful for others to converse with him, neither do others see him, and they have entrance where the wives of the King are, who are many, they are commonly eunuchs. But these are very versed in all the laws of the kingdom, for that before they enter the palace they frequent the schools, and learn very well the laws of the kingdom. In every province there are five, who among the rest are most principal, and who have a very great authority and majesty in their persons, and they are greatly reverenced and honoured, not only of the common people, but also of the other Louthias.

The principal of the five is the governor who in their language they call Tutom.[3] To him come all matters both great and small of all the province, and for the authority and majesty of his person

---

[1] 'regedores' in the original. Mandarins.

[2] Cf. Galeote Pereira, p. 10 above.

[3] Also spelt *Tutam*, *Tutão*, etc.; Viceroy or governor-general with the powers of commander-in-chief, directly responsible to Peking. Cf. Galeote Pereira, p. 6 above, n. (3).

he is not resident where the other Louthias are, that he may not be frequented of them, and so he may be more esteemed and feared. To these come all the revenues of the provinces except the ordinary expences. And by him as well the business as all the revenues which are gathered, and all that happeneth in the provinces, are referred and sent to the Court.

The second dignity of the provinces is that of the comptroller of the revenue, who in their language is called Ponchassi.[1] He hath the care to send to recover through all the province the revenues thereof, for the which he hath many Louthias under his jurisdiction, who are particular officers for the business and recoveries of the goods. He provideth all the ordinary charges of the province, and with that which remaineth he resorteth to the Tutam, that he may send it to the Court. He may intermeddle in grave matters of the other inferior officers, and hath authority over them. Likewise all the matters and affairs of the province resort unto him, to be referred by him to the Tutam.

Another chief dignity under this is the Chief Justice, who in their language they call Anchasi.[2] And though there be many other officers of justice, this is above all, and by him are the dispatches distributed to the rest, and all matters of justice resort unto him, as one that hath authority over the other inferiors. Another dignity under this is that of the Captain-Major, whom they call in their tongue Aitao.[3] To this Aitao pertaineth to command the soldiers, and all that is necessary of shipping, victuals, and all other provision against enemies and against pirates. And to this belong also the business of foreigners in cases which belong not to the Revenue.

The fifth and last of the great dignities, is that of the Captain-Major who putteth in execution the matters of war, and he commands in the fleets which the Aitao, being ashore, doth ordain. And this [Captain-Major] when it is necessary, besides the putting of matters into execution and order, if the matter require his presence, he goeth in person; and so important may the matter be,

[1] *Pu-chêng-shih.* Civil governor and comptroller, whose functions later became essentially those of a provincial treasurer. The post dates from 1376.

[2] *An-ch'a-shih.* Provincial Chief Justice or Judicial Commissioner. Also translated as Criminal Judge.

[3] *Hai-tao-fu-shih.* Commander of the provincial coastguard fleet. Sometimes translated as 'commissioner of the sea route', and sometimes as 'admiral'.

that the Aitao will go. This man is called in the language of the country Luthissi.[1] And as these five dignities are of great authority and majesty, and that of the Tutam exceeds the others, he [almost] never leaves his house, for the keeping of his authority. And when he does leave, he goes with very great pomp and with a very great train of officers and ministers. In the house of every one of these, except the Luthissi, who is the inferior of the five, are another ten who are as assistants, and who are also of very great authority. Five of these do sit at the right hand of the principal in five chairs, as we said above when we spoke of the buildings, and five do sit on the left hand. These in matters of importance are present at the dispatching with the principal of the house; and the principal dying, or by any other means wanting, one of these according to his antiquity remaineth in his stead. And if it be necessary to go through the province about some matter of importance that appertaineth to the dignity in whose house they sit, one of these do go with all the authority of the principal. The five that sit on the right hand have a greater degree and dignity than the five on the left hand. And as the dignity consisteth in their girdles and canopies, those of the right hand wear girdles of gold and canopies of yellow; and those of the left hand wear girdles of blue, or of changeable colour. The girdles are little less than three fingers broad, and an inch thick, and all about of gold or of silver very well wrought made of pieces.[2] The canopies are very large and fair, which an officer doth bear upon a fair staff, a fathom of ten spans long, and they are lined with silk.[3] Besides these assistants and the five principals, there is among the inferiors one of greater dignity, which is the chief jailer, whom they call Taissu,[4] who hath very

---

[1] The *Pei-wo-tu-chih-hui* was the title of the shore-based coastal defence commander against the Japanese pirates. Luthissi, (which word occurs only in Gaspar da Cruz and in writers deriving their information from his *Tractado*), is evidently a confused rendering of the name and the functions of Lu-t'ang, who occupied this post in Fukien in 1548–1549. Cf. Ch. XXIV, p. 195 below, and the introduction, pp. xxvii–xxviii. Possibly there is also some confusion with this official in his post of *Tu-ssŭ*, or commander of the provincial troops, which he appears to have held at the beginning of 1549.

[2] Cf. the description and illustrations of such Cantonese mandarins in the *Travels of Peter Mundy*, III. 256–257.

[3] State-umbrellas, *ló-san* in Cantonese. Cf. *Travels of Peter Mundy*, III, 259. Purchas has here translated *braça craveira* (a fathom of ten spans, or a standard fathom) as 'clove-tree', presumably through mistaking *craveira* for *cravoeira*.

[4] Identification uncertain, as explained in Galeote Pereira, p. 12, n. (3).

great houses with great courts where they have great prisons. But neither this nor any that are under may wear a girdle of gold or of silver, nor a yellow canopy, except he be an officer or captain of soldiers, who for favour of a gentleman may have a yellow canopy. The rest wear girdles of tortoise-shell or of other materials, made like them of gold or silver, and their canopies are of changeable stuff or blue. All these inferiors do speak to the five great ones when they are before them on their knees, and do kneel as long as they are with them, except the Taissu, who when he cometh in kneeleth and riseth up presently, and remaineth standing. Every one of the great ones hath many inferior officers under his juris-diction, for the matters and business necessary to the office of each one, all of whom as they are the King's officers have the title of Louthias, and their badges or signs. The five great ones with their assistants do wear for a badge the King's arms on their breasts and on their backs, which are certain serpents woven with golden thread, many of which have come to Portugal and which are often presented to churches to serve to ornament them.[1]

Every year there is one sent to every province as a justice, who is called Chãe,[2] who cometh to take account of all the Louthias, great and small, and examineth all the students, and chooseth Louthias, and visiteth the prisons, and all that is necessary to be seen and provided for in all the province. [He useth all means to spy out their bribery and injustice, and hath power to displace or prefer.][3] When he entereth newly into a city, it is not lawful for any to work in the street through which he passeth, they shut the doors and nobody walketh through the street; for to preserve his worship and authority, he will not boldly communicate in sight of the people; and many officers with banners displayed of crimson silk accompany him, and all the city Louthias both great and small are bound to go and meet him.

---

[1] Compare the *panos de China dourados*, hung in the Jesuit church at Goa for the school celebrations in October, 1559, as mentioned on p. 146 n. (2) above. It may be added that Fr. Gaspar da Cruz was apparently the first European author to describe the Chinese dragon as an imperial device; Cf. C. S. Ch'ien, 'China in the English Literature of the seventeenth century', pp. 356–357. For a discussion and illustration of the making of these 'mandarin robes' or 'dragon robes', see Schuyler Camman, *China's Dragon Robes*, New York, 1952.

[2] Censor, derived here from *Ch'a-yuan*, the Censorate in general. Cf. Galeote Pereira, p. 6 n. (4).

[3] This sentence in square brackets was added by Purchas.

The same entertainment is used to every one of the five when he cometh newly to the province where he is to administer his office. There be other dignitaries above all these, who are called Quinchais, which is to say a chop or seal of gold.[1] These are not sent but about very serious matters and of great importance to the kingdom or to the King. Every Louthia of what quality soever he be, high or low, hath for a sign or badge, besides the above-said, a high cap and round, with certain ears across, made of small thin rods woven with twist.[2]

---

[1] *Ch'in-ch'ai*, Imperial Commissioner; *Khim-chhe*, in the Amoy vernacular. Cf. Carstairs Douglas, *Dictionary*, pp. 66, 274; *T'oung Pao*, XXXI, 64.

[2] Compare the illustrations in the *Travels of Peter Mundy*, III, Pl. xiii.

CHAPTER XVII

Of how the Louthias are made, and of the studies; and how they understand each other in writing and not by speech in divers tongues.

ALL the offices are given from three to three years, and none is given for a longer time; and all are given to men who are not born in that part of the land, because they may not be moved by affection in matters of justice that belong to their offices, and also because they may not become mighty, thereby to prevent insurrections.[1] The offices are distributed by the King with the counsel of the eunuchs, according to the deserts and sufficiency of each one.[2]

The captaincies are given according to the chivalry and warlike feats of each one; none do distinguish themselves in war but they are promoted in rank more or less.[3] And because the eunuchs are those with whose counsel the offices are distributed, they are many times mightily bribed by the Louthias in order that these may receive promotion.[4] And in order that each one should do his duty in his office, and that there may be no miscarriages in the government, every year they are inspected by the Chãe; and if he findeth that they have done well in their offices, he promoteth them to higher and more honourable offices; and finding them negligent in their offices, or that they do not keep the laws of the kingdom, or that they take bribes, finding that their faults are grave and that they deserve to be deposed, he deposes them from the office and sends them to the Court, putting others in their places. The lesser Louthias are punished only by depriving them of their offices,

---

[1] Compare Galeote Pereira, p. 18 above.

[2] Eunuch advice was not the deciding (or even a legitimate) factor officially, but Cruz's statement is hardly an exaggeration for the reign of the Chia-ching emperor. The reasons for eunuch influence at Court are briefly discussed by H. Maspero, *Mélanges Posthumes*, III, 215–216.

[3] For the examination system as applied to military mandarins under the Ming dynasty, see E. Biot, *Essai sur l'histoire de l'instruction publique en Chine* (Paris, 1847), pp. 467–471.

[4] For instances of this, see G. Carter Stent, 'Chinese Eunuchs' in JNCBRAS, (New Series), XI, 143–184.

arresting them, and sending them for trial to the Court; for no officer of justice how powerful soever he may be and what authority soever he hath, can lawfully condemn any Louthia. But as the Chaem hath this jurisdiction over the Louthias and hath to enquire into their behaviour, the Louthias labour to find out before he enters their region whether he can be bribed; and if they know that he takes bribes, they relax and are at ease, being confident that if they bribe him their matter will turn out as they wish. And if they learn that the Chaem does not take bribes, then they befriend all the ministers of their households and of justice and bribe them, and order their papers in such wise that they cannot be perceived in any fault; and they bribe the scriveners and the ministers of their households because they are the chief ones who have to give evidence in the enquiry, as those with whom the officer doth everything, or in front of whom he doth everything.

The Chães whom the King doth send every three years, commonly are honest men of affairs and are not disposed to take bribes.[1] They are men of whom the King is confident that they will do in everything what is best for the realm, and for the King and for Justice. These bring commonly more authority than the rest. And these are sent in the third year, when every officer endeth his office. And because these commonly are very rigorous, and carry everything with rigorous justice, the Louthias labour more to keep themselves from being found in fault.

After that the Chães have taken the accounts of the Louthias, they visit the prisons and give audience to the prisoners, freeing those who deserve to be freed and punishing those who deserve to be punished. And finally, they order many stripes to be given to the thieves,[2] who are the most hated malefactors in the land; and the stripes are such that many die of them.

After the Chaem has inspected and provided for everything necessary in the province, he with the other principal Louthias doth examine all the scholars, and those that he findeth to have studied well he favoureth and giveth them good hopes, and those who have not studied well, if he see they have ability for it, he commandeth them to be whipped. And if already they have been whipped and

---

[1] A similar tribute will be found in Trigault-Gallagher, *The China that was*, pp. 80–82.

[2] 'ladrões' in the original. In this context, pirates, highway robbers and bandits are probably indicated rather than ordinary thieves or pilferers.

have not amended, he commands them to be put some days in prison, besides the whipping of them, that with these punishments from thence forward they may have a better care. If he findeth that they neither learn, nor have ability, he thrusts them out of the schools. This do only the Louthias who come not every three years. Those who come every three years after they have dispatched the business of the province, busy themselves in making Louthias, which is done in the following manner.

The Chaem[1] commandeth to come to the principal city of the province, all the students that have well studied, from all the cities of the province, and from all the great towns where the King hath school-masters of free schools, maintained at his charge (for the students did learn the laws of the realm, maintained at their fathers' charge). And all the principal Louthias of the province assembled with the Chaem, do there examine very well every one of the students, demanding of him many things concerning their laws; and if he answereth to all well, they command him to be put apart; and if he be not yet well instructed, either they send him to learn more, or if it be through his default they whip him, or being whipped they send him to prison, as the Portugals saw many in prison for that fault, where they were in prison also.[2] After the examination is ended the Chaem riseth up and all the Louthias, and with great ceremonies, feasts, music and playing, they give the degree to every one of them that they found sufficient, which is to give them the title of Louthias. And after passing many days in feasts and banquets, they send them to the Court to receive the badges of Louthias, which are caps with ears, and broad girdles and canopies, and there they await the distribution of offices. So that in this manner they make the Louthias who in the country are to administer justice. Those for war are made for chivalries and famous deeds which they did in war.[3] So that in this country, men are much honoured by their learning, or by their chivalry; and yet

---

[1] The reference here is presumably to the *Ti-hsüeh*, or *Hsüeh-chêng*, the provincial director of education, or 'Literary Chancellor', appointed triennially from Peking. Our friar, like Galeote Pereira, gives a very garbled account of the celebrated Chinese literary examination system. A better contemporaneous account will be found in Trigault-Gallagher, *The China that was*, pp. 55–67, and full details of the system as it functioned under the Ming in Biot, *Essai*, 422–491.

[2] Compare Galeote Pereira's account, p. 13 above.

[3] Not necessarily. Cf. p. 158 n. (3) above.

most for their learning, because of the learned do commonly come the five principal Louthias and the assistants.

Notwithstanding, there are many Louthias who are made for simple favour, either for doing some particular service to the King, or to the realm, or in some community, or for having some particular favour or quality. As they did to a young man of China, because the Portugals being in prison, he served for an interpreter, wherefor the Louthias gave him the title and badges of Louthia, because he could speak the Portugal language.[1]

But these and such others do not commonly serve offices of the King, but only enjoy the liberties of Louthias, as the Portugal gentlemen have their liberties which some enjoy by favour of the King. And these Louthias have great liberties in the country; for none can do them an injury without punishment, neither can they be imprisoned but for heinous faults; and they may order to be imprisoned any that do wrong them, and they enjoy many other liberties.

And though there were some Portugals who reported without any certainty that the Chinas did study natural philosophy, the truth is that there are no other studies nor universities in it, nor private schools, but only the schools royal of the laws of the kingdom.[2] The truth is that some are found who have knowledge of the courses of Heaven, whereby they know the eclipses of the sun and of the moon. But these if they know it by some writings that are found among them, they teach it privately to some person or persons, but of this there are no schools.[3]

The Chinas have no fixed letters in their writing, for all that they write is by characters, and they compose words of these, whereby they have a great multitude of characters, signifying each thing by a character; in such sort that one only character signifies 'Heaven', another 'earth', and another 'man', and so forth with everything else.[4]

---

[1] If this was true, he was probably made a mandarin of very inferior rank.

[2] For the organization of state-aided colleges and schools in Ming China see Biot, *Essai*, pp. 448–457. For 'laws' read 'literary classics'.

[3] There was a board of astronomy at Peking (later under the direction of and staffed in part by Jesuit missionaries) and another observatory at Nanking. Cf. Trigault-Gallagher, *The China that was*, pp. 49–52.

[4] Cf. Trigault-Gallagher, *The China that was*, pp. 42–48, and Gabriel de Magalhães, S.J., *New History of China*, pp. 68–86, for other early European

But withal you must know that they also use certain characters to write names which are or seem to be outlandish. This is the reason why in all China there are many tongues, in sort that one man cannot understand another by speech,[1] nor do the Cauchins-chinas[2] understand the Chinas nor the Japões[3] the Chinas when they speak, yet they all understand each other in writing. For example, the character which signifieth 'heaven' to them all, being written in the same way by them all, some pronounce it in one way, and others in another, but it signifies 'heaven' equally to them all.

I spoke many times with discreet men as to how it could be that so many peoples could understand each other's writing, but not each other's speech, and we could never fathom how this could be, until on one occasion when I was in a port of Cauchimchina.[4] The purser of the ship who was a China, was writing a letter to the Louthias of the country, asking them to order that we be given provisions for our money. When I saw him writing the letter, I said to him, 'Why are you writing a letter, because it will be enough to ask them by word of mouth?'

He replied to me that they would not understand him by word of mouth. I let him finish writing the letter, and then asked him to write the ABC for me. He wrote only four characters down. I asked him to write out all the letters of the ABC, and he told me that he could not do it then and there, as there were more than five thousand.[5] I at once divined what it might be, and asked him, 'What do you call this first character?'

He replied, '*Tiem*.'[6]

I asked him, 'What does *Tiem* mean?'

He answered me, '"Heaven",—and this other "earth", and this other "man".'

And thus what had previously puzzled me became clear to me. Their lines are not overthwart as in the writings of all other nations, but are written up and down.

accounts of Chinese characters and writing. There are many modern books on the subject, but Dyer Ball *Things Chinese*, pp. 719–720, will be a sufficient reference for the average reader.

[1] Cf. Appendix IV.   [2] Annamites.   [3] Japanese.

[4] Tongking—Annam, as explained in Ch. I, p. 64 n. (3) above.

[5] There are nearly 24,000 characters in all, but only about 7,000 of these are in common use.

[6] T'ien.

CHAPTER XVIII

Of the provision for the Louthias and of their ministers.

WHEN the Louthias are dispatched at the Court with offices for the provinces where they go to govern, they depart carrying nothing of their own more than the apparel they are to wear, and some few servants to serve them, even when they have no offices, neither need they carry any provision for the journey, nor carriage or shipping at their own charge; for through all the ways where he goeth are provision, as well of shipping as of necessary carriage, and necessary food for all the King's officers, which are provided of the royal rents.

In all the cities and great towns, the King hath many good and noble houses for the Louthias both great and small to lodge in (as also all those who by any means are the King's), which houses have sufficient rents for the maintenance of every person that shall dwell in the house, according to his degree. And that which is to be given to every one for his expences is already limited. Wherefore he that may lodge there being come, the officer of the house cometh to him, and asketh him if he will have his ordinary in money, or in things necessary for provision, and that which he doth demand, as far as the money doth extend he is to give him, very well and cleanly drest, either flesh, fish, ducks, or hens, or what he will. And any Louthia that doth lodge there, may command the host of the house to be whipped, if he serve him not to his will. And if any Louthia will go to lodge at the house of any acquaintance of his, he taketh the money, which the inferior Louthias do also sometimes, either to spare some money, or to be merry at their wills more freely. And in the provisions of these houses there is no want any ways, for the Ponchassis have the charge to give them sufficient provision so that nothing is wanting. And at the year's end account is taken from the officer of the house of the expences he made.[1]

Along the roads at every league, and at every two leagues, are

[1] A good description of these government hostelries will be found in Gabriel de Magalhães, S.J., *New History of China*, pp. 38–40.

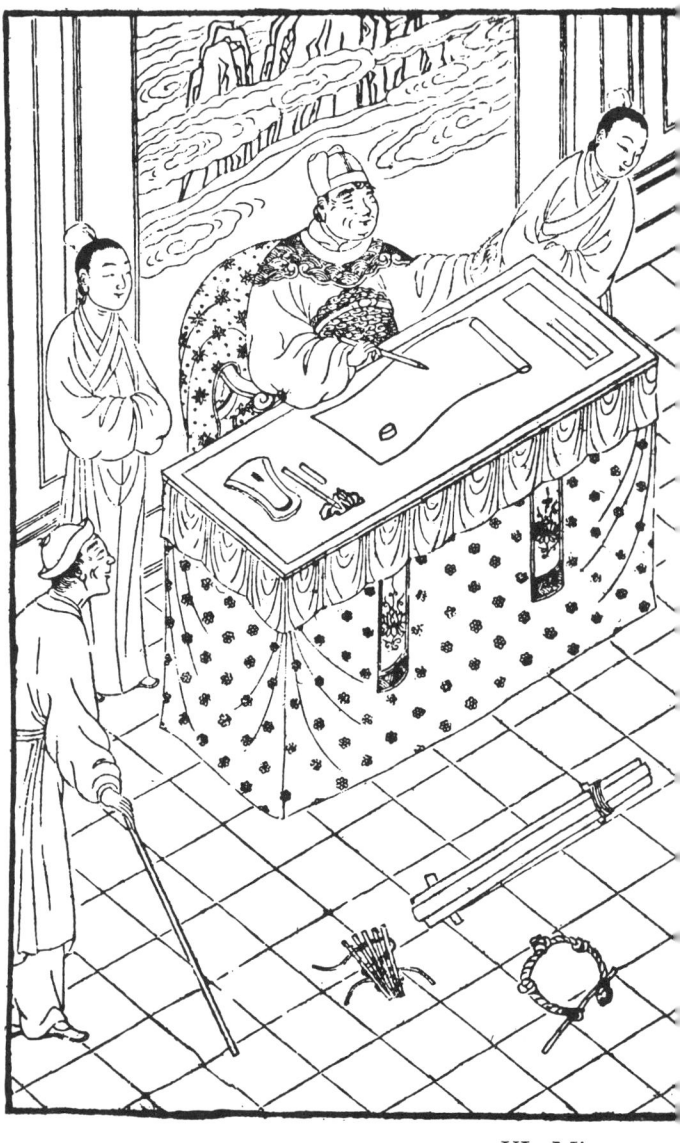

VI. Ming man[

(From the *Jên-c*

g in judgement
h'iu, 1600)

houses which only have beds and chairs for the travellers to rest and ease themselves.[1] And some of those that have care of these houses have provision for to give wine to the guests; others give nothing but *cha*, which is water with which (as we said above) everyone treats those who come to their houses.

After the Louthias come to the city where they are to be resident and execute their offices, they find the houses where they are to lodge; and according as their offices are great or small, so they find their houses greater or smaller.[2] In these houses they find all the servants necessary, scriveners, porters, and all other ministers needfull for their office. For these are continually in the houses, for to minister at all times to all the officers of the houses in which they serve. And every officer according to his house and person hath his provision necessary for his food, clothing and shoes (limited so that it sufficeth him well) which is paid to him without fail, at the beginning and end of every month. When the Louthias are old and weary in serving the King in the charges and offices of the kingdom, they are lodged in their native places or where they will, and the King alloweth them every month so much according to their quality for their maintenance till they die. And because the ordinaries of the Louthias are commonly sufficient, and with some abundance, they may always spare something to leave their wives and children.[3]

All the porters, serjeants, scriveners, executioners, and all the other ministers whom there are in each house of the Louthias, have their own ample ordinaries which are paid them very punctually each month. Before these inferior ministers, the officers do all things of their offices and matters of justice, for they are present at all things and through their evidence in the judicial enquiries the officers are condemned or absolved. Wherefore none of the officers dare to commit any irregularity in front of these inferior ministers, nor dare they on any account take bribes in front of them. If they do take a bribe, or do something outside of the laws or

---

[1] These rest-houses seem to have been more common in the south of China than in the north. Couling, *Encyclopedia Sinica*, p. 112.

[2] i.e the yamens or yamuns.

[3] Hence the formation of the *shên-shih*, 'girdled scholars', or 'scholar gentry', who exercised such an important role in Chinese society. Cf. Doolittle, *Social life of the Chinese*, I, 318; Gray, *China*, I, 182; Couling, *Encyclopedia Sinica*, p. 511.

their duty, it is so secretly and with such precaution that these inferior ministers cannot possibly suspect it.[1]

While the Louthia is sitting in his chair to hear the parties and dispatching of matters, the porters, the scriveners, the serjeant and other inferior ministers are at the door; and when any person cometh with any matter, one of the porters with a high voice that he may be heard where the Louthia sitteth (for it is far off) telleth who cometh and wherefore he cometh. And none speaketh to the Louthias but upon both their knees on the ground, and commonly they speak to him a pretty space distant from him. And from thence with a high voice that he may be well understood, the suppliant propoundeth his case, or showeth him his petition written in paper, and lifting it up in his hand desireth him to receive it and to show him justice; to whom a minister runneth, the Louthia making a sign to him, and presenteth it to him. After the Louthia readeth it, he either dispatcheth him of that which he asketh, writing it at the foot of the petition with red ink, or remitteth the party to an inferior officer to be dispatched. So I saw it done to a petition which a woman presented to the Ponchassi [*Pu-chêng-shih*].

[1] Contrast the eulogies of the Ming mandarinate by Galeote Pereira (pp. 20–21), Gaspar da Cruz, Nicholas Trigault, S.J., (*The China that was*, pp. 68–95), with the denunciations of Chinese officialdom by Christovão Vieira pp. xxx–xxxi above), and Gabriel de Magalhães, S.J., *New History of China*, p. 250.

CHAPTER XIX

Of the promptness and readiness with which the Louthias are served.

THE promptness and readiness wherewith the Louthias are served, and how feared they are, cannot be written with the pen, nor expressed with the tongue, but it must be seen with the eye for to know what it is. All obey their orders and serve them running and with great speed, not only the scriveners and serjeants, and other ministers, but also the inferior Louthias to the superior. And if any faileth never so little of his diligence and accustomed speed, or committeth the least negligence in the world before the Louthia, he hath not any remission, but immediately they put a little flag in his hand, and he must hold it in his hand kneeling until the parties be dispatched: and then the Louthia commandeth to give him the stripes that he think good: and the stripes are such as hereafter we will speak of.[1]

Whereby all the ministers in the houses of the Louthias are plastered or marked with the stripes, so that already among themselves they hold it a disgrace not to be marked with the stripes, because it is a thing generally common among them. And when the Louthia waxeth angry or is moved at anything, it is a wonder to see the trouble and fear that is in all the standers-by.

I being in the house of the Ponchassi [*Pu-chêng-shih*] with some Portugals, intreating for the deliverance of certain Portugals that were captives and imprisoned in the jail, for the which we carried him about eight ounces of amber (which at that time was much esteemed of them and now by carrying so much it is not so much esteemed)[2] we not being willing to give him the amber, without

---

[1] I have retained, with some hesitation, Purchas' translation of the Portuguese *açoutes* as 'stripes'. Alternative such as 'flogging' or 'bastinado' are no more accurate, and the nineteenth-century form 'to bamboo' or 'the bamboo', though more accurate, would nowadays be familiar only to an Old China Hand. Cf. Galeote Pereira, pp. 18–19, above.

[2] It was still worth a good deal. As late as 1637, English traders in India noted 'from Europe to China, amber in lumps, the bigger the better price and according to its largeness, sometimes valuing its weight in silver'. *Travels of Peter Mundy*, III, 485. These observations escaped the notice of the erudite B. Laufer in his article 'Historical jottings on amber'.

his giving us both the Portugals, he took an occasion for to terrify us by waxing angry against a youth, servant of a Portugal, who was in our company and acted as our interpreter. Wherefore he rose out of the chair and became red as blood, and his eyes were inflamed, and he set one foot forward, putting his thumbs on his girdle, looking at the standers-by with a terrible countenance; and stepping forward, he lifted up his foot and stamped on the ground with it, and said with a terrible voice, *Taa*,[1] which is to say 'whip'. It was a wonderful thing to see in how little space they took the youth, tied his hands behind with a cord, and laid him on his belly with his thighs bare, and two beadles placed themselves one on each side of him, with one foot forward and their whips[2] ready for to give him the stripes that they should be commanded to give him. Certainly it was all done in a moment. The merchants that came in our favour were troubled and stood aside shaking with fear. At this time, one of the prisoners said, 'Sirs, be not afraid, for he cannot whip that youth.' And in truth we knew it was so, for according to their laws there was no fault whereby he might command him to be whipped, and there was a penalty if he did it. The Louthia hearing the voice of the prisoner, commanded to carry him with speed to the jail again. And the Louthia did this for nothing else but to make us afraid, that we should give him the amber for one of the prisoners, for he could not give us the other, because he was already adjudged to die, and the sentence confirmed by the King, which was irrevocable; and he wished to have the amber, for he hoped to have of the King a greater reward than to be Ponchassi for the amber. For he did eat it to sustain life,[3] and many days were past since they had demanded it of the Portugals, but as they knew not the name we used for it, they never understood one another, till that the year after they had for the Aitão of Canton a little for delivery of a Portugal, whereby he was advanced to Ponchassi. And this man would also have for the same effect the amber at our

[1] *Ta*, 'strike!' Cf. Giles, *Glossary*, p. 139.

[2] Bamboos. Cf. the illustration in *The Punishments of China* (ed. 1804), Pl. IV.

[3] 'porque ho comia pera sustentar a vida' in the original. Neither this nor the translation make sense as they stand, but presumably the meaning is that the Emperor wanted amber for use as a compound in the elixir of long life,—the search for which killed several Chinese emperors in their endeavours to sample these Taoist nostrums.

hands for to be advanced. Notwithstanding, we seeing ourselves tied and without an interpreter by whom to speak, and the youth on the point of being whipped, we gave him the amber. Forthwith a chafing-dish was brought him for to prove it, and likewise the prisoner cast a little in the fire; and seeing the smoke ascend right up, he was contented, and scattering the smoke he set his nose over it and said '*Haoa*', which is to say 'it is very good'.[1] And he forthwith commanded to deliver us the prisoner free.

It was wonderful to see with what speed the amber was weighed, and the pieces counted and put in a paper, and noted by a scrivener before them all, the number of the pieces and the weight that was there. And after that paper another, all glued forthwith. And after that another. And in the third, the Ponchassi set his mark with red letters, and what was contained within. And at the same instant came a little box, and the amber being put therein, it was promptly sealed up, and upon the cover a paper glued, and upon it the seal of the Ponchassi. And presently came an inferior Louthia, captain of the armada, with his soldiers, and all afar off kneeled down, and there this captain received his orders on his knees, saying at every word, '*Quoo*', which is to say 'yes',[2] inclining his head and hands to the ground. And receiving his orders, just as he had come running so he returned running with the box to take shipping for to carry the amber to the Tutão, to be sent from him to the King.

I have related this incident at length, so that it may be seen with how much order and dispatch they do their business and with how much diligence they obey their commands; for all this that I have said was done in a trice before we stirred from the place where we were.

This man was also desirous to have the amber of us before the Louthia of that seat did come, who was looked for every day to come anew, for this one was only a locum tenens. When any Louthia that is not of the five, neither the Chaẽ, neither very inferior, but as they say of the meaner sort, goeth abroad into the city, he hath before him a good space two ministers with two maces that seem to be of silver, upon long staves, made almost

---

[1] *Hao*, 'good' or 'well'. It is interesting to note that the mandarin took this bribe in public, despite what Gaspar da Cruz states about the officials' reluctance to do so in Ch. XVIII, p. 166 above.

[2] *Wei*, 'yes', 'to answer promptly', would be a more likely rendering, I am told.

after our fashion. And one goeth on the one side of the street, and the other on the other side.[1] After these and at a little distance, go another two, each with a straight cane or pole in his hand. After these go another two at the same distance with two canes trailing along the pavements, which are the instruments of justice wherewith they do whip. After these go another two with two boards like two targets bowed and plastered, whereon is written the title of the officer that passeth. The foremost signify by their maces that he who passeth is in his office in the King's place. And the two straight rods represent the rectitude of the justice which he ought to do. Those who carry the instruments of whipping, do carry for a sign certain long red lances, with two great round tassels at the ends. And all do wear very gallant plumes very well made of the points [=feathers] of a peacock's tail.[2] And those that go before do now and then say with a loud voice 'Huup', which is to say, 'give place', or 'beware'.[3]

While these do pass it is not lawful in any wise for any one to cross or go in the middle of the street, under pain of being whipped without any remission. It chanced that two Portugals went walking down the middest of a street in Cantão and behind them came an inferior Louthia, who had but four ministers who came crying according to their custom that people should make way. The Portugals either gave no heed or made no regard of those that came; wherefore a minister coming, gave a great push to one of them, and the Portugal answered him with a box on the ear; and no sooner had he done so, than he was seized and his hands tied behind him on the way to be sent to prison, although the Portugal was not wanting in courage and imagination.[4] But as I have said, nobody is allowed to carry arms, no not even a knife, on pain of death. It was necessary for the Portugal to approach the Louthia

[1] This description of a provincial mandarin's procession during the Ming dynasty may be compared with similar processions under Manchu rule as depicted in Doolittle, *Social life of the Chinese*, I, 298–302, and Gray, *China*, I, 370–375, where the various insignia carried are described and illustrated in detail. Cf. also *Travels of Peter Mundy*, III, 256–261, for illustrations and descriptions of the Cantonese mandarins and their suite during the last years of the Ming.

[2] 'cabos de rabos de pavões' in the original. Cf. Galeote Pereira, p. 14 above.

[3] 'hoah', to shout loud; to bawl. Carstairs Douglas, *Dictionary*, p. 142.

[4] 'nam faltando valentia nem fantesia ao Portugues'. Purchas omitted this in his version.

and to pacify him with humble words, and he made an end of pacifying him with fourteen crowns[1] which he gave him.

I relate this affair so that it may be known what rigour there is in what I have said. Returning to our theme, after the ministers cometh the Louthia in a rich chair gilt and very fair, carried on four men's backs. These chairs are great and sumptuous, and the Louthia goeth compassed with all the scriveners and others of his ministers.[2] And all of them while he goeth by the street, go always running. And the Louthea weareth a long black gown of fine serge with long sleeves, which is the usual apparel. He carrieth his arms across like a friar, and his eyes low without looking to one side or the other; for even with their eyes they will not communicate with the common people, for to preserve their authority the more with them that they may be the more feared.

When any of the four Louthias goeth abroad, except the Tutão or the yearly Chaẽ,[3] they go in very great pomp, accompanied by many ministers, and six ministers do carry them on their backs, and they lead a spare horse with a fair saddle and a cloth of silk over it. The chair wherein they go is more sumptuous and richer; and they carry before four, five or six maces, and two or three instruments and more ministers.

When the Chaẽ that cometh every three years[4] cometh into the city, or for some important affair goeth abroad, or some Quinchay,[5] they shut up all the doors in the streets where he passeth, and no craftsman doth work, nor is anybody seen in the street when he passeth. The shops are closed and everything for sale is out of sight. The ministers with cords along the street do make three lanes, running from where the triumphal arches of the main streets are made in three arches; and through the middest passeth the Louthia only, and the ministers on the two sides, and it is not lawful for any to pass through the middle.

They are accompanied by many inferior Louthias who go on foot. And on the one side of the street and on the other are many

---

[1] *Cruzados.* See Ch. XI, p. 128 n. (6) above.

[2] Cf. Gray, *China*, I, 372–374 for confirmation.

[3] *Ch'a-yüan*, the Censorate. Here, as elsewhere, used for an individual Censor. Cf. Ch. XVI, p. 156, n. (2).

[4] Presumably the *Ti-hsüeh* (*Hsüeh-chêng*) or Literary Chancellor. Cf. Ch. XVII, p. 160, n. (1).

[5] *Ch'in-ch'ai*, Imperial Commissioner. Cf. Ch. XVI, p. 157, n. (1) above.

men-at-arms, and others with banners of red silk advanced, all standing in very good order.

In the court of the house where he is to go in, are many kettle-drums set upon high stakes to be well played upon, which are covered down to the ground with cloths of silk quartered. After these are many men placed in order with flags of silk on high. After these in the same order, are many with trumpets, and all stand in great silence. As soon as the Louthia appeareth, they all sound their instruments in order: the sound of the instruments ended, they remain again in so great a silence as if there were nobody in the court, being a great multitude of people.

The people as they come in do place themselves on the sides, the middest between the instruments remaining void, whereby the Louthia passeth. Before these Louthias go commonly many inferior Louthias, of those that carry maces when they go abroad.[1] There are also in this court many men-at-arms with long gilt lances and with very fair battle-axes. This is all in the first court.

In the second, along the gallery (whereof we spake above, when we treated of the houses of the great men, that only the Louthias pass through them) on the one side and the other are many inferior Louthias, with head-pieces on their heads, some gilt, some with silver, and with swords hanging at their belts, and with gowns or shirts made in the fashion of frocks, with studs of gold and silver, that it seemeth set upon plates, but it is a very fine work made upon very plain silk, which serveth only for bravery and ornament.[2] Some wear on their heads white head-pieces garnished with gold, but are of a very fine leaf and thin, that seeming an armour are not. In this manner also are the inferior Louthias who environ the superior Louthia. The chairs wherein these do go are very rich and of great price, and very sumptuous. The boards whereon is written the title of dignity of these grandees, are inscribed with letters of silver. And when any of these doth enter newly in any city with these feasts and entertainments, all the

---

[1] 'Yamen-runners' as they were styled in most nineteenth-century English-language books on China. Cf. Doolittle, *Social life of the Chinese*, I, 299–302.

[2] Probably the large square pieces of silk embroidered with the bird or quadruped emblematic of the official rank, which decoration was a prominent feature of Chinese official dress. Cf. Schuyler Camman, 'The Development of the Mandarin Square', in HJAS, VIII, 90 ff., and ibid., *China's Dragon Robes*, pp. 196–197.

Louthias great and small receive him at a house where he landeth, very rich and noble, and from thence they accompany him unto his lodging, and being lodged, all do take their leave of him with many courtesies. In these receptions they wear no sumptuous apparel, and the grandees at the most wear red silken gowns. In their own feasts in their houses and secretly, with one another and in banquets they wear crimson silk, and all the bravery in their apparel and in rich attire.

I was desirous of relating these things in such detail, so as to show the polity of peoples so far distant from us, and of barbarous peoples.

CHAPTER XX

Of those who are sentenced to death, and of other matters that pertain to justice; and this is a notable chapter.[1]

WHENSOEVER by way of enquiry or examination any witnesses are demanded, the Louthias do it in public before the officers and the ministers of their office, and before any other persons who by any means chance to be there present; and this so that no falsehood may be used, nor any sleight in the manner of enquiring, and by consequence in writing. And first they examine the witnesses severally, and if they disagree, they join them and cross-examine the one in front of the other, till they bring them to altercations and quarrelling by words, that by the words the one speaketh to the other, they may come to the knowledge of the truth. And if by this means they do not comprehend the truth, they give them many stripes and tortures, that by one means or another they may know the truth of the matter which they enquire or examine. They use no oath, for they esteem nothing of their gods. They have notwithstanding some respect to the testimony of persons of quality, and of whom it is presumed that they will not easily lie.[2]

When they examine any matter of great weight, or grave persons, then they write themselves the process of the examination, although they have many scriveners to take down the evidence, since they wish to trust nobody but themselves. It chanceth sometimes that some Louthias for a great bribe, or for great friendship, let some prisoner loose and put another in his place, for there never wanteth one naughty pack that will put himself in danger of stripes or death for interest, or they bring him in by deceit,

---

[1] ... 'he capitulo notauel.' So it is; but it is largely based on the experiences of Galeote Pereira and his fellow-prisoners, which is why Purchas drastically abridged it in his translation.

[2] The 'scholar-gentry' or *shên-shih* described in p. 19, n. (6) above. For the exemption of the 'eight privileged classes' from judicial torture under certain circumstances, cf. clause 404 of the Ch'ing Penal Code in Staunton's translation, and for the definition of the 'eight privileged classes' cf. Mayer's *Chinese Readers Manual* (ed. 1910), p. 353.

deceiving him with words, and making the matter light unto him, and giving him some interest, they name him as the prisoner they will let loose, that the faults and punishments of the guilty may fall upon the innocent. And when sometimes in this sort they cannot let the guilty person loose, they labour to bribe all the officers to give him for dead among those that die in the prisons.

But these inventions are not used but where the bribes are great, or the adherents very great and mighty. And for to eschew the inconveniences which sometimes fall out, when any are imprisoned for weighty matters or the prisoners have great adversaries, they set down all the distinguishing marks of the prisoners and make them sign them at the foot of the writing, so that they may not use any of the malices aforesaid.[1]

If anybody is seized for debts which he confesses that he owes, they assign him a term in which to pay them; and if he does not pay them within the stipulated term, he is whipped severely, and assigned another term in which to pay.[2] If he cannot pay at the expiration thereof, he is whipped again and given a third chance. And so the unfortunate wretch continues until he dies of the stripes, or his kinsmen pay for him, if he has not the wherewithal.

When a person wishes to move from one house and street to another, or wishes to go and live in another district, they beat a gong through the street and proclaim that so-and-so is leaving that street, and that if there is anyone to whom he owes anything then the creditor must come and see him before he leaves, that he may not lose his money. If he moves without this proclamation being made, then the neighbours are obliged to pay all his debts for him. All those who are imprisoned for being thieves or murderers, either die of starvation in the jail, or under the stripes in the yearly visitations.[3] And if they chance to escape this, either because they have means of obtaining food, or protection against the cold, or means of healing their wounds, then they die according as the lot falls on them in the way which we will relate.

All those who are already sentenced to death by a final sentence confirmed by the King, have a fixed monthly allowance of rice

[1] Purchas has omitted from here to p. 178 *infra*, 'With how much piety and leisure they kill', for the reason explained in n. (1) above.

[2] Cf. G. Staunton, *Penal Code of China*, pp. 158–160; J. F. Davis, *The Chinese* (London, 1836), I, 247–248.

[3] Cf. Galeote Pereira, pp. 21–22 above, and Gray, *China*, I, 46–74.

from the King, with the which, and with making silk shoes which they learn to make in the jail, or with some other craft, they sustain and provide for themselves while they live; whence it comes that more prisoners die of want before being sentenced, than do after they have been sentenced to death, because they are very slow in executing those who are sentenced to death.[1] So much so, that either they are executed many years after having been sentenced, or else they die a natural death; because executions are only done in the following way.

The Chaẽ[2] (who as I have said is as a judge who comes each year to examine the officers and to do other things for the good government of the provinces) demands to see the roll of all those who are condemned to death in all the jails, and the causes wherefore. These causes are reviewed by him and all the chief Louthias of the province. After having reviewed them well, they choose from among all the condemned five or six of those whom they consider deserving of death, or a few more. And late at night, when this diligence is finished, they send forthwith to the jail that they may be made ready to be led out for execution.

The Portugals who were captives there affirm that when this order is received, the noise and clamour in the jail is such that it seems as if all the devils in hell were in there, for every one of the prisoners dreadeth greatly that the lot should fall on him. When all those who are appointed to die are made ready, the Louthias do examine anew the causes of those whom they found most guilty, to see if they can find something by which they can lighten the guilt of some one of them, that he may not be so worthy of death; and when they have resolved who shall die, they command three pieces of ordnance to be shot off, which is to give warning to bring forth from the jail those that are to be executed. Then again they do anew enter into council to see if they can save any of them, and when not, they command another three pieces of ordnance to be shot off, which is the signal that the condemned are to be brought to the execution-ground. And after reviewing their sentences yet again, the Louthias command another three pieces of ordnance to bc shot off which is the signal that each one must die the death to which he has been sentenced. And it sometimes happens that after

[1] See Gray, *China*, I, 31–32, for comparison with nineteenth-century practice.
[2] Inspecting Censor.

the condemned have reached the execution-ground, one or two are sent back to the jail, because the Louthias find some excuse which lightens their guilt so that after all they are not so worthy of death. The same thing also happens in the annual visitation before this final one.

When they wish to execute this justice, as it is a thing which is done but seldom, there is great fear throughout the city and everyone goes about in awe. All the shops are shut and nothing is sold, nor doth anybody work. And the condemned prisoners are caused to sit upon a heap of ashes, with only their hands tied, and they are given plenty of food and drink.[1] And afterwards the bells do ring, which are great and of cast iron, whereon there is a great stir in the city, for this is the signal that they will now be executed. When this is done, the bodies are left on the field until near sunset. They then open the shops and begin to buy and sell.

With how much piety and leisure they kill, with so much cruelty and speed they whip, for in this case they forgive none.[2] The stripes are such that with reason it might be a sufficient punishment for to amend; for the canes wherewith they whip are platted below about four fingers broad and go straightening upward unto the end where the beadles hold them, and they are almost a finger-length thick, for there are in those parts canes as thick as a man's leg. And because in Portugal there are many knowledgeable witnesses of the same, I dare simply affirm it, and they are of eighty, ninety, and a hundred spans long. And their whips are made of these canes of the height of a middle-statured man to the breast. They give the stripes on the hams of the man's legs, being laid on his breast, and his legs laid along, and his hands tied behind. These stripes are very cruel, for the first stripe at once draws blood. One stripe is two blows by the two beadles placed one on each side, each whipping one leg. After two stripes a man cannot go on foot, and they pick him up by the arms and legs. And many die after receiving fifty or sixty stripes, for they destroy all the giblets of the hams. And since the principal intent of their justice is not to kill, save with the delay and care described above, as there is a multitude (as we will explain) of persons condemned to death, if there

---

[1] Cf. Gray, *China*, I, 63–64 for a description of this practice at Canton in 1870.

[2] Beating with the bamboo. Purchas resumes his translation of this Chapter with this sentence.

are many thieves (who are the most hated prisoners and persons) the visiting Chães make great examinations of them, ordering each of them to be given forty, fifty, or sixty stripes, whereof many of them die. When this examination takes place, they put the canes in great jars of water, the more for to whip them cruelly. And the beadles butchering, as they are commanded, the Louthias are altogether void of compassion, talking one with another, eating and drinking, and picking their teeth.

The cruelty is such that the courtyard is full of blood; and when they have made an end of whipping them, they carry them not, but drag them like sheep[1] by one leg to the prison. And when the beadles are whipping, they count the stripes with a loud voice. If the miserable prisoners who are in the prison for grievous faults at the time that this examination is to be done, can get a piece of a cord wherewith they may hang themselves, they go to buffets who shall hang himself first, that the butchery of the stripes be not executed on them.

And some Portugals who had been prisoners assured me that one day forty prisoners did hang themselves in the prison where they were, for to escape the stripes they were willing rather to lose their lives. And the Portugals assured me that the cord was so short that there was scarcely enough to go round the neck to tie it and on a stick which they stuck in the wall; and because the stick was low, they pulled one another till they were choked, coming to blows as to who should be hung first.

When any doth kill himself or dieth in the prison, it is the ordinance in China to cast him in the house of office and there to remain three days, where the rats do eat him up. And sometimes the China prisoners do eat of them with hunger. When the three days are finished, there comes an officer of justice with a scrivener and ministers, and they throw a noose round his feet and drag the body to the outer gate of the jail on the side of the field; and when they reach that gate, the officer commands him to be given three sharp blows with an iron-tipped stave on the rump. This done, the scrivener writes a certificate that so-and-so who was a prisoner for such-and-such crimes died in the jail, and in accordance with the ordinance he lay three days in the house of office, and his body was

---

[1] '. . . like butchers' in Purchas, who has mistaken the original Portuguese *carneiro* (sheep) for *carniçeiro* (butcher).

subjected to all the usual tests without any sign of life being found therein, but on the contrary it being certain that he was dead he was ordered to be thrown on the dung-hill.[1] The jailer keeps this certificate, and when the Chaẽ comes, he shows it to him, so that he may be relieved of responsibility for that prisoner. They make all these examinations of the dead bodies so that nobody can feign to be dead.

An honourable Portugal who was a prisoner, affirmed that in the jail where he lay, about two thousand people died each year, some from hunger, some from cold, and others from stripes. When they take prisoners from different parts of the province to the provincial capital city, each prisoner carries a little flag in his hand, on which is written in large characters the reason why he goes prisoner, and they make them carry them high, so that their crimes may be read and seen of all passers-by, so that everyone may thus take warning and not commit similar misdeeds.

[1] Cf. Gray, *China*, I, 48–50, for the similar practice at Canton in his day.

CHAPTER XXI

Of the prisons and jails of China.

THE prisons of China are very harsh, principally those for them who are condemned to death and those for them who have done something worthy of death. And all the jails are very strong, and each city which is the head of a province hath thirteen jails, and in six of them are the men condemned to death.

There are in Cantão alone upward of fifteen thousand prisoners.[1] There are in every jail only for those condemned to death, one hundred and twenty men that serve for watches, and have a Louthia over them as their captain, or gentleman of the round. The jails are very strong enclosures, compassed about with high stone walls. Before entering in the jails, there are three gates which must be passed, all of them closed and guarded by keepers. Within the stone wall enclosure, is another enclosure built of wood, very strong. On the inner side of the three gates are the lodgings of the Louthia who has charge of the dungeons like a jailer, which dungeons are very large.[2]

Within these lodgings is a great enclosure which has a spacious orchard and kitchen-garden with great fish-ponds. At the entrance of the Louthia's lodgings is a large courtyard paved with square flagstones. And on one of the sides of this courtyard begins one of the jails, which is closed with some gates that are not very strong, and in this jail are those who are imprisoned for small matters; and it is so large that it contains streets and market-places in which the same prisoners sell many things, both food as things needful for other purposes, which are brought them from outside for to sell there, whereby many of them earn their livelihood.[3] And others have beds there, for to hire to those who have need of them and the wherewithal to pay for them.

And this jail is never so empty but that it never has less than

[1] This number is almost certainly exaggerated.
[2] Cf. Gray, *China*, I, 46–47.
[3] Cf. H. Henry, *Ling-nam*, pp. 40–41.

eight hundred or nine hundred prisoners, some being taken out and others put in each day.

Beyond this jail is another for those who are imprisoned for weighty matters, and for those who are already condemned to death, which has a great multitude of prisoners, and which is entered through three gates of iron, one after the other. After these three gates have been passed, you enter in a very large square courtyard paved with square flagstones, and with porches round it like a cloister. In this courtyard there are eight iron gates, two on each side, which give entrance into eight very great and very long buildings. Each of these buildings has a corridor running down the middle from the entrance door to the end, with a not very high board on either side thereof. And in the corridor which runs between these two boards are two long chains with very strong iron links, in which the prisoners are chained each night, and they are placed lying on their backs, with the chain running along on top of them. Between each prisoner there is a thick iron ring through which the chain runs, and the chain crusheth them in such wise that the Portugals who were in them affirmed that in the early days before they had got accustomed to these prisons, they were left bruised and numb when taken out of the chain-gang in the morning. After all the prisoners have been laid in the chain-gang they place on top of them all a floor-board, which they lock very fast, leaving only a very narrow aperture below, just sufficient to contain the prisoners' bodies. In sort that they are so straitly crushed that they cannot by any means move or turn. And although they are so straitly crushed, they are continually very well guarded by night, with watches both outside and in. Those outside answer to those within who all night long go counting the prisoners in a loud voice, that they may be heard by the chief jailer who is lying on his bed. By day the prisoners are also counted once.

Their watches are divided into five for each night. And if any of the watch commit the least fault, or if he is found asleep, he is severely punished without fail. The jails are so strong and so well guarded, that never in China has a prisoner been known to have escaped from any of them.

There are so many prisoners in China because there is such an excess of people therein, and many of them lacking a livelihood become thieves; and hence it is that they seek many devices for to

VII. Prisoners in fetters and cangues
(From the *Jên-ching-yang-ch'iu*, 1600)

gain a living, that they may not want what is necessary for their sustenance.

Besides being chained and guarded in the above-said manner, all those prisoners who are charged with grave crimes have fetters on their feet, and on their hands they have some which they call *chucas*,[1] which are like manacles, but are made of thick wood, with two holes for to take the hands, in such sort that they can do nothing with one hand without the other following it. Those who have wherewith to bribe the chief jailer, are provided with chucas of a kind which enables them to take one hand away from it. All the prisoners seek diligently to draw one of their hands out of the chuca, and try all means to effect this; but it is necessary that they must watch very carefully lest they be found by the jailers with one of their hands free, because if they are found thus they are punished most severely.

Those who are already sentenced to death, have some boards put round their necks which hang down to their knees, plastered white, on which is written the reason why they are sentenced, and they are of little more than a span in width. All these prisoners in the morning are brought forth from the chain-gangs, and they generally all work as shoe-makers, chiefly of silken shoes embroidered with twisted thread. And with this and with the pittance of rice that the King gives to those already condemned to die (as we mentioned above) they can keep themselves. Those who are not sentenced, if they are sore oppressed by hunger, they kill themselves as best they can. And because some jails are badly roofed, and some prisoners have no clothing to cover themselves, they die of cold.

The ordinary punishment of those who have minor offences is stripes, more or less according as their crimes are. Some also for petty crimes are made to walk exposed to derision through the streets, with a thick square board of a little more than three spans wide round their neck which is put through a hole as wide as the neck in the middle of the board, which is made of two pieces of wood that can be separated for to put his neck in it.[2] And on the board is inscribed the crimes wherefore he goes thus exposed to

---

[1] *Shou-k'ao*, hand-fetters or manacles. Cf. The illustrations in the *Jên-ching-yang-ch'iu*, reproduced on pp. 165, 183; Staunton, *Penal Code of China*, p. lxxv; Doolittle, *Social life of the Chinese*, I, 165.

[2] The portable pillory, or cangue.

derision. And he goes thus for three or four days according as his crimes deserve it. Those who are charged with grave crimes and have no means whatever of keeping themselves, try to get leave sometime from some principal Louthia for to walk the street begging for alms. They are then taken under secure guard to beg in the market-places.

There be two sorts of tortures, some for the hands, others for the feet;[1] those for the hands are some sticks of the thickness of a finger and the length of a span, made cylindrical like a lathe, which are bored and traversed by two cords. They place the fingers between them and then tighten the cords in such sort that they crunch the bones.[2]

I once saw a boy of between thirteen and fourteen years who was being tortured in this way, and it was a most pitiful sight to see him thus. And they treated him in this manner because he was watching over a youth who was detained by the justice in a house, and who had fled without him seeing it, being careless; for which reason they took him around prisoner in this way, going in search of the fugitive. These are the lightest punishments.

Those of the feet are very sharp and painful, because they are two square sticks of about four spans long, joined by a hinge on one side. And they tie them with a cord on the other side, and with the ankles thus squeezed in this fashion, they hit on the top of the wood with a mallet, thus crushing the bones.[3]

[1] Cf. *Punishments of China* (ed. 1804), Pl. X; Staunton, *Penal Code of China*, p. 488; Doolittle, *Social life of the Chinese*, I, 336–337.

[2] Cf. *Punishments of China*, Pl. IX; Staunton, *Penal Code of China*, p. 488; Doolittle, *Social life of the Chinese*, I, 337; Gray, *China*, I, 34–35.

[3] The bamboo, cangue, finger- and ankle-racks, were the only official forms of torture, both under the Ming and under the Manchu dynasty. Some of the more common illegal modes of torture which were freely practiced under both dynasties are described and illustrated in Doolittle, *Social life of the Chinese*, I, 341–346. The official instruments of torture are also shown in the contemporary Ming woodcuts reproduced on pp. 164 and 183 above.

CHAPTER XXII

*With whom the King of China marrieth; and of the
ambassadors; and how every month the King is informed
of all that passeth throughout his kingdom.*

THE King in his marriages doth not mix with any person
outside of his kingdom. The custom of old time which is
now no longer kept among them, was that when the King
would give in marriage his sons and daughters, he did make a great
banquet for all the chief men and women of his court, who
brought with them the men their sons and the women their
daughters. The sons of the King were then taken among the women
and the maidens who pleased them most became their wives.
Likewise his daughters were taken among the men, and the youths
who pleased them most became their husbands. Wherefore each
one strove as to who should apparel his children most richly.[1]

The King for to preserve the greatness and authority of his
estate, never goes out. Within his gates he hath very great enclosures
with very great lodgings, great kitchen and pleasure-gardens,
orchards, and many fish-ponds in which are great store of fish.

Within are likewise many woods in the which he hath many wild
boars and deer for the chase. In sort that within his gates he hath
as many pastimes as he can wish for. No man seeth him nor doth he
communicate with any save only eunuchs through whom, as I
said, he orders and rules all his kingdom, for which reason they are
well indoctrinated in its laws.[2]

[1] This garbled story about Chinese imperial marriages is also to be found in
Galeote Pereira, p. 30 above. The idea probably arose from the fact that
Empresses (and imperial concubines still more so) were primarily selected for
their personal qualities or attractions, their family connections being a very
secondary matter. The women admitted into the imperial harem were, as a rule,
daughters of noblemen and gentlemen; but as personal beauty was the principal
qualification for an inmate of the seraglio, women from humbler walks of life
sometimes became the mothers (if not the consorts) of emperors. Cf. Gray,
China, I, 23-24.

[2] Cf. Carter Stent, 'Chinese Eunuchs' in JNCBRAS (New Series) XI,
143-184. The eunuchs were generally a corrupt and illiterate lot, but there
were exceptions of course.

They wear as a distinguishing mark some ear-pieces in their caps, made of silk and projecting upwards, the Louthias wearing them laid across, as can be seen in some of the painted hangings which come from China.[1]

The King hath as many wives as he listeth; and within doors almost all the service is of women, wherefore he hath a great multitude of them, and likewise great store of eunuchs, and there is no other people within the house.

The first son that is born unto him of any of his wives succeedeth in the kingdom. The rest he marrieth, and at such time as he marrieth them they are lodged in some of the cities that he best liketh, where they are well provided of all things necessary for their maintenance, as sons to the King. But they never see the King's face any more after they are married, neither do they leave the cities where they are lodged, as we said above concerning the kinsmen of the King.[2]

All the ambassadors that come to China with embassages from Kings or Princes, receive of the King great rewards and favours; and they give the envoy the cap and insignia of a Louthia, whereby he hath great privileges in the country.[3] They may whip and punish the Chinas themselves, so that they touch not any Louthia small or great; for to meddle with these would breed great inconveniencies.

This was the cause that Fernão Peres de Andrade going for ambassador to China, the Chinas did rise against him, and he escaped with his hands on his head, losing some ships;[4] because

---

[1] These differences in headgear can be observed in the illustrations to the *Jên-ching-yang-chiu*, and in the *Travels of Peter Mundy*, III, Pl. xiii.

[2] Cf. Galeote Pereira, pp. 40–41 above.

[3] In China, as with other Oriental countries, an ambassador or envoy was not regarded in the same light as he would have been in contemporary Europe, but merely as a king's-messenger or as a tribute-bearer. Cf. W. W. Rockhill, *Diplomatic audiences at the court of China* (London, 1905). The chief advantage accruing to foreign envoys in China was that they were given free transportation and other facilities, besides receiving imperial presents which were usually far more valuable than the tribute which they brought. Cf. T. T. Chang, *Sino-Portuguese trade*, pp. 27–30.

[4] Gaspar da Cruz, like Diogo do Couto (*Decada* V, Book 8, Ch. xii), and so many other writers on this subject, has confused Fernão Peres de Andrade with his brother, Simão de Andrade (the real culprit), and with the ambassador Tomé Pires who was made the scapegoat for Simão de Andrade's misdeeds. For the correct sequence of events, cf. Pires-Cortesão, *Suma Oriental*, I, xxx-xliv, and J. M. Braga, *Western pioneers*, pp. 62–64.

having done unaccustomed justice in China, and upon Chinas and they forbearing with him, he would stretch his hand to the Louthias.

The goods of the ambassador and of his people are free from customs, and to him and to his they give lodgings to dwell in, and all things necessary while they are in the country. No man, no not a Louthia, may disturb him in anything nor touch any of his things. Once a Louthia would have whipped a Siāo[1] for having carried a message to the prison, to some Portuguese who were prisoners there. One of the officers who was present told the Louthia that the man was one of the Siāo embassage, wherefore being satisfied therewith he let him go in peace, desiring him he would not do so again. In sort that they have great respect for ambassadors and for their people.

With China being so great as at the beginning we said and declared, the King hath such means and industry in the government thereof, that every month he knoweth all that passeth through all the realm, and he knoweth it in this manner. All matters of justice and of war, and all novelties and all that is worth the knowing in every one of the provinces is referred by the Louthias and by other persons to the Ponchassi, and the Ponchassi maketh a relation of all by writing to the Tutam. The Tutam is bound to send a post every month to the Court, which carrieth the information in writing to the King of all things that passed in that month.

They count their months by the moons, and they are to be dispatched in such sort that at the beginning of every moon the posts from all the provinces are to be at the Court, that the first day of the moon it may be presented to the King, as relations of all things happened in every province. And although some provinces are far distant from the Court, that the posts cannot come within a month to the Court, notwithstanding they are arranged in such manner that every moon the King is to have the relation of every province, though the one be of more time than another, because of the one province being far and the other near.[2] The manner of posts is as among us; they carry a horn which they wind when they come near to any place, that they may have a horse ready at every place within a fixed distance. They are bound when they hear the horn to

---

[1] Siamese.
[2] This account of the Ming courier system is evidently taken from Galeote Pereira, p. 7 above. Cf. *Ta Ming Huei-tien* (ed. 1576), pp. 145-149, 167.

have a horse ready for him, which is done with as much diligence as all the other services of the officers. And where he is to cross a river, as soon as he windeth his horn they carry him a boat with great speed, as I saw once going to the city of Cantão in a place that was by the way, called Caamão.[1] Sometimes it happeneth by the malice of some Louthias, when they have any interest in it, to keep some things concealed that the King knoweth not; but woe to them if the King come to know it, for they are grievously punished, as we shall see in a case hereafter following.

Being in India, and also in China, I was informed that sometimes the King of China doth send some men of great confidence disguised through divers parts of China, that they might see how his officers did serve him, and whether there were any novelties or changes whereof they made him not privy, or some matters for which it were necessary to provide. And because the King hath such care of the government of his kingdom and orders it so well, with its being so large as it is, he maintaineth and preserveth it united in peace since so many years, without any foreign kingdoms invading and seizing anything in China; contrariwise China subjected and hath subject many kingdoms and many peoples thanks to its singular government.[2]

[1] Probably Kongmoon or Kongmun (Chiang-mên in Mandarin), on the West River delta, about 70 miles from Canton.
[2] Trigault took a different view in 1615. Cf. *The China that was*, pp. 90–91.

CHAPTER XXIII

Of how the Portugals in former times traded with the Chinas, and of how these armed against them.

ECAUSE we spake many times before of Portugal captives in China, it will be a convenient thing that the cause of their captivity be known, where many notable things will be showed. You must know that from the year 1554 hitherto, the businesses in China are done very quietly and without danger; and since that time till this day there hath not one ship been lost but by some mischance, having lost in times past many.

Because as the Portugals and the Chinas were almost at wars, when the China fleets came upon them, the Portugal ships weighed anchor and put out to sea, and lay in places unsheltered from tempests, whereby the storms coming, many were lost upon the coast or upon some banks.

But from the year 1554 hitherto, Leonel de Sousa (born in the Algarve, and married in Chaul) being Captain-Major, made a covenant with the Chinas that we would pay their duties, and that they should suffer us to do our businesses in their ports.[1] And since that time we do them in Cantão which is the first port of China: and thither the Chinas do resort with their silks and musk, which are the principal goods the Portugals do buy in China. There they have sure havens, where they are quiet without danger, or any one disquieting them, and so the Chinas do now make their merchandise well: and now both great and small are glad with the traffic of the Portugals and the fame of them runneth through all China. Whereby some of the principal persons of the Court came to Cantão only for to see them, having heard the fame of them. Before the time aforesaid, and after the rising which Fernão Peres de Andrade did cause,[2] the businesses were done with great trouble; they suffered not a Portugal in the country, and

---

[1] Cf. introduction, pp. xxxiii–xxxv, and the sources there quoted.
[2] Should be Simão de Andrade. See p. 187, n. (4) above.

for great hatred and loathing called them *Fancui*,[1] that is to say 'men of the devil'.

Now they hold not commerce with us under the name of Portugal, neither went this name to the Court when we agreed to pay customs; but under the name of *Fangim*,[2] which is to say 'people of another coast'. Note also, that the law in China is that no man of China do sail out of the realm on pain of death.[3] It is only lawful for him to sail along the coast of the same China. And yet along the coast, nor from one place to another in China itself, is it lawful for him to go without a certificate of the Louthias of the district whence he departeth; in which is set down, whither he goeth, and wherefore, and the marks of his person, and his age. If he carrieth not this certificate he is banished to the frontier regions. The merchant that carrieth goods carrieth a certificate of the goods he carrieth, and how he paid duties for them. In every custom-house that is in every province he payeth certain duties, and not paying them he loseth the goods, and is banished to the frontier parts.

Notwithstanding the abovesaid laws some Chinas do not leave going out of China to traffic, but these never return again to China. Of these some live in Malacca, others in Sião, others in Patane, and so in diverse places of the South some of these that go without licence are scattered. Whereby some of these who live already out of China do return again in their ships unto China, under the protection of the Portugals; and when they are to dispatch the duties of their ships they take some Portugal their friend to whom they give some bribe, that they may dispatch it in his name and pay the duties.

Some Chinas desiring to get their living, do go very secretly in these ships of the Chinas to traffic abroad, and return very secretly, that it be not known, no not to his kindred, that it be not spread abroad and they incur the penalty that the like do incur. This law was made because the King of China found that the frequent communication with foreigners might be the cause of some risings, and because many Chinas on the pretext of sailing

[1] *Fan-kuei*, (Cantonese, *faan-kwai*), 'Barbarian devil'. Also romanised as *Fanqui, Fankwei*, etc. Cf. Giles, *Glossary*, pp. 6–7, 40–41.

[2] *Fan-jên* (Cantonese *faan-yân*), 'Barbarian'. Cf. Giles, op. et loc. cit.

[3] First promulgated in 1404, on the grounds that the people of Chekiang and Fukien often became pirates. This particular order was soon modified, but similar prohibitory decrees were promulgated after the death of the Yung-lo emperor in 1424. Cf. *T'oung-Pao*, XXXIV, 364–365, 388–389.

abroad became pirates and robbed the districts along the sea coast. Yet for all this diligence there are many China pirates along the sea coast. These Chinas that live out of China, and do go thither with the Portugals since the offence of Fernão Peres de Andrade[1] did direct the Portugals to begin to go to trade to Liampoo,[2] for in those parts are no walled cities nor villages, but many and great towns along the coast, of poor people, who were very glad of the Portuguese, and sold them their provisions whereof they made their gain.[3] In these towns were those China merchants who came with the Portugals, and because they were known, for their sakes the Portugals were the better entertained, and through them it was arranged for the local merchants to bring their goods for sale to the Portugals. And as these Chinas who came with the Portugals were the intermediaries between the Portugals and the local merchants, they reaped a great profit thereby.

The inferior Louthias of the sea coast received also great profit of this traffic, for they received great bribes from the one and from the other, to give them leave to traffic, and to let them carry and transport their goods.[4] So that this traffic was among them a long while concealed from the King and from the superior Louthias of the province.

After these matters had for some space been done secretly in Liampoo, the Portugals went forward little by little, and began to go and make their merchandise at Chincheo[5] and in the islands of Cantão.[6] And other Louthias permitted them already in every place for the bribes sake, whereby some Portugals came to traffic beyond Namqui,[7] which is very far from Cantão, without the King ever being witting, or having knowledge of this traffic. The business fell out in such sort, that the Portugals began to winter in the islands of Liampoo,[8] and they were so firmly settled there and with

[1] Another mistake for Simão de Andrade.   [2] Ningpo.
[3] Cf. introduction, pp. xxiii–xxiv, and sources there quoted.
[4] This is likewise confirmed by Chinese chronicles of the Ming period. Cf. W. H. Chang, *Commentary*, pp. 38, 42–43; T. T. Chang, *Sino-Portuguese Trade*, pp. 69–72; J. M. Braga, *Western Pioneers*, pp. 68–69, 72.
[5] The vicinity of the Bay of Amoy, in this context. Cf. Appendix I.
[6] 'Cantão' here, means the province (rather than the provincial capital) of Kuangtung.
[7] Nanking. 'Beyond' is rather misleading, since the Yangtze river delta region and the islands off the coast of Chekiang are presumably meant here.
[8] Shuang-hsü-chiang, 'Double island anchorage' not far from Ningpo. Cf. *Ch'ou-hai-t'u-pien*, chüan 8, p. 22; T. T. Chang, *Sino-Portuguese Trade*, pp. 76–77; W. H. Chang, *Commentary*, pp. 38–39.

such freedom, that nothing was lacking them save having a gallows and *pelourinho*.[1] The Chinas who accompanied the Portugals, and some Portugals with them, came to disorder themselves in such manner that they began to make great thefts and robberies, and killed some of the people. These evils increased so much and the clamour of the injured was so great, that it came not only to the superior Louthias of the province but also to the King. Who commanded presently to make a very great armada in the province of Fuquẽ,[2] to drive the pirates from all the coast, especially those that were about Liampoo; and all the merchants, as well Portugals as Chinas, were included in this number of pirates.

The armada being ready, it put forth to cruise along the sea coast. And because the winds served them not then for to go as far as Liampoo, they went to the coast of Chincheo, where finding some ships of the Portugals, they began to fight with them, and in no wise did they permit any wares to come to the Portugals, who stayed many days there (fighting sometimes) to see if they could have any remedy for to dispatch their business. But after many days had passed, and seeing that they had no remedy they determined to go without it. The captains of the armada knowing this, sent a message to them very secretly by night, that if they would that any goods should come to them, that they should send them something. The Portugals were very glad with this message, prepared a great and sumptuous present, and sent it by night because they were so advised. From thence forward came many goods unto them, the Louthias making as though they took no heed thereof, and dissembling with the merchants. And thus in this way was done the trade for that year, which was the year 1548.[3]

[1] A stone pillar or column which served as the emblem of a muncipality, and also as a whipping-post where public punishment was inflicted on a delinquent, somewhat after the manner of the stocks in English towns. Some typical colonial *pelourinhos* are described and illustrated by Luis Chaves, 'Os Pelourinhos de Portugal nos domínios do seu império de Além-Mar' in *Ethnos*, I, 91–112.

[2] Fukien.

[3] It is evident from contemporary Ming records that these events took place in the region of the Bay of Amoy, chiefly off Yüeh-chiang ('moon anchorage') near the modern Hai-ts'ang on the south side of Amoy Bay, and off the island of Wu-hsü, as shown in Fig. (ii). The Chinese admiral who took the bribe was probably Yao Hsiang-fêng, the acting *Hai-tao-fu-shih*, who seems to have been cashiered in consequence. Cf. W. H. Chang, *Commentary*, pp. 39–40.

How the Chinas armed again against the Portugals, and of what followed from this armada.

THE year following, which was 1549, there was a straighter watch upon the coast by the captains of the armada, and greater vigilance in the ports and entrances of China, in such sort that neither goods nor victuals came to the Portugals. But for all the vigilance and watching there was, as the islands along the coast are many (for they run in a row along the length of China) the armadas could not have so much vigilance, that some wares were not brought secretly to the Portugals.[1]

But they were not so many that they could make up the ships' ladings, and the uttering[2] those goods which they had brought to China. Wherefore they left the goods which they had not uttered in two China junks, of such Chinas as were already dismembered from China, and traffic abroad under the shadow of the Portugals; in the which they left thirty Portugals in charge with the ships and with the goods, that they might defend the ships, and in some port of China where best they could they should sell the goods that remained in exchange for some wares of China, and having ordained this they departed for India.

As the people of the China armada saw the two junks remain alone, the other ships being gone, they fell upon them, being induced by some merchants of the country, who revealed to them the great store of goods that remained in those junks, and the few Portugals that remained to guard them. They therefore laid an ambush for them, dressing some Chinas ashore, who being in arms made as though they would set upon the ships to fight with them (because they were close to the land), so that the Portugals being provoked should come out of the ships to fight with them, and thus the ships might remain defenceless to them of the armada,

[1] From the Ming records quoted by W. H. Chang (*Commentary*, p. 41), it is clear that the events narrated in this chapter took place in the coastal district of Chao-an, on the Fukien-Kuangtung border.

[2] 'Selling', or 'disposing of'.

which lay close at hand to attack them, concealed behind a promontory which jutted out into the sea.[1] Those who were left to
guard the junks being provoked in this manner, being heedless of
the ambush which they ought to have suspected was laid for them,
some of them sallied forth to fight with the Chinas ashore. On
seeing this, those of the armada who were watching in ambush,
set upon the two junks with great fury and celerity, and slaying
some Portugals that they found in them and wounding others,
they took the junks.

The chief Captain, which is the Luthissi,[2] remained so vain-
glorious and so pleased with this victory that it was a wondrous
thing to see his joy. And he forthwith used great cruelty on some
Chinas whom he took with the Portugals. He laboured to persuade
four Portugals who had more appearance in their persons than the
rest, that they should say that they were Kings of Malacca. And he
persuaded them in the end, because he promised to use them better
than the rest, and therewith he induced them. And finding among
the clothes that he took a gown and a cap, and asking one of those
Chinas who were taken with the Portugals what habit that was,
they put in his head that it was the habit of the Kings of Malacca,
wherefore he commanded forthwith to make three gowns by that
pattern, and three caps, and so he apparelled them all four in one
sort, to make his deceit true, and his victory more glorious. To this
was joined the covetousness of the Luthissi, to see if he could detain the many goods that he had taken in the junks. In sort that he
both wished to triumph over the Kings of Malacca, so that the
King might give him great rewards for the service which he wished
to show he had done him, as because he wished to help himself to
the goods which he had taken, for to make a greater display with

[1] This engagement took place at Tsou-ma-ch'i ('running horse creek') on the
T'ung-shan peninsula. Cf. Introduction, pp. xxvii–xxviii.

[2] Lu T'ang, the *Pei-wo-tu-chih-hui*, this being the title of a military commander whose chief function was to guard the coast against the attacks of
Japanese. He was a native of Ju-ning in Honan province. Chinese records differ
as to whether Lu T'ang at this date was holding this post, or if (as is probable) he
had been promoted to *Tu-ssu*, or provincial army commander, as a result of his
destruction of the pirate stronghold at Shuang-hsü-chiang a few months before.
In any event, as pointed out previously, Gaspar da Cruz has confused Lu
T'ang's name with his appointment and thus produced his hybrid *Luthissi*. Cf.
Ch'ou-hai-t'u-pien, Ch. 4, p. 12, and Ch. 8, p. 23; *Ming-shih*, Ch. 212, biography
nr. 6.

them to the people of China of his glorious victory. And in order to do this more safely, and not to be taken in a lie, he did great executions upon the Chinas whom he took with the Portugals, and killing some of them he determined to kill the rest.

These things coming to the ears of the Aitão[1] who was his superior, he reproved him severely for what he had done, and sent to him forthwith that he should kill no more of those that remained, but that he should come to see him immediately, bringing with him all the prize, as well of men who were yet alive, as of the merchandise. The Luthissi ordering his journey for to go to the Aitão as he was commanded, he ordered four chairs to be given to the four to whom he had given the title of Kings, to be carried in them with more honour. And the other Portugals were carried in pillory-coops[2] with their heads out fast by the necks between the boards so that they could not pull them in, and those who had some wounds were likewise taken along exposed to the sun and to the open air.

In this manner they took their food and drink, and thus they obeyed the calls of nature, which was no small torment and suffering to them; and they were taken seated in these coops, being carried on men's shoulders. The Luthissi went with this prize through the country with very great majesty, and carried before him four banners displayed, on the which were written the names of the four Kings of Malacca. And when he entered into the towns, he entered with great noise and majesty, with sound of trumpets, and with criers who went before, proclaiming the great victory which the Luthissi so-and-so had gotten of the four great Kings of Malacca. And all the great men of the towns came forth to receive him with great feasts and honours, and all the people came running to see the new victory.

When the Luthissi came with all his pomp and glory where the Aitão was, after giving him a particular account of all that had happened and of his victory, he revealed his plan to him and agreed

---

[1] The *Hai-tao-fu-shih*, or admiral of the coastguard fleet, who at this date was K'o Ch'iao, according to the Ming records. There is apparently some confusion in our friar's account between this Hai-tao, and the Viceroy (*Tu-t'ang*), Chu Wan. For K'o Ch'iao's biography see W. H. Chang *Commentary*, pp. 40–41. He was a native of Ch'ing-yang in Kiangnan province.

[2] The original Portuguese text has *capoeiras* ('chicken coops'), but I have retained Purchas' translation of pillory-coops as being a better description. Cf. Galeote Pereira, pp. 24–25 above.

with him to divide the goods between them both, and that he should continue the feigning of the Kings of Malacca, so that both might receive of the King honours and rewards.

This being resolved, they both agreed that to keep this in secret the Luthissi should go forward in that which he had begun, to wit, that all the Chinas who had come there captives should be killed. And forthwith they ordered that it should be put in effect, whereby they killed ninety and more Chinas, among whom were some small boys slain.[1] They left notwithstanding three or four youths and one man, that by them (bringing them to their own hand) they might certify the King all that they would, which was to make out the Portugals as pirates, concealing the goods which they took from them, certifying also by these men that those four Portugals were Kings of Malacca. And the Portugals, not having the language of the country, nor having anyone in that region who could favour or protect them, would perish.

And they being mighty would make their own tale good, following the end by them intended. And for this reason and for greater triumph of the victory, they slew not the Portugals, but left them alive. These Louthias could not do this so secretly, nor in such safety, but that their fraudulent wickednesses became known, and were generally reproved of the people. And people of all conditions chiefly reproved the executions and cruelties which they had made, since it is an unusual thing in China to kill anyone without leave of the King, as we have said above.[2] And even in inflicting death sentences the justice of this land is very slow and deliberate, as we have also shown above. Besides all this, many of those whom they slew had kindred in that region, who did grieve at the death of theirs.

Whereby, as well by these as by some Louthias who were zealous of justice and would not give consent to such great evils and fraudulent dealings, this matter came to the King's ears, and

[1] The contemporaneous *Ming shih-lu* ('Veritable records'), as quoted by W. H. Chang, *Commentary*, pp. 41–42, gives 96 men as the total number executed, 'including the bogus lieutenant, Li Kuang-tou.' The majority were Chinese.

[2] All the old Portuguese accounts have similar statements about the infliction of the death penalty in Ming China. The rule that all death sentences in normal peace time required confirmation from the Throne, and that executions could only be carried out at the annual autumn assizes, apparently dates from the reign of the first Emperor of the Sung dynasty. Cf. Giles, *Biographical Dictionary*, nr. 168, p. 70, and Couling, *Encyclopedia Sinica*, p. 467, *China Review*, XIII, 40:.

T

he was informed how the Portugals were merchants who came to
traffic with their merchandise to China, and were not pirates; and
how four of them had been given falsely the title of Kings, to the
end that the King should show them [i.e. the Aitão and the
Luthissi] great favours and do them great honours; and how these
two had usurped great store of goods, and that for to conceal these
evils they had killed men and children without fault. When the
King was informed of this, he was very angry and very grieved
thereat, and forthwith he ordered justice to be done in this matter
with great speed and diligence, as can be seen in the following
chapter which gives a full account thereof.

CHAPTER XXV

Of the diligence that was done to find out what sort of people the Portugals were; and how the judicial enquiry was made into their imprisonment.

As soon as the King was informed of all the above-said, he forthwith dispatched from the Court a Quinchay (of whom we spake before, that is to say a 'chop of gold'),[1] and such men, as we said, are never sent save on very weighty affairs. And with him he sent other two men of great authority also, of the which the one had been Ponchassi and the other Anchassi, these two as inquisitors and examiners of this matter,[2] commanding and commending to the Chaẽ[3] who that year went to visit the province of Fuquem, and to the Ponchassi and Anchassi of the same province, their aid and assistance to the Quinchay and to the two inquisitors in all things necessary for them in this business; greatly commending to all concerned in this case that they should investigate the matter as loyal servants and friends of good justice and of the good government of his Kingdom. And as this happened at a time when the provinces were all provided with new officers, all the above persons came together from the Court and they all entered into the city of Funcheo with very great pomp.

And as soon as they arrived, they all began with very great diligence and care to investigate the business on which they came, and which had been so highly commended to them. The two that came with the Quinchay as inquisitors, went forthwith to certain great houses which had in the middest a great courtyard; and on the one side of the court were certain great and fair lodgings, and on the other side others in the same sort. Each of the inquisitors entered in one of these houses aforesaid.

[1] Ch'in-ch'ai, Imperial commissioner or Legate. Cf. Ch. XVI, p. 157, n. (1) above.

[2] The supervising Censor, Tu Ju-chên, president of the Board of War (*ping-pu*) at Peking, and the Censor, Ch'en Tsung-k'uei, are the only high officiais explicitly mentioned in the *Ming shih-lu* as forming part of the commission of enquiry, but doubtless some others accompanied them. *Ming shih-lu*, Ch. 347, 363.

[3] Probably Ch'en Tsung-k'uei is meant here.

The prisoners were straightaway brought and were presented to one of them. He for courtesy remitted them to another that he should examine them first, with words of great courtesy. The other sent them back again with many thanks. So they were sundry times carried from one to another, each of them willing to give the hand to the other of beginning first, till that one of them yielded and began. And as the matter was of great import and much commended to them, all that the accused and the accusers did speak, these officers did write with their own hands.

The Portugals had for great enemies a China man and pilot of one of the ships that were taken, and a China youth who was a Christian, and who from a child was brought up among the Portugals; for they were both made of the part of the contrary Louthias, moved by gifts and promises. The Louthias were already deposed of their offices, and held for guilty of that which they were accused before the King; but though they were thus handled, they were still so mighty and so favoured that they could take from the Portugals a China youth who served them for an interpreter, so that the Portugals not having anyone who understood them would not be able to defend the justice of their cause. This youth was returned to the Portugals by means of a petition which was drawn up for them by a China prisoner, which they presented to the inquisitors, who when they had read it, immediately ordered the youth to be handed over. And this youth was the cause of their deliverance, because as through him they could make themselves understood to the officers of justice, they could prove very well that they were blameless. They examined them in this order.

The accused were first brought and examined by one of these officers, and then they carried them to another to be examined again. And while this other was re-examining the accused, the accusers were brought to him that examined first. And as well the accused as the accusers were all examined by both the officers, that afterward they both seeing the confessions of the one and the other they might see if they did agree. And first they examined everyone by himself. Afterward they examined them altogether, for to see if the one did contrary the other, or did contend and reprehend one another, that so by little and little they might gather the truth of the case.[1] In these cross-examinations the two were contrary, to wit,

[1] On the Chinese judge acting as prosecutor, cf. Dyer Ball, *Things Chinese*, p. 333.

the pilot and the Christian China youth, and they were given many stripes because they disagreed in some things.

The Louthias did always show themselves glad to hear the Portugals in their defence, which was a source of great comfort to them. It was also a great help to them that they all spoke through one interpreter and so did not contradict each other. And because the Portugals alleged in their defence, that if they would know who they were, and how they were merchants and not pirates, they should send to enquire of them along the coast of Chincheo,[1] and that there they should know the truth, which they might know of the merchants of the country, with whom they had traded for many years; and that from them they would learn that they were no Kings, for Kings do not abase themselves so much as to come with so few men to play the merchant, and if before they said the contrary it was by the deceit of the Luthissi, and to receive better usage of him in their persons.

Having this information of the Portugals, both of the inquisitors went forthwith to Chincheo, with the approval of the Quinchay and the other officers, to enquire into the truth of that which the Portugals had told them, nor was this enquiry entrusted to anyone else save only these two persons. As soon as these Louthias had finished making enquiry in Chincheo, since they learnt thereby of the truth of what the Portugals had said, and the lies of the Luthissi and of the Aitão, they dispatched immediately a post wherein they commanded to put the Luthissi and the Aitão in prisons, and in good safeguard.[2]

By this can be seen with how much power these men were invested, since they could arrest such great men; something which aroused great wonder in all the country, and many people told the Portugals that they were very lucky, since such great men had been arrested for their sakes. Wherefore from thence forward all men began to favour them very much. Notwithstanding, if this examination had been made at Liampoo,[3] instead of at Chincheo, the Portugals could not but have passed it very ill, since the evils which they had done there were great. After the Louthias returned from Chincheo, they commanded to bring the Portugals

---

[1] The region of the Bay of Amoy in this context. Cf. Appendix I.
[2] i.e., Lu T'ang and K'o Ch'iao. Cf. W. H. Chang, *Commentary*, pp. 42–43.
[3] Ningpo.

before them, and comforted them very much, showing them great good-will, and telling them that they knew already they were no pirates, but were honest men: and they examined again as well they as their adversaries, to see if they contradicted themselves in any thing of that which before they had spoken.

In these later re-examinations the China pilot, who before had shown himself much against the Portugals, and had been on the Louthias side, seeing that the Louthias were already in prison and that now they could do him no good, and that the Portugals were already favoured and that the truth was already known, he gainsaid himself of all that he had said, and stated that it was true that the Portugals were no pirates nor Kings, but were merchants and very good men, and he revealed the goods which the Luthissi[1] had taken when he surprised the Portugals. He added that if until then he had maintained the contrary, it was due to the great promises which the Louthias had made him, and for the great threats they had used to him if he did it not. But seeing they were already in prison, and that he knew they could now do him no hurt, he wished now to speak the truth.

This was a thing which made the Louthias greatly to wonder, and they gazed at each other, as if out of their wits, for a great space of time without saying a word. And recollecting themselves, they then commanded to torment him and to whip him very sore, to see if he would gainsay himself, but he still persevered in the same confession.

All the examinations and diligences necessary in this business being ended, the Quinchay willing to depart for the Court with his company, would first see the Portugals and give a sight of himself to the city. The sight was of great majesty in the manner he went abroad in the city, for he went accompanied by all the great men of it, and with many men in arms and many banners displayed and very fair, and with many trumpets and kettle-drums, and many other things which on such occasions and pomps are used. And accompanied in this manner he went to certain very noble and gallant houses. And all the great men taking their leave of him, he commanded the Portugals to come near him, and after a few words he dismissed them, since this was only for to see them.

---

[1] Lu T'ang, then apparently the *Tu-ssŭ*, or commander of the provincial troops.

Before these Louthias departed, they commanded the Louthias of the region, and the jailers, that all of them should favour the Portugals and give them very good entertainment, and should command to give them all things necessary for their persons. And they commanded every one to set his name on a piece of paper, because that while they were going to the Court and dispatching of their business, they should not craftily make some missing. And they commanded to keep the Luthissi and the Aitao[1] in strict custody, and that they should not let them communicate with any person.

Being gone from the city, they lodged in a small town, where they set in order all the papers, ingrossing only what was necessary; and because the papers were many and there was much to write, they helped themselves with three men. And having ingrossed all that they were to carry to the Court, they burned all the rest. And because these three men whom they took for helpers should not spread abroad any thing of that which they had seen or written, they left them shut up with great vigilance, that none should speak with them; commanding to give them all things necessary very abundantly until the King's sentence came from the Court and was declared. The papers being presented at Court, and all seen by the King and by all his officers, sentence was pronounced in the form and manner following.

[1] Lu T'ang and K'o Ch'iao.

CHAPTER XXVI

Which contains the sentence that the King gave against the Louthias in favour of the Portugals.

BEFORE we put down the sentence, it is convenient to note certain things. The first is that the sentence was much more extensive and lengthy than what is here summarized, and whereas the Portugals who had it in their possession curtailed it, I curtailed it still further, taking only the chief matter of it and cutting all the rest.[1] Secondly, it must be noted, for to understand some obscure points thereof, that poutoos[2] are coastguards of the sea, and are certain condemned criminals wearing red caps, who are sentenced to serve as men-at-arms in the frontier regions. Besides this, you must know that the duties of China are not paid as they are among us, but as they are paid in Sião [Siam], which is by measuring the ships which take goods to China, from poop to prow in cubits, and the payment is adjusted according to the cubits, so much for each one;[3] and the present mode of payment in China at so much per cent, was by an agreement which was made by the Portugals, with the rulers of Cantam through the advice of the Chinas who trafficked among the same Portugals, whereby the duties are heavier than they would have been if they were paid according to the custom of the country.[4] These things presupposed, the sentence is the following.

[1] I have not been able to trace the full text of the original decree, but Gaspar da Cruz's summary accords remarkably well with the much briefer extracts and references which are embodied in the *Ming shih-lu* and elsewhere, and reproduced in W. H. Chang, *Commentary*, pp. 42–43.

[2] *Pu-t,u*, 'turban-heads,' would seem to be the Chinese term indicated here, though I have not found it applied elsewhere to military convicts. For the employment of banished criminals as military convicts, see the extracts from the *Shu-yüan Tsa-chi* and the *Ming-shih*, translated in *T'oung Pao*, XXXIV, 393–394.

[3] After 1578, however, the Portuguese had to pay customs duties as well as the anchorage dues involved. Cf. Ljungstedt, *Historical Sketch*, pp. 87–90, 210–211.

[4] For the agreement made by Leonel de Sousa with the Kuangtung provincial mandarins in 1554, see J. M. Braga, *Western Pioneers*, pp. 83–89, 202–210.

Pimpu[1] by command of the King. Because Chaipuu Huchim Tutão[2] without my commandment, or making me privy thereto, after the taking of so much people commanded them to be slain. I being willing to provide therein with justice, sent first to know the truth by Quinsituam my Quinchai,[3] who taking with him the Louthias whom I sent to inform me of the truthfulness of the Portugals and also of the Aitão[4] and Luthissi[5] who had informed me that the Portugals were pirates and that they came to all the coast of my realm to rob and to murder. And the truth of all being known, they are come from doing that which I commanded them. And the papers being seen by my Pimpu and by the great Louthias of my Court, and well examined by them, they came to give me account of all. And likewise I commanded them to be perused by Ahimpu[6] and Atu Chaẽ,[7] and by Athoglissi Chuquim,[8] whom I commanded to oversee these papers very well because the matters were of great weight, wherein I would provide with justice. Which thus being seen and perused by them all, it was manifest that the Portugals had come for many years to the coast of Chincheo to drive their trade, which it was not convenient they should do in the manner they did it, but in my markets, as was always the custom in all my ports. These men of whom hitherto I knew not: I know now that the people of Chincheo went to their ships in the offing to trade, whereby I know already that they are merchants and not pirates, as it was reported to me that they were. I do not blame merchants for helping merchants, but I find great fault with my Louthias of Chincheo: because as soon as any ship came to my ports, they should have known if they were merchants, and if they wished to pay me duties, and if they would pay them, to write unto me at

[1] *Ping-pu*, The Board of War at Peking.

[2] Probably a corrupt and abbreviated verson of some of Chu Wan's official titles.

[3] Probably refers either to Tu Ju-chên, or to Ch'en Tsung-k'uei.

[4] The *Hai-tao-fu-shih*, or naval coastguard fleet commander, K'o Ch'iao.

[5] Lu T'ang, who was then either *Tu-ssŭ* or *Pei-wo-tu-chih-hui*. Cf. Ch. xxiv, p. 195 above.

[6] The *Hsing-pu*, Board of Justice, or Board of Punishments at Peking.

[7] Probably a reference to the *Tu Ch'a Yuan*, the Censorate, or Court of Censors.

[8] This defeats me, but may conceal some reference to the fact that the preliminary investigation at Peking was carried out by the Board of War in consultation with three judges. Cf. *Ming shih-lu*, Ch. 347, as quoted in W. H. Chang, *Commentary*, p. 42.

once. If they had done so, so much evil had not been done. Or when they were taken, if they had let me know it, I would have commanded to set them at liberty. And although it be a custom in my ports that the ships which come unto them be measured for to pay their duties, these being from very far off, it was not necessary but to let them do their business, and go for their countries. Besides this my poutoos[1] who knew these men to be merchants did not tell it me, but concealed it from me, whereby they were the cause of many people being taken and slain. And those that remained alive, as they could not speak, did look toward heaven, and demanded from their hearts justice of heaven [they know no other supreme God but the heaven].[2] Besides these things I know that the Aitão and the Luthissi did so much evil for covetousness of the many goods which they took from the Portugals, and paid no regard whether those whom they took, and took the goods from, were good or evil men. Likewise the Louthias along the sea-coast knew these men to be merchants and certified me not. And all of them, as evil, were the cause of so much evil. I knew further by my Quinchay that the Aitão and Luthissi had letters by the which they knew that the Portugals were merchants and no pirates; and knowing this they were not contented with the taking of them, but they wrote many lies unto me, and were not contented with killing of the men, but killed children also, cutting off the feet of some, and the hands of others, and at last the heads of them all, writing unto me that they had taken and slain Kings of Malacca. Which reason I believing to be true, grieved in my heart. And because hitherto so many cruelties have been used without my commandment, from henceforward I command they be not done. Besides this the Portugals resisted my fleet, being better to have let themselves been taken than to kill my people. Moreover it is a long time since they came to the sea of my realm to trade like pirates and not as merchants, wherefore if they had been natives as they are strangers, they had incurred pain of death and loss of goods, wherefore they are not without fault. The Tutam by whose commandment those men were slain[3] said that for this deed I should make him greater; and the people that he commanded to be slain,

---

[1] Compare p. 204, n. (2) above.
[2] The interpolation in brackets is by Fr. Gaspar da Cruz.
[3] The *Tu-t'ang* Chu Wan.

after they had no heads, their hearts, that is their souls and their blood, required justice of heaven. I seeing so great evils to be done, my eyes could not endure the sight of the papers for tears, and my heart was very sad. I know not why my Louthias having taken these people did not let them go, so that I might not come to know such great cruelties. [Note the natural clemency of the heathen King, which is still further provoked by the merciful laws of his country, which as we said are very merciful regarding the deaths of male-factors and slow in executing them. Now to continue with the sentence.]¹ Wherefore seeing all these things, I do create Senfuu² chief Louthia, because he did his duty in his charge and told me the truth. I create also chief Louthia Quinchio³ because he wrote the truth to me of the poutoos⁴ who went to traffic their merchandise in secret with the Portugals at sea.

Those who are evil I will make them baser than those who sow rice. Furthermore, because Pachou⁵ did traffic with the Portugals, and for bribes did permit the merchants of the region to go and traffic with the Portugals, and yet doing these things wrote unto me that the Portugals were pirates and that they came to my realm only to rob. And the same he said also to my Louthias, who immediately answered that he lied, for they knew already the contrary. And therefore so-and-so and so-and-so [here he nameth ten Louthias],⁶ it is nothing that all of you be degraded to red-caps,⁷ to which I hereby condemn you, but you deserve to be made baser as I do make you.

Chaẽ, for taking these men thou sayedst thou shouldest be greater, and being in the doing of so much evil thou sayedst thou didst not fear me. So-and-so [here he named nine persons] you say that for the taking of these men I would make you great, and without any fear of me you all lied [he nameth many]. I know also you took bribes. But because you did so, I make you base [he depriveth them of the dignity of Louthias] so-and-so and so-and-so [naming many].

¹ This interpolation in brackets is likewise by Fr. Gaspar da Cruz.
² Not identified.   ³ Not identified.   ⁴ Cf. p. 204, n. (2) above.
⁵ Possibly a reference to one of the local *pa-tsung*, for whose functions at this period cf. Rada's narrative, p. 243, n. (1) below.
⁶ Another interpolation by Fr. Gaspar da Cruz, as are those which follow in square brackets.
⁷ Military convicts.

If the Aitão and the Luthissi would kill so many people, wherefore did you suffer it? But seeing that in consenting you were accessory with them in their death, you are all in the same fault. Chifu and Chãchifuu,[1] you were also agreeing to the will of the Aitão and Luthissi, and were with them in the slaughter, as well of those who were guilty as of those who were not. Wherefore I condemn you all to red-caps.

Lupuu[2] had a good heart, because the Tutão being willing to kill this people, he said that they should let me first know it. To him I will do no harm, but good as he deserveth, and I command that he remain Louthia.

Sanchi[3] I make my Anchessi of the city of Cansi.[4] The Antexeo[5] I command to be deposed of his honour. Assão[6] seeing he can speak with the Portugals, let him have honour and ordinary, and he shall be carried to Chaqueã [Chekiang] where he was born. [This is the youth with whom the Portugals did defend themselves serving them for interpreter; they gave him title of Louthia and maintenance.]

Chinque,[7] head of the merchants that went to sea to traffic with the Portugals and deceived them, bringing great store of goods on shore, it shall be demanded of him and set in good safeguard for the maintenance and expences of the Portugals, and I condemn him and his four companions to red-caps, and they shall be banished whither my Louthias shall think good.

To the rest guilty and imprisoned for this matter, I command my Louthias to give every one the punishment he deserveth.

I command the Chaẽ to bring me hither the Tutão, that his faults being perused by the great men of my Court, I may command to do justice on him as I think good. This Tutão was also a consenter in the wickedness of the Aitão and the Luthissi; for the

---

[1] *Chifu* is probably *Chih-fu*. prefect, in this instance Lu Pi, the prefect of Chang-chou who was degraded for complicity in this affair. Cf. *China Review*, XIX, 50; *Chang-chou-fu-chih*, Ch. 47, p. 21.

[2] Seems to be confused with the prefect Lu Pi, who was, however, one of the guilty.

[3] Not identified.

[4] Provincial Judge or Judicial Commissioner at Kueilin.

[5] Not readily identifiable among the list of those disgraced given in the *Ming shih-lu*.

[6] Presumably A (Ah) something or other.

[7] Not identified.

Luthissi and the Aitão made him partaker, and gave him part of the booty which they took from the Portugals, that as the head he should hold for good that which they did: for in truth they durst not have done that which they did if he had not given consent and agreed with their opinion. [This man hearing what was judged against him, hung himself, saying that seeing Heaven had made him whole, that no man should take away his head.][1] The Poutoos who are yet in prison, shall be examined again, and shall be dispatched forthwith.

Cuichũ[2] shall forthwith be deprived from being a Louthia, without being heard any more.

Chibee,[3] head of six and twenty, I command that he and his be all set at liberty, for I find but little fault in them. Those who owe any money, it shall be recovered of them forthwith.

Famichim and Toumichar[4] shall die, if my Louthias do think it expedient, and if not let them do as they think best.

Afonso de Paiva and Pero de Cea [these were Portugals] Antonio and Francisco [these were slaves][5] finding them to be guilty of killing some men of my fleet, shall with the Luthissi and Aitão be put in prison, where according to the custom of my kingdom, they shall all die slowly.

The other Portugals who are alive with all their servants, who are in all fifty-one, I command them to be carried to my city of Cansi,[6] where I command they be well intreated, seeing my heart is so good towards them that for their sake I punish in this sort the people of my country. And I deal so well with them, because it is my custom to do justice to all men. The Louthias of the fleet, finding they are little to blame, I command they be set free. I

---

[1] This interpolation on the suicide of Chu Wan is by Fr. Gaspar da Cruz.
[2] Not identified.
[3] Not identified.
[4] Not identified.
[5] Words in brackets are interpolated by Fr. Gaspar da Cruz. For the Chinese translations of the Portuguese names, cf. *Ming shih-lu*, ch. 363 in W. H. Chang, *Commentary*, p. 42. As noted in the introduction, after the suicide of Chu Wan, Lu T'ang, K'o Ch'iao and others had their death-sentences commuted, and were shortly afterwards pardoned. Cf. W. H. Chang, *Commentary*, p. 43, and *China Review*, XIX, 50.
[6] Kueilin. T. T. Chang (*Sino-Portuguese Trade*, p. 84) and other commentators wrongly identify this city as Hangchow, evidently confusing the Portuguese 'Cansi' with Marco Polo's 'Quinsay'. But from the texts of Cruz and Pereira it is clear that by 'Cansi' the Portuguese meant Kuangsi.

deal in this sort with all men, that my Louthias may see that all that which I do, I do it with a good zeal. All these things I command to be done with speed. Thus far the sentence of the King.

The process of this sentence hath clearly shown the good process and order of justice which these idolatrous and barbarous peoples have in their way, and the natural clemency which God hath put in a King who liveth without knowledge of the true God. And how great diligence he putteth, and with what consideration he treateth weighty matters, seemeth to be the cause of the good government which there is in this country and the great justice thereof; forasmuch as although China is such a great kingdom as we have shown, it has been maintained in peace since a very great number of years without any rebellions; and God sustains it, because the enemies do not make raids and devestation therein, and because commonly it is sustained in great abundance, prosperity and plenty. And the rigorous justice of this land is the cause of bridling the evil inclinations and inquietudes to which the people thereof are prone, which being so strict as it is, yet withal the prisons are commonly full of prisoners, there being so many of them, as we have said. And if some year there should chance to be a famine, it is necessary, both within the land as along the seacoast, to maintain continuously many fleets to repress the depredations of the many pirates who rise up in arms.

The Portugals who were freed by the sentence, when they carried them whither the King commanded, found by the way all things necessary in great abundance, in the houses which (as we said above) the King had in every town for the Louthias when they travel. They carried them in parties, on chairs made of canes upon men's backs, and they were in charge of inferior Louthias, who caused them to have all things necessary through all the places where they came, till they were delivered to the Louthias of the city of Cansi.

From thenceforward they had no more of the King every month but one *foo*[1] of rice (which is a measure as much as a man can bear on his back), the rest which they had need of, every one did seek it by his own industry. Afterwards they dispersed them again by

[1] *fen or fun*, the $\frac{1}{100}$ part of a Chinese ounce of silver.

two and two and by three and three through divers places, to
prevent that in time they should not become mighty by joining
themselves with others.

Those that were condemned to death, were forthwith put in the
prison of the condemned. And Afonso de Paiva found a means to
give the Portugals who were free to understand that for his welcome
they had given him forty stripes straightway, which had caused him
to suffer very much, showing himself comforted in the Lord.

Those who were at liberty, now some and then some, came to
the ships of the Portugals through the industry of some Chinas,
who brought them very secretly, moved by the great bribes which
they received from the Portugal merchants who drove their trade
in the city of Cantão.

CHAPTER XXVII

Of the rites and adorations of the Chinas.

THIS people hath no knowledge whatever of God, neither among them is there found any vestige of such knowledge, which showeth it to be true that they are not given to the contemplation of natural things, nor are there among them studies of natural philosophy as some Portugals wished to maintain that there were, induced by the studies which they knew that they had; but they did not know that they were of laws and not of philosophy; albeit, as I said, some of them through some writings of the ancients, have some notice of the eclipses of the sun and of the moon, but this doth not mean that there are general studies thereof.[1]

If they had had this study, it would have sufficed them to come thereby to the knowledge of God as the old philosophers had: Saint Paul the Apostle saying in his epistle to the Romans that the invisible things of God, and his divinity, power and eternity, can be learnt from the contemplation and knowledge of things created and visible.[2]

Whereby the fact of the Chinas not having knowledge of one God is sufficient argument to show that the Chinas do not have studies of natural philosophy, neither do they give themselves to the contemplation of natural things, in spite of what some Portugals try to maintain to the contrary.[3]

When I was in the region where the Apostle Saint Thomas suffered martyrdom, which the Portuguese call São Thomé and those of the country Moleapor,[4] I learnt that an honourable Armenian had come thither on a pilgrimage from Armenia out of devotion to the Apostle, and he had deposed on oath (which was given him for greater certainty by the Portugals who served as

[1] Gaspar da Cruz is both wrong and confused here. Cf. Ch. XVII, p. 161 *ante*.
[2] Romans I. xx.
[3] Half a century later, Ricci and his followers also maintained the contrary.
[4] Meliapur or Mylapore, on the coast of Coromandel, nowadays a suburb of Madras.

major-domos in the house of the Apostle) that the Armenians had
it written in their true and authentic scriptures that before the
Apostle suffered martyrdom at Moleapor he had gone to China to
preach the gospel, and after being there certain days, seeing that he
could not do any good there, he had returned to Moleapor,
leaving in China three or four disciples whom he had made there,
—all of which was set down in the book of the house.[1] If these
disciples whom the Apostle had left, had made fruit in the land,
and through them the land came to the knowledge of God, we do
not know it; for generally among them is no notice of the evangelical
law, nor of Christianity, nor even of one God, nor a trace thereof,
save only that they believe that everything depends from on high,
both the creation of all things as the conservation and ordering of
them; and not knowing who in particular is the author of these
things, they attribute it to the same sky. And thus they blindly
grope after God.

In the city of Cantão in the middest of the river which is of
fresh water and very broad, is a little islet on the which is a kind of
monastery of their sort of priests; and within this monastery I saw
an oratory high from the ground very well made, with certain
gilt steps before it, made of carved work, in which was a woman
very well made with a child about her neck, and it had a lamp
burning before it.[2] I suspecting that to be some show of Christianity, asked of some laymen whom I found there, and of some of
the idol's priests who were there, what that woman signified, and
none could tell it me, nor give me any reason for it. It might well
be the image of Our Lady, made by the ancient Christians that
Saint Thomas left there, or by their occasion made, but the conclusion is that all is forgotten. It might also be some heathen image.
As the greatest God they have is the Heaven, so therefore the
letter that signifieth it is the principal and the first of all the
letters.[3]

They worship the sun, the moon and the stars, and all the images

[1] The question whether St. Thomas ever visited China is discussed (and
decided in the negative) by A. C. Moule, *Christians in China before the year 1550*,
pp. 10–26, where the relevant passages from Fr. Gaspar da Cruz are translated
on pp. 12 13, and by A. B. Duvigneau, C.M., *Saint Thomas a-t-il porté l'Évangile
jusqu'en Chine?* (Peking, 1936).

[2] Probably a representation of Kuan-yin, the equivalent of the goddess of
Mercy.

[3] T'ien.

u

they make without any respect. They have notwithstanding images of Louthias whom they worship for having been famous in some one thing or other.[1] And likewise statues and images of some priests of the idols and of some other men for some respects particular to them. And not only worship they these images, but whatsoever stones they erect on the altars in their temples. They commonly call these gods Omitoffois,[2] offering them incense, benjoin, eaglewood and another wood which they call Cayo,[3] Laque and other smelling things. They likewise offer them Ocha,[4] whereof is mention made afore. They all have oratories, which are at the entrance behind the doors of the houses, in which they have their principal idols, to the which every day in the morning and at evening they offer incense and other perfumes. They have in many places, as well in the towns as out of them, temples of idols.

In all the ships they sail in, they forthwith make a place for an oratory in the poop, wherein they carry their idols.[5]

In all things which they undertake, either journeys by sea or by land, they use lots and cast them before their gods. The lots are two sticks made like half a nutshell, flat on the one side and round on the other; and also larger ones as big again as a half nut, strung together on a string. And when they will cast lots, they speak first with their god, flattering him with words, and promising him some offering if he give them a good lot, and in it show them their good voyage or good success of their business. And after many words they cast the lots, and if both the flat sides fall upwards, or one up and another down, they hold it for an evil lot, and turn them toward their god very melancholy, calling him dog and many other reproaches. After they are weary of railing him,

[1] A reference to the practice of conferring minor canonisation on local worthies and notables, T'u Ti Lao-yeh, as they are colloquially called.

[2] O Mi T'o Fo, Amitābha or Amida Buddha, 'the Buddha of boundless light'. The abbreviated form of namah Amitābha, which is roughly the Chinese Buddhist equivalent of the Roman Catholic Ave. Cf. Giles, Glossary, p. 95; Werner, Dictionary of Chinese Mythology, pp. 336–338.

[3] Evidently Cayo Laque should have been printed as one word, cayolaque, the Malay-Portuguese term for the scented rosewood mentioned in Ch. XI, p. 125 n. (3) above.

[4] Ch'a, tea; apparently here derived from the Japanese form O-cha, lit. 'honourable tea.'

[5] This applies only to ocean-going ships. In the smaller river-craft, the oratory or altar is usually in the prow, where incense is burned and sacrifices offered. Cf. Doré, Manuel des superstitions chinoises, p. 98; Gray, China, II, 259.

they soothe him again with fair mild words, and ask his pardon, saying that the melancholy of not giving them a good lot, caused them to do him injury and to speak injurious words unto him; but that if he will pardon them and give them a good lot, then they will promise him more such a thing, and because the promises are for the benefit of them that promise them, they make many and great promises and offerings; and in this way they cast lots so many times until they fall both with the flat side upwards which they hold for a good lot;[1] then remaining well contented, they offer to their god that which they promised.

It happeneth many times when they cast lots about any weighty matter, if the lot fall not out good, or if launching a ship to the sea it goeth not well and some evil come to it, they turn on their gods and cast them in the water; and sometimes they put them in the flame of the fire and tread them under foot, giving them railing words until their business be ended, and then they carry them with playing and feasting, and give them their offerings. They hold for a great offering a hog's head boiled; and they also offer hens, geese, ducks and rice all cooked, and a great pot of wine. After presenting it all to the gods, they set the gods' portion apart, which is they put in a dish the small points of the hog's ears, the bills and the points of the claws of the hens, geese and ducks, a few grains of rice (but very few, and put in with great heed), and three or four drops of wine very heedfully, that there fall not many drops from the pot. These things being thus set in a bowl, they place them on the altar to their gods for to eat, and they set themselves there before the gods to eat all the rest that they bring. They worship the devil also, which they paint after our fashion; and they say that they worship him because he maketh those who are good, devils; and the evil he maketh buffaloes or kine or other beasts. And they say that the devil hath a master who teacheth him his knaveries. These things say the base people; the better sort say they worship him because he shall do them no hurt.

---

[1] This particular method of divination or casting lots (*pu-kua*) is described and illustrated in Doolittle, *Social life of the Chinese*, II, 107–108, and Doré, *Rercherches*, III, 243. It will be seen that Gaspar da Cruz's account is a trifle confused and self-contradictory. Both flat sides upwards means an indifferent answer; both flat sides downwards indicates a negative answer; whereas one flat side upward and one downward augurs an affirmative or favourable answer. Cf. *Travels of Peter Mundy*, III, 195, n. (3).

When they will launch any new ship to the sea, their priests being called by them come into the ships to do their sacrifices with long flowing garments of silk. They set about the ship many flags of silk, and they put a painting of the devil in the prow of the ship, to the which they make many reverences and offerings; and they say they do it because the devil shall do no hurt to the ship. They offer to the gods papers with divers images painted, and other sundry kinds of cuttings, and they burn them all before the idols with certain ceremonies and well-tuned songs, and while their singing doth last they ring certain small bells; and all the while there is much eating and drinking.[1]

In this country are two kinds of priests, some that have their heads all shaven, and these wear on their heads certain coarse caps like unto canopy cloth, being high and flat behind, and higher in front than behind by a hand's breadth, and made like a mitre with pinacles; their apparel is white gowns made after the laymen's fashion. These live in monasteries, and they have refectory and cells, and many pleasaunces within their walls.[2]

There be others whom commonly the people do use for their burials and sacrifices; these let their hair grow, and they wear black silk gowns, or of serge or linen, and long like the laymen, having for a token their hair tied up in a top-knot, thrust through with a stick made like a closed hand, varnished black.[3] None of these priests have wives, but they live wickedly and filthily.

The first day of the year, which is in the new moon of March, they make through all the land very great feasts, visiting each other, and the great ones do spend their time chiefly in banquets.[4] How much these people are polished in the rule and government of the country, and in their common traffic, so much they are beastly in their heathen customs and in the usage of their gods and idolatries. For besides that which is said, they have many heathenish fables and lies of men that were turned into dogs and afterwards back into men, and of snakes that were changed into men, and many

---

[1] Cf. Gray, *China*, II, 246–247, 259–261.
[2] Buddhist priests and monks. Cf. Doolittle, *Social life of the Chinese*, I, 236–246.
[3] Taoist priests and monks. Cf. Doolittle, *Social life of the Chinese*, I, 246–250.
[4] Typical descriptions of the New Year festivities in South China will be found in De Groot, *Fêtes*, I, 124–145; Doolittle, *Social life*, I, 23–34; Gray, *China*, I, 249–256.

other ignorances. There is a very good disposition in the people of this country for to become converted to the faith; one reason being that they hold their gods and their priests in small esteem,[1] whereby when they learn of the truth they esteem it, which is not the case with any of the peoples in all the regions of India.

Another reason is that they greatly like to listen to the doctrine of the truth, and they harken to it with great attention, as I found in them several times from my own experience, preaching to them on occasion in the public street, where crowds gathered to look as if at some new thing or new form of dress, until there was no room for any one to pass. As I saw that many people had gathered I preached to them, and they greatly rejoiced to hear me and asked questions that formulated their doubts very well. And being satisfied with my answers, they said that what I told them was very good, but that hitherto they had not had any one who told them thereof. This was the answer which I always received from them, both in public preaching as in private conversation.

I entered one day into a temple and came to an altar, where were certain stones set up which they worshipped; and trusting in the little estimation in which they held their gods, and in their being men who would be satisfied with reason, I threw the stones down to the ground, whereat some turned on me very fiercely and asked me angrily why I had done that? I went mildly to them, and smilingly asked them why they were so inconsiderate as to worship those stones? They asked me why they should not adore them, whereon I showed them how they were better than the stones, since they had the use of reason, feet, hands and eyes, wherewith they did divers things that the stones could not do; and that seeing they were better they should not abase and esteem so little of themselves as to worship something so vile, being themselves so noble. They answered me that I was very right, and they went out with me in company, leaving the stones on the ground; so that I found in these people this likelihood and disposition for them to become Christians.[2] And it helpeth also much to this purpose, that they do

---

[1] A fact noted by all subsequent foreign visitors to China. Cf. Trigault-Gallagher, The China that was, pp. 166–169; De Groot, Fêtes, II, 735–737.

[2] An interesting and valuable testimony to Far Eastern good manners and religious tolerance, which certainly could not have been paralleled in contemporary Europe.

not make any distinctions in their food, as do all the peoples of India. And seeing that among all the meats they esteem pork most, it is almost impossible for them to become Moors.

And thus in all China, there is not to be found a single China who is a Moor. Those who are Moors in China are not natives of the country as will be shown in the next chapter.

CHAPTER XXVIII

Of the Moors[1] which there are in China: and of the hindrances which there are against propagating Christianity therein.

THERE are some Moors in China scattered throughout divers parts thereof, who are not Chinas by nation, but who descend from the Mogores who are of the kingdom which is called Samarcham from the capital city being thus named.[2] These Moors came to China and were scattered throughout it in the manner following.

The Mogores of whom we spoke in the beginning of this work had traffic with the Chinas with whom they confined, even though there are stretches of desert in between them. A rich merchant of the Mogores in the time when these traded with the Chinas, came to have great familiarity and friendship with a chief Louthia of the city where they traded, whom he served with great gifts of things which he brought him from his own country. This Moor through the close and familiar friendship which he had with the Louthia, came to treat of the sect of Mafamede[3] with him, boasting of it, and telling him great things of Mafamede, in sort that he ended by persuading and inducing him to become a Moor. Whereby the Louthia and all his household were circumcised with great rejoicings and he ordered that no more pork should be brought to his house, and that no one of his household should eat it any more. This Louthia was such a good disciple that he at once began to persuade other Louthias and other persons of the city to likewise become Moors. Many consented but some did not wish to do so. The Louthia seeing the many whom he had converted in the city to this pestilential sect, felt emboldened (to his own ill and perdition) to promulgate a new law in all the district that no swine

---

[1] The reader will hardly need reminding that the term 'Moor', here as elsewhere, translated from the original 'Mouro', merely means 'Muslim' or 'Muhammadan'.

[2] The Mughals of Samarkand. Cf. Ch. IV, pp. 81–82.

[3] Muhammad. Cf. Galeote Pereira, pp. 36–37 above.

should be killed in the city and that all pigs should be sent outside of it, on pain of severe punishment. Those of the chief men and the commonality who had not been converted, as they were now deprived of their favourite food, and also because they saw a novelty which it was not lawful for any one to make in all the country save only the King, began to clamour and complain; and the clamour and complaint soon came to the King, that Louthia so-and-so had rebelled with the foreigners in the district, promulgating new laws. The King forthwith took measures in this matter, dispatching a Quinchay[1] with other Louthias, that they should diligently provide in this business, examining everything which was done and throwing into prison those who were found guilty, so as thus to bridle this innovation and punish all transgressors according to their misdeeds.

When the inquiry was finished and the guilty imprisoned, the business was submitted to the Court, and all the chief culprits in the affair were condemned to death, both Moors and Chinese. And the Moors who were not so much to blame in this wickedness were exiled to different parts of China, whence it comes that there are some few Moors in Cantam and other few in Cansi; and similarly a few can be found scattered here and there in other regions. And although these Moors are scattered throughout China, not a single China has become a Moor since the time they were exiled to the present day;[2] rather, those who are now living, as they are children and grandchildren of those who were exiled and are born of China women, both because of their mothers as because the country is now virtually their own, and with living among the Chinas, almost all of them eat pork and drink wine, which is forbidden for Moors, and they are almost no longer Moors, caring nowadays very little about the sect of Mafamede and its customs.

Presupposed the foregoing, it might occur to some of my readers to ask why, since the Chinas have no love for the sect of Mafamede, and have such a good readiness and disposition to receive the faith of Christ, and since my principal object (as I said at the beginning) was to go to China to propagate Christianity, why I did not remain

---

[1] *Ch'in-ch'ai*, Imperial commissioner or Legate.
[2] This, of course, is nonsense, and derived from Galeote Pereira's account, pp. 36–37 above.

there, preaching and fructifying? To this I answer that there are two very great inconveniences to make any Christians in this country. The one is that in no wise will they permit any novelty in the country, as in some sort it may be seen in the matter of the Moors. So that whatsoever novelty appeareth in the country, the Louthias take order forthwith how to repress it, and it goeth no further.

Whence it happened in Cantam that because they saw a Portugal measuring the entries of the gates, they immediately posted watches to see that none should come in without a licence, nor walk upon the walls.[1]

The second is, that no strange person may enter into China, nor remain in Cantam, save only with leave of the Louthias, who do give him licence to stay for a certain fixed time in Cantam, and when the time of the licence hath expired, they labour to make him depart. Wherefore because I and those who were with me had been for a month in Cantão, they set up written boards in the streets, that none should keep nor harbour us in their houses under pain of so much, until we held it our best cheap to go to the ships.

Add to the above-said, that the common people greatly fear the Louthias, wherefore none of them durst become a Christian without their licence, or at the least many would not do it. Therefore as a man cannot be settled in the country, he cannot continue preaching, and by consequence he cannot fructify and preserve the fruit. There is notwithstanding one way by which a man could preach freely, and whereby fruit might be made in the country, without even a dog barking at the preacher, nor any Louthia do him hurt in any way; which is, if he could have a licence for it from the King. And it might be obtained if a solemn embassage were sent with a solemn present to the King of China, in the name of the King of Portugal, religious men going with the ambassador to obtain the licence for to go about the country, showing themselves to be men without arms; and how our faith is no prejudice to his dominion and government, but a great help that all might obey him and keep his laws. This is the only remedy that there is for to reap any fruit in China, and there is no other (humanly speaking).

[1] This provides yet another proof that the ordinary Portuguese in the East were by no means so devoid of intelligent curiosity about their unfamiliar surroundings as hostile critics have main ained. Cf. Introduction, p. lv, and Ch. VI, p. 93, n. (2).

And without this it is impossible for any religious men to preach or to fructify, and because I had not this remedy, having the above-said inconveniencies, I came away from China; and therefore neither I, nor they of the Company of Jesus which undertook already this business sundry times, could fructify in China.[1]

[1] The vain attempts of the Jesuits and other Orders to found a mission in China prior to the time of Matteo Ricci are described by H. Bernard, S.J., *Aux Portes de la Chine.*

Of some punishments from God which the Chinas received in the year of fifty-six.[1]

THIS people hath besides the ignorances above said, a filthy abomination, which is that they are so given to the accursed sin of unnatural vice, which is in no wise reproved among them.[2] Notwithstanding, I preaching sometimes, as well in public as privately against this vice, they were glad to hear me, saying that I had great reason in what I said, but that they had never had any who told them that it was a sin, nor an evil thing done. It seemeth that because this sin is common among them, God was willing to send them a grievous punishment in some regions, the which was public in all China.

I being in the city of Cantão, and being willing to know of a rich China merchant the evils that had happened in the land and he not able to tell it me by word of mouth, gave me a letter which they had written unto him of what had happened, telling me to copy it and to give it him back again; but not trusting me, he copied it himself, and keeping the copy he gave me the original, which I translated into the Portugal tongue with the help of one that could speak our language and theirs, the tenour of the letter being this. The principal Louthias of Sanxi and of Savitõ[3] wrote unto the King saying that in these provinces the earth did shake terribly and the days waxed dark like night (he saith not for how long). A soothsayer told them all that should happen.

In the year before in the month of September, the earth opened in many places, and under it were heard great noises like the sound of bells; there followed a great wind with much rain, and the wind

[1] For the identification of these calamities, cf. *Variétés Sinologiques*, No. 28bis, pp. 206–209, and the *Chung-kuo li-tai t'ien-tsai Jên-huo-piao* (Shanghai, 1939), pp. 1217–1438.

[2] For the Chinese attitude to homosexuality, cf. Galeote Pereira, p. 17, n. (1) above.

[3] 'Sanxi' may stand for Shensi, which was the province most affected, although Shansi and Shantung (?Savitõ) also suffered. Cf. the sketch-map of the affected region in *Var. Sin.*, 28bis, p. 208.

ran about all the compass.[1] This was the sort of wind which is called in China a *Tufão*,[2] and many years it bloweth but once a year, and it is so raging that it driveth a ship under sail on the land and carrieth it there a great space, and the men cannot keep their feet, not even by leaning and holding on to one another, and it doth things worthy of wonder and incredible.

In the year that I was in China, in the port where the Portugals were,[3] they showed me a ship's boat of a good size, and the place where it was ashore (whence it had been carried by this wind) would be about a long stone's throw from the water, and many did affirm to me that the wind had such force that it carried it tumbling till it blew it into the sea. And all the houses which the Portugals had made of timber and covered with straw,[4] which were many and were built upon great stakes and not very high, it threw them all down, breaking the stakes. And one house being fastened with four cables, wherein many Portugals retired themselves, at the last fell also, and only one that was sheltered by a high place escaped falling down. To blow down these houses was nothing, for it doth many other great and incredible things. This wind is almost every year in China, the which within twenty-four hours that it rageth, it runneth about all the points of the compass. With this wind and the land being shaken with the earthquakes, many cities fell and were made desolate, in the which died innumerable people.

In a city called Vinhãfuu[5] in this day was a great earthquake. And on the west side a great fire burst out that swallowed up all the city, in the which innumerable people perished, escaping in one place two in another three, and so some of the Mogores escaped. In another city near to this, there happened the same, but in this none escaped. In a city called Leuchimẽ[6] the river increased in such sort that it overflowed the city, where infinite people were drowned.

---

[1] This would seem to be a garbled version of the earthquakes of 1555, mentioned in the *Chung-kuo li-tai*, p. 1347.

[2] Typhoon. Cf. *Hobson-Jobson*, pp. 947–950; Dalgado, *Glossário Luso-Asiático*, II, 389–390.

[3] Probably Lampacau (Lang-pai-kao, or Long-pai-kao), but possibly Macao.

[4] Matsheds, as they are called by foreigners in Hongkong and South China nowadays.

[5] Possibly a garbled reference to Wei-nan-hsien in Hsi-an-(Sian) fu, Shensi, which suffered particularly severely in the great earthquake of January, 1556.

[6] Not readily identifiable in the list of places affected which is given in *Var. Sin.*, 28bis, pp. 207–209.

In a city called Hiẽ[1] there was a great earthquake, with the which many houses fell which slew near eight thousand souls. In Puchio,[2] the house of a kinsman of the King fell and slew all that were in the house, except a child of seven or eight years old his son, who was carried to the King, and day and night was a noise heard under the earth like the sound of bells.

In a region called Couchue,[3] with fire from heaven and with many waters of a flood, many perished, and the land remained unable to be cultivated again. In a region called Enchinoẽ[3] at midnight the houses fell, and the city remained desolate and ruined, where perished near one hundred thousand souls. In a city called Inchumen[3] in one day and a night, the river did flow and ebb ten times, and with the great flood many people perished. Hitherto is the translation of the letter: that which followeth, was heard by word of mouth of the Portugals who were in the port of Cantão in the month of May, and I received the letter in the month of September.

In a city called Sãxi,[4] from midnight till five of the clock in the morning, the earth shook three times, on the eighteenth of January 1556, and the next day after from midnight till noon happened the same: the next day following, the 20th of the said month, the earth shook mightily after midnight with great thunder and lightning, and all the province was burnt and all the people thereof, and all the suburbs, villages and cities.[5] They say it would extend from bound to bound about fifty or sixty leagues, and that there was not saved but one small child, son to a kinsman of the King, who was carried to the King. And the 3rd February of the same year, in the city of Paquim where the King is, fell a shower of rain like blood.[6] This news was brought by a China who came to Cantão from a city near to Sanxi, to give news to a Louthia that he should resort to his own house, and he said that the city where he was a dweller was overflown, and that he knew not whether it

---

[1] Possibly Hsien-yang-hsien in Shensi, another place badly affected.

[2] Probably P'u-chou-fu in Shansi province, which was also severely damaged.

[3] Not readily identifiable in the works quoted p. 223, n. (1) above.

[4] Probably T'ai-yüan-fu the capital of Shansi province is intended here.

[5] The Chinese records date the beginning of this great earthquake, or rather series of earthquakes, on the night of the 23/24 January, 1556.

[6] I cannot trace this anecdote in such Chinese works as I have consulted.

would perish with the rest. Thus far the relation of what the Portugals heard, and of what they had noted down in writing.

It seemeth that the China who brought this news was so frightened that it appeared to him as if the whole province of Sanxi was desolated, just as the daughters of Lot, seeing the destruction of Sodom and Gomorra, thought that the whole world had perished.

What should be held for truth is that in the three provinces which commonly are said to have been destroyed, there was no more destruction than of those places of which the letter maketh mention, or little more.

The agreeing in the child, showeth that the town whereof the letter maketh mention of the child was in the province of Sanxi. This hath more appearance of truth (because the letter was written from the Court) than to say that all the three provinces perished. As to what the relation of the Portugals saith about the province of Sanxi being of some fifty or sixty leagues in extent, I do not know how true it is, because the province of Cantão which is one of the least in China, besides including in its jurisdiction the island of Ainão,[1] which is about fifty leagues, hath more leagues along its coastline than those which are given to Sanxi in this relation.

And the Portugals who were captives affirm that with their being carried always at a run, yet they took twenty days to journey from the middle of Fuquem[2] province to the end thereof. And from Cantão to where the King resides, they say that it is commonly a six months' journey; wherefore it seems to me that the Portugals did not take good note of the figures which were given them for the size of Sanxi province. What they make mention of the rain of blood, is the same wonder which happened one day when a number of Portugals were killed by the Chinas who had taken them in a ship, and who were carried ashore and there put to the sword.

After the happening of the things above-said, in the same year in the province of Cantão, a woman went to the Ponchassi, and told him that the province of Cansi[3] would be destroyed with power from heaven, the which woman after she had been well whipped

---

[1] Hainan island was administratively a part of Kuangtung province, but the aboriginal tribes in the interior were independent of Chinese control.

[2] Can this mean from Foochow to Ningtu? Cf. Introduction, pp. liii–liv.

[3] Kuangsi. I cannot trace this anecdote in the Chinese records.

was imprisoned. But in the month of May that year there fell great store of rain very hot, with the which the earth seemed to burn, and many people perished with the great heat, but the province perished not altogether; wherefore this woman was carried to the King, and she was in the prison where the Portugal prisoners were who told this.

A comet appeared in a star in the northern hemisphere, the which was visible in all the regions of India and in Portugal.[1] And it appeared almost for the space of fifteen days, likewise having been seen in China. And it appeared in the same year at almost exactly the time when the above-said things happened.

It seemeth that it gave a sign of this great punishment which God inflicted on the Chinas. It might well be that this sign was universal to all the world, and that it signifieth the birth of Antichrist; for the world showeth great signs of ending, and the scriptures in great part show that they are drawing nigh to being fulfilled. And the scripture saith that all the evil will come from the part of Aquilonar.[2] Whether it is one thing or another, or whatsoever it please God, may God in his infinite mercy open the eyes of these peoples blinded with the ignorance of the truth, so that they may come to the knowledge of Him. And let us all pray that He may open a way to His servants for them to preach to these peoples and thus draw them to the reward of His holy church. Amen.

End of the treatise of China.

[1] The comet of March 1556, whose appearance is alleged to have hastened the abdication of the Emperor Charles V; see A. G. Pingré, *Cométographie ou traité historique et théorique des comètes*, Paris, 1783, I, 502–507; E. Biot, *Catalogue des comètes observées en Chine, 1230–1640*, Paris, 1846, p. 12; J. Williams, *Observation; on comets from 611 B.C. to A.D. 1640, extracted from Chinese annals*, London, 1871, p. 83

[2] Cf. Migne, *Patrologie Latinae*, XXV (Paris, 1884), edition of St. Eusebius Hieronymus 'Commentarium in Ezechielem', col. 371–372.

APPENDIX

Relation[1] *of the chronicle of the Kings of Ormuz,*[2] *and of the foundation of the city of Ormuz, taken from a chronicle composed by a King of the same kingdom, named Pachaturunxa,*[3] *written in Arabic,*[4] *and summarily translated into the Portugal tongue by a Religious of the Order of St. Dominic who founded in the island of Ormuz a house of his Order.*[5]

WHEN King Mahometh[6] was reigning in Amão,[7] which is in the interior of Arabia Felix, at the beginning of his reign, desiring to extend his kingdom and fame, he assembled in council the chief men of his kingdom, and said to them,

[1] I have reprinted here Donald Ferguson's translation of this early version of Túrán Shāh's Chronicle, from *The travels of Pedro Teixeira with his 'Kings of Harmuz'*, edited by W. F. Sinclair and Donald Ferguson (Hakluyt Society, Second Series, Vol. IX, London, 1902), pp. 256–267. I have also reprinted that learned translator's notes, with a few unimportant variations, such as the deletion of most of his cross-references to Pedro Teixeira's own version. Any major additions or interpolations of mine are distinguished with the initials C.R.B.

[2] The writer spells the name 'Hormuz', but when the preposition *de* happens to come before it he combines the two words thus, 'Dormuz.' Cf. The *Tractado das cousas da China*, where 'Ainão' becomes 'Dainão' in the same way. I have retained the alternative spelling in the text—C.R.B.

[3] Padishāh Turán Shāh. Padishāh is a Persian title, roughly corresponding to Emperor.

[4] In point of fact it was written in Persian. The mistake (repeated later by Pedro Teixeira) probably arose from the fact that after the conquest of Persia by the Arabs, the Arabic characters were substituted for those previously used in writing Persian.

[5] As noted in the Introduction, it is not clear whether Fr. Gaspar da Cruz visited Ormuz before or after his journey to China (cf. lix–lx above), and the date of the foundation of the Dominican convent at Ormuz has not been ascertained. Cf. Silva Rego, *Documentação*, VII, 493, 511.—C.R.B.

[6] Muhammad Dirhem-Kub. No dates are given here or elsewhere in this account for the reigns of the early kings of Ormuz. Ferguson (*Travels of Pedro Teixeira*, 153–155), tentatively suggests A.D. 1100 as the approximate date of the founder Muhammad. Sir Arnold Wilson, (*The Persian Gulf. An historical sketch*, etc. Oxford, 1928, p. 104), suggests a century earlier; while Henri Cordier (Yule-Cordier, *Marco Polo*, I, 121) splits the difference at A.D. 1060—C.R.B.

[7] 'Omān. See G. P. Badger, *History of the Imams and Seyyids of 'Oman* (Hakluyt Society, First Series, Vol. 44), p. 1 ff.; A. T. Wilson, *The Persian Gulf*, pp. 77–83.—C.R.B.

that the territories on the coast of Persia had belonged to his predecessors, and through the carelessness of some of them had been
lost, depopulated and wasted; that he had determined to cross over
to them in person with the chief men of his kingdom who wished
to follow him, and with certain of the people, in order to found
some cities and towns in that country, so that it might become of
profit, since it was a good land. And thus his kingdom and fame
would be increased; and he would leave to govern Arabia his
eldest son, who was a man that would rule it well. All having agreed
that his determination seemed good to them, he at once commanded to make ready a large force, many of his chief men
following him; and setting out from Amão he came to Calciate,[1]
which is near the sea in the same Arabia.

It seemed good to him and to his followers to found in that port
a city, inasmuch as it was a place suitable for those of the country
to trade with the ships that passed that way; wherefore his son
remained there with many people, carrying out the determination
of his father and those of his council; and the city went on prospering in the course of time to such an extent, that at the present
day its ruins show the city of Calciate to have been a very great and
noble one.

King Mahometh, having given orders regarding the affairs of
Arabia and those of Calciate, embarked, with the people that he
had selected for his company, in a large number of ships that he
had commanded to be made ready, and crossed over to the coast
of Persia, arriving at the Cape of Jasques, which is where Hormuz
now is,[2] thirty leagues outside the strait.

And seeing that land and its position, it did not seem to him
suitable to make a settlement there; wherefore he continued his
journey into the strait along the coast, and arrived at a tract of
country that they then called Hormuz, which is near that which
they now call Magostam,[3] and Braamim[4] which they now call

[1] An error for 'Caliate', which is repeated in the other places below where the
name occurs. Kalhāt, a little north-west of Rās-al-Had, the eastern point of
Arabia.

[2] These words seem to have got in here by some mistake, Cape Jashk (Jask)
being a long way from Ormuz, as the writer himself shows a few lines further on.

[3] Mogistan or Mughistan, the district of Persia east of the strait of Ormuz.

[4] 'Braamim' may be represented by the Bandar Ibrahim of some maps, the
Khor Minaw (Minab) of our charts and the *Persian Gulf Pilot*, on the Persian
mainland east of Ormuz. If so, its lands would be those about Minaw or Minab.

x

Costeca;[1] it is over against what is now called Hormuz on the coast of Persia. The King and his followers being pleased with the country determined to settle and make their residence there; and they therefore at once set about building houses and improving the country. And because this King was very liberal, and showed much favour to the poor people of the country and the husband-men, and entertained strangers well, he was very greatly and uni-versally beloved by all those who had knowledge of him. And the fame of his virtues and nobility spreading to all parts round about, many people came to live under his protection and rule. This was the reason why, in a very short time, this new city became very illustrious. The fame of his virtues and goodness spreading to all the kings of that strait, both of Persia and of the other parts of Arabia, they all sent to seek him with great presents, showing the great pleasure they had at having him as a neighbour. This King, seeing himself prosperous in this country and in favour with all his neighbours, and with much people, in order the more to gain the love of all, commanded money to be coined, which was lacking in the country, the which greatly increased the love'of all towards him, and at the same time the prosperity of his country. Because of this benefit that he conferred on all that country by inventing money for it, they generally called him Deranquu which means, 'stamp of money'.[2]

After the city of Ormuz had been founded on the coast of Persia, and had become prosperous with much people and riches, the King commanded his chief men to go to the territories of Magostam and to take each one what seemed to him best, in order that he might improve it and cause it to be inhabited, by founding divers towns. This they did; and each one took the land that seemed good to him, and improved it, and caused it to be inhabited; and each one gave to the land that he occupied his own name, by which every one of those countries is called today. And because the kings that succeeded Mahometh were powerful and very good in governing, they kept the country prosperous in their succeeding reigns, increasing in population and nobility.

[1] Kuhistak of modern maps. It lies SE. of Ormuz, on the Biyaban coast, and opposite Rās Musandam.

[2] The possession of a mint and special coinage being a royal privilege through-out the East, this was an assertion of independent sovereignty. The etymology given is correct, being derived from the Persian *diram* =money, and *kob* = striking. Purchas (II, 1785) has 'seale of money'.

And the sons that descended from these were continuously
such, that the fathers in their lifetime intrusted to them the
government of the kingdom, they themselves taking their ease in
their old age.

It was the custom among these kings, in order that the memory
of their predecessors might not perish, that when they reached the
tenth generation, they began their denominations anew, the ten
following beginning to take the names of the ten preceding. So that
the first of the ten had to take the name of the founder. And thus
in order until the number of ten was completed. This order was
preserved for some years, the rule going in the direct line.[1]
Afterwards this order and custom perished, because some,
through covetousness of reigning, put to death the others, and
many were blinded by others who wished to have the rule of the
kingdom. But there is one great and notable thing about this
kingdom, that although many governed tyrannically, putting to
death the rightful kings, up to the present time there has never
reigned any one that was not of the royal line.[2] Only that, as
Hormuz was on the coast of Persia, on the death of one who then
reigned,[3] and there being in the country none of the royal family,
the Goazil, that is, the governor of the kingdom declared himself
king.[4] At this time a son-in-law of the deceased king, who was his
nephew, had gone by command of his uncle with a large armed
force against the island and city of Cays.[5] The news was brought
to him that his uncle had died, and that the Goazil had declared
himself king; whereupon he at once raised the siege of Cays and
with all the men that he had with him set out for Ormuz. Arriving
there, he was received by all with very great manifestations of
delight and rejoicings, because they were very sorrowful at having

---

[1] Teixeira's version makes no mention of any such custom, nor is the statement borne out by the names of the kings as recorded.

[2] This is not consistent with the statement in Teixeira's version (*Travels*, 160)
that 'Amir Bahadin Ayaz Seyfin', the fifteenth king of Old Ormuz and founder
of the island kingdom, was a slave.

[3] 'Mir Xabadin Molongh', the ninth king, according to Teixeira (*Travels*,
158).

[4] *Goazil* or *guazil* is the Portuguese corruption of *wazir*, an Arabic word of
Persian origin for a functionary whose power and dignity varied greatly. Here
used for the effective head of the administration; a prime minister.

[5] Kais (Qais) or Keys island, lies within the Persian Gulf, about three degrees
west of Ormuz island and half a degree south of its latitude.

for a king a man who was not of the royal family; wherefore, with great rejoicings, they proclaimed as king the nephew of the king. He at once commanded the Goazil who had set himself up as king, and all his followers, to be beheaded.[1]

After the direct line of succession to the throne had been broken, there was not such good rule in the kingdom, nor did the affairs thereof prosper, but rather they went on falling into decay, so that it no longer had such power to resist its enemies. War among the neighbouring kings increasing, it happened that the king of Cremam,[2] which is in the interior of Persia, came with many men and powerfully equipped against Hormuz to destroy it. The King Cabadim,[3] who at that time reigned in Hormuz, not daring to await the attack and power of the king of Cremam, embarked with all the people that could go, and, leaving the country abandoned, betook himself to the island called Queixome,[4] which is near to the island of Ormuz. After he had been there a few months, it appearing to him that he was not safe there, on account of its being somewhat large, so that he could not well defend himself there, he thereupon crossed over with his people to the island that is now called Hormuz, because it was more convenient, thinking that he could there better defend himself against any foes.

This island was formerly uninhabited, except by a few poor fishermen; and they called it Jarum, which means 'bush'.[5] For the whole island is as it were of salt, and the soil almost entirely impregnated with salt, because certain streams that flow through it, which come from a hilly range in the midst thereof, are of saline

---

[1] Teixeira gives a somewhat different account of these events (*op. cit.*, 157–158).

[2] Karmān, Kermān or Kirmān, one of the maritime provinces of Persia. The reference is evidently to the Mongol conquest of this province, of which Old Ormuz then formed a part, although in point of fact the Mongols hardly touched the coastal fringe. Cf. Teixeira, *Travels*, 160–161, 260; A. T. Wilson, *The Persian Gulf*, 75, 104.—C.R.B.

[3] Mir Bahdin Ayaz Sayfin, the fifteenth king of the line. The Dominican friar's 'Cabadim' is probably a printer's error for 'Bahadim'. Cf. Teixeira, *Travels*, 260; A. T. Wilson, *The Persian Gulf*, 104.—C.R.B.

[4] Kishm or Quishm.

[5] Purchas (II, 1736) has 'wood'; but I think that 'bush' conveys better the sense of the Portuguese *mato* here than either Purchas' 'wood' or Ferguson's 'jungle'. Ferguson adds that he could find no Persian word like *jarún*, meaning jungle; but that Johnson's *Pers.-Arab-Eng. Dictionary* lists *jaran* as meaning 'coarse, uneven, and stony ground' (*Travels*, 260). Sir Arnold Wilson gives Jerun (Zarun) as the original name of the island of Ormuz but offers no further explanation (*The Persian Gulf*, 104).—C.R.B.

water, and on the edges of the water is the salt as white as snow; and whoever wishes to cross the stream goes over on the top of the salt. And the tops of the hills[1] are also in some parts of salt, which the ships take as ballast to India. Nevertheless there grow in the soil some poor clumps of bush and trees, such as jujube-trees,[2] which yield certain fruit that the Portugals call little apples, like jujubes, but which are bad eating, and which obtain an existence by virtue of the rain-water. Thus because of the island being sterile, and producing only what I have said, owing to its being saline, they called it Jarum. Moreover, through being uninhabited, it was in former times smaller and more convenient than it now is; for even yet the people of the country show the places to which the sea used to come.[3]

King Cabadin then having disembarked on this island, and resolving to settle there, began to build houses for himself and his people to dwell in, and there they made shift with what they got by going to the countries round about. Moreover, because, when the king of Creman returned to his dominions, they went back again to resume possession of the lands they had formerly held, and cultivated them; and because the city founded in the island of Jarum prospered, and they made it the capital of the kingdom, those that succeeded gave it the name of Hormuz, which it retains up to the present time, which was the name of the chief city that they had on the mainland, and which was destroyed by the king of Cremam.

It is to be noted, that in this strait of Ormuz, some leagues further in than Ormuz, is an island called Cays, in which was founded in those times a very wealthy and very magnificent city, the memory of which continues even today among those of the country; and, though now the island is deserted, there are still seen the remains of the ancient buildings that existed there. This island and city were very wealthy, and very populous and prosperous, because of the great traffic of ships that came together there from all parts of

[1] I have ventured to substitute this expression for Ferguson's rendering, 'The peaks of the range,' which I feel implies high mountains rather than low hillocks. —C.R.B.

[2] 'Maceiras Danafega' in the original. According to Dozy-Engelmann's Glossaire des mots Espagnols et Portugais dérivés de l'Arabe, the word anafega is from the Arabic an-nabikat = the fruit of the lote-tree.

[3] The foregoing remarks are apparently from the Dominican friar's own observation.

India with many riches and very great quantities of merchandise; and owing to the great concourse of people from Persia and Arabia who came to that place to seek the wares that came there from India, also bringing very rich goods, in exchange for which, or for the money that they made by them, they bought those that came there from India. So that all the riches that Hormuz now has, and all the trade, were at that time possessed by the island of Cays, that which is now called Hormuz being, as I have said, uninhabited. At[1] the time that Hormuz was prosperous, on the mainland of Persia the kings were many times at war with the inhabitants of the island of Cays; and they had often come against it with great array of battle, killing many of the people, and inflicting many injuries upon it. The lord of Cays, seeing himself ill-treated by the king of Ormuz, made a treaty of peace with him, binding himself to be tributary to him. The treaty was made and confirmed, and those of Cays paid the tribute as long as the kings of Ormuz were prosperous on the mainland of Persia. But when these became weak and disorganised they were no longer willing to pay it. And because after the kings of Ormuz crossed over from the mainland to the island that they afterwards called Hormuz they continued to prosper greatly in people and in grandeur of buildings; and at the same time the ships that had regularly come from India to Cays now began to frequent Hormuz, whereby they withdrew much profit from those of Cays; the latter becoming frightened on account of their disobedience, and because they had rebelled in the matter of tribute, lest there should happen to them some evils worse than those they had received from the kings of Ormuz; and also fearing that these would prosper so in the trade as to deprive them of the whole of it (for they saw that their share was already diminishing); the lord of Cays wrote to a king of Persia to whom he was then subject, who was called the king of Xiras (which even now is a kingdom by itself),[2] that by all means and without any delay he would come with a large army to destroy the city that was in-

---

[1] All that follows, down to the end of the paragraph concluding with the words 'the conquest of Ormuz' is omitted by Purchas, who mentions this fact in a marginal note. Cf. p. 236, n. (4).

[2] Shirāz, capital of the province of Fars, which, in the Middle Ages, occupied practically the whole of the eastern coast of the Persian Gulf proper, extending from the Tab (or Hindiyan) River almost to the Strait of Ormuz. (A. T. Wilson, *The Persian Gulf*, 71.) For 'king' read 'governor'.—C.R.B.

creasing in prosperity in the island of Jarum; because if he did not do so Cays would lose the whole of its dominion, prosperity, and trade; since it was already being deprived of it by the city recently founded in Jarum. The king of Xiras gave no heed to this embassy and let it be understood that however much it might prosper it would not be difficult for him to destroy it at any time. Nevertheless the lord of Cays, seeing the danger resulting from delay, again wrote to the king of Xiras that on no account should he tarry, as great danger would result. And in order to make him understand the speed with which it was necessary that he should come, he used this metaphor: that he would know how much haste was needed, when he told him that his head remained dirty because he could not wash it.[1] The king of Xiras having seen this, at once got ready his forces, and proceeded to the island of Cays, where he prepared many boats, called by them *terradas*;[2] and in these crossed over with his forces to the island of Angam,[3] which is two leagues from Ormuz, where the king of Ormuz attacked him and gave him battle, and defeated him. And having been defeated, though not utterly, he sent a proposal to the king of Ormuz, that he should give up to him his treasures and those of his predecessors; and he would then go away and leave him in peace; and that, if he were not willing to do this, he would wage war on him with fire and sword until he had utterly destroyed him. To these words the king of Ormuz replied, asking, how a man of such low origin as he was, who was descended from merchants, dared to propose such a thing to a king who came of such an ancient race of kings, who in Amão were always most noble knights, and had always been so up to their occupation of that island which was now called Hormuz; and that he did not intend to be unworthy of his ancestry, wherefore he had nothing to fear from him. (Even yet the kings of Ormuz take to themselves much glory in being descended from such a very ancient race as the kings of Amão, and give themselves

[1] Only an Oriental could fully appreciate the significance of such a message.

[2] *Terrada* apparently derived from the Arabic *tarrād*, according to Dalgado, *Glossário Luso-Asiático*, II, 368–369. The name was applied to more than one type of sailing vessel used within the Persian Gulf. The best and fullest description of the type used in the region of Ormuz will be found in Padre Manuel Godinho's *Relação do novo caminho que fez por terra e mar vindo da India para Portugal no anno de 1663* (Lisboa, 1665), 84–85, which has apparently been overlooked by modern writers on this subject.—C.R.B.

[3] Hanjam or Henjam, just off the eastern coast of Kishm (Qishm) island.

out as related to a lord that lives in Arabia who is called Catane,[1] and despise the others, considering themselves better and nobler on account of antiquity than they.) Seeing himself thus affronted, the king of Xiras returned to Cays and reinforced himself afresh with troops, and more ships, and returned with greater force against Hormuz;[2] and, not daring to give battle to the king, strove cunningly to come to parley with him, and craftily seized him, and sent him captive to the island of Cays, and he himself proceeded to lay siege to the island of Ormuz. The siege was sustained by another, who had been elected king by advice that the king who was taken prisoner managed to send. The siege lasted several months. Then the king of Xiras, seeing that he could not take Hormuz, and that the winter was coming on, and that it would not be safe for him to go by sea, returned to Cays, with the resolve to come back once more against Hormuz in the following year.

He returned thence in six months, bringing with him the king of Ormuz whom he had captured. But on the voyage a tempest overtook him, which scattered and destroyed his fleet. And it happened in this dispersal, that the *terrada* in which was the king of Ormuz who had been captured came to land at Hormuz, where he who was acting as king was not willing to receive him with honour; wherefore after having been some days in Hormuz, he crossed over to Costeca, where Ormuz was formerly. Some days thereafter it chanced, that he who was acting as king of Ormuz found it necessary to go to war with a people that then lived where now dwell the Noutaques, who are great sea-robbers.[3] The real king, was was in Costeca, hearing of this, crossed over to Hormuz, and was received by the inhabitants as their king and lord, with great honours and rejoicings; and he reigned peacefully until his death. The king of Xiras did not care to tempt fortune again, and departed for his kingdom, abandoning the conquest of Ormuz.

The king of Ormuz,[4] seeing the evils that had come upon him

[1] Kahtán, or Joktan, from whom the tribes and districts of south-eastern Arabia traced their descent.

[2] According to Teixeira (*Travels*, 170), this was in A.D. 1315. He describes this second campaign in fuller detail than does the Dominican writer.

[3] Nōdhakī tribe of Balūchis.

[4] According to Teixeira (*Travels*, 173), this was the son of the king whose vicissitudes have just been related. Purchas resumes his translation at this point, having omitted all the foregoing details, as noted above, p. 234, n. (1).

through the Goazil of Cays, went against him with a large army, and having besieged him for some days without being able to conquer him, returned to Hormuz as the winter was approaching. He came back the following year, and took it and sacked it, and left in it a Goazil of his own choice, with many men. The defeated Goazil managed to escape, and fled in a *terrada* to the island of Barem;[1] by favour of the Goazil of Barem he equipped himself anew in Barem, and returned against Cays; and cunningly coming to parley with the Goazil whom the king of Ormuz had left there to guard the city, seized him and put out his eyes, and resumed the government of Cays. But there succeeding to the throne of Ormuz Pachaturunxa,[2] who was the author of this chronicle and who reigned some three hundred years ago,[3] a little more or less, he brought it under his rule; and from that time forward it always remained subject to the kingdom of Ormuz. And then this Pachaturunxa subjected the island of Barem as a punishment for the favour that it had given to the Goazil of Cays.

And so the kings of Ormuz went on prospering in such manner that they became rulers of all the islands in this strait, and all the country along the coast of Arabia as far as Lassa[4] and Catiffa[5] and also others on the shore of Persia, by which they formed a very great, rich and prosperous kingdom: principally because the trade of Cays passed entirely to the island that is now called Hormuz, wherefore Cays was utterly ruined, both in buildings and in wealth, so that it is now totally deserted, after having been the chief place of those parts.

And Hormuz, from having been a sterile and desert island, and a mountain of salt, is, among all the wealthy countries of India, one of the wealthiest, through the many and rich goods that come thither from all parts of India, and from the whole of Arabia and of Persia, as far as the territories of the Mogores, and even from Russia in Europe I saw merchants there, and from Venice. And thus the

---

[1] Bahrein or Bahrain, on the Arabian side of the Gulf, which was subdued by the ruler of Ormuz about A.D. 1320, as narrated below.

[2] Padishāh Tūrān Shāh, in A.D. 1347, according to Teixeira (*Travels*, 186).

[3] The original has *'reynou auera trezētos anos'*, but possibly *trezētos* is a slip of the pen for *'trinta'* (thirty). In any case, 'three hundred years ago', if the correct rendering, would not agree with the statement of Teixeira, that Tūrān Shāh reigned 1347–1378.

[4] Al Hāsa, the hinterland of Al Katif and Bahrein.

[5] Al Katīf (or Qatīf) on the Arabian mainland, NW. of Bahrein.

inhabitants of Ormuz say that the whole world is a ring and Hormuz is the stone thereof.[1] Wherefore it is commonly said, that the custom-house of Ormuz is a conduit of silver that is always running. The last year that I was in Hormuz—having been there three—the officials assured me that the custom-house had yielded 150,000 *pardaos* for the King of Portugal, besides what it is to be presumed is stolen by the Moors and the Goazil, who are officers of the customhouse.[2] And, even though this country yields no fruit, and has no water nor provisions, it has plenty of flesh, bread, rice, and much fish, and many and very good fruits, with which it is supplied from many parts, chiefly from Persia,[3] whence come many pears, and peaches, plums, apples, grapes, figs and quinces, of which they make marmalades to supply the whole of India. Thence also the whole of India is supplied with raisins for the sick, and with wine, and dried plums and almonds for the sick, and for delicious dainties. There also come thither many melons at two seasons, which are very good, with the stripes and of the appearance of those of Abrantes. The first arrive from the 15th of March onwards, up till about the end of April. Then come others that last from July to September. There is also much fruit that comes there from Persia and Arabia, which they call mangoes, which is a very good fruit.[4] The pomegranates that come from Persia are not surpassed by those of Seville. And the pears and

---

[1] The Dominican writer again quotes this well-known saying further on. Regarding it, see *Voyage of Pyrard de Laval* (Hakluyt Society ed.), II, 240, and footnote; Burton's *Camoens: Life and Lusiads*, IV, 504. Detailed accounts of Ormuz as it was under Portuguese rule, will be found in the Hakluyt Society editions of Duarte Barbosa (ed. Longworth Dames), I, 90–105; Jan Huyghen van Linschoten, I, Ch. vi; Pyrard de Laval, II, Ch. xviii; Pedro Teixeira, pp. 164–168; Tomé Pires, *Suma Oriental*, I, 19–21, to name only a few of the many sixteenth and seventeenth century travellers who have described 'the wealth of Ormuz and of Ind'.—C.R.B.

[2] Returns for the revenue of the Ormuz customs-house will be found in Simão Botelho's *Tombo do Estado da India* (ed. Lisboa, 1868), ff. 76, 78; the 'Tractate of the Portugal Indies' compiled by the Viceroy Dom Duarte de Menezes and translated under the above title in Purchas' *Pilgrimes* (ed. 1625), II, 1506–1533; cf. also the 'Regimento da Fortaleza de Ormuz', dated 20 August 1568, printed in P. Pissurlencar, *Regimentos das Fortalezas da India*, (Bastora, 1951), 164–193.—C.R.B.

[3] Here the translation in Purchas ends with an 'etc.'.

[4] Mangoes from Ormuz were extolled by Garcia d'Orta the famous Portuguese physician and botanist, in *Coloquio XXXIV* of his *Coloquios dos simples e drogas he cousas mediçinas da India* (Goa, 1563).

apples in December and January: all these fruits arriving in such condition that they appear freshly picked from the trees, and they are very good. There also come there from Persia many nuts, vegetables, oranges, lemons, and many other provisions. Of the merchandise I say nothing, because thither come all the riches of the whole world, and thence they go to all parts. So that with just reason they say, that the whole world is a ring and Ormuz the stone, though in itself it produces nothing but salt. It is very well supplied with water, both from the mainland of Persia and from the islands around.[1] So that, whilst having nothing itself, it has all the riches and abundance of everything that is brought to it from without.

[Colophon]

This treatise of China was printed in the very noble and always loyal city of Evora, in the house of André de Burgos, printer and knight of the household of the Cardinal-Infant. It was finished on the 20th day of February of one thousand five hundred and seventy.

[1] Kishm (Qishm) was one of the main sources of supply.

III. THE RELATION OF FR. MARTÍN DE RADA, O.E.S.A.

(a) *Narrative of his mission to Fukien* (*June-October*, 1575) (translated from Fr. Gaspar de San Agustín, O.E.S.A., *Conquistas de las islas Philipinas*, Madrid, 1698; pp. 313–323).

(b) *Relation of the things of China, which is properly called Taybin* (written late 1575 or early 1576, and translated from a Manila MS. of *c.* 1590 in the editor's possession).

(*a*) *Narrative of the mission to Fukien, June-October,* 1575
(translated from Fr. Gaspar de San Agustín, O.E.S.A., *Conquistas de las islas Philipinas*, Madrid, 1698)

CHAPTER XXIV

Of what happened to the Padres Fray Martin de Rada, and Fray Geronimo Marin in their embassy to China, until they returned to Manila with the Spanish Captains who accompanied them.

WE left the port of Manila on 12 June 1575, with the Captain Aumòn,[1] in a local native oared ship, because the Chinos had left theirs in Pangasinàn, when they went to interview the Governor. We had also left Sinsay[2] in Manila, so that he could take the crew and the prisoners of both sexes who had been taken in the fort, in another merchant-ship of China which was there. And we, navigating in very rough weather, took eight days to reach the islands of Bolinào, which are seven leagues on the hither side of Pangasinàn, where we found that Sinsay had arrived two days previously, since he had a better ship than we, and that he had gone on to Pangasinàn to interview the Camp-Master,[3] and to collect some money which was owed him by the soldiers for merchandise which he had entrusted to them. And we wishing likewise to go to Pangasinàn, it came on to blow so hard that we could not navigate in the ship which we brought from Manila, being forced to return to Bolinào on the same day that we left for Pangasinàn. And fearing lest the winds should increase before making our voyage (as often happens in these islands during the months of July and August), it was resolved that I should go to Pangasinàn, for one of the ships of Aumòn, and for the interpreter of the China language, whom we were to take, and who was there. And taking the smaller of the two ships, and leaving the bigger

---

[1] Wang Wang-kao, a *pa-tsung* or garrison commander over from two to three thousand men.
[2] As noted previously (p. xliv), I have not been able to identify this man.
[3] Juan de Salcedo.

243

and better to the Camp-Master, so that he could return to Bolinào, taking with me the interpreter and Sinsay, we finally left Bolinào in prosecution of our voyage to China on 26 July[1] of the said year of 1575.

After leaving the port of Bolinào, we navigated with fair winds until the following Sunday, when we sighted the land of China; and on Tuesday 5 July we entered into the port of Tiongzozou.[2] And for the honour of Our Lord I do not wish to keep secret that in the dangers in which we saw ourselves during a day and a night of storm, the Chinos told us that God had delivered them because of us Religious who were there: and they had abandoned on our account the ceremonies which they usually make in such perils to some idols which they carry in the poops of their ships, seeing that we had told them that they were vain, and that they should ask help from one true God alone. And if they did make some ceremonies to their idols, they did so in secret, without our seeing it. And the Captain Aumòn bowed deeply before our images, prostrating himself on the ground, and even saying that he would become a Christian. And, returning to our voyage, twenty leagues before we reached land, the sea-water looked very white, for we sounded the lead in less than eighty fathoms, and thenceforward it became shallower as we approached the coast.[3] In China, they already knew of our coming, through a merchant-ship which had

[1] *sic* for 26 June. A contemporary copy of Rada's narrative in the library of the Academy of History at Madrid (Codex CII, p. L of the 'Colleción Jesuitas') states that they left Pagasinàn river on 24 June and Bolinao three days later.

[2] Chung-tso-so (Tiong-tsò-só in Amoy dialect), an old name for the city of Amoy. This identification was correctly made by G. Phillips in the *China Review*, XIX, 44, 246, 325, and in *T'oung Pao* (1st series), VI, 457, but queried by Pelliot in *T'oung Pao*, (2d series), XXXIV, 194n, on the grounds that 'Phillips excellait en étymologies invraisemblables,' of which the learned French sinologue gives some typical instances. For once, however, Phillips was right and Pelliot wrong. Chinese maps of the Ming period, such as that reproduced on p. 316 from the *Ch'ou-hai-t'u-pien* of 1562, clearly depict the city and island of Amoy, under the name of Chung-tso-so. Chung-tso-so meant military defence-post, barracks, or cantonment (*lit.* 'middle-left-post'); but this military designation was also used as a place-name in this instance, as may be seen from the preface to the *Hsia-mên-chih* or *Gazetter of Amoy*. Cf. also *China Review*, XXI (1895), p. 99.

[3] The Madrid codex quoted in n. (1) above, states that they reached Amoy ('Tonçocu') on 8 July. The same source states that they estimated Amoy to be in 24° latitude, and at a distance of about 140 leagues from Bolinao. Amoy lies in latitude 24°36', but is nearly double the estimated distance from Bolinao.

arrived shortly before. The Governor of Chinchiu[1] knowing what was happening (having sent on his own account some ships in search of Limahon which had returned back again) was greatly vexed that those of Chinchiu had not found Limahon, and still more so when he heard the fine news that our men had done the pirate such harm. This Governor, knowing that Sinsay (who was from his governorship) was coming in our company, imprisoned one of his sons, and sent a captain with six ships to intercept us, and to take Sinsay prisoner by fair means or foul. Before these latter arrived, we found at the entrance to the river twelve ships on guard, six on one side and six on another. The commander of these ships came up with us for to see us, and learn what news; and he sent men ashore with letters to go post to inform the Governor of Chinchiu of our arrival at the port. On the arrival of the six ships from Chinchiu which came for Sinsay, there was a sort of skirmish about the matter, which caused us some alarm at the beginning until we learnt what it was about. However, the Chinchiu men finally went away without having effected anything.[2]

The entrance of that port was a fine sight, for besides being so large that a great number of ships could be contained therein, it was very safe, clean and deep; and from the entrance, it is divided into three arms of the sea, and so many ships were cruising under sail on each one of them that it was an amazing thing to see, for they were beyond count.[3] Before we reached the town of Tiong-zozou, (which was about three leagues up-river from the entrance of the port), whereof Aumòn was a native, three captains came out to receive us at sea, of those who are said to have a thousand men each under their charge, who told him that they came on behalf of the Governor of Chinchiu. And after many compliments (for it is a people that knows how to make them, and they weary one at times with so many compliments and ceremonies),[4] they produced

---

[1] Ch'üan-chou, as a rule, but from the context, Chang-chou may be meant in this particular connection.

[2] This episode is narrated at much greater length in González de Mendoza, *Historia*, Part II, Book I, Cap. xii.

[3] The Bay of Amoy forms one of the finest natural harbours on the China coast. The inner harbour is some two miles long, and from 400 to 600 yards broad. Both the inner and outer harbour have good depth and holding ground, but are not altogether secure from typhoons.

[4] An amusing observation from a man belonging to a race which was famous for strict observance of etiquette, protocol and punctilio.

Y

some refreshments of fruits and a collation. After this function in our ship, two of the captains returned to the town, and the third, who was called Yanlautia,[1] stayed with us, being apparently ordered to act as our guide and to accompany us on the whole journey that we were to make on shore without ever leaving us until our return. A little before we reached Tiongzozou, the whole garrison came out to receive us, being about five thousand men with their pikes, arquebuses,[2] and other weapons. They halted on a little hill, a short distance outside the town above the river; and as we approached, they left their post and marched along the shore as far as the disembarkation place. When our ship came to an anchor, she fired a salute with some pieces and arquebuses which we carried, and were answered with a return salute from the other ships which were anchored there. Forthwith the magistrate of the town sent us two written official permits, which stated that we were allowed to land as and when we pleased. And thus we landed where we found the said magistrate awaiting us, and he had brought chairs for us to be carried on men's shoulders. And as we did not wish to enter thus in the town, he ordered horses to be brought us, which we likewise declined to take, but insisted in going on foot, as we were close to the houses of the town. The concourse of people who came to see us was so great that we could not deal with them; and not only here, but in all the towns through which we passed, both going and coming, the people thronged the streets and the houses in which we lodged, although we were always in large houses with many courtyards and rooms, nor did it avail us to close the doors. Our only remedy was to drive them out forcibly, and when driven outside, they climbed on the garden walls and swarmed up the walls and roofs of the neighbouring houses, and they sometimes stayed staring at us until late at night.

This is related here at such length, so as to avoid repeating it every time that something of the sort occurs; for it was almost always thus along the whole way, at any rate in the cities and large towns. They lodged us in Tiongzozou in some chief community houses (for they have them in each town, and not one only, but

[1] Probably derived from the Fukienese, Ló-tia (Amoy), Lāu-tia (Ch'üan-chou), a mandarin, possibly with his surname prefixed.
[2] Miguel de Loarca, in his account of their arrival, expressly states that the Chinese at Amoy had no arquebuses ('Verdadera Relacion', Cap. 6).

three or four and more, according to the size of the place). There the magistrate gave us a banquet after their manner, and provided us with everything necessary in great abundance, both ourselves as the other Spaniards and our servants; as the Governor of Chinchiu had ordered should be done, not only here, but along all the road until we should arrive at the City of Hogchiu.[1]

Besides us [Religious], and the Spaniards Loarca and Sarmiento, there went in our company another Spaniard named Nicolas de Cuenca, whom the Camp-Master had sent to buy him some things there, and another lad called Juan de Triana, who had charge of the clothing and what else was necessary, and a native Christian Chino named Hernando, whom we took as interpreter,[2] besides twelve Philippine Indians as servants. In all the houses where we were lodged, there were majordomos of the same town who provided us with everything necessary, and other Chinos, who served in the kitchen and in everything else that was required.

On the day following that of our arrival at Tiongzozou, a Captain named Laulatia[3] came to visit us in great state, and he draped over the shoulders of each of us two pieces of woven silk, crossing them over the breasts somewhat after the manner of stoles.[4] The Chinos perform this ceremony with persons who have done something worthy of reward; and they did the same with Aumòn and with Sinsay, because even though this latter was a merchant he was held in esteem among them. And besides this, he had been in Pangasinàn, and been in contact with Limahon, and stayed always with our soldiers from the time that the tyrant's armada was burnt and the first attack was made on him, until returning to Manila with Aumòn and leaving with us for China. It having been decided that we should leave next day for Chinchiu, we all prepared and made ready, both we ourselves, as the Captain and other Chinos who were to go in our company.

On the morning of the next day, when we were due to start, we

[1] Foochow (Hok-chiu) in Amoy vernacular (Carstairs Douglas, *Dictionary*, p. 149).

[2] B. Laufer states that the party's spokesman was a Chinese Muslim ('Relations of the Chinese with the Philippine islands,' p. 260) but I cannot trace any such assertion in the Chinese records.

[3] Probably another confusion of *Ló-tia* or *Lāu-tia*, (mandarin), with the official's name prefixed.

[4] I cannot find any reference to this custom elsewhere, but cf. Groeneveldt, *Nederlanders in China*, p. 185, for a somewhat similar practice in 1623.

set forth from Tiongzozou, which is a town of up to three thousand householders, and went up-river in our ship of the Captain Aumòn, who did not wish to leave us until he had taken us to the Viceroy, and we arrived at a town called Tangua,[1] seven leagues distant from the port [of Amoy] as we found on the return journey by land. The whole of the garrison of Tiongzozou and the Captain Laulatia accompanied us in three ships as far as halfway and then they returned. We were greatly astonished to see so many towns on both banks of the river, and so close to each other that it could be said they were rather all one town than many.[2] And not only there, but as we found along the whole way to Hogchiu (a distance of about sixty leagues) it was populated in the same way. And they say that it is the same, or even more so, in the rest of China, save only in the province of Quantòn,[3] where the Portuguese trade, which, being a barren and mountainous region, is not so thickly peopled. The natives of these other towns through which we passed, have cultivated their land to such an extent, that even the tops of crags and rocks were sown, although it seemed as if no result of any kind could be achieved there; whence it appeared to me that this country is the most populous one in the whole world. When we reached Tangua, the *Corregidor* or chief magistrate of that city, who is called *Ticon* in their tongue,[4] behaved himself towards us as if he was of greater consequence than any person whom we had met hitherto; and I believe that he was so, since all the towns through which we had passed on our way from Tiongzozou belonged to his jurisdiction. For this reason, he did not come in person, but sent some honourable townsmen to visit us in the house where we were lodged, and to ask us that when we left on the next day, we should pass by his house and enter it to see him. On that evening there came a dispatch from the Inzuanto (for

---

[1] T'ung-an-hsien, lying at the extremity of a bay to the north of Amoy. G. Phillips gives the local pronunciation as Tang-oa. Cf. Yule-Cordier, *Marco Polo*, II, 233. Carstairs Douglas, *Dictionary*, p. 475, has Tâng-oa[n].

[2] Loarca is even more emphatic on the thickly-populated nature of this region, '. . . estaba lleno de gente y pueblos y preguntando por algunos decian que no hiciésemos caso de ellos que eran pequeñas y venido a averiguar eran de 2 mil y 3 mil casas.' ('Verdadera Relacion,' cap. vii.) T'ung-an district is still a rich and well-cultivated one.

[3] Kuangtung.

[4] *Chih-hsien*, or *Ti-koāi*[n] in the Amoy vernacular; the mandarin of a *hsien*. Cf. Carstairs Douglas, *Dictionary*, pp. 238, 490.

thus they call the Governor of Chinchiu),[1] which was a large board, whereon was written in broad characters his order or patent, in which he commanded that wherever we went, we should be supplied with everything needful.[2] It was also ordered that we Religious should be carried in large covered chairs, like litters, each one of which is borne on the shoulders of four men, and which are used by persons of quality. All of the soldiers and the servants were to be given horses, with a Chino on foot to accompany and to look after each one of them. Besides all this, each town was to provide the Chinos [coolies] who might be required to carry our baggage. And always, wherever we went, a man went ahead carrying the board with the patent, so that everyone might know how the Inzuanto had ordered us to be treated, and so that everything should be ready against our arrival. Although we Religious were very loath to be borne on men's shoulders, the Chinos who accompanied us explained that we could not refuse, for the Inzuanto would be greatly displeased with them and would order them to be very cruelly punished, unless they obeyed his orders to the letter. Moreover, they added that all beholders would regard us as base people if we were not carried in that way; for all honourable persons are carried in chairs on men's shoulders there, even when only going about the city to visit each other.[3]

On the morning of the next day which was Friday, we stopped on our way by the house of the Ticon (as he had sent to ask us to do), and we gave him thanks for the honour and entertainment which he had made for us in his town. He dressed each one of us with two little pieces of silk, as Laulatia had done. And these were the only two who girded us with them; for the others who gave us pieces of better silk and in greater quantity, namely the Inzuanto, and the Combun[4] and the Teutoc[5] (which are the names of persons

[1] *Hsing-Ch'üan-tao*, or *Heng-tsoân-tō* in the Amoy vernacular; the Governor or Inspector of Hsing-hua and Ch'üan-chou. Cf. *China Review*, XIX, 324–325; Carstairs Douglas, *Dictionary*, p. 125.

[2] *P'ai* or official rank boards. Cf. *Travels of Peter Mundy*, III, 171, 259.

[3] This was, of course, quite correct. Only servants and people of very low rank rode on horseback in South China, a litter or carrying-chair being used by people of any consequence.

[4] *Chün-mên*, or *Kun-bûn* in Amoy vernacular. Polite name for the viceroy of Min-Chê (Fukien and Chekiang) acting as commander-in-chief of the provincial troops. According to the *Ch'ou-hai-t'u-pien* of 1562 (chüan 4, p. 7a), the full title was *Tsung-tu-chün-mên*, and he was normally stationed in Chekiang.

[5] *Ti-tu*, or *Thê-tok* in Amoy vernacular. The full title was *Ti-tu-chün-wu-*

who have royal appointments as we will explain later) did not
gird us with them, and it must have been because the captains who
accompanied us informed them that we disliked being girded in
this way and laughed at it. This town of Tangua seems to contain
about ten or twelve thousand householders, and it is walled with
white square-stone. They say that this town together with its
adjacent villages contains about 150,000 vassals, and it is evidently
no exaggeration. Judging from what we saw, it seemed to us to be
the best provided of all that we passed through, and they were
many. For we passed along a street that was over half a league long,
and which throughout its length on both sides was a veritable
fish-market of different kinds of fish, although there was likewise
some meat and fruit; but most of it was stocked with fish, and in
such quantity that it seemed as if there would never be enough
people to consume what was there. They told us that this was the
ordinary state of that market, and I can well believe it; for we
found it as plentifully stocked on our return trip as if nobody had
taken anything.[1]

As soon as we left Tangua, we found many soldiers who came
to receive us by order of the Inzuanto. When we had gone about
two leagues further, we met a captain with a squadron of four
hundred men, drawn up in good order and armed with the
weapons which they use there, who had been sent by the Inzuanto
for to accompany us as far as the city of Chinchiu. And thus they
did accompany us in martial array, sounding their drums,
trumpets, shalms, and cornets, without ceasing to play until we
reached the city of Chinchiu, during the whole time of our journey
which took two days. For it is thirteen leagues from Tangua to
Chinchiu, and all as thickly peopled as we said above, and if anything rather more so.

chien hsün-fu-tu-yü-shih, and the appointment corresponded to that of a civil
governor or inspector concurrently commanding the local troops. May be
loosely translated as senior civil and military commander or Pacification Commissioner. His headquarters were at Foochow. (Ch'ou-hai-t'u-p'ien, Ch. 4, p. 7).

[1] The fishery districts of Amoy have always been noted for their abundance of
fish of various kinds. The hairtail in spring, the little sea-bream in summer
(catch about 10,000 piculs), and the sea-bream in autumn and winter (catch from
6,000–7,000 piculs) are the principal kinds of fish in the respective seasons.
Large quantities of salted and dried fish were exported from Amoy Bay to other
China ports in the halcyon days before 1937. Cf. J.G.R., Guide to China (1924)
334.

When we reached Chinchiu, they lodged us in a monastery of their friars, whom they call Huexio,[1] where, by order of the Inzuanto, they provided us with everything necessary in abundance, as they had done in the other towns. On the evening of our arrival, we went out to visit the Governor, and to give him thanks for the care which he had taken in ordering us to be received and provided for so lavishly. In the street we met the Tihu[2] (who corresponds to the civil governor of the city) who was much vexed with the [Chinese] captains who accompanied us wherever we went, because they were taking us on foot; and he made us go to his house, which he would not allow us to leave until they had brought some chairs in which to carry us. When we reached the house of the Inzuanto, they put us in one of the many ante-chambers which there are before entering into his withdrawing-room. He sent to tell us through our interpreter whom he had sent for first, that we had come thus far by his order, and that if we wished to see him, we would have to render him the same courtesy and humility that his captains made to him, which was saluting him upon their knees,—and that if we would not think of doing this, we could straightway return from whence we came. It seemed fit to us all that we should not boggle at punctilios in striving to attain the purpose for which we came and were sent; and we therefore agreed to conform to their ceremony, and they gave us entry so that we could speak to him.[3]

At the gate of the house of the Inzuanto, his guards were drawn up in two ranks with their weapons, forming as it were a way, and entering by a door, before reaching a hall where he was, there were two large courtyards, or rather one divided in the middle by a gate

[1] Ho-shang; *Hôe-siūⁿ* in the Ch'üan-chou vernacular. Buddhist monk or priest. The monastery where the Spaniards lodged was probably the K'ai-yüan temple whose celebrated twin pagodas are described and illustrated with great detail by G. Ecke and P. Demiéville, *The Twin Pagodas of Zayton* (Cambridge, Mass., 1935).

[2] *Chih-fu, Ti-hú* in Amoy vernacular. Prefect or governor of a *Fu*, the largest of the provincial sub-divisions.

[3] Loarca states categorically that he and Sarmiento were strongly opposed to performing the *kotow* (or *kowtow*),—as the Chinese ceremony of the 'three kneelings and the nine head-knockings' later came to be called by foreigners. He claims that the soldiers only reluctantly agreed to do so at the insistence of the two friars. One of the arguments on behalf of the governor of Ch'üan-chou, to induce the Spaniards to comply with his demands, was that 'asi hazian los portugueses'.

and paved walk. And besides this walk or way, which formed the principal entry, each of these courtyards had two other very broad walks or ways which ran next to the walls. The right-hand one is used by those who enter on business, and the left-hand one by those who leave; for the principal walk in the middle is used by none, save only the Governor and his servants, or those who accompany him, when he goes out in his chair. Beyond these two courtyards, there was another court or antechamber, a little higher and all paved, which was reached by some steps. On both sides of this were ranked certain heralds with their helmets, swords and shields. This is the place where the captains and warriors do their business; for even the Tihu, whom we mentioned above, (who is the second person after the Inzuanto), was in this place without entering into the hall, and the common people do not come so far, but do their business in the outer courtyard.[1] From this second courtyard we ascended by some other steps to a very large hall, in the which, a little over half-way, the Inzuanto was seated in a chair, with a table in front of him on which was a writing-desk and papers; while behind him stood a page who was fanning him with a large fan. This is the usual way in which business is conducted, not only with the Governors, but with the Viceroy, Visitor, Captain-General, Ensign-General, and all the Chief Justices; with some difference in the size of the courtyards and houses, and more or fewer men in the bodyguard, according to the rank of the personage concerned and the position which he holds. I have explained this here, so that it may not be necessary to repeat it when describing all the other officers with whom we had to negotiate. On our entering, the Inzuanto got up from his seat, and came forward as far as the steps of the hall door; and as we fell upon our knees, he made a very deep bow, and we asked him if we could get up, and we gave him the letters which we carried for him, and another which had been given us in the town, containing the list of the presents which were brought him. He forthwith ordered us to return to our lodging, saying that he would send for the present on the next day, as he did. And by the same people who came for it, he sent to summon Loarca and Sarmiento, and

---

[1] Cf. the description of a mandarin's yamen at Canton by Gaspar da Cruz, Ch. VI, p. 96–98, *supra* and the plan of an official mansion reproduced in De Groot, *Religious system of China*, I, Pl. 1.

another soldier whom the Camp-Master had sent, together with our interpreter, in order to inform himself in detail about the state in which Limahon was.[1]

On the day following, he sent to summon us to a very solemn banquet after their manner which was given in his house, at which he did not appear in person, but was represented by some captains.[2] Afterwards, he sent to summon us to take our leave, and to tell us that he wanted us to go to the Viceroy, whom they call Combun, in the city of Hogchiu; and although we wished to treat directly with him about the business on which we came, he told us that we could treat of it there with the Combun, and that the latter would give us a good dispatch. With this he dismissed us, and sent to give us captains and men who would accompany us and provide us with everything necessary until we reached the city of Hogchiu. The city of Chinchiu (where we were) has more than fifty thousand householders, exclusive of those who dwell in the suburbs of the city, which are many and great. The city is all walled round with high walls of stone, and has a most notable bridge over six hundred paces long, which is all paved with very fine flagstones, each one being about twenty paces long and a *vara* and a half thick, or a little more, and some less.[3]

We left Chinchiu on Tuesday, and it took us six days to reach Hogchiu on the Sunday, for it was a journey of about forty leagues,

---

[1] Loarca says that the resultant interview was not very satisfactory, owing to the ignorance of the interpreter employed who could not speak Mandarin ('la lengua cortesana') properly. The two soldiers protested against the Spaniards being made to kneel when interviewing senior mandarins, but did not get much satisfaction. They also got the impression that Wang Wang-kao and their own interpreter (whom they had to leave at the gateway of the yamen) were lying.

[2] Loarca gives a very full description of this banquet, as does Rada in the 'Relacion' translated below (pp. 287-290).

[3] The *Vara* was originally three Roman feet and is usually translated as 'yard'; but it varied very widely in different parts of Spain and the Spanish colonial empire, so I have preferred to leave the word untranslated. (Cf. 'Evolution of weights and measures in New Spain', in *Hispanic-American Historical Review*, XXIX, February 1949). From Loarca's more detailed account, it is clear that the bridge was the Shun-chi-ch'iao at the south side of the city, on the main road to Chang-chou, which was built about 1200, and was 1,500 feet in length. It was repaired in 1341 and 1472, and provided with stone railings, carved with figures of warriors, guardians, deities and pagodas. See G. Phillips, 'Some Fuh-kien bridges' in *T'oung Pao*, (1st Series), V, 7-8; Groeneveldt, *Nederlanders in China*, p. 149; Ecke, *Twin Pagodas of Zayton*, p. 4.

on which we passed many towns and large places.[1] Although the country was rocky and rugged, the ways were very good for the most part and the pavings very broad. We passed by the city of Linhua, which, as they told us, had been plundered a few years before by the Japanese.[2] These destroyed it in such a way, that not only did they wreck the houses in the suburbs, but even some parts of it within the principal wall are still uninhabited; and with all this, they say that there are over thirty thousand householders in the portions which are still inhabited. When we reached the city of Hogchiu, they came out to receive us by the way, as they had previous notice of our arrival, and accompanied us to our lodging which was outside the city in a very large suburb, which they say is two leagues long,[3] and by the Viceroy's order a captain came to see us here. On the next day we went to visit him, and (omitting the description of the palace wherein he lived, which looked like a great city) we went in to see the Viceroy or Combun, making him the same ceremonies as we had done in Chinchiu with the Inzuanto. However, the Combun did not move from his chair, which was a majestic throne; but he answered us with very courteous and most complimentary words, thanking us for kind usage in coming to see him from such distant lands. After receiving the letter which we brought for him, he ordered his captains to accompany us to our lodgings, which were some very beautiful and large houses next to the city wall, and on the inside thereof. He ordered the city magistrates to take care to provide us with everything which we might need, and to punish anybody who might annoy us. When we were in our lodgings, forty[4] armed soldiers arrived at nightfall and stood sentinels over us in great silence.

On the next day, the Viceroy sent for the present, and gave us a very solemn banquet, at which three of the chiefest captains were

[1] Loarca (Cap. ix) says they took seven days to go from Ch'üan-chou to Foochow and the Madrid Academy Codex says they took five. Affonso Ramires states that the Portuguese prisoners of 1549 were eight days on this stage of their journey. Cf. Appendix I below.

[2] Hsing-hua, also romanised as Hingwa. Departmental capital situated on the coast in latitude 25°28′. The Madrid Academy Codex, has 'Ynghua'. For the sack of Hsing-hua by Japanese raiders in 1562, see A. Tschepe, *Japans Beziehungen zu China*, 295, 304; Tsunoda-Goodrich, *Japan in the Chinese dynastic histories*, 138.

[3] Probably the southern suburb (Nan-t'ai). Cf. Doolittle, *Social Life of the Chinese*, I, 18.

[4] Sixty, according to Loarca (Cap. ix).

present in his name and by his order; and during the banquet all the soldiers of the company were drawn up in the courtyard of the house, and outside of it, waiting for them. On the next day we sent the Viceroy a memorial, because he had ordered it thus, in which we notified him of our arrival, and that we had not come to negotiate about human concerns, nor were we of a profession which sought the things of this world, but those of Heaven; and that, therefore, what we wanted was that he would allow us to preach the true God, in whom consisted all bliss, and that this was likewise the desire of our Catholic King of Castile, whose friendship we promised him. And forasmuch as it was impossible for us to explain to them this most important doctrine, without our first learning the language of the country, we begged and besought him to give us leave and approval to stay in his country, in the place which he should assign to us, so that we could learn the language of the country, and its manners and customs. The Viceroy received our memorial with the appearance of agreeing to everything which we asked him; but he added that as he was not empowered to make such decisions, he would have to submit the matter to the Emperor, who resides in his court at Pegkin, so that it could be reviewed by his councils there, and a decision taken as to what to do in a matter of such importance. The Viceroy asked many and very curious questions through our interpreter about ourselves, our manners, power, and customs. He was much astonished at our replies, since the China nation is so presumptuous that they consider themselves to be the first in all the world. He was greatly surprised to learn that we likewise had a script and that we used the art of printing for our books, as they do, because they used it many centuries before we did.[1] And so that he could believe it, he sent to ask us to send him a printed book, and we having no other which would serve to gratify his curiosity on this occasion sent him a Breviary, wherewith he was undeceived in his belief that they alone were those who enjoyed the ingenious invention of the printing-press. However, what appealed to him most were some representations of Christ Our Lord on the cross, and the pillar, and others of Our Lady and different saints, which served as book-markers, and so he kept them, and sent to tell us that he

[1] Cf. T. F. Carter, *The invention of printing in China and its spread westward* (New York, 1931).

would hold them in great respect. The Viceroy also asked which were the most devout and familiar prayers among us. We told him the Pater Noster, and the Ave Maria, and the Creed. He asked for them to be explained to him, and showed great pleasure in hearing them, making a show of learning them from memory; and he spent much time in this and in other questions.

When the time came to dispatch us, he first summoned for that purpose a council of the chiefest persons in that province of Fokien, and they resolved that we should return to Manila, since it was not possible for us to stay in China until the Emperor had been informed about the matter, to whom they wrote in that council. They gave the same reason in the answer which they sent to the letters which we brought from Manila. The Viceroy gave order that everything necessary for our return-journey should be given us, and appointed some captains to accompany us. After we had handed over the presents which were mentioned in the letters, we left the city of Hogchiu, having stayed therein for thirty-five days.[1] This city is the largest which we saw in China, for according to what we could learn, it has 150,000 householders, and is the capital of that province called Fokien.[2] It is entirely surrounded with a wall of coarse marble stone, about three fathoms high and four broad. All the city is built of square stone houses, roofed with tiles. In some parts of it are very deep ditches of water, and within the city are many water-channels, like those of the city of Mexico, by which boats carrying whatever is wanted can enter and leave. It has four very large suburbs, the one by which we entered being about two leagues long, and they told us that the others were larger.

We journeyed by the same cities through which we had come, everything necessary being given to us with the same punctuality as on our coming, and even more bountifully. Everywhere we went, they came out to receive us with great pomp, and served us very splendid banquets. For the journey, they gave to us Religious carrying-chairs which were borne by eight men, while Loarca and Sarmiento were given chairs carried by four men, and the other servants of our company had horses, everything else necessary for

[1] Thirty-seven, according to Loarca (Cap. xi), who gives a much fuller account of their stay in Foochow.

[2] Cf. Doolittle, *Social Life of the Chinese*, I, 18-19, where the total population is estimated at about a million in 1860.

our journey being likewise provided. For this purpose, a retainer always went in advance with a board which was inscribed with the above-mentioned edict, so that everywhere we went we should be provided at the cost of the royal exchequer with everything needful, in accordance with our standing as ambassadors. In all the places where we arrived, they came out to receive us with notably courteous ceremonies, and the mandarins and magistrates treated us to splendid banquets after their manner, with great kindliness and courtesy. This entertainment was difficult enough to bear, as it was so continuous in all the places along the road; although much more so were the extraordinary questions which they asked us through our interpreter, which were no little trouble to understand and still more difficult to answer satisfactorily.

Having left the city of Hogchiu on 22 August 1575, we reached the port [of Amoy] at the beginning of September.[1] After quickly preparing for our voyage, we set sail on the 14th of the same month, and navigating with variable winds, we reached a river which is but a short distance from the island of Pehou,[2] whither we were holding our course. And entering further in, for it was very great and mighty, we learnt from the country people that the pirate Limahon had anchored in it with his fleet over a month ago; for having left Luzon in a very shattered state he had gone thither, since it was his old haunt, to repair and refit himself from the damage he had suffered. For out of thirty-seven ships which he had taken from Pangasinàn, he had only brought eleven; of the which, only the one in which he came was of any size, another two being rather smaller, and all the others were small and ill-furnished, most of them being without sails. We were greatly vexed at this news, for we had believed that Limahon was already destroyed; however notwithstanding, we suspended our judgement until we could learn for certain the truth of what had happened. Aumòn and Sinsay summoned a council of the captains and military commanders in order to decide what should be done in this case. Some were of the opinion that information thereof should be sent to China, so that a fleet could be sent to seize him. Others said, and among them were Aumòn and Sinsay, that we should go against

---

[1] Loarca says they left Foochow on the 23rd and reached Amoy on 29 August (Cap. xi).

[2] P'êng-hu, or Pescadores island group, in the Formosa channel.

the corsair, since we were numerous enough and our ships were large and strong; and according to the story of some fishermen, Limahon did not have his fleet together, but some vessels were in the river and others in Palahoàn, to seek provisions, and to cut canes to make sails. However, our General, who was of a very different opinion, did not agree with this, giving as an excuse that he had no orders to fight; that if he had been sent for that purpose they would have given him more ships and fighting-men, and that the veteran soldiers of Limahon were very courageous, accustomed to fighting and the terror of China, whereas his own were mostly raw recruits and inexperienced. He added that he had been sent only to conduct the Padres to Luzon, and to ascertain the condition of the blockade of Limahon, and that thus he would do nothing else,—but that if the others wanted to fight, they could go and he would not prevent them, even though he would not go with them. And thus they could do what seemed best to them, since his person would be no great loss to them, and he would go in one of those fishers' boats to China, to inform the Viceroy of the state of affairs and the reason why he returned. There were various arguments and opinions among them concerning this matter, and they finally persuaded themselves (perhaps from expediency) that the news which the fishers gave of Limahon was false, and that it was not possible for him to have left Pangasinàn in the way which they related; and they therefore ordered that nobody should speak further with the fishers on this affair, and that we should hasten on our voyage, without touching at the island of Tacan,[1] for fear of the stormy weather which was threatening.

We left Pehou at midnight on 11 October, and at dawn we were off some islets called Guenio,[2] towards the south, a quarter to the South-west. The following night, it came on to blow hard, with which two ships of the fleet parted company; one of them being that of Aumòn, in which we were, and another small one. Finally, after various storms and misadventures, the whole fleet reached the island of Luzon after five days sailing, although some ships arrived on the 28 October and others on the 1 November, one of the last ships being that of the General Siahoya Oxiaguac.[3] He and the

[1] Possibly an allusion to SW. Formosa. Cf. p. 264, n. (4) *infra*.

[2] Presumably the outlying islets of the Pescadores.

[3] I cannot identify this official as his name is not given in the Chinese records to which I have had access.

other captains were greatly vexed when they learnt that the news of Limahon's escape was true; albeit subsequently, as could be gathered from their own words and behaviour, the pirate's escape did not grieve them overmuch, since if he had been killed, their charge and employment would straightaway have finished, whereas they now had hopes that it would be prolonged for some time more.

(b) Relation of the things of China which is properly called Taybin
[by Fr. Martín de Rada, O.E.S.A.]

[Introduction]

The country which we commonly call China was called by Marco Polo the Venetian the kingdom of Cathay, perhaps because it was then so called; for when he came there, which was about the year 1312, it was ruled by the Tartars.[1] The natives of these islands call China 'Sangley',[2] and the Chinese merchants themselves call it Tunsua;[3] however its proper name nowadays is Taybin,[4] which name was given it by the King, Hombu,[5] who drove the Tartars out of China; just as formerly at different times

---

[1] Marco Polo was in China 1275–1292. As pointed out in the Introduction Fr. Martín de Rada was the first modern European to identify China, correctly and convincingly, with Marco Polo's Cathay—an honour which is usually ascribed to Ricci and his Jesuit colleagues.

[2] A word of uncertain origin which has provoked a great deal of discussion. Gaspar de San Agustín (*Conquistas*, I, 253) wrote 'Llaman los de la Isla de Manila à los Chinos, *Sangleyes*, que quiere dezir Mercaderes que vienen; y sale este nombre de estas dos palabras Chinas, *xiang lay*, que significan lo mismo'. This is the explanation given by most Spanish writers, although a Manila manuscript of 1590 in my own collection (cf. Pl. opposite), contains a coloured drawing of a Sangley couple, headed by the Chinese characters meaning 'constantly coming'. B. Laufer derives the term 'from a word in the Amoy-dialect "seng-li" to trade', in his article 'Relations of the Chinese to the Philippine islands', p. 268. Cf. also, Carstairs Douglas, *Dictionary*, p. 417 in voce *seng-lí*. Pelliot (*Journal Asiatique*, IV [1914], p. 201) and H. Bernard, S.J., (*Aux portes de la Chine*, p. 106 n.) have other but no more convincing explanations. As implied in Rada's text, the word is probably of Tagalog and not of Chinese origin; but however that may be, the term was originally applied by the Spaniards to Chinese in general but more particularly to those who came from Fukien ports. In the seventeenth century, the word gradually came to mean Chinese who were resident in the Philippines (as distinct from the visiting traders to whom it had first been applied) or those who had Filipino blood in their veins.

[3] Chung-hua (Tiong-hoa in Amoy vernacular), the 'Middle Flowery' kingdom; China.

[4] Ta Ming (Tāi-bîn in Amoy vernacular), or Great Ming dynasty which ruled China from 1368 to 1644.

[5] Hung-wu (Hong-bú in Amoy vernacular), year-period or reign-title of the first Ming emperor, T'ai-tsu.

常乷 Sangley

204

VIII. Sangley merchant couple
(From a Manila MS. of *c.* 1590)

it had other names such as Hanton, Tungzonguan, Tong Gu, Cantay.[1]

The things which we will treat herein concerning this kingdom will be part of them seen with our own eyes, part taken from their own printed books and descriptions of their country, because they take an interest in themselves; for not only do they have general and particular descriptions of their country, but printed books thereof, wherein are described in detail all the provinces, cities, towns, and frontier posts and garrisons, and all the particularities thereof, and the families and tributaries and tributes, and the gains which the King derives from each one of them.[2] Seven of these books came into my hands, different editions by different authors and of different dates, so that by comparing them with each other the truth could be thus better known. Withal as they are a people who know very little geography, geometry, or even arithmetic, they draw their illustrations very crudely, and even their distances and circuits very falsely, so that it is impossible to reconcile them in many places; however, I followed that which seemed to me most truthful, comparing it all with some of their rutters which came to my hands. As regards the distances, I greatly reduced them in some places from those stated in their books, because, even taking the distances separately and afterwards adding them together, they are very wrongly added in the books.[3] Thus as regards the size of the country and the distances, what is stated hereafter will be much less than what is found in their books, but I feel it will be more exact, and I leave the truth to subsequent experience when all the country will have been travelled. But in everything else I will follow what is written in their books, and we will call the country Taybin, because that is its proper name.

[1] Transcribed as 'Han, Ton, tzon, Guan, Tou, Gu, Cantey' in the Paris-*Rev. Agust.* version. In both instances, they are corrupted renderings of the Amoy vernacular versions of earlier Chinese dynasties, the Han, T'ang, Sung and so forth.

[2] Rada is probably referring to the provincial and regional histories and topographies (*T'ung-chih, Fang-chih, Fu-chih*, etc.) which are usually lumped together by modern writers under the generic name of 'gazetteers', as they are in the present work. It is also obvious that Rada must have acquired a copy of the celebrated atlas *Kuang-yü-t'u*, or some work (or works) closely derived from it. Cf. Introduction, pp. lxxxiv–lxxxvi, xc, above.

[3] As might be expected, Rada's own figures are not always trustworthy, for successive copyist's errors have further distorted the slips of the original translators.

z

As for the name of China or Sina, I do not know where the Portuguese could have got it from;[1] unless it be from some village or point of that name which they found in those parts, and which name they gave to the whole country, just as in these islands [Philippines] the Burneyes are also called Burneyen, as the former are called China.[2] However, there is no point in arguing about names, for the first discoverer calls the land by the name which he wishes, and it is left with it for ever.

1. Of the size of the kingdom of Taybin and its situation.

The kingdom of Taybin must be almost a thousand leagues long and four hundred broad, with a circuit of nearly two thousand and five hundred leagues. It is bounded on the east and on the south side by the Eastern Indian Sea of Further India, which the ancients called Serica.[3] It is bounded on the other and western side by a very large river which rises in some lakes about fifty leagues from the sea, and running many leagues towards the north, finally passes by the end of the wall which divides China from Tartary; and running for almost a hundred leagues outside the wall, it bends towards the east and enters China, almost dividing it in the middle, and finally flows into the sea in the province of Nanquim [Nanking or Kiangnan], after having run winding in and out for more than a thousand leagues of land.[4]

[1] The generally accepted derivation is from the Ch'in or Ts'in dynasty of 221–207 B.C. Compare p. 28, n. (3) above.

[2] I am aware that this does not make sense, but neither does the original, ... 'que en estas Yslas á los Burneyes con llamallos tanbien Burneyen los llaman tanbien China'. There is obviously some copyist's error here; but I presume that Rada was trying to explain that just as the (Malay) name of Brunei town in N.E. Borneo was applied by the Filipinos to the whole island and its inhabitants, so the name of China, derived from some prominent coastal feature, was applied by the Portuguese to China and the Chinese in general. 'Burney' is the Spanish phonetic transcription of Brni or Brunei, which was in fact applied by the Chinese and Filipinos to the whole island of Borneo. Cf. Hobson-Jobson, p. 107; W. P. Groeneveldt, Notes on the Malay Archipelago and Malacca from Chinese sources (n.p., 1876), pp. 101–103.

[3] Serica was the Latin word for the country of the Seres, whence came the silk exported to the Graeco-Roman world. Originally applied to the Central Asian region through which the silk came, it soon became loosely extended to cover most of East Asia.

[4] There would seem to be some confusion here between the Huangho or Yellow river, and the Yangtse, although both rivers at this period had their respective outlets into the sea in the province of Nanking (Kiangnan). The

On the north side [of China] is a magnificent boundary-wall of square stone which is one of the most notable works which have been made in the world; for it must be about six hundred leagues long, and seven fathoms high, and six fathoms broad at the bottom and three at the top, and according to what they say it is all faced with tiles. This boundary-wall was built by the King Cincio nearly eighteen hundred years ago according to their histories.[1] And although beyond the said wall there are many cities and towns as frontier garrisons against the Tartars, in which the king of China appoints two viceroys and three captain-generals, yet because this is something acquired and added since the expulsion of the Tartars, they are not counted in the kingdom of Taybin, even though they are subject thereto.[2]

The sea-coast of this kingdom is almost eight hundred leagues in extent. Beginning in 20° latitude, it runs in a nearly east-north-easterly direction as far as 25°, where lies the city of Hocchiu,[3] and thence north-east to latitude 29°; and thence the coast bends northwards, and sometimes north-north-east, as far as about latitude 45°, whence the coast bends again to the east, forming a sea like the Adriatic or Gulf of Venice, beginning at the province of Santoan [Shantung] and running for a hundred leagues towards the north-west.[4] From the end of this gulf as far as the capital or principal city of the kingdom of Taybin where the King resides and which is called Suntien,[5] it is not more than three days journey by a

reference to the Great Wall indicates, however, that it was mainly the Yellow river which Rada had in mind. In any event, Rada's statement that this great river had its origin in some lakes about fifty leagues from the sea is very wide of the mark, even when considered in the light of Chinese maps of that period. Cf. the Ming maps from the *Kuang-yü-t'u* reproduced in Fuchs, *The Mongol Atlas and the Kuang-yü-t'u*, Pl. 1, 3, 34–36, and Purchas 'his map of China', which is crudely copied from a Ming Chinese original in his *Pilgrimes*, III, 401–402, and *Pilgrimage*, pp. 436–437.

[1] The original wall as built by Shih Huang-ti of the Ch'in dynasty (221–210 B.C.) extended from the present province of Kansu to Liaotung. It was considerably repaired and improved in the Ming dynasty, particularly during the reign of Ch'êng-hua (1464–1487). Cf. the works quoted on p. 70, n. (1) above.

[2] Cf. F. Michael, *The origin of Manchu rule in China*, (Baltimore, 1942), pp. 25–38, for a description of the Ming organization in the frontier regions of Liaotung and Liaohsi (east and west of the Liao valley), which area roughly corresponded to present-day southern Manchuria.

[3] Foochow, or Fuchou-fu; from the Amoy vernacular form Hok-chiu.

[4] The gulf of Pei-Chihli or Liaotung. Rada is well out in some of his latitudes.

[5] Shun-t'ien-fu, the official name for the city and prefecture of Peking.

river upstream, but this river cannot be navigated by large ships. In my opinion, Suntien will be in about 50° latitude.

All this coast from latitude 29° where lies the city of Nin[g]po— or Liampo as they call it in the maps[1]—is clean and has very good ports, according to what they say. At any rate from what we could see of the coast of Hocquien,[2] it afforded great store of good harbours and deep and clean anchorages. For all along the coast are innumerable islands which all belong to the country of Taybin. Many of them are inhabited and many others are un-inhabited, and thus the sea between them seems like rivers. How-ever, from Ningpo upwards until after passing all the province of Nanquim, there are many sandbanks. And from there on-wards they say that the coast is clean, although the entrance of that gulf which I said begins at the province of Santon [Shantung], is said to be a very wild and dangerous sea; in such sort that they do not dare to cross it from point to point, but only by coasting it.

Besides these islands which lie near to the coast, there are a very large number of [other] great and populous islands; these I will describe as they are depicted in their draughts. Beginning at the extremity of the province of Canton, which we said lies in latitude 20°, from thence nearly forty leagues to seaward, they say lies the great and populous island of Cauchi[3] which is tributary to China. Over against the province of Hocquien [Fukien] and beyond Tacao which we saw, as is related in our narrative,[4] lies towards the north-

---

[1] Ningpo. Cf. Galeote Pereira, p. 5 above.

[2] Fukien, or Fuchien; from the Amoy vernacular, Hok-kien.

[3] Hainan island is here confused with Annam under the Chinese name of Chiao-chih (Kau-chí in Amoy vernacular). Cf. Galeote Pereira, p. 29 above.

[4] I cannot find in the narratives of Rada and Loarca any mention of 'Tacao' having been sighted on their voyage *to* China, though Rada mentions 'Tacan' in connection with the return voyage, cf. p. 259 above. In Ch. XII of Loarca's 'Verdadera Relacion' describing the return voyage to Manila, there is mention of sighting a 'tierra [or a 'sierra' in some copies] grande y muy alta', peopled by Indians like those of the Philippines, and the name of which island is variously given as 'Tacoaticam' and 'Tangua-tzva' which is probably the same as Rada's 'Tacao' or Tacan [=Tacau?]. From the context of Loarca's 'Relacion', it is probable that this must be identified with the high hills in the southern tip of Formosa, or (less likely) with the islets of Hsiao Liu-chiu, lying south of Ta-kou (or Takao) in SW. Formosa. Any resemblance bewteen Rada's Tacao and the modern Takao, however, must be purely fortuitous, as this city is of recent origin.

east of it the island of Zuansin,[1] and from thence towards the north-east, Lusin.[1] To the east of this lies Siaugy,[1] and from here to-wards the north-west lies the Lesser Leuquiu, the which lies to the east of Hocchiu [Foochow]. Then towards the north, lies the Greater Leuquiu. These islands are called Los Lequios in our maps.[2] More towards the north is Humal,[1] over against Chetcan.[3] From thence to the northwards lies Gitpon,[4] which we call the Japones, and further north than the Japones lies Tauçian.[5] And near the strait at the entrance of the gulf of Santon [Shantung] is Tanhay[6] and at the furthest extremity of Taybin is Halecan.[7]

We had neither time nor opportunity to enable us to learn the names of the peoples and nations which border on the land of Taybin, and therefore we here make mention only of those whom we call Tartars and whom they call Tacsuy.[8] These are they with whom they have had more wars and disputes than with any other nation soever, and who have given them most cause for concern.

2. *Of the provinces into which the kingdom of Taybin is divided.*

All of this kingdom of Taybin which is bounded by the afore-said wall and by that great river and the sea, is divided into fifteen provinces which they call Çe,[9] two of which are governed by high-

[1] I cannot identify these names, which are presumably the Amoy vernacular forms of some of the islands in the China Sea depicted in the *Kuang-yü-t'u*, and in the *Ch'ou-hai-t'u-pien* of 1562.

[2] As on most Ming Chinese maps, the Lesser Liu-chiu are here identified with Western Formosa, and the Greater Liu-chiu with the modern island group of that name, better known nowadays as the Ryūkyū.

[3] Chekiang; from the Amoy vernacular, Chiet-kang.

[4] Japan; from the Amoy vernacular, Jit-pun.

[5] Chao-hsien, Chōsen, or Korea; from the Amoy vernacular, Tiâu-sién.

[6] Possibly Têng-lai, a circuit in Shantung comprising Têng-chou-fu, Lai-chou-fu and Ch'ing-chou-fu, which looks very like an island in the relevant map in the *Ch'ou-hai-t'u-pien*.

[7] Possibly a reference to the Yalu river (Ya-lü-chiang) which formed the boundary between China and Korea. Phonetically, the Hei-lung-chiang, 'Black Dragon' or Amur river is more acceptable, but Ming control did not extend so far at this time.

[8] The Chinese (Mandarin) form of the word is Ta-Ta-êrh, whence the European *Tartar*. The name was originally applied to a petty tribe (or tribes) of the north-east corner of Mongolia, probably of Tungusic stock. It was later used by the Chinese writers of all Mongols, and finally applied both by Chinese and Western writers to the tribes inhabiting Central Asia and to the Manchus. Cf. Couling, *Encyclopedia Sinica*, p. 549.

Shêng in Mandarin; *séng* in the Amoy vernacular.

courts,[1] which are Pacquiaa and Lamquia.[2] Pacquiaa or Pacquin, where the king resides, is governed by its high-court, and Lam-quiaa or Namquin is where the seat of the kings was in old times, and thus it likewise was left with its high-court. Paquiaa means 'Northern Court' and Lamquiaa means 'Southern Court'; for the principal cities of both the provinces (which are Su[n]thien and Ynthien[3]) lie due north and south of each other and are 340 leagues apart. The other thirteen provinces which are called Pechinsi[4] are governed by viceroys.

To begin with Pacquiaa which is the chief province, and one whose bounds reach to the aforesaid wall, this has towards the east the province of Santon or Suatan[5] which extends to the sea, and also to the boundary-wall since the wall begins on the sea-shore. On the west side of Pacquia is Sancij or Suancij,[6] and then Siamsay.[7] The boundary-wall ends in this last-named province, after having covered thither a distance of six hundred leagues from the sea. Southwest of Siamsay lies Susuam,[8] which is bounded on the west by the great river which we formerly mentioned. From Susuan towards the south lies Cuychiu[9] and next to it Olam or Onnam,[10] which is the last of Taybin towards the south. To the west of this province are the great lakes where rises the above-mentioned river,[11] and some high mountain ranges, and on the south side it extends to near the sea, which boundary region I

[1] 'Audiencias' in the original. The reference is to the two metropolitan provinces of Pei-Chihli (or Peking) and Nan-Chihli (or Nanking), as explained on p. 4, n. (6) above.

[2] Peking and Nanking, from the Amoy vernacular forms, Pak-kia[n] and Lâm-kia[n].

[3] Shun-t'ien-fu, Peking (cf. p. 4, n. (4) above), and Ying-t'ien-fu, another name for the southern capital of Nanking, 1356–1645.

[4] Rada has here confused the thirteen 'ambulatory departments' (or provinces) with their provincial governors and comptrollers, the *Pu-chêng-shih*. Cf. Mayers, *The Chinese government*, p. 33.

[5] Shantung; from the Amoy vernacular Soa[n]tang. From the strictly civil point of view, Liaotung was regarded as a part of Shantung for such branches of administration as could not possibly be executed under military direction. Cf. F. Michael, *Origin of Manchu rule in China*, p. 31.

[6] Shansi; from the Amoy vernacular, Soa[n]-sai.

[7] Shensi; from the Amoy vernacular, Siám-sai.

[8] Ssŭch'üan, or Szechwan.

[9] Kueichou, or Kweichow; from the Amoy vernacular, Kúi-chiu.

[10] Yünnan; Hûn-lâm in Amoy vernacular.

[11] Cf. p. 262, n. (4) above.

judge to be a rugged land and the sea-coast unpopulated since there are no inhabitants dwelling there. From Onam towards the east lies the province of Cuansij or Cansay[1] which does not reach to the sea either, although it extends to near the coast. Next lies the maritime province of Cuanton or Sayntan[2] which is frequented by the Portuguese.

Continuing eastwards along the coast is the province of Fuquien or Hoquien,[3] whither we went, and further on lies Chetcan,[4] in which the coast bends towards the north, and above it lies Namquin or Lamquiaa,[5] and next after that along the coast is the last maritime province of Santon [Shantung] which we mentioned above. These are the provinces which bound all Taybin, and there are three central provinces which are Holam,[6] Oucun,[7] and Cansay.[8] Olam is surrounded by the provinces of Paquiaa, Santon, Lamquiaa, Oucun and Sancij. And coming from Olam towards Quansij, Oucun lies in between and a little to the south-west. And going from Oucun towards Fuquien, Cansay lies in between and a little to the south-east. We have given two names to most of the provinces, the one being in the courtly language and the other in the tongue of the province of Hocquien.[9]

3. *Of the number of the cities and towns of the kingdom of Taybin.*
The fifteen provinces of the kingdom of Taybin have two kinds of cities, some called *hu* or *fu*, and others called *chuy*.[10] The most

[1] Kuangsi, or Kwangsi; Kńg-sai in Amoy vernacular.

[2] Kuangtung, or Kwangtung; Kńg-tang in Amoy vernacular. 'Sayntan' is probably a copyist's error.

[3] Fukien, or Fuchien; from the Amoy vernacular, Hok-kièn.

[4] Chekiang; from the Amoy vernacular, Chiet-kang.

[5] 'Namquin ó Lamquiaa' in the 1590 Manila MS. I suspect that here we have the origin of the mysterious province of 'Tolanchia' which figures in so many of the editions of González de Mendoza's *History*. Cf. for example the Hakluyt Society ed., I, 22–23, 36. One or other of Rada's copyist's wrote 'ó Lamquiaa' [='or Lamquiaa'] as one word, thus 'Olamquiaa', hence 'Olanchia'. The initial 'T' probably derived from a misreading of ó. As noted previously, Lâmkia[n] is the Amoy vernacular form of Nanking.

[6] Honan; from the Amoy vernacular, O-lâm.

[7] Hukuang or Hukwang; from the Amoy vernacular, Ô-kńg.

[8] Kiangsi; from the Amoy vernacular, Kang-sai.

[9] i.e., in the *kuan-hua* (or Mandarin), and in the Amoy vernacular, respectively. Rada's interpreters were obviously from the region of the Bay of Amoy. Cf. p. 247, n. (2) above, and Appendix IV below.

[10] My italics. *Fu* and *chiu* in the Paris-*Rev. Agust.* copy which is preferable

important ones are usually called *fu*, each one of which has its own governor appointed by the king, except for the capitals of the provinces wherein the viceroys usually reside. However those that are called *chiu* are usually subject to the governor of some *hu*; although there are some *chius* which are not so subject, but have a governor of their own, and contrariwise there are some *hus* which are subject to the governor of another *fu*.[1] The towns are called *coan*.[2] There are, then, in all Taybin, 15 provinces, and 390 cities, of which 155 are *hus*; and there are 1,155 towns,[3] and the number of the villages is infinite, for each city and each town has a great number of villages subjected to it, some more and others less; and these cities and towns are divided in this manner.

In the province of Paquiaa [Peking] there are 27 cities, of which 8 are *hu*, and there are 115 towns. In that of Santon [Shantung] there are 23 cities, of which 6 are *hu*, and 89 towns. In that of Sansi [Shansi] there are 23 cities of which 4 are *hu*, and 9 towns. In that of Holam [Honan] there are 20 cities, of which 8 are *hu* and 97 towns. In that of Siamsay [Shensi] there are 28 cities, including 8 *hu*, and 94 towns. In that of Susuan [Ssŭch'üan] there are 28 cities, including 8 *hu*, and 105 towns. In the province of Chetcan [Chekiang] are 12 cities, including 11 *hu*, and 75 towns. In that of Cansay [Kiangsi], 14 [? 41] cities, including 13 *hu*, and 74 towns. In that of Hocquien [Fukien], 9 cities, including 8 *hu*, and 58 towns. In that of Cuanton [Kuangtung], 17 cities including 10 *hu* and 71 towns. In that of Cuynsay [Kuangsi], 55 cities, including 12 *hu*, and 58 towns. In that of Omlam [Yünnan], 60 cities, including 22 *hu*, and 34 towns. In that of Cuynchiu [Kuei-chou], 13 cities, including 8 *hu*, and another 8 towns.[4]

here, *chiu* being the Amoy vernacular form for *chou* or *chow*. In most modern western works, *fu* is translated as 'prefecture' and *chou* as 'department', but these are only very rough equivalents. Cf. Galeote Pereira, p. 5, n. (8) above.

[1] Probably *Chihli-chou* or independent departments, and *T'ing* or independent sub-prefectures are meant here. Cf. Mayers, *Chinese government*, p. 34.

[2] *Hsien*, usually translated as 'district'; from the Amoy vernacular, *koāi*^{n}.

[3] That is, 155 *fu*, 235 *chou*, and 1,155 *hsien*. It seems obvious that Rada used a copy of the 1566 edition of the *Kuang-yü-t'u* or some work closely based on it. That edition gives the corresponding figures as 159 *fu*, 234 *chou* and 1,114 *hsien*. In the 1579 edition these are revised to read 158 *fu*, 247 *chou* and 1,151 *hsien*. Cf. Fuchs, *Mongol Atlas and the Kuang-yü-t'u*, pp. 22–23; *Fonti Ricciane*, I, 14–15.

[4] The province of Nanking or Kiangnan was inadvertently omitted by Rada from his list. Comparing Rada's figures with those given in the *Ming-shih*, those for Peking, Shantung, Shensi, Fukien and Kuangtung are remarkably close,

Besides these cities and towns there are others which are not entered in the government and account of the provinces, which are 7 *hu* cities of salt-makers,[1] and another 11 on the border regions which are called *Conmien*,[2] and 4 called *Samuysi*,[3] and 11 *Canbusi*,[4] and 15 *ambusi*[5] and 1 *cantosy*[6] and 115 *Tionco*.[6] And thus the sum total of cities and towns is 1,720, all of which are surrounded by high stone walls; and apart from these there are many other walled places which are garrisoned all along the frontiers, both by land and by sea, as we sighted on our voyage at Tinhayue,[7] a very large walled town which they say has a garrison of 10,000 men, and afterwards Ti),nçoçou[8] which we mentioned previously. These two towns are not included in the above list, and in the same way all the coastline and the frontier districts are thickly studded with garrison towns which are not included in the list of cities and ordinary towns. I could easily put down the particular name of each city and town as they were all noted, but in order to avoid prolixity and as it seemed to me an unnecessary thing, I did not record them here.

One thing which should be noted is that in each province there is a city which is the head or metropolis thereof, and although this has its own name, yet it is also often called only by the name of the province. Thus Hocchiu [Foochow] which is the metropolis of the

while those for Chekiang correspond exactly. All the others differ widely, but how far these discrepancies are due to copyist's errors, and how far to the *Ming-shih* statistics relating to a slightly later period, I do not know. Comparison with the figures given in the *Kuang-yü-t'u* (cf. preceding note) and in the text to Martino Martini's *Atlas* of 1655 also show many coincidences and some differences. I suspect the *Kuang-yü-t'u* to be the ultimate source for Rada, Ricci and Martini alike, although not necessarily the same edition.

[1] The production of salt was a government monopoly and the salt-making districts were grouped into special administrative areas, but Rada seems to have misunderstood his informants, and I cannot disentangle his errors.

[1] I cannot identify this term and do not know if Rada is referring to the NE. or the SW. borders, although the latter seems most likely. Cf. p. 277.

[3] Possibly a garbled reference to the *Hsüan-fu-ssŭ*, pacification areas, or administrative districts in regions inhabited by aboriginal tribes such as the Lolo, or the Miao etc.

[4] Possibly *Chang-kuan-ssŭ*, similar to the above.

[5] Probably *An-fu-ssŭ*, another kind of the above.

[6] I cannot identify these two terms.

[7] Comparison with Miguel de Loarca's 'Verdadera Relacion' (Ch. 4) discloses that this place must be Chên-hai-wei, a *wei* or garrison town on the promontory south of the entrance to Amoy Bay. Cf. *Ch'ou-hai-t'u-pien*, Ch. 1, map nr. 13 *verso*, and Carstairs Douglas, *Dictionary*, p. 502.

[8] Chung-tso-so, the name of Amoy during the Ming dynasty, as explained on p. 244, n. (2) above, and in *China Review*, XXI, 99.

province of Hocquien [Fukien] is also often called Hocquien; and in the province of Cuanton [Kuangtung] the capital is Quinchiu [Kuang-chou] but it is often called Cuanton.[1] Similarly, in the province where the king resides which is called Pacquin or Pacquiaa, the principal city wherein the king always lives is called Suntien [Shun-t'ien-fu], which is to say 'Heavenly Abode', and here likewise this same city is also called by the name of the province Pacquiaa [Peking]. And always in most of the writings and books it is called Quinsay or Quiansay, which is to say 'the great Court'; and thus Marco Polo also called it Quinsay, although he interpreted the name of Quinsay as being 'Heavenly City', which does not have this meaning, as does its proper name which is Suntien [Shun-t'ien].[2] It is the largest city in all China, and according to what they say in their books, it takes two days journey to cross it.[3] The palaces of the King there are so vast that it is said they occupy the space of a city, where he has every kind of pastime. And they say that he never leaves his palace, neither does anybody see him, save only those who serve him and a few very important people; and there they regard him like a demi-God, and they tell some fables such as that no bird or animal drops dung on the roof or in the grounds of the royal household.

From Hocchiu [Foochow] where we were, to Paquiaa it is 80 days journey or 612 leagues, according to their books. And I have also gathered from these books that from Cuinchiu [Kuang-chou] which is the capital of Cuanton to Zuncien [Shun-t'ien] which is Paquiaa, is a distance of 103 days' journey[4] and 783

---

[1] 'Cantonese abroad often use Kwang Tung in a general way as meaning either or both city and province': *China Review*, XIII, 225.

[2] Quinsai has been identified since the days of the Jesuit M. Martini with Hangchow, the capital of Chekiang province and from 1139 to 1276 the metropolis of the Southern Sung dynasty. Rada's statement or rather implication that Quinsay means *ching-shih*, 'the capital', is correct; but its application to Hangchow is still a matter for discussion among Sinologues. Cf. A. C. Moule, 'Marco Polo's description of Quinsai', in *T'oung Pao*, XXXIII, 106–128, especially pp. 106*n* and 121*n*. As noted previously, Shun-t'ien-fu can be translated as 'the city obedient to Heaven'.

[3] Cf. Galeote Pereira, p. 30, n. (1) and Gaspar da Cruz, p. 90, n. (1) above.

[4] Foochow is just over 2,000 miles from Peking, and Canton about 2,400 miles; but postal couriers under the imperial régime occasionally covered this last distance in 15 days. Cf. *Harvard Journal of Asiatic Studies* (April, 1938), pp. 12–46, for further details.

leagues. I do not wish to record the distances from all the other cities and towns to Paquiaa as it seems to me superfluous, although I have taken note of them all.[1]

4. Of the fighting-men, garrisons and weapons.

In all the provinces of Taybin, there is a very great number of fighting-men, some of whom are natives of the provinces wherein they serve, and who are called *Cun*, and who form the largest part.[2] These men do not wear arms, nor do they use them, nor (I believe) do they even keep them in their houses; for although we entered into many houses, we did not see weapons in any of them. They are merely men who are appointed to man the city walls for defence when necessity arises, and each one has his allotted place to which he has to repair. Where we saw this most clearly was in Hocchiu, where, as the wall is faced with bricks,[3] it has many casemates, and in each of them is inscribed the name of the squadron which has to repair thither, and each squadron consists of about ten men. These same men are responsible for rebuilding their section of the wall if the top or some other part of it falls down. At regular intervals along the wall there was a house with a garret above it; these are used as sentinels' posts or guardrooms during the time of siege; and in each one of these is inscribed the name of the captain (whom they style Cey or Çon[4]), who has to repair thither with his men. There was a distance of about one hundred ordinary paces on the wall of Hocchiu between one guardroom and another, and some seventeen, twenty, or twenty-two casemates, and similarly in the other cities and towns. Even where the wall is not faced with brick,

[1] A table of distances from each of the provincial capitals to Peking and to each other will be found in the text of Martini's *Atlas*, 1655.

[2] *Cun* is probably derived from the Amoy vernacular *kun*, meaning 'army' or 'soldiery' in general. Alternatively, it may be derived from (Mandarin) *chün*, the districts which were grouped together to form a *wei* or military guard post garrisoned by about 5,600 men of the local militia.

[3] The walls of Foochow had a circuit of about 7 miles, and were from 20 to 25 feet high, and from 12 to 20 feet wide, composed of earth and stones. The inner and outer surfaces were faced with stone or brick, and the top paved with granite flag-stones. Cf. Doolittle, *Social life of the Chinese*, I, 18.

[4] This is probably not the term for the commanders, but for the militia formations which they commanded, known as *so*, which were of two kinds, consisting of 1,120 and 112 men respectively. These *so* were subdivided into two 'general banners' of 50 or more men each, and ten 'small banners' of 10 or more men each. Cf. the works quoted in n. (2) on next page.

it has its openings in the battlements, inscribed with the names of those who have to man the walls and who are called Cun.[1] This post and duty is hereditary from father to son, and being styled soldiers they do not pay tribute.

The other sort of soldiers are strangers from other provinces who serve for wages, and among these must be counted the guards of the viceroys, governors, captains and justices, and all the men who serve these and the ministers of justice, sheriffs, constables and executioners, and likewise all the sailors who man the royal fleets and ships. As all these are reckoned among the number of fighting-men and garrisons, their number reaches an incredible total, amounting to 4,178,500 foot and 780,000 horse, distributed in the manner following,—[2]

Province	Foot	Horse
Paquiaa (Peking)	1,141,100	229,000
Canton (Shantung)	223,800	99,000
Sansi (Shansi)	152,600	32,900
Holam (Honan)	140,000	15,900
Siamcay (Shensi)	130,000	61,000
Susuan (Ssŭch'üan)	120,000	10,000
Oucun (Hukuang)	310,000	72,600
Lanquiaa (Nanking)	840,000	70,000
Chitcan (Chekiang)	160,000	40,000
Cansay (Kiangsi)	110,000	30,000
Hocquien (Fukien)	200,000	—
Cuanton (Kuangtung)	157,000	—
Holan (Yünnan)	170,000	80,000
Cunsay (Kuangsi)	100,000	12,000
Cuichiu (Kueichou)	160,000	37,400

Of these strangers, the bodyguards of the captains and governors and the guards of the city gates are continuously under arms.

---

[1] Hereditary militia.

[2] I do not know where Rada got his figures from, but for the organization of the Ming standing army and provincial militia, cf. E. Hauer, *K'ai-kuo Fang-lueh*, pp. 618–619, 645; M. H. Ch'en, *The invasion of China by Japanese pirates during the Ming dynasty*, pp. 151–154; K. M. Li, *The repulse of the Wô pirates by provincial and extra-provincial armies in the provinces of Kiangsu and Chekiang during 1551–1561* (Yenching Monograph Series No. 4, Peking, 1933); F. Michael, *The origin of Manchu rule in China*, pp. 49–50.

Their weapons are arquebusses, pikes and halberds, and other kinds of hafted weapons, some with scimitars and others made like sickles to cut the legs, and others with three prongs, as likewise scimitars and shields. They also use bows and arrows in war, both ahorse and on foot; and these archers hold a monthly review and are very skilful with their weapons.[1] We saw one in Hocchiu under two captains, each having about six hundred men, and it was admirable to see how speedy and skilful they were in what they had to do, even though their manoeuvres were not done in ordered array as we are wont to do, but in crowds and all huddled very close together.

Their artillery (at least that which we saw, and although we entered an armoury in Hocchiu) is most inferior, for it consists only of small iron guns.[2] On their walls they have neither bastions nor cavaliers[3] from which to play their artillery, but all their strength is concentrated on their gates. They make great use of incendiary bombs of gunpowder, particularly on board ship, and they put inside them many iron crowsfeet, in sort that nobody can walk thereon. They also use fire-arrows wherewith to burn the ship's timbers; also large numbers of great javelins with iron barbs on long shafts, as also broad-swords of half a fathom for boarding.[4]

[1] Miguel de Loarca ('Verd. Rel.' Part II, Cap. 5) likewise praised the dexterity of the Chinese archers in their target-practice, but added that the Chinese regular soldiery were in his opinion 'la mas vil que hay'. Rada elsewhere speaks slightingly of the Chinese as soldiers, and his praise of their martial qualities here is evidently restricted to peace-time practice. Cf. Introduction, pp. lxxvii–lxxviii and Gaspar da Cruz, Ch. XIV, p. 146, n. (3).

[2] Miguel de Loarca, as might be expected from his profession, gives a considerably more detailed account of Chinese artillery and military organization than does Rada, but his description ('Verd. Rel.', Part II, Cap. 5) is essentially the same. The Chinese had employed artillery since the beginning of the twelfth century, but Ming writers admitted that Chinese cannon were inferior to those of the 'Franks' or Fo-lang-chi. See Pelliot's erudite note on the Introduction of European cannon into China in T'oung Pao, XXXVIII, 199–207, and Carrington-Goodrich's notes in Isis, XXXVI, Pt. 2, 114–123, and XXXIX, 63–64. Cf. also Ch'ou-hai-t'u-pien (1562), chüan 13.

[3] Cavalier, 'a work generally raised . . . higher than the rest of the works . . . to command all the adjacent works and the country around', Shorter Oxford English Dictionary (ed. 1933), I, 279, quoting from a book on fortification dated 1560.

[4] Weapons of these types are described and illustrated in the Ch'ou-hai-t'u-pien of 1562, the Wu-pei-chih of 1621–1628, and E. T. C. Werner, Chinese Weapons, reprinted from JNCBRAS, VII.

5. *Of the population of the kingdom of Taybin and tributers and tributes.*[1]

Although it is not possible to state exactly the number of people that there are in such great and populous kingdoms, nor is it to be found in any of their books, yet some idea can be gained of the infinite number of people from the register of the tributers and other things which are recorded. And moreover some indication of their multitude is given by the fact that the fighting-men alone number nearly five millions. However, as regards taxes in general, it should be noted that in the provinces of Taybin the people are divided into households, some of which are gentry and the others tributers.

The gentry are known by the square bonnets which they wear, something like a clergyman's biretta, whereas the tributers have a round one. The gentry are nearly as numerous as the tributers, as we saw in all the places through which we passed.[2] Some of the tax-paying householders pay at the rate for six or eight or less tributers, although their households are much more numerous, as many of them told us, among whom was one called Jacsiu, who told us that there were seventy men in his household, and that he did not pay more taxes than for seven.[3] Another told us that there were about sixty men in his, and that he only paid taxes for four. In sort that the register of the tributers is much less [than it ought to be]; although the number of tributers is thus recorded in the

[1] i.e. Tax-payers and taxes.
[2] Rada is both confused and incorrect here. The 'scholar-gentry' ('hidalgos' in the original) as such were not exempt from taxation, but magistrates and scholars holding or awaiting official appointments were exempt from the poll-tax, as were also women and children, regular soldiers, eunuchs, Buddhist and Taoist monks, and relatives of the imperial family. The number of adult male exemptions at this period has been reckoned as high as twenty million by some authorities (cf. *Fonti Ricciane*, I, 15n) and Rada is probably confusing the scholar-gentry with the 'privileged classes' who were drawn from their ranks. Theoretically at least, all land-owners were liable to periodic assessment and tax on their holdings, with the exception of princes of the blood and some favoured high officials—a steadily increasing class at this period. Cf. H. Maspero, *Mélanges Posthumes*, III, 186–189, 211–212; *China Review*, VIII, 193–194, 259–270, 358–360, 391; IX, 129; X, 221, and XIV, 108; but the subject of Ming taxation is still obscure.
[3] I cannot identify this man, but his admission is an interesting one. Tax-evasion, in China as elsewhere, was undoubtedly widespread. Cf. p. 276, n. (2) and Gaspar da Cruz, Ch. X, p. 119, above.

馬箭

IX. Ming mounted archer
(From the *Ch'ou-hai-t'u-pien* 1600)

register of the families and tributers of each province which is reproduced herewith:[1]

Province	Households	Tributers
Paquiaa (Peking)	418,789	3,413,254
Santon (Shantung)	770,555	6,759,675
Sansi (Shansi)	589,959	5,084,015
Holam (Honan)	589,296	5,106,107
Siamsay (Shensi)	363,207	3,934,176
Susuan (Ssŭch'üan)	164,119	2,104,270
Oucun (Hukuang)	531,686	4,325,590
Lamaquiaa (Nanking)	1,962,818	9,967,439
Chetcan (Chekiang)	1,242,135	4,515,471
Cansay (Kiangsi)	1,583,097	7,925,185
Hocquien (Fukien)	509,200	2,082,677
Cuanton (Kuangtung)	483,380	1,978,022
Cuynsay (Kuangsi)	186,090	1,054,767
Onilam (Yünnan)	132,958	1,433,110
Cuyiuchiu (Kueichou)	148,957	5,132,891

Thus the total of the households which there are in all the fifteen provinces is 9,676,246, and the tributers are 60,187,047.[2] And in this accompt, the cities of the salt-makers are not included, nor the others which we said were outside the jurisdiction and register of the fifteen provinces, because they and their subjects are not in-

[1] Comparison with the corresponding figures in the copy of the *Kuang-yü-t'u* in the British Museum shows that Rada's figures coincide almost exactly with those, the few insignificant variations being due to printer's or copyist's errors. This B.M. version is apparently a Manchu reprint of a Ming edition whose exact date has not yet been ascertained, but many of the statistics in the *Kuang-yü-t'u* remained unrevised in successive editions. Cf. the figures from the 1566 and 1579 editions reproduced in W. Fuchs, *Mongol Atlas and the Kuang-yü-t'u*, pp. 22–23, where, however, the figures given for Nan- and Pei-Chihli in the first four lines of p. 22 must refer to the whole of China, as may be seen by comparison with *Fonti Ricciane*, I, 15, n. (4), and the Chinese original of 1579.

[2] According to Fuchs (*Mongol Atlas and the Kuang-yü-t'u*, pp. 22–23), the corresponding totals for households and people in the 1566 and 1579 editions of the *Kuang-yü-t'u* are 9,352,016 and 58,550,801, respectively. Carrington-Goodrich, *Short History of China*, (New York, 1943), pp. 198–199, gives the official census return for 1578 as 63,599,541, but adds that 'official figures are not satisfactory because they are based on the taxation of households and it was to the census takers' interest to withold some of the returns'. The census return for 1491 is given as 9,113,446 households and 53,281,158 persons in the Abbé Delamarre, *Histoire des Mings*, p. 406. Martini's figures in his *Atlas* of 1655 closely resemble those of Rada.

cluded in this register. Neither are many others, because they bring no profit to the king beyond sustaining the frontier garrisons of the western marches, and therefore no accompt is made of them in the books, save only their names are listed. But these contain not a few people, for in the seven cities of the salt-makers alone, an incredible number of villages are registered in the books as pertaining to them, —they say that there are 1,177,525 villages, which, even if they do not average more than thirty householders apiece, would amount to more than 35,000,000 people.[1] From this it will be seen what an infinite number of people there are in this kingdom; and in truth all the country through which we travelled was an ant-hill of people, and I do not believe that there is as populous a country in the world. The taxes which are levied each year by the king, when reduced to our weights and measures are as follows.[2]

Silver	2,863,211 ducats
hulled rice	60,171,832 *fanegas*
barley	29,391,982 *fanegas*
another kind of grain [*sic*][3]	139,535 *quintals*

[1] I cannot explain this statement about the salt-makers' cities which must be due to some misunderstanding, as stated in p. 269, n. (1) above. As regards other omissions from the census returns, these presumably refer to the aboriginal tribes in the pacification areas, and the inhabitants of the frontier garrisons.

[2] This list appears in a greatly expanded and altered form in González de Mendoza's *History*, Part I, Book 3, Ch. iv. A few items (rice, for example) are either identical or else have insignificant variations due to copyist's mistakes. Other items, however, are either wanting in Rada's list, or given in such widely differing quantities as to make it doubtful whether Rada's and Mendoza's figures are derived from the same source. The corresponding figures in Loarca's 'Verdadera Relacion' (Part II, Ch. xi) bear more resemblance to Rada's than to those of González de Mendoza, but do not coincide with either. Despite these discrepancies, I am inclined to think that our old friend the *Kuang-yü-t'u* was the ultimate source.

[3] 'De trigo llamado maíz' in González de Mendoza (*op. et loc. cit.*), who, however, gives a much larger total—20,250,000 *fanegas*. This seems to be rather an early date for the large-scale cultivation of maize in China, but González de Mendoza refers elsewhere to its growth—'between these trees they sow maize, which is the ordinary food of the Indians of Mexico and Peru' (*History*, Part I, Book 1, ch. iii). Loarca omits this item from his list. E. H. Parker (*China Review*, XIX, 192), after noting various Chinese names for maize, concludes that 'the entire absence of any uniform colloquial name for it is the best evidence that maize must be a very modern importation into China, and the frequent occurrence of the word *pan* or *p'an* suggests a foreign word'. On the other hand, the Spaniards were probably well aware of the difference between maize and millet, as the citation from Mendoza implies. The spread of maize from the New World

salt	5,990,262 *fanegas*
silken pieces of 14 varas	205,598
cotton cloth	130,870
raw silk	47,676 pounds
clean cotton ('algodon limpio')	12,856 *arrobas*
pieces of linen	3,077
petates[1]	2,590

All this is what they say belongs to the king, and is exclusive of all that is given to the judges, viceroys, governors, justices, captains and soldiers, for that is not included in this register. Only, we have included in the amount of rice, eight million fanegas, which is what is given for the rations of the king's bodyguard and for the city of Peking.[2]

6. *Of the antiquity of the kingdom of Taybin and of the changes which have occurred therein.*

In their chronicles dealing with the beginning of the population of their country (which likewise came into our hands), they tell scores of fables. For they say that the heaven, earth, and water were all joined together *ab eterno*, and that one whom they call Tayhu separated the earth from the heaven,[3] and forthwith there was born a man called Pancou[4] who never married nor had children, and after him was born Tionho with thirteen brothers, and this stock possessed the land for more than eighteen thousand years. Afterwards came Teyoncon with eleven brothers and this

to the Old merits further study. Cf. A. C. A. Wright, 'Maize names as indicators of economic contacts', in the *Uganda Journal*, XIII (March, 1949), pp. 61–81.

[1] Petate is defined as 'a liar, a cheat' in some Spanish dictionaries, and as 'a small mat', 'esterilla de palma', in others. Neither of these definitions makes sense in this context, and it would seem from a comparison with the Wan-li tribute items listed in the *Ming-shih* that 'fodder' is meant.

[2] Of the Spanish measures used by Rada, the *fanega* was usually equated with the English bushel, the *arroba* with about 25 lb. avoirdupois, and the *quintal* with the English hundredweight; but in practice they varied widely in different parts of Spain and Spanish America. Cf. p. 253, n. (3) above.

[3] T'ai Chi, the primal monad, primeval chaos, the great ultimate; T'ai I, the 'Great One', 'Great Unity.' Cf. Werner, *Dictionary of Chinese mythology*, I, 478–480.

[4] P'an Ku. Variously described as the chiseller of the universe out of chaos, he himself being the offspring of the *yang* and *yin* or dual powers of Nature, and as the actual creator of the universe. Cf. *China Review*, XI, 80–82; Werner, *Dictionary of Chinese mythology*, p. 355; Giles, *Biographical Dictionary*, nr. 1607.

family lived almost as long; and then came Sinhon with nine brothers, and they also lived a very long time. In sort that from the division of heaven and earth until there came the race of men who live nowadays, more than ninety thousand years passed, and all those beings they regard as saints.[1] After these, there fell down from heaven into the province of Santon [Shantung] a man called Ochisalan and a woman, who were nourished by heaven, and from these two are descended all the people in the world.[2]

After him came Sinon, and then Usau, who seeing that the people went about like savages, formed them into communities and taught them to build houses in trees.[3] Afterwards came a woman called Tayhou, whose son was Hoquiu Yntey, and this last had a son named Vitey who was the first king of China and reigned for one hundred years.[4]

Thus far everything is fabulous, but I consider that henceforward we have to deal with authentic history; and in order to avoid prolixity, I do not record the names of the kings, nor the time which each one of them reigned, but I will summarize briefly the changes which have occured. He and his descendants possessed the kingdom for 2,257 years and they were 117 kings.[5] After them, rose up one named Ciucion,[6] who built the boundary-wall which we described above, which is six hundred leagues long. And in order to make it, he mustered the entire nation in groups of three, first conscripting from every region one man out of three and then two out of five. As these came from such distant lands and went to such different climes, great multitudes of them died in the building

[1] Tionho, Teyoncon and Sinhon, are Rada's renderings of the Amoy vernacular forms for the series of Heavenly, Earthly and Human emperors (T'ien-huang, ti-huang and jên-huang) of the Fabulous Ages. Cf. Mayers, *Chinese Readers Manual* (ed. 1924), pp. 384–385; F. Hirth, *Ancient History of China*, p. 5.

[2] Loarca ('Verdadera Relacion') adds that 'Otzimtzalam' as he writes it, had two horns. This sounds like a version of the Fu-hsi myth, though I cannot explain how Shantung comes into it. Cf. *Chinese Repository*, XI, 173–176; Mayers, *Manual*, 385–387.

[3] Yu Ch'ao, the 'nest-having' sage, who is supposed to have induced the ancestors of the Chinese to settle in the bend of the Yellow river (in Shensi), and to have taught them to make huts of the boughs of trees.

[4] Great Yü, the legendary founder of the Hsia, or first of the official Chinese dynasties, c. 1989–1558 B.C. or 2205–1766 according to the traditional dates.

[5] Rada omits the second (Shang) and third (Chou) official dynasties from his list.

[6] Shih Huang-ti of the Ch'in, fourth of the official dynasties, 221–210 B.C.

of the wall. For this reason, a rebellion broke out against him, and they killed him and one of his sons, after he had reigned for forty years.

Next came the kingdom of Hancosau[1] and his family,—twenty-five kings who reigned four hundred and ten years. Against the last of these, called Jantey, one of his nephews, called Laupi, rose in rebellion and with the help of two very brave men, one of reddish colouring called Quanhu (whom the Chinese regard as a saint) and the other a black man called Tihunhuy, he came to the throne,— although the kingdom was then divided into three.[2] This division lasted for forty-one years, at the end of which time Chinbutey[3] rose in rebellion against the son of Laupi called Huctey,[4] and conquered the whole kingdom. There were fifteen kings of his line who reigned for 176 years.[5] The last of these, who was called Qiontey,[6] was deposed by Tzou,[7] and there were eight kings of his line who reigned for sixty-two years. The last of these, called Suntey,[8]

---

[1] Han Kao-tsu, founder of the Han, fifth of the official dynasties, which provided 27 emperors from 206 B.C. to A.D. 220. The usurpation of Wang Mang (A.D. 9–23) marks the division between the Former or Western Han and the Later or Eastern Han.

[2] The foregoing refers to the period of the 'Three Kingdoms', or three warring states which flourished A.D. 221–265, after the collapse of the Later Han dynasty. Jantey = Hsien-ti, last emperor of the Later Han. Laupi = Liu Pei, founder of the Shu-Han, sixth of the official dynasties, whose capital was at I-chou (Chengtu) in Ssŭch'üan. Quanhu = Kuan Yü, his faithful henchman who was later deified as the god of war. Tihunhuy = Chang Fei, or Chang I-tê, later deified as one of the gods of the butchers. This trio performed numerous exploits which are related at great length in the popular historical romance San-kuo-chih-yen-i, 'The Story of the Three Kingdoms.'

[3] Wu-ti, reign-title of Ssŭ-ma Yen, first emperor of the Chin dynasty which re-established the unity of China in A.D. 265.

[4] Hou-ti, grandson of Liu Pei, whose reign was ended in 263 by Wei (not Chin) conquest.

[5] The Chin, seventh of the official dynasties, had 15 emperors between 265 and 420. Divided into two branches, Western Chin (265–316) and Eastern Chin (317–420).

[6] Kung-ti (418–420).

[7] The (unofficial) Shu dynasty, with its capital at Chengtu, Ssŭch'üan. This was the first of the so-called Sixteen Kingdoms which fought among themselves in North China during the fourth and early fifth centuries. Rada naturally becomes confused here, and omits the tangled history of this period. Cf. Handbook of Oriental History, pp. 204–206, and Herrmann, Historical Atlas, 29.

[8] Shun-ti, last emperor of the Liu-Sung dynasty in Central and Southern China, who reigned 477–479. Eighth of the official dynasties.

was deposed by Cotey,[1] and there were five kings of his line
who reigned twenty-four years. The last of them, who was called
Hoctey,[2] was killed by Dian, whose line consisted of four kings
who reigned fifty-six years.[3] Then Tin rose in rebellion and there
were five kings of his line in thirty-two years.[4]

Afterwards there arose Zuy and the kingdom belonged to him,
his son and grandson, for thirty-seven years.[5] The grandson was
deposed by Tancotzou and there were twenty-one kings of his line
who reigned for two hundred and ninety-four years.[6] Then
[another] Dian rose in rebellion and he and his son after him ruled
the land for eight years.[7] The next to rise in rebellion was Outon,
who with another three of his descendents ruled for fifteen years.[8]
After this, Houtzin and his son reigned for nine years,[9] and next
came Cotzo and his son for four years[10] and then Auchiu and his
son and grandson for ten years.[11] Then Taytzou rose in rebellion
and there were seventeen kings of his line who reigned for three
hundred and twenty years.[12] The last, called Teypin,[13] fought
against Tziptzou,[14] King of the Tartars, who killed him and conquered all China, which was ruled by nine Tartar kings for the
space of ninety-three years. At the end of this time, Hombu of
the old royal line rose up and drove the Tartars out of the

[1] Kao-ti, first emperor of the Southern Ch'i, ninth of the official dynasties,
479–502. Cf. Herrmann, *Historical Atlas*, 32.

[2] Hê-ti, who reigned 501–502.

[3] Southern Liang, tenth of the official dynasties, 502–557. Cf. Herrmann,
Historical Atlas, 33.

[4] Southern Ch'ên, eleventh of the official dynasties, 557–589.

[5] Sui, twelfth of the official dynasties, 581–618.

[6] T'ang Kao-tsu, first emperor of the T'ang, thirteenth of the official dynasties,
618–906. Cf. Herrmann, *Historical Atlas*, 40.

[7] Later Liang, fourteenth of the official dynasties, 907–923.

[8] Later T'ang, fifteenth of the official dynasties, 923–936.

[9] Later Chin, sixteenth of the official dynasties, 936–946.

[10] Kao-tsu, founder of the Later Han, seventeenth of the official dynasties,
947–950.

[11] Later Chou, eighteenth of the official dynasties, 951–960.

[12] T'ai-tsu, founder of the Sung, nineteenth of the official dynasties, 960–1279.
Divided into Northern Sung (capital: K'ai-feng) and Southern Sung (capital:
Hangchow). Giles, *Biographical Dictionary*, nr. 168.

[13] Ti-ping, last emperor of the Southern Sung, 1278–1279.

[14] Shih-tsung, reign-title of Kublai (Qubilai) Khan, 1260–1294. Chinese
historians only accept the Yüan (or Mongol) as the official twentieth dynasty
from 1280, after the overthrow of the Southern Sung. Capital: Khanbalik, the
Cambaluc of Marco Polo, from 1267, on the site of the modern Peking. Cf.
Herrmann, *Historical Atlas*, 51–52.

country.[1] According to this reckoning 1,641 years elapsed from the time that the buildings of the boundary-wall was begun until the Tartars were driven out.

We could not find out exactly how long this present line had been reigning, for we could not get hold of its chronicle; but they say that the king now reigning is called Bandic,[2] that he is the twelfth of his line, and that he has reigned for three years, being about thirteen years old. They say that it is some two hundred years since they expelled the Tartars, to which if we add the 2,257 years of the kings who ruled before the wall was built, it is a wonderful thing to think that this kingdom has lasted so complete and independent of foreign peoples, save for the short time that the Tartars ruled it. If this history is true, they began to have kings shortly after the Flood, and they have been without any intermixture with foreigners since then.[3]

7. Of the manner of the people and of their customs and clothes.

The people of Taybin are all, on the one hand, white and well-built, and when they are small children they are very fair, but when they grow up they become ugly. They have scant beards and small eyes. They are proud to have a great head of hair. They let it grow long and coil it up in a knot on the crown of the head. They then put on it a hair-net, parted in the centre, to hold and fix the hair in position, wearing on top of it a bonnet made of horse-hair. This is their ordinary headgear, although their captains' bonnets are of another kind, made of finest thread, and underneath a hair-net of gold thread. They take a good time each morning in combing and dressing their hair.[4] The women do not make use of any hair-ornaments save only some garland, or jewelry of silver or gold, which they fix on the coils of their hair.

The women are very secluded and virtuous, and it was a very rare thing for us to see a woman in the cities and large towns, unless it was an old crone. Only in the villages, where it seemed that there

[1] Hung-wu, reign-title of T'ai-tsu, the first Ming emperor (1368–1398), who was not of royal blood but of very humble origin. Cf. Giles, *Biographical Dictionary*, nr. 483.

[2] Wan-li, reign-title of Shên-tsung, thirteenth Ming emperor, 1572–1620. Giles, nr. 452.

[3] Fr. Jerónimo Román, *Republicas del Mundo*, III, 226–227, has a long argument against accepting this Chinese chronology since it clashes with Biblical authority.

[4] Compare Gaspar da Cruz, Ch. XIII, p. 138, n. (1) above.

X. Ming Emperor and Empress
(From a Manila MS. of *c.* 1590)

was more simplicity, the women were more often to be seen, and even working in the fields. They are accustomed since babyhood to bind and cramp the feet in such a way that they deform them, leaving all the toes below the great toe twisted underneath.[1]

The men often let the fingernails of one of their hands grow very long, and are very proud thereof, as we saw by many of them whose fingernails were as long as their fingers.[2] Their ordinary dress is of cotton-linen,[3] dyed either blue or black, except when they wear mourning. Their dress is then made of another kind of coarse linen, and the nearer their kinship to the deceased, the coarser is the linen of their dress.[4] Their ordinary dress is a long loose upper-coat reaching down to the stockings, and a pair of long narrow drawers, and shoes made of straw. Some of them put underneath the coat, instead of a shirt, a silken net-work vest with a very wide mesh through which you can put your finger; and the captains who accompanied us, when indoors, took off their coats because of the heat, and went about in this net-work vest and their drawers. The pages of the captains ordinarily go with their hair coiled up on top and secured with a thread and bodkin thrust through. They wear stockings and straw shoes, likewise woven, but which look like nothing so much as silk mesh.[5]

The important people, and captains and governors, wear long silken gowns, usually of damask, reaching down to the ground, with very large and wide sleeves, and wide and large boots of dark colour, with the point of the toe turned up. To put them on, they first tie a large linen fillet round their feet and legs.[6] The boots and bonnets which differ serve to distinguish those who are officers of justice, or captains, and so forth. As a rule they have a great lion[7] embroidered on the breast and back of these silk gowns. The bonnets of the common people are round, and those of the gentry

[1] Cf. Gaspar da Cruz, Ch. XV, p. 149 above.

[2] Long finger-nails were a sign of gentility, as they implied that a man was above manual labour.

[3] *lienzo de algodon*, in the original. Presumably cotton-cloth is meant here. Cf. Trigault-Gallagher, *The China that was*, p. 20.

[4] Sackcloth. Cf. Gaspar da Cruz, Ch. XIV, p. 148, n. (1).

[5] For more detailed descriptions of Ming Chinese dress and footwear cf. Gaspar da Cruz, Ch. XIII, pp. 137–138 above; Trigault-Gallagher, *The China that was*, pp. 127–129; R. van Gulik, *Erotic colour prints of the Ming period*, I, 170–172.

[6] Thus looking rather like puttees.

[7] Dragon. Cf. Schuyler Camman, *China's Dragon Robes*, pp. 10–19.

square like clergymen's birettas, and all these are of horsehair, save when they wear mourning as we have said above. The viceroys, governors, captains, and ministers of justice when at home wear a bonnet like a bishop's small mitre with golden welts and embroidery. But when they go out in the streets or sit upon their thrones, they wear a kind of bonnet, the back half of which stands up nearly six inches and which moreover has, as it were, two wings or large ears sticking straight out at the sides.[1] These bonnets are worn by all the ministers of justice, and captains and viceroys. However, if any one of these captains or justices goes to interview one of his superiors, then he does not wear such a bonnet, but takes along a state-umbrella.[2]

The King's bonnet, as I have seen it depicted in many places, is of the same shape as that of the justices, save that it is square, and the two wings which we described are not so large, nor placed at the two sides, but are high on the back part, sticking up like horns. The bonnet of the secretaries or scriveners likewise has its ears, but they are made very differently from the others. The bonnets of the judges and the councillors of the king also differ from the others in the placing and shape of the ears. The bonnets of the students are shaped like letter-carriers or caskets, highly gilded and polished. Those of their friars are shaped like mitres, but differently from the captains' described above; and they fashion something like rosettes out of the folds of the front part of these bonnets, so that by the form of the bonnet you can know who a person is and what office he has.[3]

They are a plain, humble and obliging people, save only the mandarins[4] who set themselves up as gods. They are great workers

[1] 'like the bonnet of the Dodge of Venice', as Fr. Jerónimo Román aptly explains in his *Republicas del Mundo*, III, 218.

[2] *Sombrero* in the original. Parke in his 1588 edition of González de Mendoza, translates this word as 'hat'; and a broad-brimmed hat was then as now its common meaning in Europe. In Asia, however, *sombrero* (*sombreiro* in Portuguese) meant state-umbrella(s) in general and those of China in particular, as may be seen from the numerous quotations given in *Hobson-Jobson*, p. 851, and Dalgado, *Glossário Luso-Asiático*, II, 314–316.

[3] Neither Rada, Cruz, nor Trigault succeed in describing the rather complicated forms of Ming headgear with crystal clarity; readers desirous of more accurate information, should consult the wood-cuts in Ming works such as the *Jên-ching-yang-ch'iu*, or contemporary paintings of Ming scholars and officials. Cf. also Peter Mundy's drawings in his *Travels*, III, Pl. XIII.

[4] *Mandadores* in the original, which I have translated here and subsequently as 'mandarins'. The Iberian word was not, as is so often alleged, the origin of the

and very active in their trades, so that it is astounding to see how diligently they furnish their works, and in this they are most ingenious. There are to be found entire streets for each trade.

With the exception of the mandarins and soldiers in garrisons, everyone has his own proper employment. Although they have little sumpter-mules and little asses and pack-horses, they also employ men to carry burdens, like the natives of New Spain. But one Chino will carry as much as three Indians of New Spain, and thus laden they will go almost as well as a horse. It is easier to find men for carrying burdens than it is animals; nay, many times they dispute with and strike each other over who will carry the burden. Thus when we approached a place whence we were to begin the next day's journey, no sooner were we descried from the village or the ploughed fields, than many people ran out to meet us, vying with each other as to who should take some of the burdens; and many times they took them over from those who were carrying them as much as half a league before the village, in order to stake their claim to carry it on the next day, solely for the gain and pay thereof; and at times they came to fisticuffs as to who should carry it.[1] Their manner of carrying the burden is in two bundles or hampers slung at either end of a pole carried over their shoulder. If it is a very heavy burden or chest, they carry it slung from a pole between two of them. They usually travel six or seven leagues a day, and when they put down their burden they return to their own village,—I suppose that they return there to sleep.

When their principal men go out, even if it is only to visit a friend in the city, they go in large canopied chairs, carried like biers on men's shoulders.[2] The other people go either ahorse or afoot. When the sun is fiercest everyone carries his own sunshade[3]

latter term, which is really derived from the Sanskrit *mantri*, 'a counsellor', 'a minister of state'. Cf. *Hobson-Jobson*, pp. 550–552; Dalgado, *Glossário*, II, 20–22.

[1] All this will sound very familiar to anyone who travelled in the interior of South China before the Pacific War.

[2] Sedan-chairs, *chiao-tzŭ*. For their various categories, cf. Couling, *Encyclopedia Sinica*, p. 36.

[3] *Tirasol* in the original. Minsheu's *Dictionarie in Spanish and English* (London, 1599). has '*Tirasol, or Quitasol*, a kind of hat used in China verie broad, which the principall men carrie over their heads, with a short pole or staffe like a canopie, to keep the extremitie of the sun from them'. Peter Mundy retains the original Spanish and Portuguese forms in his journal; but *quitasol*, which was once anglicized as *quitasole* and *kittysol*, has long been obsolete. Cf. *Hobson-Jobson*, p. 487.

and a fly-whisk, however poor or lowly he may be. If any common man, through illness or exhaustion, wishes to go in a chair, he has to go in a lowly little chair of cane, forasmuch as only the captains and justices can go in the large and covered ones. The higher their dignity, the richer their chair. The principal persons have their chairs all decorated with broad and well-wrought bands of ivory on gilded planks which are very fine and well worth seeing. There is in each community-house a great quantity of chairs of different kinds, for the visitors who come there to make use of, according to their quality.

They are a people who use many compliments and civilities. They do not doff their bonnet or hat to anybody, but when they meet each other, instead of doffing their bonnet, they put their hands in their sleeves, and clasping them together they lift them up as high as their breast. And when they wish to be more courteous, instead of making reverence as we do, they make a deep bow, with their hands in their sleeves as described above, their hands reaching nearly to the ground, and their head lower than their knees; and then straightening up, they bring their hands close to their breast. And they are not satisfied with one of these bows, but make three or four, or more. If four or five of them meet together, each one makes his bows. Even when they are discussing business, from time to time they put their hands in their sleeves and raise them to their breast.[1]

They have scores of other kinds of ceremonies. Both in dealing with as in receiving or in going out to accompany any superior, they kneel down on both knees, and putting their hands in their sleeves and up to their breast, they bend their head down until their forehead touches ground, and this they do three times or more.[2] While they are speaking, they never get up, but listen and answer on their knees to what is said to them. Even to us, the common people sometimes spoke on their knees, and bowed their heads to the ground. And some of those who had been in Manila laughed at the Spaniards who did not bend more than one knee in church, saying that if anyone had bowed in that way on only one knee to a

[1] Cf. Gaspar da Cruz, Ch. XIII, pp. 138-139. For the way in which greetings were regulated between people of various ranks, cf. Trigault-Gallagher, *The China that was*, pp. 98-104; Gray, *China*, I, 348-361.

[2] The *kotow* or *kowtow* as foreigners later called this ceremonial prostration. Giles, *Glossary*, p. 73.

mandarin, he would have been soundly whipped. For this reason, those who have to deal very often with a mandarin are wont to carry along some knee-pads.[1] Likewise, when one goes to visit another, he usually takes a docket stating that he has come to kiss his hand, which he gives him after having made his bows. When one comes to visit another, after having made their bows and being seated, a household servant comes with a tray of as many cups of hot water as there are persons seated. This water is boiled with certain somewhat bitter herbs, and with a little morsel of conserve in the water. They eat the morsel and sip the hot water. Although at first we did not care much for that hot boiled water, yet we soon became accustomed to it and got to like it, for this is always the first thing which is served on a visit.[2]

8. *Of their manner of eating, and of their banquets.*

The principal food of all Chinos is rice, for although they have wheat and sell bread kneeded therefrom, yet they do not eat it save as if it were a fruit. Their chief bread is cooked rice, and they even make a wine from it which is comparable with a reasonable grape-wine and might even be mistaken for it. They eat seated at tables, but they do not use table-cloths or napkins; for they do not touch with their fingers anything that they are going to eat, but they pick up everything with two long little sticks.[3] They are so expert in this, that they can take anything, however small, and carry it to their mouth, even if it is round, like plums and other such fruits. At the beginning of a meal they eat meat without bread, and afterwards instead of bread they eat three or four dishes of cooked rice, which they likewise eat with their chopsticks, even though somewhat hoggishly.[4] At banquets, a table is placed for each guest, and when the banquet is a formal one, each guest gets many tables, and to explain this I would like to recount what sort of banquets they offered us, and the way in which they were served.[5]

[1] These knee-pads (Cantonese, *pau-sat*, 'wrap-knees') are described by Peter Mundy, *Travels*, III, 259. Cf. also Carstairs Douglas, *Dictionary*, p. 534 in voce *Tun (chháu-tún)*.

[2] For the serving of tea on such social occasions, cf. Gaspar da Cruz, Ch. XIII p. 140; Trigault-Gallagher, *The China that was*, p. 105.

[3] Chopsticks. Cf. Giles, *Glossary*, p. 26.

[4] Cf. the drawing of a Chinese coolie eating rice in *Travels of Peter Mundy*, III, Pl. XI.

[5] The following account is chiefly based on the official banquets which were

In a large room, at the top of the hall, they placed seven tables in a row for each one of the Religious, and along the side-walls five tables for each of the Spanish laymen who were there, and three tables for each of the Chinese captains who accompanied us. And next to the doors of the hall, opposite the Religious, sat the captains who had invited us, each one at his own table. In our room they had arranged on one side three tables bearing the covers for each one of us. All these tables were loaded as much as they could be with plates and dishes of food, save that only the principal table contained cooked meats, and all the uncooked food was on the other tables which were for grandeur and display. There were whole geese and ducks, capons and hens, gammons of bacon and other chops of pork, fresh pieces of veal and beef, many kinds of fish, a great quantity of fruits of all kinds, with elegant pitchers and bowls and other knicknacks all made of sugar, and so forth. All this which was put upon the tables, when we got up therefrom, was put into hampers and carried to our lodgings. In sort that everything which is put there for display all belongs to the guests.

Outside the door of the house where the banquet was held, was arrayed the whole bodyguard of our host, with their weapons, drums and musical instruments which they began to play when we arrived. The captains who were to be present at the banquet came out halfway into the courtyard to receive us, and without making any courtesy or bow we went together to a reception-room which was in front of the banqueting-hall, where we made our bows one by one according to their custom. With many ceremonies we seated ourselves there, each on a chair, and they forthwith brought the hot water [tea] which I have described above. When we had drunk this, we conversed for a short space, and then went to the banqueting-hall, where, after many ceremonies and courtesies which I omit to avoid tediousness, they conducted each one of us individually to the table where we were to sit. On this table the captains placed the first dish and a little cup full of wine. When everyone was seated, the music began to play, consisting of

tendered the Spaniards at Ch'üan-chou and Foochow, and which are also described in detail in Miguel de Loarca's unpublished 'Relacion Verdadera'. For other contemporaneous accounts of Chinese banquets, see Gaspar da Cruz, Ch. XIII, pp. 141–142 above, and Trigault-Gallagher, *The China that was*, pp. 106–112.

tamborets, gitterns, rebecks, lutes with a big arch, and they played continuously for as long as the banquet lasted.[1]

Other persons in the middle of the hall acted a play, and what we saw were elegant representations of old stories and wars, whose plot was explained to us beforehand, so that although we did not understand the words yet we well understood what was happening.[2] In Hocchiu [Foochow], besides the plays, there was a tumbler who did fine tricks, both on the ground and on a stick. Although the table be full of food, there is never any pause in the flow of broths and dressed meats. As long as the banquet lasts they drink healths heartily, although not with goblets but, as it were, in little saucers.[3] In drinking they are a temperate people as far as we could see. They do not drink wine continually but only water; and when they drink wine they drink it very hot, and they sip it like a broth, although they gave it us cold, as they knew that we did not drink it hot. They think it mean of the host to rise first from the table, but on the contrary as long as the guests are there, more and more dainties are continually served until they wish to get up. Even after we got up, they asked us to sit down again, begging us to wait for another one or two dishes, and this they did two or three times. Their manner of acting is with chanting, and they also usually act puppet-plays which go through all their motions, and men behind the scenes say what has to be spoken.

In their food they are not great meat-eaters, but on the contrary in our experience their principal food is fish, eggs, vegetables, broths and fruit. The things which we saw like unto our own (apart from many other different kinds) were fish, wheat, barley, rice, beans, millet and *borona*.[4] There were kine and buffaloes, and they say that there are also sheep the land inward; and we also

---

[1] Cf. Gaspar da Cruz, Ch. XIV, p. 144, n. (2) for the tentative identification of these instruments.

[2] From Miguel de Loarca's account ('Verdadera Relacion', Pt. I, Ch. ix), it is evident that this was a play based on *The Story of the Three Kingdoms*. Cf. p. 280, n. (2) above.

[3] Trigault noted that 'although their cups do not hold more wine than a nut-shell, the frequency with which they fill them makes up for their moderate content' (*The China that was*, p. 106). Cf. also *Travels of Peter Mundy*, III, 194.

[4] Minsheu's Spanish Dictionary of 1599 defines *Borona* as 'a kinde of graine in China', having evidently found the word in R. Parke's translation (1588) of González de Mendoza. Later dictionaries have 'a sort of bread made with Indian corn or millet', which does not get us much further. Cf. the note on maize in p. 277, n. (3) above.

saw pigs, goats, and hens like ours and others which have black flesh and are more tasty,[1] and likewise capons and godwits. We did not see any game, because in the region where we were there was no waste-land for them, but they say there is some the land inward. We saw birds of prey, likewise geese and royal ducks, and great store of doves and turtle-doves. Of fruits, there are white and black grapes in vines, although we did not see any wine made therefrom, and I do not believe they know how to make it. Also oranges and lemons of many kinds, and large citrons, pears, apples, wild pears, peaches, plums, mulberries, nuts, chestnuts, jujubes, pumpkins, cucumbers, water-melons, cabbages, cole-worts, turnips, radishes, garlic, onions, and many other fruits and vegetables peculiar to the country. They have much sugar and they make many and very good conserves.[2] Even in the squares and streets they have dwarf trees in pots and tubs, and I do not know with what ingenuity they grow them that though so small they can yet bear fruit, because we saw them laden with fruit. They also have a kind of tree from the fruit of which they take something like tallow, whereof throughout the whole country they make candles to give light, and which anyone would think was animal fat.[3] They have coconut-palms in the southern provinces but not in Hoc-quien [Fukien] nor north thereof.[4] They have horses although small ones, and asses, mules and donkeys. We saw good ones and droves of them.

9. *Of the buildings, husbandry, mines and other things which there are in this country.*

Their manner of building is always low without any stories, although in a very few places we saw some little houses with upper

[1] These black-fleshed fowl of Fukien are mentioned by Marco Polo, and their identification has occasioned much discussion. Cf. Yule-Cordier, *Marco Polo*, II, 226, 229; III, 98–99; *Travels of Peter Mundy*, II, 307.

[2] The production of sugar in Fukien was noticed by M. Martini, S.J., nearly a century later, as it had been by Marco Polo centuries before. Cf. Thevenot, *Relations*, III, 153.

[3] This is the vegetable tallow, *chiu-yu*, (*Sapium sebiferum*), obtained from the 'Tallow-tree', a member of the Spurge family, which occurs in all the warmer parts of China, and is remarkable for the beautiful autumnal tints of its foliage. Cf. Doolittle, *Social life of the Chinese*, I, 58; Couling, *Encyclopedia Sinica*, p. 542; *Travels of Peter Mundy*, III, 308.

[4] The commonest palm in China is the coir-palm, *Trachycarpus excelsus*, (*tsung*), which is described together with other varieties in Couling, *Encyclopedia Sinica*, p. 421.

stories, and over the gates of the cities they usually have some galleries and large halls. There are also some towers of idols, built square and of a good height, which have many fenestrations on all four sides, wherein they place their idols. We saw two of these in Chiunchiu,[1] and another two in Hocchiu [Foochow], and another three at the top of some hills. One of these last is at the very entrance of the haven, on a great hill which they call Gousou,[2] which can be seen from afar off at sea and can serve as a sea-mark for the port.

The houses of the great men, even though they are not storied, are very large and they occupy a great space, for they have court-yards and more courtyards, and great halls and many chambers and kitchen-gardens. These halls are ordinarily higher up than the ground by three or four steps of very large and beautiful flag-stones. The foundations are usually of square stone, and are built on the ground of each room to the height of about a *vara*.[3] They then place thereon some pillars or posts of pinewood on bases of stone; the keystones on top are very well wrought and the ceiling covered with tiles. The floor is well paved with bricks set very close together, although without lime, and sometimes paved with flagstones. Between the pillars they have thin walls of lath and plaster over wattle frames strengthened with great bars of wood and first daubed with clay on both sides and then plastered. The walls of the courtyards and kitchen-gardens are of tamped earth plastered on the outside. We saw one house in Tangoa[4] which was well worth seeing, with a very fine pond all paved with flagstones, and with arbours and paths above the water, and very fine tables made from

[1] Ch'üan-chou. The twin octagonal stone pagodas of the K'ai-yuan temple (also called the Temple of the Purple Cloud) at Ch'üan-chou were built during the thirteenth century. Cf. Ecke-Demiéville, *The twin pagodas of Zayton*, for a full description and illustrations of these famous monuments. Rada's account is the earliest mention of them in European literature, as neither Marco Polo nor Galeote Pereira allude to them.

[2] Wu-hsü (Gō-sū in Amoy vernacular) island, at the south side of the entrance to the Bay of Amoy. Although there may have been a stone tower on this island (the Dutch chart of *c.* 1630 reproduced herewith, calls it 'Gaussiu or Pagoda island'), Rada is, I think, confusing the name of the island with the much more prominent stone tower on the summit of Nan-t'ai-wu on the mainland opposite. Cf. Appendix I, especially pp. 322–323.

[3] For *vara*, cf. p. 253, n. (3) above; and for the architecture of Chinese houses, Gaspar da Cruz, Ch. VI, pp. 96–100, and Trigault-Gallagher, *The China that was*, pp. 31–32.

[4] T'ung-an; from the Amoy vernacular, Tâng-oaⁿ. Cf. p. 248, n. (1) above.

single slabs of stone. Of similar form are the royal community-houses which we said above were in all the towns, some being larger and others smaller.[1] The houses of the common people are like the little houses of the Moriscos.[2] Each one occupies about fourteen feet of street frontage, and they usually consist of two rooms with a small courtyard in between. The room which abuts on the street is divided into two, the front part serving as a shop.

The main streets are very broad, and they all have a large number of triumphal arches, some of very well wrought stone and others of wood. For every great man prides himself on leaving as a memorial such an arch, inscribed with his name and the year it was built, and other notable things which he did.[3] These main streets serve as market-places, and there are to be found in them every kind of meat, fish, fruits and vegetables; and stalls selling books, paper, knives, scissors, bonnets, shoes, straw sandals, etc. As these main streets are so wide, there is a good space left in the middle, with room to pass between the stalls and the houses, although the stalls stretch from one end of the street to the other. The other streets are all filthy little alleys. Their way of building walls has been described above. They are all of square stone, although daubed with clay without lime, and then the joints are plastered over on the outside. Their lime is made from oyster-shells and mussels. Their highways are paved with flagstones, and there are many well wrought bridges of stone.[4] The tombs of the principal people are usually outside the towns and cities, and are built of stone. In front of the grave, facing the road, is a very large flagstone erected on a tortoise or some other animal, hewn from one large stone slab. On the tombstone are inscribed the achievements of the man who is buried there.[5]

[1] He has not described these previously, but a good account of them (at a somewhat later date) will be found in Magalhães, *New History of China*, pp. 38–40. Cf. Carstairs Douglas, *Dictionary*, 239, 245

[2] Moors who remained in Spain after the Christian reconquest. They were finally expelled *en masse* in 1609.

[3] *P'ai-lou*. Cf. Galeote Pereira, p. 10, n. (2), and Gaspar da Cruz, Ch. VII, p. 103 above.

[4] Fukien was famous for its monolothic bridges which have no equal in China or elsewhere in the world. Cf. Appendix III for details.

[5] *Pei* (or *p'i*); large sepulchral tablets of stone, high and broad, standing apart, in an upright position, close by the tombs of actual or titular office-bearers and their wives, either exactly in the middle of the open ground in front of the tomb, or a little to the right or left. They display in large characters the names and

Most of their husbandry is by irrigation, in so far as we could see, and greatly abounds in rivers and waters. With certain buckets fixed to wooden water-wheels, they easily irrigate all their crops, and even on top of the hills they have irrigated crops.[1] I think they give the land but little rest, for when we went to Hocchiu [Foochow] we found all the land tilled in this way. Some of the rice had not yet been transplanted, some had just been, some was more advanced, some was fairly grown, and some was being harvested. On our return, we saw the same kind of activity, for another crop was already planted where the first had been harvested, and elsewhere another was being gathered in.[2] They till the soil with hoes and ploughs. They have mills both to cleanse the rice from the straw as to make meal, and they are hand-mills, although we saw a few water-mills.

There is a great abundance of silk and cotton, sugar and musk throughout all the country, as also many drugs.[3] There are mines of all kinds of metals, iron, steel,[4] copper, latten[5] in great abundance and very cheap, and also lead and tin. They say that there are mercury mines in the province of Namquin. The mines of gold and silver which are listed in their books are as follows.[6]

Province	District	Mines
Paquiaa [Peking]	Poam	Silver
Santon [Shantung]	Tinchiu	Gold

dignities of the occupant(s) of the grave. If erected for an officer of one of the three highest ranks, such a tablet stands on the back of a tortoise, in all other cases on a square pedestal or monolith. Cf. De Groot, *Religious system of China*, III, 1140–1164, Pl. xxxvi and Fig. 25 for full description and illustration of typical specimens.

[1] For Chinese water-wheels and endless-chain pumps see p. 121, n. (4) above. Similar praise for Fukienese methods of irrigation will be found in the text of Martini's *Atlas*, where it is stated that such methods were brought to a higher pitch of perfection than in any of the other provinces. Thevenot, *Relations*, III, 151.

[2] Cf. F. H. King, *Farmers of forty centuries*, pp. 23, 73, 87–92, 233–237 for Chinese methods of multiple cropping.

[3] *drogas* in the original. Here used in the sense of 'spices', 'medicinal plants', etc.

[4] [*Sic*] 'acero' in the original.

[5] *laton* in the original. A term used to denote both brass and tin-plate.

[6] Rada does not give his sources and I have not tried to identify all the districts concerned, for the production of precious metals in China was not comparable to that of Mexico and Peru, as the Spaniards seem to have imagined. Cf. Couling, *Encyclopedia Sinica*, 367–375.

Province	District	Mines
Oucum [Hukuang]	{River Buchian	Silver
	River Sinchiu	Gold
Namquien [Nanking]	Linquoy	Silver
Chetcan [Chekiang]	Unchiu	Gold
Hocquien [Fukien]	{Hocchiu [Foochow]	Silver
	Ciuchiu [?Ch'üan-chou]	Gold and silver
Cuinsay [? Kuangsi]	Quinoan	Silver
Quanton [Kuangtung]	Yanchiu [Lien-chou]	Pearl-fishery

Despite all this, most of the people are poor, as there are so many of them; and thus everything is very cheap, and all things are sold by weight, even birds and firewood. We did not see any kind of money save only in the district of the city of Cunchiu [Ch'üan-chou] and its appendages, where there was a stamped copper money with a hole bored through the middle of it.[1] They gave us 312 and 320 of these pieces for four rials.

Everywhere else (and also there) everything is bought by weight with little bits of silver which weigh what they call a *Nio*. One of these *nio* weighs eleven rials in our money; and one *nio* equals ten *lacuns* and one *lacun* equals ten *phou* and one *phou* equals ten *dis*, in sort that they divide eleven rials of our weight into a thousand parts.[2]

We also saw poor people who went begging through the streets, especially blind. Although they are so numerous a people they do not throw anything away. They do not waste a bone or horn, but make a thousand things thereof, as also of straw and grass, and they make use of everything in some way or other.

Their ships are somewhat slow and ill-made, although they sail very well before the wind and well enough close-hauled. They do not have sea-cards but they do have some manuscript rutters.[3]

---

[1] 'Cash' made of base metal. Cf. Gaspar da Cruz, Ch. XI, p. 128, n. (2) above.

[2] These are our old friends, taels (*liang*), mace and candareens, under Fukienese variants of their proper names. *Nio* = *liang* (tael); *lacun* = mace; *phou* = *fên*; *dis* = 'cash'. Cf. Gaspar da Cruz, Ch. XI, pp. 128-129 above.

[3] The Chinese did have charts ('sea-cards') as well as written sailing-directions ('rutters') during the Ming dynasty, and some typical examples are discussed in the following articles: J. V. Mills, 'Malaya in the *Wu-pei-chih* charts' (JMBRAS, December 1937, pp. 1-48); J. J. L. Duyvendak, 'Sailing Directions of Chinese voyages' (*T'oung Pao*, XXXIV, 230-237); W. Z. Mulder, 'The Wu Pei Chih charts' (*T'oung Pao*, XXXVII, 1-14). Mulder's article contains the reproduction of one of the *Wu-pei-chih* charts depicting the China coast from Hainan to Nanking.

They also have a compass-needle, but not like ours, for it is only a very sensitive little tongue of steel which they touch with a load-stone. They place it in a little saucer full of sea-water and on which the winds are marked. They divide the compass into twenty-four parts, and not into thirty-two as we do.[1]

As regards their paper, they say it is made from the inside pith of canes. It is very thin, and you cannot easily write on both sides of the paper, as the ink runs through.[2] They sell the ink in little slabs, and write with it after moistening it in some water.[3] For pens they use extremely fine little brushes. Their letters are the most barbarous and difficult of any which have yet been discovered, for they are characters rather than letters. They have a different character for every word or thing, in sort that even if a man knows ten thousand characters he cannot read everything.[4] Thus he who can read the most is the wisest among them.

There came into our hands printed books of all the sciencies, both astrology and astronomy, as physiognomy, chiromancy, arithmetic, and of their laws, medicine, fencing, and of every kind of their games, and of their gods.[5] In all of these (save only in medicinal matters, wherein like herbalists they know from experience the virtues of herbs and depict them as we do in the book of Dioscorides),[6] in everything else there is nothing to get hold of, since they have nothing more than the smell or shadow of the substance. For they do not know anything of geometry, nor do they have compass-dividers, nor can they reckon beyond simple addi-

[1] The Chinese mariner's compass-card at this period was divided into 24 points, on the traditional basis of relating all directions to the five primordial essences of *mu* (wood), *huo* (fire), *t'u* (earth), *chin* (metal), *shui* (water). Cf. the detailed explanations by S. Wada, *Memoirs of the Research Department of the Toyo Bunko*, No. 4, pp. 152–153, and W. Z. Mulder, *T'oung Pao*, XXXVII, 6–7.

[2] Rada is evidently referring to the finer class of Chinese paper which is made from bamboo pulped after not more than two years' growth. Cf. Couling, *Encyclopedia Sinica*, p. 423, and Carter, *Invention of printing in China*, Ch. I, for this and other varieties of paper used for books.

[3] R. H. Van Gulik, *Mi Fu on ink-stones* (Peking, 1938), is the standard work on ink-slabs.

[4] Cf. Gaspar da Cruz, Ch. XVII, pp. 161–162, and Trigault-Gallagher, *The China that was*, pp. 42–48.

[5] The list of these books, arranged in categories, is reproduced in the introduction, pp. lxxxiv–lxxxvi.

[6] M. Martini, S.J., (*c.* 1650) made the same comparison between Chinese herbals and European editions of Dioscorides. Cf. Thevenot, *Relations*, III, 9.

tion, subtraction and multiplication.[1] They think that the sun and the moon are human, that the sky is flat, and that the earth is not round. It is true that, like the natives of these islands,[2] they recognize many of the stars, and by their relative positions they calculate the seasons for sowing and harvesting; and they know thereby when the north-east and south-west monsoon winds begin, and when it is the season for storms or heats,—but since these Indians, although savages, know such things, it is obvious that the Chinos know them much better. I also saw sundials in the city of Hocchiu [Foochow], but they were ill-made, as if by ignorant people, and did not give the exact hour. All their divination is usually done by casting lots.[3]

When they know that someone of good family can read really well, he is examined by one called a Ja Ju, and if he is found sufficiently able he is given what we would call a bachelor's degree.[4] They place two silver nosegays in his ears, and he is taken on horseback in procession through the city with flags and minstrels in front.[5] We saw one of these in Hocchiu [Foochow], and

[1] Cf. Trigault-Gallagher, *The China that was*, pp. 49–53. Rada is unfair in his cursory dismissal of Chinese mathematics and astronomy. It is true that mathematical studies were in a dormant condition at this time; but some of the older works contained material which, in some respects at least, was actually in advance of the methods that were later introduced by Ricci and the Jesuits. Geometry was altogether new to Ming China, but the ancient Chinese were acquainted with trigonometry, both plane and spherical, as well as with algebra and other branches of mathematics. A. Wylie, *Notes on Chinese Literature* (ed. Shanghai, 1922), pp. 106–119; Dyer-Ball, *Things Chinese*, p. 355.

[2] I.e. the Philippines, where Rada wrote his report after returning from Fukien.

[3] Cf. Gaspar da Cruz, Ch. XXVII, pp. 214–215; Trigault-Gallagher, *The China that was*, pp. 140–141; Doré, *Manuel des superstitions chinoises*, pp. 98–106.

[4] A better and fuller contemporaneous Western account of the celebrated Chinese literary examination system will be found in Trigault-Gallagher, *The China that was*, pp. 55–67. The *hsiu-t'sai* ('licentiate') is usually translated as B.A., and *chü-jên* ('promoted man') as M.A., but there was scarcely any similarity between Chinese and European degrees throughout the respective systems. For a full account of how the Chinese system functioned under the Ming dynasty, see Biot, *Essai*, pp. 422–491, 577–582. Rada's *Jaju* may be the *Chiao-yü*, or provincial director of studies. Cf. Mayers, *Chinese government*, nr. 305.

[5] For the celebrations organised in honour of successful *chü-jên* at Foochow, cf. Doolittle, *Social life of the Chinese*, I, 412–420. Rada's 'nosegays' are evidently those connected with 'the cap of ceremony, on two sides of which (those which come by his ears) has been fastened a kind of artificial flower, professedly made of gold-leaf, but really of brass foil, fastened to a wire. These project up several inches above the cap perpendicularly' (*ibid.*, p. 414). Cf. also Carstairs Douglas, *Dictionary*, pp. 233 and 575, in voce *Tsam-koà* and *Tsam-hoe*.

he was a noble youth. When they receive that degree they are thenceforth fitted to exercise some office of justice; for nobody who cannot read and write well (and knows the court language besides) can become a governor or his deputy.[1]

In each province they have a different speech, although they are all rather similar—just as those of Portugal, Valencia and Castile resemble each other.[2] The script of China has this peculiarity, that since not letters but characters are used, then the same document can be read in all the tongues of China; although I saw documents written in the court script which was different from that of Hocquien [Fukien]. However, the one style and the other can be read in both tongues.[3]

10. *Of their Justices and ways of government.*

They say that in all the kingdom of Taybin there are no lords of vassalls, for everyone is subjected directly to the King.[4] However, there are slaves of the same natives of the country, for they also say that they do not admit foreigners [as slaves]. Some of the slaves are born in servitude, some sell themselves into slavery on account of crimes which they have committed.[5]

The number of people who have offices in the administration of justice is so great as to be almost infinite,—at least judging by the way in which the province of Hocquien [Fukien] is governed. The other provinces which have viceroys must be ruled in the same way, but the provinces of Pacquien [Peking] and Namquien [Nanking] have different kinds of offices and are administered by high-courts.[6] In Hocchiu [Foochow] which is the chief city of the province of Hocquien [Fukien], there is always resident the viceroy, whom they term Commun;[7] and the second person after

---

[1] It may be added that office was normally conferred on a successful graduate only after he had taken the third or *chin-shih* examination at Peking. The 'court language' was the *kuan-hua*, or 'Mandarin'.

[2] Cf. Appendix IV below.

[3] For differences in the forms of Chinese characters, which have, however, nothing to do with provincial boundaries, cf. C. C. Hopkins, *The six scripts* (Amoy, 1881); Dyer Ball, *Things Chinese*, p. 920.

[4] i.e. there is no feudal system in China.

[5] Cf. Gaspar da Cruz, Ch. XV above.

[6] Provinces of Pei-Chihli and Nan-Chihli. See Galeote Pereira, p. 4 and n. (6), and Gaspar da Cruz, Ch. V, p. 90.

[7] *Chün-mên*, or *Kun-bûn* in Amoy vernacular. Cf. p. 249, n. (4) above.

him is the Tontoc,[1] who is the captain-general of all the fighting-men. These two have authority over all the people and officials of the whole province. After these come the chief standard-bearer, whom they call Cancunto,[2] and the Pauchiu who is the royal treasurer, the Pouchinsi who is the lieutenant-treasurer,[3] the Sanchian or deputy captain-general,[4] the Ansasi who corresponds to our *corregidor*,[5] the Viancay answering to our *alcalde-mayor*,[6] and three called Tihu who are like ordinary *alcaldes*.[7]

All these are justices who can punish offenders, although it is very seldom that the greater justices ever inflict punishment, unless it be on some captain or important man, or in an affair of great import. For they remit all other offenders with a note to the ordinary magistrates, signifying therein the punishments which they should be given, as we saw several times. It is an amazing thing to see the solemnity which they keep, both in their houses and when they go out in public. Each one is accompanied by a number of bailiffs, whose device is a plume from a peacock's tail-feathers, as also by many executioners with their whips, sticks and cords. Their whips are as it were broad rods made from the stems of [bamboo] canes, for the canes of this country are very large and thick. Each rod would be about six spans or more in length and about four fingers wide, and a thumb in thickness. It is very heavy,

---

[1] *Ti-tu*, or *Thê-tok* in Amoy vernacular. Commander of the provincial troops. Cf. p. 249, n. (5) above.

[2] I cannot identify this dignitary, and suspect some confusion with a *Fên-hsün-tao*, Intendant or Inspector of a circuit, (*Bên-sûn-tō* in Amoy vernacular).

[3] There is more confusion here, since 'Pauchíu' and 'Pouchinsí' seem to be variants of the same title, *Pu-chêng-shih*, civil governor and provincial comptroller: *Pò-chèng-si* in Amoy vernacular. Cf. Galeote Pereira, p. 6, n. (1).

[4] 'Sanchian' is apparently derived from *Ts'an-chiang* (*Chham-chiong* in Amoy vernacular), a military route (or route-army) commander, of whom there were three in Fukien, Cf. *Ch'ou-hai-t'u-pien*, ch. 4.

[5] The Spanish *corregidor* is usually translated as 'civil governor', although he had much wider judicial functions than the English equivalent. The official here indicated is the *An-ch'a-shih*, provincial judge, or judicial commissioner.

[6] I cannot identify the 'Viancay', but as we are dealing with the senior officials of the provincial hierarchy, and in view of the high-ranking Spanish equivalent which is given, I suspect it may be another reference to the *Fên-hsün-tao*, or Intendant of a circuit, colloquially known as *Tao-t'ai*, or *Taotai* to foreigners under the Manchus.

[7] *Chih-fu* (*Ti-hú* in Amoy vernacular). The title of the mandarin governing the largest of the provincial subdivisions; prefect. The Spanish *Alcalde* had a wide range of equivalents in English, 'justice', 'sheriff', 'magistrate' and 'mayor', all figuring in the dictionaries.

and they commonly whip with this. However, when they wish to punish more severely, they whip with some cudgels or round sticks as thick as the arm.

Their way of whipping is that when the mandarin gives a shout, five or six executioners hurl themselves on the poor victim, throw him on the ground in a trice and take off his drawers. When he is thus lying face downwards, one holds him fast by the feet, another by the head, while another with the said cane or cudgel held on high beats him with all his strength on the hind muscles of the thighs, until he is told to stop. Every five strokes they turn the body so as to beat it on the other side. Meanwhile, another of the executioners who is on his knees, counts out loud the number of the strokes, which are so savage that those who receive more than sixty very rarely escape death. Those whom they wish to torture more, are first straitly bound by their hands and feet in a way much worse than what is called *ley de vayona*,[1] and they then whip him when thus bound. There is no distinction of persons made in whipping *si no es que el mayor en haziendo*, for they whip inferiors however honourable they may be and even if they have a crown office. When we were in Hocchiu [Foochow], the Tontoc had an honourable captain whipped for a mere trifle, ordering him to be given eighty strokes, of which he died the next day.

Every morning, when they wish to open their gate, which is usually about eight or nine of the clock, the whole bodyguard is already drawn up outside the gate. They first fire three small iron cannon, sound their trumpet and beat a great drum[2] and then the minstrels strike up, and the mandarin is seen seated in that majesty which we have already described of [the] Inzuantou in the narrative of our journey in Chinchiu [Ch'üan-chou], or even in greater state according to the dignity of his rank. Forthwith many captains enter to perform their obeisance as described above, kneeling afar off and bowing down three or four times. When the captains have finished their obeisances, then the whole of the bodyguard

---

[1] A Spanish friend informs me that this was some kind of a naval punishment, but neither he nor anyone else I have consulted can carry the identification any further. Nor can I cope with the next phrase left in Spanish.

[2] In front of the yamens of the highest provincial mandarins was a small octagonal building, called the drum-pavilion or drum-tower, occupied by the band of music attached to the mandarinate. Doolittle, *Social life of the Chinese*, I, 303-304; *China Review*, XVII, 39.

likewise perform theirs in unison from outside the gate, which would be about an arquebus-shot from where the mandarin is seated. When the captains have finished their obeisance to the Comcum, all those who have not got to stay there, or who have no business there, make another to the Tontoc and to the other dignitaries.

Besides these mandarins who are the principal ones, there is one whom they call the Tanpoa[1] who is the overseer of victuals, who is responsible for seeing that there is always a supply thereof and punishes those who do not bring in time the victuals which they have been ordered to bring. There is also another, called Choyqua,[2] who punishes vagabonds. In every ward there are other lesser mandarins who hear complaints and judge minor offences, and who make the rounds at night. These are they to whom the higher mandarins send evil-doers to be punished. The other cities of the province have their own governors, although with different names according to their respective official ranks. One is termed Insuanto,[3] another Hayto,[4] another Peipito,[5] and another Tiacto[6] etc. They have instead of the Vauchiu[6] one whom they call Soupu,[6] the magistrates and overseers being the same as those in the provincial capital. However, in the towns there is one corresponding to a *corregidor* who is called Ticon,[7] and his chief magistrate

[1] I cannot trace anything like this term in Carstairs Douglas, *Dictionary of the Amoy vernacular*, but the functions described would seem to be those of the *Liang-tao* or provincial grain-intendant. Cf. Mayers, *Chinese government*, nr. 278.

[2] Phonetically, the Amoy vernacular *Chhe-kha*, 'hangers-on who go along with constables to serve warrants', seems fairly close; but the context indicates an official of higher rank.

[3] Our old friend the *Hsing-Ch'üan-Tao*, or Governor (*Taotai*) of the prefectures of Hsing-hua and Ch'üan-chou. Cf. p. 249, n. (1) above.

[4] *Hai-tao-fu-shih*, naval coastguard-fleet commander; admiral. Cf. p. 154, n. (3) above.

[5] *Pei-wo-tu-chih-hui*, military coast-defence commander against Japanese pirates.

[6] I cannot identify 'Tiacto' and 'Vauchiu', although I suspect that this latter has something to do with the Viancy whose identification is discussed on p. 298, n. (6). 'Soupou' may possibly be derived from *shou-fu*, a literary term for the head prefect of a province, but I admit this is not very likely. Cf. Mayers, *Chinese government*, nr. 281.

[7] From the Amoy vernacular, *Ti-koâi^n*; the mandarin of a *hsien*-district, or *chih-hsien*. Cf. Carstairs Douglas, *Dictionary*, p. 490; Mayers, *Chinese government*, nr. 289.

termed Cansin,[1] together with one like a *alcalde de hermandad* called Tensu[2] and his overseer, as also lesser justices in the various wards. The villages have their magistrates, constables and mandarins subordinated to their chief city. Thus the towns and their justices are subordinated to those of the cities, and each city and town has many villages subordinated thereto. All these justices have their own executioners with their canes for to whip, who always go in front of them whithersoever they go, shouting for everyone to make way, and anyone who fails to do so is promptly ordered to be whipped.

These mandarins have so great authority over all the other people, that when they pass anybody on horseback he has to dismount and stand to one side, and anybody in a chair has to have it put down on the ground and gets out of it, while he who carries a sunshade lowers it, and he who carries a fly-whisk hides it up his sleeve. They say that no justice can pass a death-sentence, save only the captains in time of war. In all other cases, if anyone is found to merit a death-sentence he is kept in prison until the king is informed of his case and he is condemned to death by him. For this reason they have many prisons and some people who have been in them for many years.[3]

Those of their fetters which we saw were some wooden manacles on the hands, as also a great board round the neck after the fashion of a pillory, although the prisoner can walk about with it on and carry a fair load and work; the reason for his punishment is inscribed thereon.[4]

They say that the prisons are very dark and stinking. The ordinary punishments which the judges and justices award besides a term of imprisonment are the whippings described above, which

[1] Amoy vernacular, *koāin sêng*; the mandarin of the sub-division of a district, or *hsien-ch'êng*. Carstairs Douglas, *Dictionary*, p. 238; Mayers, *Chinese government*, nr. 291.

[2] Probably from the Amoy vernacular, *Tién-sú*, a petty mandarin; district police-master, or jail-warden. Carstairs Douglas, *Dictionary*, p. 500; Mayers, *Chinese government*, nr. 294.

[3] Cf. Galeote Pereira, pp. 21–25, and Gaspar da Cruz, Ch. XX, p. 177 above. This practice formed a striking contrast with the state of affairs in contemporary Japan, where there were no prisons and 'each man does justice on those of his household', killing offenders out of hand. Cf. the Portuguese eyewitness quoted in my *Christian Century in Japan*, pp. 34–35.

[4] Cf. Gaspar da Cruz, Ch. XXI, p. 184.

are given to people of all classes without distinction, and some little sticks which they put between the fingers and which are pulled very tight with cords, thus squeezing the fingers and causing the wretched victim to scream with pain, until the judge orders him to be released.[1] This device is also used as a form of torture. Women are more commonly punished with these little sticks then with whipping, although they are sometimes whipped, as we were told. They also customarily punish the children and kinsmen of offenders whom they cannot find, as we saw and heard of some of them.[2] And according to what we were told, if the offence is a very serious one, they not only punish the offender if they catch him, but all his kith and kin likewise.

All these justices and governors have to be from another province and not from that which they administer, and they are relieved every three years. Besides this, the king sends yearly to each province an inspector called Çauli,[3] who redresses wrongs and investigates whether the viceroy, captain-general, and governors do their duty faithfully, and he can send them or take them to the king. This inspector also investigates whether the provincial officials take bribes, for in this they are most circumspect although they are very fond of them, and it is difficult to deal satisfactorily with them without greasing their palms. However, this bribery has to be done most secretly, for in public they receive nothing. What I say about this is derived from our own experience, and it may well be that there are many others of another sort.[4]

They punish all vagabonds severely which makes everyone work hard; and they are great enemies to merchants whom they say are a vagabond lot, and that they allow them to subsist for fear lest they might become robbers, of whom they say that there are many the land inward, as also pirates at sea.[5] Nobody can leave the districts

[1] Cf. Gaspar da Cruz, Ch. XXI, p. 185.

[2] Correct. Cf. Doolittle, Social life of the Chinese, I, 330–331; Gray, China, I, 83.

[3] Tao-li, cenor(s) or inspector(s) of the thirteen circuits or Tao. Cf. Trigault-Gallagher, The China that was, pp. 80–82; Fonti Ricciane, I, 60, (n).

[4] As indeed there were. For popular recognition of honest mandarins on completion of their term of office, see Doolittle, Social life of the Chinese, I, 327–328; Gray, China, I, 44–45.

[5] Confucian contempt for and dislike of the merchant-class relegated the trader to near the bottom of the social scale. Trade was regarded as a necessary evil, whereas agriculture was considered the only source of permanent wealth. For a discussion of the effect of these views on the development of China, see H. Maspero, Mèlanges Posthumes, III, 163.

of his own city, even if it is for another place in the same province, without a written permit; and if he does so, he is forthwith flung into prison and punished. Usually they give these permits on paper with many seals and certificates of the magistrates and other authorities.[1] But when somebody goes on public business, or they wish to honour him, they give him a patent on a board like the one I mentioned above which they gave to us.[2] The post-riders that they send with dispatches, besides having a distinctive apparel, go on horses which have a collar of heavy hawks-bells.

They do not admit foreigners into the country, although they say that in Suntien [Peking], which is the seat of the court, there are many different kinds of nations, each one living in its own ward, on the gate of which is inscribed the name of the nation concerned.[3] They gave me a note listing these nations that were there. Cauchin, Lonquia, Chienlo, Malacca, Payni, Campuchi, Chausin, Tata, Cauli, Gitpon, Vyue, and they say that these last are Moors who live in the land inward between China and Bengal.[4] They say that all these nations pay tribute to the king of China. In Hocchiu [Foochow] we saw some men from Lauquiu, whom we call Lequios, who came to bring their tribute.[5]

Besides these mandarins, there are many other inferior ones and different kinds of captains, amongst whom are many of those whom they term Pettzon.[6] These likewise have jurisdiction and are authorised to go in large chairs, and to have their executioners going before them with canes to whip and cords to bind, and they can also punish; and all this not only in the place where they live, but

[1] 'Chinese policy strongly sets its face against anything in the nature of *liu* or wandering, even from one district or province to another,' *China Review*, VIII, 261.

[2] Cf. p. 249, n. (2) above.

[3] An allusion to the practice of confining foreign envoys (tribute bearers) and their suites in certain hostelries or guest-houses during their stay in the capital. Their location at different periods is discussed by Pelliot in *T'oung Pao*, XXXVIII, 253–272.

[4] The list reads in order, Annam, Liu-chiu, Siam, Malacca, W. Borneo (?), Cambodia, Korea, Tartary, Kao-li [=Koryö or Korea again], Japan, and Uighúrs from Central Asia.

[5] Luchuans from the Liu-chiu, or Ryūkyū islands.

[6] From the Amoy vernacular *pé-tsóng* (*pa-tsung*), garrison commander, who was in command of a force of about two thousand men during the Ming dynasty. Under the Manchus, the term came to denote the equivalent of a junior officer or senior N.C.O. Cf. *Ch'ou-hai-t'u-pien*, Ch. 4, pp. 9–10; Carstairs Douglas, *Dictionary*, p. 362.

they furthermore are empowered to punish the poor people everywhere, and thus they hold them in subjection.

11. *Of the Gods, Idols, Sacrifices and Feasts.*

So great was the number of idols which we saw everywhere we went that they were beyond count, for each house has its own idols besides the multitude which they have in temples and in special houses for them. In one temple at Hocchiu [Foochow] there were over a hundred idols of different kinds, some with six, eight, or more arms, others with three heads (which they say is prince of the devils), and others were black, red, and white, both men and women. There is not a house but has its little idols, and even in the hills and along the highways and byways, there is hardly a large rock which does not have idols carved thereon. With all that, the one which they hold as the true God is the Heaven, for all the others they consider to be merely intercessors through whom they pray to Heaven (which they call Thien)[1] to grant them health, wealth, dignity, or a prosperous voyage. They believe that Heaven created and made all things.

The greatest of those who is in Heaven they call Yohon, or Yocon Sautey,[2] of whom they say that he was *ab eterno* like Heaven, although he is inferior thereto and has no body. This being has a servant called Sancay, who was made from Heaven and who likewise has no body.[3] They say that he has charge of everything under Heaven, including life and death. He has three servants who rule this world by his orders, Tianquan who has charge of the waters,[4] Cuicuan of the sea and mariners,[5] Teyquan of the men and fruits of the earth.[6] They also revere one whom they say is the gatekeeper of Heaven, and many others of this sort.

[1] *T'ien*; the material Heaven being confused with the spirits supposed to reside there. See Werner, *Dictionary of Chinese mythology*, p. 502.

[2] Yü Huang Shang Ti, 'The Pearly [or Jade] Emperor supreme ruler', for whose worship at Foochow, see Doolittle, *Social life of the Chinese*, I, 257–258; Werner, *Dictionary of Chinese mythology*, pp. 598–600.

[3] This seems to be another corrupted version of Shang Ti. Cf. Werner, *op. cit.*, pp. 410–411.

[4] Probably T'ien-kuan, the first of the Three Rulers, Agents, or Transcendent Powers, collectively known as the San-kuan. Cf. Werner, *Dictionary of Chinese mythology*, pp. 400–403; J. J. M. de Groot, *Fêtes*, I, 9–10.

[5] Probably Shui-kuan, the 'ruler of water', and third of the Three Transcendent Powers, or 'Lords of the Three Worlds'.

[6] Probably Ti-kuan, the 'ruler of earth', and second of the Three Transcendent Powers.

Besides these, they have many others whom they revere as saints, some of whom they call Fut[1] and others Pousat.[2] They worship some of these because they were very brave—as for instance a red one called Quanhu whom we mentioned previously as having aided Laupi to rebel and conquer the kingdom.[3] Yet the one whom they honour most is a woman called Quanyin, daughter of a king called Tonçou, who led a solitary life and a holy one after her fashion.[4] However, mariners prefer another woman called Nemoa, born in the province of Hocquien [Fukien], in a village near Hinhua [Hsing-hua] called Puhuy.[5] They say that she led a solitary life in the uninhabited island of Vichiu (where they say there are horses) which lies about three leagues off the coast.[6] They also worship the devils[7] lest these should do them any harm.

They usually place together three images of one and the same person; and when asked why, they say that those three are really one. We saw an example of this in Laulo,[8] with three great images of Nemoa [Niang-ma] placed together and a grating in front with its altar, and just at the side an image of a red man and another of a

[1] Buddha, whose Chinese characters are pronounced *Fo* in Peking, *Fuh* in Nanking, and *Put* in Amoy.

[2] *P'u-sa* (*p'o-sat* in Amoy vernacular); colloquial term for a Bodhisattva, one whose essence (*sattva*) has become intelligence (*bodhi*). Includes Buddhas who are not yet perfected by entering Nirvana. Cf. Werner, *Dictionary*, p. 386; De Groot, *Fêtes*, I, 181.

[3] Kuan Yü and Liu Pei, two of the three heroes of the famous 'oath in the peach-orchard' in the popular *Story of the Three Kingdoms*. Cf. p. 280 n. (2).

[4] The Bodhisattva Kuan Yin, often called in Western books on China, the goddess of mercy. She was third daughter of a ruler of a northern kingdom nowadays identified with Chuang Wang (696–81 B.C.) of the Chou dynasty. Cf. De Groot, *Fêtes*, I, 178–200; Werner, *Dictionary of Chinese mythology*, pp. 225–227; Eliot, *Hinduism and Buddhism*, III, 238–239.

[5] *T'ien-hou Niang-niang* (*Thien-hō Niû͘ niû͘* in Amoy vernacular) the Heavenly Concubine, or the Lady Empress of Heaven, for whose legend and cult, cf. Doré, *Recherches*, XI, 914–920; De Groot, *Fêtes*, I, 260–267; Werner, *Dictionary*, p. 503; Duyvendak in *T'oung Pao*, XXXIV, 344, and XXXIX, 188–191. Rada's 'Nemoa' is derived from *Niang-ma*, a Fukienese appellation for this Celestial Spouse. For Puhuy, see next note.

[6] Mei-chou (Bî-chiu in Amoy vernacular) in P'u-t'ien-hsien, near Hsing-hua. Cf. De Groot, *Fêtes*, I, 261; Duyvendak in *T'oung Pao*, XXXIV, 344*n*.

[7] *Kuei*, or disembodied spirits. The deceased who are not *shên* or genii.

[8] Identified from Loarca ('Verdadera Relacion', I, xii) as Liāu-lô, the S.E. corner of Quemoy island in the Bay of Amoy. Cf. Appendix I, p. 323 below.

black who received the sacrifices.[1] What they usually offer, after making their obeisances and prayers, are perfumes, scents, and a great quantity of paper-money, which is afterwards all burnt amid the ringing of bells. They likewise often burn this money over the dead, and if the deceased was a rich man they also burn pieces of silk.

They have their little lamps burning before their idols, although they are not a very devout people. They also sacrifice to their idols whole cows, pigs, ducks, fish and fruits, which are all placed raw upon an altar. After many ceremonies and prayers, they take three little cups of wine with great obeisances, and throw away one for their God (who is the Heaven) and they then drink the others, and divide all that food among themselves, eating it as something sanctified.[2] Besides these rites and ceremonies, they have others which are very ridiculous, as we saw in the ship in which we went when we were already near the islands.[3] Because they said that they had to give a send-off to Nemoa [Niang-ma] who had accompanied us thus far in order to give us a prosperous voyage.

They made a ship-model of cane with sails and a rudder, and they placed a small grilled fish and a scrap of cooked rice inside it with many ceremonies, and thus they launched it in the sea. And in order to expel the devil from the ship, they all line the gunwales with a stave in each hand. Then come two men, each with a large saucepan of cooked rice which they scatter over the ship's side into the sea, starting at the prow and ending at the poop. Behind them come another two men, armed with scimiters and shields, who go along brandishing their weapons and gesticulating, what time the ship's company beat very noisily upon the gunwales with their staves, and doing many other foolish things.[4]

Likewise, they often make vows, promises and offerings. We saw

[1] The heavenly Concubine's two assistants were 'Favourable-wind-ear' and 'Thousand-mile-eye', and were often portrayed as described by Rada. Cf. Doolittle, *Social life of the Chinese*, I, 264.

[2] Sacrifices of food and wine, whether to household or other gods, or to the ancestral tablets, were always feasted upon. Cf. Doolittle, *Social life of the Chinese*, II, 230–231, 388–389; Doré, *Manuel*, pp. 85–86.

[3] The text is remarkably ambiguous here, but from comparison with Loarca's 'Verdadera Relacion', it is probable that the reference is to the return voyage and that 'the islands' are the Philippines.

[4] Cf. Gray, *China*, II, 259–261, for identical practices on ocean-going junks three centuries later.

some fasting devotees who had vowed not to eat flesh, eggs or fish for many days, but only rice, herbs and fruits. Others had as it were silken altar-cloths which they had sent as votive-offerings, whereon was inscribed the name of the petitioner, and why he offered it and to whom. They are a people much given to omens, and thus wherever they are, even along the roads, they seek omens before their idols. They first of all make their prayer to these, then take a great quantity of little sticks, and spinning them round take the first one [which falls?] without looking at it; and they then look at the word which is written thereon, and then according to its meaning go to a table whereon all the answers are placed. Alternatively they write on a little stick which is squared off on all sides, and after praying they erect an altar complete with thurible and then they throw the stick thereon, and what is written on the side which comes uppermost they think will befall, and so forth and so on.[1]

They hold feast-days on the first days of the moon and the fifteenth days; but their chief feast-day is their New Year which now falls in February. According to what they say, their year has twelve moons for two years in succession and thirteen in the third. If they always follow this reckoning, they never correspond to our years, for in fifty-seven of our years they will come to have two moons less, and thus their year is always behind.[2]

They also keep as a very great feast the fifteenth day of their seventh month. We saw this feast in Hocchiu [Foochow] because they keep it in all the houses of the community, and so they celebrated it likewise in the inn where we were lodged. It is the feast of the dead in honour of Siquiag, who was the founder of such religious orders as there are in China.[3] They erected in one of the halls an image of Siquiag with many other images which were on their knees around him. There was also a large altar with seven or eight separate tables all loaded with food. At nightfall three men began

[1] For a full description of these and other common methods of divination as practised in Fukien, see Doolittle, *Social life of the Chinese*, II, 106–114, 384–385.

[2] The Chinese lunar calendar is made up of 12 lunar months of 29 or 30 days each. For a succinct explanation of Chinese calendars and systems of dating, see *Handbook of Oriental History*, pp. 196–200; and for a concordance of Far Eastern with European dates, M. Tchang, *Synchronismes Chinois* (Shanghai, 1935).

[3] Sakyamuni (Shih-chia Fo), the fourth Buddha of the present *kalpa*. Cf Werner, *Dictionary of Chinese mythology*, p. 278.

to sing from their book, one of them being a priest and the other two cantors. Sometimes they sang after the manner of psalms, and at other times like hymns, always playing on some small hand-bells and a tambourine. From time to time, the priest took a little dish of food from the tables, said a prayer, and placed it on the altar. This continued until all the dishes were finished, which was nearly midnight.[1]

12. *Of the friars, hermits and nuns which there are in Taybin.*

There are in the kingdom of Taybin two kinds of friars after their manner of religion, some who do not eat meat nor eggs nor fish, but sustain themselves only with rice, herbs and fruits.[2] Many of these live like hermits, like one we saw on a hill adjoining the wall of Hocchiu [Foochow]. He was in a tiny little grot with three little idols therein, and he looked as if he was wrapped in contemplation. Around the cell was his little garden which he had planted with gourds, cucumbers, water-melons, egg-plants and other vegetables, and there was a brook of running water. On the outside, it was bounded by a high and thick cane plantation, being distant about an arquebus-shot from the houses of the town.[3] There are others in the mountains and hills, and we saw some of these carrying rosaries larger and differently divided from ours.

There is another kind of friar who lives in community in the towns. According to what we were told, the king has given them possessions on which they live, although we also saw some in Hocchiu [Foochow] who walked through the streets begging for

---

[1] For a detailed description of the 'Festival of hungry ghosts' as celebrated in Fukien, see De Groot, *Fêtes*, II, 403–435. Cf. also Doolittle, *Social life of the Chinese*, II, 61–63; Bredon, *Moon Year*, pp. 376–390.

[2] This applies, theoretically at least, to all Buddhist priests and monks. Rada may have been thinking either of the difference between Buddhist and Taoist monks, or else of the *Lü-shih*, Buddhist 'Disciplinists' who go barefoot and follow rigidly the old injunctions for leading an ascetic life. Cf. Werner, *Dictionary* pp. 32–33; Eliot, *Hinduism and Buddhism*, III, 331.

[3] Gautama Buddha discouraged solitary asceticism, and the true Buddhist leads a celibate monastic life. Rada may have seen a Taoist hermit; but, on the other hand, there are some Buddhist monks who voluntarily withdraw from the fellowship of the community to which they usually belong, and take up their abode, sometimes under a vow of silence, in solitary hermitages. Cf. R. F. Johnston, *Buddhist China*, (London, 1913), pp. 277, 297. From what follows, it would seem most likely that Rada was referring to Buddhist rather than to Taoist monks and hermits, despite his remark that some of them 'eat of everything'. Buddhist discipline was notoriously lax at that period.

alms. These went singing and playing on some little bells, and carrying a large fan which they bend to one side and the other, so that anyone who wishes to give alms can place or throw them thereon. These eat of everything. We stayed in one of their houses at Chinchiu,[1] where they usually got up two hours before dawn to chant their matins, and while they sang they played on a great bell and on a drum with its little bells; and it was the same tune as the one which we described in the feast of the dead. We did not see them chant anything else save only those matins which they finished just before daybreak.[2] They burnt incense before their idols night and day. They told us there there were also monasteries of nuns but we did not see any.[3] Both monks and nuns have their heads shaven, and the monks also shave their beards. They are called Huxio.[4]

They have what corresponds to a general who lives at the court and is called Cecua.[5] He appoints as it were a provincial to each province, who is called Toncon.[6] The head or prior of each house is called Tionlo.[7] The founder of these orders is called

---

[1] Ch'üan-chou. Probably one of the outlying buildings belonging to the K'ai-yuan temple, to which establishment the celebrated twin pagodas belonged. Cf. Ecke-Demièville, *Twin Pagodas of Zayton*, pp. 84–85.

[2] The Buddhist service 'consists of versicles, responses and canticles, and, though strangely reminiscent both in structure and externals (such as the wearing of vestments) of the offices of the Roman Church appears to be Indian in origin'. Eliot, *Hinduism and Buddhism*, III, 331.

[3] Chinese Buddhist nunneries, both then and later, had a widespread reputation for immorality; but it is not clear how far these charges were exaggerated, and in any case nunneries were not numerous at this period. Cf. Doolittle, *Social life of the Chinese*, I, 253–254; Gray, *China*, I, 131–133; Van Gulik, *Erotic colour-prints of the Ming period*, I, 157.

[4] *Ho-shang*; *Hê-siū^n* in Amoy vernacular, whence the forms 'Hexio' or 'Huexio', etc., found in Portuguese and Spanish sources. This word, which hs no derivation in Chinese, is thought to be a corruption of some vernacular form of the Sanskrit *Upâdhyâva* current in Central Asia. Cf. Eliot, *Hinduism and Buddhism*, III, 330, n. (2).

[5] The President of the Board of Rites at Peking (*Li-pu Shang-shu*) was ex-officio superintendent of all the Buddhist monasteries, temples, and priests in China. Rada's Cecua (*Cisua* in other copies) is presumably derived from the Amoy vernacular form, *siū^n-si*, of *Shang-shu*. For the organisation of the Buddhist hierarchy in Ming China, see *Ming-shih*, Ch. 74. It remained substantially unchanged under the Manchus. Cf. Mayers, *Chinese government*, pp. 84–85.

[6] *Sen-kang;* Cheng-kong in Amoy vernacular, and *Chöng-kong* in Ch'üan-chou. Carstairs Douglas, *Dictionary*, p. 34; Mayers, *Chinese government*, nr. 493.

[7] *Sêng-lu;* Cheng-lék or *Cheng-liók* in Amoy vernacular. Superior.

2C

Siquag,[1] whom they revere as a saint. He was a foreigner, and said to be from the region of Tiantey,[2] although one of his friars told us that he was from Syria.

The Chinese believe that souls are immortal, and that the good and the holy[3] go to Heaven. As regards the others, a Huexio [Ho-shang] told us that they become demons.[4] Their friars are held in scant respect and regard; only the captains and the mandarins are respected on account of the punishments they can inflict. Finally, the land is very fruitful, abundant and populous, although with people who are heathen and thus suffer from the evils which afflict those who do not know God, to whom be honour and glory for evermore, and may He convert and bring them to the knowledge of Himself. Amen.

[1] Sakyamuni. The Portuguese and Spaniards distorted the Chinese versions of this name into Siecqua, Sicquaq, Sciacca, etc. Cf. p. 307, n. (3) above.

[2] From the Amoy vernacular *Thien-tiok* (Mandarin, *T'ien-chu*) an old name for India. Buddhism was officially introduced from India in the reign of the Emperor Ming Ti of the Han dynasty, A.D. 58–76, but there is no doubt that it had arrived in a more modest way some time before. Cf. H. Maspero, *Mélanges Posthumes*, I, 197–211.

[3] *shên*, genii, spirit. For more accurate definition and fuller discussion, cf. Werner, *Dictionary*, p. 417.

[4] *kuei*, spirits who are not *shên*; demons. Cf. Werner, *Dictionary*, p. 231.

APPENDIXES

Appendix I

'CHINCHEO'

ALTHOUGH it is now generally accepted that the 'Zayton' of Marco Polo and other medieval travellers is to be identified with Ch'üan-chou,[1] there is far less agreement about the identity of the 'Chincheo' of their Portuguese and Spanish successors. Among the most recent writers who have had occasion to discuss this topic, A. Kammerer claims that the Portuguese invariably identified 'Chincheo' with Ch'üan-chou;[2] whereas J. M. Braga affirms with equal conviction that the Portuguese carto-graphers distinguished between 'Chincheo' and 'Zaiton' as early as 1529 to mean Chang-chou and Ch'üan-chou respectively.[3] It is the object of this article to show that such categorical claims are untenable; and that, in fact, 'Chincheo' had a wide range of meanings to both Portuguese and Spaniards, although it was most often used to denote the Bay of Amoy and its hinterland. The quotations which follow are not, of course, exhaustive; but they suffice to show that by the term 'Chincheo', or some variant thereof, the Portuguese and Spaniards did not invariably denote either Chang-chou or Ch'üan-chou, and that they often confused the two.

The earliest mention of this word which I have been able to find occurs in the *Suma Oriental* of Tomé Pires which was compiled about 1512–1515. His brief references to 'Chamcheo' might indicate either the province of Fukien as a whole, or one of its ports in particular; but, con-trary to what his editor asserts, there is nothing to show whether it was Chang-chou or Ch'üan-chou which his informants had in mind.[4] Dr. Cortesão endeavours to prove that the 'Chamcheo' of Tomé Pires is identical with Chang-chou, on the grounds that Portuguese portulans of 1554–1580, 'show clearly that *Chincheo* is Chang-chou, situated at the inner end of a bay dotted with several islands.' These portulan charts

[1] G. Ecke and P. Demiéville, *The Twin Pagodas of Zayton*, p. 1, and the works quoted there in support of this assertion.

[2] A. Kammerer, *La Découverte de la Chine par les Portugais au XVI siècle et la cartographie des portulans*, p. 103, and index s.v. 'Chincheo'.

[3] J. M. Braga, *The Western Pioneers and their discovery of Macao*, p. 72, and index s.v. 'Chincheo'. Mr. Braga has used the Cantonese romanisation for these two towns.

[4] A. Cortesão, *The Suma Oriental of Tomé Pires*. I, 119, 126, 265. The last reference . . . 'there is a Xabamdar for the Chinese, Lequeos, Chancheo and Champa', implies that 'Chancheo' here indicates the province of Fukien as a whole.

are on such a small scale, however, that their evidence on this point is by no means conclusive. Moreover, Pires' information was evidently acquired from Asian traders at Malacca and not from Portuguese navigators who had visited the China coast. The Portuguese first reached Fukien in 1518, and the evidence deduced from portulans compiled forty or fifty years later is not really relevant to a work written in 1512–1515.

The next references to 'Chincheo' occur in the accounts of Fernão Peres de Andrade's expedition to China in 1517–1518. During his stay in the Pearl River, Andrade detached Jorge Mascarenhas to make a reconnaissance voyage to the Liu-chiu islands, in the company of some returning Liu-chiu junks and provided with Chinese pilots. Contrary winds prevented Mascarenhas from getting beyond the coast of Fukien, 'which province', wrote João de Barros, 'our people generally call Chincheo from a maritime city which is situated there, and where some of them later went to trade.'[1] Barros adds that Jorge Mascarenhas drove a very profitable trade at this 'city Chincheo' before he was recalled to the Pearl River by Peres de Andrade, who was anxious lest he should miss the monsoon for the return voyage to Malacca at the end of September, 1518. Another contemporary Portuguese chronicler, Fernão Lopes de Castanheda, also alludes to Jorge Mascarenhas' visit to Fukien, where 'he came to a city called Chincheo, in which it seemed to him that there were richer people than in Canton, and who were more civil than those of Canton, . . . and as long as he stayed there he found much friendship and good treatment from the people of that land, who are heathen and white and handsome, and do themselves very well'.[2] A third contemporary chronicler, Damião de Goes, states that Jorge Mascarenhas started from Canton with Chinese pilots and an interpreter, 'with whom he sailed along the coast of Chincheo, which is clean and peopled with many towns and villages: in this voyage he met many local ships which were sailing to different parts, and in a port where he anchored, they told him about the great city of Fuquiem,[3] whither he set sail, but in approaching the mouth of the river where it is situated, he received letters from Fernão Perez, which he sent him by land, in which he ordered him to return as it was time to sail for India, which he did and gave him an account of what he had done and seen in this voyage, and of the great fertility of those provinces and the abundance of every-

[1] João de Barros, Decada III, livro 2, cap. viii. Though first published in 1563, this Decada was finished about 1549, from internal evidence.

[2] Fernão Lopes de Castanheda, Os liuros quarto e quito da historia do descobrimento and conquista da India (Coimbra, 1552), Cap, XL. From the context of this brief account, it is clear that Castanheda was confusing hearsay reports about the Liu-chiu and their inhabitants with Mascarenhas' actual experiences in Fukien.

[3] Foochow, the capital of Fukien, 35 miles up the Min river.

thing, both of merchandize as of domestic animals and foodstuffs, where pepper is worth more than in China, and the goods which they give in exchange for those which they take thence are much better and cheaper than those of China'.[1]

In these extracts we find 'Chincheo' variously indicated as a name for Fukien province, and as the name for one of its ports, although the references are too imprecise to allow us to decide whether Chang-chou or Ch'üan-chou was meant in this connection. Barros states explicitly that it was a 'maritime city', and this might indicate Ch'üan-chou, which is only about six miles from the sea-coast, rather than Chang-chou which is some twenty-five miles up-river, but we cannot be sure of this.

Another allusion to the trade of the Liu-chiu islanders with Fukien at this time will be found in the letter of Vasco Calvo, written from the jail at Canton towards the end of 1524.[2] 'Then in the province of Foquem there is a city that is called Camcheu: it is a fine and large city. It stands on the sea, and is rich in silk and taffetas, and in camphor and much salt, and is of great traffic, and has in it a great number of junks, which can come and go in all seasons.' Here again, it is anybody's guess whether the writer was referring to Chang-chou or to Ch'üan-chou in this context. The same can be said of Diogo do Couto's vague references to 'the port of Chincheo', when relating the accidental discovery of Japan by some Portuguese in a junk which was blown off its course by a typhoon when bound for this port in 1542.[3]

The references to 'Chincheo' in the narratives of Galeote Pereira and his companions will be found in the text of the present work, and it is only necessary to repeat two of them here. At the beginning of his 'Tratado' Galeote Pereira remarks that the city of Fukien province which was best known to the Portuguese was 'Chincheo, in respect of a certain haven below it, whither in time past they were wont for merchandise to resort'.[4] The 'certain haven' is obviously Amoy Bay, or some

---

[1] *Quarta e ultima parte da chronica do felicissimo Rei Dom Emanuel* (Lisbon, 1567), cap. xxiv. In this extract, Goes evidently meant Canton, or the province of Kuangtung, where he wrote 'China'; unless he, like Castanheda, confused reports about the Liu-chiu islands with Mascarenhas' experiences in Fukien.

[2] D. Ferguson, *Letters from Portuguese captives in Canton*, pp. 92, 152. As noted previously, Dr. A. Cortesão has adduced good reasons for believing that these letters were written in November 1524; and not, as later copyists' errors led Ferguson to believe, in 1534–1536. (*Suma Oriental of Tomé Pires*, pp. xlv–xlviii.)

[3] Diogo do Couto, *Decada Quinta* (Lisbon, 1612), livro 8, cap. xii.

[4] ... 'Chincheo de que os purtugueses tem mais noticia e conhecimento, por aver muitos annos que vinhão a hum porto abaixo dela, a fazenda', in the original Portuguese, first printed in the *Archivum Historicum Societatis Iesu*, Vol. XXII, (1953), pp. 57–92.

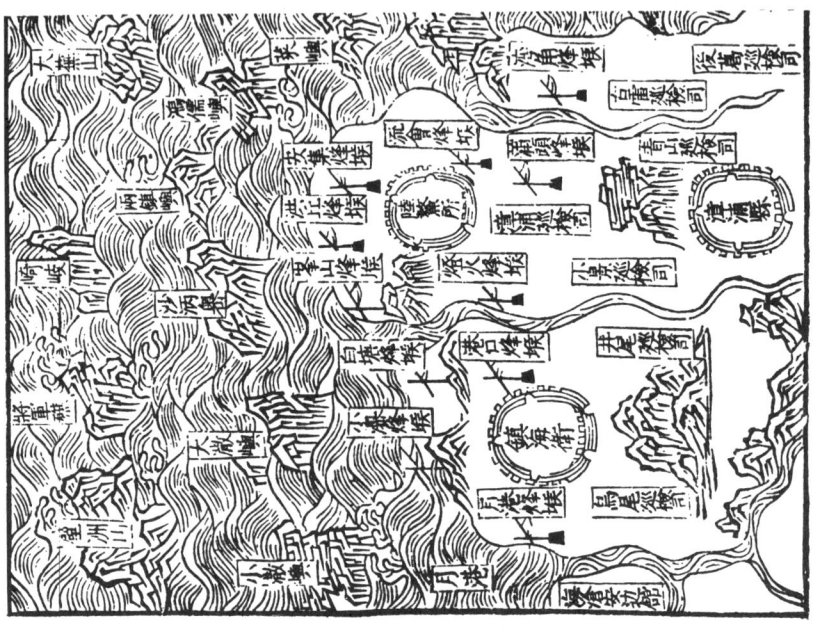

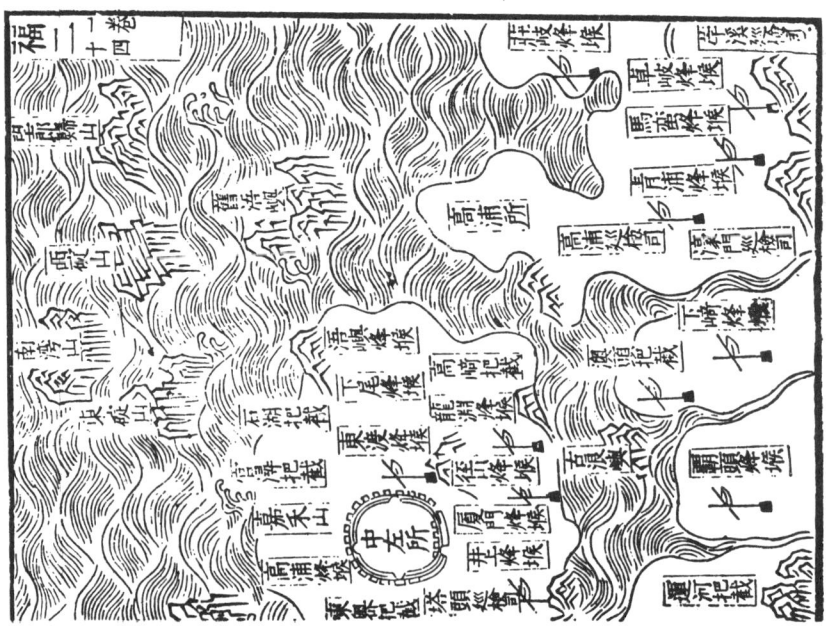

XI. Ming map of the Bay of Amoy, 1562
(From the *Ch'ou -hai-t'u-pien*)

Tos-tan-su

Wu-pai I

Yüeh-ch'iang

Chen-pai-wei

Chung-tso-so
(Amoy)

Toa-tan-su

Yüeh-chiang

Chên-hai-wei

Wu-hsü I

Chung-tso-so
(Amoy)

B. An-hai

C. Granite Bridge

D. Hui-i-tau

E. Quemoy

F. Lieh-hsü

G. 'Taotta' islands (Toa-tan-su)

A. Amoy

I. Kulangsu

K. Tower Island

L. Nan-t'ai-wu H. Wu-hsü I.

D. Hui-tau

B. An-pai

C. Granite Bridge

E. Öwanyö

F. Lieh-pai

G. "T'osotö' Islands (Tos-tau-su)

A. Amoy

I. Kulangsu

K. Tower Island

H. Nan-t'i-wu

L. Wu-pai

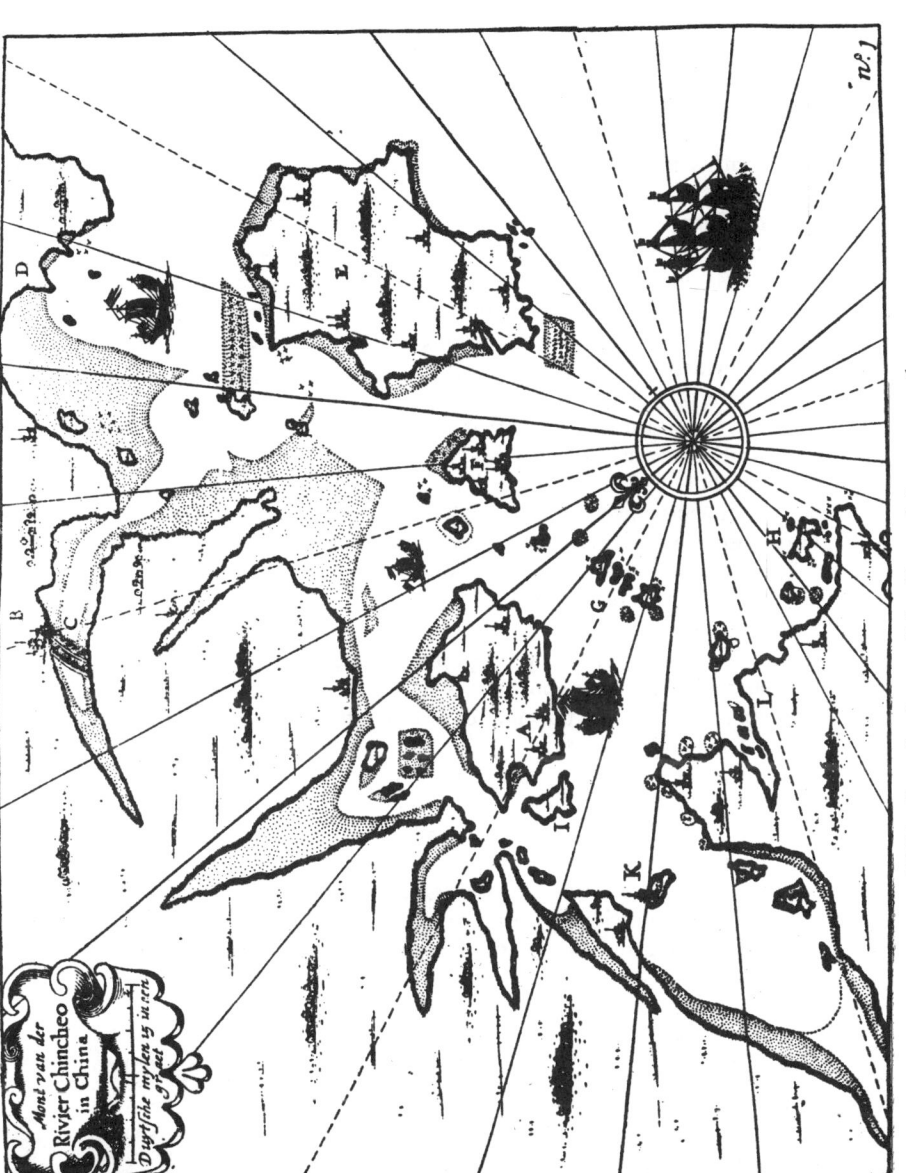

XII. Dutch chart of the Bay of Amoy, c. 1630
(From the *Begin ende Voortgangh*, 1645)

part of it; but it is less obvious whether 'Chincheo' stands here for Chang-chou or for Ch'üan-chou, since Amoy harbour can be said to be 'below' both these ports in terms of sixteenth-century geographical usage. More definite is Affonso Ramiro's statement that 'Chincheo' city, through which the Portuguese prisoners of 1549 were taken on their way to the provincial capital, was eight days journey from Foochow.[1] As previously mentioned, and as set forth in fuller detail below, the Spanish party in 1575 took seven days to cover this distance; the Dutch party of Cornelis Reyersen in 1623 took nine days, two of which, however, were spent in resting owing to the festivities connected with the Chinese New Year. These are very strong indications that the 'Chincheo' of Galeote Pereira and Affonso Ramiro is Ch'üan-chou, since during the sixteenth and seventeenth centuries a week or eight days was evidently the normal time for a road journey between Ch'üan-chou and the provincial capital.

Against this, it can be argued that G. Phillips, who spent some time as consul in Fukien, stated that in his time (1880) it was a five day journey from Foochow to Ch'üan-chou, and another five days from Ch'üan-chou to Chang-chou via T'ung-an.[2] This would mean that the Portuguese prisoners *could* have been carried from Chang-chou to Foochow in eight days by forced marches, which would identify 'Chincheo' with Chang-chou in this particular instance. But as we know that the Portuguese prisoners (or some of them) were dressed up as 'kings of Malacca' and exhibited as a spectacle to the populace in the towns through which they passed (pp.195–196 above), it is rather more likely, in view of the distances involved,[3] that the eight days which they took must have been counted from Ch'üan-chou.

At this point it will be as well to turn to the Chinese records and see what light they can throw on this problem. The *Chang-chou Gazetteer* under the date of Chia-Ching 26 [1547] records the visit of *Fo-lang-chi* (Portuguese) ships near Yüeh-chiang and Wu-hsü in the region of the Bay of Amoy, and the unsuccessful (and half-hearted) measures taken by the local authorities to prevent merchants from Ch'üan-chou and Chang-chou from trading with the foreigners.[4] The use of Wu-hsü and

[1] Cf. p. lii, n. (1) above.

[2] *T'oung Pao* (1st ser.), I, 227; Yule-Cordier, *Marco Polo*, II, 233.

[3] A Chinese Ming gazetteer gives the distance from Foochow to Ch'üan-chou as 410 *li*, and from Foochow to Chang-chou as 700 *li*, according to my colleague, Mr. O. B. van der Sprenkel. The approximate distances in a straight line are 100 miles and 160 miles, respectively.

[4] *Chang-chou-fu-chih*, chüan 31; *China Review*, XIX, 50; W. H. Chang, *Commentary*, p. 39. Wu-hsü is pronounced Gō-sū in the Amoy vernacular, and Yüeh-chiang as Gèh-kang, whence the corrupted versions which are found in European works. Wu-hsü at one time had been a coast-guard garrison station

other islands near Amoy as smuggling-bases by the Portuguese ships which frequented the Fukien coast at this time is amply attested by the other Chinese records which have been quoted previously (pp. xxiii–xxiv) and need not be repeated here. This fact did not escape the notice of G. Phillips, who, after vainly trying to find traces of the actual settlement *in situ* wrote, 'There is however frequent mention made in Chinese history of Portuguese ships resorting to the island of Gawseu [Wu-hsü] and the late Dr. Douglas with whom I had many conversations upon the subject, told me that he thought it not improbable for the Portuguese to have had a small settlement on shore at Ting-hai [= Chên-hai?] a place on the mainland, nearly opposite Gawseu, as the country people there were full of traditions of foreigners having lived among them many, many years back.'[1]

The references in the Chinese annals prove abundantly that the Portuguese traded in the outer waters of Amoy harbour and frequented several other islands there besides Wu-hsü; but they give no indication that their ships proceeded up-river as high as either Chang-chou or Ch'üan-chou, and I for one agree with Phillips that it is exceedingly unlikely that they did so. It is possible that Jorge Mascarenhas visited one of these two ports in 1518, and the tantalisingly brief and vague accounts of his visit to Fukien which are given by Barros, Castanheda and Goes, certainly imply that he did so. But it is odd that no description whatever is given of this city of 'Chincheo', whereas all these chroniclers give detailed accounts of Canton. Phillips wrote in 1891, 'As the Portuguese were only allowed to trade in the neighbourhood through the connivance of the authorities they doubtless never saw the famous port.[2] They simply traded in the outer waters, now known as Amoy harbour, to which they gave the name of Chincheo, a corruption of Chiangchiu, the local pronounciation of Changchow.' The learned Consul was perhaps a little hasty in his identification of Chincheo with Chang-chou. It might equally well be a corruption of Chüan-chou; or of Chin-chiang, which was another name for Ch'üan-chou in its capacity of district city (Chin-chiang-hsien).[3]

---

which was transferred to Chung-tso-so (Amoy) early in the Ming dynasty. The island then became a resort of pirates and smugglers (and hence of the Portuguese), and after 1550 a favourite rendezvous for the Wako or Japanese raiders (*Ch'ou-hai-t'u-pien*, chüan 4, p. 17).

[1] *China Review*, XVIII, 48.

[2] i.e. Zayton, which Phillips mistakenly identified with Yüeh-chiang, the seaport of Chang-chou at this period. *China Review*, XVIII, 44.

[3] Cf. for instance the confused references to these ports in the earliest Spanish report on China, compiled about 1565, printed in Sanz Arizmendi, 'Capítulo', pp. 447–449, where 'Chancheo' seems to be Chang-chou, and 'Tzuychiu' to be Ch'üan-chou. Other renderings are 'Chanchou', 'Chinchon.'

One important point to remember is that part of the north shore and many of the islands in the Bay of Amoy were not in Chang-chou prefecture at this time, but in that of Ch'üan-chou, as indeed they were for long afterwards. The name of Ch'üan-chou would in Chinese parlance, apply equally to the city and to any part of the *fu* or prefecture. It would seem that at one period the island of Wu-hsü was even incorporated in the Ch'üan-chou administrative area, though this may have been only for defence purposes.[1] Amoy itself was, as we have seen, purely a military station during most of the Ming dynasty and it did not achieve any great commercial importance until the seventeenth century. As the Portuguese traded indiscriminately with smugglers from both Chang-chou and Ch'üan-chou, but seldom if ever (save as prisoners) visited either port, it must have been very difficult for them to distinguish between two places with names so alike (to the untrained European ear) and so closely connected, administratively, strategically and commercially, with the islands in the Bay of Amoy. Small wonder that they continually confused the two, and that the chroniclers and cartographers in Europe perpetuated the confusion.

E. H. Parker has given us another valuable Chinese contribution to this question when he quotes from the *Tung-hsi Yang-kuo*, to the effect that the *Fên-hsün-Hsing-Ch'üan-tao* or governor of Hsing-hua and Chüan-chou, applied for permission about 1560, 'to establish duties in Chung-tso-so [Amoy] belonging to Ch'üan-chou, just as they were in Chang-chou.' He adds that it was proposed to make the Ch'üan-chou people deal solely with Japan, Luzon and Taiwan, and the Chang-chou people solely with the western barbarians; but this idea was, after discussion, dropped as impracticable.[2] In other words, merchants from both ports continued to trade, illegally or otherwise, with the foreigners who naturally did not make any distinction between them but lumped them all together under the designation of 'Chincheos'.

With the contemporary Spanish accounts of the 1575 mission, we reach somewhat firmer ground. From Rada's own itinerary, and still more from the detailed 'Relacion Verdadera' of Miguel de Loarca, it is crystal clear that the city of 'Chinchiu' which they twice visited on their way between T'ung-an and Foochow was Ch'üan-chou.[3] But this does not mean that the confusion was at end, and that the name 'Chincheo' or 'Chinchiu' henceforth designated Ch'üan-chou alone. Far from it. In Loarca's narrative we have a further perpetuation of this confusion. When giving a brief description of the principal ports of Fukien from

[1] Cf. p. 318, n. (4) above, and W. H. Chang, *Commentary*, p. 40.
[2] *China Review*, XVIII, 325.
[3] This fact was first convincingly demonstrated by E. H. Parker, and finally accepted by Phillips, *China Review*, XX, 25.

north to south, he enumerates first 'Ucheo' (Foochow), next 'Yngoa' (Hsing-hua), and then proceeds,—

'Chincheo is two leagues from the sea, and has at the mouth of the river Ahoinningui, a walled town. It has two thousand soldiers in garrison here and along the coast.' . . . 'From Chincheo to the sea is ten leagues along the river. At the mouth of the haven it has Tinahue with a garrison of ten thousand soldiers.'[1]

The first 'Chincheo' is obviously Ch'üan-chou, which is in fact about six miles from the sea; Ahoinningui is probably a very corrupted form of An-hai or Ngan-hai, which, although not connected with Ch'üan-chou by river, is only some twenty miles from this place, and then as now handled much of the trade with Ch'üan-chou.[2] The second 'Chincheo' is obviously Chang-chou, which is indeed about twenty-five or thirty miles from the sea; Tinahue, as explained previously, is probably a copyist's corruption of Ting-hai or Chên-hai-wei, which was situated on the promontory south of the entrance to Amoy harbour and was then a garrison headquarters. The strength of the garrison is considerably exaggerated, but here as elsewhere the Chinese were probably doing their best to impress and intimidate their Spanish visitors. Finally, it may be added that the story related by Loarca and Mendoza about the ships sent by the governor of 'Chincheo' to intercept and seize Wang Wang-kao's junk with the Spaniards on board at the entrance to Amoy harbour in July 1575, makes no sense at all unless it is assumed that 'Chincheo' in this case refers to Ch'üan-chou and Chang-chou alternately, and that their governors were mutually jealous of each other.[3]

Miguel de Loarca in his 'Verdadera Relacion' of 1575–1576, mentions that the Portuguese charts of the China Sea showed 'Chincheo' as situated in about 24° latitude,[4] and this would apply almost equally well either to Chang-chou or to Ch'üan-chou, which are in Lat. 24°31', and Lat. 24°49' respectively. Here as elsewhere, however, 'Chincheo' was primarily intended for the Bay of Amoy, whither the Spaniards were then bound; decisive proof of this is to be found in the Portuguese sailing-

---

[1] 'Verdadera Relacion', Part II, Ch. 5. In one variant of this MS. the first 'Chincheo' is spelt 'Chinchio' and the second 'Chincheo', but this does not affect my argument as 'chio' and 'cheo' are both attempts to render the Chinese -chou (chiu in Amoy vernacular), suffix denoting a departmental city.

[2] For the importance of An-hai as an outlet for the trade of Ch'üan-chou, cf. Yule-Cordier, Marco Polo, II, 240; L. Richards, Comprehensive Geography, p. 223.

[3] 'Verdadera Relacion', Part I, Ch. 5; González de Mendoza, History, Part II, Book I, Ch. xii.

[4] . . . 'segun las cartas portuguesas Chincheo está en 24 grados y Bulinao está en 16 poco mas ó menos' ('Verdadera Relacion', Parte I, cap. iv). Cf. also p. lxx above.

directions dating from *c.* 1550 to 1588, which were collected by Lin-schoten at Goa in 1583–1589, and printed as part of his celebrated *Itinerario*, first published at Amsterdam in 1595–1596.[1]

Chapters 30–43 of this invaluable compilation consist of translations of Portuguese *Roteiros* or rutters for the coasts of China and Japan, in which frequent mention is made of the Bay of Amoy and its approaches. Then as now the first object which struck the mariner on nearing this magnificent natural harbour was the splendid landmark of Nan-t'ai-wu, on the south shore, consisting of an old stone round tower at a height of some 1700 feet.[2] The Portuguese pilots when referring to this landmark usually likened it to the *Varella* or pagoda on the coast of Champa.[3] In these rutters of *circa* 1550–1588, it is stated that the Portuguese often traded or wintered at various islands in the Bay of Amoy, this Bay being indifferently called 'the haven of Chinchon', 'the haven of Chincheo', 'the islands of Chincheo', or 'the river of Chincheo'. Mention is made of Diogo Pereira having wintered with his ship off an island which was evidently Wu-hsü; and although the year is not given, it may well have been in 1548, when we know from other accounts that he was there.[4] It is also clear from these rutters that the Portuguese frequented Wu-hsü and other islands in company with the Japanese pirates. Another island much frequented by the Portuguese was Lieh-hsü (Léh-sū), or 'Little Quemoy', 'where often times the Portingales ships have lain to lade their wares and merchandises, such as are there to be had', as the Elizabethan translator of 1598 puts it.[5] Other places can be identified with fair certainty from a comparison of these various *Roteiros*, including Hai-mên island, 'where the Portingales have often dressed their ships', and where 'great store of victuals and other provisions' were readily available.[6] The

---

[1] The quotations which follow are taken from the English edition of 1598, checked with the reprint of the original Dutch edition as edited by J. C. M. Warnsinck for the Linschoten Society (Vols. IV and V of the Series XLIII, 1939), where the orthography of the original is preserved.

[2] *Itinerario* (ed. Warnsinck), V, 174, 212, 224, 239, 264 for typical examples. The tower itself is about sixty feet high, and it is said that on a clear day the mountains of Formosa are visible from it.

[3] Cape Varella (Mui Nai, Pagoda Cape), lat. 12° 55' N., and long. 109° 26' E. so called because on the top of the hill behind it is a large perpendicular rock, which mariners mistook for a pagoda. Cf. *Travels of Peter Mundy*, III, Pt. I, pp. 155–156 and Pl. X., fig. 25, for Peter Mundy's interesting and accurate description of this rock, 'one of Natures Wonders' as he terms it, which also formed the boundary-mark between Champa and Annam.

[4] Cf. Introduction, p. li above; *Itinerario* (ed. Warnsinck) V, 175; *Discours of voyages*, (1598), p. 365; *China Review*, XVIII, 45.

[5] *Discours of voyages*, p. 366; *Itinerario* (ed. Warnsinck), V, 175.

[6] *Discours of voyages*, p. 366; *Itinerario* (ed. Warnsinck), V, 176. The island's name is not mentioned in the text, but from the context it would seem that Hai-mên must be the island intended (Hái-mn̂g in Amoy vernacular).

Bay of Liao-lo or *Lialoo*, *lailo*, as it appears in the charts and *Roteiros*, on the south coast of Quemoy island, was also recommended as a good anchoring place in rough weather.[1] None of these rutters which are often very detailed—sometimes too much so for anyone who is not a professional navigator—make any mention of the Portuguese having proceeded either to Chang-chou or to Ch'üan-chou city. It is quite obvious that they never did so (with the possible exception of Jorge Mascarenhas in 1518), and that they simply traded off the islands in the outer harbour of the Bay of Amoy, which was what they meant, in nine cases out of ten, by the terms 'enseada de Chincheo' or 'rio de Chincheo'.

The late Mr. A. Kammerer, has tried hard to show, by quoting from a single one of these *Roteiros* (that reproduced in ch. 30 of Linschoten's work), that the Portuguese, unlike the Spaniards, reserved the word 'Chincheo' exclusively for Ch'üan-chou,[2] but this theory is quite untenable. Whatever may be the wording of the French edition of 1619 from which Kammerer quotes, the original Dutch edition of 1596 uses the words 'haven van Chinchon' and 'haven van Chincheo', quite indiscriminately to designate Amoy Bay in this very chapter.[3] It is true that in one instance (and in one only) does the original text describe the approaches to Ch'üan-chou which it terms 'Chencheu';[4] but elsewhere 'Chincheo', 'Chinchon' and 'Chincheu' are used indifferently to describe the Bay of Amoy and its outer approaches, of which the 'varella de Chincheo' is always cited as being the most conspicuous.[5]

We now come to two clear-cut cases where 'Chincheo' can only be identified with Chang-chou. The first of these is the 'Relación' by Fr. Agustín de Tordesillas O.F.M., of the journey which this friar with a number of others made to China in 1579, on an abortive attempt to found a Franciscan mission there. The party miraculously reached Canton without being intercepted by the Chinese, but from there they were eventually sent overland to Chang-chou and Amoy, where they

[1] Lailo appears on the Mappemonde of Lopo Homem (1554) with the inscription *Lailo onde se fez a veniaga* ('Lailo where the trade is carried on'). Cf. A. Kammerer, *La Découver e de la Chine*, pp. 152, 170, 223; *Discours of voyages*, p. 366; *Itinerario*, (ed. Warnsinck), V, 177, 265; Lailo is also mentioned by Rada (cf. p. 305 above), and Loarca, 'Verdadera Relacion', Parte I, Cap. xii, under the name of 'Laulo', which approximates more to the Amoy vernacular form of Liāu-lô. It is likewise marked on the chart of Amoy harbour in O. Dapper, *Tweede en Derde Gesandschap*, pp. 130–131; cf. *Ch'ou-hai-t'u-pien*, chüan 1, map nr. 14.

[2] A. Kammerer, *La Découverte de la Chine*, pp. 103–105, 170–171, 223–224.

[3] *Itinerario* (ed. Warnsinck), V, 174–177, 212, 224, 239, 252, 259, 262, 264–265; *Discours of Voyages*, pp. 365–366, 381, 386, 392–393, 399, 401, 403–404.

[4] *Itinerario* (ed. Warnsinck), pp. 174–175; *Discours of Voyages*, p. 367.

[5] Cf. for example *Itinerario* (ed. Warnsinck), pp. 174, 212; *Discours of Voyages*, pp. 365, 381.

were embarked for Manila early in 1580. The details of their itinerary show beyond dispute that their 'ciudad de Chincheo' was none other than Chang-chou.[1] The second identification occurs in the unpublished Portuguese-Chinese dictionary compiled by Father Matteo Ricci S.J., where, in front of the word 'Chincheo', he has written the Chinese characters for Chang-chou.[2]

The Dutch navigators who followed the Portuguese into the China Sea at the beginning of the seventeenth century naturally made great use of Linschoten's translation of the sailing-directions of their Portuguese predecessors, and so likewise perpetuated the confusion over 'Chincheo'. We find this name, with variants such as 'Chincheuw', 'Chinchiu', and 'Sinseau', applied indifferently to designate Fukien province, Ch'üan-chou city, Chang-chou city, and, most commonly of all, the region of the Bay of Amoy, under the designation of 'the river of Chincheo'.[3]

Mention has previously been made of the journey of Cornelis Reyersen overland from the Bay of Amoy to Foochow and back in 1623, along the same coast road over which the Portuguese prisoners of 1549 were taken.[4] In one entry in his journal he writes Chang-chou as 'Chincheuw', and in another entry he refers to the same city as 'T'schangchu'.[5] Ch'üan-chou, which the Dutch party by-passed on the way, both going and coming, is referred to as 'Chouysuy' and as 'T'souytsou', as well as the more normal 'Chincheuw'.[6] Obviously the Dutch, like the Portuguese and Spaniards, were very careless in their use of the word 'Chincheo', and their ears were seldom able to distinguish between Ch'üan-chou and Chang-chou on the tongues of their interpreters.

This confusion in the minds of the men on the spot was, of course, reflected and perpetuated in the maps and charts of the China coast drawn by cartographers in Europe, and based on information supplied by people who had only hazy (and often conflicting) ideas concerning the identification of 'Chincheo'. This word appears on Portuguese portulans and *mappemondes* from about 1550 onwards, both as the designation of Fukien province, and of a port or bay therein.[7] We have

---

[1] *Sinica Franciscana*, II, 155–157; *T'oung Pao*, XXXIV, 191–194, 208.

[2] *Fonti Ricciane*, I, 350, n. (2).

[3] Cf. W. P. Groeneveldt, *De Nederlanders in China*, pp. 16, 35, 37, 46, 139, 163.

[4] Printed in full by W. P. Groeneveldt, *De Nederlanders in China*, pp. 141–162.

[5] W. P. Groeneveldt, *De Nederlanders in China*, pp. 146, 161.

[6] *Ibid.*, pp. 144, 148–149, 160.

[7] A. Cortesão, *Cartografia e cartógrafos portugueses*, II, 76; A. Kammerer, *La Découverte de la Chine par les Portugais*, pp. 103–104. As stated above, I disagree with Kammerer's conclusions; but I agree with his remark that deductions drawn from a study of these maps form an 'argument de peu de poids il est vrai à cause de l'échelle réduite des dits portulans, qui a embarrassé les dessinateurs e trendu les précisions difficiles'.

seen that Miguel de Loarca observed that 'Chincheo', in the sense of a port or bay, was placed by the Portuguese in about lat. 24° in their charts, and this is confirmed by the *Roteiros* translated by Linschoten, where 'Chincheo' harbour is located in lat. 24¼°, or in 24½°. It would, however, be a mistake to argue from this that Chang-chou (in lat. 24° 30′) is necessarily indicated here rather than Ch'üan-chou (in lat. 24° 49′). It may have been so in a few specific cases; but from the evidence adduced above, the reader will see that it was usually the Bay of Amoy which was intended by the 'enseada de Chincheo', in the sailing-directions on which the maps themselves were largely based. Moreover, as noted previously, the scale of these portulans is far too small to show the accurate location of the places indicated. Even the Portuguese settlement of Macao was located on the wrong side of the Pearl River estuary in most sixteenth-century portulans; this grave error is perpetuated in Linschoten's map[1] despite the fact that it is contradicted by the text of the *Itinerario*. The only thing that can be said with confidence is that the Portuguese located 'the haven of Chincheo' in about latitude 24°, and this line does in fact run through the southern half of Amoy harbour.

The seventeenth-century Dutch cartographers were more skilful than their Portuguese predecessors, and more of their large-scale charts have survived, so the identification of the 'haven [or river] of Chincheo' presents no problem on their maps. For proof that it was Amoy harbour, the reader need only turn to the chart of the 'Mont van der Revier Chincheo in China', which is annexed to the Journal of Seyger van Rechteren (1629–1632) as printed in Deel II of the *Begin ende Voortgangh* (Amsterdam, 1645),[2] and to the still larger-scale chart of Amoy harbour and its outer approaches which is to be found between pp. 130–131 of O. Dapper's *Tweede en Derde Gesandschap na het Keyserryck van Taysing of China* (Amsterdam, 1670). The landmark of Nan-t'ai-wu, the island of Wu-hsü and other places where the Portuguese traded in 1547–1548, as the Dutch did seventy-five years later, are clearly marked on these charts.

A seventeenth-century Chinese chronicle which was quoted by Phillips and Parker in their controversy concerning Chincheo, states that 'from T'ai-wan you can come in two days and nights to the inland sea which leads to both Chang-chou and Ch'üan-chou',[3] in other words

---

[1] Cf. A. Cortesão, *Cartografia e cartógrafos Portugueses*, II, 288.

[2] pp. 45–5 of this journal. The scale is 15 German miles to a degree. The journal was first printed at Zwolle in 1635, together with the map, but I have not access to a copy of this exceedingly rare first edition, although another two editions, dated 1639, are in the British Museum. Cf. p. 317 above.

[3] *China Review*, XVIII, p. 325, where the Chinese characters for this expression are reproduced, as they likewise are on pp. 365 *infra* (Chang-ch'üan-nei-chiang).

2D

the Bay of Amoy. It is exactly in this sense that the Portuguese, Spaniards and Dutch used the expression 'the haven [or islands, or river] of Chincheo', while Chincheo *per se* was applied indifferently to both Chang-chou and Ch'üan-chou. This was all the more natural since the north shore and the islands adjoining it, including Amoy, fell within the jurisdiction of Ch'üan-chou prefecture, whereas the southern shore came under that of Chang-chou. As the Europeans had few opportunities of penetrating to either of these two cities, it is not surprising that they were seldom able to distinguish between them, and that confusion over the name and application of 'Chincheo' lasted for centuries.

Appendix II

'Aucheo'

GONZÁLEZ DE MENDOZA when describing the expedition of the Austin friars to Fukien in 1575, gives a lengthy account of their reception by the viceroy of 'Aucheo',[1] which city, as we have seen, is indisputably the provincial capital of Foochow. In his account of the pioneer Franciscan mission to China in 1579, Mendoza likewise describes the visit of these friars-minor to the viceroy of 'Aucheo', which he identifies with the 'Aucheo' of Rada and his companions in Fukien.[2] In this he was badly mistaken, as it is clear from the accounts which he reproduces that the 'Aucheo' of 1579 was reached by the Franciscans sailing for five days up the West River from Canton. This Aucheo, then, cannot possibly be Foochow but must be identical either with Wu-chou or with Chao-ch'ing-fu.

As regards Wu-chou, the position was correctly stated by Christovão Vieira in 1524, when he wrote from his prison at Canton that the senior provincial officials of Kuangtung province normally resided 'in a city called Vcheu [Wu-chou] which lies at the border of both those provinces. This city belongs to Queançy [Kuangsi]. They reside there most of the time, because they carry on war there, and from there they govern both. Sometimes they come to Cantão [Canton], and stay two or three months, now one, now another; and sometimes two years pass without anyone's coming. In this province of Quēçy [Kuangsi] a very large part is perpetually in a state of insurrection, without their being able to remedy it. This is the cause why they stay there for most of the time. This city lies to the west of Cantão a matter of thirty leagues by river,[3] because there are no roads by land and the country is all intersected by rivers. They go there in five days travelling post-haste with many people for towing, and come in three, going night and day. The water flows from there to Cantão'.[4]

It is curious that Miguel de Loarca transformed Hok-chiu (*Hocchiu* for Foochow) into 'Ucheo', and Mendoza into 'Aucheo', just as the Spaniards sometimes wrote 'Ochian' for Hok-kien (Fukien). Whether this was due to the peculiarities of some Fukien vernacular or to the

---

[1] Part II, Book I, Chs. xxi–xxviii.
[2] Part II, Book II, Chs. vii–x.
[3] Wu-chou is really about 220 miles from Canton by river.
[4] D. Ferguson, *Letters from Portuguese captives in Canton*, pp. 79, 135.

carelessness of their copyists, I cannot say. But as Loarca wrote about the 'viceroy of Ucheo' (meaning Foochow), González de Mendoza, when writing his *Historia* evidently confused this functionary with the Viceroy of the Two Kuang who had his seat first at 'Vcheo' (Wu-chou), and then at 'Soquin' (Chao-ch'ing).[1]

In his account of the Franciscan expedition to China in 1579, which is confessedly based largely on that of Fr. Agustín de Tordesillas,[2] González de Mendoza relates how the party miraculously arrived at Canton from the Philippines, and were brought before a local magistrate who cross-examined them as to who they were and why they had come. He then proceeds, 'when this examination and talk was finished, he commanded them to return unto their ship, promising them for to write unto the viceroy (who was thirty leagues from that place), and to give him to understand that they were men without any suspicion, and that he might well give them licence for to come to his presence: upon which relation he would command what should be done, either to tarry or to go unto him.'[3]

The friars were told a few weeks later that the Portuguese of Macao had memorialised the local authorities, warning them against the Spaniards as undesirable and unauthorised intruders who had come to spy out the land. The examining magistrate forwarded the Macaonese memorial 'unto the viceroy of the province of Aucheo, that he might see and peruse it; who when that he had easily perceived it, and understood the intent of him that presented the same, and the innocency of them that were therein complained of, he sent and commanded the governor of Canton for to give them good entertainment, and not to permit any harm or hurt to be done unto them, and that he should send them unto the city of Aucheo, for that he would see them, for that it was told him that they seemed to be holy men, and although that they had their apparel in the same form of the Austin friars, (whom he had seen), yet their garments were of another colour and more asper'.[4]

Reference to Fr. Agustín de Tordesillas' account shows that here, for once, González de Mendoza has taken unwarrantable liberties with his original which does not mention 'Aucheo' at all. The relevant passage in the original version reads simply 'according to what we were told, the viceroy took no notice of the [Macaonese] memorial; on the contrary, he

[1] Wu-chou was made the general headquarters of the viceroyalty of the two Kuang in 1469; Delamarre ed., *Histoire de la dynastie des Ming*, pp. 340–341. I have not been able to ascertain when these headquarters were transferred to Chao-ch'ing-fu, but they were still at Wuchou in 1575.

[2] First printed correctly in *Sinica Franciscana*, II, 103–160.

[3] *History* (Hakluyt Society ed.), II, 154. Cf. *Sinica Franciscana*, II, 124–125.

[4] *History* (Hakluyt Society ed.), II, 159.

said that he wanted to see us, because he had already seen the Austin friars when they went to Chincheo, where he was then viceroy'.[1]

González de Mendoza having here wrongly identified 'Aucheo', persists in the same error for the rest of his account of the 1579 expedition. He thus makes the friars go to Foochow, instead of up the West River in the direction of Wu-chou, which is what they actually did do. They did not, apparently, get as far as Wu-chou; since their interview with the viceroy of the Two Kuang took place at Chao-ch'ing-fu on the 21 August, as related in detail by Fr. Agustín de Tordesillas who calls it 'la ciudad de Soquin'.[2]

The friars remained for a week or ten days in Chao-ch'ing-fu, before they returned to Canton where they arrived on 2 September 1579. Apropos of their stay in Chao-ch'ing-fu, González de Mendoza introduces another gratuitous and unwarranted interpolation, when, referring to this city as 'Aucheo', he adds 'The mightiness of this city, and the great admiration they had, with the multitude of people, and a wonderful great bridge the which they passed, with many other things of the which they made mention, we do let pass, for that it is declared into you more at large in the relation given by the Augustin friars, in the book before this, at their entry into the said city'.[3]

We are not concerned with the doings of the Franciscans after their return to Canton, and it will suffice to state that some of them went to Macao, where they founded a convent of their Order, and the others returned via Chang-chou (here called 'Chincheo') to Manila in Dec. 1579–January 1580, as already mentioned.[4] González de Mendoza's mistaken identification of Chao-ch'ing-fu with 'Aucheo' is all the more surprising as his chief authority, Fr. Agustín de Tordesillas, always writes of this city as 'Soquin'; nor does he mention any bridge at 'Soquin', and does not describe the city nor allude to its population. Francisco de Dueñas, another member of the 1579 expedition, described Chao-ch'ing-fu as being 'a small city that would have about twelve thousand householders' (vezinos). After describing its exact situation on the West River, he explains that this city had been selected as the seat of the viceroyalty of the Two Kuang partly because of its natural strength and partly because it was 'in the middle of the two provinces'.[5] González de

[1] *Sinica Franciscana* II, 128. Liu Yao-hui was governor of Foochow in 1575 and viceroy of the two Kuang in 1579.
[2] *Sinica Franciscana*, II, 135–143.
[3] *History* (Hakluyt Society ed.), II, 167.
[4] pp. 323–324.
[5] . . . 'en medio de las dos provincias,' *Sinica Franciscana*, II, 136, n. (3). This last statement is, on the face of it, more applicable to Wu–chou which lies just on the Kuangsi side of the provincial border, another hundred miles or so up-river; but from other indications it is evident that Chao-ch'ing (or Shiu-hing as

Mendoza's *gaffe* has been overlooked by his editors and commentators, and has misled at least one of them very badly.[1] I cannot explain why Mendoza, usually so careful and conscientious an editor, should have substituted 'Aucheo' for 'Soquin'. I can only tentatively suggest that the reference to the 'viceroy' who had been in 'Chincheo' in 1575 confused him; and that he did not realise that this mandarin [Liu Yao-hui] had since been transferred from the capital of Fukien to that of the Two Kuang, so he deliberately altered 'Soquin' to 'Aucheo'.

While on the subject of 'Aucheo' or Foochow, it may be recalled that both Portuguese and Spanish accounts of this city as it was in the sixteenth century imply that it was situated on a river, or at least traversed by numerous canals which reminded the foreign visitors of Mexico City and Venice.[2] Marco Polo went even further, and wrote 'there flows through the middle of this city a great river, which is about a mile in width, and many ships are built at the city which are launched upon this river'.[3] The Venetian traveller has been taken severely to task for this by several of his commentators, who point out that the river Min does not flow through the middle of the city, nor even under its walls. It was for this reason, among others, that Phillips suggested that Polo's 'Fuju' was not Foochow, as was generally thought, but Ch'üan-chou.

The identification of Fuju with Foochow was stoutly maintained by Yule, who pointed out that the suburbs at any rate extended to the river, and that Fortune, who was there in 1845, so spoke of it.[4] He did not, however, quote Galeote Pereira and Martín de Rada in this connection, so it is worth pointing out that they had much the same impression as 'Il Milione' had. A similar impression is given by the narratives of the Dutch envoys who visited Foochow in 1663–1666,[5] and the testimony of so many independent sources cannot be disregarded.

it is also called nowadays) was really the city visited by the friars. This would indicate that the transfer of the seat of government of the Two Kuang from Wu-chou to Chao-ching, took place in 1575–1579.

[1] A. Kammerer, *La Découverte de la Chine*, pp. 104–105, where his n. (4) requires drastic revision.

[2] pp. 28 and 256 above.

[3] Yule Cordier, *Marco Polo*, II, 231.

[4] Yule-Cordier, *Marco Polo*, II, 232–233. Yule might have quoted the description of Foochow in Doolittle, *Social Life of the Chinese*, I, 17–32, in support of his view.

[5] O. Dapper, *Tweede en Derde Gesandschap*, p. 204, where, however, the editor has wrongly placed Foochow on the southern bank of the Min. Yule (*op. cit.* p. 233, n.) remarks, 'I do not know the worth of the old engravings in Montanus. A view of Fu-chau in one of these shows a broad creek from the river penetrating to the heart of the city.' Comparison with the originals indicates that the Dutch engravers took some liberties with the drawings from which they worked, but the main features are usually reflected with fair accuracy. Cf. P. A. Tiele, *Nederlandsche Bibliographie*, p. 179.

Although the walled city proper lies about three miles north of the Min River, the suburb of Nantai lies on both sides of its northern channel, and in their general descriptions of the city the old travellers evidently made no distinction between the city and the southern suburb, which are connected by a long straggling street.[1] In Ming times, there may well have been more canals in the city than there are nowadays, and two of the sluice-gates mentioned by Pereira still survived up till recently at least.[2] Miguel de Loarca in his account of the city ('Verdadera Relacion', Parte I, Ch. ix) also states that it was liable to heavy flooding, and signs of flood damage were very evident at the time of the Spaniards' stay there in August, 1575.

Although the comparisons with Venice and Mexico City might have been a trifle far-fetched, I have no doubt that the 'Fuju' of Marco Polo, the 'Fucheo' of Galeote Pereira, and the 'Ucheo' of Miguel de Loarca are all to be identified with Foochow. The 'Aucheo' of González de Mendoza, on the other hand, refers to Foochow when he is dealing with the Augustinian mission of 1575, and to Ch'ao-ching-(Shiu-hing)-fu when he is dealing with the Franciscan mission of 1579.

[1] Cf. pp. 255–257 above.

[2] Moreover, old maps of Foochow, such as the one reproduced from an eighteenth-century edition of the *Fu-chou-fu-chih* on pp. 26–27 of this work, likewise depict the city as traversed by several streams and canals.

Appendix III

THE GREAT GRANITE BRIDGES OF FUKIEN

GALEOTE PEREIRA'S reference to the great stone bridges of Fukien province is the earliest mention of these granite monoliths which I have found in European accounts of Ming China, but his wording is so vague and ambiguous that it is difficult to say which two bridges he had in mind.[1] In effect, he says that before you come to 'Chincheo' you come to two populous and well-walled cities, equal in size with 'Cinceo', and with a gigantic bridge at the entrance to either one of them. Since the Portuguese captives traversed this part of Fukien from south to north after their capture in 1549, when they were taken from 'Chincheo' to Foochow, one might infer that he means the *southern* entrance to each city, although there is no positive proof of this. But on their way to Kueilin in 1550–1551, the Portuguese might have gone over this road in the contrary direction, so he might have been thinking in terms of north to south. It may be thought that the estimation which he gives of the number of arches (forty) in one bridge might help definitely to identify this one at least; but later accounts of these bridges diverge so markedly from each other in important details, that its identification is problematical, as can be seen from a comparison with the following.

Miguel de Loarca, in his 'Verdadera Relacion'[2] of the Spanish envoys' journey overland from Amoy to Foochow in 1575, mentions a bridge at the entrance to Ch'üan-chou, 'with a drawbridge at the end; the bridge would be about 800 paces[3] long and all its stones are about twenty-two feet long and five broad, and it is certainly a sight worth seeing. There were many ships made fast to the bridge which sail from the sea up the river, and other large boats which pass up the river to the city'. This bridge can hardly be any other than the Shun-chi bridge built in 1211 at the site of Ch'üan-nan, in the days of Zayton's grandeur a settlement for traders from all parts of the medieval East,[4] and which is still (or was up till 1938) a mooring-place for junks.

Loarca further relates that on the morning that the Spanish party left

[1] pp. 7–8 above.

[2] Part I, Ch. 7.

[3] 'Pasos', the *paso* is defined in Minsheu's Spanish–English Dictionary of 1599 as 'a step, a pace in going or striding, the measure of two feet and a half'.

[4] Ecke-Demiéville, *Twin Pagodas of Zayton*, p. 4. Phillips, *T'oung Pao*, V, 7–8, says this bridge was originally built in 1190, was repaired in 1341 and 1472 and was 1,500 feet in length.

'Megoa' [= Hegoa = Hsing-hua] for 'Ucheo' [= Fucheo = Foochow], 'we passed a bridge of stone work which was about 1,300 paces long, and all the stones thereof measured 17 and 18 paces.' I cannot identify this bridge; and it is all the more surprising that Loarca describes this bridge to the north of Hsing-hua, and briefly alludes to the famous bridges over the Min River at the southern approach to Foochow,[1] but makes no mention of the celebrated Loyang bridge, some six miles north-east of Ch'üan-chou, which is often styled the most famous bridge in all China. He does not allude to any bridges at all during the return trip over the same coast road; but the account in González de Mendoza's *History* (Part II, Book I, ch. xxi) describes the same bridge as does Loarca, adding that the Spaniards stayed there a good time, 'measuring it all from one end to another, that it might be put amongst the wonders of that country, which they took a note of', some of the stones being twenty-two feet long. Possibly the Spanish accounts wrongly placed the Loyang bridge to the north of Hsing-hua, instead of outside Ch'üan-chou.[2] Alternatively, there may then have been an imposing bridge just north of Hsing-hua which has since fallen into ruin and disappeared, as have several of the great granite bridges of Fukien.[3]

Marco Polo does not mention the Loyang bridge either, and this surprising omission has likewise puzzled his commentators, some of whom suppose that he must have taken another route between Foochow and 'Zayton'.[4] However this may have been, there can be no doubt that both Galeote Pereira and his companions in 1549, and the Spanish envoys of 1575, travelled over the coastal high-road, so an account of this celebrated bridge may well find a place here. I may add that the

[1] . . . 'crossing the river by three bridges, whither large ships can come and pass up-river by lowering their masts.' 'Verdadera Relacion', Part I, Ch. ix. The bridges were really two, of which the longest, measuring some 1,300 feet, crossed the north channel of the Min river and the other one the south channel, an island in mid-river serving as a base for the two, conjointly known as the 'Bridge of Ten Thousand Ages'.

[2] The location of this bridge in Mendoza's account likewise confused G. Phillips, who, when finally agreeing with E. H. Parker that Mendoza's Chincheo was Chüan-chou and not (as he had at first maintained) Chang-chou, adds: 'I myself thought so at first, but the description of the route from Megua to Aucheo presented a difficulty to one who has travelled over the road so frequently as I have done. I refer particularly to the description of the bridge of 1,300 feet long crossed by the embassy the day they left Megua. I know of no bridge answering to this description between Hinghwa [Hsing-hua] and Foochow. This to my mind seems most probably to refer to the Loyang bridge, and if its description were placed immediately after that relating to the city of Chincheo, I should never have hesitated about Mendoza's Chincheo as Chinchew' [Chüan-chou]. *China Review*, XX, 25.

[3] Cf. *T'oung Pao*, V, 10; Fugl-Meyer, *Chinese Bridges*, p. 79.

[4] Yule-Cordier, *Marco Polo*, II, 231.

Loyang bridge is briefly described in Cornelis Reijersen's account of his overland journey from Amoy to Foochow in 1623,[1] and much more fully and accurately by the Dutch visitors to Fukien in 1663–1664.[2]

Medhurst in his *Dictionary of the Hok-keen Dialect*, (Macao, 1832) pp. xxii–xxiv, describing this bridge from Chinese sources, states that 'it is built of a black kind of stone, supported by about 250 strong columns or buttresses, 125 on each side. These columns are sharpened towards the upper part, in order better to break the impetuous egress and regress of the current; they are capped with five stones, of an equal breadth, each twenty feet long and two broad, which successively touch one another at each buttress, and thus form a pathway to walk upon, at least 2,500 feet in length; on each side, rails of the same kind of stone are put for safety, adorned with lions and other images'. These are probably the 'Roman works' mentioned in Galeote Pereira's account.

The legend connected with the building of this bridge is a very interesting one and is worth reproducing here, together with the account of the structure itself by a Protestant missionary who examined it in 1877.[3] 'It is built across an estuary which at low tide is a mud flat, covered with oyster-beds. The river, at this point about forty yards wide, runs rapidly near the centre of the expanse of mud. When the tide is in the whole is completely covered from shore to shore. The bridge is a thousand yards long. I timed myself to nine and a half minutes' quick walking in crossing it. One hundred and twenty piers, which rise to nearly forty feet above high water mark, support the long masses of granite which span the space between the shores. The buttresses on the north side are very massive, in order to resist the pressure of the spring torrents. After 800 years of wear the roadway is in very good condition. Five blocks of stone, each twenty feet and more in length, and two feet in breadth, form the road, which is therefore about ten feet broad, though it varies somewhat. On either side, is a heavy balustrade, or railing, of massive granite, held in position, not by cement, but block fitting into block in sockets.

'The story of its origin is substantially written on a tablet at one end of the structure. Before the bridge was built, travellers and market people were compelled to cross this estuary in the ferry-boats, or they must needs make a long *détour* which would be a good part of a day's journey. But there are hills to the north at which they used to look with gruesome awe, because sudden squalls would come down upon the water in spring and summer, and many lives were lost by the upsetting

---

[1] W. P. Groeneveldt, *De Nederlanders in China*, p. 150.

[2] O. Dapper, *Tweede en Derde Gesandschap*, pp. 204–205.

[3] E. J. Dukes, *Everyday Life in China; or scenes along river and road in Fuhkien* (London, 1885), pp. 144–150.

of the boats. These squalls did not arise like common breezes. They were caused by two wicked fairies who lived up there among the hills, shaped like a tortoise and a snake, or at the bottom of the river, in the form of a boat and a man. . . . When they had come down from the hills and had transformed themselves into a man and a boat, the boat and man used to appear at the ferry to seek for fares. There was no telling them from ordinary boats and men; so they took their passengers into mid-stream, and then came the terrible "squall of the fairies"; the boat sank; the man and boat became a snake and a tortoise, and devoured the poor people at their leisure.

'Now it happened that about the year 1000 A.D. a boat full of market folk was nearing the fatal spot where so many people had been carried off by the fairies. The wind began to blow all ways at once. The waves broke into the midst of the passengers, who cried out that the tortoise and the snake were upon them. Amid the lamentations, however, a voice was heard distinctly saying, "Chhah, the mandarin in the boat, must build a bridge." No sooner were the words uttered than the winds subsided, and the boat reached the shore in safety. Great and grave was the discussion as to the mysterious voice. There was clearly something supernatural about it. "Who among us bears the surname Chhah?" No one replied, until at length a woman timidly confessed that her husband's surname was Chhah, and that she had married him a few months before. With one consent all declared that she would become the mother of a man whose work should be to build a bridge over this dangerous creek and so defeat the wicked fairies.

'Not long after this a son was born to her, whom she named Siang, and she vowed that Chhah Siang[1] should obey "the heavenly command". He proved to be an intelligent child. His mother wrought upon his youthful imagination by constantly describing what a fine thing it was to be a mandarin, and rule over large masses of people. She gave him a good education which would fit him for office. And as he grew into youth, she revealed to him the remarkable facts that had heralded his birth. The boy was powerfully impressed by the story she told of the voice from the air. He resolved to spare no efforts to fulfil his mission.

'He had, however, to face a very great difficulty. There is an ancient law in China that forbids any magistrate to hold office in the neighbourhood where he was born. What was to be done? How could he overcome this formidable barrier to his noble ambition? He had passed his early

---

[1] Ts'ai Hsiang in Mandarin. H. A. Giles, *Chinese Biographical Dictionary*, nr. 1974, says that he was a native of Hsien-yu in Fukien, where he was born in 1011. He distinguished himself as a poet and official under the Emperor Jen Tsung of the Sung dynasty, and rose to be President of the Board of Rites before his death in 1066. Cf. p. 337, n. (2) below.

examinations, and was ready for office. He determined now to proceed to Peking,[1] to seek employment in the Imperial palace, and then to wait his opportunity. He was about fifty years of age, and in daily attendance upon the emperor, when he matured his plans for carrying out his life-long project. Knowing that the emperor was intending to take a walk in the palace grounds, Chhah Siang went down the grove an hour before, and having previously chosen a tree with an ant's nest at its foot, he wrote in large characters with a brush and a pot of honey, 'Chhah Siang, the learned, be magistrate in your native prefectural city'. He then returned to the palace to accompany the emperor on his walk.

'The party soon set out, and passing down the grove, the emperor caught sight of a mass of ants marshalled in squadrons which shaped them on the trunk of the tree into Chinese characters. In breathless astonishment the emperor stood still and read aloud, "Chhah Siang, the learned, be magistrate in your native prefectural city!" In a moment Chhah Siang, pretending not to notice that the emperor was only read-ing what was on the tree, fell upon his knees and thanked him for the appointment. In vain the emperor protested that he had not intended to nominate him for office. The Celestial prince was reminded that he could not recall the words he certainly had uttered. The law was over-ruled for this once, seeing that there seemed to be a divine omen in it. Chhah Siang returned to the southern province of Fuh-kien, and became prefect of Chinchew [Chüan-chou], the city whose authority governs Lo-iu [Loyang]. At once Chhang Siang began to gather funds, and to make needful preparation for the great work he had before him. He devoted all his leisure time to arousing the enthusiasm of the people in regard to the proposed bridge. He called on the whole prefecture for voluntary subscriptions. The towns and villages caught their governor's enthusiasm, and responded heartily.

'The task was gigantic. After many years of labour, in which vast sums of money had been spent, it seemed likely to fail because of the impossibility of laying the foundations of the centre piers, where still the stream flows rapidly at low tide. If the river were to run almost dry the thing might be done; but unfortunately even a long period of drought scarcely affected this part of the stream at all. After suffering distress of mind for many months, and trying every imaginable scheme, a happy thought occured to Chhah Siang. He resolved to write a letter to the god of the sea, and to ask his Marine Majesty to be so kind as to draw off all the water. When the letter was ready, Chhah, sitting on his magistrate's bench, said, "Who is able to descend to the sea?" A man in the chamber at once said, "Here am I, your Excellency." Now, it should be explained

---

[1] [sic] for K'ai-fêng, which was the capital of the Sung dynasty at this period.

that Chinese names are usually translatable, and on this occasion it happened that in the hall was a man whose name was Ui Loh-iu ("Able Descend-sea"), who thinking himself called, replied to Chhah's question. They laughed a little at the mistake, but regarded it as a good omen, and Mr. "Able Descend-sea" was compelled to make good his name.

Ui Loh-iu took the letter, and proceeded to seek an interview with the god of the sea. He chose a spot at low tide that was moderately clean, and lay down to wait for the tide to return and cover him. Here he fell asleep, and when he awoke he found himself still in the same place and quite comfortable; but his letter to Neptune was gone, and in its place was another addressed to the prefect. It did not occur to him that this was the answer required, but he thought it best to bring it to Chinchew, and deliver it to his master. Opening it, Chhah Siang found only one large character written inside,—the word *Ts'o* or vinegar.

'This was indeed most confusing. Long and earnestly did the prefect gaze upon it, till he felt himself turning sour and angry. But a lucky fortune-teller made a happy hit by suggesting that the character *Ts'o* could be taken to pieces to read *Twenty-first day, at evening*. The explanation was at once clear. The laconic reply was from Neptune himself. Preparations were made in anticipation of the water being very low on the evening of the twenty-first of the month, and were not made in vain. The water all ran off, and the foundations of the central piers were successfully laid before the tide returned. No further hindrance delayed the progress of the work. The Lo-iu bridge was completed before Chhah Siang's death,—a million and a half pounds of our money having been spent upon it.

'In 1877, when the writer spent some days in Lo-iu, the monument to the memory of Chhah Siang was being renovated. This must have been at or near the 800th anniversary of its erection.'

These two nineteenth-century accounts of the Loyang bridge, tally pretty closely with the facts and figures given in the seventeenth-century Dutch descriptions of this great structure; but they are not easy to reconcile with the briefer Spanish and Portuguese accounts, nor even with the following one by Phillips who often travelled over this road in the eighteen-eighties.[1] 'This bridge, called also the Wangan bridge, lies about six miles from Chinchew. It was constructed in 1023[2] over an arm of the sea; it is over 3,600 Chinese feet in length and fifteen feet in breadth. The openings between the buttresses forty-seven in number are not arched, but, like the other Fuh-kien bridges, flat. There are generally five stone sleepers placed close alongside each other, which,

[1] 'Some Fuh-kien bridges', in *T'oung Pao*, V, 1–10.
[2] This date does not fit in very well with those of its builder, 1011–1066.

lying on the buttresses form the roadway. There is a stone railing on either side of the bridge, let into stone posts upon which are carved lions, pagodas and other objects, which add greatly to the beauty of the bridge. On one or two of these pagodas are to be seen four Sanskrit characters. The bridge is built of slabs of dark blue granite, cunningly morticed into each other without lime or iron to keep them together. It is wonderful how it has stood so many years without falling. There are some four or five guard-houses on it.'

I cannot explain why Pereira (assuming that he had this bridge in mind) and Phillips should give some forty odd buttresses as the total, and the other eye-witnesses some two hundred and fifty. The fact that the original bridge has undergone major repairs at intervals, when new buttresses have been inserted to reduce the spans where the huge deck stones have failed, is not of itself a sufficient explanation. Pereira and Phillips, though separated by some three centuries, agree as well with each other as do our seventeenth-century Dutchmen and nineteenth-century missionaries on the other side.

Turning to more modern accounts of the Loyang bridge, a guide-book of 1924 states that it was built early in the eleventh century and measured 3,600 feet long by 15 feet wide. 'The enormous size of its monoliths (of which there are 120), from one abutment to another, is a source of wonder to all visitors.'[1]

Unfortunately none of the libraries to which I have access at the time of writing has got G. Ecke's detailed study on the great granite bridges of Fukien;[2] but a later, if more popular work dealing with the same subject gives the total length of the Loyang bridge as 3,780 feet, and average width as 16 feet.[3] This authority likewise gives the number of spans as 47, thus agreeing with Pereira (again on the assumption that he had this bridge in mind) and Phillips. Personally, I should have thought that forty-seven piers would be far too few for the great length of this bridge, and that the other estimates of 250 (125 on each side) would be far more likely; but in view of the conflicting evidence on this point, I must leave the riddle to be solved by some constructional engineer.

Of the other bridges described or alluded to by our Portuguese and Spanish travellers, the following can be identified with relative ease and certainty. The 'Bridge of ten thousand ages' over the Min river at the southern approach to Foochow has already been mentioned above. The northern portion of this bridge is 1,270 feet long and 14½ feet wide, and it has 35 intermediate piers and 36 spans. The southern portion, leading

---

[1] JGR, *Guide to China*, p. 339.

[2] G. Ecke, 'Zaytonische Granitbruecken', in *Sinica*, VI, 270 *et seq.*–296 *et seq.*

[3] H. Fugl-Meyer, *Chinese Bridges* (Shanghai, 1937), p. 77. The accompanying illustration is unfortunately of such poor quality that it is quite useless.

from 'Middle island' to the other bank of the river is considerably shorter, the whole structure being built in 1297–1323 during the Yüan or Mongol dynasty.[1]

The Shun-chi bridge over the Chiu-chiang at the southern entrance to Ch'üan-chou has also been mentioned above; but another famous bridge in this city which our travellers presumably saw was the 'Bridge of charitable help', built in the middle of the eleventh century by the monk Fa-ch'ao, a native of Ch'üan-chou. This bridge had 130 arches and a length of 800 feet, and there were six pavilions with pagodas and Buddhist images at intervals along it.[2]

Our Spanish travellers did not traverse the country between T'ung-an and Chang-chou, but as the Portuguese prisoners of 1549 (or some of them) may have done so, we may mention the 'bridge of monks', so-called because it was built by Buddhist monks (or at their expense) in 1294 on the road to Chang-chou. This bridge was about 1,000 feet long and had 18 openings.[3] Chang-chou-fu itself contained three notable bridges, of which the most famous was the Chiang-tung bridge, over the Dragon river about six miles from the east gate of the city. This superb structure, which was built about 1240 and which vies with the Loyang bridge for the title of the most famous bridge in all China, is 1,100 feet long and some of the spans are more than seventy feet. These spans are each composed of three long stones, five feet high and six feet wide. Such monoliths each weigh more than 200 tons, and the secret of handling these enormous stones has long been lost.[4]

In several places in Fukien, ruins of other giant stone bridges are to be found (or were until recently) which attest the remarkable development in the construction of stone truss bridges which took place in this province from the Sung to the early Ming dynasty. It is still a problem where and how these huge stones were quarried, and how they were transported and put in place. The construction of these gigantic granite bridges of Fukien is unique, for no other bridges of this kind exist elsewhere in China, or anywhere else in the world as far as I know. When I motored with some friends from Amoy to Foochow in April, 1938, the surviving bridges were then being prepared for demolition in view of an anticipated landing by the Japanese in that region.[5] If memory serves me rightly, the Shun-chi bridge at Ch'üan-chou was blown up on the

---

[1] H. Fugl-Meyer, *Chinese Bridges*, p. 79.

[2] Ecke-Demiéville, *The Twin Pagodas of Zayton*, p. 94.

[3] Ecke-Demiéville, *op. et. loc. cit.*, *T'oung Pao*, V, 9.

[4] Fugl-Meyer, *Chinese Bridges*, p. 75. Also called the 'Tiger Ferry' and 'Poh-lam' bridge. Rather different measurements are given by Ecke-Demieville, *op. cit.*, p. 22.

[5] H. S. P. Hopkinson, 'Motoring in South China' in *The Rifle Brigade Chronicle for 1938* (London, 1939), pp. 175–201, especially pp. 187–190.

morning that our party left the city, and I have not been able to learn what happened to the other bridges during the Pacific War and the subsequent Communist occupation.

From the fact that these giant bridges were found only in the province of Fukien, and that they were all built within a relatively short period, it has been argued that they were all the works of a single genius, a great master of primitive bridge building, and a few of his disciples. The credit for their construction is usually given to a local magistrate or governor; or in some cases to Buddhist monks, who, at that time and in that province at least, belied their Confucian reputation of being nothing but a swarm of lazy drones. The local governors and district magistrates were, of course, all learned literati who owed their posts to their familiarity with the classics (or to their purchase of a literary degree) and there is no reason to suppose that any of them had the engineering skill necessary to design or construct such outstanding works. Some of the monks seem to have been competent technicians, but the real credit for these great bridges evidently belongs to some unknown artisans who had the technical responsibility but who were never mentioned in the official report of the work.[1]

To our Portuguese and Spanish travellers belongs the credit of first revealing these imposing structures to the knowledge of Europe, for Marco Polo makes no mention of those between Foochow and Chang-chou.[2] It is true that their accounts leave a good deal to be desired on the score of clearness and accuracy, and they evidently confused the different bridges which they passed on their way. But the general impression which they give is fair enough, and those who have had the good fortune to see these gigantic structures *in situ* can echo Galeote Pereira's commendation, 'this causeth us to think that in all the world there be no better workmen than the inhabitants of China.'

---

[1] Fugl-Meyer, *Chinese Bridges*, pp. 21–22.

[2] He does mention some bridges at Chien-ning-fu in northern Fukien, but these have long since disappeared. Cf. Yule-Cordier, *Marco Polo*, II, 225, 228.

Appendix IV

SINCE Fukien and the Fukienese played such a prominent part in the history of early Portuguese and Spanish intercourse with China, some account of the languages spoken in this province, and their relationship to those spoken elsewhere in China, may be of interest to the reader. The following remarks are condensed from the introduction and appendices to the *Dictionary* of Carstairs Douglas who lived for many years in Fukien. Though written in the nineteenth century, these remarks are generally applicable to the sixteenth, and they therefore help to clarify the rather hazy observations of our travellers about the spoken languages of China. These observations were derived, in part at least, from information supplied by Fukienese interpreters, such as the 'Sangleys' who helped Fr. Martín de Rada. These came from the region round the Bay of Amoy, so we will concentrate on that area.

The vernacular or spoken language of Amoy is also termed the 'Amoy dialect', or the 'Amoy colloquial', but such words as these give an erroneous conception of its nature. It is not a mere colloquial dialect or patois; it is spoken by the highest ranks, just as by the common people, by the most learned just as by the ignorant. Nor does the term 'dialect' convey anything like a correct idea of its distinctive character. It is no mere dialectic variety of some other language. It is a distinct language, one of the many and widely-differing languages, which divide among them the soil of China.

The so-called 'written language' of China is indeed uniform throughout the whole country; but it is rather a *notation* than a language; for this universal written language is pronounced differently when read aloud in the different parts of China, so that while as written it is *one*, as soon as it is pronounced it splits into several languages. And still further, this written language, as it is read aloud from books, is not *spoken* in any place whatever under any form of pronounciation. The most learned men never employ it as a means of ordinary communication even among themselves. It is in fact a *dead language*, related to the various spoken languages of China somewhat as Latin is to the languages of south-western Europe.

The spoken languages of China, such as the Mandarin [or Court language as our writers term it], the Hakka, the vernaculars of Canton and Amoy and several others, are not dialects of one language. They are cognate languages, bearing to each other a relation similar to that which subsists between English, German, Dutch, Danish, Swedish, etc. Another serious objection to the use of the term 'dialect' as applied to these languages is that within each of them there exist real dialects. For instance, the Mandarin, the greatest of all, contains within itself at least three very marked 'dialects', the northern or Peking variety; the southern or Nanking; and the western which is spoken in the provinces of Ssŭch'üan, Hupeh, etc. In like manner the so-called Amoy vernacular contains within itself several real dialects, including those spoken at Chang-chou, Ch'üan-chou, T'ung-an, and of Amoy itself. These varieties may be said to form one language which is spoken widely (but not exclusively) throughout three prefectures and two departments in Fukien.

The language spoken in the region of Ch'ao-chou-fu (or Chau-chau-fu) in Kuangtung province, near the Fukien border, is nearly related to the Amoy vernacular. As Swatow was the original treaty-port for that region, the language is often called the 'Swatow dialect'. The ancestors of the people in this area emigrated many centuries ago from Fukien, and to this day they are distinguished from the other inhabitants of Kuangtung by the appellation 'Hok-lo', that is persons from Hokkien or Fukien. This 'Swatow dialect' differs from the Amoy much as Dutch differs from German, or Portuguese from Spanish, so that those who understand one or other of the 'dialects' well, can make out the greater part of what is said in the other.

The provincial capital of Foochow is the seat of another 'dialect', which is largely spoken in the centre and north of Fukien. It has many points of resemblance to the Amoy, but is quite unintelligible to the Amoy Chinese with the exception of an occasional word or phrase.

Hsing-hua (Heng-hoà), has a 'dialect' or language of its own, which appears to be an importation from Kuangtung province. It is spoken in an egg-shaped piece of territory about thirty-five miles from north to south, and sixty miles from east to west.[1] Speakers of the Amoy and the Foochow vernaculars have the greatest difficulty in making themselves understood in this region.

T'ung-an, or Tâng-oa, though in the same district as Amoy and thus in the prefecture of Ch'uan-chou, yet has a very marked variety of dialect for itself. It is said to have originally belonged to the prefecture of Chang-chou, which may perhaps partly explain its peculiarities. Moreover, the dialect spoken at the city of Ch'üan-chou itself differs from that spoken in the island of Amoy almost as much as that of Chang-chou does.

The Amoy vernacular—or 'Hok-kien dialect' as it used to be called—

[1] E. J. Dukes, *Everyday Life in China*, p. 155.

has certain affinities with the language spoken by the Chinese, as distinct from the aboriginal inhabitants of Hainan island; but it is widely different from Cantonese and the other spoken languages of China. All these Chinese languages evidently spring from one common stock; but that common stock is *not* the modern Mandarin dialect, but the ancient form of the Chinese language as spoken about three thousand years ago.

In conclusion, it may be mentioned that the Amoy vernacular was carried overseas by emigrants from Fukien. Thus Formosa was mainly colonised by emigrants from Chang-chou, Amoy and Ch'üan-chou; Java and the Straits Settlements largely by emigrants from Chang-chou; and Manila and the Philippines by emigrants from Ch'üan-chou.

Bibliography

I. TEXTS TRANSLATED IN THE PRESENT WORK

(i) *Galeote Pereira.*

Jesus Maria. Algũas cousas sabidas da China por purtugeses que estiverão lá catiuos e tudo na verdade que se tirou dum tratado que fez Galiote Pereira homem fidalgo que lá esteue catiuo alguns annos e vio tudo isto passar na verdade o qual he de muito credito. Jesuit Archives Rome; Japsin. 123, folios 214–226. Written in a contemporary hand by one or other of the 'meninos' of the Jesuit Seminary at Goa in 1561. Endorsed by Padre Luis Frois S.J., and included as an appendix to the annual Jesuit missionary report from Goa to headquarters at Rome, where it was received in 1562. A partial Italian translation was printed in the *Nuoui Auisi Delle Indie Di Portogallo . . . Quarta parte* (Venice, 1565), whence the English translation by Richard Willis in the *History of Trauayle in the West and East Indies* (London, 1577), folios 237–253 [251], which, as explained in the introduction (pp. vii, lvi) forms the basis of my own translation. The manuscript copy of 1561 at Rome was first published in full in the *Archivum Historicum Societatis Iesu*, St. Francis Xavier commemoration number, Vol. XXII, pp. 57–92 (Rome, January, 1953). In preparing the present translation, the 1561 text has been compared and collated with a later version in the Ajuda Library at Lisbon, Codex 49–IV–50, folios 388–399. For the location of other copies see Schurhammer, *Die zeitgenössischen Quellen*, p. 462 nr. 6154.

(ii) *Fr. Gaspar da Cruz O.P.*

Tractado em que se / cõtam muito por estẽso as cousas / da China, cõ suas particulari- / dades, & assi do reyno dormuz / cõposto por el. R. padre frey / Gaspar da Cruz da orde / de sam Domingos. / Dirigido ao muyto poderoso Rey dom / Sebastiam nosso señor. [title beneath the Royal Arms; the whole within a woodcut border] *Impresso com licença*, 1569.

4to.—88 leaves—30 lines to a full leaf—Gothic letter—no catchwords; *collation by signatures;* a—l, each 8 leaves; total 88 leaves.

The colophon [on fl. 88] reads:- *Foy impresso este tratado da / China, na muy nobre & sempre leal cidade de Euora / em casa de Andre de Burgos impressor & caua- / lleiro da casa do Cardeal Iffante. Acabou / se aos. xx. dias de Feuereiro de mil qui- / nhentos & setenta.*

For further bibliographical details cf. A. J. Anselmo, *Bibliografia das obras impressas em Portugal no século XVI* (Lisbon, 1926), p. 108, nr. 399;

Early Portuguese books, 1489–1600, in the library of His Majesty the King of Portugal, London, 1935, Vol. III, pp. 2–3, item nr. 121.

As explained in the preface (pp. vii, lxvii), my translation has been based on that made by (or for) Samuel Purchas and printed in *Purchas his Pilgrimes,* Part III (London, 1625), pp. 166–198; with the restoration of the chapters and paragraphs which were omitted or abridged by Purchas. I might add, however, that a careful comparison of Purchas' translation with the original Portuguese text of 1569, does not bear out the oft-repeated allegation that 'a comparison of what he has printed with such originals as remain shows that he was very far indeed from a faithful editor or a judicious compiler'.[1] In this instance, at least, this judgement is over-harsh. Most of Purchas' omissions can be accounted for by the fact that the material he omitted (or abridged) was derived from Galeote Pereira, whose narrative was also reprinted in the same volume of the *Pilgrimes.* It is not clear whether the actual translation was the work of Hakluyt or of Purchas, or of one of the translators whom they both employed. The translation is a good one on the whole, which is the chief reason why I have retained the wording of it wherever possible; most of the obscurities in the text are due to the fact that the original Portuguese is anything but clear in those places. Proof-reading was not taken very seriously in those days; and in any event Fr. Gaspar da Cruz was succouring plague victims at Lisbon and Setubal (at the cost of his own life) while his book was going through the press at Evora, so he presumably never saw the proofs.

(iii) *Fr. Martín de Rada O.E.S.A.*

(a) *Relacion verdadera de las cosas del reyno de Taibin, por otro nombre China, y del viage que a el hizo el muy reverendo padre fray Martin de Rada, provincial que fué del orden de St. Augustin, que lo vio y anduvo en la provincia de Hocquien año de* 1575 *hecha por el mismo* [n.d.n.p. but written at Manila or Cebú between Nov. 1575 and May 1576]. Sixteenth-century copy in the Bibliothèque National, Paris; *Fonds Espagnol* nr. 5. folios 16–31.

As explained in the introduction (pp. lxxviii–lxxix), I have not seen this codex myself, but it was published serially in the *Revista Agustiniana,* VIII (Valladolid, 1884), pp. 51–53; 112–122; 293–300; IX (*Ibid.* 1885), pp. 231–237. I have utilised this printed version for comparison and collation with the two following sources which form the material for my own translation.

(b) Gaspar de San Agustín O.E.S.A., *Conquistas de las islas Philipinas*

---

[1] Cf. Sir John Laughton in the *Dictionary of National Biography*, XVI, 488, and Sir William Foster in *Richard Hakluyt and his successors* (Hakluyt Society 2nd Series, No. XCIII), p. 49.

SOUTH CHINA IN THE SIXTEENTH CENTURY

(Madrid, 1698), Lib. II. Cap. XXIV, pp. 313–323, *De lo que les sucedio à los Padres Fray Martin de Rada, y Fray Geronimo Marin en su embaxada de China, hasta que bolvieron à Manila con los Capitanes Españoles que los acompañaron.*

Fr. Gaspar de San Agustín explicitly states that 'todo lo sucedido en la embaxada referida, escrivió el P. Fr. Martin de Rada, cuya relacion es la siguiente, sin mas mutacion que la de algunas palabras algo confusas'. I see no reason to doubt this assertion after comparing this version with that mentioned above, and with another MS. preserved at Madrid of which I have obtained photostats.[1] This whole chapter is printed in inverted commas, which further implies that Fr. Gaspar de San Agustín was copying *ad verbum* from a manuscript and not summarising or paraphrasing it. This part deals only with the voyage to and from China, and the Spaniards' stay in Fukien, June–October, 1575. As explained in the introduction (p. lxxviii) Fr. Gaspar de San Agustín did not print the second part, which I have therefore supplied from a sixteenth-century manuscript copy in my own possession, the relevant portion being entitled:

(c) *Relacion De las cosas de china que propriamente se llama Taybin,* leaves 213–239 of an anonymous codex, which, from internal evidence, was compiled at Manila about 1590. A full description of this curious codex has been given elsewhere,[2] and it will be sufficient to state here that it comprises about 270 pages of MS. text, with 75 coloured drawings of various races in the Far East, including Filipino Indians, Chinese, Indochinese and Malays, etc., and 88 smaller coloured drawings of birds and fantastic animals, mostly copied from contemporary Ming Chinese works. The title-page, if there ever was one, has been removed; but the latest date mentioned in the text, whether directly or by inference, is 1590, and the calligraphy is also of that period.

For further bio-bibliographical details of Fr. Martín de Rada and his account of China cf. pp. lxviii–xc of the introduction to this work; Santiago Vela, *Ensayo de una Biblioteca Ibero-Americana,* III (Madrid, 1917), pp. 226–231; VI (ibid. 1922), p. 455; Streit, *Bibliotheca Missionum,* IV (Aachen, 1928), pp. 311–312, 519.

[1] Academia de la Historia, Madrid, Collección Jesuitas, C II, pap. L: copy in sixteenth-century handwriting. Cf. *Boletín de la Academia de la Historia,* Tomo XCVIII (Madrid, 1931), pp. 423–424.

[2] C. R. Boxer, 'A late sixteenth-century Manila MS.', in *Journal of the Royal Asiatic Society* (April, 1950), pp. 37–49.

II. Fuller titles of authorities quoted in the
introduction and footnotes to the texts

(a) *Manuscripts.*

(i) LOPEZ, GASPAR. Fragment of a letter from Gaspar Lopez to his friend and brother, dated from the prison at Canton, 14 October, 1551. The first part of the letter is missing, and much of the remainder too damaged to read. Torre do Tombo, Lisbon, Fragmentos, maço 30. Original. Cf. Schurhammer, *Die zeitgenössischen Quellen*, nr. 4694.

(ii) ANON. *Enformação de algũas cousas acerca dos costumes e leis do Reyno da China q̃ hũ homẽ onrado q̃ la esteue cativo seis annos cõtou no Collegio de Malaca ao P^e M^{te} belchior año de 1554.*

Seventeenth- or eighteenth-century copy in the Biblioteca da Ajuda, Lisbon; Cod. 49–iv–49, fls. 193v–197.

Fr. G. Schurhammer S.J. (*Die zeitgenössischen Quellen*, nr. 6062), tentatively ascribes this *Enformação* to Manuel de Chaves, but as explained in the introduction (p. lvii), I am rather dubious of this identification. The original was first printed, in translation and in an abridged form, in *Copia de unas cartas de algunos padres y hermanos dela compañia de Iesus que escriuieron dela India, Iapon y Brasil* (Lisbon, 1555), and at greater length in the *Auisi Particolari Delle Indie di Portugallo* (Rome, 1556), fls. 30–37, whence various later French, Spanish and Italian editions. An English version by R. H. Major will be found in the Hakluyt Society edition of González de Mendoza, *History*, I. xxxix–li. Cf. Streit, *Bibliotheca Missionum*, IV, p. 516 nr. 1918.

(iii) RAMIRO, AFFONSO. *Treslado de hũa carta q̃ Afonço Ramiro catiuo na China escreveo aos portugeses q̃ estavão fazẽdo fazẽda ẽ o porto da China, Año de 1555.*

Seventeenth- or eighteenth-century copy in the Biblioteca da Ajuda, Lisbon; Cod. 49–iv–49, fl. 233v–234v. There is another copy in the library of the Academia de Ciências, Lisbon; Cod. *Cartas do Japão*, I. fls. 255v–257. Fragments of the original in Torre do Tombo, maço 24. Cf. Schurhammer, *Die zeitgenössischen Quellen*, p. 457, nr. 6107.

(iv) PEREIRA, AMARO. *Enformaçã da china q̃ ouue de hũ p̃tugues p̃ nome Amaro pereira q̃ esta preso ha 14 annos ẽ cantã a q̃l vay no ç̃erto.* Padre Balthazar Gago S.J.'s covering letter to this report is dated Goa, 10 Dec. 1562.

Contemporary copy in the Jesuit Archives, Rome (Goa, 31, fls. 167v–170v). There is a later copy in the Biblioteca da Ajuda, Lisbon; Cod. 49–iv–50, fls. 460–463. Cf. Schurhammer, *Die zeitgenössischen Quellen*, p. 463, nr. 6159.

(v) LOARCA, MIGUEL DE. *Verdadera Relacion de la grandeza del Reyno de China con las cosas mas notables de allá hecha por Miguel de Loarca,*

soldado, uno de los que fueron alla desde las Islas de Luçon que aora llaman philipinas. Año de 1575.
Late sixteenth-century copy in the Academia de la Historia, Madrid; Colección Salazar letra N, Tomo IV, fls. 113 (134)—150 (171). For the location of other MS. copies see *Boletín de la Academia de la Historia*, XCVIII. 424; Santiago Vela, *Ensayo*, III. 230–231.

As with Fr. Martín de Rada's narrative, this *Verdadera Relacion* is divided into two parts. The first deals with the voyage to Amoy, journey in Fukien and return to Manila, and is entitled, 'Relacion del viage que hizimos a la China desde la ciudad de Manila en las [islas] del Poniente año de 1575, con mandado y acuerdo de Guido de Lavazaris gouernador y Capitán general que a la sazon era en las islas Philipinas.' The second, and much shorter part, is the actual description of China, divided into 12 chapters. Their order, arrangement and contents are not identical with those of Rada's *Relacion*, but closely resemble them for the most part.

Nos. (i) and (iii) of the above were printed and edited by Fr. G. G. Schurhammer, S.J., in AHSI, Vol. XXII, pp. 43–56, after this book went to press.

(b) *Printed works.*
Archivum Historicum Societatis Iesu, Rome, 1932 to date. (AHSI).
ATKINSON, GEOFFROY. *Les Relations de voyages du XVIIe siècle et l'évolution des idées*, Paris, 1924.
—— —— *Les nouveaux horizons de la Renaissance française*, Paris, 1935.
AYMONIER, E. *Le Cambodge*, 3 vols., Paris, 1900–1904.
BARBOSA MACHADO, DIOGO. *Bibliotheca Lusitana, historica, critica e cronologica*. 4 vols., Lisbon, 1741–1759. Reprinted 4 vols., Lisbon, 1930–1935.
BARROS, JOÃO DE. *Terceira Decada da Asia*, Lisbon, 1563.
BEFEO. *Bulletin de l'Ecole française d'Extrême-Orient*, Hanoi, 1901 to date.
Begin ende Voortgangh van de Vereenighde Nederlantsche Geoctroyeerde Oost-Indische Compagnie, 2 vols., Amsterdam, 1645.
BERNARD-MAÎTRE, HENRI, S.J. *Aux portes de la Chine. Les missionaires du seizième siècle, 1514–1588*, Tientsin, 1933.
—— —— *Les Iles Philippines du grand archipel de la Chine. Un essai de conquête spirituelle de l'Extrême-Orient 1571–1641*, Tientsin, 1936.
BIOT, E. *Essai sur l'histoire de l'instruction publique en Chine et de la corporation des Lettrés depuis les anciens temps jusqu'a nos jours; ouvrage entièrement rédigé d'après les documents chinois*, Paris, 1847.
BLAIR, E. H., AND ROBERTSON, J. A. [eds.]. *The Philippine islands, 1493–1898*, 55 vols., Cleveland, Ohio, 1903–1905.
Boletim do Instituto Português de Hongkong, 3 vols., Macao, 1948–1950.

Boletín de la Academia de la Historia. See Rodríguez Moñino.

BOXER, C. R. *Fidalgos in the Far East, 1550–1770. Fact and fancy in the history of Macao,* The Hague, 1948.

—— —— *The Christian Century in Japan, 1549–1650,* University of California and Cambridge University Press, 1951.

—— —— *Macao three hundred years ago,* Macao, 1942.

BRAGA, J. M. *O primeiro accordo Luso-Chines de 1554,* Macao, 1939.

—— —— *The Western pioneers and their discovery of Macao,* Macao, 1949.

BREDON, J., AND MITROPHANOW, S. *The Moon Year. A record of Chinese customs and festivals,* Shanghai, 1927.

BRETSCHNEIDER, E. *Mediaeval researches from East Asiatic sources. Fragments towards the knowledge of the geography and history of Central and Western Asia from the 13th to the 17th century,* 2 vols., London, 1910.

BROOMHALL, MARSHALL. *Islam in China,* London, 1910.

BROWN, DELMER M. *Money economy in medieval Japan. A study in the use of coins,* New Haven, Connecticut, 1951.

CABATON, A. *Brève et véridique relation des événements du Cambodge por Gabriel Quiroga de San Antonio, O.P. Nouvelle édition du texte espagnol avec une traduction et des notes,* Paris, 1914.

CAMMAN, SCHUYLER. *China's Dragon Robes,* New York, 1952.

CARSTAIRS, DOUGLAS. See Douglas.

CARTER, T. F. *The invention of printing in China and its spread westward,* New York, 1931.

CHANG, T. T. *Sino-Portuguese trade from 1514 to 1644. A synthesis of Portuguese and Chinese sources,* Leiden, 1934.

CH'IEN, CHUNG-SHU. 'China in the English literature of the seventeenth century', in the *Quarterly Bulletin of Chinese Bibliography* (English edition), New Series, Vol. I, pp. 351–384, Kunming, 1940.

The China Review, or, Notes and queries on the Far East, Hongkong, 1872–1901.

The Chinese Repository, Canton and Hongkong, 1832–1851.

CORTESÃO, ARMANDO. *Cartógrafia e cartógrafos portugueses dos séculos XV e XVI. Contribuição para um estudo completo,* 2 vols., Lisbon, 1935.

—— —— *The Suma Oriental of Tomé Pires and the Book of Francisco Rodrigues,* Hakluyt Society, Ser. II, Vols. 89–90, London, 1944.

COULING, S. *The Encyclopedia Sinica,* London, 1917.

COUTO, DIOGO DO. *Decada Quinta da Asia,* Lisbon, 1612.

—— —— *Decada Setima da Asia,* Lisbon, 1616.

—— —— *Decada Outava da Asia,* Lisbon, 1673.

CRUZ, FR. GASPAR DA, O.P. *Tractado em que se cõtam muito por estẽso as cousas da China, cõ suas particularidades, e assi do reyno dormuz*, Evora, 1569–1570. Reprinted: Lisbon, 1829, and Barcelos, 1937. See Part I of this Bibliography, p. 344.

DALGADO, S. R. *Glossário Luso-Asiático*, 2 vols., Coimbra, 1919–1921.

DAPPER, OLFERT. *Gedenkwaerdig Bedryf der Nederlandsche Oost-Indische Maetschappye, op de kuste en in het Keizerrijk van Taising of Sina; Behelzende het tweede gezandschap . . . en het derde gezandschap . . . Beneffens een Beschryving van geheel Sina*, Amsterdam, 1670. Cited in this work by the half-title, *Tweede en derde gezandschap*.

DELAMARRE [ABBÉ] [ed.]. *Histoire de la dynastie des Ming composée par l'empereur Khian-loung*, Paris, 1865. For the Chinese work from which this is translated, see W. Franke, *Preliminary Notes*, nr. 262.

D'ELIA, PASQUALE M., S.J. *Fonti Ricciane. Documenti originali concernenti Matteo Ricci e la storia delle prime relazioni tra l'Europa e la Cina, 1597–1615*, 3 vols., Rome, 1942–1949.

DOOLITTLE, JUSTUS. *Social life of the Chinese; with some account of their religious, governmental, educational, and business customs and opinions, with special but not exclusive reference to Fuhchau*, 2 vols., London, 1866.

DORÉ, H., S.J. *Manuel des superstitions chinoises, ou petit indicateur des superstitions les plus communes en Chine*, Shanghai, 1926.

—— —— *Recherches sur les superstitions en Chine, avec nombreuses chromolithographies, d'après les originaux chinois*, 15 vols., Shanghai, 1911–1934.

DOUGLAS, CARSTAIRS. *Chinese-English Dictionary of the vernacular or spoken language of Amoy, with the principal variations of the Chang-chew [Chang-chou] and Chin-chew [Ch'üan-chou] dialects*, London, 1873.

DUKES, E. J. *Everyday life in China; or, scenes along river and road in Fuh-Kien*, London Missionary Society's edition, [1885.]

DUYVENDAK, J. J. L. *China's discovery of Africa*, London, 1949.

DYER BALL, J. *Things Chinese; or, notes connected with China. 5th edition. Revised by E. Chalmers Werner*, Hongkong, 1925.

ECKE, G., and DEMIÉVILLE, P. *The Twin Pagodas of Zayton. A study of later Buddhist sculpture in China*, Harvard University Press, 1935.

EDEN, R., and WILLIS, R. [eds.]. *The History of Trauayle in the West and East Indies and other countreys lying eyther way towards the fruitfull and ryche Moluccas*, London, 1577.

ELIOT, SIR CHARLES. *Hinduism and Buddhism. An historical sketch*, 3 vols., London, 1921.

ESCALANTE, BERNARDINO DE. *Discurso de la Navegacion que los Portugueses hazen à los Reinos y Provincias del Oriente, y de la noticia que se tiene de las grandezas del Reino de la China*, Seville, 1577. See also under Frampton, John.

Ethnos. Revista do Instituto Português de Arqueologia, história e etnografia, 2 vols., Lisbon, 1935–1942.

FENN, C. H. *The Five Thousand Dictionary. A Chinese-English pocket dictionary*. Revised American edition, Harvard University Press, 1944.

FERGUSON, D. *Letters from Portuguese captives in Canton, written in 1534 and 1536 [alias 1524]. With an introduction on Portuguese intercourse with China in the first half of the sixteenth century*, Bombay, 1902.

—— and SINCLAIR, W. F. *The travels of Pedro Teixeira; with his 'Kings of Harmuz' and extracts from his 'Kings of Persia'*, Hakluyt Society, Ser. II, Vol. 9, London, 1902.

FERRAND, GABRIEL. *Les poids, mesures et monnaies des mers du Sud aux XVIe et XVIIe siècles*, Paris, 1921.

FRAMPTON, JOHN. *A Discourse of the navigation which the Portugales doe make to the Realmes and Provinces of the East partes of the world, and of the knowledge that growes by them of the great things, which are in the Dominions of China. Written by Barnadine of Escalante, of the Realme of Galisia Priest*, London, 1579. For the Spanish original, see Escalante.

FRANKE, WOLFGANG. *Preliminary notes on the important Chinese literary sources for the history of the Ming Dynasty (1368–1644)*, West China Union University, Studia Serica Monograph Series A, No. 2, Chengtu, 1948.

FUCHS, WALTER. *The 'Mongol Atlas' of China by Chu Ssu-pen and the Kuang-yü-t'u. With 48 facsimile maps dating from about 1555*, Peking, 1946. (Monumenta Serica. Monograph VIII.)

FUGL-MEYER, H. *Chinese Bridges*, Shanghai, 1937.

GEIL, W. E. *The Great Wall of China*, London, 1909.

—— —— *Eighteen Capitals of China*, London, 1911.

GILES, H. A. *A Glossary of Reference, on subjects connected with the Far East*, Hongkong, 1878.

—— —— *A Chinese Biographical Dictionary*, Shanghai, 1898.

—— —— *A Chinese-English Dictionary*, London, 1892; 2nd ed. 1912.

GILES, LIONEL. *Short Glossary of Chinese*. 1st edition, Jan. 1943; General staff, War Office, London.

GONZÁLEZ DE MENDOZA, FR. JUAN, O.E.S.A. (a) *Historia de las cosas mas notables, ritos y costumbres del Gran Reyno de la China, sabidas assi por los libros de los mesmos Chinas, como por relacion de Religiosos y otras personas que an estado en el dicho Reyno*, Rome, 1585. There being numerous editions and reprints of this work, of which the latest was published at Madrid in the series *España Misionera* in 1944, citations and references are usually made by Part, Book and Chapter, irrespective of whether they refer to any of the Spanish editions or to either of the English editions mentioned below.

—— —— (b) *Historie of the great and mightie kingdome of China, and the situation thereof; together with the great riches, huge citties, politike governement and rare inventions in the same.* Translated by R. Parke, London, 1588.

—— —— (c) *History of the great and mighty kingdom of China* etc. edited by Sir G. T. Staunton, with an introduction by R. H. Major. Hakluyt Society. Ser. I, Vols. 14–15; 2 vols., 1853–1854.

GRAY, J. H. *China. A history of the laws, manners and customs of the people.* 2 vols., London, 1878.

GROENEVELDT, W. P. *De Nederlanders in China. De eerste bemoeiingen om den handel in China en de vestiging in de Pescadores, 1601–1624,* The Hague, 1898.

GROOT, J. J. M. DE. *Les Fêtes annuellement célébrées à Emoui (Amoy). Etude concernant la religion populaire des Chinois* (Annales du Musée Guimet, Vols. XI and XII), 2 vols., Paris, 1886.

—— —— *The Religious System of China. Its ancient forms, evolution, history and present aspect. Manners, customs and social institutions connected therewith,* 6 vols., Leiden, 1892–1906.

GULIK, R. H. VAN. *The Lore of the Chinese Lute. An essay in Ch'in ideology,* Tokyo, 1940.

—— —— *Erotic colour prints of the Ming Period, with an essay on Chinese sex life from the Han to the Ming dynasty,* 3 vols., Tokyo, 1951. (Privately printed.)

Handbook of Oriental History. By members of the Department of Oriental History, School of Oriental and African Studies, University of London. General editor, C. H. Philips. London, 1951.

HJAS=*Harvard Journal of Asiatic Studies,* Cambridge, Mass., 1936 to date.

HARVEY, G. E. *History of Burma from the earliest times to the beginning of the English conquest,* London, 1925.

HAUER, E. *Huang-Ts'ing K'ai-Kuo Fang-Lüeh. Die Gründung des Mandschurischen Kaiserreiches,* Berlin, 1926.

HENRY, B. C. *Ling-nam, or interior views of Southern China including explorations in the hitherto untraversed island of Hainan,* London, 1886.

HERRMANN, ALBERT. *Historical and Commercial Atlas of China*, Harvard University Press, 1935.

HOANG, PIERRE, S. J. *Catalogue des tremblements de terre signalés en Chine d'après les sources chinoises 1767 B.C.–1895 A.D.*, 2 vols., forming vols. 28 and 28 *bis* of the *Variétés Sinologiques*, Shanghai, 1909–1913.

—— —— *Quelques mots sur la politesse chinoise*, Shanghai, 1906. Vol. 25 of the *Var. Sin.*

HUDSON, G. F. *Europe and China. A survey of their relations from the earliest times to 1800*, London, 1931.

Isis. An international review devoted to the history of science and civilization. Vols. 35–39, Burlington, Vermont, 1944–1948.

J[APANESE] G[OVERNMENT] R[AILWAYS] (ed.), *Guide to China. Second (revised) edition*, Tokyo, 1924.

JNCBRAS. *Journal of the North China Branch of the Royal Asiatic Society*, Shanghai, 1858–1952.

JRAS. *Journal of the Royal Asiatic Society*, London, 1834 to date.

KAMMERER, A. *La Découverte de la Chine par les Portugais au XVIᵐᵉ siècle et la cartographie des portulans. . . . Avec des notes de toponymie chinoise par Paul Pelliot*, Leiden, 1944. (Supplement to *T'oung Pao*, XXXIX.)

KING, F. H. *Farmers of forty centuries. Or, permanent agriculture in China, Korea and Japan*, London, 1926.

LAUFER, B. 'Relations of the Chinese to the Philippine islands', reprinted from the *Smithsonian Miscellaneous Collection*, vol. 50, pp. 248–284, Washington, 1908.

—— —— 'The domestication of the cormorant in China and Japan', in *The Field Museum of Natural History*, Publication 300: Anthropological Series, Vol. XVIII, no. 3, pp. 205–262, Chicago, 1931.

LE BOULANGER, PAUL. *Histoire du Laos Français*, Paris, 1930.

LECLÈRE, A. *Le Buddhisme au Cambodge*, Paris, 1899.

—— —— *Histoire du Cambodge depuis le 1ᵉʳ siècle de notre ère d'après les inscriptions lapidaires, les annales chinoises et annamites et les documents européens des six derniers siècles*, Paris, 1914.

Libro y Relacion de las grandezas del Reyno de la China. Hecho por un Frayle descalço de la Orden de Sant Francisco, de seys que fueron pressos en el dicho Reyno en la isla de Haynam en el año de 1585, [n.d.n.p Madrid, 1587?]. I only know of two copies of this very rare work. One in the British Museum (pressmark, C.32.e.25) and the other listed in Maggs Bros. *Catalogue* no. 519, item no. 157, London, 1929.

LINSCHOTEN, JAN HUYGHEN VAN. *Itinerario ofte schipvaert van Jan*

354   SOUTH CHINA IN THE SIXTEENTH CENTURY

Huyghen van Linschoten naer Oost ofte Portugaels Indien, 1579–1592, Amsterdam, 1595–1596. Citations in this book are taken from the 5-vol. edition by the Linschoten Vereeniging, The Hague, 1910–1939, (of which the last two volumes were edited by J. C. M. Warnsinck), and from the English translation by John Wolfe:

—— —— *John Huighen Van Linschoten his discours of voyages into ye Easte and West Indies*, London, 1598.

LJUNGSTEDT, A. *An historical sketch of the Portuguese settlements in China; and of the Roman Catholic church and mission in China. [With] A supplementary chapter entitled Description of the city of Canton*, Boston, 1836. The work was previously published at Macao and Canton in 1832, but the American edition is cited in this work as being more accessible.

MAGALHÃES, GABRIEL DE, S. J. *A new history of China, containing a description of the most considerable particulars of that vast empire*, London, 1688. Translated from the French edition of 1688, both versions deforming the Portuguese author's surname into 'Magaillans'.

MAILLA, J. A. M. DE MYRIAC DE. *Histoire générale de la Chine*, Vol. X, Paris, 1779. For the Chinese records on which De Mailla based this volume cf. W. Franke, *Preliminary Notes*, p. 24, note (34). Cf. also under Delamarre.

MARTINI, MARTINO, S.J. *Novus Atlas Sinensis*, Amsterdam, 1655. See also under Thevenot, *Relations*, Paris, 1666.

MASPERO, GEORGES. *Le Royaume de Champa*, Paris–Bruxelles, 1928.

MASPERO, HENRI. *Mélanges posthumes sur les religions et l'histoire de la Chine*. I, *Les Religions Chinoises*. II, *Le Taoïsme*. III, *Études Historiques*. 3 vols., Paris, 1950.

MAYERS, W. F. *The Chinese government. A manual of Chinese titles, categorically arranged and explained, with an appendix.* 3rd edition, revised by G. M. H. Playfair, Shanghai, 1896.

—— —— *Chinese Reader's Manual*, Shanghai, 1910.

MEYER, B. FR., and WEMPE, T. F. *The Student's Cantonese-English Dictionary*, Hongkong, 1935.

MICHAEL, F. *The origin of Manchu rule in China. Frontier and bureaucracy as interacting forces in the Chinese empire*, Baltimore, 1942.

MILNE, W. C. *Life in China*, London, 1858.

MINSHEU, JOHN. *A Dictionarie in Spanish and English, first published into the English tongue by Ric. Perciuale Gent. Now enlarged and amplified with many thousand words*, London, 1599.

Missionalia Hispanica. Revista cuatrimestral, Vols. 1–4, Madrid, 1944–1947.

MORGA, DR. ANTONIO DE. *Sucesos de las islas Filipinas*, Mexico, 1609.

Citations in this book are taken from the annotated reprint by W. E. Retana, Madrid, 1909.

MOULE, A. C. *Christians in China before the year 1550*, London, 1930.

—— —— 'A list of the musical and other sound-producing instruments of the Chinese' in JNCBRAS, XXXIX (1908), pp. 1–160.

MUNDY, PETER. *The Travels of Peter Mundy in Europe and Asia, 1608–1667*. Vol. III, Pt. I; *Travels in England, Western India, Achin, Macao and the Canton River, 1634–1637*. Hakluyt Society, Ser. II, Vol. 45, London, 1919.

NIEUHOF, J. *An Embassy from the East-India Company of the United Provinces to the Grand Tartar Cham, Emperor of China . . . Englished . . . by John Ogilby*, London, 1669. The original Dutch edition was published in 1665.

Nuoui Auisi Delle Indie Di Portogallo, Venuti nuouamente dalli R. padri della compagnia di Giesu, & tradotti dalla lingua Spagnola nella Italiana, Quarta parte, Venice, 1565. Fls. 63–87 contain the first printed version of Galeote Pereira's narrative, with a separate heading—*Alcune cose del paese della China sapute da certi Portughesi, che iui furon fatti schiaui, & questo su cauato da un trattato, che fece Galeotto Perera, gentil huomo persona di molto credito, il quale stette priggione nel sudetto luogo per alcuni anni.* It was this section of the *Nuovi Avisi* which was mistaken by Barbosa Machado for a separate work, thus misleading many subsequent bibliographers.

PASTELLS, PABLO, S.J. *Labor Evangélica de los obreros de la Compañía de Jesús en las islas Filipinas, por el P. Francisco Colín de la misma Compañía*. Annotated edition, by P.P., 3 vols., Barcelona, 1903–1904.

—— —— *Catálogo de los documentos relativos á las islas Filipinas existentes en el Archivo de Indias de Sevilla por D. Pedro Torres y Lanzas*, edited by P. P., Barcelona, Vols. I–III, Barcelona, 1925–1927.

PIRES, TOMÉ. See Cortesão, A.

PLAYFAIR, G. M. H. *The cities and towns of China. A geographical dictionary*, Hongkong, 1879.

[ANON.,] *The Punishments of China, illustrated by twenty-two engravings; with explanations in English and French*, London, 1804. First published in 1801, in a slightly different form.

PURCHAS, SAMUEL. *Hakluytus Posthumus, or Purchas His Pilgrimes, contayning a History of the World in Sea Voyages and Lande Travells*, 4 vols., London, 1625.

—— —— *Purchas his pilgrimage. Or Relations of the world and the religions observed in all ages and places discovered*, London, 1626.

Revista Agustiniana, Año IV, Vol. VIII, Valladolid, 1884; Año V, Vol. IX, Valladolid, 1885.

RICCI, MATTEO, S.J. *See D'Elia, and Trigault.*

RICHARDS, L. *Comprehensive Geography of the Chinese Empire and dependencies.* English translation by M. Kennelly, S.J., Shanghai, 1908.

RODRÍGUEZ MOÑINO, A. R. 'Bibliografía hispano-oriental. Apuntes para un catálogo de los documentos referentes a las Indias Orientales (China, Japón, Cochinchina, etc.) de las colecciones de la Academia', in *Boletín de la Academia de la Historia*, Tomo XCVIII, (Madrid, 1931), pp. 417–475.

ROMÁN, FR. JERÓNIMO, O.E.S.A. *Republicas del Mundo. Divididas en tres partes*, 3 vols., Salamanca, 1595. The account of China is in Vol. III, fls. 210*v*–235*r*.

SAN AGUSTÍN, FR. GASPAR DE, O.E.S.A. *Conquistas de las islas Philipinas; la temporal, por las armas del Señor Don Phelipe Segundo El Prudente; y la espiritual, por los religiosos del Orden de San Augustin*, Madrid, 1698.

SANSOM, G. B. *The Western world and Japan*, London, 1950.

SANTIAGO VELA, FR. GREGORIO, O.E.S.A. *Ensayo de una Bibliotheca Ibero-Americana de la Orden de San Agustín*, 7 vols., Madrid, 1913–1925.

SANTOS, FR. JOÃO DOS, O.P. *Ethiopia Oriental e varia historia de cousas notaueis do Oriente*, 2 parts in 1 vol., Evora, 1609.

SANZ ARIZMENDI, DON CLAUDIO. 'Un capítulo para la historia de Felipe II (Relaciones entre España y China)', in *Actas y Memorias, Congresso de historia y geografía Hispano-Americanas, Sevilla, Abril, 1914*, pp. 429–472, Madrid, 1914.

SAYER, G. R. *Ching Tê-Chên T'ao Lu or The Potteries of China. Being a translation with notes and an introduction by G. R. S.*, London, 1951.

SCHURHAMMER, GEORG, S.J. *Fernão Mendes Pinto und seine 'Peregrinaçam'.* Reprinted from *Asia Major*, Vol. III, Leipzig, 1927.

—— —— *Die zeitgenössischen Quellen zur Geschichte Portugiesisch-Asiens und seiner Nachbarländer zur Zeit des hl. Franz Xaver,* Leipzig, 1932.

—— —— [and J. WICKI, S.J., eds.,] *Epistolae S. Francisci Xaverii aliaque eius scripta*, 2 vols., Rome, 1944–1945.

—— —— 'O Descobrimento do Japão pelos Portugueses no ano de 1543', in the *Anais da Academia Portuguesa da História*, 2^d ser. Vol. I, pp. 1–172, (Lisbon, 1946).

SCHUYLER CAMMAN. *China's Dragon Robes*, New York, 1952.

SCHURZ, W. L. *The Manila Galleon*, New York, 1929.

SEN, SURENDRANATH. *Indian Travels of Thevenot and Careri. Being the third part of the travels of M. de Thevenot into the Levant and the third part of a voyage round the world by Dr. John Francis Gemelli Careri*, New Delhi, 1949.

SILVA REGO, P. ANTÓNIO DA. *História das missões do padroado português do Oriente. India*, 1° vol. (*1500–1542*), Lisbon, 1949.

SILVA REGO, P. ANTÓNIO DA. *Documentação para a História das missões do padroado português do Oriente. India, 1500–1559*, 7 vols., Lisbon, 1947–52.

Sinica Franciscana. Volumen II. Relationes et epistolas Fratrum Minorum saeculi XVI et XVII. Edited by A. Van den Wyngaert O.F.M., Quaracchi-Firenze, 1933.

STAUNTON, G. T. [translator], *Ta Tsing Leu Lee; being the fundamental laws, and a selection from the supplementary statutes of the penal code of China*, London, 1810.

—— —— [ed.], *The History of the great and mighty kingdom of China and the situation thereof. Compiled by the padre Juan Gonzalez de Mendoza and now reprinted from the early translation of R. Parke. Edited by Sir George T. Staunton, Bart. With an introduction by R. H. Major Esq*ʳᵉ. 2 vols., London, 1853–1854. Hakluyt Society, Ser. I, Vols. 14–15.

STREIT, ROBERT, O.M.I. *Bibliotheca Missionum*. Vol. IV, *Asiatische Missionsliteratur 1245–1599*, (Aachen, 1928); Vol. V, *Asiatische Missionsliteratur 1600–1699*, (Aachen, 1929).

THEVENOT, MELCHISEDECH. *Relations de divers voyages curieux . . . Troisième partie*, Paris, 1666. Contains the *Description géographique de l'empire de la Chine par le Père Martin Martini*, 216 pp., being the French translation of the descriptive text of the *Novus Atlas Sinensis*, Amsterdam, 1655.

The T'ien Hsia Monthly, 11 vols., Shanghai, 1935–1941.

T'oung Pao. Archives concernant l'histoire, les langues, la géographie, l'éthnographie et les arts de l'Asie Orientale, Leiden, 1890 to date. (Sub-title varies slightly in 1st and 2nd series.)

TRIGAULT, NICHOLAS, S.J. *The China that was. China as discovered by the Jesuits at the close of the sixteenth century. From the Latin of Nicholas Trigault*. Translated by L. J. Gallagher S.J., Milwaukee, 1942. A translation of the first book of Trigault's *De Christiana Expeditione apud Sinas*, Augsburg, 1615.

TSCHEPE, S.J. *Japans Beziehungen zu China seit den ältesten Zeiten bis zum Jahre 1600*, Jentschoufu, 1907.

TSUNODA, R., and CARRINGTON-GOODRICH, L., [trans.]. *Japan in the Chinese Dynastic Histories, Later Han through Ming Dynasties*, Pasadena, 1951.

VALIGNANO, ALESSANDRO, S.J. *Historia del principio y progresso de la*

Compañia de Jesús en las Indias Orientales, 1542–1564. Herausgegeben und erläutert von Josef Wicki, S.J., Rome, 1944.

VORETZSCH, E. A. 'Primeira Embaixada Portuguesa a China', article in *Nichi-Po kōtsū* or *Boletim da Sociedade Luso-Japonesa*, I, pp. 50–69, Tokyo, 1929.

WADA, SEI. 'The Philippine Islands as known to the Chinese before the Ming period', in *Memoirs of the Research Department of the Toyo Bunko (Oriental Library)*, No. 4, pp. 121–166, Tokyo, 1929.

WAGNER, H. R. *Juan Gonzalez de Mendoza: Historia de las cosas mas notables, ritos y costumbres del gran Reyno de la China and El viaje que hizo Antonio de Espejo.* Fifty copies reprinted from *The Spanish Southwest*, Berkeley, California, 1924.

WERNER, E. T. C. *A Dictionary of Chinese mythology*, Shanghai, 1932.

———— *Chinese Weapons*, Shanghai, 1932 (extra volume of the JNCBRAS). See also under Dyer Ball.

WILSON, A. T. *The Persian Gulf. An historical sketch from the earliest times to the beginning of the twentieth century*, Oxford, 1928.

WOOD, W. A. R. *A History of Siam from the earliest times to A.D. 1781*, Bangkok, 1933.

YULE, H. and CORDIER, H. (eds.). *The Book of Ser Marco Polo, the Venetian, concerning the kingdoms and marvels of the East*, 3 vols., London, 1903–1920.

———— and BURNELL, A. C. *Hobson-Jobson. A glossary of colloquial Anglo-Indian words and phrases, and of kindred terms.* New edition by W. Crooke, London, 1903.

(c) *Chinese and Japanese Books and Periodicals.*
(The characters for the names and titles will be found in the glossary, section 6, pp. 373–374.)

1. Akiyama, Kenzo, *Nisshi kōshō-shi kenkyu*, Tokyo, 1939. Studies in the history of Sino-Japanese relations down to Hideyoshi's invasion of Korea (1592). Reproduces many extracts from Chinese texts.

2. *Ao-mên-chih-lüeh.* Compiled in 1745–1746, and first printed in 1751 or shortly afterwards. Cf. Boxer, *Fidalgos in the Far East*, pp. 283–284; S. C. Chu, *Catalog*, p. 416. A Portuguese translation by Luis G. Gomes, *Ou-Mun-Kei-leok. Monografia de Macao por Tcheong-ö-lâm e Ian Kuong-Iâm*, was published at Macao in 1950.

3. *Chang-chou-fu-chih.* Chang-chou Gazetteer. Compiled during the Ch'ing dynasty, and published in 1877. S. C. Chu, *Catalog*, p. 400.

4. Chang Hsing-lang, 'The Real "Limahong" in Philippine History', in *Yenching Journal of Chinese Studies*, No. 8 (Dec. 1930), pp. 1473–1491.

5. Chang, Wei-hua, *Ming-shih Fo-lang-chi, Luzon, Holan, Italia, szu-chüan-chu-shih, A Commentary of the four chapters on Portugal, Spain, Holland and Italy in the History of the Ming Dynasty.* Yenching Journal of Chinese Studies, Monograph Series No. 7, Peking, 1934. Cited as W. H. Chang, *Commentary.*

6. Ch'en, Mao-heng, *Ming-tai Wo-k'ou k'ao-lüeh. The invasion of China by Japanese pirates during the Ming dynasty.* Yenching Journal of Chinese Studies, Monograph Series No. 6, Peking, 1934.

7. *Ch'ou-hai-t'u-pien* by Hu Tsung-hsien. Original preface dated 1562. Re-edited with a preface dated 1624, towards end of Ming. W. Franke, *Preliminary Notes,* nr. 211.

8. Chu, Shih-chia, *Kuo-hui-t'u-shu-kuan ts'ang Chung-kuo Fang-chih mu-lu, A Catalog of Chinese local histories in the Library of Congress,* Washington, D.C., 1942. Cited as S. C. Chu, *Catalog.*

9. *Ch'üan-chou-fu-chih.* Ch'üan-chou Gazetteer. The British Museum possesses an edition of 1612 which is not recorded in S. C. Chu, *Catalog,* p. 398.

10. *Chung-kuo li-tai t'ien-tsai jên-huo-piao,* Shanghai, 1930. Record of natural and heavenly calamities in the Middle Kingdom compiled from dynastic histories and provincial gazetteers.

11. *Fu-chien [Fukien] -t'ung-chih.* Fukien Gazetteer. Compiled during the Ch'ing dynasty, and first printed in 1737. S. C. Chu, *Catalog,* p. 395.

12. *Fu-chou-fu-chih.* Foochow Gazetteer. Edition of the Ch'ien-lung period. S. C. Chu, *Catalog,* p. 396.

13. *Hsia-mên-chih.* Amoy Gazetteer. Compiled by 1832 and published in 1839. S. C. Chu, *Catalog,* pp. 399–400.

14. *Jên-ching-yang-ch'iu.* ('Chronicles of model human beings'.) Although the text of this work refers to a much earlier period, the illustrations are faithful portrayals of the people, costumes, architecture etc. of the Wan-li period in the Ming dynasty, when the book was published. Chinese artists never troubled about historical accuracy of detail, and depicted the surroundings of their own age, irrespective of the periods to which the books they were illustrating referred.

15. *Kuang-yü-t'u,* by Lo Hung-hsien. 'Universal Atlas' of China and the adjacent countries with short accompanying text and statistics, mainly based on the 'Mongol Atlas' of Chu Ssu-pen. First printed edition *c.* 1555, followed by others dated 1558, 1561, 1566, 1572, 1579, 1799. W. Franke, *Preliminary Notes,* nr. 242.

16. Li Ch'ang-fu, 'Critical Notes on "The Real Limahong" in Philippine History', in *Yenching Journal of Chinese Studies,* No. 9 (June, 1931), pp. 1869–1871.

17. Li Kuang-ming, 'Further Notes on the identity of Limahong in the History of the Philippine islands', in *Yenching Journal of Chinese Studies*, No. 10 (Dec. 1931), pp. 2061–2081.

18. Li Kuang-ming, *The Repulse of the Wo pirates by provincial and extra-provincial armies in the provinces of Kiangsu and Chekiang during 1551–1561*. Yenching Monograph Series No. 4, Peking, 1933.

19. *Ming-shih*, Official History of the Ming dynasty, compiled in 1723–1739. Numerous current editions. W. Franke, *Preliminary Notes*, nr. 257.

20. *Ming Shih-lu*. 'Veritable Records' of the Ming dynasty forming the raw material for the official history. The MS. sections covering the Cheng-tê, Chia-ching and Wan-li periods were compiled between 1525 and 1630. First printed in 1940. W. Franke, *Preliminary Notes*, nr. 1.

21. *Nanking Journal. Chinling hsüeh-pao*.

22. *Nichi-Po kōtsū. Boletim da Sociedade Luso-Japonesa*. 2 vols. Tokyo, 1929–1943. Text of first volume mostly in Japanese, but with one article and some summaries in Portuguese. The text of the second volume is entirely in Japanese.

23. *San-kuo-chih-yen-i*. Romance of the Three Kingdoms. An historical novel dealing with the period A.D. 168–265, but written during the Yüan dynasty. Cf. A. Wylie, *Notes on Chinese Literature* (ed. Shanghai, 1922), p. 202.

24. Shimizu, Taiji, 'A Study of the manors of the Ming period', in *Tōyō Gakuhō*, XVI (1927), pp. 334–350, 463–544.

25. *Ta Ming Hui-tien*. Collected statutes of the Ming Dynasty. First printed in 1511; revised, and several times reprinted, in the Wan-li period. Cf. W. Franke, *Preliminary Notes*, nr. 121.

26. *Tōyō Gakuhō, Reports of the Oriental Society of Tokyo*, 1911 to date.

27. *Tung-hsi-yang-k'ao*, by Chang Hsieh. Preface dated 1618. W. Franke, *Preliminary Notes*, nr. 206.

28. Wang Ch'ung-wu, 'Population changes during the Ming dynasty', in *Yenching Journal of Chinese Studies*, No. 20 (Dec. 1936), pp. 331–373.

29. *Wu-pei-chih*, by Mao Yüan-I. Author's preface dated 1621. W. Franke, *Preliminary Notes*, nr. 150.

30. *Yenching Journal of Chinese Studies. Yenching hsüeh-pao*.

CHINESE GLOSSARY

1. Chinese dynasties and emperors.
2. Geographical names and terms; administrative areas.
3. Personal names.
4. Official ranks, titles, and organisations.
5. Miscellaneous.
6. Titles of books and articles in Chinese and Japanese.

1. Chinese Dynasties and Emperors
(a) The Dynasties of China, 1989 B.C.–A.D. 1912

Official Number	Name	Character	Approximate Dates
1.	Hsia	夏	1989–1558 B.C.
2.	Shang	商	1558–1051 B.C.
3.	Chou	周	1050–249 B.C.
4.	Ch'in (Ts'in)	秦	221–207 B.C.
5.	Western Han	西漢	206 B.C.–A.D. 8
	Wang Mang (usurper)	王莽	A.D. 9–23
5.	Eastern Han	東漢	A.D. 25–220
	[Three Kingdoms (San Kuo)]	三國	A.D. 220–265
6.	minor Han (Shu Han)	蜀漢	A.D. 221–263
	Wei	魏	A.D. 220–265
	Wu	吳	A.D. 222–280
7.	Chin (Tsin)	晉	A.D. 265–420
	West Chin	西晉	A.D. 265–316
	East Chin	東晉	A.D. 317–420
	[Sixteen Kingdoms including the Shu (unofficial)]	十六國	4th and early 5th centy.
		蜀	A.D. 302–347
8.	Liu-Sung	劉宋	A.D. 420–479
9.	Southern Ch'i	齊	A.D. 479–502
10.	Southern Liang	梁	A.D. 502–557
11.	Southern Ch'ên	陳	A.D. 557–589
12.	Sui	隋	A.D. 589–618
13.	T'ang	唐	A.D. 618–906
14.	Later Liang	後梁	A.D. 907–923
15.	Later T'ang	後唐	A.D. 923–936

Official Number	Name	Character	Approximate Dates
16.	Later Chin	後晉	A.D. 936–946
17.	Later Han	後漢	A.D. 947–950
18.	Later Chou	後周	A.D. 951–960
19.	Sung	宋	A.D. 960–1127
20.	Southern Sung	南宋	A.D. 1127–1279
21.	Yüan	元	A.D. 1280–1368
22.	Ming	明	A.D. 1368–1644
23.	Ch'ing (Ts'ing)	清	A.D. 1644–1912

(b) *The Ming Emperors who ruled* A.D. 1506–1619

Wu-tsung	武宗	Chêng-tê	正德	A.D. 1506–1521
Shih-tsung	世宗	Chia-ching	嘉靖	A.D. 1522–1566
Mu-tsung	穆宗	Lung-ch'ing	隆慶	A.D. 1567–1572
Shen-tsung	神宗	Wan-li	萬曆	A.D. 1573–1619

(c) *Other imperial designations mentioned in the text or notes*

Ch'ien-lung	乾隆	Ming-ti	明帝
Hê-ti (Ho-ti)	和帝	Shih-tsu	世祖
Hou-ti	後帝	Shun-ti	順帝
Hsien-ti	獻帝	T'ai-tsu	太祖
Hung-wu	洪武	Ti-ping	帝昺
Jen-tsung	仁宗	T'ien-shun	天順
K'ang-hsi (Kanghsi etc.)	康熙	Wu-ti	武帝
Kao-ti	高帝	Ying-tsung	英宗
Kao-tsu	高祖	Yung-lo	永樂
Kung-ti	恭帝		

2. GEOGRAPHICAL NAMES AND TERMS: ADMINISTRATIVE AREAS

Alumangia	阿魯(祜)尼阿	Chiang-nan (Kiang-nan)	江南
A-ma-ao ⎫ Macao	阿媽澳	Chiang-tung-ch'iao	江東橋
A-ma-kung ⎭	阿媽宮	Chiao-chih (Giao-chi, Kōchi, Annam)	交趾
Amoy (Hsia-mên)	厦門	Chien-ning-fu	建寧府
An-fu-ssŭ	安撫司	Chihli	真隸省
An-hai (Ngan-hai)	安海	Chihli-chou	直隸州
Anhui (Anhwei)	安慶省	Chin-chiang-hsien	晉江縣
Annam	安南國	Ching-shih	京師
Ao-mên (Macao)	澳門	Ching-tê-chên	景德鎮
		Ch'ing-yang-hsien	青陽縣
Bun-lai (Brni, Brunei, Borneo)	文萊	Chou	州
Canton. See Kuang-chou, and Kuangtung		Chou	洲
Chang-chou (Chang-chow-) fu	漳洲府	Chü-chiang (Ku-kiang, Kiu-kiang)	珠江
Chang-Ch'üan-nei-chiang	漳泉内港	Ch'ü-chiang- (Ku-kong-) fu	曲江府
Chang-shui	章水	Ch'üan-chou- (Chin-chew-) fu	泉州府
Ch'ang-an	長安	Ch'üan-nan	泉南
Ch'ang-chou-hsien	長洲縣	Chün	郡
Ch'ang-kuan-ssu	長官司	Chung-hua	中華(國)
Chao-an- (Chau-ngan) hsien	詔安縣	Chung-tso-so (Amoy)	中左所
Chao-ch'ing- (Chau-king-) fu	肇慶府		
Chao-hsien (Chōsen, Korea)	朝鮮		
Ch'ao-chou-fu	潮州府	Fo-lang-chi (Fo-lan-ki; Franks)	⎧ 佛郎機 佛朗機 拂狼機 ⎫
Chêkiang (Chê-chiang)	浙江省		
Chên-hai-wei	鎮海衛		
Ch'êng-tu	成都	Foochow (Fu-chou, Fu-chau, Fucheo, etc.)	福州府
Chiang	江	Fu	府
Chiang	港	Fukien (Fu-chien, Fo-kien, Hok-kíen)	福建省

Lai-ma-tao (Lema islands) 來馬烏

Lai-ma-chai-tao (Lamock island) 來馬街烏

Lang-pai-kao (Lampa-cau) 浪白澳(澳)

Liao-lo (Liāu-lô) 料羅(頭)

Liao-hsi 遼西

Liao-tung 遼東

Lieh-hsü (Lēh-Sū) 裂嶼

Lien-chou-fu 廉州府

Ling-nam (Ling-nan) 嶺南

Liu-chiu (Loochoo, Lew-chew, Ryūkyū) 琉球

Lolo 猓猓(玀玀)

Lo-man-shan (Ladrone islands) 老萬山

Loyang 洛陽

Loyang-ch'iao 洛陽橋

Lung-ch'i-hsien 龍溪縣

Lung-kiang (Lung-chiang) 龍江

Macao 阿媽宮(澳門)

Manchu 滿州

Mei-chou (Bî-chiu) 湄州

Meiling pass 梅嶺山

Miao-tzu (Miaotse) 苗子

Min 閩

Min-Chê 閩浙

Min-chiang (Min-kiang) 閩江

Mongol 蒙古

Namoa (Nan-o) 南澳

Nanchang- (Nan-ch'ang-) fu 南昌府

Nan-Chihli 南直隸省

Nanking (Nan-ching) 南京

Nan-kuan 南關

Nan-t'ai 南臺

Nan-t'ai-wu (t'a) 南太武(塔)

Nan-t'ou (Nantau, Nantao) 南頭

Ningpo-fu 寧波府

Ning-tu 寧都

Pa-chiu-tu 八九都

Pao-ting-fu 保定府

Pei-chi-ch'iao 悲濟橋

Pei-chiang 北江

Pei-Chihli 北直隸省

Pei-ching (Peking) 北京

Pei-ping 北平

P'êng-hu (Pescadores) 澎湖

P'u-chou-fu 蒲州府

P'u-t'ien-hsien 莆田縣

Quemoy (Chin-mên; Kin-mên) 金門

Sai (Hsi, Si) 西

Sai-kuan 西關

San-shui-hsien 三水縣

Shang-ch'uan 上川

Shantung 山東省

Shansi 山西省

Shao-chou-fu (Shau-chau-fu) 韶州府

Shensi	陝西省	T'ing	廳
Shêng	省	Tongking	東京
Sheng-ch'eng	省城	Ts'ê-ao	賊澳
Shiu-hing-fu (Chao-ch'ing-fu)	肇慶府	Tsou-ma-ch'i	走馬溪
Shuang-hsü-chiang	雙嶼港	T'un-mun (T'un-mên)	屯門
Shun-chi-ch'iao	順濟橋	Tung-ao	東澳
Shun-t'ien-fu	順天府	Tung-kuan	東關
Si-kiang (Hsi-chiang)	西江	T'ung-an-hsien	同安縣
Siang-kiang (Siang-chiang)	湘江	T'ung-shan	銅山
Sien-lo (Siam)	暹羅		
Soochow (Su-chou, Su-chow)-fu	蘇州府		
Ssǔ-ch'uan (Szechwan)	四川省	Ui Lóh-iu^n	爲落洋
Swatow (Shan-t'ou)	汕頭	Uigurs	回黑 回紇 回回
Tak-ou (Takow, Takao)	打狗		
Ta-Mi [-kuo]	大明國	Wa (Wo)	倭
Ta-Ming-jên	大明人	Wako (Wo-k'ou)	倭寇
Ta Shih (Arabs)	大食	Wan-gan-ch'iao	萬安橋
Ta-Ta (-erh)	達達兒 韃靼 達子	Wei-nan-hsien	渭南縣
		Wu	吳
Ta-tu	大都	Wu-chou-(Wuchow)-fu	梧州府
T'ai-wan (Taiwan)	臺灣	Wu-hsü (Go-si)	浯嶼
T'ai-Yüan-fu	太原府		
Tanka	蛋家	Ya-lü-chiang (Yalu river)	鴨綠江
T'ang	唐	Yangtze-chiang	揚子江
T'ang-jên	唐人	Ying-t'ien-fu	應天府
Tao	道	Yüeh-chiang (Geh-kong)	月港
Têng-Lai-Ch'ing-tao	登萊青道	Yünnan	雲南省
T'ien-chu (Thien-tiok)	天竺	Yünnan-fu	雲南府

3. PERSONAL NAMES

Anda (Altan, Yenta) Khan	俺答可汗	Limahon	李馬鴻
		Lin-A-Fêng	林阿風
		Lin Hsi-yüan	林希元
Chang Fei	張飛		
Chang T'ien-tsê	張天澤	Liu Pei	劉備
Chang Wei-hua	張維華	Liu Yao-hui	劉堯海
Ch'ên Chiu-tê	張九德	Lo Hsien-hao	羅先浩
Ch'ên Chih-jang	陳志讓	Lu Pi	盧璧
Ch'ên Tsung-k'uei	陳宗夔	Lu T'ang	盧鐘
Chhah Siang (Ts'ai Hsiang)	蔡襄		
Ch'ien Chung-shu	錢鍾書	Ma-tso-po (Ma-tsu-p'o)	媽祖婆
Chu Ssu-pen	朱思本	Mi Fu (Mi Fei)	米芾
Chu Wan (Chu Huan)	朱紈		
		Niang-ma	娘媽
		Nü Kua (Nü Wa)	女媧
Fa-ch'ao	法超		
Fo (Fuh, Put; Buddha)	佛	O-mi-t'o-fo	阿彌陀佛
Fu Hsi	伏羲		
		Pang Níng	邦寧
Han Kao-tsu	漢高祖	P'an Ku	盤古
		P'usa	菩薩
K'o Ch'iao	柯喬		
Kuan Yin (Kwan-yin, Kwannon)	觀音	Shih-chia-fo	釋迦佛
Kuan Yü	關羽	Shih Huang-ti	始皇帝
		Shou Chien	守謙
Lê (Li)	黎氏	Shui-kuan	水官
Li Kuang-t'ou	李光頭	Ssŭ-ma-yen	司馬衍

Ta Yü	大禹	Wang Mang	王莽
T'ai Chi	太極	Wang Po	汪柏
T'ai I	太一	Wang Wang-kao	王望高
T'ang Kao-tsu	唐高祖	Wu Kuang-ching	吳光清
T'i-kuan	地官		
T'ien-hou-Niang-niang	天后娘娘		
T'ien-kuan	天官	Yao and Shun	堯舜
Tu Ju-chen	杜汝禎	Yao Hsiang-fêng	姚翔鳳
		Yu Ch'ao	有巢
		Yü	禹
Wang Hung	汪鋐	Yü-huang-shang-ti	玉皇上帝

4. OFFICIAL RANKS, TITLES, AND ORGANIZATIONS

An-ch'a-shih	按察使	Fên-hsün-tao	分巡道
		Fên-hsün-Hsing-Ch'üan-tao	分巡興泉道
Ch'a-yüan	察院	Hai-tao-fu-shih (Haitão, Aitão, etc.)	海道副使
Chhe-kha	差脚	Ho-shang (Hôe-siün Huexio, etc.)	和尚
Chi-ti-p'u	急遞鋪	Hsien-ch'êng	縣丞
Chiao-yü	教諭	Hsing-Ch'üan-tao (Heng-tsoân-to)	興泉道
Ch'ien-hu-so	千戶所	Hsing-pu	刑部
Chih-fu	知府	Hsiu-ts'ai	秀才
Chih-hsien	知縣	Hsüeh-chêng	學政
Chin-chiang-wang	靖江王	Hsün-fu-tu-t'ang	巡撫都堂
Chin-shih	進士		
Ch'in-ch'ai	欽差	I (Yi, Iah)	馬驛
Chü-jên	舉人	I-chan	馬驛站
Chün	軍		
Chün-mên (Kun-bûn)	軍門		
		Li-pu-shang-shu	禮部尚書

Liang-tao	糧道	T'ai-shou	太守
Lo-tia	老爹	T'ai-tsun	太尊
Lü-shih	律師	Tao-li	道吏
		Tao-t'ai	道台
Pa-tsung	把總	Ti-tu	提督
Pei-wo-tu-chih-hui	備倭都指揮	Ti-tu-chün-wu-chien- hsün-fu-tu-yü-shih	提督軍務兼 巡撫都御史
Ping-pu	兵部		
Po-hu-so	百戶所	T'i-hsüeh	提學
Pu-cheng-shih	布政使	Tien-shih (Tién-sú)	典史
Pu-t'u (or pu-tao)	色頭	Ts'an-chiang (Chham- chiong)	參將
Pu-t'ing	捕廳		
		Tsung-tu-chün-mên	總督軍門
Sêng-kang (Cheng- kong)	僧綱	Tu-ch'a-yüan	都察院
Sêng-lu	僧錄	Tu-chih-hui	都指揮
Shang-shu (siūⁿ-si)	尚書	Tu-ssŭ	都司
Shên-shih	紳士	Tu-t'ang	都堂
Shing-wong-miu (ch'êng-wang-miao)	城隍廟		
Shou-fu	守府		
So	所	Wei	衛

5. MISCELLANEOUS

A-(Ah-)	阿	Chin	金
		Ch'in	琴
		Chiu	酒
Cha (Ch'a)	茶	Chiu-yu	柏油
Chang	樟	Chüan	卷
Ch'ao-fan	朝飯		
Chêng	箏		
Ch'eng-jên	城人	Fán (fan)	飯
Chhat (Ts'at, ch'i)	漆	Fan	番
Chia	枷	Fan-jên	番人
Chiao-tzu	轎子	Fan-kuei (Fan-kwei, Fanqui, etc.)	番鬼

Fen (fun, foon, etc.) 分

Fêng-shui (fung-shui) 風水

Fo-lang-chi (Folanki; 佛郎機
  Franks) 佛朗機 拂狼機

Hao 好

Hao-a 好阿

Ho (Hoah) 喝

Hsiao-mai 小麥

Hu-ch'in 胡琴

Huo 火

Kin 斤

Kotow (kowtow) 磕頭 (叩頭)

K'uai-tzǔ 快子 (筷子)

Kuan 管

Kuan-hua 官話

Kuei (kwei) 鬼

Kumquat (cumquat) 金橘

Liang (tael) 兩

Lichih (lichee, lychee) 荔枝

Liu 流

Lo-san (lōh-saàn) 羅傘

Lǒ-lǒ (lu-lu) 櫓 (艣)

Lü-shih 律師

Mace 錢

Miao 廟

Mu 木

Muitsai (mei-tzu) 妹仔

Nien-hao 年號

Paau-sat 色膝

P'ai 牌

P'ai-lou (pailow) 牌樓 (坊)

Pei (p'i) 碑

P'i-p'a 記 琶

P'u-kua 卜卦

P'usa 菩薩

Seng-lí { 生理 常求 (?)

Shê 嫂

Shên 神

Shên-shih 紳士

Shou-k'ao 手銬

Shui 水

Ta 打

Tael (liang) 兩

Tëĕ-tseen-yün (tieh- 疊前韻
  ch'ien-yün)

Teng-chieh 燈節

T'ien 天

T'ien Hsia 天下

T'ien-hsiao-tê 天曉得

Ts'o { 醋 / 二十一日酉

Tsung 椶

Tu-ch'eng 度秤

T'u 土

T'u-ti-Lao-yeh 土地老爺

Wan-shou-kuan 萬壽宮

Wang-fu 王府

Wei 唯

Wo-k'ou (Wako) 倭冦

Yamen (yamun) 衙門

Yang and yin 陽陰

Yeh-fan 亱飯

Ying-pi 影壁

Yuloh (yao-lu) 搖櫓

6. TITLES OF BOOKS AND ARTICLES
Listed in Section II (c) pp. 358–360.

1. 秋山謙藏, 日支交涉史研究

2. 澳門記畧

3. 漳州府志

4. 張星烺, 斐律賓史上"李馬奔"Limahong 之真人考 附林道乾事蹟考 (燕京學報之八)

5. 張維華, 明史佛郎機呂宋和蘭意大里亞四傳注釋 (燕京學報專號之七)

6. 陳懋恆, 明代倭冦考畧 (燕京學報專號之六)

7. 胡宗憲, 籌海圖編

8. 朱士嘉, 國會圖書館藏中國方志目錄

9. 泉州府志

10. 中國歷代天災人禍表

11. 福建通志

12. 福州府志

13. 廈門志

14. 人鏡陽秋

15. 羅洪光,　廣輿圖

16. 李長傳.　"斐律賓史上 Limahong 之真人考" 補遺
　　　　　　　(燕京學報之九)

17. 黎光明.　"斐律賓史上 Limahong 之真人考" 補正
　　　　　　　(燕京學報之十)

18. 黎光明.　嘉靖禦倭江浙主客軍考 (燕京學報
　　　　　　　專號之四)

19. 明史

20. 明實錄

21. 金陵學報

22. 日蜀交通

23. 三國志演義

24. 清水泰次,　明代莊田考 (東洋學報)

25. 大明會典

26. 東洋學報

27. 張燮,　　東西洋考

28. 王崇武,　明代戶口的消長 (燕京學報之二十)

29. 茅元儀,　武備志

30. 燕京學報

Index

(The first syllable of a Chinese name is treated as a separate word, whether followed by a hyphen or not.)

388 INDEX

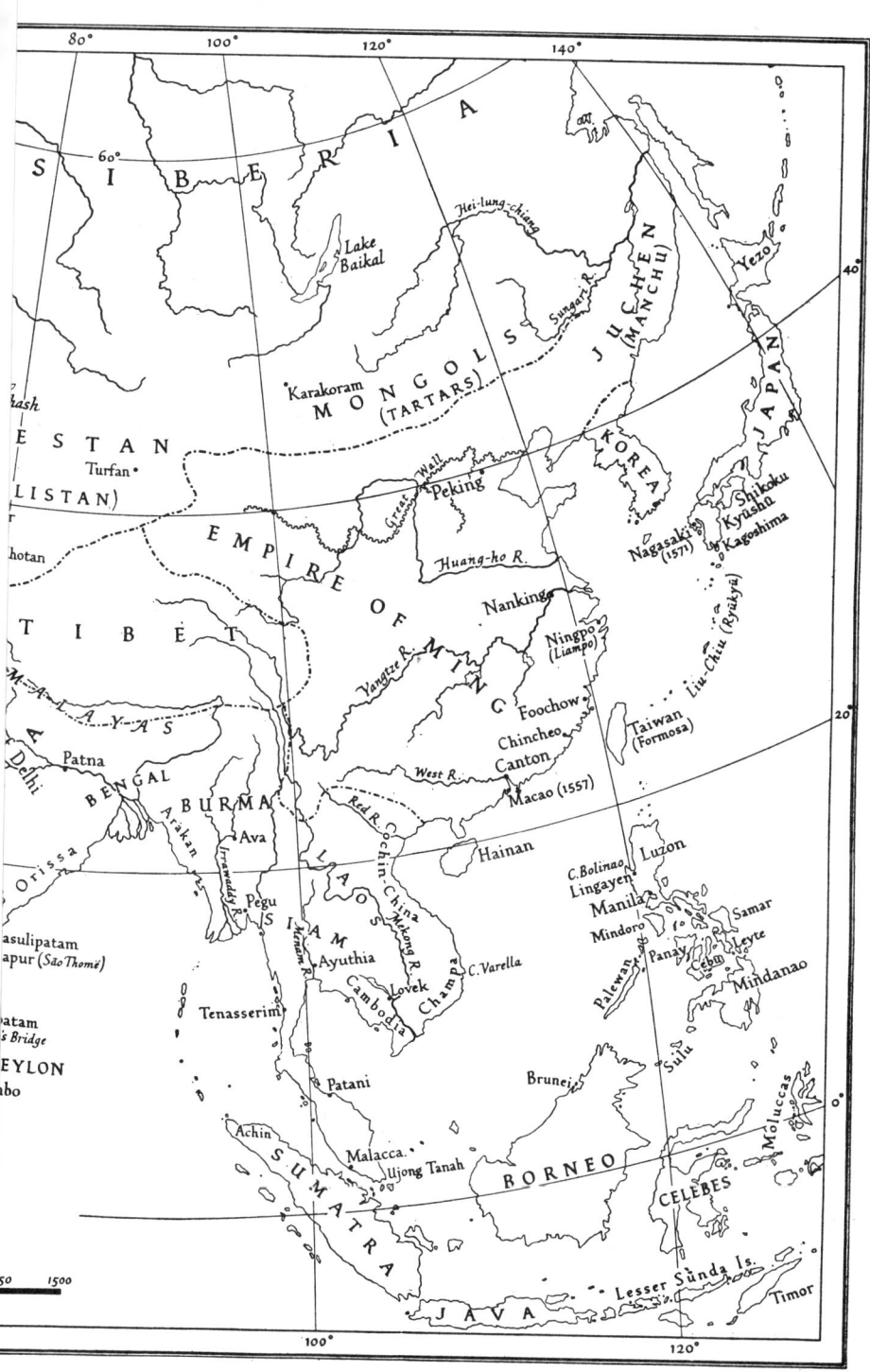

80° 100° 120° 140°

60°

S I B E R I A

S I B E R I A

Lake Baikal

Hei-lung-chiang

J U C H E N
(MANCHU)

Yezo

40°

kash

E S T A N

Karakoram

M O N G O L S
(TARTARS)

Sungari R.

Turfan

LISTAN)

E M P I R E

Great Wall

Peking

KOREA

JAPAN

Shikoku
Kyushu
Nagasaki Kagoshima
(1571)

hotan

T I B E T

O F   M I N G

Huang-ho R.

Nanking

Ningpo
(Liampo)

Liu-Chiu (Ryūkyū)

20°

M A L A Y A S

Patna

Yangtze R.

Foochow

Chincheo

Taiwan
(Formosa)

Delhi

BENGAL

B U R M A

West R.

Canton

Macao (1557)

Orissa

Arakan

Ava

Irrawaddy R.

Red R.

Cochin-China

Hainan

C.Bolinao Luzon
Lingayen
Manila

asulipatam
apur (São Thomé)

Pegu

S I A M

Ayuthia

Mekong R.

Mindoro

Samar

Panay Leyte
Cebu

L A O S

Menam R.

Lovek

C.Varella

Palawan

Mindanao

atam
's Bridge

Tenasserim

Cambodia

Champa

EYLON
bo

Patani

Brunei

Sulu

Moluccas

Achin

Malacca

Ujong Tanah

B O R N E O

CELEBES

0°

50   1500

S U M A T R A

J A V A

Lesser Sunda Is.

Timor

100° 120°